THE EIGHTY-FOUR HYMNS OF HITA HARIVAMŚA

THE EIGHTY-FOUR HYMNS OF HITA HARIVAṂŚA

An Edition of the Caurāsī Pada

RUPERT SNELL

MOTILAL BANARSIDASS
PUBLISHING HOUSE • DELHI
Email: naraina@mlbd.in • Website: www.mlbd.in
@mlbdofficial
+91 89 2999 9000

Reprint: Delhi, 2024

First Published: Delhi, 1991

ISBN: 978-93-5971-880-4 (Hardcover)
ISBN: 978-93-5971-536-0 (Paperback)

Published in
Europe and North America by
the School of Oriental and African
Studies (University of London),
Thornhaugh Street,
London WC1H OXG

Printed & Published by
Rajendra P Jain *for*
Motilal Banarsidass Publishing House
A-44, Naraina Industrial Area, Phase I,
New Delhi–110 028 (INDIA)
Email: naraina@mlbd.in Website: www.mlbd.in
Tel.: (+91-11)4751 1592

Delhi Showroom:
4637/20, F-2, Hari Sadan, First Floor, Ansari Road, Daryaganj
Delhi–110 002 (Opp. Fire Station) ***Tel.***: (+91-11)4559 7999

Bengaluru Showroom:
1st Floor, 1/2 Rathnavilas Road, Basvanagudi, Next to Pai Vista
Convention Hall, South End Circle Bengaluru - 560004 (India)

To

Śrī Lalitā Caraṇ Gosvāmī,

rasika ananya

बानी हित हरिबंश की सागर तें गंभीर ।
कही गई मोपें जिती तितौ गहै षग नीर ।।

धरणीधरदास

TABLE OF CONTENTS

TABLES

PREFACE

Of the numerous Braj bhāṣā devotional texts written or compiled during the 16th and 17th centuries, the *Caurāsī pada* (CP) has a particular importance between of its attribution to Hita Harivaṃśa, regarded as the 'founder' of one of the Kṛṣṇaite *sampradāyas* established at that time. The Rādhāvallabha *sampradāya* does not boast the specifically theological treatises which are found in related traditions, and sectarian theology is largely deduced from works attributed to Hita Harivaṃśa, especially the lyrics of the CP. Consequently, a tradition of *ṭīkā*-writing has accompanied the transmission of the CP, and manuscripts with and without *ṭīkā* abound in the private and institutional collections of Vrindaban and its environs. Although comparatively little known outside the *sampradāya*, the *Caurāsī pada* continues to be an important living work within the Rādhāvallabhī community, and its currency in temple worship as well as in individual devotions lends an especial interest to its study.

The language of the CP contains a high proportion of *tatsamas* and semi-*tatsamas*, and even the *tadbhava* forms present few difficulties of etymology or meaning: consequently an index verborum has not been included here. Problematic forms are discussed in the annotations to the translation in chapter V, with cross-references to other occurrences where appropriate; such forms are itemized in the index.

My first debt of gratitude is to members of the Rādhāvallabha *sampradāya* in Vrindaban, not least because access to privately-owned manuscript collections had made the present work possible: In particular I owe much to Śrī Lalitā Caraṇ Gosvāmī, to whom this book is dedicated; to Śrī Hitānanda Gosvāmī, to Bābā Hit Dās, and to the *samājīs* of the Choṭī Sarkār temple. The vivisection of a much-loved work is poor requital for the cordial welcome which I received in Rādhāvallabhī temples and homes: but if a laying bare of text and tradition appears ruthless, it intends no disrespect, and some reassurance may be offered in a phrase from *Caurāsī pada* 82, *binu bhūṣana bhūṣita braja gorī*, 'without adornment is the fair lady of Vraja adorned'.

The staff of the Vrindaban Research Institute have given generously of their assistance, both in the procuring of texts and in the providing of personal contacts within the labyrinthine religious communities of present-day Braj.

The greater part of this study was written[1] under the guidance of

1. This study was first undertaken as a PhD thesis: R. Snell 1984.

Professor J.C. Wright, whose awesome knowledge of Indo-Aryan language and literature has been both an inspiration and an invaluable support throughout. I am also indebted to Dr. J.D. Smith and Dr. D.R. Widdess, who have made helpful comments on the contents of Chapter VI; and to Dr R.D. Gupta, Dr R.S. McGregor, Professor C. Shackle and Mr S.C.R. Weightman, who have commented on specific points and advised on the general organization of material. I also thank the Publications Committee of the School of Oriental and African Studies for meeting part of the cost of publication.

Textual editing easily becomes an all-engaging obsession equal to that shown to a *parakīyā*; to my *svakīyā*, Mary, I owe the traditional vote of thanks for keeping her displays of *māna* to a minimum. I am very grateful to Acharya Sripad Baba, of the Vraja Academy, for permitting the reproduction of the painting on the dust-jacket; and also to Dr. Grahame Niemann for kindly providing the photograph.

RUPERT SNELL

NOTE ON REFERENCES AND ABBREVIATIONS

References in the text or in footnotes give author's name, date of publication and page number; date of publication is omitted when only one work by a given author is listed in the bibliography (where full publication details will be found).

Cross-references are to chapter number, section and sub-section, as 'IV.3.(iii)'; in the case of references to the edition, stanza number and line number are cited, as '27.9'. When cited without a line number being specified, references to an individual stanza are preceded by the siglum CP (for *Caurāsī pada*), as 'CP 27'.

Abbreviations

(Universally established abbreviations are not listed. Sigla referring to published texts are listed separately below.)

Ap.	Apabhraṃśa
BrBh.	Braj bhāṣā
CP	*Caurāsī pada*
Dhar.	Dharaṇīdharadāsa (CP commentator)
foll.	following; followed
H.	Hindi
HvP.	*Harivaṃśa purāṇa*
KhB.	Khaṛī bolī
LCG	Lalitā Caraṇ Gosvāmī (as CP commentator)
Lok.	Lokanātha (CP commentator)
m.	*mātrā*
Pers.	Persian
prec.	preceding; preceded
Prem.	Premadāsa (CP commentator)
Rasik.	Rasikalāla (CP commentator)
RvS.	Rādhāvallabha sampradāya
sec.m.	*secunda manu*
Sk.	Sanskrit
v.	*varṇa*

Abbreviations referring to published texts

(Full details of the works referred to here are given in the bibliography.)

BBhSK	Prem Nārāyaṇ Taṇḍan, ***Braja bhāṣā sūra kośa.***
BhK	Hermann Jacobi, ***Bhavisatta kaha von Dhaṇavāla.***
CDIAL	Turner, R.L., ***A comparative dictionary of the Indo-Aryan languages.***
GG	Stella Sandahl-Forgue, ***Le Gītagovinda.***
GHL	S.H. Kellogg, ***A grammar of the Hindī language.***
GNG	C. Shackle, ***A Gurū Nānak glossary.***
HGA	Ganesh Vasudev Tagare, ***Historical grammar of Apabhraṃśa.***
HŚS	Śyāmsundar Dās, ***Hindī śabdasāgara.***
LB	Dhirendra Verma, ***La langue Braj.***
LIO	R.S. McGregor, ***The language of Indrajit of Orcchā.***
MW	M. Monier-Williams, ***A Sanskṛit-English dictionary.***
Platts	John T. Platts, ***A dictionary of Urdū, classical Hindī and English.***
SS	Nandadulāre Vājpeyī (ed.), ***sūvasāgara.***
SV	Lalitā Caraṇ Goṣvāmī (ed.), 1975: ***Śrī Sevaka vāṇī.***
SVL	[***Siddānta vicāra, līlā,*** in] Lalitā Caraṇ Goṣvāmī (ed.), 1971: *Śrī bayālīsa līlā.*

CHAPTER I

HITA HARIVAMŚA AND THE RĀDHĀVALLABHĪ TRADITION

1. The Sectarian Background

The names of devotional poets such as Sūradāsa, Mīrābāī and Rasakhāna are known to every Indian child, and the legends associated with them form as much a part of the fabric of the culture of Northern India as do those of the God Kṛṣṇa whom their poems eulogize. In a convenient shorthand which parries the question of whether it is the literary or the spiritual aspect of such figures which should be regarded as paramount, they are often designated 'poet-saints'; and their verses comprise not only some of the greatest examples of the 'classical' period of Hindi literature, but also the daily hymnal of Vaiṣṇava Hindus in the modern age. Yet some of the most influential of the Kṛṣṇa-poets have been denied their share of the limelight, and remain little known outside the narrow confines of sectarian and academic interests. Among this group are those Kṛṣṇa-poets who show a special preference for the dalliance of Kṛṣṇa with his consort Rādhā, and who find a special enjoyment in restricting the contexts of their verse to this one exalted theme; while not for a moment negating the validity of the broader Kṛṣṇaite narrative such as that relayed by the *Purāṇa* tradition, these poets look to Kṛṣṇa's *nikuñja līlā* or 'bower-sport' as the source of the most potent form of the *rasa* or essential aesthetic flavour which forms the basis of their spiritual experience. In recognition of this predilection, these poets are themselves referred to as *rasikas,* aesthetes of the spirit who reproduce in themselves and in their verses the nature of the experience of Kṛṣṇa's love for Rādhā. Their lyric verse is typically more rhapsodic than narrative in content and style, and its rhetoric rests on a clear assumption that the 'reader' or hearer of the text will share the poet's devotional attitudes and will approach the text not as he would a secular work but rather with all the deference due to *vāṇī*, which is sacred or inspired utterance.

One such *rasika* is Hita Harivaṃśa (often given the title 'Gosvāmī' which is to this day assumed as a surname by his descendants), whose lyric verses in Braj Bhāṣā and Sanskrit form the theological basis of the Vaiṣṇava sectarian community known as the Rādhāvallabha *sampradāya*. Hagiographers of successive centuries provide *post facto* contextualizations of the circumstances in which Harivaṃśa was instructed by Rādhā, through the device of a dream visitation, to instigate in Vrindaban the worship of the eponymous deity Rādhāvallabha. The worship of their deity still provides the basis for devotional activity within the sect, whose line of scriptural authority derives from the devotional verse of Harivaṃśa, and in particular from his most cherished work the *Caurāsī pada* (CP) or 'Eighty-four Hymns'.

Antecedents of this poetry include the 14th/15th century Maithilī songs of Vidyāpati, the Braj Bhāṣā or 'Gvāliyarī' verse of Viṣṇudāsa from the same era, the little-studied poetry of the Brajabūlī tradition, and the earliest strata of *padas* attributed to Sūra, Mīrā and their contemporary Kṛṣṇa-*bhaktas* of the opening years of the fifteenth century; at a further remove, the CP looks back to literary and prosodic models in Middle Indo-Aryan, to a mythological framework relayed by the *Bhāgavata Purāṇa* and elaborated by Jayadeva's *Gītagovinda,* and to an intensely emotional mode of devotion traceable ultimately to the Āḷvār poets of the Tamil tradition.

Though the text of the CP bears no date, the sectarian hagiographers place its author in the first half of the sixteenth century A.D., thus locating him in that most extraordinary period of devotional activity which saw a great flowering of vernacular poetry all over Northern India. Having been composed at a time when the Vaiṣṇava *sampradāyas* based on the *tīrthas* of Vrindaban were in a seminal state, the CP was itself influential in the moulding of the new devotional traditions of Braj Bhāṣā poetry, especially in respect of the newly proclaimed status attributed to Rādhā. Had the text been associated with a dynamic proselytizing tradition such as the Vallabha *sampradāya*, whose following pervades Northern India and the far-flung countries of the diaspora, it would no doubt enjoy the widespread prominence of texts such as the *Sūrasāgara*; but the fate of the CP has been one of relative obscurity outside the circle of its own sectarian following, and though literary critics of the present century invoke comparisons with the lyrical poetry of Jayadeva and Vidyāpati, the name of neither Hita Harivaṃśa nor his text register much recognition with even the more pious representatives of today's Hindi-speaking literati.

Within the Rādhāvallabha *sampradāya*, (RvS) of course, a different picture obtains. Here, the CP holds a position of unrivalled prestige, since its alleged author is regarded as the founder (or rather 'instigator', *pravarttaka*) of the sect; in the absence of works of formal theology, the CP is looked to as the authoritative basis of sectarian doctrine. Yet while later Rādhāvallabhī poets derive much of their style and inspiration from the CP, the content of the text itself could hardly be described as explicitly sectarian: the epithet 'Rādhāvallabha', for example, does not occur once in the whole text, and the ascendancy of Rādhā over Kṛṣṇa[1] which is a special feature of the *sampradāya*'s doctrinal stance is by no means fully developed here. Furthermore, the word *hita,* prominent in later Rādhāvallabhī literature as a technical term denoting the sectarian conception of divine love, does not have this special sense in the CP.

In common with other *rasika* traditions, the RvS directs its worship towards a joint form (*yugala svarūpa*) of Rādhā and Kṛṣṇa. While the *sampradāya* takes its name from an epithet of Kṛṣṇa, it is Rādhā who enjoys predominance in the developed theology of the sect, holding a position superior to Kṛṣṇa's.[2] As a *rasika sampradāya,* the RvS concentrates almost exclusively on the *nikuñja vihāra* aspect of the Kṛṣṇa myth, adopting *mādhurya bhāva* as its preferred devotional approach; a distinction is maintained between *nikuñja līlā,* in which the sublimated passion of Rādhā and Kṛṣṇa provides the focus of the devotee's attention, and *vraja līlā,* the generality of puranic Kṛṣṇa mythology, regarded as inferior as a source of *rasa* since its diversity is detrimental to the experiencing of single-minded absorption (*ananya bhāva*) in the sport of the joint deity. The role of the *sakhī* in promoting (but not participating in) the *nikuñja vihāra* is to be emulated by the devotee, whose highest aim is to achieve the vicarious delight of being an on-looker in the *nikuñja.*[3] An *alaukika* Vṛndāvana[4] is the setting for this divine activity, and takes the place of other Vaiṣṇava conceptions of paradise such as Vaikuṇṭha and Goloka.

The RvS does not claim affiliation to the 'classical' Vaiṣṇava *catuḥ-sampradāya,* nor does it specifically profess any one of the major philosophical positions of classical Hinduism. Its claim to autonomy as a *sampradāya* in its own right rests on its following a particular mode or style of *bhakti,* and in the maintaining of distinct lines of authority descending from Hita Harivaṃśa himself. Only latterly has any attempt been made to support this claim for autonomy by producing sectarian *bhāṣyas* on the *Brahmasūtras* (Snātak 1968:121 ff.). The main centre of sectarian activity is the Rādhāvallabha temple in Vrindaban, which is in the authority of Gauḍa Brahmins who claim patrilineal descent from Harivaṃśa through his eldest son Vanacandra, and who assume the

1. The name 'Kṛṣṇa' is used here as being that most generally applied in studies of literature and religion. It is worth recording, however, that this name occurs rather rarely in sectarian sources, more endearing epithets such as 'Nandanandana', 'Śyāmasundara' etc. being preferred. The name *kṛṣṇa* appears only once in the CP, and then only in the formulaic compound *kṛṣṇa rasāmṛta sāra* (30.17).

2. Even so, the shrine of the temple of Rādhāvallabha in Vrindaban contains no anthropomorphic representation of Rādhā, who is worshipped in the form of a tablet bearing her name and placed, suitably adorned, on Kṛṣṇa's left in lieu of an image.

3. The concept of the *nikuñja* as a sacred realm is discussed in R. Snell 1989.

4. The Sanskrit spelling 'Vṛndāvana' is adopted here when referring to the concept of the eternal *dhāman* of Kṛṣṇa and Rādhā, while the form 'Vrindaban' designates the modern town.

title *gosvāmī* as their family name. Since the latter part of the seventeenth century this *gosvāmī* dynasty has been split into two branches, following a disputed succession to the *ācārya*-ship of the *sampradāya*. The historical origins of this rift are obscure, but the tension between the two branches (called *Rāsa vaṃśa* and *Vilāsa vaṃśa* after the two rival claimants, Rāsadāsa and Vilāsadāsa) is still in evidence today and has been the subject of protracted litigation in recent years; rights to *sevā* in the temple have sometimes been allocated by an officially appointed receiver.

The *gosvāmī* lineage represents the main channel of sectarian authority, and its members are held in very great esteem by their lay disciples and followers. In addition to the *gṛhastha* tradition, the sect also has an ascetic branch, which holds some of the sectarian sites in its custodianship; in common with other Vaiṣṇava *sampradāyas,* however, the RvS does not regard renunciation as being a necessary part of its *sādhanā.* The *gosvāmī* and ascetic branches of authority are known by the names *bindu parivāra* and *nāda parivāra* respectively, representing the conception that the authority of the ascetic branch is an emanation from the central authority of the *gṛhastha* line (and therefore ultimately subservient to it).

According to the *Rasika ananya māla*, a 17th century hagiography, the original temple housing the image of Rādhāvallabha was built during the incumbency of Harivaṃśa's son Vanacandra.[1] During the incursions of the iconoclast Aurangzeb, many of the Vrindaban temple images were removed for safekeeping in neighbouring Hindu kingdoms, and the image of Rādhāvallabha is said to have been spirited away to Kāmavana (Kaman) in Rajasthan; it was eventually reinstalled in a new temple[2] in Vrindaban in v.s. 1739 (Mītal 1968: 411). Worship of the deity is carried out on the *aṣṭayāma* pattern, and in accordance with a cycle of seasonal festivals. Special importance is attached to the singing of appropriate texts in *samāja,* and a large body of sectarian literature, mostly in Braj Bhāṣā, exists for this purpose; few texts are published (though a hymnal entitled *Śṛṃgāra rasa sāgara*[3] is in circulation, and the main works of the principal poets are available at least in bazaar editions), and even today the *mukhiyā* who leads the singing in *samāja* will on occasion have recourse to manuscripts for his text. The use of Vedic ritual, and the observance of certain generally accepted Vaiṣṇava practices such as the *ekādaśī vrata,* are spurned as irrelevancies. The RvS has a considerable following in the Braj area, as well as a number

1. Lalitāprasād Purohit (ed.) 1960:47.
2. The old temple, slightly damaged, now stands empty alongside the later one; it is one of the oldest buildings in Vrindaban, and was much admired by Growse (1883:254).
3. Bābā Tulsīdās, 1956-62. Also an abridged edition in three volumes under the title *Śrī Rādhāvallabha jī kā varṣotsava* [Lalitā Caraṇ Gosvāmī (ed.) 1978].

of devotees in Gujarat, Madhya Pradesh and other parts of Northern India. The sect is formally opposed to caste restrictions, though attitudes vary.

In addition to the CP, the following works are attributed to Harivaṃśa: (i) *Rādhāsudhānidhi*, a Sanskrit *stotrakāvya* in 270 stanzas; (ii) a Sanskrit *Yamunāṣṭaka;* (iii) a further collection of BrBh. *padas*, usually entitled *Sphuṭa vāṇī*; (iv) two brief letters in BrBh. prose, written to a disciple named Viṭhaladāsa. Discussion of these texts follows in Section 4.

2. Materials relating to the life of Hita Harivaṃśa[1]

The hagiographic nature of all available data relating to Harivaṃśa's life precludes the possibility of assembling any historical biography, and a survey of such data must begin by acknowledging this fact. Vaiṣṇava hagiographies cannot be regarded as objective historical statements, and the temple records of the Rādhāvallabhī tradition, which would no doubt yield much genealogical information, have so far remained inaccessible to outside researchers. Secondary sources, comprising the academic endeavours of scholars writing mostly in Hindi or English, are based almost entirely on primary sources still directly accessible to us, and so add little new information.

It is not possible, therefore, to present an authoritative biography of the *bhakta* to whom the CP is ascribed. This section has instead a threefold objective: firstly, to trace the development of Harivaṃśa's hagiography and thereby to illuminate the sectarian background to the compilation and transmission of the CP; secondly, to note such incidents and dates as *can* be shown to be plausible by external evidence; and thirdly to disentangle the extraordinary profusion of quasi-biographical information propounded by the various primary and secondary sources. Barely a single aspect of Harivaṃśa's life as related by any one source—save perhaps his devotion to Rādhā—remains uncontested by some contradictory statement elsewhere; and yet the roots of these inconsistencies are not inaccessible to research and may often be traced to confused interpretations of extant texts.

(i) *Early eulogistic references*

The earliest references to Harivaṃśa are not biographical, but rather in the form of salutations in texts written by his contemporaries and followers. An example is the *Śrīhitaharivaṃśacandrāṣṭaka* ascribed to Prabodhānanda Sarasvatī, allegedly a contemporary of Caitanya (S.K. De, p. 130). The sixth *śloka* of this work describes Harivaṃśa as belonging to the 'dynasty of Vyāsa':

1. Much of the material presented in sections '2' and '3' has been published as: 'History versus hagiography in early Hindi literature: the biography of Hita Harivaṃśa', *Purvadesh*, Vol. 1, No. 2 (Winter 1980), pp. 109-135.

hṛdayanabhasi śuddhe yasya kṛṣṇapriyāyāś caraṇanakharacandrā
bhānty alaṃ cañcalāyāḥ;
tadatikutukakuñje bhāvalabdhālimūrtiḥ sa jayati harivaṃśo
vyāsavaṃśapradīpaḥ.[1]

'All hail to that Harivaṃśa, luminary of the Vyāsa dynasty, in the clear sky of whose heart shine the toenail-moons of Kṛṣṇa's capricious beloved, and who for love of her has taken [as it were] the form of a bee in her most wondrous grove.'

Vijaypāl Siṃha and Candrabhān Rāvat (p. 21, n. 2) cite a further reference to Harivaṃśa in the works of Prabodhānanda; the reference, from *śataka* 17 of the *Vṛndāvanamahimāmṛta,* begins *tvam asi śrī harivaṃśa śyāmacaṃdrasya vaṃśa*, but is not found in the available edition of the text (Prabodhānanda Sarasvatī, vol. IV).

A second and somewhat more explicit reference to 'Vyāsa' is found in the first *śloka* of the *Karṇānanda* of Kṛṣṇadāsa, who is identified in sectarian tradition as the second son of Harivaṃśa:

sphuradvadanapaṅkajaḥ kanakakūṭadehadyutiḥ
praśastasukhasaṃpadāṃ nidhir apūrvamānapradaḥ;
sakṛṣṇavṛṣabhānujācaraṇamādhurīcañcuraḥ
sadā madhuravākpaṭur jayati sādhu vaiyāsakiḥ.[2]

The *Karṇānanda's* editor N.S. Shukla translates:

'Son visage est épanoui comme un lotus; l'éclat de son corps est comme un mont d'or; il est un trésor de joie et de richesse parfaites; il est enclin à faire de rares honneurs et il est habile à goûter la douceur des pieds de la fille de Vṛṣabhānu, accompagnée de Kṛṣṇa, c'est lui, le toujours diligent à la voix douce; que le fils de Vyāsa triomphe!'[3]

The patronymic *vaiyāsakiḥ*[4] is glossed by the *Karṇānanda's Arthakaumudī* commentary (itself ascribed to the author of the *mūla*) as *vyāsanandanaḥ śrīharivaṃśākhyaḥ,*[5] identifying the 'son of Vyāsa' as Harivaṃśa. The form *vyāsanandana* is taken up by later vernacular hagiographers as an epithet for Harivaṃśa, and appears frequently in the colophons of Rādhāvallabhī texts as part of the salutation to him. No early text, however, offers a view on the identity of 'Vyāsa', and it is left

1. Lalitāprasād Purohit (ed.), 1960:100 (appendix *a*).
2. N.S. Shukla (ed.), p. 157.
3. *Ibid.*, p. 93.
4. The patronymic *vaiyāsaki-* designates Śukadeva in the earlier literature: attestations are found in the *vārttika* on the *Vyākaraṇa mahābhāṣya* 4.1.97 (F. Kielhorn, p. 253) and in *Bhāgavatapurāṇa* 10.1.14 etc. I owe the former reference to Dr. J.D. Smith.
5. N.S. Shukla (ed.), p. 158.

to the later hagiographers (of the seventeenth century) to supply this information. Confirmation of the fact that Harivaṃśa is Kṛṣṇadāsa's father appears in *śloka* 188, where the poet refers to Harivaṃśa as '*guru* twice over'—i.e. both *guru* and father; the *śloka* also identifies Kṛṣṇadāsa's mother as Rukmiṇī.[1]

Shukla's interpretation of *praśastasukhasampadāṃ nidhiḥ* as 'un trésor de joie et de richesse parfaites' enables him to see in this phrase a historical statement about the wealth owned by Kṛṣṇadāsa's father; but the phrase must be interpreted as a *tatpuruṣa* compound expressing a formal panegyric ('a treasury of perfect manifestations of joy') without any implication of material wealth. A similar imposition of the specific onto the general occurs in the sectarian interpretation of the phrase *sadā madhuravākpaṭuḥ*, explained by a member of the Rādhāvallabhī community as alluding to Harivaṃśa's musical prowess (said to have been manifested in his singing of the CP stanzas). Here again there is no real reason to suppose that the reference is in any way specific. These traditional interpretations of allusions in Kṛṣṇadāsa's text illustrate how detailed 'biographical' narratives may derive from general references in panegyrical contexts.

The *Karṇānanda* is one of the first Rādhāvallabhī texts to bear a date of composition; the date *Śaka* 1500 (A.D. 1578) appears in the final *śloka*. Shukla asserts, on the basis of 'quelques-uns des manuscrits de langue indigène',[2] that Kṛṣṇadāsa was born in A.D. 1531: he would therefore have been 47 years old at the time of this text's composition. Assuming for the moment that Kṛṣṇadāsa was indeed the son of Harivaṃśa, this dating provides the first pointer towards a likely floruit for the latter poet.

The *padas* of Harirāma Vyāsa, a BrBh poet of the late 16th–early 17th centuries, contain a number of eulogistic references to Hita Harivaṃśa, often linking his name with that of Svāmī Haridāsa.[3] A clear past tense reference in the opening line of *pada* 24 (Vāsudev Gosvāmī, p. 196) shows that Vyāsa outlived Hita Harivaṃśa, and mourned his passing:

> *hutau sukha rasikani kau ādhāra*;
> *binu haribaṃsahi̇̄ sarasa rīti kau kāpai calihai bhāra.*

These references provide some attestation of the alleged relationship between Harivaṃśa, Harirāma Vyāsa and Haridāsa; yet they are of

1. *sadā rādhājāneś caraṇabhajanānandatucchīkṛtānyo*
   guruḥ yasya dvedhā sumatiharivaṃśo mahātmā prasiddhaḥ;
   prasūḥ śrīrukmiṇy apratimasahajā cābhidhā kṛṣṇadāso
   girāṃ tasya krīḍā hariratiyujāṃ sādhu cittaṃ dhinotu. (N.S. Shukla, p. 314.)
2. N.S. Shukla (ed.), p. 21.
3. E.g.: *āsū kau haridāsa rasika haribaṃśa na mohī bisārau*;
   ihi patha calata syāma syāmā ke vyāsahī borau bhāvahī tārau.
(Vāsudev Gosvāmī, p. 196).

little help in establishing any historical dates or facts. Vyāsa's own floruit is itself uncertain, and the arguments on which Vāsudev Gosvāmī (pp. 41, 104) asserts dates for Vyāsa's life (b. v.s. 1567, with v.s. 1675 as a *terminus ad quem* for his death) are to some extent based on an assumption of Harivaṃśa's floruit being determined beyond doubt. Similarly, in summarizing the evidence for the dates of Haridāsa, R.D. Haynes (p. 68) finds that 'all that one can say for sure is that Haridāsa was born in the last two decades of the fifteenth century and had died by 1596 [A.D.]'; and even this cautious conclusion rests to some extent on an assumption that dates in Vyāsa's life in turn provide fixed points for a comparative chronology.

One of the earliest texts of the *bhaktamāla* genre to refer to Harivaṃśa is the undated *Bhaktanāmāvalī* of the Rādhāvallabhī poet Dhruvadāsa. 42 short texts and a collection of *padas* are attributed to Dhruvadāsa; five of the 42 are dated, indicating a floruit of at least 48 years—v.s. 1650-1698 (A.D. 1593-1641).[1] Since a floruit significantly longer than this already lengthy span would seem unlikely, the *Bhaktanāmāvalī* also may reasonably be allocated to this period. Dhruvadāsa is himself described as a disciple of Gopīnātha, third son of Harivaṃśa according to sectarian sources,[2] by the *Rasika ananya māla* of Bhagavat Mudita:

> *kāyatha kula devana ke vāsī; paramparāi ananya upāsī.*
> *(śrī) gopīnātha ke śiṣya ju śreṣṭha; sevata rādhāvallabha iṣṭa.*[3]

> 'A resident of Devana [modern Deoband, Saharanpur District, U.P.] of *kāyastha* stock, a traditional worshipper of single-minded dedication. Most excellent disciple of Gopīnātha, he worships Rādhāvallabha as his personal deity.'

The 114 *dohās* of the *Bhaktanāmāvalī* make brief mention of 123 devotees; while many of these are associated with Vṛndāvana modes of *bhakti* and belong to the present *kaliyuga*, the text also alludes to several characters from Puranic sources associated with earlier *yugas* and thus has a panegyrical rather than a historical tenor. The text has no apparent sectarian bias, giving as much prominence to adherents to the Gauḍīya and Vallabhite traditions as to those whose allegiance was to the Rādhāvallabha *sampradāya*. The text opens, however, with a salutation to Harivaṃśa as the revealer of a *rasa* unattainable to the Vedas, and continues with an eulogy of Vanacandra, Kṛṣṇacandra, Gopīnātha and

1. The dates are as follows (page references are to Lalitā Caraṇ Gosvāmī (ed.), 1971): *Rasānanda līlā*, v.s. 1650 (p. 251); *Premāvalī līlā*, v.s. 1671 (p. 180); *Sabhā maṇḍala līlā*, v.s. 1681 (p. 146); *Vṛndāvana sata līlā*, v.s. 1686 (p. 21); *Rahasya mañjarī līlā*, v.s. 1698 (p. 187).
2. An example is the *Hitakulaśākhā* of Jayakṛṣṇa, discussed below.
3. Lalitāprasād Purohit (ed.), 1960:78.

Mohana[-candra], whom sectarian sources identify as the four sons of Harivaṃśa:

(śrī) harivaṃśa nāma dhruva kahata hī bāḍhai ānaṃda beli;
prema raṅga ura jagamagai yugala navala rasa keli. **1.**
nigama brahma parasata nahī̃ jo rasa saba tẽ dūri;
kiyo pragaṭa harivaṃśa jū rasikani jīvana mūri. **2.**
(śrī) banacaṃda carana aṃbuja bhaju mana krama vacana pratīti;
vṛndābana nija prema kī taba pāvai rasa rīti. **3.**
kṛṣṇacanda ke kahata hī mana ko bhrama miṭi jāi;
bimala bhajana sukha siṃdhu mẽ rahai citta ṭhaharāi. **4.**
(śrī) gopīnātha pada ura dharai mahā gopya rasa sāra;
binu bilamba āvai hiye adbhuta yugala bihāra. **5.**[1]

1. 'As soon as Dhruva utters the name of Harivaṃśa, the creeper of bliss grows;
   the love-impassioned sports of the young pair shine in the heart.
2. The Vedas cannot touch that Spirit, that *rasa* which is concealed from all;
   [But] Harivaṃśa jī has made it manifest, the root-of-life of *rasikas*.
3. Worship the lotus feet of Vanacandra with mind, deed, word and faith;
   then you attain the joyful path of Vṛndāvana's innate love.
4. Immediately on uttering the name of Kṛṣṇacandra the mind's delusion is erased;
   and the consciousness remains founded in an ocean of the joy of pure adoration.
5. When one holds to one's breast the feet of Gopīnātha—a most mysterious quintessence—
   the wondrous sport of Rādhā and Kṛṣṇa enters the heart without delay.'

Harivaṃśa is further mentioned in connection with five of the devotees included in the *nāmāvalī*: [Dāmodaradāsa] 'Sevaka' (*dohā* 44), Naravāhana (46), Nāharamalla (56), Mohanadāsa (57) and Nehī Nāgarīdāsa (63). In the last two references Harivaṃśa is referred to by the patronymic Vyāsananda[-na].

(ii) The developing hagiography

The first text to make more than passing reference to Harivaṃśa's parentage is probably the *Sevaka vāṇī* of Dāmodaradāsa 'Sevaka'. This text in sixteen chapters (*prakaraṇa*) is devoted to the eulogy of

1. Lalitā Caraṇ Gosvāmī (ed.), 1971: 26-27. The first *pāda* may intend 'On uttering the refrain (*dhruva*) of the name of Harivaṃśa...'.

Harivaṃśa and his teaching. The text bears no testimony to its date or the circumstances of its composition, though a tradition promoted by the hagiographies of Bhagavat Mudita and Uttamadāsa (described below) maintains that Dāmodaradāsa was a contemporary of Harivaṃśa and a resident of the village of Gaḍhā (near Jabalpur, Madhya Pradesh). According to Bhagavat Mudita's account [Lalitāprasād Purohit (ed.) 1960:31-35], Dāmodaradāsa 'Sevaka' and his friend Caturbhujadāsa became attracted to Rādhāvallabhī *bhakti* when a devotee came to Gaḍhā and told them about Harivaṃśa and the following which he was attracting in Vrindaban. The two resolved to become disciples of Harivaṃśa, but their prospective *guru* passed away before they could travel to Vrindaban. 'Sevaka' would accept no other *guru*, and stayed in Gaḍhā where his devotion was rewarded by the granting of initiation by Harivaṃśa himself in a dream. Caturbhujadāsa, meanwhile, went to Vrindaban and became a disciple of Harivaṃśa's son and successor Vanacandra.

The *Sevaka vāṇī* enjoys canonical status in the *sampradāya*; its somewhat prosaic verses enshrine what are considered to be the principal tenets of Harivaṃśa's *bhakti* and often quote verbatim from the CP. The text is regarded as the first real statement of Rādhāvallabhī doctrine, Harivaṃśa's own works lacking any explicit exposition; Lalitā Caraṇ Gosvāmī (1957: 437) goes so far as to call the *Sevaka vāṇī* the principal doctrinal authority of the *sampradāya*. It is commonly found in manuscripts and printed books as a companion text to the CP, being generally preferred as a 'commentary' on the latter to any of the actual *ṭīkās*. According to Bhagavat Mudita's *Rasika ananya māla*, the tradition of the linking of these two texts was instigated by Vanacandra:

> *taba taĩ ajñā daī gusāĩ; pothī doū milī likhāĩ;*
> *caurāsī aru sevaka vānī; ika saṃga likhata paḍhata sukhadānī.*[1]
>
> 'From then on the Gosvāmī had both books written together by order; writing and reading the *Caurāsī* and the *Sevaka vāṇī* together is felicitous.'

These two legends or traditions—that of Dāmodaradāsa's would-be discipleship of Harivaṃśa, and the decree of Vanacandra—seem to indicate that Dāmodaradāsa was indeed a contemporary or near-contemporary of Harivaṃśa. The account of his friendship with Caturbhujadāsa, however, raises some doubts since a work ascribed to the same Caturbhujadāsa bears the date V.S. 1686 (A.D. 1629).[2] Since the *Rasika ananya māla* account clearly implies that Caturbhujadāsa had reached adulthood by the time of Harivaṃśa's death, then either the authenticity of this account or the accuracy of the traditional dates of Hari-

1. Lalitāprasād Purohit (ed.), 1960:35.
2. Lalitāprasād Purohit (ed.), 1971:25.

vaṃśa's life discussed below—A.D. 1502-1552—must be called into question: if Caturbhujadāsa had reached maturity by 1552 then he would have been a centenarian by the time he composed his own text in 1629.

Harivaṃśa's birth is described in the first *prakaraṇa* of the *Sevaka vāṇī*, where he is identified as an incarnation of Viṣṇu. The fourth and fifth stanzas describe the prevailing conditions of *kaliyuga* which finally moved Viṣṇu to become manifest in the world as Harivaṃśa, for the sake of *dharma;* the earth is described as 'suffering under the burden of non-Aryans' (*mlecchani bhāra dukhita*, stanza 5)—a reference, presumably, to the ascendancy of Muslim power. The sixth stanza refers to the place, month and day (but not the year!) of Harivaṃśa's birth, and names his parents:

mathurā maṃḍala bhūmi āpanī jahā̃ bāda pragaṭe jaga dhanī
bhanī avani vara āpa mukha;
śubha bāsara śubha ṛkṣa vicāra mādhava māsa gyāsa ujiyāra
nārinu maṃgala gāiyau.
tacchina deva duṃdubhī bājiye jai jai sabda surani mili kiye
hiye sirāne sabani ke;
tārā janani janaka ṛṣi vyāsa jasa baranaū̃ harivaṃśa vilāsa
śrī harivaṃśahi gāihaū̃.[1]

'In the Mathura region, his own land, where [lies the village of] Bād, the lord of the world became manifest and spoke with his own lips in that fine place.
Calculating an auspicious day and lunar mansion, in the month of Mādhava [Vaiśākha] on the eleventh day of the bright fortnight, women sang a song of celebration [at his birth].
At that moment the kettledrum of the gods was sounded, and together [the gods] declared 'Hail! Hail!', comforting the hearts of all;
Tārā was his mother, his father the *ṛṣi* Vyāsa. I describe the glory of Harivaṃśa's sport. I shall sing [the praises] of Śrī Harivaṃśa.'

The first *prakaraṇa* continues by describing the ubiquitous delight caused by Harivaṃśa's appearance in the world, and the miraculous events which spontaneously follow the birth of the saintly: nature is restored to plenty, even *mlecchas* proclaim the glory of Hari now that the *kaliyuga* is over, Brahmins attend once more to their appointed duties, and so on. The remainder of the *prakaraṇa* (stanzas 11-14) is dedicated to a summary of Harivaṃśa's teaching of *bhakti.* The four stanzas suggest four successive stages in his teaching, from that of the

1. Lalitā Caraṇ Gosvāmī (ed.), 1975:8.

general tenets of *bhakti* to his own special path. The first lines of stanzas 11-13, and the second line of 14, show this progression:

11.1 *aba upadeśa bhakti kau kahyau jaisī vidhi jāke cita rahyau*
lahyau ju mana vā̃nchita saphala;
12.1 *aba avatāra bheda tina kahe sakala upāsaka tina mana rahe*
kahe bhakti sādhana sabai;
13.1 *aba ju kahī saba braja kī rīti jaisī sabani naṃdasuta prīti*
kīrti sakala jaga vistarī;
14.2 *aba niju dharma āpanaū̃ kahata tahā̃ nitya vṛndābana rahata*
bahata premasāgara jahā̃;[1]

'Now he gave instruction in *bhakti* in accordance with the hearts of each, [and each] adopted that by which his desires were fulfilled.'
'Now he told of the categories of *avatāra*, all worshippers being borne in his mind; he told of all the means of *bhakti*.'
'Now he told of all the [devotional] ways of Braj, according to the [various kinds of] love held by all for the son of Nanda; his renown spread throughout the world.'
'Now he tells of his own eternal *dharma*; therein subsists an eternal Vṛndāvana, where surges an ocean of love.'

The change from perfective forms in the first three quotations (*kahyau, kahe, kahī*) to the imperfective (*kahata*) in the fourth may be understood as implying that Harivaṃśa was still alive when the text was composed; equally though, *kahata* may be construed as a historic present, or as an 'atemporal' imperfective parallel to the *bahata* in the last foot of the line.

The *Sevaka vāṇī* is the first eulogistic text to append the *upanāma 'hita'* to the name of Harivaṃśa; with the exception of the passages already quoted, however, it yields little biographical or hagiographical data.

The earliest non-Rādhāvallabhī hagiographer to refer to Harivaṃśa appears to be Nābhādāsa ('Nābhā jī'), whose *Bhaktamāla* is generally held to date from the early years of the seventeenth century.[2] Two devotees by the name of Harivaṃśa appear in this text. *Chappaya* 167[3] describes a Harivaṃśa who was a devotee of Govinda and a servant of *sādhūs*; nothing in this stanza suggests a connexion with Hita Hari-

1. *Ibid.*, pp. 11-14.

2. In his study of the *Bhaktamāla*, G. Pollet maintains that the text was composed between A.D. 1594 and 1624 (p. 11); one of his arguments for positing the former date is that 'Harivaṃśa Gosā̃ī, who is dealt with in v. 90, flourished in A.D. 1585'. While not seeking to postulate an earlier date for the composition of the *Bhaktamāla*, one may consider this argument an unreliable indicator of a *terminus a quo*, since the claim that Harivaṃśa was alive in A.D. 1585 is far from proven; the point is discussed further in section 3(i) below.

3. Narendra Jhā (ed.), p. 61.

vaṃśa, who is the subject of *chappaya* 85[1] and who is mentioned also in the stanza describing Caturbhuja (*chappaya* 116).[2] *Chappaya* 85 is regarded by Rādhāvallabhīs as a succinct summary of Harivaṃśa's *bhakti;* indeed, it is so frequently quoted as such by Rādhāvallabhī writers that its function may now be regarded as prescriptive:

((śrī) harivaṃśa gusāī̃ bhajana kī rīti sukṛta kou jānihai.)[3]
śrī rādhā caraṇa pradhāna hṛdai ati sudṛḍha upāsī;
kuṃjakeli daṃpati tahā̃ kī karata khavāsī.
sarvasu mahāprasāda prasidha tāke adhikārī;
vidhi niṣedha nahī̃ dāsa ananya utkaṭa bratadhārī.
vyāsa suvana patha anusarai soī bhalai pahacānihai;
(śrī) harivaṃśa gusāī̃ bhajana kī rīti sukṛta kou jānihai.

'(Few will understand the pious mode of worship of Harivaṃśa Gosvāmī.)
The feet of Śrī Rādhā are pre-eminent in his heart, he is a most staunch worshipper;
he performs attendance of the couple in their bower-sport.
The *mahāprasāda*,[4] of which he is a well-known claimant, is his entire property;
not [concerned with] precepts and prohibitions,[5] he is a single-minded servant and a fervent votary.
He who follows the path of Vyāsa's son, he alone will comprehend it fully;[6]
few will understand the pious mode of worship of Harivaṃśa Gosvāmī.'

The most important commentary on the *Bhaktamāla* is the *Bhaktirasa bodhinī* of Priyādāsa, written in V.S. 1769 (A.D. 1712).[7] *Kavittas* 364-366 of this text expand on the account given by Nābhādāsa. Stanza 364 is a general statement on Harivaṃśa's *bhakti*, providing a gloss on Nābhādāsa's *mūla*; 365 and 366 extend the account, referring to Harivaṃśa's marriage and to his instruction from Rādhā to propagate the service of Rādhā and Kṛṣṇa:

1. *Ibid.*, p. 31.
2. *Ibid.*, p. 42.
3. Each *chappaya* in the *Bhaktamāla* is prefaced by its own final line, which here (as typically) bears the name of the devotee under discussion; the six-line *chappaya* is therefore presented as a seven-line form.
4. Pollet (p. 229) translates *sarvasu mahā prasāda* as 'He is a great blessing for all people': yet *sarvasu* is for Sanskrit *sarvasva*, and the overriding sense of *mahāprasāda* in a Vaiṣṇava context is of 'a great present (of food etc. distributed among the persons present at the worship of an idol)' (*MW*).
5. Pollet (*loc. cit.*) translates *vidhi niṣedha* as 'forbidden rites': but established *dvaṃdva* usage renders such a reading unlikely.
6. Pollet (*loc. cit.*) interprets *bhale* (*bhalai* in the quoted text) as a noun, yielding 'he...will discriminate virtue', which again does not seem tenable.
7. R.D. Gupta, p. 24.

364 *hitajū kī rīti koū lākhani maĩ eka jānaĩ*
rādhā hī pradhāna mānai pāche kṛṣṇa dhyāiyai;
nipaṭa bikaṭa bhāva hota na subhāva aiso
unahĩ kī kṛpādṛṣṭi neku kyaũ hũ[1] *pāiyai.*
bidhi au niṣedha cheda ḍāre prānapyāre hiye
jiye nija dāsa nisi dina vahai gāiyai;
sukhada caritra saba rasika bicitra nīke
jānata prasiddha kahā kahikai sunāiyai.

365 *āye ghara tyāga rāga baḍhyau priyā prītama sõ*
bipra baḍabhāga hari ājñā daī jāniyai;
terī ubhai sutā vyāha devau levo nāma merau
inako jo baṃsa so prasaṃsa jaga māniyai.
tāhī dvāra sevā bisatāra nija bhaktana kī
agatina gati so prasiddha pahicāniyai;
māni priya bāta gahagahyau sukha lahyau saba
kahyo kaise jāta yaha mata mana āniyai.

366 *rādhikāballabhalāla ājñā so rasāla daī*
sevā mo prakāsa au bilāsa kuṃjadhāma kau;
soī bisatāra sukha sāra dṛga rūpa piyau
diyo rasikani jina liyau paccha bāma kau.
nisi dina gāna rasa mādhurī kau pāna ura
aṃtara sihāna eka kāma syāmāsyāma kau;
guna so anūpa kahi kaise kai sarūpa kahai
lahai mana moda jaise aura nahī nāma kau.[2]

364 'One in hundreds of thousands may know the way of Hita jī—
he accepts Rādhā as pre-eminent, and Kṛṣṇa is worshipped secondly;
most formidable is the manner of his being—there is no [other] nature like this
and through his grace alone may it perhaps be attained a little.
Casting off precepts and prohibitions, [with] the beloved in his heart
living as [the beloved's] servant he sings of him constantly,
all his joyous deeds are impassioned, wonderful and good;
I know them to be famous—how could they be described?

365 'He left his home and came [to Braj?] and his passion for lover and beloved grew;

1. For *kyaũ hũ*, Growse's text (1883:201) gives the metrically preferable reading *kihũ*, which is followed in the translation here.
2. S.Ś. Bhagvān Prasād (ed.), pp. 600-601.

it is known that Hari had given a command to a most fortunate brahmin:
"Give your two daughters in marriage, taking my name:
their offspring will be held worthy of fame in the world.
Through them the worship [performed] by my devotees will spread,
and will be considered famous as a path for the pathless";
obeying this sweet command, he was thrilled and all were delighted—
how could it be told? Accept this sentiment in your mind.

366 'Rādhā's dear beloved gave the joyous command:
"Make known my worship and the delights of the bower-abode";
spreading that [teaching], [Harivaṃśa] drank with his eyes its essence of joy,
and gave it to those devotees who allied themselves with the female [deity].
Day and night he relished the delight of singing praises,
infatuated in his heart with his one passion for Śyāmā-śyāma;
describing their qualities as unparalleled, how could he describe their form?
He delights in his mind as at no other name.'

A probable source for the account given by Priyādāsa is a text of uncertain title attributed to Uttamadāsa and also, erroneously, to Bhagavat Mudita. The confusion over this text's authorship stems from the fact that Uttamadāsa's text usually follows Bhagavat Mudita's *Rasika ananya māla* in manuscripts, and has consequently been identified by some as a part of that work. The two texts will be discussed here in turn.

Two BrBh. works are attributed to Bhagavat Mudita. The first is a translation of one *śataka* from the Sanskrit *Vṛndāvanamahimāmṛta* ascribed to Prabodhānanda Sarasvatī: this translation is dated V.S. 1707 (A.D. 1650).[1] The second work, *Rasika ananya māla*, is dedicated almost entirely to accounts of the lives of Rādhāvallabhī devotees. The author shows nominal allegiance to the Gauḍīya tradition, to which he allegedly belonged,[2] by first paying homage to Caitanya and Nityānanda in the first *dohā* of the *maṅgalācaraṇa*, but the eulogy of Harivaṃśa which follows is notably more protracted.

1. Vrindaban Research Institute, Hindi MS 61, f. 32v:
saṃvatu daśa sai sāta (saī) aru sāta varaṣa haĩ jāna;
caita māsa mai catura vara bhāṣā kīyo baṣāna.

2. Bhagavat Mudita is described as a disciple of Haridāsa, *adhikārī* of the Govindadeva temple, in *kavitta* 626 of Priyādāsa's *Bhaktirasa bodhinī:* S.Ś. Bhagvān Prasād (ed.), p. 920.

The *Rasika ananya māla* is undated, but the date of the other work noted above gives an indication of Bhagavat Mudita's floruit. A complication arises from the fact that Bhagavat Mudita is himself the subject of a stanza in the *Bhaktamāla* of Nābhādāsa, which is thought to date from the early years of the 17th century. In the introduction to his edition of the *Rasika ananya māla* (p. 9), Lalitā Prasād Purohit casts doubt on the authenticity of the *Bhaktamāla* stanza in question, and in a recent edition of the latter text (Narendra Jhā, p. 74) the stanza is relegated to an appendix as an interpolation.

The *Rasika ananya māla* gives accounts of incidents in the lives of 37 devotees. Its narrative style contrasts sharply with the enigmatic references of Nābhādāsa's *Bhaktamāla* and Dhruvadāsa's *Bhaktanāmāvalī*. The 37 'biographies' (called *paracaī*) necessarily include many references to Harivaṃśa (though he is not himself the subject of any one of them) and his descendants. Of the 37 described, the first 13, listed here, are specifically mentioned as contemporaries of Harivaṃśa; those who are described as his initiated disciples are marked here with an asterisk: Naravāhana*, Vyāsa*, Chabīladāsa, Nāharamalla*, Viṭṭhaladāsa*, Mohanadāsa*, Navaladāsa*, Haridāsa Tulādhāra*, Paramānandadāsa, Prabodhānanda, Karmaṭhī Bāī*, Dāmodaradāsa 'Sevaka', Caturbhujadāsa. The remaining devotees are the disciples of Harivaṃśa's descendants, ending with those of his great-grandson Dāmodaracanda. Some of those mentioned are described as officers of the Mughal administration, while others appear to have suffered persecution at the hands of the Muslims.

In some of the *paracaīs*, the name of the *guru* (which may provide a key to the approximate dates of the devotee) is not stated, being represented instead by some general title such as *gusā̃ī*. An example is the *paracaī* of the two sisters Gaṅgā Bāī and Yamunā Bāī.[1] The *guru* from whom they receive initiation in the narrative is usually interpreted as being Harivaṃśa himself, yet the same *paracaī* refers to a visit to Raja Man Singh at Agra, who was still in his early infancy at the alleged time of Harivaṃśa's death. If the normally accepted date of Harivaṃśa's death (A.D. 1552) is correct, then the *gusā̃ī* mentioned by Bhagavat Mudita must be one of Harivaṃśa's descendants. The example is alluded to here because it illustrates the inexplicit style of narrative found in this hagiography, and the chronological confusion engendered.

The lack of an actual 'biography' of Harivaṃśa in the *Rasika ananya māla* is made good by Uttamadāsa's text. The colophon of a manuscript in the Vrindaban Research Institute including both texts suggests a joint authorship of the two:

1. Lalitāprasād Purohit (ed.), 1960:51-55.

atha uttimacaṃda kṛta tathā bhagavaṃta mudita kṛta
rasika māla liṣyate. śrī harivaṃśa caritra liṣyate.[1]

The words *harivaṃśa caritra* here do not, however, denote the title of the whole work, but of the first section of it; this is followed by four further sections:

śaranāgatina kī kathā (comprising several separate *prasaṃgas*);
śrī jī kau janama utsava samaya varnana;
Sevaka jī ke guna varnana;
Hita jū ke kṛpāpātra.

The colophon at the end of the V.R.I. manuscript[2] reads simply *iti rasika paracarī*, and is immediately followed by the text of the *Rasika ananya māla* headed *atha rasika ananya māla likhyate.*

The colophon of an incomplete manuscript of this text in the Nāgarī Pracāriṇī Sabhā's Māyāśaṅkara Yājñika collection gives the title *śrī hita caritra* in place of the *śrī harivaṃśa caritra* of the V.R.I. manuscript.[3] It does not name the author of the text. The folios bearing the latter part of the text, including the colophon at the end of the *Hita caritra* and the beginning of the consecutive *Rasika ananya māla*, are missing from the manuscript. The colophon at the end of the *Rasika ananya māla*[4] gives only the title of the text, omitting the name of the author.

A second manuscript in the Nāgarī Pracāriṇī Sabhā lacks the first folio, but the colophon between the two texts clearly identifies them as discrete works:

iti śrī hita caritra saṃpūrṇa. śrī rādhāvallabhojayati. atha rasika māla liṣyate.[5]

The Nāgarī Pracāriṇī Sabhā's published findings of their search for Hindi manuscripts[6] describes a copy of the '*Ananyamāla*' of 'Hita Uttamadāsa' in the collection of Rūpalāla Gosvāmī of the Rādhāvallabha temple, Vrindaban. The colophon is reported as giving the title *Śrī hita harivaṃśa candra caritra ananyamāla.* An earlier volume of the 'search reports'[7] lists manuscripts of three texts by Bhagavat Mudita: *Hita caritra, Sevaka caritra* and *Rasika ananya māla.* The *Sevaka*

1. Vrindaban Research Institute, Hindi MS 4398 f.1ᵛ. (The transliteration) 'ṣ' is retained for scribal ष, even when representing the phonome/kh/.)
2. *Ibid.*, f. 34ᵛ.
3. Nāgarī Pracāriṇī Sabhā (Āryabhāṣā Pustakālaya, Māyāśankar Yājñik collection) MS 4822, f. 1ʳ. The MS is dated v.s. 1817.
4. *Ibid.*, f. 107ᵛ.
5. Nāgarī Pracāriṇī Sabhā (Āryabhāṣā Pustakālaya, Māyāśaṅkar Yājñik collection) MS 332, f.33ʳ. The MS is dated v.s. 1837.
6. Vidyābhūṣan Miśra (ed.), p. 379. The Rūpalāla collection still exists in the safekeeping of Rūpalāla's descendants, but access has proved problematic.
7. Shyam Behari Misra (ed.), pp. 48-50.

caritra is perhaps merely a part of the *Hita caritra* constituting the section entitled *sevaka jī ke guna varnana* in the V.R.I. manuscript described above.

The attribution of Uttamadāsa's work to Bhagavat Mudita is perhaps based on the final stanza of the text. This last section, *hita jū ke kṛpāpātra,* lists briefly most (but not all) of the devotees described more fully in the *Rasika ananya māla*: Uttamadāsa provides here a synopsis of Bhagavat Mudita's text. He concludes with the following *dohā*:

it[e] rasika kī paracaī bhagavāta mudita vaṣāni;
d[i]gadarasanavata eka ṭhā̃ uttama kīne āni.[1]

An interpretation of this couplet reading *uttama* as adjectival may lead to the mistaken conclusion that Bhagavat Mudita is being referred to as the *author* of the work. Since an author would be unlikely to preface his own text with a prolonged synopsis of that same text, a more feasible interpretation would be:

'Thus many are the devotees' biographies related by Bhagavat Mudita;
Uttama has brought them together in one place as a survey [of Mudita's text].'

A further reference to the *Rasika ananya māla* is found at the end of the section entitled *sevaka jū ke guna varnana*:

adhika kahī bhagavaṃta nai uttama sevaka rīti;
paḍhai sunai śraddhā sahita vaḍhai jugala sau prīti.[2]

Interpretation of this couplet hinges on a *śleṣa* in the word *uttama*:

'Bhagavat has said more (a) of the ways of the excellent Sevaka [Dāmodaradāsa];
(b) and Uttama's way is that of a servant [to him];
When one reads and hears this with reverence, love for the couple grows.'

One is led to accept the conclusion proposed by Lalitā Caraṇ Gosvāmī (1957: 22) that the text of Uttamadāsa was written to complement the *Rasika ananya māla* by adding, principally, the *caritra* of Harivaṃśa himself. It seems that a separate title was not given to the work by its author, who consequently became confused with the author of the original text.

The date of the *Hita caritra* is not known. Kiśorīśaraṇ 'Ali' (p. 38) includes Uttamadāsa in a list of writers of the eighteenth century of the Vikrama era and attributes a second text, *Śrīrādhānāma pratāpa līlā*,

1. Vrindaban Research Institute, Hindi MS 4398 f. 34ᵛ.
2. *Ibid.*, f. 32ᵛ.

to the same author. Lalitā Caraṇ Gosvāmī (1957:24) reports that Uttamadāsa was a disciple of Gosvāmī Kuñjalāla who was born in v.s. 1696 (A.D. 1639), and contends that the *Hita caritra* must therefore date from c. v.s. 1740-45 (A.D. 1683-88).

With the exception of the controversial date of birth of Harivaṃśa, to be discussed below, the 'biography' recounted by Uttamadāsa is accepted as authoritative by most later members of the *sampradāya*. The following is a précis of Uttamadāsa's account, based on Vrindaban Research Institute Hindi MS 4398:

> Harivaṃśa's home was in the town of Devana [Deoband, Saharanpur District, U.P.], in a family of Gauḍa brahmins—Yajurvedīs of the *mādhyaṃdinī* branch, members of the Kaśyapa *gotra*. His father, Vyāsa Miśra, was a wealthy and renowned astrologer whose fame had reached the king. Vyāsa Miśra was summoned to court, where he was given great wealth and received the king's favour in full measure. After some time at court, he returned home laden with wealth, yet unhappy because of his childlessness. Soon, Kṛṣṇa appeared to Vyāsa's ascetic brother Nṛsiṃhāśrama in a dream and announced his intention of becoming incarnate as the joint form of Hari and *vaṃśa* (= *vaṃśī*, flute). Vyāsa's wife Tārā Rānī was soon with child; Vyāsa was overjoyed, and resumed his position at court. On Monday, the 11th day of the bright half of the month of Vaiśākha, in the year v.s. 1559 [A.D. 1502], in the village of Bāda near Gokula, Harivaṃśa became manifest as the crown-jewel of *rasikas*; he was to be a refuter of *karma* and *jñāna* and a proponent of the way of *prema bhakti*. The joy of his birth was like the joy of Kṛṣṇa's birth described by Śuka. At an early age Harivaṃśa thrilled to hear the name of Rādhā; his childhood acts were beyond description. At the age of seven his *yajñopavīta* ceremony was performed, and later he became married to a girl named Rukmiṇī. He began to teach *bhakti* in such a way that each person's devotion to a particular form of the deity increased. Rādhā appeared to Harivaṃśa in a dream and told him that the *yugalamantra* was written on the topmost leaf of a peepul tree near his door, and that he was to make it known in the world.[1] Rādhā further ordered him to look in the well in his father's garden, where he would find a two-armed image [of Kṛṣṇa] in the flute-holding pose. Harivaṃśa followed these commands, and established the image in a temple in Devana which he then served for some time. On the death of his father Vyāsa Miśra, Harivaṃśa was summoned to court in his father's place; but he

1. The imparting of this instruction through the favourite hagiographic device of a dream resembles an incident in the hagiography of Vallabha, to whom revelation of the image of Śrīnātha jī was similarly initiated (Barz p. 28). The two traditions also share certain other parallels, such as the alleged births of Vallabha and Harivaṃśa both taking place while their respective parents were on a journey.

refused the summons, rejecting the worldly status which the royal post entailed. He fathered three sons and a daughter, all of whom married; they were all initiated by him as his disciples. On receiving a further command from Rādhā, Harivaṃśa left home and set out for Vrindaban, leaving his family behind. Again Rādhā appeared to him in a dream and told him that in the village of Caḍathāvali [understood as Charthawal, near Muzaffarnagar, U.P.] he would encounter a wealthy brahmin who would offer Harivaṃśa his two daughters in marriage; Harivaṃśa was to accept them, counting them as colleagues in the devotional life. He was also to take from the brahmin a second image of Kṛṣṇa, which he was to take to Vrindaban and worship there. Accordingly, Harivaṃśa went on with his two new brides Kṛṣṇadāsī and Manoharī to Vrindaban, where he was delighted by the transcendental beauty of the natural surroundings. He went to a high spot by the bank of the Yamunā, where there was a throng of Braj people who were thrilled to realise that he had come to live there. They[1] put a bow and arrow into his hands, and offered him as much land as he could cover in a bow-shot; he fired the arrow, which flew 'from the old building' (*purānai bhavana tai*) as far as Cīraghāṭa. He built a beautiful temple and consecrated the image of Rādhāvallabha there[2] on the 13th day of the bright half of the month of Kārttika, V.S. 1592 [A.D. 1535].[3] He established the service of the deity with seven food-offerings (*bhoga*) through the eight periods of the day (*yāma*), according to the season. He rejected all orthodox precepts and prohibitions in favour of pure devotion, and renounced fast-days because they denied him the consumption of *prasāda*. He ignored the ten rites

1. Snātak (1968:102) reports a tradition which maintains that the protagonist who addresses Harivaṃśa here is Naravāhana, the zamindar-bandit who later became Harivaṃśa's disciple and to whom two stanzas of the CP (11 and 12) are allegedly 'dedicated'; Snātak also maintains that the 'high place on the bank of the Yamunā' is the modern 'Madan Ṭer'. Uttamadāsa, however, does not mention these details in the present passage.

2. Sectarian tradition holds that the place where the image of Rādhāvallabha was first established was the grove called Sevākuñja (still an important sectarian centre). The image was later installed in the new temple built, according to the *Rasika ananya māla* [Lalitāprasād Purohit (ed.), 1960:44-48] by Sundaradāsa Bhaṭanāgara—a *kāyastha* disciple of Harivaṃśa's fourth son Gopinātha, in the employ of Abdur Rahīm K͟hānk͟hānā in Delhi—during the incumbency of Harivaṃśa's eldest son (and successor) Vanacandra. See p. 32, n. 2.

3. Vrindaban Research Institute, Hindi MS 4398, ff.8v-9r.
paṃdraha sai vānava ju suhāyau; kātiga sudi terasa suṣa ch[*āyau*].
paṭṭa mahotsava tā dina kīnau; jācika dvija guniyani dhanu dīnau.

In an unattributed quotation of the same text, Baldev Upādhyāy (1953: 423 n. 2) gives a reading which yields the date V.S. 1591 (A.D. 1534):
pandraha sau ikyānabe suhāyo: kātiga sudi terasa sukha chāyo;
paṭa mahotsava tā dina kiyo; yācaka guniyana bahu dhana diyo.

The V.R.I. text is metrically more correct (although *ju* is superfluous).

of passage (*saṃskāra*) and defeated ceremonialists, Śaivas, Śāktas and the followers of other doctrines; many people came for his *darśana*, and so populated Vrindaban.

This account is followed by the *śaranāgatina kī kathā*, as described above; then comes a short section in which the major dates of Harivaṃśa's life are recapitulated. This section, *śrī jī kau janama utsava samaya varnana*, is quoted here in full:

atha śrī jī kau janama utsava samaya varnana. dohā.
saṃvata paṃdraha sai adhika unasaṭhi kau vaiśāṣa;
sudi ekād[aś]i pragaṭa hita pujaī rasa abhilāṣa. caupaī.
varaṣa vatīsa vahi krama jānau; pragaṭa vāsa vana kau mana mānau.
varaṣa aṭhāraha lau vana vase; vahura nikuṃja mahala mai lase.
mānasarovara ḍhiga ramanīya; bhǎvara bhǎvaranī ati kamanīya;
priyā jaunha mai yau mili gaī; sahacari saṃga lagī chavi chaī.
aisaiī śrī hariva[ṃ]śa gusāī; mahala padhāre so sava gāī. dohā.
saṃvata soraha sai ru nava kātiga pūnyo svakṣa;
tā dina śrī harivaṃśa vapu dīsata nahi jaga akṣa. iti prasaṃga.[1]

'Now begins the description of the dates of celebration in the life of Śrī jī [Harivaṃśa].[2]

In the year 1559 [A.D. 1502], on the eleventh day of the bright half of Vaiśākha,

Hita became manifest, fulfilling [humanity's] yearning for *rasa*. Know this to be the order [of events], that at the age of thirty-two he realized his heart's desire of living in the grove [Vrindaban]; For eighteen years he lived in the grove, and then sported in the arbour-palace [i.e. died].

As on the bank of the lovely Mānasarovara, charming with bees, the Beloved merged with the moonlight with her companions amidst great splendour, just so did Śrī Harivaṃśa Gosvāmī enter the palace, as all have recounted.

On that bright full-moon night of Kārttika in the year 1609 [A.D. 1552], the body of Śrī Harivaṃśa was seen no more by the eyes of the world. Here the section ends.'

The major dates of Harivaṃśa's life as given here appear again in another text, the *Hitakulaśākhā* of Jayakṛṣṇa dated V.S. 1760 (A.D. 1703). Manuscripts of the text having proved elusive, quotations given from it here are taken from the passages cited by Snātak (1968; 100 ff.) and Lalitā Caraṇ Gosvāmī (1957: 23 ff.). Certain portions of Uttama-

1. Vrindaban Research Institute, Hindi MS 4398 ff.31r-31v.
2. The title 'Śrī jī' is used in Braj tradition to refer to Rādhā, Kṛṣṇa, or a saintly individual. It is clear from the present context that the last sense applies here.

dāsa's account, such as the finding of the image of Kṛṣṇa in the well, are absent in Jayakṛṣṇa's brief version, while others are alluded to only in passing. Jayakṛṣṇa does, however, supply the dates of birth of Harivaṃśa's children, which are not found in Uttamadāsa's text. The relevant section of the text is given by Snātak (*loc. cit.*) as follows:

jinakī saṃtati saba kou jānai; beṭī sāhiba de su bakhānai.
sutā eka suta tīna sudhāma; tinake janma dyausa puni nāma.[1]
pandraha sai panacāsiyā anta; chahau ritu me riturāja basanta.
caitra vadī chaṭha maṃgala gāyau; śrī vanacandra janama jasa chāyau.
pandraha se satāsiyā jānau; dvai aru bīsa māsa laghu mānau.
māgha māsa navamī ujiyārī; kṛṣṇacandra janma sukhakārī.
pandraha sai aṭhāsiyā āyau; teraha māsa uraha jasa chāyau.
phāguna māsa lagata kī pūnau; gopīnātha janama sukha dūnau.

'Of his offspring everybody knows; his daughter is described as Sāhib De.
One daughter and three handsome sons, their dates of birth and names [follow].
At the end of 1585 [A.D. 1528] in the spring—king of the six seasons—it is recounted that on Tuesday the sixth day of the dark half of Caitra the glory of Vanacandra's birth spread around.
Know that in 1587 [A.D. 1531]— a short [?] twenty-two months later—on the ninth day of the bright half of Māgha Kṛṣṇacandra's joyful birth [took place].
1588 [A.D. 1532] came, and thirteen months [after Kṛṣṇadāsa's birth] glory pervaded the heart;
precisely on the full-moon day of the month Phālguna was the doubly joyous birth of Gopīnātha.'

A further reference to Vanacandra is made elsewhere in the text, where Jayakṛṣṇa gives the date of Vanacandra's succession to his father's *gaddī*:

saṃvat soraha sai nava sahī; kātika sudi terasa dṛḍha gahī.
āsana para baiṭhe gururāja; śrī banacandra suhṛda siratāja.[2]

In 1609 [A.D. 1552], on the thirteenth day of the light half of Kārttika, the king amongst *gurus* Vanacandra, crown-jewel of the kind-hearted, ascended the throne.

These accounts by Nābhādāsa, Priyādāsa and Uttamadāsa are apparently the sources for most of the later hagiographers. Most later versions are extremely derivative, as will be shown by selected examples.

1. The relative and correlative pronouns are perhaps reversed in this *caupāī*.
2. Lalitā Caraṇ Gosvāmī, 1957:52.

Approximately contemporary with the *Bhaktirasa bodhinī* of Priyādāsa is the *Bhaktamāla* of Rāghavadāsa (Rāghodāsa) the Dādūpanthī.[1] This text includes entries on two Harivaṃśas—evidently the same two that appear in the better-known text of Nābhādāsa. *Chappaya* number 255 is devoted to Hita Harivaṃśa, and is virtually a paraphrase of Nābhādāsa's *chappaya* quoted above:

(yaū bhakti sīra sakṛta kauü jānata hita haribaṃsa kī.)
rākhata caraṇa pradhāna āpa śrīrādhājī ke;
syā̃mā syā̃ma byahāra kuṃja madha sādhe nīke.
sevata mahāprasāda sadā brata tapa nahī̃ mā̃naī
bidhi niṣedha bhrama sakala chāḍi utma dharma ṭhā̃naī.
rāgho byāsa bicitra suta karanī pālata haṃsa kī;
bhakti sīra sakṛta kou jā̃nata hita haribaṃsa kī.[2]

Few understand the devotion of Hita Harivaṃśa.[3]
He holds as principal the feet of Śrī Rādhā jī,
and worships full well the actions of Śyāmā and Śyāma in the grove.
He ever partakes of the *mahāprasāda*, not following vows or austerities;
Casting aside all precepts and prohibitions as delusion
he sets his heart upon the highest *dharma*.
O Rāghava, Vyāsa's wondrous son observes the actions of an enlightened soul; few understand the devotion of Hita Harivaṃśa.

The *ṭīkā* of Caturadāsa which follows this *chappaya* in Nāhaṭā's edition (*loc. cit.*) is no more original in content than the *mūla*, being merely a paraphrase of Priyādāsa's *kavittas* 364-6 (though Caturadāsa's stanzas are in the *Indava* metre). The only other significant change made by Caturadāsa is in the order of the stanzas' subject-matter: for Priyādāsa's order '1, 2, 3' Caturadāsa's reads '2, 3, 1'.

Two other late examples of the *bhaktamāla* genre may be mentioned briefly. The section devoted to Harivaṃśa in the undated *Bhaktamāla* of Pratāpasiṃha,[4] begins by paraphrasing Nābhādāsa and then gives an account of Harivaṃśa's life which appears to derive from Uttamadāsa. The second example is the *Bhaktamāla*[5] or *Rāmarasikāvalī* of

1. Though this text does bear a date, its interpretation is disputed. The couplet bearing the date appears as follows in the edition of Agarcand Nāhaṭā (p. 246):
saṃbat satraha sai satrahaū̃tarā sukala pakṣa sanibāra;
tithi tritīyā āṣāḍa kī rāgho kiyau bicāra.
Nāhaṭā interprets *satrahaū̃tarā* as seventeen (p. *ś*, introduction), dating the text to v.s. 1717; W.M. Callewaert (p. 7) objects to this interpretation on etymological grounds as well as on the basis of internal evidence, and conjectures a reading of v.s. 1777. Neither party offers any comment on the grossly unmetrical structure of the line in question (to be improved by excising *saṃbat* ?).
2. Agarcand Nāhaṭā, pp. 128-129.
3. *sīra* remains obscure. Reading as *rasa kṛta* leaves *sī* unresolved.
4. Kālīcaraṇ Caurasiyā Gauḍ (ed.), pp. 70-72.
5. Raghurājasiṃha, pp. 710-711.

Raghurājasiṃha (V.S. 1880-1936; A.D. 1833-1897), Maharajah of Riwa; the relevant section of this text begins with a Sanskrit *praṇāma* to Harivaṃśa, and then gives a short account of Harivaṃśa's *bhakti* and of his coming to Vrindaban, evidently drawn from Nābhādāsa and Priyādāsa.

The anthology of chronicles of the Vallabha *sampradāya* entitled *Caurāsī vaiṣṇavana kī vārtā* includes a reference to one 'Harivaṃśa'. This prose text is attributed to Gokulanātha (A.D. 1551-1716), but owes its present form to Harirāya (A.D. 1591-1716).[1] The fifth *prasaṃga* of the *vārtā* of Kumbhanadāsa,[2] one of the *aṣṭachāpa* poets, describes how Harivaṃśa, Haridāsa and other saintly men from Vrindaban went to meet Kumbhanadāsa at Girirāja (Govardhan) in order to discuss with him the composition of verses dedicated to Svāminījī (Rādhā). This text has been translated by R.K. Barz, who interprets this Harivaṃśa as Hita Harivamśa[3]. The fact that the name is associated here with Haridāsa does indeed support Barz's contention; there is, however, no mention of this incident in the Rādhāvallabhī sources. The traditional dates of Kumbhanadāsa given by Vallabhite sources are A.D. 1469-1584[4]; this lifespan of 115 years, though obviously unrealistic, does encompass the traditionally accepted lifetime of Hita Harivaṃśa (1502-1552); the incident described in the *vārtā* is therefore chronologically possible.

Certain editions of the *Caurāsī vaiṣṇavana kī vārtā*[5] contain a second reference to Harivaṃśa, this time in the *vārtā* of another *aṣṭachāpa* poet, Kṛṣṇadāsa. Here, Harivaṃśa and a certain 'Vyāsa' are described meeting Kṛṣṇadāsa at the house of the Rajasthani poetess Mīrā Bāī in Aghana. If the 'Vyāsa' referred to is Harirāma Vyāsa of Orcha, then it would seem possible that the name Harivaṃśa refers to the Rādhāvallabhī poet, with whom the former is said to have associated. As in the case of Kumbhanadāsa, the traditional dates of Kṛṣṇadāsa (A.D. 1497-1580)[6] allow of the possibility of the incident described, (though Mīrā Bāī, whose dates are uncertain, may antedate the other devotees mentioned here).

Clearly it is unreasonable to regard the *vārtā* texts as historical chronicles; and even in a hagiographic context it is not possible to prove that the two references described here do actually allude to Hita Harivaṃśa. The name 'Harivaṃśa' is common in Vaiṣṇava circles, and indeed one Vallabhī 'Cācā Harivaṃśa' is described in the second anthology of

1. R. Barz, p. 4.
2. Dvārkādās Parīkh (ed.), p. 499.
3. R. Barz, p. 183, n.l.
4. *Ibid.*, p. 104.
5. See for example the lithographed edition entitled *Caurāsī kī vārtā* (author not named), Aligarh, 1868, p. 393.
6. R. Barz, p. 104.

Vallabhite hagiography, the *Do sau bāvana vaiṣṇavana kī vārtā.*[1] However, the fact that these incidents are not mentioned in Rādhāvallabhī sources does not rule out their validity, since one would not expect such sources to give prominence to any association that Hita Harivaṃśa may have had with members of a 'rival' *sampradāya.*

One account which clearly does not derive from Nābhādāsa or the Rādhāvallabhī hagiographers is that found in the Bengali *Bhaktamāla* of Kṛṣṇadāsa Bābā (also known as Lāladāsa). This text is undated, but another text attributed to the same author, the *Upāsanā candrāmṛta*, is dated Śaka 1684 (A.D. 1762).[2] Though the publisher's preface to an edition of the *Bhaktamāla*[3] maintains that it is based loosely on the *Bhaktamāla* of Nābhādāsa and its *Bhaktirasa bodhinī* commentary by Priyādāsa, the account of Harivaṃśa in the Bengali version bears no resemblance to the account in these Hindi texts apart from the mention of Harivaṃśa's predilection for *prasāda*; yet it is likely that the 'Harivaṃśa' to whom Kṛṣṇadāsa refers is indeed Hita Harivaṃśa, since he is specifically described as being a Rādhāvallabhī *gosvāmī*. Kṛṣṇadāsa devotes only ten couplets to the *caritra* of Harivaṃśa, though the *caritras* immediately following—those of Svāmī Haridāsa and Harirāma Vyāsa—are three and five times as long respectively. The comparative brevity of Harivaṃśa's *caritra* may be explained by its controversial subject matter, since Kṛṣṇadāsa's claim that Harivaṃśa was a disciple of the Gauḍīya Gopālabhaṭṭa is inevitably the cause of much consternation in the Rādhāvallabhī camp.[4] The text of Harivaṃśa's *caritra* by Kṛṣṇadāsa is as follows:

śrīmān harivaṃśa gosvāmi caritra; jagate vyāpita haya parama pavitra.
śrīmān gopālabhaṭṭajīra śiṣya tẽha; mahābhaktivān tẽha rādhākṛṣṇa premavaha.
eka ekādaśīdine tāmbūla prasādi; khāilā baliyā guru kailā aparādhī.
antare gosāñi ruṣṭa nāhi ta hailā; bāhya lokaśikṣā hetu śāsana karilā.
harivaṃśa gosāñira śiṣya anukrame; ebe rādhāvallabhi gosāñi vrajadhāme.
śrīmān gopālabhaṭṭa śāsana karila; tāhāte kichui mātra doṣa nāhi chila.

1. Nirañjandev Śaran Gauḍ (ed.), pp. 41-46.
2. Bimānbihārī Majumdār (ed.), p. 568.
3. Upendranāth Mukhopādhyāy (ed.), introduction.
4. According to Gopālprasād Śarmmā (*Bhramocchedana* n.d., p. 48), an editor of the Bengali *Bhaktamāla* named Durgādās Lāhaḍī added an emendment to later editions of the text, admitting the allegation of Harivaṃśa's discipleship to be false. Śarmmā also recounts (p. 46) how another Bengali author, Rādhācaraṇ Gosvāmī, similarly retracted the same allegation, showing his good faith by publicly paying a fine of Rs. 5 to the Inspector of Police at Vrindaban: printed copies of the retraction were widely distributed. The furore is indicative of the depth of feeling provoked by sectarian rivalries of this kind.

ācārya gopālabhaṭṭa tāhāte praṇālī; phirāilā ki hetuka nā jāni ki bali.
yehetuka anya anya sampradāya sane; vyavahāra āhāra paramārthe nāhi bane.
biccheda haila eka-pataṅga nā haya; rājā jayasiṃha vahu vicāra karaya.
se sava kahāte ebe phala kichu nāi; koṭi koṭi daṇḍavat sabhākāra ṭhāi.[1]

'The deeds of *śrīmān* Harivaṃśa Gosvāmī are known the world over as most pure.
He was a disciple of *śrīmān* Gopālabhaṭṭa;
greatly imbued with devotion, he bore the love of Rādhā and Kṛṣṇa.
One *ekādaśī*[2] [fast] day he ate the *prasāda* betel,
and because of this his *guru* pronounced him guilty.
Though the Gosvāmī [Gopālabhaṭṭa] was not angry in his heart,
he outwardly chastised [Harivaṃśa] as an example to others.
Rādhāvallabhī *gosvāmīs* in the lineage of Harivaṃśa's disciples live even now in the domain of Braj.
Śrīmān Gopālabhaṭṭa chastised him; there was not the least fault in this—Gopālabhaṭṭa was the preceptor, and moreover [this was] the system; I do not know why he [Harivaṃśa?] turned [against the tradition?].
Since [the Rādhāvallabhīs] do not agree with the various other *sampradāyas* in social intercourse, the partaking of food and in metaphysics,
A schism occurred and there is not [now] commensality [with the other *sampradāyas*]; Rājā [Savāī] Jayasiṃha closely consulted [the scriptures].[3]
There is no advantage in describing all these incidents now; tens of millions of obeisances to everyone.'

The purport of the seventh couplet is not clear, though it appears to continue the theme of the preceding couplet, in which Kṛṣṇadāsa justifies Gopālabhaṭṭa's right to punish his disciple. The tone of this excusing of Gopālabhaṭṭa's action suggests that such a chastisement might ordinarily give offence, and perhaps therefore that Harivaṃśa, though described as the disciple of Gopālabhaṭṭa, also enjoyed some high status in his own right. Kṛṣṇadāsa seems anxious to avoid any prolonged discussion of the

1. Upendranāth Mukhopādhyāy, pp. 224-225. I am indebted to Dr. T. Mukherjee for his interpretation of these lines.
2. *Ekādaśī* is widely observed as a fast-day by orthodox Vaiṣṇavas.
3. Sawai Jai Singh is said to have convened a 'conference' of the various *sampradāyas* in 1780, in an attempt to restrict the proliferation of non-*smārta* sectarianism (P.D. Mītal 1968:422).

friction between the *sampradāyas*, and rapidly dismisses the topic in the last couplet.

The list of Rādhāvallabhī texts which allude in some way to the life of Harivaṃśa is a long one; yet most later texts are extremely derivative, merely embroidering the accounts given by earlier sources. The existence of such works, including for example the *Hitaharivaṃśa sahasranāma* and other texts of the prolific 18th century poet Vṛndāvanadāsa 'Cācājī', demonstrates the continuity of allegiance to Harivaṃśa over the centuries; yet the works themselves add little information to illuminate the circumstances of Harivaṃśa's establishment as a religious teacher and poet. The apotheosis of this tradition of sectarian hagiography may be said to have been achieved in the *Rādhāvallabha bhaktamāla* by Priyādāsa Śukla of Caubepur. This long book, mostly in prose but quoting piecemeal from many verse works, was written in V.S. 1968 (A.D. 1911) and published 18 years later. It draws from many of the primary sources discussed above (usually without any acknowledgement), and gives lengthy accounts of the lives of Rādhāvallabhīs from the 16th to the 19th centuries.

(iii) *Summary of the primary sources*

The development of Hita Harivaṃśa's hagiography in the available extant sources may be summarised as follows:

16th century:
- (a) Prabodhānanda refers to Harivaṃśa as 'luminary of the Vyāsa dynasty'.
- (b) Kṛṣṇadāsa refers to his father Harivaṃśa as 'son of Vyāsa' and names his own mother as Rukmiṇī.

16th-17th century:
- (a) Harirāma Vyāsa eulogises Harivaṃśa in his *padas*, linking his name with that of Svāmī Haridāsa.
- (b) Dhruvadāsa eulogises Harivaṃśa and subsequently in the same text (*Bhaktanāmāvali*) praises 'Banacaṃda', 'Kṛṣṇacaṃda' and 'Gopīnātha', later to be identified as Harivaṃśa's sons.
- (c) Dāmodaradāsa 'Sevaka' uses the *upanāma* '*hita*' in conjunction with the name *harivaṃśa*. He identifies the place, month and day of Harivaṃśa's birth, and names his parents as 'the *ṛṣi* Vyāsa' and 'Tārā'. Four successive stages in the teachings of Harivaṃśa are alluded to, and the basis of sectarian theology is laid down.

17th century:
- (a) Nābhādāsa's *Bhaktamāla* outlines the main aspects of Harivaṃśa's *bhakti*.
- (b) Bhagavat Mudita's *Rasika ananya māla* re-

counts narratives concerning many disciples of Harivaṃśa.

(c) Uttamadāsa lays the foundation of a standard hagiography by giving a detailed account of Harivaṃśa's birth, life, marriages, offspring and devotional career; the major dates are established.

18th century: (a) Jayakṛṣṇa's *Hitakulaśākhā* corroborates Uttamadāsa's version and adds the dates of birth of Harivaṃśa's children.

(b) The Bengali *Bhaktamāla* alleges that Harivaṃśa was a disciple of Gopālabhaṭṭa.

Details of the hagiography develop and expand in the later literature.

(iv) *Secondary Sources*

Most later writers have been content to derive their material from one of two 19th century English sources: H.H. Wilson's *Essays and lectures chiefly in the religion of the Hindus* (1862) and F.S. Growse's *Mathurā: a district memoir* (1883). A mistake in the latter book regarding the number of *ślokas* in the text *Rādhāsudhānidhi*[1] is repeated throughout much of the critical literature of the 19th and 20th centuries: not only Western writers but also many Indian historians of Hindi literature have evidently considered Growse's 15-page account of the Rādhāvallabha *sampradāya* too thorough to make any further glance at the original sources necessary. The fact that few Rādhāvallabhī texts had, until recent years, been available in anything but local bazaar editions no doubt accounts in part for the derivative nature of the secondary material.

Wilson's discussion of the *sampradāya* is for the most part limited to the status of Rādhā. This discussion is based largely on the *Brahmavaivarta purāṇa*—a work of only slight relevance to the Rādhāvallabhī tradition.

Growse keeps more closely to the traditional sources for his discussion of the life of Harivaṃśa. He quotes the accounts of Nābhādāsa and Priyādāsa, and fills them out with material evidently drawn from Uttamadāsa—though this source is not cited. Growse also gives the text and translation of the first 25 *ślokas* of the *Rādhāsudhānidhi* and of the first 12 stanzas of the CP. These extracts remained until very recently the only published English translations of Harivaṃśa's works.[2] Growse's comments on these verses and on the *bhakti* of Harivaṃśa are, naturally,

1. Growse (1883:203) gives the number of *ślokas* as 170, whereas the manuscript evidence discussed below in section 4(ii) shows 270 to be the correct number.

2. Growse's translations of CP 1-12 are very probably the source for a German version of CP 1-3, 9-12 (Hermann Goetz and Rose Ilse-Munk, pp. 93-99).

strongly imbued with the attitudes of the Victorian age: he refers to the contents of the CP as 'the language of the brothel' (p. 215), and to Rādhā as 'the goddess of lust' (p. 200), noting with some surprise that 'the Gosains, who accept as their Gospel these sensuous ravings of a morbid imagination, are for the most part highly respectable married men, who contrast rather favourably, both in sobriety of life and intellectual acquirements, with the professors of rival sects that are based on more reputable authorities' (p. 215). The relevance of this attitude to the present study is that it has in no small part contributed to the reticence shown today by members of the *sampradāya* towards the researches of outsiders. Growse himself noted the difficulty of gaining access to privately-owned manuscript collections,[1] and the experiences of Professor Snātak[2] show that this is not a difficulty limited to Europeans.

Sir George Grierson mentions Harivaṃśa in two books, of which the first is his *The modern vernacular literature of Hindustan* (1889), wherein he accredits his information to the '*Rāg-Sāgarodbhab rāg-kalpadrum*' of Krishnānand Byās Deb (1843). A later edition[3] of this voluminous anthology of *padas* by various authors does not yield the information given by Grierson (which will be discussed later), though it does include several stanzas attributed to Harivaṃśa. Grierson's second discussion of Hita Harivaṃśa and the Rādhāvallabhīs is to be found in James Hastings' *Encyclopaedia of religion and ethics*, where Grierson gives slightly contradictory information under two headings—'Bhakti mārg' and 'Rādhāvallabhīs'. Further reference to these sources will be made later.

Much of the critical literature in Hindi merely reiterates information taken from Growse and others. There are, however, notable exceptions to this tendency. The pioneering studies of Lalitā Caraṇ Gosvāmī (1957), written from within the sectarian tradition, and Vijayendra Snātak (1968) have jointly inherited the mantle of Growse and Wilson, and are now regarded as the standard Hindi authorities on the *sampradāya*. Vāsudev Gosvāmī gives much original information on the background to the *sampradāya* in the introduction to his edition of the *Vyāsa vāṇī* (1952). Baldev Upādhyāy's two surveys of Rādhāvallabhī *bhakti* (1953, 1978) are based on primary sources and deserve mention. Prabhudayāl Mītal, though acknowledging the authorities of Lalitā Caraṇ Gosvāmī and Snātak, adds much original material of his own in his discussions of the Rādhāvallabhīs (1968, 1975).

The most detailed published accounts of the Rādhāvallabhīs in European languages are also the most recent. The first is N.S. Shukla's

1. F.S. Growse 1878:98.
2. Vijayendra Snātak 1968:302.
3. Nagendranāth Vasu (ed.), 1914-16.

edition and French translation of the Sanskrit poem *Karṇānanda*, ascribed to Hita Harivaṃśa's son Kṛṣṇadāsa; the text is prefaced by a lengthy introduction in which Shukla discusses the theological background of the *sampradāya*, basing his account on the *Karṇānanda* itself and on the *Rādhāsudhānidhi*. Shukla specifies his English sources, but not the (presumably) Hindi sources from which such details as the birth dates of Harivaṃśa's children must have been taken.

A study of the CP was recently made by Charles S.J. White (1977). The introduction to the text moves uneasily between short statements on the background of the sect (based largely on Snātak's study, with due acknowledgement) and sections on the history and characteristics of Hindi literature in general; little of the information given on the *sampradāya* is original. The account of Harivaṃśa's life given here is based on an oral report by a Rādhāvallabhī *gosvāmī*, and does not refer to written sources. A second translation of the CP has been undertaken as a BA dissertation by Grahame Niemann (1977).

3. Areas of Dispute in the Hagiography of Hita Harivaṃśa

Although the account of Harivaṃśa's life provided by Uttamadāsa has become regarded as an 'authorised' biography within the *sampradāya*, many parts of it are disputed by secondary sources. The discussion of these areas of dispute which follows cannot hope to resolve the biographical questions with any degree of certainty, but it may at least expose the roots of the more ill-founded claims and trace the origins of some of the confusions and contradictions in the various versions of the 'biography'.

(i) *The dates of Harivaṃśa's birth and death*

Two dates are proposed for the year of Harivaṃśa's birth: v.s. 1559 (A.D. 1502) appears in the texts of Uttamadāsa and Jayakṛṣṇa cited above, while the acceptance of a rival date of v.s. 1530 (A.D. 1473) is advocated by many later writers.

Among the most determined proponents of the earlier date is Gopālprasād Śarmmā, who cites a reference to this date in a *śloka* (from an unspecified text) attributed to Gosvāmī Kṛṣṇacandra (understood as Harivaṃśa's son Kṛṣṇadāsa).[1] In accordance with this dating, the alleged quincentenary of Harivaṃśa's birth was celebrated enthusiastically by most members of the Rādhāvallabhī community in A.D. 1973. Contributors to the souvenir volume of this event frequently re-affirm the v.s. 1530 date, but nowhere is convincing evidence put forward to

1. *viyadguṇeṣuśubhrāṃśu saṃkhye saṃvatsare śubhe.* [1] 530
mādhave māsi śuklaikādaśyāṃ ca somavāsare;
gosvāmī harivaṃśākhya[*ḥ*] *śrīmanmāthuramaṇḍale*
bādagrāme śubhasthāne prādurbhūto mahān guru[*ḥ*].
(Gopālprasād Śarmmā 1915:12.)

support it. The editor of the volume, Vijayendra Snātak, avoids any statement on this important question in his own contribution;[1] in his own major study of the *sampradāya*, however, Snātak argues strongly for acceptance of the later date.[2] Here he maintains that astrological calculations show the exact date given by Uttamadāsa for Harivaṃśa's birth—Monday the 11th day of the bright half of Vaiśākha—to be consistent with v.s. 1559 but not with v.s. 1530, when the '11th day' fell on a Saturday.

In his article on 'The Rādhāvallabhīs' (p. 559), Grierson gives A.D. 1502 as the date of Harivaṃśa's birth (though elsewhere[3] he gives the year as A.D. 1559). This appears to be a simple confusion of calendars, 1559 being the date of birth according to the Vikram, and not the Christian, calendar. The same mistake appears again in H.C. Conybeare's gazetteer of the North-West provinces (p. 103).

The lack of attested dates as points of reference makes it impossible to settle the question of Harivaṃśa's date of birth; none of Harivaṃśa's own works, and few other texts regarded as contemporary to his *floruit*, are dated. Given this lack of evidence in support of either of the proposed dates, one may postulate two judicious if somewhat cynical reasons for preferring the later of the two. Firstly, it is difficult to see why hagiographers of the Rādhāvallabhī *sampradāya* itself—Uttamadāsa and Jayakṛṣṇa—should deliberately postdate the birth of the revered author of their own tradition; secondly, the fact that the early date (A.D. 1473) neatly precedes the dates of birth of both Vallabha (A.D. 1479)[4] and Caitanya (A.D. 1486)[5] shows that there is some sectarian advantage to be gained by an antedating.

The v.s. 1609 date is given by Uttamadāsa for the death of Harivaṃśa, and is endorsed by Jayakṛṣṇa in the extract quoted above wherein Vanacandra is described as acceding to the sectarian *gaddī* in this year. Lalitā Caraṇ Gosvāmī reports (1957:52) that this date is also confirmed by extant temple records which show that Vanacandra was *adhikārī* of the shrine of Rādhāvallabha from v.s. 1609 to 1665 (A.D. 1552 to 1608).

Various claims have been made, however, that Harivaṃśa lived beyond A.D. 1552. Rāmacandra Śukla maintains (p. 124), without citing any authority, that in v.s. 1622 (A.D. 1565) Harirāma Vyāsa of Orcha became Harivaṃśa's disciple; and according to Vāsudev Gosvāmī (p. 88), the two devotees could not have met before v.s. 1612. But Snātak (1968:117) refutes the latter assertion, and shows on the basis of the *Rasika ananya māla* that Harirāma Vyāsa first came to Vrindaban

1. Vijayendra Snātak (ed.), 1975:31-40.
2. Vijayendra Snātak 1968:92.
3. G.A. Grierson 1909:546.
4. F.S. Growse 1883-283.
5. S.K. De, p. 68.

in V.S. 1591, thus allowing ample time for the association with Harivaṃśa to take place.

An early British source also suggests that Harivaṃśa lived beyond A.D. 1552. H.H. Wilson states that Harivaṃśa 'erected a temple there [in Vrindaban] that still exists, and indicates, by an inscription over the door, that it was dedicated to *Śrī Rādhā Vallabha* by Hari VANŚ, in Samvat 1641, or A.D. 1585'.[1] Since the gateway referred to no longer exists, it is not now possible to evaluate Wilson's interpretation of the inscription it carried. However, it is doubtful that the inscription stated categorically that the temple was dedicated by Harivaṃśa himself, since the accomplishment of any such major work would surely have been seized upon by the hagiographers. An inscribed dedication would naturally have included Harivaṃśa's name at some point, and it is tempting to speculate that the wording of Wilson's report conceals the true implications of the inscription. According to the *Rasika ananya māla*[2] and to sectarian tradition generally, the temple of Rādhāvallabha was built *after* the death of Harivaṃśa, during the incumbency of his eldest son and successor Vanacandra.

Few sectarian texts refer to the manner of Harivaṃśa's death. Uttamadāsa's allusive or metaphorical description of this event has already been referred to; the Bengali work *Premavilāsa* by the Gauḍīya author Nityānanda apparently gives a more specific and rather remarkable account, which is probably apocryphal since nothing like it appears in any early source. (The *Premavilāsa* has not been available for inspection at first hand: its contents are discussed by Lalitā Caraṇ Gosvāmī 1957: 45-51.) The text states that Harivaṃśa forfeited his life on the offence of eating *prasāda* on the *ekādaśī* fast day; the account seems to be an elaboration of the episode described in Kṛṣṇadāsa Bābā's *Bhaktamāla* discussed earlier. Gopālabhaṭṭa, identified in the text as *guru* to Harivaṃśa, allegedly took pity on his deceased 'disciple' and granted him salvation posthumously. This far-fetched account has little credibility, since the *Premavilāsa* is known to have been subject to accretion on a large scale.[3]

1. H.H. Wilson, 1862: 177.

2. Lalitāprasād Purohit (ed.), 1961:44-48. According to the *Rasika ananya māla* account, the temple of Rādhavallabha was built by a *kāyastha* named Sundaradāsa Bhaṭanāgara, a *dīvān* in the service of (Abdur Rahīm) K͟hānk͟hāna at Akbar's court. Many would-be patrons of the temple building, including Rājā Mānsingh who built the temple of Govindadeva (Growse 1883:243), were put off by a prediction made by Vanacandra that whoever undertook the project would die a year after its completion; Sundaradāsa accepted this stipulation and went ahead (with the financial backing of his employer). The prediction proved true, and Sundaradāsa breathed his last within the completed temple during the singing of CP 49 in *samāja*.

3. Bimānbihārī Majūmdār (p. 507), discussing the accretions to this text, remarks that 'the *Premavilāsa* grew bigger day by day in Vaiṣṇava homes just as Kṛṣṇa grew bigger day by day in the house of Nanda'.

(ii) *Harivaṃśa's parentage*

The tradition that Harivaṃśa's father was named Vyāsa is consistently asserted in the texts discussed in the above pages. Certain secondary sources do give some variations on the name: the 19th century history of Hindi literature *Miśrabandhuvinoda*[1] gives the name as 'Vyāsa Svāmī', and adds the *upanāma* 'Harirāma Śukla'. Baldev Upādhyāy, on the other hand, holds that Harivaṃśa's father was called Keśavadāsa and that his *upanāma* was 'Vyāsajī'.[2] Neither authority betrays the source of these allegations. In *The modern vernacular literature of Hindustan* (pp. 28-29), Grierson identifies Harivaṃśa's father, 'Byās Swāmī alias Hari Rām Śuk'l', with the poet (Harirāma) Vyāsa: there is no justification for this assertion (which has been followed by Pollet, p. 346) since no early source suggests a blood relationship between Harivaṃśa and Harirāma Vyāsa. Grierson follows a more orthodox line in his article on 'The Rādhāvallabhīs' (p. 559), where he states that Harivaṃśa was 'the son of a Gauḍ Brāhmaṇa living in the Sahāranpur district'.

Though we may accept the plausibility of the claim that Harivaṃśa's father was Vyāsa of Deoband, little more can be said about his forbears. His mother is identified as 'Tārā' by Dāmodaradāsa 'Sevaka' and Uttamadāsa, as shown in section 2(ii) above; Priyādāsa Śukla (p.19) claims to have found a rich source of information on Vyāsa's family in a text entitled *Hitacandrikā* (V. S. 1714, A.D. 1657) by one Jamunādāsa, but no copy of this text appears to be extant today. Śukla himself, writing at the beginning of the present century, reports that he was working from a single tattered copy of the text.

The identity of the monarch at whose court Vyāsa is said to have been employed is also uncertain. If Uttamadāsa's dates for the life of Harivaṃśa, A.D. 1502–1552, are even approximately correct, then the monarch ruling in Delhi at the time of Harivaṃśā's birth would have been Sikandar Lodi, who died in A.D. 1517.[3] As Lalitā Caraṇ Gosvāmī (1957:27) points out, there is considerable difficulty in believing that a fervent Muslim iconoclast such as Sikandar Lodi[4] would have shown much favour towards a Hindu *paṇḍita* such as Vyāsa, though some authorities hold that it was indeed Sikandar who was Vyāsa's patron. It is more likely that the monarch to whom Uttamadāsa refers was one of considerably lesser stature, for although Uttamadāsa refers to him by the words *pṛthvīpati*, *nṛpa*, *nariṃda* and *pātisāha*, there is no reason why such lofty titles should not refer to a local ruler in the hyperbolical context of hagiography. Two sources, Priyādāsa Śukla and Bābā Hit Dās,

1. Gaṇeśbihārī, Śyāmbihārī and Śukdevbihārī Miśra, Vol. I, p. 294.
2. Baldev Upādhyāy 1953:422.
3. Vincent A. Smith, p. 262.
4. 'It is said that in Mathura "and other places" [Sikandar] turned temples into mosques, and established Muslim Sarais, colleges and bazars in the Hindu places of worship.' Kishori Saran Lal, p. 191.

do name the monarch. Śukla (p. 23) maintains that he was Vijaya Bahādur, a courtier of the emperor Homayoun and grandson of Kīrticandra. The court to which Vijaya Bahādur summoned Vyāsa was, according to Śukla, at Bijnaur—in the same (modern) district as Vyāsa's alleged home of Deoband. But the chronology proposed by Śukla is confused: he states that it was Kīrticandra who defeated Sher Shāh and reinstated Homayoun to the Delhi throne. Homayoun's return to power took place in A.D. 1555[1]: how then could Kīrticandra's *grandson* have been ruling at Bijnaur at the supposed time of Harivaṃśa's birth 53 years earlier? A more feasible proposition is put forward by Bābā Hit Dās (p. 31) who maintains that Vyāsa was *guru* to Kīrticandra himself, and not his grandson; but it is still impossible to assess the validity of the proposed account without knowing the source whence it came. It may be pointed out, finally, that Saharanpur itself must have held a court capable of offering patronage of the kind described by Uttamadāsa, as it was one of the eight *sarkārs* (sub-divisions) of the *sūbah* of Delhi during Akbar's reign; and Deoband was one of the 36 *mahāls* (revenue divisions) constituting that *sūbah*.[2] Though Akbar's reign had not yet begun at the alleged time of Harivaṃśa's birth, it is clear that Saharanpur was a centre of some importance during the sixteenth century.

(iii) *Harivaṃśa's Offspring*

The number of children born to Harivaṃśa's various wives is another aspect of his life to be disputed. Most sectarian authorities maintain that three sons–Vanacandra, Kṛṣṇacandra (or Kṛṣṇadāsa) and Gopīnātha—and a daughter Sāhiba De were born to his first wife Rukmiṇī, and that a fourth son Mohanacandra was born to one of the two wives taken by him during his journey from Deoband to Vrindaban. The offspring of the first marriage are mentioned by Uttamadāsa, though not by name; in the passage from Jayakṛṣṇa's text quoted in section 2(ii) above, the dates of birth of Rukmiṇī's sons are given as V.S. 1585, 1587 and 1588; Snātak (p. 112) also reports Jayakṛṣṇa as giving Mohanacandra's birthdate as V.S. 1598. Jayakṛṣṇa appears not to mention the birthdate of Harivaṃśa's daughter.

Harivaṃśa's four sons are again mentioned in *dohās* 3 to 6 of Dhruvadāsa's *Bhaktanāmāvalī*, also quoted above. Various other sources give conflicting details as to Harivaṃśa's children; Pratāpasiṃha's *Bhaktamāla* (p. 70), which in most other respects follows Nābhādāsa and Uttamadāsa, mentions only two sons and a daughter as the offspring of Harivaṃśa's first marriage. Growse follows suit (1883; 199, 202) saying that Mohan Chand, Gopīnāth and a daughter were the offspring of Harivaṃśa's first marriage, while his later marriages produced Braj

1. Vincent A. Smith, p. 324.
2. H.S. Jarrett (trans.), Vol. II, pp. 105 and 292.

Chand and Krishan Chand. Nityānanda's Bengali *Premavilāsa* (discussed by Lalitā Caraṇ Gosvāmī, 1957: 47) gives the names of Harivaṃśa's children as Kṛṣṇadāsa, Sūryadāsa, Vanacandra and Vṛndāvanacandra respectively. That these last two sources are incorrect is shown by the fact that it was Vanacandra who inherited the *gaddī* from his father, and from whom the present *adhikārīs* claim descent; Vanacandra must therefore have been the eldest son of Harivaṃśa. This vindicates Jayakṛṣṇa's version, and it is reasonable to suppose that he is also accurate with respect to the other three children. The date given by Jayakṛṣṇa for the birth of Kṛṣṇadāsa, A.D. 1531, is not inconsistent with the date of composition of Kṛṣṇadāsa's *Karṇānanda*, A.D. 1578, discussed above.

One undisputed area of Harivaṃśa's biography may also be included here for the sake of completeness, and that is the question of his place of birth and his family home. In the texts discussed in section 2(ii), Dāmodaradāsa 'Sevaka' and Uttamadāsa give the village of Bād (some six miles south of Mathura) as the birthplace of Hita Harivaṃśa. All sectarian sources agree on this point, and no other evidence is forthcoming to challenge them. The alleged birthplace is now marked by a small Rādhāvallabhī settlement called Vyās Bhavan, which is in the hands of the ascetic branch (*nāda parivāra*) of the *sampradāya*. Vyās Bhavan consists of a small temple and a *rāsamaṇḍala* (a round stone platform used as a stage for *rāsalīlā* dramas) in a pleasant site on the border of Bād village, on a rise above a large pond. The interior of the temple doorway is surmounted by a painting which depicts the birth of Hita Harivaṃśa in an idealized setting, reflecting Uttamadāsa's comparison of the birth of Harivaṃśa with the appearance of Kṛṣṇa in the house of Nanda.

There seems to be little doubt that the family home of Harivaṃśa was, as Uttamadāsa states, in Deoband. No early text contradicts this, and the image of Kṛṣṇa as 'Raṅgīlāla jī' which Harivaṃśa reputedly consecrated and worshipped there is to this day attended by a family of Harivaṃśa's descendants.

(iv) *Harivaṃśa's Original Sectarian Allegiance*

The final controversy in the biography of Harivaṃśa is the vexed problem of his original sectarian allegiance; the question of who had been his *guru* before he established his own path of *bhakti* is still hotly contested. Harivaṃśa has been variously described as associated with the Nimbārka, Mādhva, Vallabha and Gauḍīya traditions. Two of the least sensible claims may be dismissed without deliberation: firstly that of the Rev. M.A. Sherring who maintains (p. 261) that 'the founder of the [Rādhāvallabha] sect was Vallabha Swāmī'; secondly the fantastic statement of A.K. Majumdar (p. 51) that 'Nandadāsa [was] the founder of the Rādhā-Vallabhī sect and author of the Hita-Harivaṃśa'. The first of these statements may perhaps be based on a simple confusion of the names 'Vallabha' and 'Rādhāvallabha'; the second appears to be entirely fanciful, since no connection at all is apparent between Nandadāsa (the celebrated member of the Vallabhite *aṣṭachāpa* group of poets) and the Rādhāvallabha *sampradāya*. Furthermore, Majumdar has evidently been mislead by the title of the Sanskrit text *Harivaṃśa* into supposing that 'Hita Harivaṃśa' must also be the title of a literary work.

A third claim as to Harivaṃśa's sectarian allegiance, that he was a member of the Nimbārkī sect, can also be shown to be ill-founded. This claim stems from an error perpetrated by the mid-19th century Hindi littérateur 'Bhāratendu' Hariścandra in his *Vaiṣṇava sarvasva*. In a list of the *guru paramparās* of the Viṣṇusvāmī, Madhva, Caitanya, Rāmānuja and Nimbāditya *sampradāyas*, the fourth *śākhā* of the Nimbāditya *paramparā* includes the name of Hita Harivaṃśa. The *śākhā* is listed as follows: 'Vyāsadeva, Paraśurāma, Hitaharivaṃśa, Nārāyaṇahita, Vṛndāvanahita, Śrī Govindahita'.[1] But for the title '*hita*' which appears in four of the names, the list constitutes exactly the Nimbārkī *guru paramparā* descended from Harivyāsa Deva.[2] It seems that Hariścandra has erroneously used the Rādhāvallabhī title '*hita*' in place of the Nimbārkī, '*deva*', and that the Harivaṃśa referred to is thus the Nimbārkī Harivaṃśa Deva, who inherited the *gaddī* at Salimabad from his celebrated *guru* Paraśurāma.[3]

The contention that Harivaṃśa was a Mādhva comes from Growse (1883:200): 'Originally he had belonged to the Madhvāchārya Sampradāya, and from them and from the Nimbāraks, who also claim him, his doctrine and ritual were professedly derived'. Unfortunately Growse does not name the professors of this theory.

The only other specific statement about Harivaṃśa's sectarian background which differs from the Rādhāvallabhī view is that made first by the Bengali *Bhaktamāla* and endorsed later by the *Premavilāsa* of Nityānanda: these texts maintain that Harivaṃśa was a disciple of Gopalabhaṭṭa—a claim not found in any but Bengali sources.

Uttamadāsa's account of Harivaṃśa's life proposes a harmonious and feasible chronology, and as such is generally accepted—with the exception of the disputed date of birth—by sectarian writers and historians of Hindi literature as a historical record. The fact is, however, that the account will remain largely speculative until it can be substantiated by real historical evidence The occurrence of a piece of information in more than one hagiographic source often suggests collusion rather than corroboration, though the typically more reverential view of most Indian writers on such subjects would no doubt regard this circumspection as unduly cynical. It is greatly to be hoped that the temple archives of the Rādhāvallabhī tradition will one day become accessible

1. Vrajaratan Dās (ed.) p. 563.
2. Nārāyaṇ Datt Śarmā, p. 49.
3. *Ibid.*, p. 53.

for study, so that the biographical and historical questions raised here may be discussed on the basis of rather more sound evidence.

4. Further texts attributed to Hita Harivaṃśa

(i) The '*Sphuṭa vāṇī*'

In addition to the CP, a second anthology of BrBh. stanzas is attributed to Hita Harivaṃśa. In the edition of Lalitā Caraṇ Gosvāmī (1972), given the siglum W for the purposes of this discussion, the anthology has the title *Sphuṭa vāṇī* and consists of 27 stanzas. '*Sphuṭa vāṇī*' is taken as a working title here, but the sources discussed below show a number of variations: it is apparent that this and other appellations are intended as descriptive labels rather than as formal titles deriving authoritatively from a single author or compiler.

The *Sphuṭa vāṇī* does not appear in manuscripts as commonly as does the CP. Two manuscripts in the Vrindaban Research Institute's collection are analysed here. The first, given the siglum X, is V.R.I. Hindi MS 7848, a 20th century manuscript including among a number of sectarian works the *Sphuṭa vāṇī* with a commentary by Priyādāsa. A discrepancy exists between the title of the text as it appears at the head of the text and as it appears in the colophon, as can be seen from the following transcription (copied verbatim):

Begins (f.1^r): *śrī rādhāvallabho jayati. śrīhitaharivaṃśacandro jayati. atha śrīhitaharivaṃśa jū ke phuṭakara padõ kī ṭīkā likhyate. priyādāsa jū kṛta.*

Ends (f.230^v): *iti śrīmaddhitaharivaṃśacandracaraṇāraviṃdamaṃda makaraṃdamadhuvrata priyādāsakṛta sphuṭapadaṭīkā samāpta. phālguna kṛṣṇa 4 vikramī saṃvata 1961 hitadāśākṣarāṇi. māgha sudī 4. saṃvata 1982.*

In this manuscript the order of *dohās* 25 and 27 is inverted *vis-à-vis* the order in W. An additional 8-line *pada*,[1] bearing the *chāpa* of Harivaṃśa but introduced as *bheṭa kau pada* and therefore not actually attributed to him, concludes the text. X defines the contents of the anthology as comprising two component sections[2] (although a single numbering sequence subsists throughout) by interposing the following colophon between stanzas 9 and 10:

(ff. 92^v–93^r): *iti siddhāṃta pada. atha rasa ke pada prāraṃbha.*

Vrindaban Research Institute Hindi MS 4410 (siglum Y), which provides text E for the present edition of the CP and which also contains

1. See Appendix III.
2. A similar division into *rasa* and *siddhānta* contexts occurs in the *vāṇī* of Haridāsa, comprising the anthologies *Kelimāla* and *Aṣṭādaśa siddhānta* respectively (Prabhudayāl Mītal 1971).

the text of the *Rādhāsudhānidhi* discussed below, contains 14 stanzas corresponding to stanzas 10-23 of the sequence in W; this group of stanzas comprises the so-called '*rasa*' section as identified by X, but omitting the four final *dohās* (which return to *siddhānta*[1] material). The stanzas are headed:

īte śrīhita jū ke pada codaha liṣyate

The siglum Z is given to the final source to be evaluated here: this is also the published source of CP text 'G' in the present edition (Vijaypāl Siṃha and Candrabhān Rāvat, 1971). Here again the anthology is divided into two component sections. Under the heading *atha śrī jī kī bānī liṣyate* (*ibid.*, p. 199) appears the *rasa* sequence corresponding to stanzas 10-23 in W, followed by the colophon *iti sphuṭa pada pūrṇa* (*ibid.*, p. 204); this is followed by the heading *atha kabitta kuṃḍaliyā arilla chappai* (*loc. cit.*) and the 10 *siddhānta* stanzas (in a new numbering sequence) corresponding to W's stanzas 1-9, 24. The final colophon reads *iti śrī kabittādi pūrṇa. śrī śrī.* (*ibid.*, p. 206). The final three *dohās* of W's text (25-27) are thus absent from Z.

The contents of the four sources are tabulated below in a concordance.

Table 1: Concordance of *Sphuṭa vāṇī* texts

	X	Y	Z	
W1 :	1		1	(2nd sequence)
W2 :	2		2	,, ,,
W3 :	3		3	,, ,,
W4 :	4		4	,, ,,
W5 :	5		5	,, ,,
W6 .	6		6	,, ,,
W7 :	7		7	,, ,,
W8 :	8		8	,, ,,
W9 :	9		9	,, ,,
W10 :	10	1	1	
W11 :	11	2	2	
W12 :	12	3	3	

1. The so-called *siddhānta* stanzas are in fact more didactic than exegetical. The difference in style between the *siddhānta* and *rasa* sections can be seen by comparing stanzas 9 and 23 (the latter being close in style to the CP):

Sphuṭa vāṇī 9 (Lalitā Caraṇ Gosvāmī 1972:151)
mānuṣa kau tana pāya bhajo brajanātha kõ;
darbī laikai mūḍha jarāvata hātha kõ.
(*jai śrī*) *hita harivaṃśa prapaṃca viṣaya rasa moha ke;*
(*hari hā̃*) *bina kaṃcana kyaū̃ calaī pacīsā loha ke.*

Sphuṭa vāṇī 23 (*Ibid.*, p. 166)
doū jana bhī̃jata aṭake bātana;
saghana kuñja ke dvāṛe ṭhāṛhe aṃbara lapaṭe gātana.
lalitā lalita rūpa rasa bhījī bū̃da bacāvata pātana;
(*jai śrī*) *hita harivaṃśa paraspara prītama milavata ratirasa ghātana.*

	X	Y	Z	
W13 :	13	4	4	
W14 :	14	5	5	
W15 :	15	6	6	
W16 :	16	7	7	
W17 :	17	8	8	
W18 :	18	9	9	
W19 :	19	10	10	
W20 :	20	11	11	
W21 :	21	12	12	
W22 :	22	13	13	
W23 :	23	14	14	
W24 :	24		10	(2nd sequence)
W25 :	27			
W26 :	26			
W27 :	25			

The Nāgarī Pracāriṇī Sabhā's report on the searches for Hindi manuscripts in the year 1909-1911 (Shyam Behari Misra 1914: 180) lists an undated manuscript in a temple collection in Mirzapur. Catalogued as *Phuṭakara báni*, the text is quoted as being headed *śrī hita ju* [*sic*] *kī bānī*. The extent of the text is recorded as being 101 *ślokas*, but this is evidently a misprint as the number of folios is given as only four. The text begins with W 1, and a citation from the middle of the text is of W 15; the text ends with a *pada* numbered 13 (!) which does not appear in W, X, Y or Z.

In comparison with the CP, contexts in the *Sphuṭa vāṇī* show less concentration on the *nikuñja vihāra* and a greater concern with a broader mythology and with the external manifestations of Vaiṣṇava *sādhanā*.[1] Stanzas 3, 4, 7, 8, 9 and 20 comprise exhortations to turn away from the world and worship Kṛṣṇa, and so to make the most of a valuable human birth: this is a theme familiar from the *vinaya* sequences of the *Sūrasāgara*, but notably absent from the CP. Stanzas 18 and 19 describe the *āratī* of Kṛṣṇa in terminology much more closely related to the actuality of temple worship than occurs in CP contexts. Other themes not found in the CP include the celebratory songs of the birth of *Rādhā* (stanza 16) and of Kṛṣṇa (stanza 11), and the eschatological preoccupations of stanza 4.[2] While doctrinal points made in the poems of the so-called *siddhānta* sequence are mostly quite general and applicable in a wide Vaiṣṇava context, certain references have a more restricted sectarian intention; an example is the first of the four *dohās* (text W), which catalogues the essential elements of life as a devotee and includes the sectarian catchwords *hita* and *rādhāvallabha*:

1. Compare a similar feature in four additional stanzas bearing Harivaṃśa's *chāpa*, but not actually attributed to him, given in Appendix III.
2. Especially in 4.3 (Lalitā Caraṇ Gosvāmī 1972: 147):
(jai śrī) hita harivaṃśa naraka gati durabhara
yamadvāre kaṭiyata naka chīke.

saba sõ hita niṣkāma mati vṛndābana viśrāma;
(śrī) rādhāballabhalāla kau hṛdaya dhyāna mukha nāma.[1]

'Repose in Vṛndāvana with a mind beneficent to all and free from desire; reflection on dear Rādhāvallabha in the heart, and his name on the lips.'

The *Sphuṭa vāṇī* includes many stanzas in metres not represented in the CP; among these are the composite metres *chappaya* (stanzas 3, 7) and *kuṇḍaliyā* (stanzas 5, 6). Many of the stanzas have a rather imperfect scansion in the texts seen.

In vocabulary also a distinction is apparent between this text and the CP. Many words may owe their inclusion here to a difference in genre (in the didactic, doctrinal and eschatological contexts) rather than to a difference in authorship; but this does not explain such distinctions as exist in the epithets used to refer to Kṛṣṇa in the two texts. Whereas the name *kṛṣṇa* itself occurs in the CP only in the single formulaic compound *kṛṣṇa rasāmṛta sāra* (CP 30.17), in the *Sphuṭa vāṇī* it occurs seven times (1.4, 4.1, 7.6, 8.1, 8.5, 18.5, 25.2); cf. also the epithets *brajapati* (8.3), *brajanātha* (9.1), *govardhanadhara* (17.1) and significantly *rādhāvallabha* (24.2, 26.2), which do not appear in the CP at all.

A morphological peculiarity of the text *vis-à-vis* the CP is the prominent use of double consonants, as in *yaddi* (1.2), *nikajja* (5.1); their inclusion alongside more usual Hindi forms is apparently *metri causa.*

In more general terms the *Sphuṭa vāṇī* is characterised by a more colloquial and vernacular style than that found in the CP. The CP's Sanskritic compounds are not so common here. Many of the didactic stanzas have an admonitory tenor which is quite foreign to the CP style: an example is the blunt *tū bālaka nahī̃* which constitutes the opening phrase of stanza 4[2]; cf. also the colloquial use of vocative *bhaiyā* in 8.1.

While it is not possible to reach any definite conclusion about the history of the *Sphuṭa vāṇī* on the basis of the available manuscript evidence, the autonomy of the *rasa* sequence (W 10-23) suggests that this group may derive from a different source from the remainder of the text. The fact that *padas* in the *siddhānta* section (including the four *dohās* 24-27) contain more specifically sectarian material than the *rasa padas* suggests that the former may derive from a later stratum in sectarian tradition; while Snātak (1968:303) concludes that the *Sphuṭa vāṇī* is likely to be a later work than the CP, he does not venture the logical conclusion that the two texts are likely to be the work of two distinct authors.

(*ii*) *The 'Śrīmukha patrī'*

Two letters in BrBh. prose are ascribed to Hita Harivaṃśa. No manu-

1. *Ibid.*, p. 166.
2. *Ibid.*, p. 147.

script copy has been available for inspection; Snātak reports the same difficulty in his discussion of the letters (1968:330), but subsequently cites variants from 'old copies' (*ibid.*, p. 331). The letters are commonly included in 'bazaar' editions of Harivaṃśa's works; such editions are clearly unreliable, but *faute de mieux* must form the basis of discussion here.[1]

Both letters are addressed to a devotee named Vīṭhaladāsa. One Viṭ(h)ṭhaladāsa is the subject of a section of the *Rasika ananya māla*, where he is identified as an employee at the court of Junagarh (Kathiawar) and a disciple of Hita Harivaṃśa (Lalitāprasād Purohit (ed.) 1960:13-14); this reference mentions correspondence between *guru* and disciple. The language of the letters is not inconsistent with the Sanskritized BrBh. of the CP, allowing for the difference between prose and verse styles (especially in the greater use in the former of the auxiliary verb in composition with participles). A reference to CP 29.1 appears in the phrase *braja nava taruṇi kadamba* in the second letter. Occurrence of the form *rādhe* in a non-vocative context in the same sentence reflects a widespread tendency in BrBh. usage to apply this form generally without consideration of case.

In content the two letters consist mainly of the formulas of correspondence, interlarded with such blessings and assurances as a *guru* might be expected to extend to his disciple. The first letter concludes with messages of goodwill to other devotees (suggesting perhaps that the Rādhāvallabhī foothold in Gujarat, which is a feature of the modern sect, had an early beginning); the second includes in the fourth sentence (see note 1) a slightly terse reminder that lack of faith is

1. The letters are brief enough to be quoted in full. The texts given here are taken from Snātak (1968:331), who cites them from a sectarian anthology entitled *Śrī hitāmṛta sindhu* edited by Hit Gobardhandās (Vrindaban).

I श्री सकल गुण सम्पन्न रस रीति बढ़ावन चिरंजीव मेरे प्राणन के प्राण वीठलदास योग्य लिखित श्री वृन्दावन रजोपसेवी हरिवंश जोरी सुमरिन बंचवौ । जोरी सुमरिन मत्त रहा । जोरी जोहै सुख बरषत है। तुम कुशल स्वरूप है । तिहारे हस्ताक्षर बारंबार आवत है। सुख अमृत स्वरूप है। पत्री वांचत आनन्द उमड़ि चलै है। मेरी बुद्धि कों इतनी शक्ति नहीं जो कहि सकों पर तोहि जानत हों। श्री स्वामिनी जी तुम पर बहुत प्रसन्न हैं। हम कहा आशीर्वाद देंय, हम यही आशीर्वाद देत हैं कि तिहारो आयुष बढ़ौ और तिहारी सकल सम्पत्ति बढ़ौ । तिहारे मन को मनोरथ पूरण होहु, हम नेत्रनि मुख देखें, हमारी भेंट यही है। यहाँ की काहू बात की चिन्ता मत करो, तेरी पहिचान तैं मोंकूं श्री श्यामाजू बहुत सुख देत हैं। तुम लिखी हो दिन दश में आवेंगे सोई आशा प्राण रहे हैं । श्री श्यामाजू वेगि ले आयें। चिरंजीव कृष्णदास कौ जोरी प्रसन्न है, श्याम वन्दिनी विहार चन्दन लेनों। गोविन्ददास, सन्तदास की दंडौत, गांगू मेदा को कृष्ण सुमिरन बांचनौ, कृष्णदास मोहनदास को कृष्ण सुमिरन, रंगा की दंडौत, वनमाली धर्मशाला को कृष्ण सुमिरन बांचनो ।

II श्री वृषभानु नन्दिनी जयति । जोग्य लिखित श्री हरिवंश वीठलदास के कोटि-कोटि अपराध में सेवी आगले पाछिले। वीठलदास मेरे प्राण हैं। जो शास्त्र मर्यादा सत्य है और गुरु महिमा ऐसे ही सत्य ह तो ब्रज नव तरुणि कदम्ब चूड़ामणि श्री राधे तिहारे स्थापे गुरुमार्ग विषै अविश्वास अज्ञानी कों होत है तातैं यह मर्यादा राखनौ। तुम दोऊ सफल आनन्द बरसौ । बीठलदास को अहो सींचनौ ॥ इति ।

the product of ignorance. The letters do not betray any specifically sectarian drift; the term *hita* does not occur (either as *upanāma* or independently), and references to the deity are to Rādhā (as *rādhe, vṛṣabhānunandinī, śyāmā* and *svāminī*), to Kṛṣṇa, or to 'the couple' (*jorī*), and not to Rādhāvallabha.

In the absence of manuscript evidence, the attribution to Hita Harivaṃśa of these letters remains speculative; but the attribution is certainly plausible, and given the rather unremarkable contents of the letters it is unlikely that they represent sectarian forgeries.

(*iii*) *Rādhāsudhānidhi*

This Sanskrit text is a *stotrakāvya* in 270 *ślokas*. Numerous manuscripts of the text exist in libraries in the Braj area and further afield, and (with some exceptions discussed below) the attribution of the text is to Hita Harivaṃśa. An example is MS 4410 in the Vrindaban Research Institute's collection[1]; this manuscript also contains the text of the CP given the siglum 'E' in the present edition, and is described under II.1 below. The *mūla* of the *Rādhāsudhānidhi* is preceded by the dedication *śrīrādhāvallabho jayati* (f.1r)[2], and is followed by the colophon:

iti śrīvṛṃdāvaneśvarīcaraṇakṛpāmātravijṛṃbhitaṃ
śrīrādhāsudhānidhistavaḥ śrīhitaharivaṃśagosvāminā
viracitaḥ saṃpūrṇaḥ.

(The scribal colophon, giving the date v.s. 1825, has been transcribed in the description of CP text 'E' in section II.1 below.)

Some manuscripts bear the alternative title *Rādhārasasudhānidhi*. An example is Vrindaban Research Institute 2309[3]; this is a complete manuscript of 55 folios of which ff. 1, 31, 45 and 46 are replacement folios in a different hand from that of the remainder. The 270 *ślokas* of the text are followed by the colophon:

iti śrīvṛṃdāveśvarīcaraṇakṛpāmātravijṛṃbhita[ṃ]
śrīmadrādhārasasudhānidhiḥ stavaḥ śrīmad hitaharivaṃsa
caṃdragosvāmīnā viracitaḥ samāptaḥ. 18.48 posa vadī 9.

The former of these titles, *Rādhāsudhānidhi*, appears in the colophons of V.R.I. manuscripts 3263[4] and 4358, while the latter, *Rādhārasasudhānidhi*, appears in 344[5] and 8836[6] (dated v.s. 1956). The compound

1. Cat. no. 5472: R.D. Gupta and J.C. Wright (eds.) 1978:302.
2. As noted in the description of this manuscript in section II.1, each of its component texts bears a separate pagination sequence.
3. Cat. no. 1338-E: R.D. Gupta and M.L. Gupta (eds.) 1976:160. (Catalogued as *Rādhāsudhāṇidhi.*)
4. Cat. no. 2260: R.D. Gupta and M.L. Gupta (eds.) 1976:270.
5. Cat. no. 2259 (*loc cit.*).
6. Cat. no. 8786: R.D. Gupta and J.C. Wright (eds.) 1981: 312. (Catalogued as *Rādhāsudhānidhi.*)

rasasudhānidhi appears in the final *śloka* of the text,[1] but this cannot of itself be regarded as proof that *rasa* has a place in the original title. Thus it is not possible to resolve the discrepancy in the title on the basis of the presently available material. Widespread usage in discussions of Rādhāvallabhī literature establishes *Rādhāsudhānidhi* as the generally preferred title; the inclusion of *rasa* in the compound, on the other hand, yields a logical semantic link between *rādhā* and *sudhānidhi* without which the title is to some extent elliptical. (Use of suffixed *caṃdra* with the poet's name in the second colophon quoted may, incidentally, be an extension of the *sudhānidhi* image.) No available manuscript supports Growse's statement (1883:203) that the text consists of 170 *ślokas*: this seems to be a printing error.

A rival claim as to the authorship of the *Rādhāsudhānidhi* is made by the Gauḍīya *sampradāya*, in which tradition the text is attributed to Prabodhānanda Sarasvatī. One manuscript in the Vrindaban Research Institute collection bears a colophon bearing this attribution (almost certainly fraudulently, as a late imposition), and another (incomplete) manuscript begins with a Gauḍīya dedication. These will now be discussed in turn.

MS 6626[2] is complete in 50 folios. The original invocation preceding the text, written in red ink, is still legible as *śrīrādhāvallabhojayati*; but the original *akṣaras* —*vallabho*— have been covered in black ink by the replacement —*ramaṇo*—, yielding the Gauḍīya invocation *śrīrādhāramaṇojayati*. In addition, a *śloka* in praise of Caitanya[3] has been added above the text. The final folio is a complete replacement of the original, written in a different hand; the folio number of f.50 is preceded by the siglum *su. ni.* instead of the *su.* which appears in ff. 1-49. Following the *mūla* of the text as it appears in the manuscripts discussed above, a salutation to Caitanya is given as an extra *śloka*,[4] and is finally followed by the colophon attributing the whole text to Prabodhānanda:

> *iti śrīpravodhānaṃdagosvāmiviracitaṃ rādhāsudhānidhi-*
> *stotraṃ saṃpūrnaṃ śrīrādhāramaṇojayataḥ. rāma*

The *akṣaras* of the words *rādhāsudhānidhistotraṃ saṃpū-* of this

1. *adbhutānandalobhaścennāmnā rasasudhānidhiḥ;*
stavo [']yaṃ karṇakalaśairgṛhītvā pīyatāṃ budhāḥ.
(Bābā Hit Dās (ed.) p. 163.)
2. Cat. no. 5475: R.D. Gupta and J.C. Wright (eds..) 1978:302.
3. *niṃdaṃtaṃ pulakotkareṇa vikasannīpaprasūnachaviṃ*
prordhvīkṛtya bhujadvayaṃ harihariīty uccair vadaṃtaṃ muhuḥ;
nṛtyaṃtaṃ drutam aśrunirjharacayaiḥ kurvaṃtam urvītalaṃ
gāyadbhir nijapārṣadaiḥ parikṛtaṃ śrīgauracaṃdraṃ stumaḥ.
(Literal transcription.)
4. *sajayati gaurapayaudharmāyāvādārkatāpasaṃtaptaṃ;*
sannabhaüda śītala padyorādhārasasudhānidhinā. 271.
(The *akṣaras* of *sannabhaüda*, evidently corrupt, are written over damage to the folio, perhaps by a later hand.)

colophon appear to have been re-written over damage to the folio, but apparently in the same hand.

MS 3263 is incomplete; ff. 1, 3-9, 11-22 survive, bearing the text of *ślokas* 1-5 (part), 19-83 (part), and 91 (part)–187 (part). The text is preceded by the invocation *śrī[rā]dhā[kṛ]ṣṇā[ya]namaḥ* (in which alternate syllables have been left blank, intending completion in red ink). The first *śloka* of the text is the same encomium to Caitanya which appears as an addition to MS 6626 (see note 3, page 43); this is here incorporated into the *mūla* and followed by the numeral '1'. Subsequent *śloka* numbering in the remainder of the folio is subsequently one in advance of the usual order, but this discrepancy has disappeared by the beginning of f.3 (*śloka* 19), showing that one *śloka* from the sequence 6-18 has been omitted from the missing second folio.

The evidence of these manuscripts is consistent with the conclusion drawn by S.K. De (p. 132 n. 3) as to the authorship of the text. On the basis of the colophons of manuscripts held in the India Office Library, the Bodleian Library and the Asiatic Society of Bengal, De concludes that the attribution of the text to Prabodhānanda 'is obviously a case of appropriation by the Caitanya sect of a work composed by Hitaharivaṃśa of the Rādhāvallabhī sect!'. Other scholars of the Gauḍīya tradition, however, have identified passages in the *Rādhā*[-*rasa*-]*sudhānidhi* showing correspondences with passages from other texts attributed to Prabodhānanda: *Saṅgītamādhava, Vṛndāvanamahimāmṛta* and *Caitanyacandrāmṛta*. Śakuntalā Agravāl (p. 65 n.1) cites, for example, the following *ślokas* from *Rādhārasasudhānidhi* and the unpublished *Saṅgītamādhava*:

gatā dūre gāvo dinamapi turīyāṃśamabhaja-
dvayaṃ dātuṃ kṣāṃtāstava ca janani vartmanayā;
akasmāttūṣṇīke sajalanayane dīnavadane
luṭhatyasyāṃ bhūmau tvayi nahi vayaṃ prāṇiṇiṣavaḥ.
Rādhārasasudhānidhi 229
(=228 in Rādhāvallabhī sources).

gatā dūre gāvo dinamapi turīyāṃśamabhaja-
dvayaṃ kṣutkṣāmāḥ sma stava ca janani vartmanayaḥ;
akasmāttūṣṇīke sajalanayane dīnavadane
tvayi tyaktvā khelāṃ nahi nahi vayaṃ prāṇiniṣavaḥ.
Saṅgītamādhava 50.

Further correspondences are cited by Agravāl, by Sundarānanda Dāsa 'Vidyāvinoda' (pp. 93-96), and by Anantadāsa Bābājī (p. viii).[1] A

1. Anantadāsa repeats much of Sundarānanda Dāsa's material *verbatim*, without acknowledgment.

detailed discussion of these citations is beyond the scope of the present study, though it may be noted that in many instances the correspondences cited as proof of common authorship are actually quite formulaic; an example is the recurring conceit of *rādhāpadanakhajyoti*, allegedly a favourite of Prabodhānanda, which Sundarānanda Dāsa (p. 95)[1] cites as below:

> *śrīrādhāpadanakhamaṇi jyoti*
> (*Caitanyacandrāmṛta* 68)
> *yasyāḥ sphūrjjatpadanakhamaṇijyotiḥ*
> (*Rādhārasasudhānidhi* 136)
> *tadpādāmbhojarājannakhamaṇivilāsajyotiḥ*
> (*Rādhārasasudhānidhi* 147)
> *vṛṣabhānujāpadanakhajyotiḥ*
> (*Rādhārasasudhānidhi* 268)

These conceits are standard rhetoric, such as forms the stock-in-trade of devotional poets, and cannot prove identity of authorship. The parallels between the two *ślokas* quoted earlier, however, cannot be dismissed lightly and clearly do demonstrate some kind of relationship between the two texts. While seized upon by the Gauḍīya camp as proving the Prabodhānanda attribution, such correspondences may, however, equally well lead to quite different conclusions: it is possible that the *Saṅgītamādhava* contains plagiarized passages from the *Rādhā*(*-rasa-*) *sudhānidhi*, or vice versa, or that both texts include plagiarisms from a third source. In their anxiety to substantiate a foregone conclusion, Agravāl and the other authors here mentioned spoil their case by introducing weak or false arguments. Agravāl, for example, insists that since Harivaṃśa wrote no other Sanskrit work except the unsubstantiated *Yamunāṣṭaka,* he 'cannot' have been the author of the *stotra* to Rādhā (p. 67): that the absence here of the *chāpa* of Harivaṃśa, which is so persistent a feature of the CP, is significant (!): that the *vandanā ślokas* showing allegiance to Caitanya are 'invariably' present in the old manuscripts.

A piece of circumstantial evidence consistent with the attribution to Harivaṃśa is the existence of an imitative text entitled *Upasudhānidhi*, whose unchallenged attribution is to Harivaṃśa's son Kṛṣṇadāsa; this text is included in MS 4410, discussed on p. 42 above.

Given the uncertainties surrounding the biographical and bibliographical data relating to both Harivaṃśa and Prabodhānanda, it is possible that the fiercely debated attribution of this Sanskrit text cannot finally be resolved. A full survey of all available manuscripts, and of the contents of the various texts mentioned in this discussion, has, however, yet to be undertaken. At the present time absolute conviction

1. Repeated by Anantadāsa, p. viii.

in favour of one or other attribution can be held only by those who are content to be swayed by sectarian allegiance.

While general correspondences in theme are commonplace between the *Rādhāsudhānidhi* and the CP, it is not possible to locate specific passages in the former which reflect in any detail those passages in the CP showing a Sanskritic diction; thus authorship of neither text can be verified or disproved by comparison with the other. In context and style the *Rādhāsudhānidhi* bears a rather different stamp from the CP taken as a whole, although it is not dissimilar from those CP stanzas in which Rādhā holds the predominant role; in the Sanskrit text, however, the subservient and secondary position of Kṛṣṇa is much more clearly asserted. As in the CP, the servile position of the poet is equated with that of the devotee/*sakhī*, but here the descriptive praise of Rādhā is expressed in terms of plangent and anguished longing, in marked contrast to contexts in the CP where the *sakhī*'s vicarious enjoyment of the *nikuñja vihāra* is reported in a more neutral tone as a *fait accompli*. The need to receive Rādhā's grace, an idea barely present in the CP (except perhaps in isolated passages such as 73.5) is often expressed here; similarly, the desire for a vision of Rādhā (visible 'only in Vṛndāvana'[1]) here takes the place of the CP's preoccupation with the joint form of Rādhā and Kṛṣṇa united.

The relevance of the *Rādhāsudhānidhi* to the sectarian interpretation of the CP is discussed in Chapter VII.

(iv) The Yamunāṣṭaka

The Sanskrit text *Yamunāṣṭaka* portrays the Yamunā personified as a beautiful woman. The eight *ślokas* are followed by a ninth comprising the *phalaśruti*. This short text does not enjoy the currency of the *Rādhāsudhānidhi* or Harivaṃśa's BrBh. works, and appears in manuscripts only rather rarely. An undated MS in the collection of the Nāgarī Pracāriṇī Sabhā (Āryabhāṣā Pustakālaya MSS 8983) bears the text with the following colophon:

[f.3] *iti śrīmaddhitaharivaṃśacaṃdragosvāmin*[*ā*]
viracitaḥ śrīyamunāṣṭaka saṃpūrṇa.

1. *Śloka* 76 exemplifies this, and also stands as an example of the tenor of the text as a whole:

yadvṛndāvanamātragocaram aho yannaśrutīkaṃśiro
[']*pyāroḍhuṃ kṣamate na yacchivaśukādīnāṃ tu yaddhyānagam;*
yatpremāmṛtamādhurīrasamayaṃ yannityakaiśorakaṃ
tadrūpaṃ pariveṣṭumeva nayanaṃlolāyamānaṃ mama.

(Bābā Hit Dās (ed.) p. 47.)

CHAPTER II

MANUSCRIPTS OF THE CAURĀSĪ PADA

1 Manuscripts of the CP collated for the present edition

The sources collated for the present edition of the CP are described in detail below under the sigla A–M. Two of these sources, G and H, are not manuscripts but printed texts: these have been included on the principle that published texts may reasonably be regarded as a direct continuation of the manuscript tradition; indeed, they offer a further insight into the transmission of the text. The text labelled G is in fact based on a single MS, as described below.

I am indebted to Ācārya Śrī Hitānanda Gosvāmī for his permission to photograph MS A, a particularly valued manuscript since it is the only known extant copy of the CP commentary by Dharaṇīdharadāsa, and also is the oldest dated CP manuscript procured for this edition. Similar acknowledgment is due to Ācārya Śrī Lalitā Caraṇ Gosvāmī for his kind permission to photograph MS B; to the authorities of the Municipal Museum, Allahabad, for permission to photograph that portion of MS C bearing the text of the CP; to the Librarian of the Houghton Library, Harvard University, for providing a microfilm of MS I; to Dr. G.R. Niemann, for pointing out the existence of MS M in the Honner Collection of Corpus Christi College,[1] and to the Library authorities for providing a microfilm of the MS; to the authorities of the Vrindaban Research Institute, for providing the facilities for the study of the remaining manuscripts; and to the authorities of all the libraries mentioned here, for permission to reproduce specimens of the respective manuscripts.

MSS IJKLM have been studied on microfilm only.

Since there are few variations in the order of the 84 stanzas, a full concordance is not necessary; a concordance of the stanza order peculiar to MS A is given in the description of that manuscript. A tabulation of the basic structure of each stanza is given in section VI.5; the allocation of *rāgas* to the text is shown in a table in VII. 3 (i). Following the descriptions of the sources collated for the present edition is given a catalogue of further MSS of the CP which have been inspected but not collated; in common with sources A to M, all these are in the Devanāgarī script.

The manuscript descriptions given below often make reference to

1. For a handlist of the Honner Collection, see G.R. Niemann 1980.

three stanzas of *phalaśruti* which follow the *mūla* in many sources; the first two are *chappayas* praising the efficacy of the CP, and the third is a *kavitta* listing the *rāgas* allocated to the 84 stanzas. The text of these three stanzas is given below in section II.3.

MS A

From the private collection of Ācārya Śrī Hitānanda Gosvāmī, Baḍavālā Muhallā, Aṭhakhambhā, Vrindaban.

Folios:	72.
Size:	13.5 by 23.5 cm.
Lines:	19 to 20 per page.
Date:	V.S. 1749 (A.D. 1693).
Scribe:	Pāṭhaka Paramānanda.
Place:	Udaipur.

The manuscript is complete and is written in black ink on badly water-stained paper. The folios have been roughly sewn together as a book; the first folio is badly insect-damaged on the left-hand side. *Daṇḍas*, verse numbers, *rāga* and metre headings are in red ink, and the text is enclosed by double red margins; the *mūla* is indented.

The MS contains the CP with the verse commentary of Dharaṇīdharadāsa. Stanza 13 and its commentary are omitted from the main body of the text and added in the margin of f.10ʳ. The handwriting of this marginal addition is broadly similar to that of the main text, but three features do suggest a different hand: (a) conjunct *ry* is written र्य here, र्‍य elsewhere (see III.2. (xi) for a discussion of this feature); (b) *dhu* is here written with the vowel sign attached to the right of the consonant (धु), rather than in the conventional subscript manner (धु) found elsewhere; (c) *a-kāra* is here written with a single semicircular stroke as its left-hand portion (अ), whereas elsewhere in the manuscript this portion is written as two more or less straight strokes (अ). (The commentary on CP 13 is only partially legible in the photograph, being necessarily written in a very cramped hand; and the circumstances in which this privately-owned manuscript was photographed did not allow a detailed examination of the manuscript at that time.) The numbering of stanzas subsequent to CP 13, and of the *dohās* and *savaiyās* of their commentary, presupposes the non-inclusion of this stanza.

The order of stanzas here differs from that found elsewhere, though the groupings of stanzas under *rāga* headings is maintained; the differences in order can be seen in the concordance given below. The *rāga* allocations in this MS correspond to those used in the majority of MSS, with three exceptions: Lalita in place of Vibhāsa; Gujarī in place of Devagandhāra; Gorī (Gaurī) in place of Gauḍamalāra. These discrepancies are tabulated in VII. 3 (i).

The text begins:

[f.1r] *śrī rādhāvallabho jayati. śrī vyāsanandano jayati. śrī dāmodaramani jayati.*[1]

Ends:

[f.71r] *iti śrī caurāsī saṭīka saṃpūrnaṃ. śubhaṃ bhavata maṃgalaṃ dadāt.*

This is followed by the commentator's formulaic apology for the shortcomings of his work, occupying seven *dohās*; then follows the colophon:

[f.71r–71v] *saṃvatu 1749 phālguna māse sukala pakṣe 15 punyo saṃṇaü kau saṃpūrṇa. leṣaka nāma pāṭhika paramānanda asthāna udaipura. subhamastu. śrīrastu. suhasta dharanīdharadāsa suta śrī jagajīvanadāsa ke.*

This is followed by a single *pada* of eight lines, bearing the *chāpa* '*dharanīdhara*', followed at the end of the folio by the syllable *saṃ* [*-pūrṇa*] in red ink. Folio 72r bears a stanza of *phalaśruti* in a later, untidy hand; this begins with the words *bhava jalanidhi* (see II.3 for the full text). This *chappaya* occupies less than half the page, the rest being left blank. The verso of the folio bears in the same scrawled hand, the following account of the *rāgas* used in the text (the text is in *dohās*, but the final *dohā* is corrupt):

lalita bilāvala rāga rasa ṭoḍī juga paribāna;
āsāvarī basaṃta puni ye bivi pahicāna.
dhanāsirī aru gūjarī riṣi samudra samāna;
sā̃rāga sadā sīgāra he eka adhika paribāna.
malāra barana ṣaraṣai sadā gorī disa saba āhi ritu kalyāna;
nidhi kānharo kedāro veda baṣāna.

Nāgarī numerals written above each *rāga* name interpret the symbolic numbers, which yield the following totals of *padas* allocated to each *rāga*:

Lalita	6	Sāraṃga	17
Vilāvala	6	Malāra	4
Toḍī	4	Gaurī	10
Āsāvarī	2	Kalyāna	6
Vasanta	2	Kānharau	9
Dhanāśirī	7	Kedāra	4
Gūjarī	7		

1. Lalitā Caraṇ Gosvāmī (n.d.: 11) attests that Dāmodara was the grandson of Hita Harivaṃśa (implying that *-maṇi* is merely an honorific suffix in this context), and that Dharaṇīdharadāsa, author of the commentary, was a disciple of Dāmodara.

This listing corresponds to the *rāga* headings in the manuscript's text, but for the transposition of the headings Gūjarī and Dhanāsirī.

This stanza is followed by the *kavitta* enumerating the *rāga* allocations of MSS other than A (see section II.3 for the text): this is written in yet another hand. Finally the manuscript ends with part of *Sphuṭa vāṇī* 20,[1] apparently in the same hand as the preceding stanza but written with a different pen. The folio ends after the first syllable of the word *maryādā* (line 4).

Concordance showing stanza order unique to MS A

The stanza order here designated as 'standard' is that which is found in all the manuscripts except A, with two exceptions: in C, CP 3 and CP 4 are transposed (as in A); and in I, CP 65 is omitted. *Rāgas* listed against the 'standard' stanza order are subject to greater variation, as is shown in the Table in Chapter VI.

Table 2: Concordance of MS A

Rāga	*MS A*	*Standard*	*Rāga*	*MS A*	*Standard*
Lalita	1	1		32	24
	2	2		33	25
	3	4		34	26
	4	3	Sāraṃga	35	36
	5	5		36	37
	6	6		37	38
Bilāvala	7	7		38	39
	8	8		39	40
	9	9		40	41
	10	10		41	42
	11	11		42	43
	12	12		43	44
	(margin)	13		44	45
Ṭoḍī	13	14		45	46
	14	15		46	50
	15	17		47	47
	16	16		48	48
Asāvarī	17	19		49	49
	18	18		50	51
Vasaṃta	19	27	Malāra	51	52
	20	28		52	53
Gūjarī	21	29		53	54
	22	30		54	55
	23	31	Gorī	55	56
	24	33		56	57
	25	32		57	58
	26	34		58	59
	27	35		59	60
Dhanāsrī	28	20		60	62
	29	21		61	61
	30	22		62	63
	31	23		63	64
	64	65		75	76

1. I.e. the stanza designated '20' in text W, discussed in section I.4.(i).

Kalyāna	65	66		76	77
	66	67		77	78
	67	68		78	79
	68	69		79	80
	69	70	Kedārau	80	81
	70	71		81	82
Kānarau	71	72		82	83
	72	73		(83, unnumbered)	84
	73	74			
	74	75			

Rāga	*'Standard'*	*MS A*	*Rāga*	*'Standard'*	*MS A*
Vibhāsa	1	1		43	42
	2	2		44	43
	3	4		45	44
	4	3		46	45
	5	5		47	47
	6	6		48	48
Vilāvala	7	7		49	49
	8	8		50	46
	9	9		51	50
	10	10	Malāra	52	51
	11	11		53	52
	12	12		54	53
	13	(margin)		55	54
Ṭoḍī	14	13	Gauḍamalāra	56	55
	15	14	Gaurī	57	56
	16	16		58	57
	17	15		59	58
Āsāvarī	18	18		60	59
	19	17		61	61
Dhanāśrī	20	28		62	60
	21	29		63	62
	22	30		64	63
	23	31		65	64
	24	32	Kalyāna	66	65
	25	33		67	66
	26	34		68	67
Vasaṃta	27	19		69	68
	28	20		70	69
Devagaṃdhāra	29	21		71	70
	30	22	Kānharau	72	71
	31	23		73	72
	32	25		74	73
	33	24		75	74
	34	26		76	75
	35	27		77	76
Sāraṃga	36	35		78	77
	37	36		79	78
	38	37		80	79
	39	38	Kedārau	81	80
	40	39		82	81
	41	40		83	82
	42	41		84	(83, unnumbered)

MS B

From the private collection of Ācārya Śrī Lalitā Caraṇ Gosvāmī, 'Yamunā Pulin', Baḍavālā Muhallā, Aṭhakhambhā, Vrindaban.

Folios:	98.
Size:	29 x 14.5 cm.
Lines:	9 per page.
Date:	V.S. 1881 (A.D. 1825).
Scribe:	Hīrālāla.
Place:	Parasauna (modern Palson, near Govardhan).[1]

The manuscript is complete and is written in black ink, with red ink for *daṇḍas*, stanza headings (*atha pada mūla* etc.) and, in a rather random fashion, for parts of the colophon. The verso of the first folio, where the text begins, is ornamented with wide double-ruled margins, the space between the two rulings being cross-hatched and dotted. Folio 98^{r} is similarly decorated, and has only seven lines of text. Folio 55^{r} bears a single *dohā* and a roughly-drawn floral decoration in the centre of the page; neither feature appears to be connected with the surrounding text on ff. 54^{v} and 55^{v} (which bear the *mūla* of CP 48). Folio 55^{r} shows signs of ink having smudged from another folio, and is not used for the continuation of the main text. Folio 79 is wrongly numbered 78, and all sub,equent folios are correspondingly one behind the correct numbering; this mistake has been clumsily corrected in a later hand. Several corrections or emendments to the text have been made in the margin by both the scribe and a later hand.

The MS contains the CP with the prose commentary of Lokanātha. The order of stanzas is that followed by all sources except MSS A and C: the *rāga* headings are also in agreement with the majority of sources, with the exception that the heading *Kalyāna* does not appear here.

The text begins:

[f.1^{v}] *śrī gaṇeśāyanama. śrī rādhāvallabho jayati. śrī vyāsanaṃdano jayati. atha śrīmac caurāsī ṭikā sahita liṣyate ṭīkā śrī lokanātha jī kṛta.*

The commentary ends:

[f.97^{r}] *iti śrī caurāsī pada kau* [sic] *ṭīkā lokanātha jī kṛta saṃpūrnaṃ.*

There then follow 12 lines of further exegetical material in prose and 2 *dohās*. This is followed by the two *chappayas* of *phalaśruti*, and the *kavitta* listing the *rāga* allocations. The first two words of the *kavitta*, *cha pada*, have been written by the scribe as a heading in red ink and

1. Growse (1883 : 333) proposes the derivation *parasurāma gānw*>*parsagānw*>*parsānw*>*parson*>*palson*, and quotes a popular legend which interprets '*parson*' as 'the day before yesterday'!

enclosed by double red *daṇḍas*, by analogy with the heading *chappaya* preceding the *phalaśruti*. Following this stanza is the colophon as below:

[f.99v] *iti śrī caurāsī ṭīkā sahitam saṃpūrṇa pustaka liṣyatam śrī vṛṃdāvana madhye śrī jamunā taṭe. prata saṃpūrnaṃ phāguna sudi. 5. saṃvat. 1881. mukāma nagra parasauna madhyai liṣītaṃ paṃ* [*-ḍita*] *śrī vrahmana hīrālāla ju avadikṣa jathā prata tathā liṣyate mama doso na dīyate śubhaṃ bhavat*[*u*] *dadāt*[*u*] *6.5.6.5.*

The final part of the colophon appears to be in a different hand:

[f.99v] *paṭhanārtha paṃ*[*-ḍita*] *śrī vaisanava rādhikādāsa vasiyau parakai īṣṭa upāsanā śrī rādhāvallabha mahāsahāya śrī rādhāvallabha śrī haravaṃśa śrī vriṃdāvana śrī vanacanda śrī śrī śrī*

Finally a recent addition records the presentation of the manuscript to its present owner in V.S. 2015 (A.D. 1958):

[f.99v] *śrī carana sevaka ghamaṃḍī agravāla ne mitī māgha śuklā paṃcamī bhaīṭa kī saṃ*[*-vat*] *2015*

While the collocation of such generalities as *rādhāvallabha*, *vṛṃdāvana* and *vanacandra* leaves the colophon open to various interpretations, sectarian sources always identify Vanacandra as the son of Harivaṃśa (as discussed in the previous chapter). The formula 6.5.6.5., which fills space until the end of the line, remains unresolved, as does the phrase *vasiyau parakai īṣṭa upāsanā*. The readings *bhavat*, *dadāt* (for *bhavatu*, *dadātu*) apparently represent scribal misreadings of *u-kāras* as *virāmas*.

MS C

Municipal Museum, Allahabad; Hindi MS no. 23. (Previously owned by Lalit Kṛṣṇa Gosvāmī, now resident in Allahabad but previously of Vrindaban.)

Folios: 120.
Size: 11.5 by 21cm.
Lines: 18 per page.
Date: V.S. 1794 (A.D. 1737).
Scribe: —
Place: —

This badly-worn MS is written in black ink in a neat square hand on brittle brownish paper. Red ink is used for headings, double margins, and *daṇḍas*. The MS has been roughly bound; many repairs obscure or replace original readings. The last folios are badly insect-damaged, much of the text (but no part of the CP) being lost thereby. At least one folio at the end of the MS is lost, as is folio 3 (bearing 6.3–9.3). Of the folios carrying the CP, repairs have been carried out to ff. 15r,

15ᵛ, 21ᵛ, 22ᵛ. Folio 20 is a complete replacement for the original, evidently lost: this carries CP 55.3–57.14; the lower half of f. 23 is also a replacement: this carries CP 62.6–63[i].4 and 63[ii].4–63[iii].5. The replacement text is in an untidy hand with great variations in the thickness of ink leaving the pen.

The MS contains five Rādhāvallabhī works:

f.1ᵛ:	CP
f.32ᵛ:	*Sevaka vāṇī* of Dāmodaradāsa 'Sevaka'.
f.71ʳ:	*Śṛṃgāra sata* of Dhruvadāsa
f.105ʳ:	*Rasānaṃda līlā* of Dhruvadāsa
f.116ʳ:	*Manaśīkṣā sāra* of Dhruvadāsa

The MS begins with the following invocation to the titular deity:

[f.1ᵛ] *śrī rādhāvallabho jayati.*

The CP ends on f.32ʳ:

iti śrī corāsī pada saṃpūrṇa.

This is followed by the first of the two *phalaśruti chappayas,* and concludes:

[f.32ᵛ] *iti śrī corāsī saṃpūraṇa. subhamastu. śrī.*

The remaining four texts then follow in the same hand and in the same pagination sequence, as listed above. Each folio number is preceded by a siglum indicating its contents: *cau* for *caurāsī* etc. The concluding colophon is partially obscured by a tape repair:

[f.120ᵛ] *iti śrī manaśikṣā sāra saṃpūrṇa. saṃvat* 1794
varṣe māgha saravada 10 *likhyate śubhamastu.*
śrīrastu. śrī rādhāvallabho [///]

This MS shares with MS A an inversion in the order of CP 3 and CP 4 *vis-à-vis* all other MSS; another feature shared with MS A is the use of the *rāgas* Lalita and Gujari.

MS D

Vrindaban Research Institute, Vrindaban; Hindi MS 4412 (Cat. no. 822).[1]

Folios:	116.
Size:	14.2 by 10.5 cm.
Lines:	8 per page.
Date:	—
Scribe:	—
Place:	—

1. Catalogue references in this section are to R.D. Gupta and M.L. Gupta (eds.) 1979.

This is an incomplete MS written in a clear but rough hand in black ink, with red ink for *daṇḍas* and headings. The paper is badly worn. Folios 2, 3 and 20 (bearing CP 1.4–6.2; 32.7–34.6), and the end of the MS (bearing part of the *Sevaka vāṇī*) are missing.

The MS bears the CP and the *Sevaka vāṇī* (incomplete). The CP begins and ends as follows:

[f.1v] [///] *rādhāvallabho jayati. śrī vyāsanaṃdano jayati. atha śrīmata caurāsī pada liṣyate.*

[f.53r] *iti śrī caurāsī pada saṃpūrṇa. atha phalastuti liṣyate.*

The two *phalaśruti* stanzas and the *rāga kavitta* are given, followed by:

[f.54r] *iti śrī caurāsī pada kau rāga pramāṇa saṃpūrṇa. śrī rādhāvallabho ja*[*ya*]*ti.*

This is followed by the beginning of the *Sevaka vāṇī*.

MS E

Vrindaban Research Institute, Vrindaban; Hindi MS 4410 (Cat. no. 824).

Folios: 229 (3+78+124+24).
Size: 14 by 8.8 cm.
Lines: 7 per page.
Date: V.S. 1829 (A.D. 1762).
Scribe: —
Place: —

This is a bound manuscript written in black ink on paper of various colours. Red ink is used for *daṇḍas* and, occasionally, for headings. The MS is complete, though the first and last folios are badly worn.

An index on the first folio identifies the various texts contained in the manuscript, and their respective folio numbers:

[f.1v]	*śrī yamunāṣṭaka*	1–3.
	śrī rādhāsudhānidhi	1–78.
	śrī sevaka vānī	1–68.
	śrī caurāsī pada	69–123.
	phalaśruti	124.
	śrī hita jū ke pada	1–15.
	śrī upasudhānidhi	16–24.

The CP text begins and ends as follows:

[f.69v] *śrī rādhāvallabhāya namaḥ.*

[f.123r] *iti śrī caurāsī saṃpūrṇa.*

The date of the MS appears in the colophon to the *Rādhāsudhānidhi*; while it cannot be certain that this date applies to the whole MS, the fact that all the texts are in the same hand suggests that this is likely. The colophon reads:

[f.78v] *iti śrīvṛṃdāvaneśvarīcaraṇakṛpāmātravijṛṃbhita śrī rādhāsudhānidhi stavaḥ śrīhitaharivaṃśagosvāminā viracitaḥ saṃpūrṇa. śubhaṃ. śrīrastu lekhaka pāṭhakayoḥ. saṃvat. 18.29. mārgaśīrṣa śuklapakṣe tithau dvitīyāṃ śanivāsare. bhagnipṛṣṭi kaṭigrīvā vadhamuṣṭir adhomukhāḥ. kaṣṭena likhyataṃ graṃtha yatnena pariyālayet. śivamastu. bhadrabhūyāt. oṃ svasti prajābhyāṃ. śrī gusāī śrī govarddhana svāmī viṃśottara śataṃ ciraṃjīvituḥ śrī rādhāvallabho jayati oṃ.*

Folio 104r bears the words *śrī hari* at the bottom right-hand corner; the verso bears the words *śrī kṛṣṇa* at the bottom left-hand corner.

MS F

Vrindaban Research Institute, Vrindaban; Hindi MS 8372 (Cat. no. 827).

Folios: 253.
Size: 10 by 14.7 cm.
Linnes: 11 per page.
Date: —
Scribe: —
Place: —

This is a complete MS, bound in coloured striped silk which is badly dilapidated and frayed. The thick white paper is slightly foxed and damaged by damp. The text is written in black ink, with red ink for *daṇḍas*; headings have alternate characters in red. The text on each folio is enclosed within a square ruled in red, black and yellow lines; *mūla* is distinguished from *ṭīkā* by being indented within a second, smaller square within the outer boundary. The first folio is decorated with a cupola-like shape drawn above the text. The original numbers on ff. 214, 215 and 237 are incorrect and have been corrected by a later hand: the overall numbering sequence is not affected. This MS does not include the *rāga* headings *Vilāvala* and *Sāraṃga*.

The MS bears the CP with the prose commentary of Lokanātha. The texts begins and ends as follows:

[f.1r] *śrī vyāsanaṃdano jayati.*
[f.250r] *iti śrī caurāsī pada kī ṭīkā lokanātha jī kṛta saṃpūrṇa.*

After this colophon there follows the same exegetical supplement referred to in the description of MS B above, and the two *phalaśruti chappayas*. This section ends on f.252v. The recto of the final folio bears in a scrawled later hand the text of the *rāga kavitta* (here *kavitā*).

Text G

This copy of the CP with the prose *ṭīkā* of Premadāsa is a published edition edited by Vijayapāl Siṃha and Candrabhān Rāvat, based on a single MS in the collection of the Nāgarī Pracāriṇī Sabhā. The MS, undated but complete, is not fully described or identified in the published text, though a photograph of the first folio is given opposite the transcribed text of that folio: a comparison of this folio with its transcription reveals a number of inconsistencies, representing either standardizations (*rasikana* for °*ni*, *dohā* 1) or inaccuracies of transcription or of printing (*agyau* for *ūgyau*, *dohā* 2).

The text begins as follows (from the photographed folio, facing p.1):

śrī rādhāvallabho jayati. śrīmad harivaṃśa caṃdro virājate mama manasi. śrī hitena kṛta caturāśīti padasya akṣarārtha mana saṃbodhanārtha likhyate.

The final stanza of the text is followed by the following colophon (from the published transcribed text, as are all subsequent quotations)—p.191:

iti śrīmad harivaṃśa caṃdra gosvāminā kṛtasya caturāśīti padasyākṣarārtha bahurasāṃkura ṭīkāyāṃ premadāsena kṛta suratāṃta samaye caturāśītitamo nikuṃja vilāsaḥ saṃpūrṇaṃ. 84. śubham astu.

The *phalaśruti* which follows is preceded by a rubric attributing the first of the two *phalaśruti* stanzas to Vanacandra:

śrīmac caturāśī saṃpūrṇa bhaī tākī phalastuti biṣẽ śrīmat gosvāmī śrī hita banacaṃda jī kachu kahata haĩ. śrī rādhākṛṣṇa.

The second *phalaśruti* is attributed to Rūpalāla, in recognition of the *chāpa rūpalāla hita* in the last line of the stanza (p. 195):

jaba śrī jugala kiśora jū kõ nirakhe taba kahā avasthā hoi, tāhi śrīmat gosvāmi śrī rūpalāla ne prakāśita kiyau hai, iti. śrī rādhāhari.

The *rāga kavitta* also has an attribution, to Hita Hari Malla (p. 196):

śrī mac caturāśī ke pada jini rāgani mẽ haĩ. tini kī gaṇanā
śrī hita hari jī malla jī ne karī hai, tāhi likhiyata hai.

The two *phalaśruti* stanzas and the *rāga kavitta* (which does not acknowledge the omission of the *rāga* heading *Vilāvala* in this MS) all have commentaries by Premadāsa himself. They are followed by a short sequence of *dohās* and *kavittas* by the same author, and ending with a *dohā* which dates the whole work as having been composed in *saṃvat* 1791 (A.D. 1734); the text is concluded with a brief colophon (p. 198):

satraha sai ikyānabai saṃbata mādho māsa;
yaha prabaṃdha pūraṇa bhayau śukla dvaija budhabāsa.
iti śrī saṃpūrṇa śubham astu śrī. śrī.

A number of variants is given below the text in most stanzas from CP 34 onwards; the source of these is not stated, and they have not been reproduced in the apparatus of the critical edition.

The MS on which this published edition is based also contains the *Sphuṭa vāṇī* attributed to Hita Harivaṃśa. As noted in section I.4(i), the composition and order of the *Sphuṭa vāṇī* as it appears here differs somewhat from that found in other MSS. The colophon at the end of this section describes the circumstances of the copying of this MS; the date of the MS is not mentioned: (p. 207)

pothī śrī mahaṃta caturadāsa rādhāballabhī, tinike śiṣya rādhācarana dāsa jī tina ke śiṣya gulābadāsa jī jānaī pothī likhāī. śrī gosvāmi haribaṃśa jī kṛta padya caurāsī jī kī pothī likhāī. naṃdagrāma koṭā madhye. lekhaka rādhākṛṣna ne. śrī rādhā.

Text H

This copy of the CP is a printed book published in Mathura in v.s. 1993 (A.D. 1936) by Svāmī Śrī Nārāyaṇadāsa, under the auspices of Gosvāmī Hita Rūpalāla of the Rādhāvallabha temple, Vrindaban. It contains the following texts under the general title *Śrī hita vāṇī jī*:

(*a*) *Yamunāṣṭaka* (with Hindi prose translation);
(*b*) *Rādhāsudhānidhi* (with Hindi verse translation *Hita hārda prakāśinī* by Kiśorīlāla;
(*c*) *Sphuṭavāṇī* (here, *Hita sphuṭa vāṇī*);
(*d*) CP (here, *Caturāśī*);
(*e*) *Sevaka vāṇī*;
(*f*) *Aṣṭayāma sevā vidhi* (66 Sanskrit verses, with Hindi prose translation).

No mention is made of the source from which the texts are taken. The text is preceded by the following:

[9.161] *śrī rādhāvallabho jayati. śrī hita harivaṃśa candro jayati. adhikārī śrī hita guru kiśorīlālo vijayate. śrīmad gosvāmī śrī hita harivaṃśa candra mahāprabhū viracita śrīmac caturāśī jī.*

Each stanza is preceded by a brief contextualization, as for example in CP 1:

(*śrī priyā jī hita sakhī—paraspara saṃbhāṣaṇa*) *śayyā samaya.*

The text is followed by the two stanzas of *phalaśruti*, the *rāga kavitta*, and a single *pada* bearing the *chāpa* of Nāgarīdāsa.

MS I

Houghton Library, Harvard University, MS Indic 1754.

Folios:	184 (48+49+87).
Size:	15.5 by 11.5 cm.
Lines:	8 per page (CP only).
Date:	V.S. 1860 (A.D. 1803) (in colophon of *Nāmamālā*).
Scribe:	Harirāma Rāvala (in colophon of *Nāmamālā*).
Place:	—

The MS is written in black ink in two different hands: one for the CP, a second for the two subsequent texts. Red ink is used for *daṇḍas*, margins and *rāga* headings; *daṇḍas* and margins, however, are discontinued from the ninth folio bearing the CP, and are resumed only at the beginning of the subsequent text. The MS is bound as a book; the folios have been trimmed, perhaps at the time of binding, and folio numbers and some margin corrections have consequently been wholly or partially cut off; duplicate folio numbers are written on the bottom left hand corner of the folio, apparently in the original hand.

The MS contains three texts: the CP (CP 64 is erroneously numbered 65; CP 65 is subsequently omitted, and the text jumps from CP 64 to CP 66), the *Nāmamālā* (of Nandadāsa, though no attribution is made in the MS itself), and an untitled anthology of devotional verse attributed to poets of the Vallabha *sampradāya*. Each text has a separate numbering sequence.

The text of the CP begins and ends as follows:

[f.1r] *śrī rādhākṛṣṇa jī. atha śrīma*[c] *caurāsī prāra*[*ṃ*]*bha.*

[f.47v] *iti śrī caurāsī saṃpūrṇam.*

This colophon is followed without a break by two *padas*, concluded:

[f.48r] *iti bhavatu. rāma rāma rāma rāma rāma*

The remainder of this folio is left blank, as is the whole of the following folio. The *Nāmamālā*, in a different hand and with a new numbering sequence, begins and ends as follows:

[f.1r] *śrī gaṇeśāya namaḥ. atha nāmamālā likhyate.*

[f.49v] *iti śrī nāmamālā saṃpūrṇam. saṃvat 1860 nā jyeṣṭa vidi 2 gujarāti harirāma rāvala. vrāhmaṇa udicya likhitaṃ ga. rāmacaṃdrāya nama tubhyaṃ. śrī hariharāya namaḥ. rāmacaṃdrāya nama*

1½ blank folios are followed by the final text, apparently in the same hand, with a new numbering sequence. The text begins:

[f.1r] *śrī rāmacaṃdrāya namaḥ.*

The *padas* which follow are arranged under *rāga* headings; various folios are left half-empty in order to start a new *pada* at the top of a fresh page. The text ends abruptly on f.86[r], without a colophon; the remaining two folios (ff. 87, 88) are numbered but left blank. This anthology is apparently a compilation of the 8th *gaddī* of the Vallabha *sampradāya*, since it contains *padas* with the *chāpas* of Kevala/Kevalajana, and Lāladāsa, as well as a genealogy of 'Śrī Lāla jī' (as discussed by A.W. Entwistle, p. 481).

The lack of any of the usual Rādhāvallabhī salutations in this copy of the CP, together with the fact that the other two texts which complete the MS are of the Vallabha persuasion, suggests that neither the scribe nor his patron was a follower of the Rādhāvallabhī tradition.

MS J

Vrindaban Research Institute, Vrindaban; Hindi MS 4360 (Cat. no. 820).

Folios:	45.
Size:	20.3 by 11.1 cm.
Lines:	7 per page.
Date:	—
Scribe:	—
Place:	—

A complete, unbound MS; the text is written in black ink, with red ink for margins, *daṇḍas* and colophon. The first four *rāga* headings, and the sixth and seventh, are written in red ink; the fifth is written with alternate *akṣaras* in red, and the remaining seven are in black ink. The verso of each folio bears the siglum *cau*[*-rāsī*] before the folio number in the top left-hand corner, and the word *śrī* precedes the repeated folio number in the lower right-hand corner. Several emendments have been made in the margins by a later hand.

The MS bears the CP *mūla* only. The text begins:

[f.1[v]] *śrī rādhebhāya namaḥ. śrī rādhāvallabho jayati. śrī hita harivaṃśa caṃdro jayati. atha śrīmac caurāsī pada liṣyate.*

Ends: [f.44[v]] *iti śrīmac caurāsī pada saṃpūrṇam. śrī rādheśyāma. atha phalastuti liṣyate.*

The two stanzas of *phalaśruti* are followed by:

[f.45[v]] *iti śrī phalastuti saṃpūrṇam. atha rāga saṃkhyā liṣyate.*

Following the *rāga kavitta* is a fragment of verse in a later hand; the second line is followed by the word *ṭeka,* indicating that this is the beginning of a *pada*. The fragment ends abruptly at the end of the folio:

[f.45[v]] *namo namo caturāsī bānī; jā madhi hita rasa kahata na āvai jugala taraṃga siṃdhu hita jānī. ṭeka. namo namo*

MS K

Vrindaban Research Institute, Vrindaban; Hindi MS 8378 (Cat. no. 828).

Folios: 241.
Size: 16.7 by 25.7 cm.
Lines: 19 per page.
Date: V.S. 1965 (A.D. 1908).
Scribe: Rādhāmohana.
Place: —

The MS is complete. The text is written in a square and rather clumsy hand, in black ink; red ink is used for the *daṇḍas*, colophons, margins and *rāga* headings. Some words and phrases have been blocked out by the application of a light-coloured substance: such is the case in the first two lines of f.4[r], which carries duplicated material. The top left-hand corner of each folio (verso) bears the folio number preceded by the siglum *cau.ṭī.* (for *caurāsī ṭīkā*), sometimes simply *cau.*

The MS contains the CP with the commentary of Premadāsa and begins as follows:

[f.1[v]] *śrī rādhāvallabho jayati. śrī hita harivaṃśa caṃdro jayati. atha śrī hitena kṛta caturāśīti padasya akṣarārtha mana saṃvaṃdhanārthāya likhyataṃ.*

The sequence of *phalaśrutis* and *rāga kavitta* is the same as in text G described above. The scribal colophon follows on f.241[v]:

> *iti śrī premadāsa jī kṛta śrī caurāsī vaṃdha ṭīkā saṃpūrṇam. mi hastākṣara rādhāmohana mālā miti bhādo vadī 11 sanivāra saṃ*[*vat*] *1965. śloka saṃkhyā 4500.*

MS L

Vrindaban Research Institute, Vrindaban; Hindi MS 10501 (Cat. no. 830).

Folios: 206.
Size: 9.8 by 7.8 cm.
Lines: 7 per page.
Date: —
Place: —
Scribe: —

This MS is bound as a book, in a worn cloth cover. There is slight damage to the first folio, but otherwise it is in good condition (though listed as incomplete in the V.R.I. catalogue, p. 158). The text is written in black ink, with red ink used for margins, *daṇḍas*, colophons and *rāga* headings.

The MS contains the CP and the *Sevaka vāṇī*. Damage to the first folio has removed part of the invocatory text, as shown:

[f.1^{r}] *[///]vallabho jayati. śrī [///]naṃdano jayati. atha śrīmac caurāsī liṣyate.*

The CP ends:

[f.84^{r}] *iti śrīmat caurāsī saṃpūrṇaṃ.*

This colophon is followed by the two *phalaśruti* stanzas, and the *rāga kavitta,* followed by:

[f.84^{v}] *subham astu śubha bhavatu śrīrastu.*

The remaining space on f.84^{v} is decorated with dotted circles. This MS has only been studied on microfilm, and the text of the *Sevaka vāṇī* which follows the CP has not been available for inspection; the V.R.I. catalogue (p. 241) records that the *Sevaka vāṇī* is complete but undated.

MS M

Corpus Christi College (Cambridge University Library) OR.MS.C9
Folios: 11+288.
Size: 16.3 by 25 cm.
Lines: 18 per page.
Date: —
Scribe: —
Place: [Collected in Jaipur, Rajasthan.][1]

This is a complete, bound manuscript, written in black ink with red ink for the double margins, *daṇḍas*, *rāga* headings and colophons. The MS has been written by three different scribes: the first hand, neat and consistent, continues up to f.210^{v}; the second, less well formed, continues to the end of the text with one interruption, where folios 252^{v} to the middle of 253^{v} are written in a third and more erratic hand. The distribution of text among these folios is as follows:

Scribe 1	ff.1–210^{v}	CP 1–62;
Scribe 2	ff.211^{r}–252^{v}; 254^{v}–end	CP 63–72; 74-84;
Scribe 3	ff.252^{v}–253^{v}	CP 73.

The top left-hand corner of each folio (verso) bears the siglum *ṭī.*[-*kā*] and the folio number. The convention of indenting *mūla* text to distinguish it from the *ṭīkā*, adopted by the first scribe from CP 5 onwards, has been followed by the other two scribes, though only the first scribe has enclosed the *mūla* within a second margin of double red lines. All three scribes fill any space remaining on the last line carrying the *mūla* of each stanza by repeating the formula *śrī* the requisite number of times.

1. G. R. Niemann, 1980:8.

The MS bears the CP with the commentary of Premadāsa. The text is preceded by 11 unnumbered folios in which the first lines of the 84 stanzas are listed with their folio numbers; this index is in a scrawled hand different again from the three styles found in the text, and is headed *śrī rāma jī*. The text begins on the first numbered folio:

[f.1r] *śrī rādhāballabho jayati. śrīmad haribaṃśa caṃdro birājate mama manasi. śrī hitena kṛta caturāsīta padasyākṣarārtha mana saṃbodhanārthāya liṣyate.*

The final stanza of the text is followed, erroneously, by a repeat of the colophon to CP 79; this has been lightly crossed through, and replaced by the correct colophon added in the margin by a later hand. This replacement is the same as the equivalent colophon quoted in the description of text G above, except that it lacks the phrase *bahurasāṃkura* and has the folio number following, and not preceding, the formula *śubham astu.*

The sequence of *phalaśrutis* and *rāga kavitta* is the same as that described under G and K above: the *rāga kavitta* does not reflect the absence of the heading *Devagaṃdhāra* in the text. The text ends with the following colophon:

[f.285r] *iti śrī saṃpūrṇa. śubhamastu. śrī śrī.*

The remaining folios are left blank until the last folio (f.288v), which bears an anonymous stanza headed *kabitta*, again in a different and erratic hand. This stanza has no apparent connexion with the main text or commentary.

Summary of the sources collated for the edition

Siglum	V.S. *date*	*Commentator*	*Provenance and library number*
A	1749	Dharaṇīdharadāsa (Dhar.)	Collection of Śrī Hitānanda Gosvāmī
B	1881	Lokanātha (Lok.)	Collection of Śrī Lalitā Caraṇ Gosvāmī
C	1794	—	Allahabad Museum Hindi MS 23
D	—	—	Vrindaban Research Institute (V.R.I.) 4412 (Cat. no. 822)
E	1829	—	V.R.I. 4410 (Cat. no. 824)
F	—	Lok.	V.R.I. 8372 (Cat. no. 827)

G	—	Premadāsa (Prem.)	Nāgarī Pracāriṇī Sabhā edition
H	1993	—	Svāmī Nārāyaṇadāsa edition
I	1860	—	Houghton Library, Harvard, Indic 1754
J	—	—	V.R.I. 4360 (Cat. no. 820)
K	1965	Prem.	V.R.I. 8378 (Cat. no. 828)
L	—	—	V.R.I. 10501 (Cat. no. 830)
M	—	Prem.	Cambridge University Library, OR MS. C9

MS A

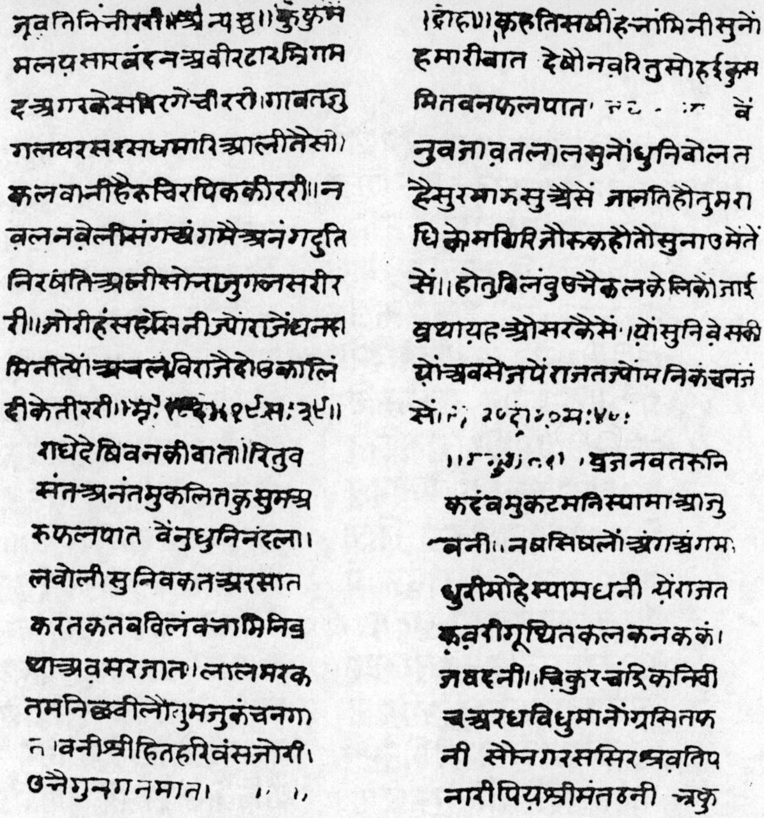

नृवतिनिंनीरवी ... न्यसु॥कुंकुंम
मलयसारबंदनअवीरटायग्निगम
दअगरकेसमिरगेचीररी।गाबतहु
गलयरसरसधमारिआलीनेसो।
कलवानीहैकविरपिककीररी॥न
वलनवेलीसिंगच्छंगमैअनंगदुति
निरषतिअनीसोनजुगलसरीर
री॥गोरीहंसहंसिनीज्यांराजेंघनस
मिनीत्यांअबलविराजैदोउकालिं
दीकेतीररी।...॥१९स:३९॥
राधेदेषिवनकीवात।रितुव
संतअनंतमुकलितकुसुमअ
रुफलपात वेंनुधुनिनंदला।
लबोलीसुनिवकतअरसात
करतकतबविलंबभामिनिव्र
था...अवसरजात।लालमरक
तमनिछवीलौतुमजुकंचनगा
...वनीश्रीहितहरिवंसजोरी।
उनैगुनगनमात।

।दोहा।।कहतिसषीहसामिनीसुनो
हमारीबात देषोनवरितुसोहईकुसु
मितबनफलपात ... वें
नुवजावतलालसुनोंधुनिबोलत
हैसुरमारुसुऐसें जानतिहोतुमरा
धिकेमधिरनौलककहौतोसुनाउमैंतें
सें॥होतुबिलंबुछनेकलकेलिकोजाई
ब्रथायहओसरकैसें।येंसुनिवेसकी
येंअवसेजपेंराजतज्योंमनिकंचनजं
सें।...
...।व्रजनवतरुनि
कदंबमुकटमनिस्यामाआजु
बनी॥नषसिषलोंअंगअंगम
धुरीमोहेस्यामधनी येंराजत
कवरीगूथितकलकनककं।
जबदनी॥चिकुरचंद्रिकनिवी
चअरधविधुमानोंग्रसितफ
नी सोनगरससिरश्रवतिप
नारीपियश्रीमंतठनी अकु

MSB

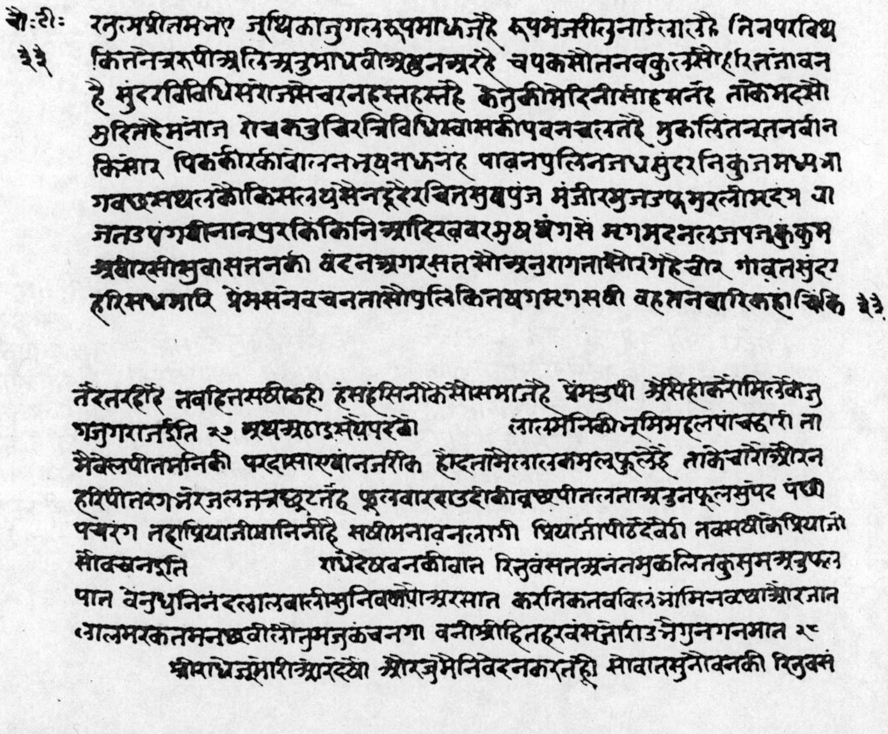

सोरीः ३३
रतुअपीतमनए जूथिकानुगलरूपमाअजैहे रूपमंजरीजुनोउयाजैहे तिनपरविथ
कित्तेनअरूपीअलिअनुमायवीअजुनअरहे चपकसोतनवकुतसोहरितजावन
हे मुंदरविविधिसेराजेसेबरनहस्तहस्तेहे केतुकीमेदिनीसाहसनेर ताकेमदसो
मुदितहेमनोज रोचककुविरनिविविधिस्वामकोपवनचलततै मुकलितनतनवीन
किसार पिककीरकोवालनमधुपनफनेंहे पावनपुलिननजपमुंदरनिकुंजमधुमा
गवछअमथलकोकिसलयसेनहूरैरचितमुखपुंज मंजीरमुजउपमुरलीमदेम या
जतउपंगवीनानपुरकिंकिनिआसिरवरमुषचंगसे मगमदनलजपनकुंकुम
अबीरसीमुवासतनको वंदनअगरसतसोअनुरागनासोरंगहेचीर गावतसुंदर
हरिसधमारि प्रेमसनेवचननतासोपुलिकितषगमगसषी वहमनबारिकहा रिंकि ३३

तेरतरहोरे नवहितसषीकहे हसहंसिनीकेसीसमाजेहे प्रेमरूपी ऐसिहीकोरामिलेकेजु
गजुगराजईति २७ अथअठाइसयेंपरको सातमेनिकोनमिमहलपावहूरी ना
मैवेलपीतमनिकी परदसारवानजरीके हेमदनामिलालकमलफूलेहे ताकेचारोओरन
हरिपीतरंगनेरजलनअछूटतेहे फूलवारबउदाकोवृछपीनतनाअनुनफूलसुपर पंछी
पचरंग नराप्रियाजीमानिनीहे सषीमनावनलागी प्रियाजीपीठदेवेठी नवसषीकेप्रियाजी
सोवचनईति राधेदेषवनकीवात रितुवसनअनंतमकलितकुसुमअनुफल
पात वेनुधुनिनंदलालबालीसुनिवकपोअरसात करतिकतवविलंभामिनवथाओरजात
लालमरकतमनछवीलोतुमजुकंचनगा वनीश्रीहितहरवंसजोरीउनेगुनगनमात २८
श्रीराधेजुमारीआरस्यो ओरजुमैनिवेरनकरतेहो सोवातसुनोवनकी रितुवसं

MS C

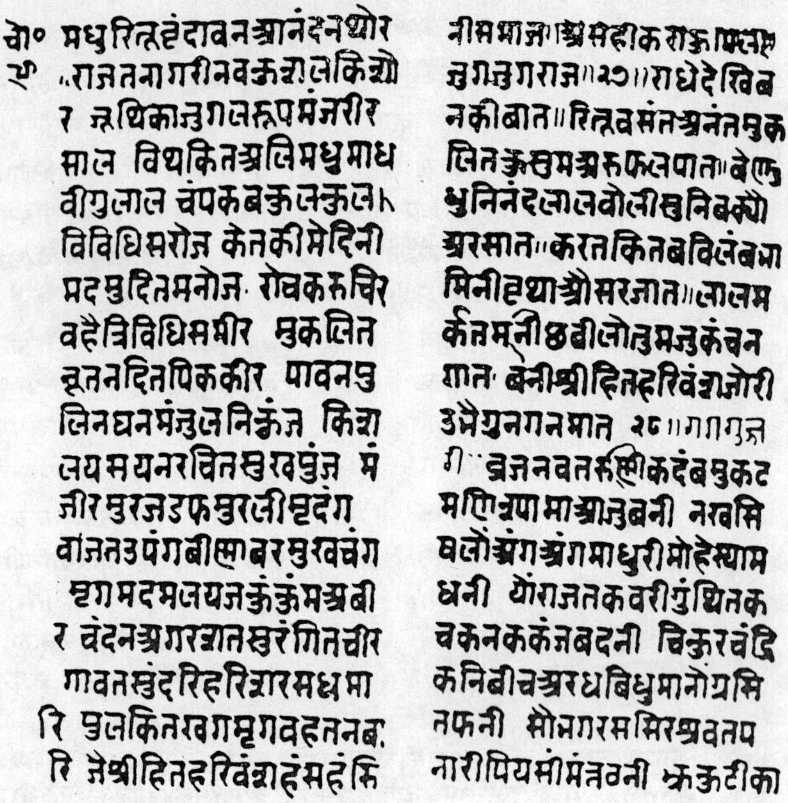

चौ० मधुरितुवृंदावनआनंदनथोर
४९ ॥राजतनागरीनवकुसलकिसो
र जूथिकाजुगलरूपमंजरीर
साल विथकितअलिमधुमाध
वीगुलाल चंपकबकुलकुल॥
विविधिसरोज केतकीमेदिनी
मदमुदितमनोज रोचकरुचिर
वहैत्रिविधिसमीर मुकलित
नूतनदितपिककीर पावनपु
लिनघनमंजुलनिकुंज किश
लयसयनरचितसुखपुंज मं
जीरमुरजडफमुरलीमृदंग
बाजतउपंगबीनाबरमुखचंग
मृगमदमलयजकुंकुमअबी
र चंदनअगरजातसुरंगितचीर
गावतसुंदरिहरिरागमधमा
रि पुलकितखगमृगबहतनब
रि जैश्रीहितहरिवंशहंसहंसि

नीसमाज ॥ असहीकरौमिलिजु
जुगजुगराज ॥ २७ ॥ राधेदेखिब
नकीबात ॥ रितुबसंतअनंतमुक
लितकुसुमअरुफलपात ॥ वेणु
धुनिनंदलालबोलीसुनिबक्यौ
अरसात ॥ करतकितबविलंबभा
मिनीहथाऔसरजात ॥ लालम
र्कतमनीछबीलोतुमजुकंचन
गात ॥ बनीश्रीहितहरिवंशजोरी
उभैगुनगनमात २८ ॥ रागगुज
री ॥ ब्रजनवतरुनिकदंबमुकट
मणिश्यामाआजुबनी नखसि
खलौंअंगअंगमाधुरीमोहेस्याम
धनी यौंराजतकबरीगुंथितक
चकनककंजबदनी चिकुरचंद्रि
कनिबीचअरधबिधुमानोंग्रसि
तफनी सौभगरससिरश्रवतप
नारीपियसीमंतठनी भृकुटीका

MS D

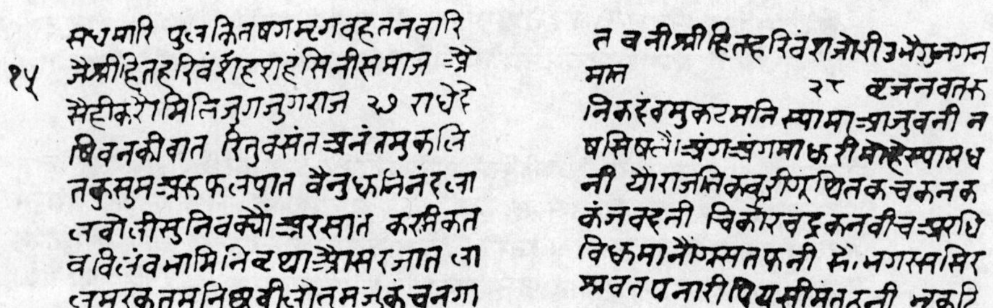

सुखमारि पुलकितखगमृगवहतनवारि
१५ जैश्रीहितहरिवंशहंसहंसिनीसमाज ऐसे
सैहीकरौमिलिजुगजुगराज २७ राधेदे
खिवनकीवात रितुवसंतअनंतमुकलि
तकुसुमअरुफलपात वेनुधुनिनंदला
लवोलीसुनिवक्यौंअरसात करतिकित
वविलंवभामिनिवथाऔसरजात ला
लमरकतमनिछवीलौतुमजुकंचनगा

त वनीश्रीहितहरिवंशजोरीउभैगुनगन
मत्त २८ ब्रजनवतरु
निकदंवमुकटमनिस्यामाआजुवनी न
खसिखलौंअंगअंगमाधुरीमोहेस्यामध
नी यौराजतिकवरीगुंथितकचकनक
कंजवदनी चिकुरचंद्रकनवीचअरधि
विधुमानौग्रसतफनी सौभगरससिर
श्रवतपनारीपियसीमंतठनी भ्रकुटि

MS E

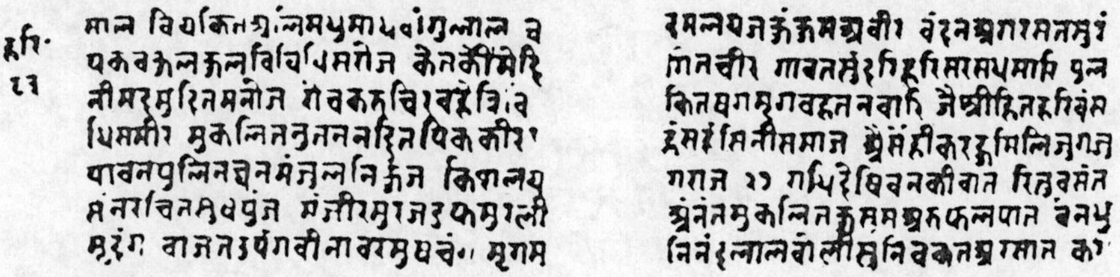

MS F

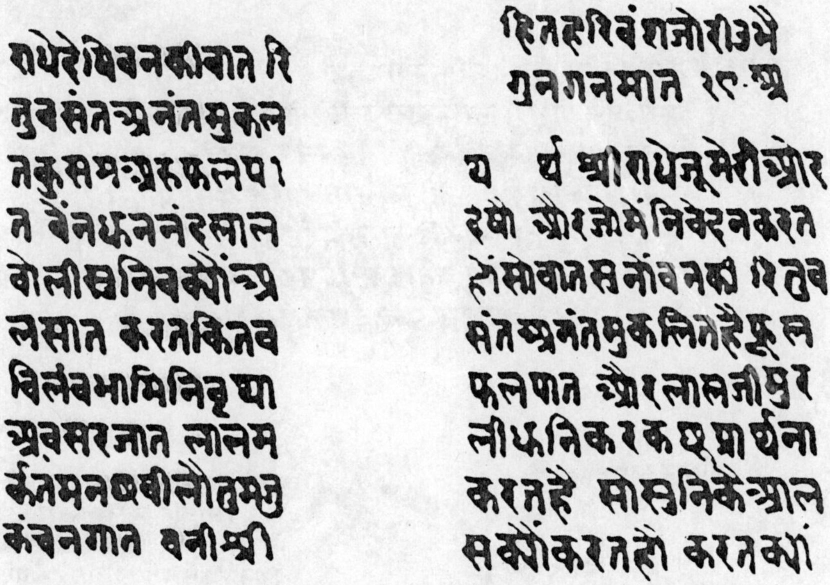

MS I

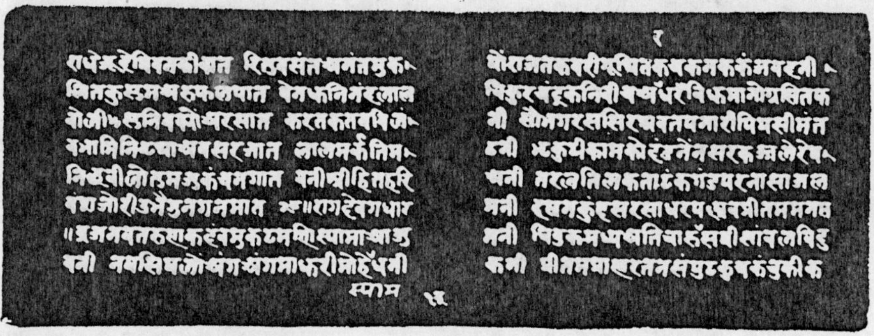

MS J

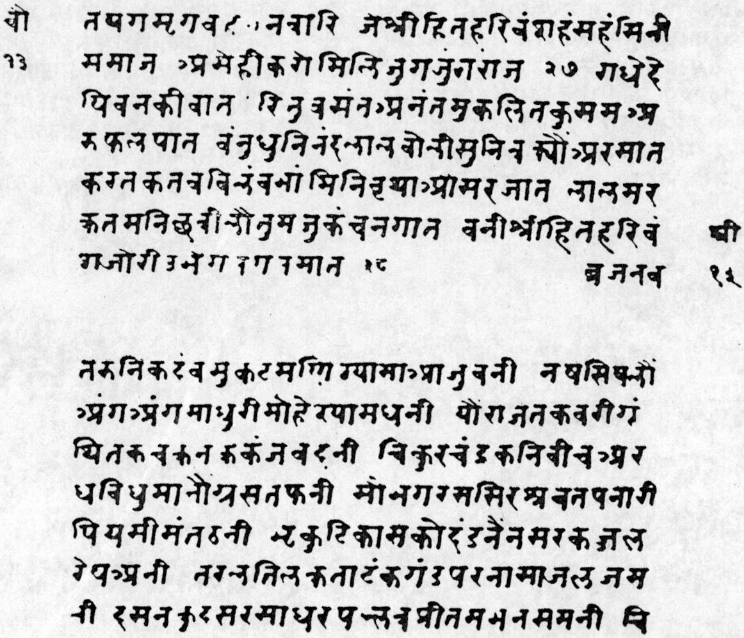
छौ नथगमगवत ।नवारि जेश्रीहितहरिवंशहंसहंसिनी
३३ समान ऽप्रेमहीकगे भिलि जुगलजुगराज २७ गधेरे
पिवनकी बात रितुबसंतऽप्रनंतमुकलितकुसमऽप्र
रुफलपात वेनुधुनिनंदलाल बोलीमुनिव स्यौंऽप्रसमात
करतकतबविलंबभांमिनिवृथाऽप्रासरजात लालसर
कतमनिछवीतौनुमनुकंवनगात वनीश्रीहितहरिवं छौ
शजोरीउभेगरगनमान २८ वजनव १९

तरुनिकदंवमुकटमणि स्यामाऽप्राजुवनी नखसिखलौं
ऽप्रंगऽप्रंगमाधुरीमोहेस्यामधनी छौरा जतकवरीगं
थितकचकुन कंजवदनी चिकुरचंद्रकनिबीचऽप्रर
धविधुमानौग्रसतफनी सौभगरसमिरऽप्रवतपनारी
पियसीमंतठनी भ्रकुटिकामकोदंडनैनसरकजल
रेपऽप्रनी तरलतिलकताटंकगंडपरनासाजलजम
नी दसनकुंदसरसाधरपल्लवप्रीतमऽमनसमनी वि

MS K

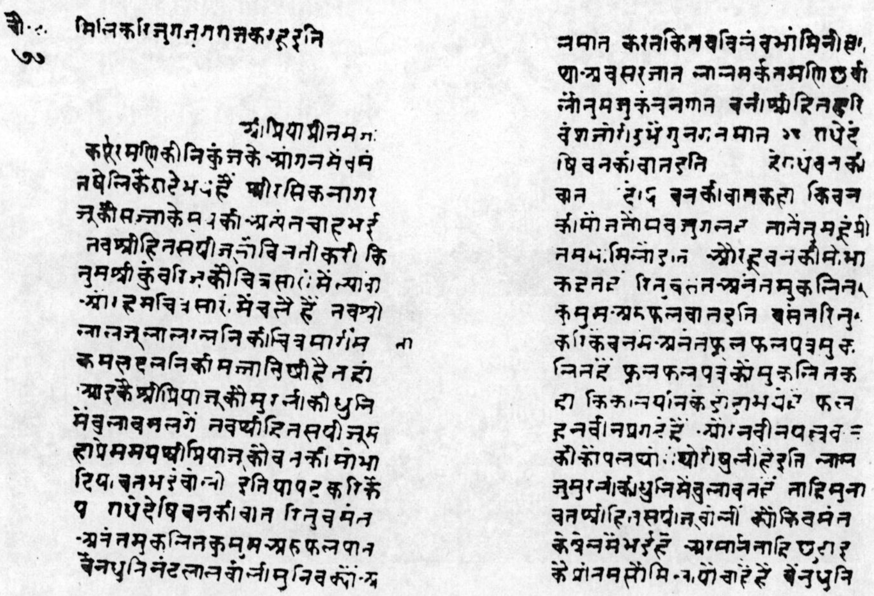

MS L

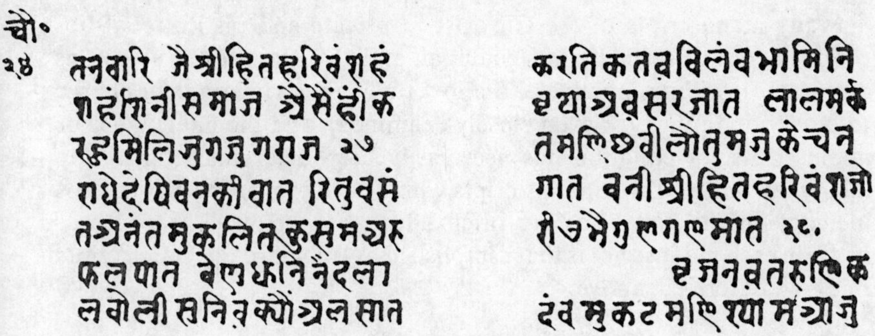
चौ०
२४ तनवारि जै श्री हितहरिवंश हं
शहंशानी समाज ऐसैं ही क
रहु मिलि जुगजुग राज २७
राधे देषि वन की वात रितु वसं
त अनंत मुकुलित कुसुम अरु
फल पात वेणु धुनि नंदला
ल वोली सुनि क्यों अलसात
करति कत वृविलंव भामिनि
वृथा अवसर जात लाल मर्क
त मणि छवीलो तुम जु कंचन
गात वनी श्री हितहरिवंश जो
री उभै गुण गण मात २८
वृजनवृतरुणिक
दंव मुकट मणि श्याम आजु

MS M

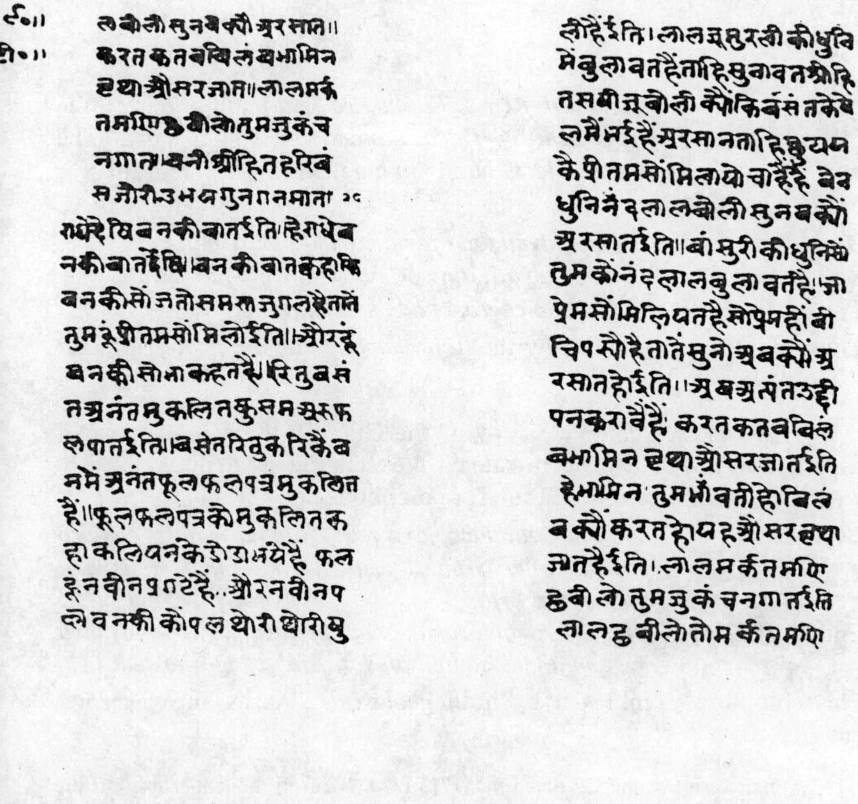
९०॥ ल बोली सुनि क्यों अरसात॥
टी०॥ करत कत बविलंब भामिन
वृथा औसर जात॥ लाल मर्क
त मणि छबीलो तुम जु कंच
न गात॥ बनी श्री हित हरिवं
स जोरी उभय गुन गन माता २८
राधे देषि बन की बात ई ति। हे राधे ब
न की बात देषि। बन की बात कहा कि
बन की सोंभा तो सम्र जुगल है ताते
तुम हूं प्रीतम सों मिलो इति॥ और हूं
बन की सोभा कहत हैं। रितु बसं
त अनंत मुकलित कुसुम अरु फ
ल पात ई ति॥ बसंत रितु करि कें ब
न में अनंत फूल फल पत्र मुकलित
हैं॥ फूल फल पत्र को मुकलित क
हा कलियन के डोडा भये हैं फल
हूं नवीन प्रगटे हैं.. और नवीन प
ल्लवन की कोंपल थोरी थोरी सु
ली हैं इति। लाल जु मुरली की धुनि
में बुलावत हैं ताहि सुनावत श्री हि
त सषी जु बोली कैं कि बंसी तके षे
ल में भई हैं अरसानता हि कुयम
के प्रीतम सों मिलायो चाहें हैं वेन
धुनि नंदलाल बोली सुनि क्यों
अरसात इति॥ बांसुरी की धुनि सों
तुम कों नंदलाल बुलावत हैं। जा
प्रेम सों मिलि चहत है सो प्रेम ही वी
चिप्यो है ताते सुनो अब क्यों अ
रसात हो इति।। अब असंत उद्दी
पन करावें हैं करत कत बविलं
ब भामिन वृथा औसर जात इति
हे भामिन तुम औ बती हो बिलं
ब क्यों करत हो यह औसर वृथा
जात है इति। लाल मर्कत मणि
छबीलो तुम जु कंचन गात इति
लाल छबीलो तो मर्कत मणि

3. Other manuscripts of the CP[1]

Many manuscripts of the CP exist in private and institutional libraries in India, especially in Vrindaban and the Braj area. Custodians are often unwilling, however, to allow the manuscripts in their charge to be photographed (or even closely examined), and the final choice of manuscripts for collation has necessarily been determined largely by their availability. Those manuscripts which have been inspected but not included in the collations are briefly described below. The order of *padas* in each manuscript is that established as 'standard' by manuscripts B, D–M described above.

(*i*) *Manuscripts in the Municipal Museum, Allahabad*

(These manuscripts were donated to the Museum by Śrī Rādhā Kṛṣṇa Gosvāmī of Mahājanī Ṭolā, Allahabad, formerly of Vrindaban.)

(a) MS 225. A complete bound manuscript in 191 folios, bearing the following texts: *Rādhāsudhānidhi*

CP

Sevaka vāṇī

Sphuṭa vāṇī (here *Phuṭakara pada*), followed by three folios of different paper bearing *Dādasa mantra* in a later hand. The text is written in a consistent hand in black ink, with red ink for colophons etc.

Begins: [f.1r] *śrī rādhāvallabho jayati. śrī hita harivaṃśa caṃdro jayati. atha śrīmac caurāsī pada liṣyate.*

Ends: [f.122v] *iti śrīmac caurāsī pada saṃpū*[*rṇa.*]

This colophon is followed by the first *chappaya* of the *phalaśruti*, and the *rāga kavitta*.

(b) MS 232. A complete copy of the CP with the commentary of Lokanātha. 289 badly worm-eaten folios, bound as a book. Neatly written in black ink with red ink for colophons etc.

Begins: [f.1r] *śrī rādhāvallabho jayati. śrī hita harivaṃśa caṃdro jayati. atha śrīmati caurāsī ṭīkā samasta liṣyate. lokanātha kṛta.*

Ends: [f.289v] *iti śrī vṛṃdāvana madhye hastākṣara vaiṣṇava jagannātha dāsa ke. saṃvata* 18.48. *aghena sūdī* 11.

This colophon is followed by both *phalaśruti* stanzas and the *rāga kavitta*.

1. A manuscript of the CP dated V.S. 1713 (A.D. 1656) in the collection of the K.M. Hindi Institute, University of Agra, and reported by J.S. Hawley (1984:52 n.37), came to my notice too late for inclusion here. The manuscript includes a *Sūrasāgara* text.

(c) MS 236. Another copy of the CP with the commentary of Lokanātha. Incomplete: lacks ff. 1–6; early folios badly damaged. Written in black ink with red ink for colophons etc.

Ends: [f.233v] *iti yaha pustaka śrī vṛṃdāvana mẽ liṣī saṃvata* 1810. *pauṣa kṛṣṇa* 9 *maṃgalavāra pūrṇa bhaī. prema sõ paḍhai vicārai suṣa prīti hoi. śrī jī ke āsarai śrī vṛṃdāvana vāsa.*

This colophon is followed by both the *phalaśruti* stanzas, and the *rāga kavitta.*

(*ii*) *Manuscripts in the Nāgarī Pracāriṇī Sabhā, Varanasi*

(a) 530. A complete manuscript of the CP in 58 bound folios. A very clear hand in black ink with red ink for colophons etc.

Begins: [f.1r] *atha śrīmad caurāsī pada liṣyate.*
Ends: [f.58r] *iti śrīmad gosvāminā śrī hita harivaṃśa caṃdra viracitāyāṃ caturāsī pada vilāsa saṃpūrṇam.*

This colophon is followed by the first *phalaśruti* stanza, and the *rāga kavitta.*

(b) 1234. A complete manuscript of the CP in 60 bound folios. Written in an erratic hand, with black ink for text and red ink for colophons etc., enclosed in a red and yellow border.

Begins: [f.1r] *śrī rādhāvallabho jayati. iti śrīmata cavarāsī liṣyatai. śrī hita harivaṃśo jayatī.*

The text is followed immediately by the first stanza of the *phalaśruti,* and ends:

[f.60v] *iti śrī harivaṃśa gusāĩ jī kṛta caurāsī saṃpūrṇa. śrī rādhāval[l]abha śrī harivaṃśa. śrī vṛṃdāvana śrī vanaca[ṃ]dra. śrī kṛṣṇaghano*[*?*] *namaḥ.*

This colophon is followed by an illegible scribble in a later hand.

(c) 1244. An incomplete manuscript of the CP and the *Sevaka vāṇī* bound together. Ff.1-87 carry the CP; f.1 is a later replacement and ff. 2-4 are missing. A neat hand in black ink, with red ink for colophons etc.

Begins: [f.1r] *śrī rādhāvallabho jayati. atha śrī caurāsī jī likhyate.*
Ends: [f.87v] *iti śrīmac caurāsī pada saṃpūrṇa.*

This colophon is followed by the two *phalaśruti* stanzas and the *rāga kavitta.*

(d) 1773. A complete manuscript of the CP, in 80 folios. A very clear hand in black ink, with red ink for colophons etc.

Begins: [f.1r] *śrīmad hita harivaṃśa caṃdro jayati śrī hita rādhāvallabho jayati śrīmac caurāsī pada prāraṃbha.*

Ends: [f.80r] *iti śrīmad ācāryya śiromaṇi śrīmad hita harivaṃśa caṃdra gosvāmī kṛta śrī caturāśī pada samāptaḥ.*

The colophon is followed by the first stanza of the *phalaśruti,* and the *rāga kavitta*; the former is here ascribed to Gosvāmī Vanacandra in the following words:

[f.80v] *ātha* [*sic*] *gosvāmī śrī vanacandra jū kṛta phalastuti chappai.*

(e) 2447. A lithographed handwritten text of the CP with the title *Premalatā*, published in Agra in v.s. 1945. Cover damaged. Imprint from cover reads:

premalatā, arthāt śrī rādhā kṛṣṇa caraṇāraviṃdānugāmī parama ananya bhakta śiromaṇi śrī vṛndāvana nivāsī śrī hita harivaṃśa jī mahārāja racita caurāsī pada. āgarā. a[*tu*]*la ulāhī presa mẽ chapā*[///]*samvat* 1945.

(f) 2248. An incomplete, roughly-written copy of the CP in a slightly cursive hand, written in black ink with red ink for colophons etc. The first 5 of the 48 bound folios are missing. Badly damaged throughout by smudging of ink, and made almost illegible in parts by a very clumsy attempt at lamination. No date, though accompanying library label gives date as v.s. 1859.

Ends: [f.47v] *iti śrīmat caturāsī saṃpūrṇa.*

This colophon is followed by the first of the *phalaśruti* stanzas, and the *rāga kavitta.*

(g) 4825. A manuscript of the CP in 31 folios, the first two of which are a replacement of the original, written in a later hand on modern milled paper of a colour similar to that of the remainder of the manuscript. The text on ff. 3-31 is in black ink, with red ink for colophons etc. A change to a finer hand from f.17 onwards suggests a change of scribe and perhaps of exemplar; the second scribe's orthography shows a marked preference for *-u* endings in substantives (*rāgu* etc.).

The text of the first two folios is crude but clear, in a brown ink with no decorative red. These folios bear the text of CP 1-9.3, and show the following noteworthy features:

i) In the colophon quoted below, the name of Kṛṣṇa precedes that of Rādhā—a most unusual occurrence in sectarian texts. The lack of extended honorifics in the reference to Harivaṃśa is also remarkable.

ii) The honorific slogan *jai śrī* attached to the *chāpa* of Harivaṃśa in *all* other manuscripts inspected is not found in the stanzas carried by these two folios.

iii) Each stanza, and the occasional individual line, is followed by the first syllable of the first word of that stanza, presumably as a *da capo* instruction for the singing of the text.

iv) Each stanza bears a *rāga* heading, whereas in other manuscripts only the first stanza in each *rāga* group is so headed.

The inference is that these replacement folios may have been copied from a manuscript written specifically as a 'performance' copy, probably (in the light of (i) above), from a tradition other than the Rādhāvallabha *sampradāya*.

This manuscript is also unusual in having a distinctive allocation of *rāgas*; the groupings, which may be compared with those of the collated MSS on pp. 48-63. are as follows:

CP	1–13	Vibhāsa
	14–16	Toḍī
	17–18	Guā̃varī (?)
	19–26	Dhanāsirī
	27–28	Vasaṃta
	29–30	Gujarī
	31–35	Devagaṃdhāra
	36–51	Sāraṃga
	52–55	Malāra
	56	Gaurī malāra
	57–65	Gaurī dhamārī
	66–71	Kalyāna
	72–80	Kānharau
	81–84	Kedārau.

The text begins: [f.1r] *śrī kṛṣṇa rādhe jayati. caurāsī harivaṃśa jū kī.*

Ends: *iti śrī caurāsī pada saṃpūrṇa.*

This colophon is followed by the first *phalaśruti* stanza and, notwithstanding the distinctive arrangement of *rāgas* listed above, the usual *rāga kavitta*.

(*iii*) *Manuscript in the Rajasthan Oriental Research Institute, Udaipur Palace Museum*

3179. A complete manuscript of the CP followed by an anonymous text entitled *Dhyānalīlā*. 51 folios, written in a rough hand in black ink, with red ink for colophons etc. First folio has heavily decorated margins. *Rāga* headings are not given.

Begins: [f.1r] *śrī rādhāvallabho jayata. atha haravaṃśa caurāsī liṣyate.*

Ends: [f.51r] *ite śrī hita harivaṃśa kṛta caurāsī saṃpūrṇa samāpta.*

The two *phalaśruti* stanzas precede the following colophon:

[f.51v] *phala astuta saṃpūrna samāpta. mitī jeṭha sudī* 4 *saṃvata* 1824 *mukāma maharāja nagara caraṣārī liṣyatama*
vrajabhūṣana bhajanī. jo kou vā̃cai sunai tākau jai rādhaikṛsna jai rādhaikṛsna jai rādhaikṛsna.

iv) Manuscripts in the collection of Hit Dās Bābā, Vrindaban

(a) CP with the commentary of Ratanadāsa, followed by the *Nāgarī aṣṭaka* of Nāgarīdāsa with commentary. A modern copy on milled foolscap paper, bound as a book.

Begins: [f.1r] *śrī rādhāvallabho jayati. śrī hita harivaṃśa candro jayatī. atha śrīmad harivaṃśa candra gosvāmī kṛta śrīmad hita caurāsī jī saṭīka śrī kṛpāpātra parma vaiṣṇava śrī hita ratanadāsa jī kṛta likhyatai.*

Ends: [f.167r] *iti śrī śrīmat harivaṃśa caṃdro gosvāmī kṛtasya caturāsīti pada akṣarārtha saṃpūrna. śubham astu.*

This colophon is then followed by the first *phalaśruti chappaya*; this is here attributed to Vanacandra, the second *chappaya,* which follows, being attributed to Rūpalāla:

[f.167v] *yaha tau śrīmata gosvāmī śrī hita vanacaṃda jū nai kahī. yāhī saũ ava śrī hita rūpalāla jī gosvāmī jū kahata hai.*

(b) A manuscript of 97+68+125 folios, bearing the *Rādhāsudhānidhi*, CP, *Sevaka vāṇī* and (in the same pagination as this last) the *Nāgarī aṣṭaka*. Written in a clear and consistent hand in black ink, with red ink for colophons etc. Folio 61 of the CP sequence is missing: CP 77-79 carried on this lost folio have been added to the margins of ff.60v and 62r. The colophon following the *Rādhāsudhānidhi* is dated Samvat 1877:

[f.97v] *iti śrīvṛṃdāvaneśvarīcaraṇakṛpāmātravijṛṃbhita śrīmad rādhāsudhānidhistava śrimad hitaharivaṃśacaṃdragosvāminā viracitāḥ samāptaḥ. saṃvat.* 1877. *mitī vaiśākha sukle* 14. *vṛhaspatavāre śubham astu bhūyāt. śrī śrī śrī śrī śrī hitāya namo namaḥ.*

The CP begins [f.1r, new sequence]:

śrī rādhāvallabho jayati. śrī hita harivaṃśa caṃdro jayati. atha śrīmata caturāsī liṣyate.

The colophon following the text cannot be read, since the folio bearing it is stuck fast to the first folio of the *Sevaka vāṇī*.

4. The Phalaśruti

The text of the *phalaśruti* stanzas, which follow the *mūla* in many of the manuscripts, varies little except in orthography; thus variants are not given in the transcription below. The text given here is taken from source G (Vijaypāl Siṃha and Candrabhān Rāvat, pp. 195-197).

[*chappaya* 1.] Appears in A (*sec. m.*), BCDEFGHJKLM.
bhava jalanidhi ko nāva kāma pāvaka kõ pānī;
prema bhakti ko mūla moda maṃgala sukhadānī.
nigama sāra siddhāṃta saṃta biśrāma madhura bara;
rasakani ko rasa sāra sakala akṣara rasa ko ghara.
caurāśī (*śrī hita*) *haribaṃśa kṛta paṛhe sune niśi bhora;*
chuṭe caurāśī bhramani tẽ nirakhe jugala kiśora.

[*chappaya* 2.] Appears in BDFGHJKLM.
nirakhe jugala kiśora bhora aru raina na jāne;
pie rūpa rasa matta bhayau kachu manahi na āne.
prema lakṣaṇā bhakti hoi hiya ān̐dakārī;
aru bṛṃdābana bāsa sakhī sukha ko adhikārī.
kuṃja mahala kī ṭahala sukha saṃpati daṃpati pāihai;
(*jai śrī*) *rūpalāla hita prīti sõ jo caurāsī gāihai.*

[*kavitta.*] Appears in A (*sec. m.*), BD, F (*sec.m.*), GHJKLM.
cha pada bibhāsa mãjha sāta haĩ bilāvala mẽ
ṭoḍī māhĩ catura āsābarī mẽ dvai bane;
sapta haĩ dhanāsirī mẽ jugala basaṃta keli
devagaṃdhāra paṃca doi rasa sõ sane.
sārãga mẽ ṣoḍasa haĩ cāri hī malāra eka
gauḍa mẽ suhāyo nava gaurī rasa mẽ bhane;
ṣaṭa kalyānahi nidhi kānhare kedāre beda
vāṇī hi ⟨t⟩ a jū kī saba caudaha rāga mẽ gane.

As discussed under the description of MS G above, Premadāsa attributes these three stanzas to Vanacandra (son of Harivaṃśa), Rūpalāla[1] and Hita Hari Malla[2] respectively. The *rāga* allocations given by the *kavitta* are discussed below in section VII.3.(i); it is not apparent why symbolic numbers (*nidhi* = 9, *veda* = 4) should be resorted to for the final two *rāgas* only.

5. The Ṭīkās[3]

Three *ṭīkās* are represented in the CP manuscripts collated for the edition, and a fourth, that of Rasikalāla, has been examined from a manuscript not containing the *mūla*. Frequent reference to readings in these commentaries is made in the annotation to the text in Chapter V,

1. The traditional dates for Rūpalāla are v.s. 1775-1875 (A.D. 1718-1818): Lalitā Caraṇ Gosvāmī 1957: 482.
2. Discussed in Chapter VII.
3. The commentaries are surveyed in an article published at an earlier stage in the preparation of this study: R. Snell 1980 (b).

and a summary of their interpretations is offered in VII.3.(ii) and (iv); examples of the four *ṭīkās* can be seen in Appendix I, which comprises transcriptions of glosses on CP 5. The present section discusses the date and formal composition of the commentaries.

Vijayendra Snātak (1968:303) lists 16 commentaries on the CP. According to this list, the oldest is that of Rasikalāla (Rasik.), dated V.S. 1734 (A.D. 1677). Rasik. is identified by Mītal (1968:441) as the second son of Vilāsadāsa Gosvāmī (V.S. 1665-1725[1]), a descendant of Harivaṃśa. Kiśorīśaraṇ 'Ali' (p. 19) includes Rasik. in a list of authors of the 18th century of the Vikrama era and attributes to him commentaries on the *Karṇānanda* and the *Gītagovinda* as well as the CP *ṭīkā* and a *padāvalī*. The copy of Rasik. on which discussion here is based is incomplete and lacks the colophon folio.[2] The commentary is in verse (mostly *dohās* with occasional *soraṭhās* and, rarely, other metres); the gloss on each stanza is preceded by an introductory sequence of couplets, and is followed by a formula on the following model, yielding the title *Rahasya artha samaya nirūpana:*

[f.6v] *iti śrī corāsī pada rahasya artha samaya nirūpana*
śrī rasikalāla kṛta dohābaddha bhāṣāyāṃ dvitiya
vilāsa sa[ṃ]pūrṇaḥ. 2.

This formula is frequently abbreviated, e.g.:

[f.26v] *iti śrī trayodasa vilāsa pūrṇa.* 13.

The *ṭīkā* of Dharaṇīdharadāsa (Dhar.) is borne by MS A, copied in V.S. 1749 (A.D. 1693). As noted in the description of that manuscript, the commentary contains a salutation to Dāmodara, understood as Hita Harivaṃśa's grandson: but Dharaṇīdharadāsa does not appear in a list of the disciples of Dāmodaradāsa given in the *Rādhāvallabha bhaktamāla* of Priyādās Śukla (p. 122). In this commentary the *mūla* of each stanza is followed by a *dohā* which introduces the context, and a gloss in *savaiyās*. Content of the gloss is limited to a paraphrase of

1. Prabhudayāl Mītal 1968: 410.

2. The manuscript is a bound, incomplete copy in the collection of Bābā Hit Dās of Vrindaban. The manuscript is paginated f. 5-196, lacking ff. 1-4 and the last folios; the commentary on CP 1 and the beginning of the commentary on CP 2 is missing, as is the end of the commentary on CP 84 and the colophon. A crudely executed drawing of Kṛṣṇa and Rādhā attended by a *sakhī* occupies f. 51r (following the commentary on CP 25), the adjacent folios 50v and 51v being left blank; similarly a drawing of Kṛṣṇa as *muralīdhara*, accompanied by two *gopīs* and a herd of cows, occupies f. 65r (in the middle of the commentary on CP 29), the adjacent folios 64v and 65v again being left blank. Folio 119 is also left blank. Ff. 139v to 159v are in a neat hand which is in contrast to the remainder of the manuscript and is apparently the work of a different scribe; the remainder is written in a very erratic hand with great changes of character size, number of lines per page and thickness of pen. The *mūla* text is not given in this manuscript, nor are *rāgas* indicated; stanza order shows an inversion of CP 2 and 3 *vis-à-vis* the 'standard' order.

the *mūla* with the minimum of exegetical comment, and in this respect Dhar.'s treatment of the text differs markedly from that of the other commentators. Dhar.'s interpretations often tally with those of Rasik., to the exclusion of the two later commentators discussed below.

The *ṭīkā* of Lokanātha (Lok.) is of uncertain date. According to the *Rādhāvallabha bhaktamāla* (Priyādās Śukla pp. 412-413), Lok. was a Brahmin from Patna who became a disciple of Vilāsadāsa (mentioned above as father of Rasik.); but a *dohā* at the beginning of this commentary[1] salutes the name of Sukhalāla, identified by Mītal (1968:416) as grandson of Vilāsadāsa, from which it appears that the Lok. *ṭīkā* was written some considerable time after Vilāsadāsa's death in V.S. 1725. The prose *ṭīkā* introduces each stanza with an *ābhāsa*, giving a conventional[2] and stylized description of each 'grove' setting. Similarities of interpretation with Prem.'s commentary suggest that Lok. may have been the model for Prem.

The *ṭīkā* of Premadāsa (Prem.) appears in MSS GKM; as noted in the description of MS G, the *ṭīkā* is dated V.S. 1791 (A.D. 1734). In a sequence of *dohās* introducing the prose *ṭīkā*, Prem. praises the name of his *guru* Rūpalāla,[3] whose dates are given by Mītal (1968:421) as V.S. 1738-1801 (A.D. 1681-1744). In the same *dohā* sequence Prem. records his intention of giving a *literal* rendering of the text,[4] and his glosses do give more discussion of lexical meanings than is found elsewhere. Prem. also explains his use of prose rather than verse as being intended to render meanings more readily accessible;[5] but similarities with the Lok. gloss (including a similar use of *ābhāsas* to each stanza) suggest that his use of prose is not an innovation in the CP tradition.

In addition to the four commentaries discussed here, the modern Hindi rendering of the CP by Lalitā Caraṇ Gosvāmī (1972) is also referred to in Chapter V, under the siglum LCG.

1. *śrī sukhalāla saroja pada tinakau nija sira dhāri;*
   śrī vyāsa suvana śubha girā (kī) ṭīkā liṣata bicāra.

(MS B ff. 1v -2r.)

2. Lok.'s frequent references to watershoots etc. (e.g. *hauda nahara jalajaṃtra jala bhare chūṭata haĩ*, App. I) do not, however, derive from the Sanskritic tradition but show familiarity with Rajput palaces such as that at Deeg, inspired ultimately by the Indo-Islamic garden palaces of the Mughals.

3. *jayati jayati ānaṃda ghana śrī guru pūraṇa caṃda;*
   udaya rahau mama hṛda gagana tama bhrama kiyẽ nikaṃda. 9.
   sākṣāta hita rūpa śrī rūpalāla sukha puṃja;
   jorī jū ke keli kī jinike naina nikuṃja. 10.

(Text G, p. 1.)

4. *jayati jayati haribaṃśa jū tinike pada cita lāi;*
   caturāśī pada ko kahõ akṣara artha banāi. 17.
   ati agādha hita kī girā samajhe ko sāmartha;
   mana saṃbodhana hita karõ kachu ika akṣara artha. 18.

5. *kīje tilaka kabitta bādha samajhata hoi abāra;*
   tātẽ bacanana mẽ kahaũ līje sadya bicāra. 25.

(*loc. cit.*)

CHAPTER III

MANUSCRIPT AFFILIATIONS AND THE LANGUAGE OF THE TEXT

1. Affiliation of Manuscripts and Editorial Procedure

There is no question of an autograph copy of the CP ever having been in existence, since even the sectarian attribution of all 84 stanzas to Hita Harivaṃśa does not maintain that the text existed as a unified compilation in Harivaṃśa's own lifetime. It is likely that the CP, as a consolidated text to which the symbolically significant number '84' lends a formal coherence, originally comprised a loose anthology of *padas* not conceived *ab initio* as forming a discrete text; an early corpus may have been complemented by the addition of other material from other sources, or of new material composed especially to complement the existing stanzas. The original anthology may have been transmitted from an early stage through oral tradition, though in view of the relatively complex metrical forms discussed in Chapter VI it seems unlikely that the text itself derives directly from a transcription of sung verses. The canonical status attributed to the CP as sectarian tradition gathered momentum will have ensured the transition of a broadly standardized text which, although subject to various corrupting influences, has successfully maintained the appearance of a uniform composition.

Since the archetype of the received CP clearly postdates the collection of its component parts, orthography in the manuscripts must reflect a stage in the development of the language rather later than that at which the *padas* themselves were originally composed. Influences bearing on the archetype during the copying process are threefold. First is the tendency towards commentatorial amendment or accretion for the sake of semantic clarity[1] or sectarian advantage. Secondly, the text may have been subject to the requirements of musical performance, the effects of which are discussed in VI.6. Finally, and most conspicuously, is the process of Sanskritization evident in the orthography of the manuscripts: it is clear that the language of the CP is characterized by a high number of *tatsama* and semi-*tatsama* forms (in comparison with contemporary texts such as the *padas* of Sūradāsa), and many of the scribes,

1. Cf. a similar tendency in the *vāṇī* of Haridāsa, where the accretion of pronouns and proper names has taken place to 'indicate the direction of action and otherwise resolve ambiguities' (R.D. Haynes, p. 268).

emboldened by this characteristic, have 'upgraded' old forms in the direction of Hindi/Sanskrit norms, often thereby robbing the text of intended meanings, rhetorical effects or grammatical features. It is apparent that this process of Sanskritization is not necessarily transmitted through the copying process alone, but is to a large extent spontaneous: as a result, a veneer of late Sanskritization tends to obscure genetic affiliations between manuscripts. In the case of *padas* having an easily perceived and readily recognized prosodic form (such as the 16+11/12 *mātrā* types Sarasī and Sāra), errors of transmission have to some extent been restricted by scribal compliance with familiar metrical patterns; but in the case of more complex prosodies of the *varṇavṛtta* type, the scribes have often lost sight of the original metrical constructions, and corruptions and accretions have affected the text more freely.

The aim of the edition is to reverse the processes of corruption and to edit back through the manuscripts towards the (hypothetical) archetype. In order to identify correspondences and affiliations between the manuscripts, the evidence of each manuscript is assessed below. In advance of section III.2 which discusses script, it must be noted here that the transliteration graph ṣ represents both /ṣ/ and /kh/ (yielding *ghoṣa* and *ṣeta,* etc.): the graph ष is maintained in the edited text in Chapter IV.

MS A. This is the manuscript with the highest number of exclusive readings; it also has a different stanza order from the other manuscripts, and differences in *rāga* allocations. A minority of readings exclusive to MS A are equal in metrical or semantic value to the 'majority' readings:

13.4 A *kāko mana rahata* for *kaise mana rahata;* (cf. the reading *kāko* in the *Sūrasāgara* version of this stanza, given in Appendix II.)

26.4 A *subhaga pāvana pulina* for *parama pāvana pulina* (Cf. further collocations of *subhaga* and *pulina* at 36.2, 64.2, 68.2 and 72.1, to which the MS A reading is perhaps assimilated.)

Most readings exclusive to A, however, are inferior—

(a) in metre:

21.6 A *rasika* for *rasikinī;*

27.1 A *ghora* for *na thora;*

or (b) in sense:

24.4 A *dija* for *braja* in *braja juvatina kī bhīra;*

25.4 A *badati* for *bidita* in the adjectival phrase *sakala bidyā bidita;*

or (c) in sense *and* metre:

16.3 A *lāgati,* by haplography for 5-*mātrā lāga gati*

83.2 A *karata,* for 2-*mātrā kata,*

It is curious that out of 9 occurrences in the CP, the name *hari* is omitted three times in MS A— at 27.15, 58.6 and 65.1 (and at 9.3 *hari* in A replaces an erased reading). In each of the three instances the A reading is unmetrical; no reason for the omissions is apparent.

Of the readings found in A and shared by certain of the other manuscripts, some are apparently authentic (i.e. have not been subject to corrupting influences found in the remaining group), while others must be rejected as corrupt. Examples of such corrupt forms are given below:

10.2 AC *lāsa rāsa,* E *rāsa*, for *rāsa lāsa*; the AC reading may reflect an erroneous restoration after the omission of *lāsa* in E.

11.2 A *druti*, CEGM *druta*, for *duti*. *duti* for *dyuti* 'brightness' is the intended sense; *dr°* is nonsensical in the context, and has not been borne out by the commentaries in A (Dharaṇīdharadāsa) or GM (Premadāsa).

20.3 ACE *upara* for *ūpara*. A four-*mātrā* form is required for metre. The ACE reading reflects a general use of *upara* in the language of the scribes: cf. the same feature in *LIO*, para 2.14.

27.2 AE *kusala* omitted.

31.7 ABI *ghana ghora* for *ghana ṣora*. *ghora* 'thunder' has no place in the context, a description of the *kuṃja: ṣora* 'covered lane', is apposite.

58.1 AC *māī ho* prefixes the full line, superfluously. The phrase is probably incorporated from the sung version, where it may be used as a musical *mukhaḍā* (as discussed in section VI.6(iii)).

59.3 AC *jaba ru* (?), for absolutive *jori*.

66.9 ACEGLM *byāpita*; BI *byāpyo*, DJ *byāpyau*, for (FHK) *byāpata*. *byāpita* appears to have been formed, by analogy with true participial adjectives, from intransitive Hindi *vyāp-*. *byāpata*, as a semi-*tatsama* orthography for *vyāpta*, is more likely to be the authentic form. The BrBh. participle in BI and DJ perhaps derives from a commentatorial paraphrase.

74.1 AFJ *hau*, BD *he*, I *ho*, for *hai*. The *hau/ho* form implies a *plural* subject, who is Rādhā; but in all other contexts Rādhā is addressed in the singular, as is apparent from the use of the singular pronoun *tū* etc.

75.1 ABIJKL *ḍarāti*, for *ḍārati* which is correct for both sense and end-rhyme.

83.4 ACE *ḍaribau* for *ḍharibau* (<**dhalati*).

MS A therefore contains many corrupt forms, whether exclusive to this manuscript or shared with others.

A correspondence between A and C, and to a lesser extent between A and E, is a recurring feature and can be seen in the above examples; A and C both have *kata* for *kyaū* (28.3) and also share the inversion of CP 3 and 4, and two exclusive *rāga* allocations: the use of Lalita at the beginning of the text and of Gujarī for the stanzas headed by Devagandhāra or Vasanta in other manuscripts. This group is occasionally joined by GM, as seen in the examples *drut-* and *byāpita* above.

MS B. This manuscript contains various intrusions into the *mūla* of the Lokanātha *ṭīkā* which it contains. At 66.1, *kuṃja* is followed by *ke madhya*, from the gloss on that line; at 63[iv].5 the two words *magana sahelī* are separated by a long phrase taken from the subsequent gloss on 63[i].1; the phrase *priyā jī so bacana* which follows *bacana* at 83.2 derives from the *ābhāsa* to the *mūla* of CP 84.

MS B has a large number of lacunae: words, *akṣaras* or parts of *akṣaras* are quite frequently omitted, often by haplography. Examples are 1.4 and 27.17 *haṃsinī* for *haṃsa haṃsinī*; 11.6 *bharata* for *bhara bharata*; 49.2 *ṣori ka* for *ṣori ṣiraka*. Most divergent B readings detract from the sense of the line, though a number do so without disturbing the metrical construction. The following are metrically satisfactory but semantically implausible readings:

7.7 B *mukaṭa* for *mukara* in *hari ura mukara*;
11.4 B *cāhu* for *cāṭu* in *cāṭu baina*;
31.7 B *mani* for *bana* in *bana biharata*;
52.2 B *ati* for *adha-* in *karata adhagrīvā*.

This manuscript has a tendency, albeit an inconsistent one, to show final short *-a* rather than the predominant *-i* in absolutive forms: 47.3 *dura* (other MSS *duri*); 53.2 *niraṣa* (other MSS *niraṣi*).

Correspondences in a corrupt mode of transmission are suggested by the following readings shared by B and other manuscripts:

1.3 BDJ *prāna prāna*, F *prāna te prāna*, I *prāṇa prāṇa*, for *prāna*;
16.2 BK omit *bhalaī*;
26.5 BDIJ *banata* for *banita*;
26.6 BDHI prefix the third *pāda* with the metrically superfluous *jai śrī*: (*jai śrī*) *ubhai kalahaṃsa haribaṃśa bali dāsu rī*;
27.5 BJ omit *kula*, by haplography, from *bakula kula*;
50.4 BI *calī*, by metathesis for *lacī*;
66.9 BI *byāpyo*, DJ *byāpyau*, for *byāpata*;
68.8 BDFHIJ add the superfluous *jai śrī* to the third *pāda* as in 26.6 above: (*jai śrī*) *ubhai kala haṃsa haribaṃśa ghana dāminī*.

There is a tendency for B readings to be found also in D and J and to a lesser extent in I and K. D differs from B more frequently than does J, as in 1.3 where D, with ACHKL, reads *mere*, resisting the intrusion of the commentatorial particle *to* (*mere to*) found in BFGIJM. The loosely affiliated group BDIJK tends to be differentiated from ACE readings on the one hand, and from GM readings on the other.

MS C. Examples of variant readings given above under MS A show a correspondence between A and C, and this correspondence endures throughout most of the evidence. C also shares readings with E; these are usually shared by A also, (as already demonstrated) but sometimes exclude A, as in CE *kabahuka* for *kabahu* (34.9), CE *citu* for *cita* (35.4). This is consistent with the hypothesis that A and C both derive from E, suggested by the crux referred to above in which AC restore but wrongly locate *lāsa* (10.2), omitted in E. C also imposes its own errors on the text, typically by lengthening *-i* to *-ī* unmetrically (as discussed in section 2); another example of error exclusive to this manuscript is the imposition of the words *jai śrī hita* for *dina* immediately before the *chāpa* of *haribaṃśa* at 34.10.

MS D. This manuscript has few exclusive readings. D shares with I a lengthening of *u* to *ū* in *prabhū* at both 11.5 and 12.5. A limited correspondence exists between D and BJ, and to a lesser extent with I; though rarely forming an autonomous group, these manuscripts have a general correspondence of readings tending to set them apart from the ACE and GM groups. The BDIJ affiliation is seen not only in its avoidance of corruptions found in those groups, but also in corrupt readings of its own, as already demonstrated under the description of B above.

In some instances, D has a better reading than other members of the BDIJ group—perhaps having resisted commentatorial intrusion into the text. Examples are:

- 1.3 D, with ACHKL, reads *mere* where BFGIJM read *mere to*/*tau*;
- 27.5 BJ omit *kula;*
- 62.2 BDEF *kini,* ACHKL *kina*, in a two-*mātrā* context where GM read *kyaũ na* and IJ *kyõ na*.

MS E. MS E has a number of lacunae not apparent in other manuscripts. Examples are the omission of *lāsa* (10.2), *rī* (15.2), *syāma* (29.17), *kata* (40.4, by haplography from *karata kata*), and the whole of line 61.5 The dance term *sudhaṃga* is corrupted to *sugaṃdha* in most occurrences, leaving nonsensical readings. At 41.1 the verb *jānai* is prefixed by the particle *na*, negating the intended sense.

As shown above in the description of MS A, E has correspondences with A and with C, often showing agreement in a mode of corruption. Orthographic agreement with A is fairly common, especially in reading *ra* (less commonly *ri*) for *ṛ*: AE *braṃdā* (26.3), AE *brathā* (28.4). Agreement with C to the exclusion of A tends towards Sanskritized orthographies: CE *syāmala*, L *śyāmala* (1.4, for *sā̃vala*), DEFH *caṃdra* (6.3, for *caṃda*).

MS F. Exclusive readings are few. For *prāna* (1.3) F reads *prāna te prāna*, an unmetrical reading probably derived from BDJ *prāna prāna*. *raṃga bharī* is omitted from the end of 84.1, robbing this metrically irregular *ṭeka* of its rhyming syllables. An affiliation with M is suggested by the omission from both manuscripts of *karata* (7.10, by haplography from *karata kara*), and by the FGLM reading *ika bāta* for *niju bāta* in 83.5 (cf. *ika bāta* at 75.1). The affiliation with M is often not exclusive, often also including G as exemplified in the following:

1.3 BFGIJM *mere* foll. by *to/tau*;
12.6 F *bilasau*, GM °*o*, for *bilasahu* (A °*ahi*);
33.5 AFGIM *naina aruna* for *aruna naina*;
42.3 CFGHL *saritā*, M *saratā*, Sanskritized from *saliṭā*;
58.6 FGM *tana* omitted (and GM read *tana* for *tava*).

F does not usually share readings with G to the exclusion of M (though (D)FG do omit the *rāga* heading *Bilāvala* from CP 7); F is however frequently excluded from a correspondence between G and M, and the fact that such exclusive GM readings are usually corrupt (as is shown in the discussion of G below) shows that F holds a place higher in the stemma than GM.

When F shows readings different from those in M, it usually falls into a group including K, and slightly less frequently including also B, H, I, J:

11.2 F *duta*, BDHIJKL *duti*, against the incorrect reading *druta/i* in other manuscripts;
65.2 BFHJK *surataru ke nikaṭa* for *sura ke taru nikaṭa*;
66.9 FHK *byāpata* correctly, against ACEGLM *byāpita*, BI *byāpyo*, DJ *byāpyau*;
68.8 BDFHIJ *jai śrī* suffixed to third *pāda* superfluously.

The superiority of the majority of readings shared with F by other manuscripts shows this affiliation to be a mode of authenticity; when F falls in with M, however, unsatisfactory readings result (as shown above). Again the situation is not clear-cut, and in some instances F shares readings with manuscripts other than those identified in the two groups discussed:

57.3 DF °*ata* for °*ana* in *sī̃cana* (the finite participle *sī̃cata* is plausible in the context, but does not improve on the sense carried by the verbal noun in the other manuscripts);
79.2 CF *paga* for *pada*.

MS G. Certain inaccuracies in the transcription of this manuscript into its published form have already been pointed out: its orthographies must therefore be regarded with circumspection. A number of lacunae exist, exemplified by *aṃga* (3.2), *kāma kī* (39.4), *hita* (46.4), *bica* (60.5). G shows a number of Sanskritized orthographies found also in H: *śyāma* for *syāma* (10.3), *svara* for *sura* (37.3, 48.4); but this correspondence with H does not appear to be genetic. G is closely affiliated to M, as is shown by a number of readings either exclusive to these two manuscripts or shared with certain others:

10.3 GM *ghoka* for *ghoṣa*: the corrupt GM reading may be founded on pronunciation, or simply on miscopying;

18.6 GIM *tāpara* for *tāpai:* the GIM reading is perhaps an imposition of a *graphically* bisyllabic orthography meant to sustain the prevalent dactylic rhythm of the couplet 18.5-6;

–⏑⏑– ⏑⏑ –⏑⏑ –– –⏑⏑ –⏑ ⏑–⏑ ⏑––
jāhi biraṃca umāpati nāye tāpara taĩ banaphūla bināye.

57.11 GM *tahā̃*, *jahā̃* in other manuscripts; neither form is correct metrically, since only two *mātrās* are required; but the majority reading with relative *ja*° gives the better sense;

58.6 FGM *tana* omitted; GM *tana* for *dhana*;

58.6 G *bhaje*, M *bhajaĩ*, for *bhajahi*;

67.6 GHM *kvaṇita*, Sanskritization for *kunita*.

70.7 GM *tinike,* K *tinakai,* for (alliterative) *jinakai*;

73.3 GM *race haĩ* for *race*; auxiliary *haĩ* is incorporated from the Premadāsa *ṭīkā* (carried by G,K,M), which reads: *kahā̃ sõ race haĩ.*

The above examples show readings shared by GM, to the exclusion of other manuscripts, to be corrupt.

Text H. This printed text is characterized by a high degree of Sanskritization in its orthography. This does not seem to derive consistently from any one manuscript or group of manuscripts, but rather to occur spontaneously. Examples of Sanskritic forms not found in the other manuscripts are:

1.4 and *passim*, H *jaya* for *jai*;

19.14 H *ramaṇa* for *ravana*;

35.4 H *nayana* for *naina.*

The Sanskritization process is occasionally applied wrongly, showing ignorance of the etymology of a semi-*tatsama* form:

11.6 H *pāminī* for *pāvanī*; 63[iv].3 *svara*° for *surasuṃdari.*

H often imposes honorific *śrī* or *jaya* (*jai*) *śrī* superfluously:

18.1 HI *śrī rādhā* for *rādhā*;
25.1 HI *śrī rādhikā* for *rādhikā*;
26.6 BDHI *jai śrī* prefixes third *pāda*;
68.8 BDFHIJ *jai śrī* prefixes third *pāda.*

Although these readings suggest an affiliation with I, such an affiliation is not borne out elsewhere; this shows the imposition of the honorific *śrī* to be spontaneous and non-genetic.

MS I. This manuscript has several exclusive readings and, as discussed above, has apparently been copied outside the Rādhāvallabhī fold. Certain features of the manuscript, however, connect it with others collated here and thus show that it does not belong to a discrete recension. Several of the accretions in I, for example, may be traceable to the *ṭīkā* of Premadāsa—though not specifically with MSS G, K, M which are the three collated manuscripts bearing this *ṭīkā*. Examples are:

7.4 I *syāma* is followed by *tamāla* in the phrase *tāpara syāma nivesita gaurī:* cf. Premadāsa's *abhāsa* to the stanza, which includes the phrase *suṃdara syāma tamālani sõ kanaka latā lapaṭī haĩ*;
43.4 I *kadalī* is followed by *ṣaṃbha* in the phrase *kadalī jaṃgha*: cf. Premadāsa's gloss *kadalī ṣaṃbha kī jaṃghā haĩ*. (Assimilation to *kadali ṣaṃbha* at 29.14 may also be involved.)
48.5 I *banyo* is followed by auxiliary *hai* in the phrase *banyo samāja:* cf. Premadāsa's gloss *samāja banyo hai.*

A connection with the Premadāsa *ṭīkā* manuscripts G and M (but not K) may be apparent in the following readings:

18.6 GIM *tāpara* for *tāpai*;
33.5 AFGIM *naina aruna* for *aruna naina.*

Affiliations with GM are not, however, a recurrent feature of I readings; rather, as already noted, MS I has a tendency to fall in with the BDJ group. Thus MS I appears to share with BDJ a common exemplar, but to have taken on some corrupt readings from the Premadāsa *ṭīkā* manuscripts; it has also developed a number of exclusive readings, exemplified in the following list:

11.3 *anila bāyu* for *anila*;
12.1 *guna nidhāna* for *suṣa nidhāna*;
19.11 *kusuma deva muni harṣata* for *kusuma*;
35.1 *ye doū jhūlata* for *jhūlata doū*;
44.4 *śrīphala juga kuca* for *śrīphala kuca*;
CP 65 whole stanza omitted.

The fact that so many of the accretions in MS I are of the nature of commentatorial synonyms or paraphrases, but not traceable to any of the commentaries examined for the present study, suggests that this manuscript may have been subject to corruptions from yet another *ṭīkā* tradition.

MS J. This manuscript has very few exclusive readings; they are generally attributable to scribal error, and many have been corrected by marginalia. Examples are:

10.3 J *mathura* for *madhura;*
14.1 J *kai* omitted;
23.1 J *syārī* for *pyārī*;
24.5 *braja* for *brata.*

Correspondences of J with B and D have already been noted under the discussions of those manuscripts. The affiliation between B and J is particularly close, but all three manuscripts have developed separately. Instances of disagreement between J and B or D do not show any consistent pattern of conflation from any of the other manuscripts collated.

MS K. Exclusive readings in this manuscript are again mostly limited to scribal errors. Examples are:

7.4 K *supela* for *supesala*;
9.5 K *nilola* for *nicola*;
19.1 K *brajamaṃḍala* for °*maṃḍana*;
50.1 K *navala nāgarī* is repeated;
50.3 K *macī* omitted.

K has an affiliation with L; although these two rarely comprise a group to the exclusion of other manuscripts, they seldom differ in their readings (though L consistently shows the more Sanskritic orthographies). Conspicuous exceptions to the KL affiliation are:

65.2 ACDEGLM *sura ke taru nikaṭa*, BFHJK *surataru ke nikaṭa*:
83.5 ABCDEHIJK *nija bāta,* FGLM *ika bāta.*

K shows occasional correspondences with M, but more generally shares readings with BDIJ (though excluding many errors shared by these). Readings in BDIJ and K tend to be authentic, though K does not guarantee correctness—B and K omit *bhalaī* (16.2), I and K prefix *bṛṃdābana* with the superfluous honorific *śrī* (64.2).

MS L. The previous section has demonstrated an affiliation between K and L. Since Sanskritized forms suggest a later stage of development it may be assumed that L derives from a later stage in the transmission than K. Furthermore, L has a number of variant readings not found in K:

13.4 L *rahai* for *rahata* (C *rahe,* E *rahi*; cf. *rahai* in the *Sūrasāgara* version of this stanza, Appendix II);
25.4 L *śrī* prefixed to *haribaṃsa*;
43.3 L *rasa* for *guna* (by assimilation to 82.4?);
75.2 L *ravana* omitted;
84.2 L *sithala kaṭi kī ḍorī* omitted;
84.4 L *pulaki prema parasa* omitted.

L's fondness for Sanskritic orthographies is most commonly seen in the use of *ś* for *s*: *aṃśa* (25.3 etc.), and even *haṃśa* (26.6 etc.); also *ṇ* for *n*: *pariraṃbhaṇa* (31.6 etc.). This tendency sometimes seems to equate L and C readings, but more fundamental differences elsewhere show this to be non-genetic.

MS M. The affiliation between F and M has already been demonstrated. M has a number of exclusive or near-exclusive readings, exemplified by the following:

11.1 M *kala* omitted;
11.4 M *saina* omitted;
30.8 DM *prāna* for *pāni*;
39.2 M *sudhāryo* for *sāvāryau*;
45.10 M *bana* omitted;
48.4 M *sura* omitted;
63[ii].5 M *sura* for *dhuni*; (by assimilation to 25.3?);
78.4 M *liyau hai* for *liyau* (auxiliary *hai* from *ṭīkā*).

G and M have developed independently of each other in terms of orthography, with G tending towards Sanskritized forms (as already noted), while M is characterized by a haphazard representation of unstressed vowels—particularly in cases of *a* for *i* and vice versa. Non-orthographic differences between the two manuscripts are for the most part limited to cases where one or the other manuscript has an exclusive reading: such readings, exemplified in the list above, are therefore late and independent developments, and do not affect the genetic affiliation petween the two manuscripts. Only rarely are G and M divided over readings varying at an earlier stage in the transmission: exceptions are slightly more common towards the end of the text, indicating that a change of exemplar may have accompanied a change of scribe in M from CP 63.

The date summarized here enable us to form a view of the relationships between the 13 sources. The discussion of manuscript correspondences has dealt mainly with shared error, since it is in this mode of corruption that the autonomy of the various apparent groupings appears most clearly. Many of the corrupt readings have been traced to the accretion of commentatorial text from the *ṭikās*, suggesting a relatively late date for even this degree of divergence between the sources; other features, such as the varying degrees of Sanskritization found in orthographies, are even more superficial and are unreliable as indicators of genetic affiliations.

The resolution of the summarized data into a structured stemma may give an overly explicit impression of homogeneity and straightforwardness in the transmission of the text. It is important to emphasize that the number of removes which separate the various hypothetical exemplars from the archetype cannot be conjectured, and that actual patterns of conflation are likely to be more complex than those identified. With this caveat, three main groupings may be identified:

(i) the ACE group, of which A includes many variants and peculiarities of stanza order *vis-à-vis* all the other sources;

(ii) the FGM group;

(iii) the BDIJ group, related also to KL, and related comparatively closely to group (ii) versus group (i).

(i) E is close to AC in many readings; partial correspondences between A and C in *rāgas* and in stanza order are not, however, shared by E and may be considered a later development. A, C, E thus seem to share a common exemplar, with AC distanced from it by an unknown stage in the transmission; A is also influenced by another unknown source, from which its many exclusive readings derive.

(ii) The correspondence between F, G and M has been demonstrated, with GM shown to be particularly close. FG rarely exclude M; GM agreement is usually agreement in error (against correct F), showing GM to be corrupt derivations of F.

(iii) B in general falls in with DIJ, but has a large number of corrupt readings not found elsewhere in the group and therefore appears to belong to a later stage in the stemma than the other three. B's correspondence with J is rather closer than its correspondence with DI, but this is not a consistent feature.

MS I has correspondence (in error) with BJ, but also shows evidence of corruption from the Premadāsa *ṭīkā* associated with group (ii), and also from another *ṭīkā* not represented among the collated manuscripts.

D also has correspondence with BJ, and has few exclusive readings; BD agreement to the exclusion of J is rare, suggesting that D occupies a place level with J and above B. Agreements between DJ excluding I, and between DI excluding J, both occur.

K is loosely connected to this group as against groups (i) and (ii), but is excluded from a number of BDIJ readings; it therefore appears to share a common exemplar with BDIJ but to have developed separately. L is a Sanskritized derivative of K's exemplar.

H derives loosely from the same group but has no consistent connexion with any one of the manuscripts collated; it is characterised by a highly Sanskritic orthography, interpreted as a spontaneous assimilation to modern KhB. and therefore not based specifically on any orthography transmitted by the manuscripts.

A graphic representation of these relationships yields the following stemma:

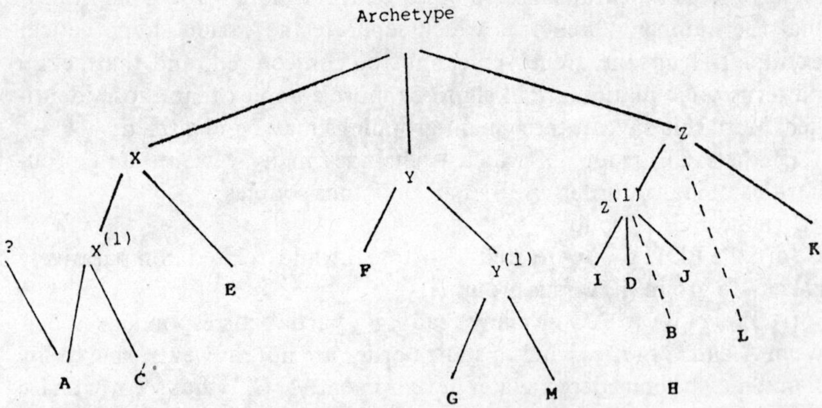

No single group recommends itself as consistently showing authentic readings, and the edition cannot therefore be based on any one manuscript or group of manuscripts. Group (iii), although characterized by many shared errors as shown above, often preserves authentic readings lost in group (i) or (ii), and therefore generally carries greater weight than these other groups; of group (iii), readings found in both D and K are favoured, since these two represent independent derivations from the group exemplar. As a general editing principle, then, readings found in D and K (or either one of these) *and* supported by manuscritps in early positions in the stemmata of groups (i) and (ii) are usually to be regarded as authentic.

This principle cannot, however, be applied rigidly, and must often yield to other considerations. Since D and K are themselves both subject to Sanskritization (often in common with, but not necessarily showing genetic affiliation with, other manuscripts), many of their orthographies are considered unreliable. Similarly, semantic, syntactic and metrical factors may override readings found in these manuscripts and demand a choice of text which has weak support in terms of the stated principle. Metrical emendation is the most common of these exceptions; this typically consists of revision of vowel length (as at 4.4, where the ABCFGHJKLM reading *kachū* is inferior to two-*mātrā kachu*, which appears in E and I only), or of the excision of commentatorial accretion (as in 4.1, where two genitive case-markers appearing in *all* the manuscripts have to be excised from the *pāda*, *piya* (*ke*) *saṃgama* (*ke*) *sūcata* in order to restore its lost 10-*mātrā* value). More drastic examples of metrical revision are to be seen in CP 2 and CP 84, where the vulgate text is given below the edited text to facilitate comparison.

A distinction must continually be made between modes of authenticity and of corruption in group (iii). When a reading is found in a majority of group (iii) manuscripts but is unsupported by either group (i) *or* group (ii), it is likely to be a corruption inherited from the group (iii) exemplar and is therefore to be rejected. An example is the reduplication of *prāna* (1.3) in BDIJ (with further debased *prāna te prāna* in F). This corrupt reduplication has been resisted in K, which is supported by groups (i) and (ii).

Support by group (i) *or* group (ii) of a reading found in group (iii) manuscripts does not automatically indicate an authentic reading, but rather may show a conflation of (iii) with (i) or (ii). Thus the reading *mere tau/to* in DFGIJM for *mere* (1.3) appears to show a conflation of DIJ with the group (ii) manuscripts (B follows J but corrupts *mere* to ungrammatical *merau*). Here again, the satisfactory reading is found in K, and is supported here by group (i).

Caution has to be taken when allowing stylistic criteria to influence editorial decisions. The danger is that in attempting to achieve some degree of consistency in the edited text, one may unwittingly advance the process of standardization already apparent in the work of the scribes; preference of one reading to another on metrical grounds alone, or for the sake of a more effective rhetorical device, may constitute nothing more than the blind pursuit of an ideal model of *chandaḥśāstra* or *alaṅkāraśāstra*. Similarly, the selection of a reading on the grounds that it echoes an established reading elsewhere in the text may be a continuance of a process of assimilation, already under way in some of the manuscripts, which erodes a possible authentic diversity of style (and perhaps of source) in the archetype.

Examples of editorial decisions made on the principles outlined here are given below. Major exceptions to the procedure discussed are, necessarily, dealt with on an *ad hoc* basis, and are usually discussed in the annotations to the translated text (as are various hypothetical emendations to the text regarded as being too speculative for inclusion in the edition).

12.5	*nihāri* (ACDEFKL):	preferred to	BGHIJM *nihāra*;
19.2	*juvatini* (ACEGKL):	-do-	BJ °*inu*, DFHIM °*ina*;
20.5	*arujhātī* (BDFIJKL):	-do-	ACEGM *ara*°, H *ura*°;
21.6	*rasikinī* (CDEHJK):	-do-	A *rasika*, BLM *rasakanī*, FGI *rasikanī*;

37.3	*birahākula pulakita* (CEFGKLM)	preferred to	ABDHIJ *pu*° *bi*°;
45.3	*majjana* (CEFGHKL)	-do-	A *maṃjjana,* BDIJM *maṃjana*;
57.28	*trana* (ABEFKL):	-do-	DIJ *tṛna,* CGHM *tṛṇa*;
59.3	*pai* (BDEHJK)	-do-	ACFGILM *para;*
72.1	*–dāika* (CEFGKM) (A – *dāīka*)	-do-	BDHIJL *–dāyaka.*

2. Script, phonology and orthography

For the most part the manuscripts are written in a 'standard' Devanāgarī; the present section is limited to the reporting of scribal peculiarities and to discussion of certain features closely relevant to the edition, and does not attempt a full analysis. Some further orthographic points are discussed in the sections on morphology and syntax.

(i) ***ā-mātrā***. When space at the end of a folio line in MS L does not allow the writing of the usual *mātrā* for intrasyllabic *ā*, *ā* falling in that position is rendered by a superscript sign ; thus CP 1.1 *bhāve* is rendered भ॑/वे(f. 1^{r} lines 4-5). A single occurrence (53.4 *kahā*, f. 50^{v} line 5) is found in the *middle* of a folio line, and evidently represents an emendment by the scribe of *kaha* to *kahā*.

(ii) ***i-mātrā***. Use of *i-mātrā* in conjunction with *i-kāra* (i.e. िइ) is found occasionally in A and B alongside more general use of standard इ.

(iii) ***ū-mātrā***. In J, syllabic *ū* is written with a superscript hook over the *u-kāra*, on the model of ई, thus: उ॑. The first scribe of M$_{1}$ has a distinctive shape for the *u-kāra*, resembling the graph associated with the *praṇava oṃ*: ३. /ru/and/rū/are written with a subscript hook in B and E: रु, रू

(iv) *Vocalic* ***ṛ***. ⟨ṛ⟩ is generally maintained by most manuscripts except A, which usually (but inconsistently) prefers *ri*, less commonly *ra*. In all seven occurrences of *bṛṃdā*, E has *ra* and is followed in this by A in three occurrences. *ri* and *ra* occur sporadically in all manuscripts (though rarely in IJ); B has *daga* alongside *draga* (⟨*dṛga*), perhaps as a simple miscopying.

An exception to the general retention of ⟨ṛ⟩ occurs in readings for *tṛṣita*: here *ri* occurs quite widely, perhaps through confusion with *tatsama tri-* forms. (Conversely, in the seven occurrences of words with *tatsama tri-*, ⟨ṛ⟩ occurs three times in J and once in C.) *ra* also appears in *graha* ⟨*gṛha,* at 4.6 and 63[ii].3 (though in the latter, confusion with *tatsama grahapati* may be involved).

The only word whose *tatsama* form has /ṛ/ in initial position is *ritu* (27.1 and 28.2); here ⟨ṛ⟩ is found in only one reading (K, 27.1), *ri* being uniform otherwise. Thus the graph ऋ has very limited application.

(v) ***e, ai** and **o, au** vowels.* MS A shows considerable inconsistency in distinguishing between mono- and diphthongal forms, as discussed in section (xv) below. Metrical considerations suggest that diphthongal spellings in *-ai* may have been archetypal possibilities in masc.pl. perfective participles and oblique sg. participles (*diyai* etc.), where only disyllabic forms fully accord with established metrical patterns:

30.6b dharai dharani para heja (all MSS *-e*)

31.3a aṃsani para bhuja diyai bilokata (ACEFGIJKM *-e*)

33.2b uṭhai unīde bhora (all MSS *-e*)

42.4a jyaũ nādahi mana diyai kuraṃgani (AGM *-e;* CEF *-ẽ*)

61.2b diyai bimala bhujadaṃḍana (ACEGIJM *-ẽ*; FK *-e*)

66.10a satvara uṭhai mahā madhu pīvata (ABCDFGHIJKLM *-e* (foll. by *ju* in A); E *-i*)

67.8c kiyai rasa bibasa ghanasyāma piya gorī [first *gaṇa* ⏖ ⏑ ⏖] (ABCDEFGHIJKL *-e*;M *-ẽ*)

Manuscript readings overwhelmingly support *-e* readings here, such that general (hyper–)correction to *-ai* on metrical grounds cannot be justified as an editorial practice. Furthermore, by contrast to the above there are also metrical contexts where a requirement for a short vowel in the participle lends some support to the *-e* spelling; in the following examples the only instance of *-ai* is in K, for *mile* (21.2):

4.5b palate prītama cīra [10 *mātrā gaṇa*]

4.5c basa kiye syāma siṣai sata maina [15 *mātrā gaṇa*]

13.5b citavani kau bhaye naina cakora

21.2b mile haĩ kuṃjabihārī (K milai)

Disyllabic *-au* is often encountered in masc.sg. perfective participles, and is here regularly maintained in the majority of the manuscripts:

—/⏑⏑ ⏑ ⏑/⏑ ⏑ —/⏑
35.8b ānā̃da baḍhy**au** na thora (I –*o*)

—/⏑⏑ ⏑ ⏑/⏑ ⏑ —/⏑
48.5b nīk**au** bany**au** samāju (A –*ŏ*; CGIM –*o*)

⏑⏑/⏑ ⏑ —/ ⏑⏑ —/⏑
66.9b diy**au** sudhādhara dhīra (IM –*o*)

⏑ ⏑/⏑ ⏑ ⏑⏑/⏑ ⏑⏑⏑/ ⏑⏑ —/—
82.2b barabasa kiy**au** citai muṣa morī (E –*ai*; IM –*o*)

Finally it can be noted that rhyme contexts mostly distinguish *e* from *ai* and *o* from *au*.

(vi) ***kṣ***. ⟨kṣ⟩ appears to be authentic in its sole example, 25.3 *dakṣina*, since the reading *–ch–* in CDEGJKL is metrically wanting and there are no *ccha* readings here. *Tadbhava* derivatives are exemplified by the commonplace BrBh forms *ṣeta* (/*kh*/⟨/*kṣ*), *china* ⟨*kṣaṇa* etc.

(vii) ***kh***. The graph ख appears commonly only in the printed texts G and H; it appears occasionally in C, and individual occurrences are found in E (4.1 *sukha*) and J (7.9 *dekhata*). With these exceptions, the graph ष is used for etymological /kh/, as well for /ṣ/, throughout. Those sources which do use the graph ख do so etymologically, without consideration of actual BrBh phonology in which the pronunciation of an original retroflex sibilant approximates to that of a velar fricative. Since it is not possible, on the manuscript evidence, to reconstruct an authentic phonology, the single graph ष has been used throughout in the edition, (transliterated as *ṣ* in the apparatus criticus), without reference to individual manuscript readings.

(viii) ***ṇ***. In nearly every instance, /n/ is clearly authentic for *tatsama* /ṇ/. All manuscripts Sanskritize to ⟨ṇ⟩ in at least one instance, and in GHIL this is commonplace. Support for ⟨ṇ⟩ is strong only in *praṇaya* (7.10, 50.6, 72.10), *kṛṣṇa* (30.17) and three instances of *maṇi* (29.1, 30.14, 41.2); even here, of course, graphic retention of the *tatsama* form does not guarantee its realization as a retroflex in the language of the text.

(ix) ***t***. In B, ⟨t⟩ is written with an initial horizontal stroke which gives the character the appearance of ⟨tt⟩ : त्त. ⟨tt⟩, however, is written with a horizontal stroke as a distinct member adjoining the vertical stroke: this latter usage is also standard in C, D, E, F, K, L, M.

(x) **b** *and* **v**. All sources except EIJK, which use the single graph व in all contexts, distinguish graphically between (i) unstressed/intervocalic contexts, probably having the phonetic value [w], and (ii) initial and stressed syllables in which an approximation exists between [v] and [b]. The latter category includes, of course, both original /b/ and original /v/: *badhū*, *bakra*. The two categories appear in the manuscripts as shown:

(i) ABDFLM ब CGH व
(ii) ABDFLM व CGH ब

No manuscript is totally consistent in maintaining the distinction, but the evidence is sufficiently strong for the distinction to be maintained in the edition and the apparatus: here, without reference to manuscript readings in individual cases, the transliteration scheme *v* for (i), *b* for (ii) has been adopted.

Exceptions to this usage are in the pronoun *ve* and the verb *vār–*, regularly maintained in the manuscripts (and hence in the edition) with group (i) spellings.

(xi) ***y*** ⟨y⟩ is dotted (य़) in A, except in conjuncts. In the absence of undotted ⟨y⟩ (with the exception noted), however, the dotting can retain no phonological significance: in instances of stressed syllables in *tadbhava* and semi-*tatsama* words, A falls in with the other manuscripts and reads ⟨j⟩ (*jāminī, jūtha*). The dotting may therefore be considered a redundant archaism, inherited from a tradition where a phonological distinction existed between the graphs य़ and य.

In conjunct *ry*, superscript *repha* appears in the printed texts G and H only. In A, and occasionally in G, the conjunct is formed by a horizontal stroke adjoining the centre of following य (as noted by Grierson, 1916:13): -य. In BCDEFIJKLM (i.e. all actual manuscripts except A), the *r* component of the conjunct is written as a full graph, the *y* component being joined to it on the model of the usual *dy* conjunct द्य : र्‍य .

(xii) ***r***. *r* for etymological *l* follows established BrBh. usage, as exemplified by *dhūri* (confirmed by rhyme with *pūri*, 57.21-22) etc. Both *jhakajhol-* and *jhakajhor-* are confirmed by rhyme as being authentic readings (30.16 and 67.6 respectively); at 34.9, the only non-rhyme context, *jhakajhol-* has the stronger manuscript support.

(xiii) ***ś***. Etymological ⟨ś⟩ is favoured by most scribes in a number of words (e.g. *kiśora, haribaṃśa*, with only ABEM reading ⟨s⟩ here with any regularity) alongside other words in which ⟨s⟩ is almost universal among the manuscripts (*nisi, sira*). Retention of a Sanskritic orthography does not necessarily imply retention of the phonetic value of *tatsama* /ś/ (cf. the discussion of ⟨ṇ⟩ above): collocations such as *haribaṃśa haṃsa* suggest rather that ⟨ś⟩ is here realized as a dental. Some clear cases of the imposition of *tatsama* spellings are noted, such as the IL reading *haṃśa* at 1.4 and in readings of *prasaṃś-* at 5.6, 29.17, 35.10, seeking alliteration with *haribaṃśa*; but the strength of the manuscript evidence elsewhere suggests that ⟨ś⟩ as an orthography is not to be dismissed as a Sanskritization out of hand.

(xiv) ***ṣ***. *Tatsama* ⟨ṣ⟩ appears very widely (though its phonological value is uncertain, as discussed in section (vii) above): in the total 25 instances furnished by the forms *ākaraṣ- baraṣ-, bhūṣana* and *bhūṣita*, for example, a single manuscript reading of ⟨s⟩ is found (4.3 L *bhūsita*).

Thus the manuscript evidence suggests that here again the appearance of the *tatsama* form, as an orthography at least, may be regarded as authentic.

(xv) *Nasality. Candrabindu* does not appear in DEI; vowel nasality is shown by *anusvāra* in these manuscripts, and also quite commonly in the remaining manuscripts. All of the scribes show some inconsistency in the extent to which they indicate nasality, be it original, conditioned or spontaneous. In order to restrict the bulk of the critical apparatus, only original nasality has generally been admitted in the edition and shown in the variants; exceptions to this are in the direct object marker *kau/kau*, and verb terminations. Use of *candrabindu* (transliterated by a tilde) indicates vowel nasality or, in the case of homorganic nasals, indicates that a syllable which is long by position must be counted as short for metre.

An analysis of nasality of all three types in the manuscripts yields the following points.

(a) MS A has a very strong tendency to nasalize *e* and *o* vowels in nasal contexts, but not *ai* and *au*; this leads to random orthographies, ẽ appearing alongside *ai* even in rhyme contexts (similarly õ, *au*).

(b) MS A consistently reads *hẽ* for auxiliary *hai/haĩ* (except in two instances where A has second person *hau* for 3rd person *hai*). Other manuscripts fairly consistently show nasality with the auxiliary in pl. contexts only.

(c) Nasalization of stressed vowels before nasal consonants occurs frequently in all sources except B, H and M (first scribe). Nasalization *following* nasal consonants is rather less common.

(d) Two manuscripts show a distinction between the orthographies of *au* in direct case *kauna* and in instrumental *kaune* (a single occurrence at 59.1), perhaps reflecting an interpretation of analytical construction (pronoun *kau* followed by case-marker *ne*) and consequently not envisaging the *au* vowel as being enclosed by a nasal consonant: ms I reads *kaũna/kõna*, but *kone*; J reads *kaũna*, but *kaune*.

3. Morphology and Syntax

This section outlines the main grammatical forms represented in the text, treating in detail only those features which depart from established BrBh. usage or which have particular implications for the editorial process. A full analysis is not attempted. As in the previous section, much of the discussion here takes *LIO* as a model. Various individual points, particularly regarding variant manuscript readings and commentatorial interpretations of the syntax of the *mūla*, are discussed in the annotations to the text.

(i) *Substantives in -ā, -au, -e.*

Fem. sg. substantives in *-ā* are common and regular. Masc. substantives in *-ā* occur in stanzas 19 and 63, where they are *-a* stems arbitrarily lengthened for rhyme and metre: examples are 19.8 *anaṃgā* and 63[i].3 *gupālā* (AE *gupāla*).

Masc. sg. direct *-au* stems are also represented only rarely, (though *-au* occurs quite frequently in adjectives showing masc. sg. agreement); *pyārau* occurs at 1.1 (CDGIM *pyāro*) and at 1.2 (IM *pyāro*), and *lāḍilau* at 51.2 (CDIM *-o*). Alongside these may be mentioned two nominal forms derived from verbs: perfective participles such as *bhayau*, discussed in section (viii); and infinitives in *-ibau*, discussed in section (xiii).

Masc. forms in *-e* are as follows:

honorific pl. :	1.1	*pyāre*	(AD *pyārai*);
	2.1	*pyāre*	(in vulgate);
grammatical pl.:	1.2	*tāre*;	
locative sg.:	77.2	*hĩḍore*	(B *hidorai*; DKL *hĩḍorai*);
genitive pl. :	1.2 and 39.6 *pyāre*.[1]		

A further category comprises two perfective participles used nominally: 16.1 *kahe* (ABDHIJL *kahai*), 33.5 *roke* (EI *rokai*).

Fem. vocative *-e* is attested in *rādhe* (28.1) and *rādhike* (12.1, 26.2) alongside vocative *-ā* in *rādhā* (18.1), *rādhikā* (15.2).

(ii) *Substantives in* ***-i***, *-ī*

Substantives in *tatsama -ī* appear in this form unless metre requires a shortening of the final vowel, which is quite commonly the case. Thus *bhāminī* occurs five times in the text, *bhāmini* eight times. The strength of the final long *-ī* vowel, often reinforced by rhyme, ensures that erroneous *-i* readings are kept to a minimum; 10.1 *nāgari* in A is a rare example. C very commonly shows a preference for *-ī* even when the other manuscripts bow to the metrical requirement for *-i*: 26.3 C *rajanī*, 37.1 C *māninī*.

Final *-i*, representing either *tatsama -i* or *-ī* shortened for metre, is very frequently represented by *-a* in M, less often so in F and comparatively rarely elsewhere: 10.2 FM *kela* for *keli* (despite alliteration with *meli*), 30.9 FM *kāmina* for *kāmini* (C *kāminī*). There is a tendency for final *-i* to be represented by *-a* more often in words containing a long syllable than in words of two or more short syllables: thus no *-a* reading appears in the 14 occurrences of *gati*, and only one *-a* reading in the 11 occurrences of *ali* (33.5 B *ala*), whereas M regularly prefers *kela* to *keli*, *kāmina* to *kāmini*. Though this is by no means a totally consistent phenomenon, a similar observation can be made with other *-i/-a* examples, and the feature is not related to gender[2] or number.

1. *pyāre* at 39.6 may be read as singular: adjectival and verbal forms agreeing with Kṛṣṇa are found in both numbers in the text.

2. This does not imply, however, that *no* sense of gender attaches to the *-i/-a* distinction. It may be, for example, that in the phrase *haribaṃśa dāsi* at 34.10, those MSS (EFIKL) with the reading *dāsa* envisage a masculine subject, while the *-i* reading in ABCDGHJM is founded upon the traditional identification of Harivaṃśa with *sakhī*.

It is difficult to establish to what extent this feature exists with forms in *-u* (discussed below), since the sample is very small; but the manuscripts seem not to show the tendency, with readings of *siṃdha* for *siṃdhu* being balanced, for example, by readings of *tara* for *taru*.

(iii) *Substantives in* ***-u***

Substantives in *-u* are of two types: (a) *tatsama -u* stems, such as *taru*; (b) *tadbhava -a* stems in which the Ap. direct case *-u* termination is maintained (or imposed), examples occurring principally in the *-āju* rhyme of CP 48.[1] *-u* of the first type is sometimes unmetrically lengthened to *-ū*: 12.5 DI *prabhū*, 14.4 C *iṃdū*; the reading *prabho* (for *-u*) in A at 65.4, which repairs the deficient scansion of the line, may reflect a familiarity with *tatsama* vocative forms or may represent the Ap. lengthening of *-u* to *-o* (and not *-ū*) when metre requires a long final vowel (*BhK* para 22).

By far the highest number of *-u* readings for direct case *tatsama -a* stems occurs in MS A. Such readings tend to occur in sequences: A has *bacanu, rasu* (three times), *rūpu* and *jasu* in CP 18, and *rāgu, raṃgu, bratu* in CP 24—but always alongside other direct forms in *-a*, which remains predominant. Even in A, retention of the Ap. declension is fragmentary, and it appears that weakening of the unstressed final vowel had, by the time of the text, removed the phonetic distinction between the cases (while orthography lagged variously behind).

Distinctions between *-u* and *-a* are not, therefore, consistently maintained in the text. In certain contexts, such as 57.7-8 where *tatsama bandhu* is asked to rhyme with *sugaṃdha,* weakness of manuscript support for *-u* spellings suggests that *-a* spellings for *-u* are authentic (*sugaṃdha, baṃdha*). Elsewhere, such as in the adverbial expression *palu palu* 'at every moment', a generalizing of the direct case form to embrace oblique usage appears to have taken place at the expense of the Ap. declension: here (16.4 and 17.4), only HM read *pala pala.*[2]

(iv) *Substantives with suffix* ***-na***, ***-ni***, ***-nu***

Substantives with suffixed *-na, -ni, -nu* are oblique plurals; such suffixes perhaps derive from Prakrit genitive pl. pronoun endings (*amhāṇa, tumhāṇa*) borrowed into Ap. alongside the regular Ap. forms (*amahā̃, tumhahā̃*: *BhK* para 29), since they are not apparent in the Ap. noun paradigm. The text contains examples in stems *-a, -i, -ī,* and *-iyā*. The

1. The same Ap. declension (with *-a* for oblique cases) may have been imposed erroneously on some occurrences of *-u* stems, particularly in A. Thus we find locative *siṃdha* in A (12·6), ablative *dhena* in ACM (63[iv]·3) alongside majority *-u* readings. Straightforward weakening of the final vowel may alternatively account for the loss of *-u* in these readings.

2. H and M show the 'correct' form only accidentally: H in conformity with KhB. (Sanskritized) usage, M within a general tendency to represent unstressed vowels as *a*, particularly those in final position.

-ni ending is favoured by all the manuscripts as the regular oblique plural form for all classes in both genders; occurrences of *-na* are also common, however, being represented by at least one manuscript in nearly every instance.[1] Evidence for original *-na* is found in the end-rhyme of CP 61, where the rhyming of plurals *daṃḍana, gaṃḍana* with *maṃḍana* etc. presupposes an original identity of the two forms.

MS B shows a strong tendency to read *-ni* for masc., *-na* for fem. oblique plurals; this observation stands only for samples from the *ṭikā* in B, and does not appear to apply to the *mūla*.

The *-nu* suffix is uncommon, and is restricted to substantives (of both genders) in *-i*, *-ī*, *-iyā* stems. *-nu* occurs sporadically in most MSS, most commonly in B, D and J (five instances in each), with no examples in G or K. In no occurrence of an oblique pl. *-i*/*-ī*/*-iyā* form, however, is the *-nu* reading totally unrepresented. Occurrences of *-nu* are shown below, alongside the sigla of the manuscripts in which they appear (other manuscripts show *-ni* or *-na*); the first two instances and the last are of masc. nouns, the remainder of fem. nouns:

13.2	BCDEJ	*haũ apane* ***motinu*** *lara povata*
20.4	CD	*ṭūṭī lara laṭakata* ***motinu*** *kī*
24.4	BFJ	*braja* ***juvatinu*** *kī bhīra*
36.4	BJM	***juvatinu*** *maṃḍala*
57.27	ABCDFHIJLM	*niju* ***cerinu*** ura
72.3	BD	*sītala haṃsasutā rasa* ***bīcinu*** *parasi*
84.3	(D)IJ[2]	***motinu*** *lara ṭūṭī*

All but the example from 72.3 are genitive forms, either analytical (*juvatinu kī bhīra*) or compounded (*motinu lara*). The *-u* termination can therefore be said to represent the genitive pl. endings of Ap. (*BhK* paras 27-28), attested in *-i* stems in both fem. (*dēvihu*) and masc. (*aggihu*/*-hũ*). It is of no great surprise to find *-u* occurring also in the accusative context of 72.3, by analogy with the genitive examples: what is significant is that nowhere in the CP does an *-a* stem show this termination. The popularity of the spelling *cerinu* (57.27) may be explained by the support of assonance with adjacent *niju* and *ura*; elsewhere occurrences of *-nu* are very sporadic, and therefore it seems more likely that they represent impositions of an archaic orthography than that they derive from the archetype. The fact that the seven examples embrace only four different nouns shows even this restricted usage to be formulaic.

1. In some contexts there may be some ambiguity as to whether a final *-na* syllable represents an oblique plural suffix or simply the last syllable of a word in direct case: thus at 70·5 MS I reads *alaka nabaṃdha*, presumably intending *alakana baṃdha*, for correct *alaka nibaṃdha*. Cf. discussion on the phrase *nībī baṃdhana* at 7·6.

2. D reads *mutiyanu*; other spellings involving the extended *-iy-* form appear in other manuscripts. The stanza exhibits some metrical corruption.

(v) *Pronouns*

All the pronominal forms occurring in the text, and no others, are given in the following paradigm, based on the model of *LIO* 3.55. Forms are singular unless shown otherwise.

(a) *Demonstrative of near reference*

Direct	*yaha*	pl. *ye*
Oblique	*yā*	pl. *ina*
Instrumental	*ihi*	

(b) *Demonstrative of distant reference*

Direct		pl. *ve*

(c) *Demonstrative-correlative*

Direct	*so, su*	
Oblique	*tā, tihi*	pl. *tina*
Object	*tāhi*	

(d) *Relative*

Direct	*jo, ju*
Oblique	*jā*
Object	*jāhi*

(e) *Personal* (1st)

Direct	*haũ*
Oblique	*mo*
Object	*mohi, mokau*
Possessive	*merau/-e/-ī, mora,* (*mama*)
Instrumental	*maĩ*

(f) *Personal* (2nd)

Direct	*tū*	pl. *tuma*
Oblique	*to*	
Possessive	*terau/-e,* (*tava*)	
Instrumental	*taĩ*	

(g) *Interrogative* (1)

Direct	*kauna, kavana, ko*
Instrumental	*kaune*

(h) *Interrogative* (2)

Direct	*kahā*
Oblique	*kā, kāhe*

(i) *Indefinite*

Direct	*kou*
Oblique	*kāhū*

a) *yaha* is regular in all MSS, though A has one reading of *yahu* (59.6), maintaining the masc. sg. *-u* termination of Ap. *ēhu* (*BhK* para 30). At 54.6 A reads *cira jiyȍ īhu bhūtala jorī* for *cira jīvau bhūtala yaha jorī*, replacing nom. *yaha* with loc. *īhu.*

b) *ihi:* found only once in the text, at 63 [ii].2, represented by *iha* in I and by unmetrical *īhi* in A. The final vowel is nasalized in DHL, perhaps preserving the nasality of Ap. instrumental (pl.) *ehĩ*/*ihĩ* (*BhK* para 30). *ihi* is a relatively rare form in BrBh, being cited by neither Grierson nor Verma; it is listed by Kellogg, Table X, in Kanauji, as an oblique form (with *ko*) and as an agentive (with *ne*); and a single occurrence of agentive *iha* is cited in *LIO* 3.78.

The instrumental force of this pronoun is clear in its single occurrence in the CP:

63[ii].2 *mohana benu bajāvai; ihi rava nāri bulāvai.*

ye: always written *e* in A, and once (31.5) in C also.

ve: represented by *vai* in C in all three occurrences: 32.5, 58.6, 75.4; *LB* (para 120) cites this *-ai* form, which is also listed for BrBh. in *GHL*, as showing Awadhi influence.

c) Demonstrative-correlative. *so* without enclitic *-i* occurs at 14.4 and, as a variant in EFHLM, for *su* at 73.6. *so* with enclitic *-ī* occurs once, reduplicated, in the first line of the text.

d) *jo* occurs only once without enclitic *-ī* (18.7), though IL also show *jo* for *ju* in the metrically uncertain context of 2.2. *ju* most frequently occurs without a correlative, as at 75.1:

75.1 *haũ ju kahati ika bāta saṣī suni*

A further weakening of the relative sense of *ju* is apparent in the following, where its only real function is that of a metrical filler:

26.6 *tuma ju kaṃcanatanī lāla marakatamanī*
'you the golden-bodied one, Lāla the emerald'.

e)–f) *haũ* and *hȍ* are both equally well represented in the MSS for the 1st nom., the former sometimes being left without nasalization in ABE. CGIM fairly regularly prefer simplified *hȍ*, and JKL *haũ*; other manuscripts show both forms without consistency.

Alongside the more usual possessive *merau*/ *-e*/ *-ī* occur the two forms *mora* and *mama*. The former is standard for Eastern Hindi dialects, and is attested in rhyme contexts in Sūradāsa (*LB* para 161): the two occurrences in the CP are also from end-rhymes—13.1 and 31.8. *mama* has a rather limited currency in BrBh., and here (66.14) serves as a metrically convenient archaism to lend distinction to Kṛṣṇa's speech.

Instrumental *maĩ* and *taĩ*, reflecting accusative/instrumental/locative forms in Hemacandra's Ap. paradigm (*BhK* para 29), occur in the perfect tense construction with transitive verbs discussed in section (ix) below. *maĩ* appears only once (66.11). Simplification of the vowel to *-e*/ *-ẽ*is commonplace, especially in C.

Possessive *tava,* an Ap. borrowing, occurs occasionally alongside *terau.* Noted by Verma as rare in BrBh. (*LB* para 167), it is perhaps introduced in the CP as a metrical alternative, and to instil an archaic flavour into such contexts as 66.14 in collocation with Sk. *mama.* At 74.3 the *tatsama* nature of this borrowing is underlined by its showing sandhi with following *ākṛti.*

g) *kauna* is the usual form for direct cases, and occurs once with postposition *pai* (59.3); the spelling *kona* appears in C, and sporadically in AEFI. Synonymous *ko* occurs once (42.2, DK *kau*). *kavana* appears twice (39.4, 40.4), both times for *-avana* rhyme; also once again in Λ for *kauna* at 59.3. *kavana* is of course the regular Awadhi form, not cited for BrBh. by *LSI*, *LB* or *LIO* but occurring in Sūradāsa (*BBhSK*) and Nandadāsa (*HŚS*); it need not be regarded as an Awadhi loan since *kavaṇa* is the Ap. source for H. *kauna.*

Instrumental *kaune* has been discussed in section (xv) above; this is an oblique form of *kauna*, and probably derives from the Ap. sg. instrumental *kavaṇeṃ* (*BhK* para 30).[1] The single occurrence in the CP is in the rhetorical question *kaune sacu pāyau* (59.1).

h) Direct *kahā* is regular. Its inflected form *kā-* is represented in *kāhe, kāsu* and *kāsʊ̃.*[2] *kāhe* is usually strengthened by *kaũ*, as in *kāhe kaũ karata bādhā* (58.2), occurring alone only in *kāhĕ na pratipārati* (75.6). *kāsu* and *kāsʊ̃* occur once each, in almost synonymous clauses:

26.5 *upamā kahaũ kāsu rī*
52.6 *kāsʊ̃ paṭatariyai*

i) *kou* occurs once only (52.3), with (unmetrical) strengthened final vowels in most manuscripts: A *koī,* BCDFGHIJKL *koū.* (*koī* is cited in *LB* para 191 as occurring less frequently than *koū* in old BrBh. Since the *-ī* suffix (< *api, HGA* para 128) is present in the Ap. indefinite noun, however, A's reading *koī* need not be interpreted as showing the influence of KhB.; rather, it is *koū* which should be regarded as the 'modern' form (Bloch p. 202)).

Oblique *kāhū* occurs once only, in the genitive phrase *kāhū kī kāni* (42.1); BDEK have the spelling *kāhu*, perhaps intended as a metrical emendation (though the metrical composition of the *ṭeka* makes this uncertain).

(vi) *Subjunctive-present tense*

In the first person, *a*-stem verbs have the regular termination *-aũ* (*kahaũ* etc.);[3] this is often simplified to *-ʊ̃*, particularly in CFGM.

1. The form *kaune* is a possible source for the modern H. postposition *ne.*
2. The form *kāsu*/*kāsʊ̃*, though understood as an analytical formation (oblique pronoun + postposition) may alternatively reflect the Ap. ablative sg. form *kāsu* (*HGA* para 127A).
3. An exception to this pattern is *pranaũ* (57·1), from *pranav-*. (E has *pranaũ*, G *praṇāũ*, M *praṇa.ũ*)

ā-stem verbs have *-āũ* (*jāũ*, 56.1); the final vowel is lengthened in the rhyme context of CP 14 (*durāũ* etc.). Nasality is often dropped, especially in ABEJK.

The second person is not represented.

In the third person the regular termination is *-ai* (*kahai* etc.); a tendency to simplify to *-e* is common in G, occurs sporadically in AC, and is found less frequently elsewhere. Nasalization of the termination is largely dependent on nasal environments and, as noted in *LIO* 3.137. is not indicative of number. *ā*-stems have intervocalic *-v-* (*bulāvai* etc.).

Many contexts are ambiguous as to mood. When a subjunctive sense is strongly implied, the number of *-e* readings tend to increase; thus ACFGIKLM all have *bane* (*-ẽ* in ACFK, *-i* in E) in the following rhetorical context:

35.8 *bepathajuta kyaũ banai bibecita*

A contrast between subjunctive and indicative moods is apparent in readings for the rhyme words in 41.1 and 41.2, where ACFJK perhaps understand the two lines as having subjunctive and indicative force respectively:

41.1 *prīti kī rīti raṃgīlauī jānai*; (ACFJK jānẽ, G jāne)
41.2 *jadyapi sakala loka cūḍāmani dīna apanapau mānai.* (G māne)

(In the remainder of this stanza, however, this distinction is lost.)
The fact that the distinction in moods in the above example is at odds with consistency of rhyme suggests that the preference for *-e* spellings in subjunctive contexts may show the influence of modern KhB. In the first-quoted example, the metrical pattern established as standard in section VI.3(i) confirms diphthongal *-ai* as the authentic spelling here:

— ⏑ ⏑⏑⏑ | ⏑⏑ ⏑ ⏑ | ⏑⏑ — | ⏑⏑
35.8a *bepathajuta kyaũ banai bibecita*

Although many examples of the subjunctive-present used with indicative force do occur, they are greatly outnumbered by the general present (with imperfective participles as finite verbs). Occasionally the two forms may occur in the same context with little or no difference of sense, as in *bāj-* below:

19.4 *madhura madhura muralī kala bājai*
19.7 *bājata tāla mṛdaṃga upaṃgā*

(vii) *Imperfective participles: stem* + ***-ta***, (***-tu***), ***-ti***, ***-tī***; ***-te***

There are over 300 examples of imperfective participles in the text, the majority being active finite verbs without auxiliary. The auxiliary appears in conjunction with imperfective participles in only three instances:

30.1 *lāgata hai ati cāru*
61.1 *nācata haĩ brajamaṃḍana*
74.1 *kāhe kaũ māna baḍhāvata hai*

The fact that all three instances are from the first line of a stanza may be coincidental, though it is likely that the dactylic rhythm supplied by long verb root+participle ending+auxiliary is a significant factor in the construction of the line in the first two examples.

The auxiliary also appears with two of the three passive participles found in the text, though not with the third:

21.4 *ura naṣa reṣa pragaṭa dĕṣiyata hai*
84.1 *āju deṣiyata hai pyārī raṃga bharī*
(19.12 *suniyata diva duṃdubhi kala ghoṣā.*)

None of the manuscripts is fully consistent in its showing of participial concord; *-ta* for fem. participles is found with great frequency alongside *-ti*. MS A has the highest number of *-ti* spellings (about 75% of all occurrences of fem. participles), while among the remaining sources only D and J show *-ti* for more than 50%. A relatively high score of *-ti* spellings is attained in first and second person contexts (again with the highest number appearing in A); number does not appear to be a factor. There is no basis for a universal editorial 'emendment' to *-ti* in fem. contexts; each instance has been assessed independently on the manuscript evidence.

Fem. *-tī* occurs in a few instances, occasionally as scribal error but more commonly for metre; end-rhyme requires participles in *-tī* in 15.2, 3, 4, 6 and 20.2, 5,8.

The termination *-ti* in masc. contexts occurs sporadically, with at least one example in each source; only in I, however, with 20 examples, is the tendency at all common and it should not be seen as a regular alternative form. It may occasionally be induced by alliteration, as at 26.2 where FIL read *karati ratirāja*.

The termination *-tu* occurs in only the following instances, alongside majority readings of *-ta* except in the fem. context of 66.15 (*kahati*). 57.19 has a joint masc. and fem. subject, the remainder being masc. sg.:

8.3	A	*mṛga **sakatu** cali na rī* (E *-ti*)
30.1	AE	*nikuṃja . . **lāgatu** hai ati cāru* (DI *-ti*)
32.8	A	*hita haribaṃśa āju tṛṇa **ṭūṭatu*** (I *-ti*)
57.7	A	***bahatu** pavana rucidāyaka*
57.19	B	*doū karatārinu paṭakata **laṭakatu** ita uta jāta*
59.3	AFL	*dvai turaṃga para jora **caḍhatu***
59.3	L	***paratu** kauna pai dhāyau*
66.15	G	*priyā **kahatu*** (E *-tī*; FHLM *-ta*)
81.5	A	*urasi **rājatu** hāru*

Alliteration with other *u* forms within the line may perhaps account for the appearance of *-tu* in 30.1, 32.8, 57.7, 57.19, 59.3 and 81.5. Since A is the only manuscript to show *-tu* in more than one line of the whole text, it is clearly not to be regarded as a regular variant of *-ta* in the language of the text.

The only occurrence of *-te* in the whole text is in the substantive verb, masc. pl.: *kahā̃ hute piya* (66.15); cf. *LIO* 3.115, where *hatau* 'is presumed to have variants of the morpheme group *-au* in adjectival *au*-stems, viz. *hate*, etc., *hatī*'.

In some contexts individual manuscripts confuse participial adjective (root+*ita*) with imperfective participle. An example is found at 57.5 (*aruna nūta pallava para* ***kūjata*** *kokila kīra*), where CEFL read *-ita* for *-ata*. It is likely that some such readings derive from an expectation that the participle is non-finite and forms part of an adjectival compound ('with warbling cuckoos and parrots'), though in the present example the locative case of the preceding phrase ('on fresh reddish sprays') requires that the participle be finite. In other instances, where the form is more obviously incorrect, the form must be explained as a corruption, sometimes metathetical, consequent upon the weakness of the penultimate syllable. Most manuscripts show approximately five instances of this feature; D has only one example, and H none at all, while F has 10 and L 14.

(viii) *Perfective participles: stem*+ **(*y*)*au***, **(*y*) *ai*/*e***, ***-i***

For the verbs *kar-*, *de-* and *le-* the perfective participles *kiyau* °*e*, *diyau* °*e*, and *liyau* are attested. There is also a single occurrence of *kīne* (alongside *kiye*), but this appears to represent, or be involved in a *śleṣa* for, *kīn-* < *krīṇāti* (as discussed in the note to *kīne*, 34.6).

The substantive verb occurs as an auxiliary with the perfect participle only twice, both occurrences being in the same stanza: 21.2 *mile haĩ kuṃjabihārī*; 21.5 *parī hai pīka*.

Perfective participles have the following functions:

a) Adjectival usage, e.g. *gaura syāma abhirāma raṃga* ***bharĕ*** (5.2).

b) Usage in independent participial constructions,[1] involving both transitive and intransitive verbs: *aṃsani para bhuja* ***diye*** *bilokata* (31.3); *ye*...[*naina*]...***aṭake*** *anata ne jāta* (60.2).

c) Usage in intransitive finite constructions, showing agreement with sentence subject, e.g. ***milĕ*** *haĩ kuṃjabihārī* (21.2).

d) Usage in transitive finite constructions, showing agreement with sentence object, e.g. ***palaṭĕ*** *prītama cīra* (4.5); this is discussed in section (xiii).

1. As noted in *LIO* 4·42, this independent participial usage is semantically equivalent to usage of the absolutive; this is shown very clearly by the similar contexts of participial *kiye*.. *diye* and absolutive *kai*.. *dai* in consecutive couplets (lines 67.2, 67.4).

e) Nominal usage, discussed in section (xiii).

(ix) *Perfect tense construction with transitive verbs*

Transitive construction using the perfective participle in concord with grammatical subjects represents a transitional stage between old instrumental forms and the agentive construction of modern KhB. and BrBh. Vestiges of the instrumental construction are seen in the pronouns occurring here: *maĩ, taĩ, kaune*, all deriving from Ap. instrumental forms. In most examples from the CP, participles show appropriate agreement with grammatical subjects;[1] in the first occurrence of *taĩ*, however, there is no finite verb involved, and the force of the construction is more clearly instrumental:

4.3 *sira sīm̐ta bhūṣita manu taĩ na.*

Other nominal forms associated with this construction are mostly singular substantives with endings incapable of showing their oblique case, as exemplified by *śruti* in the following:

18.7 *jo rasa neti neti śruti bhāṣyau*

An exception is found at 13.1, where the genitive case-marker *ke* in concord with *lāla* shows sg. oblique case (the verbal form *gayau* governed by *lāla* in 13.2 shows the latter to be conceived as sg., and not honorific pl., here):

13.1 *naṃda kĕ lāla haryau mana mora*

Oblique pl. forms in this construction are exemplified by *laṭani*, 31.5:

31.5 *chūṭī laṭani lāla mana karaṣyau.*

In certain instances where a plural might be expected, a gnomic singular is found:

24.5 *brata chāḍyau muni dhīra*
36.3 *ṣaga mṛga sacu pāyau.*

The verb *bola-*, normally intransitive in BrBh. and KhB., appears to be used transitively in two contexts involving the instrumental agentive construction:

2.1 *pyāre bolī bhāminī* (in the vulgate text only)
'The Beloved has called [you], passionate lady';
28.3 *benu dhuni nm̐dalāla bolī*
'Nandalāla has called [you] with the sound of his flute';

1. The only instance of concord not being shown as expected is at 65·3: *taĩ na śravana sunyau benu bajaṇī.* Apparently *bajanī* is conceived as adjectival (allowing verbal concord with masc. *benu*), though a more usual usage would be nominal: cf. KhB. *karanī, kahanī*, both nominal forms. (Although the pleonastic expression *śravana sun-* occurs 11 times in the text, all other examples involve either the absolutive, or the imperfective participle: a possible interpretation of the present example as showing concord between *sunyau* and *śravana* (m. 'a hearing') therefore remains untested.)

and perhaps again in the elliptical first line of CP 44:

44.1 *cali suṃdari bolī bṛṃdābana*
'Come, beautiful one, [he] has called [you] to Vṛndāvana'.

Cf. transitive *bulā-* in a single instance only (present tense):

63[ii].2. *ihi rava nāri bulāvai.*

The parallel usage of *bola-* and *bulā-* as transitives perhaps reflects the identity in application of the Ap. forms *vollai* and *vollāvai* (*BhK* p. 199), suggesting that at the time of our text the functions of the *-a* stem and its extended form had not yet been clearly defined as respectively intransitive and transitive.

(x) *Absolutives*

The only form found commonly is the Ap. *-i* form (*suni* etc.); suffixed *-kai* occurs only once (58.2 *bheṭikai*), *-kari* not at all. The absence of the latter form accords with Verma's view (*LB* para 221) that it appears in late BrBh. through the influence of KhB. The absolutive forms of *de-* and *le-* are *dai*, *lai* respectively.

The stem form is normally represented by *-i*, though BFIM and very occasionally other MSS show *-a* sporadically. (To a certain extent the choice of final vowel is dependent upon euphony, but this is a tendency only.) As noted in *LIO* 3.159 the weak final *-i* of the absolutive may occasionally be represented by *-ya* (in roots with a long final vowel): 7.8 DHIM *janāya*, 30.10 HM *dhāya*. A's two readings in *-ī* at 7.8 (*praloī, janāī*) are unmetrical and cannot be construed as anything but incorrect spellings of the *-i* absolutive; the long *-ī* in 82.2 *morī* (all MSS) represents absolutive *-i* lengthened for rhyme.

Since the stem form is also regularly used as a singular imperative, and also with an auxiliary in compound verb formations, certain contexts may allow a limited degree of ambiguity. An example is the following collocation of absolutive *ḍāri* (FJ *ḍāra*) with finite *gayau* where, as discussed in the note to 13.2, some commentators read *gayau* as having intensive force:

13.2 *kāṃkara ḍāri gayau*
'he threw pebbles and went'.

Absolutives occur most frequently in association with finite verbs, as in the above example or on the following pattern, where absolutive *nirași* follows finite *deta:*

70.7 *deta asīsa nirași juvatī jana*

(xi) *Imperatives in* ***-i, -a***

The most frequent context in which imperatives occur is in sentences where the poet/*sakhī* addresses Rādhā: consequently the majority of examples are 2nd sg. forms. Most examples are of root +*-i*, following the common Ap. form (*HGA* para 138), the suffix being represented sporadically by *-a* in BHM and very occasionally so in other MSS. Except in H, there is no consistent pattern in the choice of *-a* in preference to *-i*: as in other contexts, the variation must be attributed to the weakness of the final vowel. H appears to favour *-a* readings when the imperative is in close collocation with a verbal-stem absolutive, as though to differentiate between the two forms. Thus H (here with BGIJM) reads *nihāra* (imperative) and *bhari* (absolutive, FI *bhara*) in the following context, where *locana bhari* has adverbial force:

12.5 *narabāhana prabhu nihāri locana bhari ghoṣa nāri.*

(xii) *Imperatives in* ***-ahi***, ***-ahu***, ***-au***

a) *2nd sg. and pl.*

2nd sg. imperatives in *-ahi*, according with the Ap. *karahi* form cited in *BhK* para 34, are sparsely represented in the text. Three of the examples are occurrences of the same word, *calahi* (12.1, 38.1, 39.5); the remainder are 38.4 *karahi,* 58.6 *bhajahi,* 44.2 *rājahi.* This last example occurs in collocation with rhetorical *kina* (Sk. *kiṃ na*).

Spellings in *-ahī* are found in C in all but the 12.1 and 58.6 examples, showing again the tendency for the unmetrical lengthening of short vowels already noted for this manuscript. The reading *calihi* found in M at 12.1 and in L at 38.1 reflects the indeterminate phonetic value of unstressed vowels: cf. M's spelling *harabaṃsa* alongside *hari*°, 34.7 *bilulata* for °*lita*, etc. and L's spellings *prayā* for *priyā* at 35.4, etc. (Anticipation in the stem of the final *-i* vowel may also be a factor here, though this is not apparent as a consistent feature in any MS.) 58.6 *bhajahi* shows four variants: F *bhajajahi*, J *bhajaha* (emended to *-hi*), G *bhaje,* M *bhajaĩ*; the first two of these are clearly scribal errors, while the GM termination probably represents loss of *-h-*. This development may have been assisted by the existence of subjunctive-present forms in *-ai*, cited in *LIO* 3.149 as being parallel in function with subjunctive-future forms in *-ahi*. Further examples of *-aĩ* imperatives are *milai* (16.2), and *rājai* in FGM for *rājahi* (44.2).

The *-ahu* termination appears in the CP with both singular and plural reference, though as noted in *LIO* 3.153 this is historically a plural form. Loss of *-h-* in FGM's spelling *rājai* noted above occurs in this form also: F reads *bilasau,* GM *bilaso*, for *bilasahu* at 12.6; A reads *bilasahi* in the same instance.

The rhetorical *kina* noted above occurs again with the *-ahu* form at 62.2 and 62.4; rhetorical *na* follows *karahu* at 56.4.

Imperatives in *-au* are a development of the *-ahu* form (*LIO* 3.139), and denote plural number in most examples.

b) *3rd sg. and pl.*

A single example reflecting the Ap. 3rd sg. imperative in *-au* is found in 54.6 *jīvau* (A *jīyō*, BDFGL *jīyau*, CI *jīvo*):

54.6 *cira jīvau bhūtala yaha jorī.*

The same form occurs with plural (or rather dual) number in the following occurrence of *karau* (AGM *karo*, C *karaū*, IL *karahu*):

57.30 *karau dina doū acala bihāra.*

karau may here represent a development of *karahu* on the regular pattern, since the extension of the *-ahu* imperative from the 2nd pl. to the 3rd pl. is attested in Ap. (*HGA* para 138; cf. *-ahu* as 3rd pl. in *LIO* 3.156). Alternatively, since the *BhK* paradigm (para 34) cites only *karau* (sg.) and *karantu* (pl.) for the third person, it is possible that the *karahu* form appearing in MSS IL here may represent an analogical 'restoration' of *-h-* to the *-au* form.

(xiii) *Verbal nouns*

a) The verbal noun in *-ibau*, from the Ap. gerundive in *-ivvau* etc. (*BhK* para 38) is represented in the end-rhyme context of CP 83, where consistency in the *-au* spelling is almost fully maintained.

b) Participles in *-(y)au* are also used nominally. At 1.2 *bhayau* (DGIM *bhayo*) is the object of *cāh-* in a usage giving the sense 'wishes to' cited in *LIO* 4.21; another example of the same usage is with *ṣelyau* (ADI *ṣelyo*, M *ṣelo*) at 39.1. At 59.3 nominal *dhāyau* (IM *dhāyo*) is the subject of *parata*; at 59.5 *ṣāyau* (B *dhāyau*, IM *ṣāyo*) is the predicate of *saba*. Oblique usage occurs in 16.1 *kahe* and 33.5 *roke*.

c) The verbal stem + *-na* is another form used nominally, as for example in 55.5 *tina kī calana* (here showing a divergence from the usual masc. gender), 7.10 *kara dhūnana*. *-na* is often represented by *-ni* in the manuscripts: all but M read *ḍolani* at 34.1, *-olani* rhyme then being maintained throughout the stanza; CEK alone read *sīcani* at 56.3.

(xiv) *Postpositions*

kari appears with specifically postpositional force only at 59.1 *eka mana bahuta ṭhaura kari*, other occurrences being of verbal absolutives. ***kai***, as a variant of *kari*, appears once (for rhyme with *dai*) at 67.4 and also pleonastically after *kaise* at 14.1 and 14.5 (cf. KhB. *kyȍkar* etc.)

kau (1), (***kaũ***), ***kī***, ***ke***: a quarter of all occurrences of the genitive postposition appear in the first line of a stanza: analytical construction is perhaps favoured here, where a *pada* theme is being 'labelled' and introduced, whereas the more descriptive contexts which typically prevail later in the stanza allow greater use of compounded or elliptical expressions. *ke* occurs also in the compound postpositions ***ke kārana*** (13.5) and ***ke sãga*** (79.1).

kau (2): the oblique case marker is not consistently distinguished in its orthography from the genitive postposition (masc.), though slightly wider support for the *ko* form is found here.

tana 'towards' occurs at 73.5 and 75.3 only (though the commentators show some confusion of this with nominal usage of *tana*).

tīra 'near, up to': the only specifically postpositional use is at 37.7 *capala calī piya tīra*; in other instances (mostly following *kalapataru*), *tīra* is understood as nominal.

tẽ has the sense 'from' (e.g. *bana tẽ*, 58.1) three times, and occurs in comparative contexts four times (e.g. *tana. . tẽ pritama priya*, 1.3).

nikaṭa: postpositional usage at 12.3 and 65.2.

para has regular locative usage in all instances except 22.1 *nainani para* 'for the sake of'.

pai: shows agentive usage at 18.6, genitive or sociative at 51.5, instrumental at 59.3 and ablative (*mo pai na durata* 'is not hidden from me') at 84.2.

prati: 53.4 only.

binu, ***bina*** 'without' precedes the word to which it relates in five out of a total 10 occurrences. The sense 'apart from, but (for)' applies in rhetorical contexts: 39.4 *to binu. .kavana* 'who but you?' 42.6 *mohana binu* 'who but Mohana?'.

bīca 'between, amidst' occurs four times as a postposition. Cf. adverbial usage at 71.2, with the sense 'in the middle', and at 35.4, reduplicated, with the sense 'at intervals'.

madhya and derivatives: *madhya* 'amidst' occurs four times, with the following variants: *maddhi* A, 11.2 and 29.9; *madhi* C, 11.2; *maddha* F, 66.11. The *tadbhava* forms ***māhī*** (63[iii].1 and 6) and ***mā̃jha*** (66.19) occur in rhyme contexts only. Much more common, and with the more general sense 'in', is ***maĩ*** with 24 occurrences.

misa: usage in 66.7 *lālana misa ātura* may be understood as postpositional.

lagi 'for the duration of, up to': 52.3 only. ***laũ*** occurs twice, 29.2 and 73.2.

saṃga 'with' occurs three times in this form, a further three as ***sãga***. Twice (64.5 and 68.3), *saṃga* precedes the words to which it relates. Further occurrences are in the compound postposition ***ke sãga*** (79.1) and the adverbial expression *eka saṃga* 'together' (11.2).

samāna: three occurrences.

sameta: 43.6 only.

sahita 'with, along with' occurs four times, preceding the word to which it relates at 26.3 and 62.2. A third occurrence, *mohe mṛga dhenu sahita surasuṃdari* (63[iv].3) is ambiguous in this respect.

saũ, sõ occurs most frequently in expressions of speaking, meeting, or comparison (as KhB. *se*), e.g. 58.4 *haũ tosaũ kahata hārī*: 16.2 *piya saũ milai*; 52.6 *kāsǒ paṭatariye*. There is one instrumental use, 75.4 *kara saũ..ṭārati*; occasionally the sense is equivalent to that of *sahita*, as in 39.3 *saurabha saũ sītala pavana* (cf. 26.3 *anila..sahita bāsu*). A more general sense, 'in respect of', applies in contexts such as 75.2 *prāna ravana saũ kyaũ ba karata*. ***su*** occurs as a variant (for ***sũ***? cf. *LIO* 3.177), appearing in the CP only in the ***-āsu rī*** rhyme context of 26.5.

hita 'for the sake of' appears at 48.2, and twice forming a compound postposition after genitive *tere* (12.1 and 58.1).

heta 'for the sake of': 50.3 only.

(xv) *Miscellaneous Forms and Usages*

a) *ba*. This is an elided form of *aba* 'now'. H normally reads '*ba*, showing *avagraha*; I substitutes the rhetorical negative particle *na* at 39.5. The semantic value of *ba* is virtually nil in many contexts (particularly after *āju* in the vulgate of 84.1), and often calls for no translation equivalent; its function seems to be that of a metrical filler (whose inclusion at 84.1 is consequent upon an erroneous understanding of that stanza as having a syllabic construction).

b) *mano* 'as though'. *mano* 'as though' (KhB. *māno*) derives ultimately from the Sk. 1st sg. *ātmanepada* form *manye*, through Ap. *manne*, *maṇe* 'methinks' ('indeclinable particle of consideration', *CDIAL* 9857), *mannaũ* 'I deem' (used as a finite verb in *Sanatkumāracaritam* 482.2 (H. Jacobi 1921:30)). The short *a* of the unstressed particle is only sporadically represented among the many different orthographies which appear in the MSS. In the CP and in BrBh. generally, *mano* etc. is used only in the sense 'one would think', 'as though'.[1]

Two-, three-, and four-*mātrā* contexts are found in the CP according to metrical convenience, showing a continuing process of reinstating a stressed finite verb followed by further weakening. As one would expect, the more recently coined alternative spelling has, by the time of the manuscripts, been generalized at the expense of the most archaic formation, so that requisite two-*mātrā* orthographies are rarely achieved. Among contexts requiring four *mātrās*, only once is a metrically 'light' form found: 3.3 M *mano*.

The other possibility, that the archetype was written without regard for prosody, does not work out attractively (*mane*>*mān*-, generalized to *man*- very sporadically). (A third possible hypothesis, that the various orthographies represent random usage in the archetype, is not convincing since this would imply a corollary of random scribal interference.)

c) The *chāpa*. Resolution of the syntactic involvement of the

1. But cf. Tulasīdāsa, *mānahū mori karata hahĩ nindā* 'methinks (they) are speaking ill of me' (Saksena 1971:274).

chāpa is a familiar problem in the vernacular *pada* form. In the CP a number of different contexts exist, calling for various resolutions in the translation.

Occasionally a sense of *haribaṃśa* as 'the *Harivaṃśa purāṇa*', or 'literature of the *HvP* type' seems a possibility (in respect of which cf. the 'patronymic' *vaiyāsaki-* discussed on p. 6); an example is *haribaṃśa prasaṃsita* (35.10), capable of interpretation as 'as lauded in the *Harivaṃśa*'. Elsewhere, the sectarian tradition whereby Hita Harivaṃśa is regarded as an incarnation as the flute of Kṛṣṇa (Hari, *vaṃśī*) may have some basis in the common collocation of the *chāpa* with forms of the verb *sun-*, as in the final couplets of CP 37 and 38. It seems unlikely, however, that either of these contexts could underlie general application, even if they might individually offer a glimpse of an early usage in which the *chāpa* had more semantic and syntactic weight than is generally the case in the later, more stereotyped usage.

A predominant context is that in which the main body of the poem comprises the words of a *sakhī* to Kṛṣṇa or Rādhā, with the final line or couplet often offering a detached comment or observation made, as it were, by the poet himself. Thus in CP 16 the first two couplets, bearing the *sakhī*'s exhortation to Rādhā to join Kṛṣṇa, are followed (with a change from present to past tense) by a final couplet reporting the subsequent union. Here the *chāpa* is most conveniently represented as a vocative, although it may equally well be regarded as having no syntactic or semantic connexion with the remainder of the line. Vocative usage is more clearly intended in *hita haribaṃśa suni* (46.4).

By contrast, another favourite context is that in which the *chāpa* is woven into the line by a conceit which involves the poet in the action of the stanza. This usage conforms with (or rather justifies) the sectarian view of Harivaṃśa as *sakhī*.[1] Examples are *palu palu haribaṃśa pivata naina caṣaka jheli* (17.4) and *hita haribaṃśa asīsa deta muṣa* (54.6). These examples must be seen alongside parallel contexts in which it is the *sakhīs* who are described as relishing, and offering blessings to, Rādhā and Kṛṣṇa: *praṇayamaya rasika lalitādi locana caṣaka pivata makaraṃda suṣa rāsi aṃtara sacī* (50.6); *deta asīsa niraṣi juvatī jana* (70.7).

Occasionally '*haribaṃśa*' may be read as referring to Kṛṣṇa himself, as in the line *hita haribaṃśa karata apanau jasa pragaṭa aṣila brahmaṃḍana* (61.6). Elsewhere, the name refers quite specifically to the poet, as in *hita haribaṃśa jathāmata baranata* (30.17); taking this sense, reference to Kṛṣṇa can be achieved only when *prabhu* is suffixed to the poet's name as in 71.5. In a single occurrence at 53.6, *hita* appears in the same line as *haribaṃśa* without being adjacent to it: here the independent nominal sense of *hita* applies.

1. This concept is discussed in the final chapter.

A traditional usage in which the *chāpa* is compounded with following *prabhu* to yield the sense 'X's lord, Kṛṣṇa' appears in CP 11, 12, 65 and 71. In the first two of these instances, the *chāpa* concerned is not (*hita*) *haribaṃśa* but *narabāhana*; the significance of this is discussed in section VII.3.(i).

While most occurrences of the *chāpa* fall into one or other of the categories discussed, a few examples remain in which the *chāpa* cannot be accommodated in the syntax of the translated line. Thus *in extremis* a usage adopted by A.W. Entwistle for the *padas* of Kevalarāma, wherein the *chāpa* is set apart from the remainder of the line by a colon, has been followed in some instances. Occasionally, a traditional function of the *bhaṇitā* has been made explicit by the addition in square brackets of a finite verb, as for example in 84.4 '[declares] Hita Harivaṃśa'.

CHAPTER IV

THE CAURĀSĪ PADA: EDITED TEXT AND APPARATUS CRITICUS

Introductory notes

i) The use of single and double *daṇḍas* in the text (after odd and even lines respectively) does not represent a consistent usage in the manuscripts, but is incorporated in recognition of the couplet-based construction of the text.

ii) *Rāga* headings are not shown here, but are fully tabulated in section VII.3 (i).

iii) A brief indication of the metrical construction of each stanza follows the apparatus. This is meant simply as an aid to reading the text: a full discussion of the metrical forms follows in Chapter VI.

iv) For a note on the showing of nasality in the manuscripts, see section III.2 (xv).

v) Two further standardizations have been adopted in order to reduce the bulk of the apparatus: occasional use of nasal consonants in conjunct forms in H has not been shown; nor has the spelling *jaya*—which occurs throughout H in the excised honorific slogan *jai śrī* (which commonly precedes the *chāpa*)—been given as a variant.

vi) The annotations given in chapter V, following the translated text, are headed by line numbers, and may therefore be approached directly from the *mūla* as well as via the translation.

CP 1.

१ जोई जोई प्यारौ[1] करै[2] सोई मोहि[3] भावै
भावै[4] मोहि जोई[5] सोई[6] सोई[7] करै[8] प्यारे[9] ।
२ मोकौ[10] तौ[11] भावती[12] ठौर[13] प्यारे के[14] नैननि[15] मैं[16]
प्यारौ[17] भयौ[18] चाहै मेरे[19] नैननि[20] के तारे ।।
३ मेरे[21] तन मन प्रान[22] हू तें[23] प्रीतम प्रिय[24]
अपने[25] कोटिक प्रान[26] प्रीतम[27] मोसों[28] हारे ।
४ हित[29] हरिबंश[30] हंस[31] हंसिनी[32] साँवल[33] गौर[34]
कहौ[35] कौन[36] करै[37] जल तरंगनि[38] न्यारे[39] ।।

1 CDGIM pyāro; 2 CEG kare; 3 B [omitted]; 4 M bhāva [follows next]; 5 AM joi; 6 A soi; 7 A soi; 8 FHIJL karaĩ; G kare; 9 AD pyārai; 10 CDFGIM °ko; 11 DFIM to; 12 AGJKL bhāvati; 13 DM ṭhora; 14 C kai; L [omitted, added *sec.m.*]; 15 CD nenani; I nenana; 16 ABE mai; GHK mẽ; 17 DI pyāro; 18 DGIM bhayo; 19 E merai; 20 CDE nenani; I nenana; 21 B merau tau; E [omitted: *merai to* added *sec.m.*]; FGJ mere tau; IM mere to; L merai; 22 BDJ prāna prāna; C [2nd *prāna* added *sec.m.*]; F prāna te prāna; GHL prāṇa; I prāṇa prāṇa; 23 AB tai; C [*tē* foll. by one illegible *akṣara*]; J te; L taĩ; 24 A prīya; 25 A [folio damaged: *apa-* remains]; B apanai; 26 FGHI prāṇa; 27 A [1st syllable replaces original]; 28 BJ °sau; CEHL °saũ; 29 all MSS jai śrī hita; 30 A [folio damaged; *haribaṃ-* remains]; BM harabaṃsa; EG haribaṃsa; 31 B [omitted]; IL haṃśa; 32 DFIJM haṃsanī; L haṃśinī; 33 AF sāvala; CE syāmala; D [folio missing: text resumes at 6.2]; L śyāmala; 34 A [folio damaged: *gau-* remains]; M gora; 35 IM kaho; 36 CE kona; I kahĩ [indistinct: marginal *kona*, *sec.m.*]; 37 G kare; I [omitted]; 38 A [folio damaged: *taraṃga-* remains]; BCEF taraṃginī; I taraṃgana; 39 A [folio damaged: *-āre* remains.].

Metre: Irregular *mātrika.*

CP 2.

१ आजु[1] नीकी जामिनी[2]
भेंटि[3] नवीन मेघ सौदामिनी[4] ।
२ मोहन[5] रसिक राइ[6] ता सौं[7] जु[8] मान[9] करै[10]
ऐसी[11] कौन[12] कामिनी[13] ।
३ हित[14] हरिबंश[15] श्रवन[16] सुनत[17] राधारवन[18]
सौं[19] मिली गजगामिनी[20] ॥

[Folio missing in D.]

[To facilitate comparison, the vulgate text (with orthography standardised) is given opposite.]

1 HIM āja; all MSS [prec. by *pyāre bolī bhāminī*; -°*anī* in M]; 2 B [foll. by double *daṇḍa*]; H yāminī; M jāmanī; 3 GJ bheṭi; M bheṭa; 4 CEHJKL saũdāminī; FGIM sõdāminī; 5 A mauhana; 6 ABC rāī; M rāya; all MSS [foll. by *rī māī*; ~*rāi* in A]; 7 AFGIM sõ; BK sau; 8 A [omitted]; IL jo; 9 A mānu; 10 G kare; 11 AC esī; 12 C kona; 13 FM kāmanī; 14 all MSS jai śrī hita; 15 AE haribaṃsa; M harabaṃsa; 16 GIL śravaṇa; 17 all MSS [foll. by *pyārī*]; 18 ABCEFGIKLM rādhikāravana; HJ rādhikāravaṇa; 19 ABK sau; EFGIM sõ; 20 M gajagāmanī.

Metre: 10+10+12 *mātrās* (first line irregular).

Vulgate text.

१ प्यारे बोली भामिनी आजु नीकी जामिनी
भेटि नवीन मेघ सौदामिनी ।
२ मोहन रसिक राइ री माई ता सौं जु मान करै
ऐसी कौन कामिनी ।
३ जै श्री हित हरिबंश श्रवन सुनत प्यारी राधिकारवन
सौं मिली गजगामिनी ॥

CP 3.

१ प्रात समै[1] दोऊ[2] रस लंपट
सुरत[3] जुद्ध[4] जै-[5] जुत[6] अति फूल ।
२ श्रम[7] बारिज घन[8] बिंदु[9] बदन पर[10]
भूषन[11] अंगहि अंग[12] बिकूल ॥
३ कछु[13] रह्यौ[14] तिलक सिथल[15] अलकावलि[16]
बदन कमल[17] मानौ[18] अलि भूल ।
४ हित[19] हरिबंश[20] मदन रँग रँगि[21] रहे[22]
नैन[23] बैन[24] कटि सिथल[25] दुकूल ॥

[Folio missing in D.]

1 G same; H samaya; 2 AE dou; 3 M [this and foll. 2 words obscured by blot: also line (2) *bārija ghana biṃdu*]; 4 CH yuddha; 5 EFGHLM jaya; 6 B jata; 7 B [*śra-* omitted]; 8 G [*bārija ghana* printed as *bāri jaghana*]; 9 G bidu; 10 M pari; 11 GH bhūṣaṇa; 12 G [omitted]; 13 L kachū; 14 CIM rahyo; 15 AEF sithila; H śithila; J sathala; M sthila; 16 FJ alikāvali; M alakāvala; 17 F kavala; 18 CFG mānõ; I māno; M mano; 19 ABCEFGHJKLM jai śrī hita; I śrī hita [*jai* added in margin, *sec.m.*]; 20 ABEM haribaṃsa; 21 GIM rāga; 22 C rahai; 23 ACEFI nena; 24 CEI bena; 25 A sithila; H śithila.

Metre: 16+15 *mātrās*.

CP 4.

१ आजु[1] जुवति[2] तेरौ[3] बदन[4] आनँद भर्‌यौ[5]
पिय[6] संगम[7] सूचत[8] सुष चैन[9] ।
२ आलस[10] बलित बोल[11] सुरंग रँगे कपोल
बिथकित अरुन[12] उनीदे दोउ[13] नैन[14] ॥
३ रुचिर तिलक लेस[15] किरत[16] कुसुम[17] केस[18]
सिर[19] सीमँत[20] भूषित[21] मनु[22] तैं[23] न ।

४ करुनाकर[24] उदार[25] राषत[26] कछु[27] न सार
दसन[28] बसन[29] लागत[30] जब दैन[31] ॥
५ काहे[32] कों[33] दुरत[34] भीर[35] पलटे प्रीतम चीर[36]
बस[37] किये[38] स्याम[39] सिषै[40] सत[41] मैन[42] ।
६ गलित उरसि[43] माल सिथल[44] किँकिनि[45] जाल
हित[46] हरिबंश[47] लता ग्रह[48] सैन[49] ॥

[Folio missing in D.]

1 ABCEFGJKL āju tau; H āja tau; IM āja to; 2 F juvata; H yuvati; 3 EIM tero; 4 A badanu; 5 I bharyo; M bharayo; 6 ABCEGHIJKLM piya ke; F pīya ke; 7 all MSS saṃgama ke; 8 E sucita; 9 ACE cena; 10 L ālasya; 11 I boli; 12 GHIL aruṇa; 13 A doī; B dohū; CFGHJKLM doū; E ve dou; 14 ACEK nena; 15 BCHL leśa; 16 I kīrata; M kirati; 17 B kumasu; CL kuśuma; FM kusama; 18 CGHILM keśa; 19 GHM śira; 20 A śrī°; L śīmāta; 21 L bhūsita; 22 AEIM māno; BGHJKL mānau; CF mānõ; 23 ABCEFIK tẽ; HM tai; 24 ABFK karunākari; CGLM karuṇākara; HIJ karuṇākari; 25 C uddāra; 26 EJL rāṣati; 27 ABCFGHJKLM kachū; 28 L daśana; 29 C baśana; 30 AJL lāgati; 31 CEJ dena; 32 E kāhi; 33 BK kau; HJL kaū; 34 ACEL durati; 35 CH bhīru; 36 C cīru; 37 C baśa; M basi; 38 I kīye; 39 GHL śyāma; 40 C siṣa; 41 GH śata; 42 CEJ mena; 43 M ūrasa; 44 AG sithila; H śithila; 45 CEFI kīkinī; GHL kikiṇī; M kīkanī; 46 all MSS jai śrī hita; 47 AEM haribaṃsa; 48 HI gṛha; 49 CEIJ sena; H śaina.

Metre: 10+10+15 *mātrās*.

CP 5

१ आजु[1] प्रभात लता मंदिर[2] मैं[3]
सुष बरषत अति हरषि[4] जुगल[5] बर ।
२ गौर[6] स्याम[7] अभिराम रंग भरे[8]
लटकि[9] लटकि[10] पग[11] धरत[12] अवनि पर ॥
३ कुच कुंकुम[13] रंजित मालावलि
सुरत नाथ श्री स्याम[14] धामधर[15] ।
४ प्रिया प्रेम[16] के अंक अलंकृत
चित्रित[17] चतुर सिरोमनि[18] निजु[19] कर ॥
५ दंपति अति[20] अनुराग मुदित कल[21]
गान[22] करत मन हरत[23] परस्पर[24] ।
६ हित[25] हरिबंश[26] प्रसंस[27] परायन[28]
गायन[29] अलि सुर[30] देत मधुरतर[31] ॥

[Folio missing in D.]

1 HM āja; 2 M maṃdara; 3 ABE mai; FGHIJ mẽ; 4 CIM haraṣa; E

haraṣata; 5 EHM yugala; 6 I gora; 7 GH śyāma; 8 AEGHJM bhari [E emended to *bhare*]; 9 M laṭi [*-ka* added, *sec.m.*]; 10 M laṭika; 11 C pagu; 12 A dharati; 13 B [*-ku-* omitted, added *sec.m.*]; HIJ kumakuma; M kuṃkama; 14 GH śyāma; 15 B ghamaghara; 16 AB praima; 17 FM citrata; 18 B śriromaṇi; EM siromaṇi; GH śiromani; L śiromaṇi; 19 C nīju; GHM nija; 20 E [omitted, added *sec.m.*]; 21 B kalu; I kali; 22 C gānu; 23 E [one extra *akṣara* between *hara-* and *-ta*, now erased]; J harana; 24 M parasapara; 25 all MSS jai śrī hita; 26 AEM haribaṃsa; 27 AE prasaṃsi; C prasaṃśa; GI praśaṃsa; HL praśaṃśa; 28 A parāīna; GL parāyaṇa; 29 A [omitted, added *sec.m.*]; FG gāina; 30 H svara; 31 I madhurabara.

Metre: 16+16 *mātrās*.

CP 6.

१ कौन[1] चतुर[2] जुवती[3] प्रिया[4] जाहि[5]
मिलत[6] लाल[7] चोर[8] ह्वै रैंन[9] ।
२ दुरवत[10] क्यौं[11] ब[12] दुरै[13] सुनि[14] प्यारे[15]
रंग[16] मैं[17] गहिले[18] चैन[19] मैं[20] नैन[21] ॥
३ उर नष चंद[22] बिराने[23] पट अटपटे से बैन[24] ।
४ हित[25] हरिबंश[26] रसिक[27] राधापति प्रमथित[28] मैन[29] ॥

[D: text resumes in line (2) after missing folio.]

1 CEFI kona; 2 E [*-ra* omitted, added *sec.m.*]; 3 AEFG juvati [E emended to *juvatī*, *sec.m.*]; H yuvatī; 4 AF prīyā; 5 I tāhi; 6 L meḷata [emended to *milata, sec.m.*]; 7 K [foll. by 2 *akṣaras,* now erased]; 8 BC caura; 9 AE rena; CF raini; 10 A durata; 11 AK kyau; EHIM kyõ; 12 H 'ba; 13 ACEM durẽ; BI dure; GL duraï; 14 B [*su-* omitted, added *sec.m.*]; 15 A pyārī [emended to *pyāre, sec.m.*]; 16 D [text resumes with °*ga* after missing folios]; 17 ABK mai; EFGHJ mẽ [C folio bearing remainder of stanza is missing; text resumes at 9.4]; 18 BF gahale; KM gahilai; 19 AE cena; 20 ACEHJK mẽ; B mai; 21 ACI nena; G na; 22 DEFH caṃdra; 23 ABL birānai; M birāna; 24 AEI bena; G bainana; 25 all MSS jai śrī hita; 26 AE haribaṃsa; M harabaṃsa; 27 A surata; 28 BJ pramathata [J emended to *pramathita, sec.m.*]; 29 AEFI mena.

Metre: irregular *mātrika*, basic 16+(X).

CP 7.

१ आजु निकुंज मंजु[1] मैं[2] षेलत
नवल किशोर[3] नवीन किशोरी[4] ।

२ अति अनुपम[5] अनुराग परस्पर[6]
सुनि अभूत भूतल[7] पर जोरी ॥
३ बिद्रुम फटिक[8] बिबिधि[9] निर्मित धर[10]
नव कर्पूर[11] पराग न थोरी ।
४ कोमल[12] किशलय[13] सैन[14] सुपेसल[15]
ता पर स्याम[16] निवेसित[17] गोरी[18] ॥
५ मिथुन हास[19] परिहास[20] परायन[21]
पीक कपोल कमल[22] पर झोरी ।
६ गौर स्याम[23] भुज कलह मनोहर
नीबी बंधन मोचत[24] डोरी ॥
७ हरि उर मुकर[25] बिलोकि[26] अपनपौ[27]
बिभ्रम[28] बिकल[29] मानजुत[30] भोरी ।
८ चिबुक[31] सुचारु प्रलोइ[32] प्रबोधत[33]
पिय[34] प्रतिबिंब जनाइ[35] निहोरी[36] ॥
९ नेति नेति बचनामृत[37] सुनि सुनि
ललितादिक देषत[38] दुरि चोरी ।
१० हित[39] हरिबंश[40] करत[41] कर धूनन[42]
प्रणय[43] कोप मालावलि[44] तोरी ॥

[Folio missing in C.]

1 A muṃja; BM maṃja; 2 ADFGHIJ mẽ; B mai; 3 AM kisora; 4 AE kisorī; 5 AM anūpama; 6 B [*-ra-* omitted]; M parasapara; 7 B bhratala; 8 AH sphaṭika [*s-* crossed out in A]; E sphuṭika; 9 H bibidha; 10 B ghara; K [*-ra* omitted, added *sec.m.*]; I dhari; L dharu; 11 DJ karapūra; 12 M komila; 13 AKM kisalaya; 14 ADEFIK sena; H śayana; 15 BDGHJL supeśala; K [*-sa-* omitted]; 16 GHJL śyāma; I [foll. by *tamāla*]; 17 DF nivesata; GHL niveśita; M navesata; 18 E [line is followed by numeral *1*]; 19 A hāsi; 20 FLM parahāsa; 21 A parāīna; F parāina; G parāiṇa; L parāyaṇa; 22 F kavala; 23 D [*-ma* omitted, added *sec.m.*]; GJL śyāma; 24 A mocana; 25 B mukaṭa; E [*-ra* omitted, added *sec.m.*]; HK mukura; 26 FJ biloka [emended to *biloki* in J, *sec.m.*]; 27 A āpunapai; B apunapau; DIM apanapo; 28 B bibhuma; F bibhṛma; 29 E [*-ka-* omitted, added *sec.m.*]; 30 H °yuta; 31 A cibuku; B cibaka; 32 A praloī; H praloya; 33 AEFGIJKLM prabodhita; 34 A pīya; K priya; 35 A janāī; DHIM janāya; 36 I nahorī; 37 A bacanāmrata; 38 ABDH deṣati; 39 ABDFGHIJKLM jai śrī hita; E [*jai śrī* added *sec.m.*]; 40 AEG haribaṃsa; M harabaṃsa; 41 FM [omitted, added *sec.m.* in M]; 42 AFI dhūnani; B dhunana; 43 A pranai; DEFI pranaya; 44 M mālāvala.

Metre: 16+16 *mātrās*.

CP 8.

१ अति ही अरुन[1] तेरे नैन[2] नलिन[3] री ।
२ आलसजुत[4] इतरात[5] रँगमगे[6]
    भये[7] निसि[8] जागर[9] मषि[10] न मलिन री ॥
३ सिथल[11] पलक मैं[12] उठत[13] गोलक गति[14]
    बिधयौ[15] मोहन मृग[16] सकत[17] चलि[18] न री ।
४ हित[19] हरिबंश[20] हंसकल[21] गामिनि[22]
    संभ्रम देत[23] भवरन[24] अलिन री ॥

[Folio missing in C.]

1 GHI aruṇa; 2 ADEIK nena; H nayana; 3 A nalini; D [-*na* omitted, added *sec.m.*]; 4 H °yuta; 5 M ītarāta; 6 ABIKL ragamage; 7 ABDGJ bhae; 8 FM nisa; H niśi; 9 D jāgarana; E jagara [emended to *jāgara*, *sec.m.*]; 10 M maṣa; 11 AG sithila; H śithila; 12 AB mai; DGHIJK mẽ; 13 DEHIL uṭhati; 14 M [foll. by *ye*]; 15 DGI bidhayo; E bīdhayo; H bīdhayau; M bīdhiyõ; 16 A mriga; 17 A sakatu; E sakati [emended to *sakata*]; 18 ABI cala; 19 all MSS jai śrī hita; 20 AEM haribaṃsa; 21 L haṃśa; 22 M gāmina; 23 A deti; 24 A bhãvarina; DE bhavarani; KL bhramarana; G bhavarāna [for °*ani*?]; H bhrãmarani; J [changed to *bhavarani, sec.m.*].

Metre: 16+16 *mātrās*.

CP 9.

१ बनी राधा[1] मोहन की जोरी ।
२ इंद्रनीलमनि[2] स्याम[3] मनोहर सातकुंभ[4] तन[5] गोरी ॥
३ भाल बिसाल[6] तिलक हरि[7] कामिनि[8] चिकुर[9] चंद्र[10] बिच[11] रोरी ।
४ गज नायक[12] प्रभु चाल[13] गयंदनि[14] गति बृषभान[15] किशोरी[16] ॥
५ नील निचोल[17] जुवति[18] मोहन[19] पट पीत अरुन[20] सिर[21] षोरी ।
६ हित[22] हरिबंश[23] रसिक राधापति सुरत[24] रंग मैं[25] बोरी ॥

[C: text resumes in line (4) after missing folios.]

1 AHI śrī rādhā; 2 BGHIL iṃdranīlamaṇi; M īṃdranīlamaṇi; 3 GHJL śyāma; 4 HJ śāta°; 5 FJ tanu; 6 DFGHIJLM biśāla; 7 A [*hari* replaces original reading]; 8 L kāmine [emended to *kāmini*]; M kāmina; 9 D cikora; 10 AEFIL caṃda; 11 E bicā; M bici; 12 AEFGK nāika; 13 AJ cāli; 14 B gayadani; D [-*ni* omitted]; FIM gayaṃdana; K gayaṃdini; C [text resumes with -*danī* (emended to -*dani*) after missing folio]; 15 A braṣabhāna; DH bṛṣabhānu; 16 AB kisorī; 17 K nilola; 18 B javati;

HL yuvati; 19 I mauhana; 20 GHIJKL aruṇa; 21 GHI śira; 22 all MSS jai śrī hita; 23 AE haribaṃsa; 24 IM surati; 25 ADFGHJ mē̆; B ma; IKL mai.

Metre: 16+12 *mātrās.*

CP 10.

१ आजु[1] नागरी[2] किशोर[3] भावती[4] बिचित्र जोर[5]
कहा कहौं[6] अंग अंग परम[7] माधुरी ।
२ करत केलि[8] कंठ मेलि[9] बाहुदंड गंड गंड
परस सरस रास[10] लास[11] मंडली[12] जुरी ॥
३ स्याम[13] सुंदरी[14] बिहार बाँसुरी[15] मृदंग[16] तार[17]
मधुर[18] घोष[19] नूपुरादि[20] किंकिनी[21] चुरी ।
४ देषत[22] हरिबंश[23] आलि[24] निर्त्तनी[25] सुधंग[26] चालि[27]
वारि[28] फेरि[29] देत[30] प्रान[31] देह सौं[32] बुरी ॥

1 M āja; 2 A nāgari; 3 AB kisora; 4 B [-*va*- omitted, added *sec.m.*]; 5 C jori [emended to *jora*]; 6 ABJK kahau; CDEFGIM kahõ; 7 B [-*ma* omitted]; 8 FM kela; 9 E mile [emended to *meli, sec.m.*]; M mela; 10 AC [follows next]; 11 E [omitted, added *sec.m.* after *rāsa*]; H lāsya; 12 C maṃḍilī; 13 GH śyāma; 14 I [-*rī* omitted]; 15 DFGIL bāsurī; K [foll. by double *daṃḍa*]; 16 A mridaṃga; B mradaṃga; 17 I cāla [emended to *tāla, sec.m.*]; 18 J mathura; 19 GM ghoka; 20 EM nūparādi; 21 GHL kiṃkiṇī; IM kiṃkanī; 22 A jai śrī deṣati; BCDEFGHIJKLM jai śrī deṣata; 23 EM haribaṃsa; 24 D āla; E ālī; 25 ADEM nṛttanī; BCJ nirtanī; L nṛtyanī; 26 H sugaṃdha; 27 CEFGHKM cāla [E emended to *cāli*]; 28 FKM vāra; 29 EFGHLM phera; 30 AE deti; 31 BCGHL prāṇa; 32 AEFGIM sō; B so; K sau.

Metre: (7 x /⏓⏓⏑⏓⏓⏑/) + /—/.

CP 11.

१ मंजुल कल[1] कुंज देस[2] राधा हरि बिशद[3] बेश[4]
राका नभ कुमुदबंधु[5] सरद[6] जामिनी[7] ।
२ स्यामल[8] दुति[9] कनक अंग बिहरत[10] मिलि[11] एक संग
नीरद[12] मनि[13] नील[14] मध्य[15] लसत[16] दामिनी[17] ॥
३ अरुन[18] पीत नव दुकूल[19] अनुपम[20] अनुराग मूल[21]
सौरभजुत[22] सीत[23] अनिल[24] मंद गामिनी[25] ।
४ किशलय[26] दल रचित सैन[27] बोलत पिय चाटु[28] बैन[29]
मान[30] सहित प्रतिपद[31] प्रतिकूल कामिनी[32] ॥
५ मोहन[33] मन मथत मार[34] परसत कुच[35] नीबी[36] हार
बेपथ-[37] जुत[38] नेति[39] नेति[40] बदति[41] भामिनी[42] ।

६ नरबाहन प्रभु[43] सुकेलि[44] बहुबिधि[45] भर[46] भरत[47] झेलि[48]
सौरत[49] रस रूप नदी जगत पावनी[50] ॥

1 I kali; M [omitted, added *sec.m.*]; 2 B dasa; CHJL deśa; 3 AEIM bisada; 4 AEFM besa; 5 BFLM kumada°; 6 CGHK śarada; 7 M jāmanī; H yāminī; 8 GH śyāmala; J sā̃vala; 9 A druti; CEGM druta; F duta; 10 A bihirata; 11 BF mila; 12 E nirada; 13 A madhini [*-dhi-* replaces original reading]; BJ manau [J emended to *mani, sec.m.*]; F manõ; GHLM maṇi; I mano; 14 B [*nī-* omitted]; 15 A maddhi; C madhi; 16 ABCJ lasati; 17 M dāmanī; 18 GHIL aruṇa; 19 B duphūla; C dūkula; 20 M anūpama; 21 M maula; 22 CHJL °yuta; 23 GHIKL śita; J [omitted, added in margin]; 24 I [foll. by *bāyu*, crossed out]; 25 M gāmanī; 26 ABHKM kisalaya; 27 CEFI sena; M [omitted, added *sec.m.*]; 28 B cāhu; M cāṭa; 29 CE bena; 30 C mana; G [this and next printed as *mānasa hita*]; 31 M pratapada; 32 EM kāmanī; 33 I mauhana; 34 I mari [emended to *māra*]; 35 B [*-ca* omitted]; M kucī [emended to *kuca*]; 36 ABEFJK nībī; C [emended to *nībi, sec.m.*]; 37 B bapatha; 38 B jata; CGHL yuta; 39 FI neta; 40 FI neta; 41 CGHKM badata; M badita; 42 M bhāmanī; 43 DI prabhū [foll. by *nihāri locana* (crossed out) in I]; 44 M sukela; 45 C bahūbidhi; 46 B [omitted]; I bhari; 47 CKL bharita; 48 M jhela; 49 KLM sorati; 50 H pāminī; KL pāvinī.

Metre: (7x / ⏕⏑⏕⏑ /) + /—/.

CP 12.

१ चलहि[1] राधिके सुजान तेरे हित सुष[2] निधान
रास[3] रच्यौ[4] स्याम[5] तट कलिंदनंदिनी[6] ।
२ निर्त्तत[7] जुवती[8] समूह[9] राग रंग अति कुतूह[10]
बाजत[11] रस मूल मुरलिका[12] अनंदिनी[13] ॥
३ बंशीबट[14] निकट[15] जहाँ परम रवन[16] भूमि[17] तहाँ
सकल सुषद मलय[18] बहै[19] बायु[20] मंदिनी[21] ।
४ जाती ईषद बिकास[22] कानन[23] अतिसै[24] सुबास
राका निसि[25] सरद[26] मास बिमल चंदिनी[27] ॥
५ नरबाहन प्रभु[28] निहारि[29] लोचन भरि[30] घोष नारि
नषसिष[31] सौंदर्ज[32] काम दुष निकंदिनी[33] ।
६ बिलसहु[34] भुज ग्रीव मेलि[35] भामिनि[36] सुष सिंधु[37] झेलि[38]
नव निकुंज[39] स्याम[40] केलि[41] जगत बंदिनी[42] ॥

1 M calihi; 2 I guna; 3 A rāsu; 4 DI racyo; 5 GHL śyāma; 6 BIM naṃdanī; 7 AEHM nirtata; BDJK nirttati; M nṛtata; 8 CH yuvatī; 9 E samuha; 10 ABDF katūha; 11 DJ bājati; 12 C muralīkā; M murilikā; 13 B ānaṃdinī; M anaṃdanī; 14 ABEM baṃsī°; 15 M

nikaṭi; 16 A ravani; J [changed to *ravani, sec.m.*]; D ramani; H ramaṇi; 17 A bhumi; 18 A male; 19 B bahe; 20 A bāī; 21 IM maṃdanī; 22 H bikāśa; 23 A kānani; 24 B atasaya; GH atiśaya; I atise; JLM atisaya; 25 BM nisa; GH niśi; 26 GH śarada; 27 AIM caṃdanī; F cā̃dinī; 28 DI prabhū; 29 BGHIJM nihāra [J emended to *nihāri, sec.m.*]; 30 FI bhara; 31 GH naṣaśiṣa; 32 A suṃdarajja; B saudarjja; CE sauṃdarya; HL sauṃdaryya; K saudaryya; M soṃdarja; 33 BEFIM nikaṃdanī; 34 A bilasahi [emended to *bilasahu*]; C bilaśahu; F bilasau; GM bilaso; 35 FM mela; 36 A [*-nī* omitted, added *sec.m.*]; B bhāmana; CF bhāminī; M bhāmina; 37 A siṃdha; C siṃdhū; 38 F jhela; 39 B nikaṃja; M nakuṃja; 40 GH śyāma; 41 FM kela; 42 M baṃdanī.

Metre: (7x/6m/) + /—/

CP 13.

१ नंद के लाल हर्‌यौ[1] मन मोर[2] ।
२ हौं[3] अपने[4] मोतिन[5] लर पोवत[6]
काँकर[7] डारि[8] गयौ[9] सषि[10] भोर ॥
३ बंक बिलोकनि[11] चाल[12] छबीली[13]
रसिक सिरोमनि[14] नंदकिशोर[15] ।
४ कहि कैंसे[16] मन रहत[17] श्रवन[18] सुनि
सरस मधुर मुरली की घोर ॥
५ इंदु[19] गोंबिद[20] बदन के कारन[21]
चितवनि[22] कौ[23] भये[24] नैन[25] चकोर ।
६ हित[26] हरिबंश[27] रसिक रस जुवती[28]
तू[29] लै मिलि[30] सषि[31] प्रान[32] अकोर ॥

[Text absent in A: *mūla* and *ṭikā* added in margins.]

1 ADIM haryo; 2 M moro; 3 ACEFGIJKM hõ; B hau; 4 A [*a-* omitted]; BL apanai; 5 B mautinu; CDEJ motinu; GL motini; 6 ABCDEH povati; 7 ACEIL kaṃkara [E emended to *kā̃kara*]; J kākara; 8 FJ ḍāra; K ḍari [emended to *ḍāri*]; 9 A gae; DEIJM gayo; 10 BFM saṣī; 11 D bilokini; KM bilokana; 12 ADIJ cāli [J emended to *cāla, sec.m.*]; 13 E chabilī; I chabīlo [emended to *chabīlī*]; 14 B siromaṇi; E śiromani; FM siromana; GHIL śiromaṇi; 15 BKL °kisora; 16 A kāko; BDHJLM kaisai; I kese; 17 C rahe [*-ta* added *sec.m.*]; E rahi [*-ta* added *sec.m.*]; L rahai; M harata [emended to *rahata* by numerals above *akṣaras*]; 18 GHIL śravaṇa; 19 AM iṃda; B iṃtu; E iṃdra; 20 AE gubiṃda [E emended to *gobiṃda*]; I [omitted, added *sec.m.*]; 21 B kārani; GH kāraṇa; 22 ABGHILM citavana [I emended to *citavani*]; 23 AFGIKM ko; 24 ABDEGJ bhae; 25 AEIJ nena; C nayana; 26 all

MSS *jai śrī hita*; 27 EM haribaṃsa; 28 A jūvatī; H yuvatī; 29 E tū̃ [followed by one erased *akṣara* (*-ma*?)]; 30 BEFH mila; L mele [emended to *mili*]; 31 ABEFHIJKM saṣī; 32 GHIL prāṇa.

Metre: 16+15 *mātrās*.

CP 14.

१ अधर[1] अरुन[2] तेरे कैसैं[3]- कै[4] दुराऊँ[5] ।
२ रबि ससि[6] संक[7] भजन कियौ[8] अपबस[9]
अद्भुत[10] रंगनि कुसुम[11] बनाऊँ[12]।।
३ शुभ[13] कौशेय[14] कसि[15] ब कौस्तुभ[16] मणि[17]
पंकज[18] सुतनि[19] लै अँगनि[20] लिपाऊँ[21] ।
४ हरषित[22] इंदु[23] तजत जैसैं[24] जलधर
सो[25] भ्रम ढूंढि[26] कहाँ[27] हौं[28] पाऊँ[29] ।।
५ अंबुन[30] दंभ कछू[31] नहि[32] ब्यापत[33]
हिमकर[34] तपै[35] ताहि कैसैं[36]-कै[37] बुझाऊँ[38] ।
६ हित[39] हरिबंश[40] रसिक नवरँग[41] पिय
भृकुटी[42] भौंह[43] तेरे षंजन लराऊँ[44] ।।

1 D adharana [emended to *adhara*]; 2 GHIJKLM aruṇa; 3 AI kese; CEG kaise; 4 B ke; J [omitted]; 5 AC durāū; B durāi; 6 CGHIM śaśi; 7 GHM śaṃka; 8 D kīyo; J [emended to *kiye*]; L keyau [emended to *kiyau*]; M kiya; 9 C apabaśa; 10 B adabhuta; 11 DFIM kusama; 12 ABC banāū; 13 AKL subha; 14 ACDFGH kauseya; E kausaya; M koseya; 15 BDIJM kaśi; 16 A kaustibha; FM kaustabha; J kostubha; 17 ACE mani; 18 B paṃgaja; 19 ABIJ sutana; 20 A aṃgana; 21 AC lipāū; B lapāū; DEFGHIJKLM lupāū̃; 22 B harasati; I haraṣata; L harasita; 23 AM iṃda; C iṃdū; 24 ACEFG jaise; 25 AE sõ; 26 A ḍhuḍhi; BCDFIM ḍhūḍhi; J ḍhūḍha [emended to *ḍhūḍhi*]; 27 BDE kahā; 28 ACDEFGJKM hõ; B ho; 29 ABC pāū; 30 DI aṃbana; J [emended to *aṃbani*]; M aṃbuni; 31 AEIL kachu; 32 D nahī; FH nahī̃; J nahī; 33 ACE byāpita; BM byāpati; 34 C hīmakara; 35 G tape; 36 A kaisau; BCGJ kaise; I kesai; 37 I ke; 38 ACDE bujhāū; 39 all MSS jai śrī hita; 40 AEM haribaṃsa; B harabaṃsa; 41 A navarāgā; 42 AEGM bhrakuṭī; B bhrakuṭi; JL bhṛkuṭi; 43 ACEG bhõha; 44 ABC larāū.

Metre: 16+16 *mātrās*.

CP 15.

१ अपनी[1] बात मोसौं[2] कहि[3] री भामिनी
औंगी[4] मौंगी[5] रहत[6] गरब[7] कौं[8] माती ।

२ हौं[9] तोसौं[10] कहत[11] हारी सुनि[12] री[13] राधिका प्यारी
निसि[14] कौ[15] रंग[16] क्यौं[17] न कहति[18] लजाती ।।
३ गलित कुसुम[19] बैनी[20] सुनि[21] री सारंग नैनी[22]
छूटी लट अँचरा[23] बदति[24] अरसाती[25] ।
४ अधर निरंग[26] रंग[27] रच्यौ[28] री कपोलनि[29]
जुवति[30] चलति[31] गजगति अरुझाती[32] ।।
५ रहसि रमी छबीले रसन बसन ढीले
सिथल[33] कसनि[34] कंचुकी[35] उर राती ।
६ सषी सौं[36] सुनि श्रवन[37] बचन मुदित मन
चली हरिबंश[38] भवन[39] मुसकाती[40] ।।

1 A apinī; 2 ACEFGIM °sõ; B °sau; 3 J [*kaha* emended to *kahi*]; 4 ACFGI õgī; B [omitted]; 5 ACFG mõgī; K maugī; 6 ACDEL rahati; 7 BDK garba; 8 A kā; 9 ACDEFGIM hõ; 10 ACEFGIM °sõ; 11 ABCDIJL kahati; 12 BM suna; 13 E [omitted, added *sec.m.*]; 14 C nisī; H niśi; M nisa; 15 AGILM ko; 16 AC raṃgu; 17 AIJ kyõ; B kyau; D kyo; 18 B [-*ha*- omitted]; GHIKM kahata [emended to *kahati* in K]; 19 D kukusuma; FIJM kusama; 20 ACEKM benī; G beṇī; 21 BIM suna; 22 ACEIK nenī; 23 A ā̃carā; M acarā; 24 FGM badata; L badita; 25 H alasātī; 26 A niraṃgu; G [printed with prec. as *adharani raṃga*]; M naraṃga; 27 A [omitted]; 28 ADIM racyo; 29 C kapolanī [emended to *kapolani, sec.m.*]; FH kapolana; 30 A juvatī; H yuvati; 31 B caliti; EFKM calata; 32 ACEGM arajhātī; B arujhata; F arasātī; 33 A sithila; H śithila; 34 M kasana; 35 C kaṃcūkī; 36 ADFGM sõ; BC sau; 37 GL śravaṇa; 38 ABEM haribaṃsa; 39 C bhuvana; 40 DHJL musikātī; I muśikātī.

Metre: 8+8+13/14 *varṇas* (first line irregular).

CP 16.

१ आजु[1] मेरे[2] कहे[3] चलौ[4] मृग-[5] नैनी[6] ।
२ गावत[7] सरस[8] जुवति[9] मंडल[10] मैं[11]
पिय[12] सौं[13] मिलै[14] भलै[15] पिकबैनी[16] ।।
३ परम प्रबीन[17] कोक बिद्या मैं[18]
अभिनय[19] निपुन[20] लाग[21] गति लैनी[22] ।
४ रूप रासि[23] सुनि नवल किशोरी[24]
पलु[25] पलु[26] घटति[27] चाँदिनी[28] रैनी[29] ।।
५ हित[30] हरिबंश[31] चली[32] अति[33] आतुर
राधारवन[34] सुरत[35] सुष दैनी[36] ।
६ रहसि[37] रभस[38] आलिंगन[39] चुंबन[40]
मदन कोटि[41] कुल भई[42] कुचैनी[43] ।।

1 BM āja; 2 A merai; 3 ABDHIJL kahai; GM kahẽ; 4 AM calo; 5 AEF mriga-; 6 AEFJ nenī [emended to *nainī* in J, *sec.m.*]; 7 ACDEIL gāvati; 8 K [*-ra-* omitted, added *sec.m.*]; 9 C juvatī; H yuvati; 10 B maṃḍila; D maṃḍalī; I maṃḍalai; J maṃḍali; 11 ACFGHK mẽ; BJ mai; I [omitted: see prec.]; 12 A pīya; 13 ACFGM sõ; B sau; 14 ABKM milaĩ; CEFG milẽ; 15 BK [omitted, added *sec.m.* in K]; 16 CE pikabainī; 17 B prībīna; 18 ABF mai; GH mẽ; 19 A abhine; M abhanaya; 20 GH nipuṇa; M napuni; 21 A lāgatī [but foll. *gati* omitted]; 22 CE lenī; 23 BF rāsa; H rāśi; 24 B kisosorī; 25 HM pala; 26 HM pala; 27 FGIKM ghaṭata; 28 ABGIM cā̃danī; D cādinī; 29 ACEFIJK renī; 30 all MSS jai śrī hita; 31 AEM haribaṃsa; B harabaṃsa; 32 E [omitted, added *sec. m.*]; 33 A ati ati; 34 H °ramaṇa; 35 B surata ata; L surati; 36 CDE denī; 37 B rahasa; 38 AEHIL rabhasi; 39 A ālīgana; 40 C cūṃbana; 41 F koṭa; 42 A bhae; E bhaĩ; 43 B kubainī; CEI kucenī.

Metre: 16+16 *mātrās*.

CP 17.

१ आजु[1] देषि[2] ब्रज[3] सुंदरी[4] मोहन[5] बनी केलि ।
२ अंस[6] अंस[7] बाहु[8] दै[9] किशोर[10] जोर[11] रूप रासि[12]
मनो[13] तमाल अरझी[14] रही सरस कनक बेलि[15] ॥
३ नव निकुंज[16] भवर[17] गुंज मंजु[18] घोष[19] प्रेम[20] पुंज
गान करत मोर पिकनि[21] अपने[22] सुर[23] सों[24] मेलि ।
४ मदन मुदित अंग अंग बीच[25] बीच[26] सुरत[27] रंग
पलु[28] पलु[29] हरिबंश[30] पिवत[31] नैन[32] चषक[33] झेलि ॥

1 HM āja; 2 F deṣa; 3 BCDIKL bṛja; 4 H suṃdirī; 5 D [*-na* omitted, added *sec.m.*]; 6 L aṃśa; 7 L aṃśa; 8 K [*bā-* omitted, added *sec.m.*]; 9 C dẽ; I de; 10 B kisora; C kiśori; 11 C jori; 12 FM rāsa; 13 A mana; BHJ manau; CEF manõ; DKL manaũ; 14 DHIL arujhi; E [*-ra-* omitted, added *sec.m.*]; M arajha; 15 B bela; D belī; 16 M nakuṃja; 17 GLM bhā̃vara; H bhrā̃vara; 18 A muja; 19 B ghoṣu; 20 B praima; 21 B pikana; 22 BCDL apanai; 23 H svara; 24 A sa; BDEHJL saũ; 25 M bīci; 26 M bīci; 27 I surati; 28 HM pala; 29 HM pala; 30 A [*-baṃ-* omitted]; EFM haribaṃsa; 31 ADFLM pīvata; 32 AEIK nena; C nayana; 33 A caṣaga; B caṣaraka.

Metre: (7x/ ⏓⏓⏑ ⏓⏓⏑ /)+/ – ⏑/.

CP 18.

१ सुनि[1] मेरौ[2] बचन[3] छबीली राधा[4] ।
२ तैं[5] पायौ[6] रस[7] सिंधु[8] अगाधा ॥

३ तू वृषभान[9] गोप की बेटी ।
४ मोहनलाल रसिक हसि[10] भेटी[11] ॥
५ जाहि बिरंच[12] उमापति[13] नाये[14] ।
६ तापै[15] तैं[16] बनफूल[17] बिनाये[18] ॥
७ जो रस[19] नेति[20] नेति[21] श्रुति[22] भाष्यौ[23] ।
८ ताकौ[24] अधर[25] सुधारस[26] चाष्यौ[27] ॥
९ तेरौ[28] रूप[29] कहत[30] नहि[31] आवै[32] ।
१० हित[33] हरिबंश[34] कछुक[35] जस[36] गावै ॥

1 M suna; 2 AEGIM mero; 3 A bacanu; 4 C pyārī rādhā; HI śrī rādhā; 5 ABK tai; CDEFJ tẽ [J emended to *taĩ, sec.m.*]; 6 DIM pyāro; 7 A rasu; B rasi; 8 M siṃdha; 9 ABE braṣabhāna; H bṛṣabhānu; 10 BHJKM hãsi; 11 B bhaiṭī; JK bhẽṭī; 12 ACHIJL biraṃci; 13 B [*u*- omitted]; M [one *akṣara* (*ma*?) erased between *u*- and *-māpati*]; 14 ACFGJ nāe; B nae; 15 ACEF °pe; GIM °para; 16 ABCFIJM tẽ [J emended to *taĩ, sec.m.*]; E te; 17 E °phula; 18 ADFGJL bināe; B bināai; C bānāye [emended to *bināye, sec.m.*]; 19 A rasu; 20 F neta; 21 F neta; 22 M śruta; 23 CDIM bhāṣyo; 24 A tini; CFGIM tāko; 25 [*adhara* is preceded by: A *terau;* B *te*; CEFIJ *tẽ* (J emended to *taĩ, sec.m.*); DGHLM *taĩ*; K *tai*]; 26 A °rasu; 27 ACIM cāṣyo; 28 ACEGIJM tero; 29 A rūpu; 30 IJ kahati [J emended to *kahata*]; 31 HJM nahĩ; 32 A āve; B pāvai; 33 all MSS jai śrī hita; 34 AEM haribaṃsa; B harabaṃsa; 35 C kachūka; 36 AE jasu; H yaśa.

Metre: 16 *mātrās.*

CP 19.

१ षेलत रास रसिक ब्रजमंडन[1] ।
२ जुवतिनि[2] अंस[3] दिये[4] भुज[5]-दंडन[6] ॥
३ सरद[7] बिमल नभ[8] चंद[9] बिराजै[10] ।
४ मधुर मधुर मुरली कल बाजै[11] ॥
५ अति राजत घनस्याम[12] तमाला ।
६ कंचन बेलि[13] बनी[14] ब्रजबाला[15] ॥
७ बाजत ताल मृदंग[16] उपंगा ।
८ गान मथत मन[17] कोटि अनंगा ॥
९ भूषन[18] बहुत[19] बिबिधि[20] रँग सारी ।
१० अंग सुधंग दिषावत[21] नारी ॥
११ बरषत[22] कुसुम[23] मुदित सुरजोषा[24] ।
१२ सुनियत[25] दिव[26] दुंदुभि[27] कल घोषा[28] ॥
१३ हित[29] हरिबंश[30] मगन मन[31] स्यामा[32] ।
१४ राधारवन[33] सकल सुष धामा ॥

1 K °maṃḍala [emended to °*maṃḍana*]; 2 BJ juvatinu; C yuvatini; DFIM juvatina; E [*juvatini* changed to *juvatina*]; H yuvatina; 3 HL aṃśa; 4 DHL diyai; G dië; 5 D [*-ja* omitted]; 6 D daṃḍani; 7 GH śarada; 8 A nabhi; 9 H candra; 10 C bīrājai; G birāje; 11 D gājai [emended to *bājai sec.m.*]; G bāje; 12 CGHL °śyāma; K [*-syāma* omitted, added *sec.m.*]; 13 BFI bela; 14 B [*banī* omitted, added same hand]; 15 I bṛja°; 16 A mridaṃga; B mradaṃ [*-ga* omitted]; H mṛdaṃgā; 17 CEI mano; D [*mana* changed to *mano*, *sec.m.*]; 18 GHL bhūṣaṇa; 19 C bahūta; 20 F bibidha; 21 ADG diṣāvati; 22 H barasata; 23 CFM kusama [follows *mudita* in M]; I [*kusuma* is followed by *deva muni harṣata*, these words being crossed out by short vertical strokes through top line]; 24 H °yoṣā; K [*surā*°, emended to *sura*°]; 25 AIL suniyati; 26 CEGHLM divi; 27 D duṃdubhī; I dudabhī; M duṃdabhi; 28 A ghoṣa; B joṣo; 29 all MSS jai śrī hita; 30 BEM haribaṃsa; 31 B ghana [probably understood as forming compound with foll. *syāma*]; E [*-na* omitted, added *sec.m.*]; 32 B syāma; GHJL śyāma; 33 CEL śrī rādhāravana; GL rādhāravaṇa; H rādhāramaṇa.

Metre: 16 *mātrās*.

CP 20.

१ मोहनलाल के रस माती[1] ।
२ बधू[2] गुपत[3] गोवति[4] कत[5] मोसों[6] प्रथम[7] नेह सकुचाती ।।
३ देषि[8] सँभारि[9] पीत[10] पट ऊपर[11] कहाँ[12] चूनरी[13] राती[14] ।
४ टूटी लर[15] लटकत[16] मोतिन[17] की नष बिधु[18] अंकित[19] छाती ।।
५ अधर बिंब षंडित मषि[20] मंडित[21] गंड चलति[22] अरुझाती[23] ।
६ अरुन[24] नैन[25] घूमत[26] आलसजुत[27] कुसुम[28] गलित लट पाती ।।
७ आजु[29] रहसि[30] मोहन[31] सब लूटी बिबिधि आपनी थाती ।
८ हित[32] हरिबंश[33] बचन सुनि[34] भामिनि[35] भवन[36] चली मुसकाती[37] ।।

1 G bhātī; 2 B baṃdhū; 3 BDHIJK gupati; CEFG gupita; 4 AFIKLM govata; J [omitted: *govati* added *sec.m.*]; 5 C kita; F kati; 6 BDHJL °saũ; 7 I [*-tha-* omitted, added *sec.m.*]; 8 HJ deṣa; 9 AL samhāri; BCDEJ sabhāri; FGHM sãbhāra; 10 A prīta; 11 ACE upara; 12 ABI kahā; 13 E cunarī; 14 D rā rātī; 15 A lara lara; 16 ACDEJ laṭakati; L [*laṭakata* changed to *laṭakati*]; 17 AGL motini; CD motinu; 18 M bidhi; 19 B aikita; 20 IM maṣa; 21 M maṃḍata; 22 FGJKM calata; 23 ACEGM arajhātī; H urajhātī; 24 GHIL aruṇa; 25 ACEIK nena; 26 A ghumata; C dhūmata; I [omitted, *ghumata* added same hand]; 27 H °yuta; 28 FJM kusama; L kuśuma; 29 H āja; 30 B rahasa; J rahata [emended to *rahasi sec.m.*]; M rahisa; 31 I mauhana; 32 all MSS jai śrī hita; 33 AEM haribaṃsa; 34 B suna; 35 B bhatini; C bhāminī; M bhāmina; 36 C bhuvana; E [*-na* omitted, added *sec.m.*]; 37 B masakātī; DGHL musikātī; I musikyātī.

Metre: 16+12 *mātrās*.

CP 21.

१ तेरे नैंन[1] करत दोउ[2] चारी ।
२ अति कुलकात[3] समात[4] नहीं[5] कहुँ[6] मिले[7] हैं[8] कुंजबिहारी ॥
३ बिथुरी माँग कुसुम[9] गिरि[10] गिरि[11] परैं[12] लटकि[13] रही लट न्यारी ।
४ उर नष रेष[14] प्रगट देषियत[15] है[16] कहा दुरावत[17] प्यारी ॥
५ परी[18] है[19] पीक सुभग[20] गंडनि[21] पर[22] अधर निरँग[23] सुकुवारी[24] ।
६ हित[25] हरिबंश[26] रसिकिनी[27] भामिनि[28] आलस अँग अँग[29] भारी ॥

1 ACEI nena; 2 BCDFGHIJKL doū; 3 ADIM kulakāti; 4 AD samāti; I samāna [emended to *samāta*, *sec.m.*]; 5 CEFGHILM nahī̃; 6 BFGHIJLM kahū̃; E kahu; 7 B mila; K milai; 8 ACIJ hẽ; BE hai; 9 BM kusama; 10 I gira; 11 IM gira; 12 ACJM parẽ; DKL paraĩ; EG pare; 13 M laṭika; 14 F [*reṣa* and foll. *pragaṭa* are unclear replacements, *sec.m.*, of obscured original reading]; 15 BCDEL deṣiyati; 16 A hẽ; C haĩ; 17 A darāvati; BCDJL durāvati; 18 C pari; 19 A hẽ; I he; 20 M śubhaga; 21 IJLM gaṃḍana; 22 I pari; 23 M narãga; 24 AEHLM sukumārī; GK sukūvārī; 25 all MSS jai śrī hita; 26 AEM haribaṃsa; 27 A rasika; BLM rasakanī; FGI rasikanī; 28 AC bhāminī [C emended to *bhāmini*]; M bhāmina; 29 I [*-ga* omitted].

Metre: 16+12 *mātrās*.

CP 22.

१ नैननि[1] पर[2] वारौं[3] कोटिक[4] षंजन ।
२ चंचल चपल[5] अरुन[6] अनियारे अग्रभाग बन्यौ[7] अंजन ॥
३ रुचिर मनोहर[8] बक्र बिलोकनि[9] सुरत समर दल गंजन ।
४ हित[10] हरिबंश[11] कहत[12] न बनै[13] छबि[14] सुष[15] समुद्र मनरंजन[16] ॥

1 A nenani; I nenana; 2 I pari; 3 AIJM vārõ; BCK vārau; 4 AI koṭi; 5 M [*ca-* omitted, added *sec.m.*]; 6 GHIL aruṇa; 7 AD banyõ; CIM banyo; EFHJL banyaũ; 8 B manauhara; 9 A bilokini; H bilokana; 10 all MSS jai śrī hita; 11 AEM haribaṃsa; B harabaṃsa; 12 DF kahati; 13 AEF banẽ; CGM bane; DL banaĩ; 14 C chabī [emended to *chabi*, *sec.m.*]; 15 C sūṣa; 16 J mano° [emended to *mana*°, *sec.m.*].

Metre: 16+12 *mātrās*.

CP 23.

१ राधा प्यारी[1] तेरे नैंन[2] सलोल ।
२ तैं[3] निजु[4] भजन कनक तन जोवन[5] लियौ[6] मनोहर मोल ॥
३ अधर निरंग[7] अलक[8] लट छूटी रंजित पीक कपोल ।

४ तू रस मगन भई[9] नहि[10] जानत[11] ऊपर[12] पीत निचोल ।।
५ कुच जुग[13] पर नष रेष प्रगट मनो[14] संकर[15] सिर[16] ससि[17] टोल ।
६ हित[18] हरिबंश[19] कहत[20] कछु[21] भामिनि[22] अति आलस[23] सों[24] बोल[25] ।।

1 I syārī; 2 ACEIJ nena; 3 ACDEFIJ tẽ [J emended to *taĩ*, *sec.m.*]; K tai; 4 GHKM nija; 5 C jauvana; 6 A lae; FGM liye; I liyo hai; 7 A niraṃgu; M naraṃga; 8 G ālaka [for *alika*?]; M alika; 9 AE bhaï; 10 C nahī; FL nahī; HM nahī; 11 AEI jānati; 12 A upara; 13 B jaga; DH yuga; 14 AK mānau; CE manõ; DF mānõ; G mānõ; HJL mānaũ; 15 CGHLM śaṃkara; E [*saṃ-* omitted, added *sec.m.*]; 16 GHI śira; 17 GH śaśi; K sisi [emended to *sasi*]; M saśi; 18 all MSS jai śrī hita; 19 AE haribaṃsa; B harabaṃsa; M harabaṃśa; 20 AFIJK kahati; 21 B [*-chu*, and *bhā-* from foll., omitted, added *sec.m.*]; CFIJ kachū; 22 CEG bhāminī; M bhāmina; 23 A ārasa; 24 B sau; DEHL saũ; 25 E bāla.

Metre: 16+11 *mātrās*.

CP 24.

१ आजु[1] गुपाल[2] रास रस षेलत
पुलिन कलपतरु[3] तीर[4] री सजनी[5] ।
२ सरद[6] बिमल नभ चंद बिराजत[7]
रोचिक[8] त्रिबिधि[9] समीर री सजनी ।।
३ चंपक बकुल[10] मालती मुकलित
मत्त[11] मुदित पिक[12] कीर री सजनी ।
४ देसी[13] सुधँग[14] राग[15] रँग[16] नीकौ[17]
ब्रज[18] जुवतिन[19] की भीर री सजनी ।।
५ मघवा[20] मुदित निसान[21] बजायौ[22]
ब्रत[23] छाड्यौ[24] मुनि धीर री सजनी ।
६ हित[25] हरिबंश[26] मगन मन[27] स्यामा[28]
हरत[29] मदन घन पीर री सजनी ।।

1 E [*-ju* omitted, added *sec.m.*]; M āja; 2 HM gopāla; 3 HM kalpataru; 4 B nīra; 5 A janani; 6 GH śarada; 7 C bīrājata; 8 ABCDEH rocaka; 9 F tṛbidhi; J tribidha; 10 C bakūla; M bakala; 11 J mata [emended to *matta, sec.m.*]; 12 C pīka [emended to *pika, sec.m.*]; 13 IL deśī; 14 EM sugãdha [M roughly emended to *sudhãga, sec.m.*]; 15 A rāgu; 16 M rãgu; M [*-ga* omitted, added *sec.m.*]; 17 ACGIM nīko; 18 A dija; D [*-ja* omitted, added *sec.m.*]; KLM bṛja; I [*braja* is followed by *desa,* crossed out by short vertical strokes through top line]; 19 AEG juvatini; BFJ juvatinu; C juvatīni; H yuvatina; 20 M maghuvā; 21 C nīśāna; L niśāna; 22 AGIM bajāyo; 23 ACF bratu; DIKM bṛta; J braja; 24 B

chāḍau; I chāḍyo; 25 all MSS jai śrī hita; 26 AEM haribaṃsa; B harabaṃsa; 27 B [omitted]; 28 GHL śyāmā; 29 ACDEL harati [E emended to harata]; B harita.

Metre: 16+17 *mātrās*.

CP 25.

१ आजु[1] नीकी बनी[2] राधिका नागरी[3] ।
२ ब्रज[4] जुवति[5] जूथ[6] मैं[7] रूप अरु चतुरई[8]
सील[9] सिंगार[10] गुन[11] सबनि[12] तैं[13] आगरी[14] ॥
३ कमल दक्षिन[15] भुजा बाम[16] भुज अंस[17] सषि[18]
गावति[19] सरस मिलि[20] मधुर सुर[21] राग री ।
४ सकल[22] बिद्या[23] बिदित[24] रहसि[25] हरिबंश[26] हित
मिलत[27] नव कुंज बर स्याम[28] बडभाग[29] री ॥

1 A āju ba [*ba* cancelled by application of yellow paste]; HM āja; 2 A [omitted: *yānī* (? unclear) added above line, *sec.m.*]; 3 HI śrī rādhikā; 4 A brija; LM bṛja; 5 A juvatī; H yuvati; 6 E jyutha; H yūtha; I jutha; 7 AB mai; CFGHJKM mẽ; 8 E caturaï; M caturāï; 9 GHIJL śila; 10 HI śṛṃgāra; 11 GH guṇa; 12 HM sabana; 13 AB tai; H taī; L te; 14 A ogarī; 15 BM dakṣaṇa; CDEGKL dachina; F dakṣana; H dakṣiṇa; J dachana [emended to *dachina, sec.m.*]; 16 I syāma; 17 HL aṃśa; 18 K saṣī; 19 C gāvati; 20 F mila; 21 H svara; 22 B kamala; 23 F [*bidyā* unclear: apparently replaces original]; 24 A badati; 25 E rahisi; 26 BEM haribaṃsa; L śrī haribaṃśa; 27 CK milita; 28 GHJLM śyāma; 29 K baḍabhāgī [emended to *baḍabhāga*].

Metre: 4x/ ⏕⏑⏕, ⏕⏑⏕ /.

CP 26.

१ मोहनी मदन गोपाल[1] की बाँसुरी[2] ।
२ माधुरी श्रवन[3] पुट सुनत[4] सुनि[5] राधिके
करत[6] रतिराज के ताप कौ[7] नासु[8] री ॥
३ सरद[9] राका रजनि[10] बिपिन[11] बृंदा[12] सजनि[13]
अनिल अति मंद सीतल[14] सहित[15] बासु[16] री ।
४ परम[17] पावन पुलिन भृंग[18] सेवित[19] नलिन
कलपतरु[20] तीर बलबीर कृत[21] रासु[22] री ॥
५ सकल मंडल[23] भली[24] तुम[25] जु हरि[26] सौं[27] मिली[28]
बनी बर[29] बनित[30] उपमा कहौं[31] कासु री ।
६ तुम[32] जु[33] कंचनतनी[34] लाल[35] मर्कत[36] मनी[37]
उभै[38] कलहंस[39] हरिबंश[40] बलि[41] दासु री ॥

1 F gupāla; 2 AIKL bāsurī; 3 DK sravana; GHIL śravaṇa; 4 K sanata; 5 B suna; 6 FIL karati; 7 AGIM ko; 8 M nāsa; 9 E saradā; GHM śarada; 10 B rajana; C rajanī; 11 AG bipini; M bipana; 12 AE braṃḍā; 13 BF sajana; C sajanī; 14 HL śītala; K [omitted: *śītala* added *sec.m.*]; 15 C sahīta [emended to *sahita, sec.m.*]; 16 H bāsa; 17 A subhaga; M parma; 18 ACE bhraṃga; 19 all MSS sevata [E: *se-* is replacement of original]; 20 HJM kalpa°; 21 A krita; B krata; 22 M rāsa; 23 A maṃḍalī; L maṃḍali; 24 H bhalī̃; 25 B [precedes foll.: *ju tuma*]; 26 K harī; 27 AFGIM sõ; BEK sau; 28 GHL milī̃; 29 M baru; 30 BDIJ banata [J emended to *banita, sec.m.*]; 31 ACFGIM kahõ; BEJK kahau; 32 A tū ba [see foll.]; 33 A [omitted]; 34 C °tani [emended to °*tanī, sec.m.*]; 35 A lālu; 36 ABDJ marakata; 37 C mani [emended to *manī, sec.m.*]; E mānī; GHL maṇī; M maṇi; 38 BDHI jai śrī ubhai; 39 L haṃśa; 40 BEM haribaṃsa; 41 M bala.

Metre: 4x/ ⏓⏓ ⏑ ⏓⏓, ⏓⏓ ⏑ ⏓⏓ /.

CP 27.

मधुरितु[1] बृंदाबन[2] आनँद न[3] थोर[4] ।
राजत[5] नागरी[6] नव[7] कुशल[8] किशोर[9] ॥
जूथिका[10] जुगल[11] रूपमंजरी रसाल[12] ।
बिथकित अलि मधुमाधवी[13] गुलाल ॥
चंपक बकुल कुल[14] बिबिधि[15] सरोज ।
केतुकी[16] मेदिनी[17] मद मुदित मनोज[18] ॥
रोचक[19] रुचिर बहै त्रिबिधि[20] समीर[21] ।
मुकलित[22] नूत[23] नदित पिक कीर ॥
पावन पुलिन घन मंजुल निकुंज[24] ।
किशलय सैन[25] रचित सुष[26] पुंज ॥
मंजीर मुरज डफ मुरली मृदंग ।
बाजत उपंग[27] बीना[28] बर मुषचंग ॥
मृगमद मलयज कुंकुम[29] अबीर
बंदन अगर सत[30] सुरँगित[31] चीर ॥
गावत[32] सुंदरि[33] हरि[34] सरस[35] धमारि[36] ।
पुलकित[37] षग मृग बहत न बारि[38] ॥
हित[39] हरिबंश[40] हंस[41] हंसिनी[42] समाज ।
ऐसे[43] ही करहु[44] मिलि[45] जुग[46] जुग[47] राज ॥

1 C °ritū; E °rita; K °ṛtu; 2 ABE braṃdābana; K śrī bṛṃdābana; 3 A [omitted]; 4 A ghora; 5 J rājati; 6 H nāgirī; 7 B navala; 8 A kusala; D [*-la* omitted, added in scribe's own hand]; E [omitted, added *sec.m.*] 9 B kisora; 10 H yūthikā; J jūthakā; 11 H yugala; 12 L raśāla; 13 D

mādhuvī; 14 BJ [omitted, added *sec.m.* in J]; 15 GL bibidha; 16 CEGHM ketakī; 17 F modanī; M medanī; 18 I [*ma-* and *-noja* separated by *bhā*, which lacks top line]; 19 AFGIKM rocika; L [changed to *rocika*]; 20 F tṛbidhi; 21 B [*sa-* omitted]; 22 L mukulita; 23 B [*-ta* omitted]; E nutana; L nūtani; 24 B kuṃja; 25 AEI sena; CFL sayana; H śayana; 26 M [*-ṣa* omitted, added *sec.m.*]; 27 A pīpaṃga [?? unclear]; 28 CEGHL bīṇā; 29 DHIJ kumakuma; M kuṃkama; 30 C śata; 31 A suragita; 32 L gāvati; 33 BFGIKM suṃdara; 34 A [omitted]; 35 C śarasa; 36 FIM dhamāra; 37 FM pulikita; 38 FI bāra; 39 all MSS jai śrī hita; 40 BEM haribaṃsa; 41 B [omitted]; DL haṃśa; 42 BI haṃsanī; L haṃśinī; 43 BCDHJLM aisai; I ese; 44 BDGHIJ karau; C karauhu; M karo; 45 C milī; 46 H yuga; 47 H yuga; J [*juga* replaces original reading (perhaps *juta*)]; M jaga.

Metre: 14 *varṇas*.

CP 28.

१ राधे[1] देषि[2] बन की बात ।
२ रितु[3] बसंत अनंत मुकलित कुसुम[4] अरु फल पात ॥
३ बेनु[5] धुनि[6] नँदलाल बोली[7] सुनि[8] ब क्यौं[9] अरसात[10] ।
४ करत[11] कत[12] ब बिलंब[13] भामिनि[14] बृथा[15] अवसर[16] जात ॥
५ लाल मर्कत-[17] मनि[18] छबीलौ[19] तुम जु कंचन गात[20] ।
६ बनी हित[21] हरिबंश[22] जोरी उभै[23] गुनगन[24] मात ॥

1 E rādhi; I rādhe jū; M rādhā; 2 BH deṣa; 3 C ritū; 4 FJM kusama; 5 CGHL beṇu; D bainu; EFI bena; K baina; M beṇa; 6 F dhuna; H dhvani; 7 B bālī; I [*bolī* followed by one illegible *akṣara*]; 8 M suna; 9 AE kata; BC kyau; GI kyõ; 10 FKL alasāta; 11 BL karati; D [emended to *karati, sec.m.*]; E kararata; 12 CFK kita; E [*kaba ta* for *kata ba*]; 13 B [*-ba* omitted]; 14 BM bhāmina; CK bhāminī; 15 AE brathā; 16 B aura [for *ausara*]; CDGJM ausara; 17 ABDEJ marakata; I markati; 18 BF mana; C manī [emended to *manī, sec.m.*]; GHKLM maṇi; 19 CGIM chabīlo; H chabīlī; 20 B [*-ta* omitted]; 21 ABCDEFGIJKLM śrī hita; H jaya śrī hita; 22 AEM haribaṃsa; B harabaṃsa; 23 GHM ubhaya; 24 GHL guṇagaṇa.

Metre: 14+10 *mātrās*.

CP 29.

१ ब्रज[1] नव तरुनि[2] कदंब मुकट[3] मणि[4] स्यामा[5] आजु[6] बनी ।
२ नष सिष लौं[7] अँग अंग माधुरी मोहे[8] स्याम[9] धनी ॥
३ यौं[10] राजत[11] कवरी गूँथित[12] कच[13] कनक कंज बदनी ।

४ चिकुर[14] चंद्रिकनि[15] बीच[16] अरध[17] बिधु[18] मानौं[19] ग्रसित[20] फनी ॥
५ सौभग[21] रस सिर[22] स्रवत[23] पनारी पिय[24] सीमंत[25] ठनी ।
६ भृकुटि[26] काम कोदंड[27] नैन[28] सर[29] कज्जल[30] रेष अनी ॥
७ तरल तिलक[31] ताटंक[32] गंड पर नासा[33] जलज[34] मनी[35] ।
८ दसन[36] कुंद सरसाधर[37] पल्लव[38] प्रीतम[39] मन समनी[40] ॥
९ चिबुक मध्य[41] अति चारु सहज[42] सषि[43] साँवल[44] बिंदुकनी[45] ।
१० प्रीतम[46] प्रान[47] रतन संपुट कुच[48] कँचुकी[49] कसि[50] ब तनी[51] ॥
११ भुज मृनाल[52] बल[53] हरत[54] बलय[55]-जुत[56] परस सरस श्रवनी ।
१२ स्याम[57] सीस[58] तरु[59] मनो[60] मिडबारी रची रुचिर रवनी ॥
१३ नाभि गँभीर मीन मोहन मन षेलन[61] कौं[62] हृदनी[63] ।
१४ कृस[64] कटि[65] पृथु[66] नितंब किंकिनि[67] बृत[68] कदलि[69] षंभ जघंनी ॥
१५ पद अंबुज जावकजुत[70] भूषन[71] प्रीतम उर अवनी ।
१६ नव नव भाइ[72] बिलोभ[73] भाम इभ[74] बिहरत[75] बर करनी[76] ॥
१७ हित[77] हरिबंश[78] प्रसंसित[79] स्यामा[80] कीरति[81] बिसद[82] घनी ।
१८ गावत स्रवननि[83] सुनत सुषाकर बिश्व[84] दुरत[85] दवनी[86]

1 DLM bṛja; 2 C taruṇī [emended to *taruṇi, sec.m.*]; GHL taruṇi; I taruṇa; M taruna; 3 B jukaṭa; H mukuṭa; 4 B [-*ṇi* omitted]; ADEFM mani; 5 CGHJ śyāmā; FL śyāma [emended to *śyāmā, sec.m.*]; 6 HM āja; 7 ACI lõ; BL lau; M lo; 8 B mohai; 9 BGHJL śyāma; I [omitted, added *sec.m.*]; 10 A yẽ; B yau; CGIM yõ; 11 DL rājati; 12 CEFGHM guṃthita; 13 A kala; 14 A cikara; D cikora; 15 B caṃdrakanī; DK caṃdrakana; FIJLM caṃdrakani; 16 M bīci; 17 D aradhi; FI adhara [emended to *aradha, sec.m.*]; H ardha; K adharadha [emended to *aradha, sec.m.*]; 18 B bidha; M bidhi; 19 ACFGIM mānõ; E mānahu; 20 BDJM grasata; F gṛsata; 21 B sobha [-*ga* added *sec.m.*]; E saubhāga; 22 GHM śira; L sara; 23 A śravati; BCDEFGHIKLM śravata; 24 E priya; F pīya; 25 A śrīmaṃta; 26 AG bhrakuṭi; BFIL bhṛkuṭī; C bhrakuṭī; 27 A kuvaṃḍa; DE kaudaṃḍa; 28 AEI nena; CH nayana; 29 C śara; 30 I kajjale; 31 M [-*ka* omitted, added *sec.m.*]; 32 E tīṭaṃka [emended to *tāṭaṃka*]; 33 CL nāśā; 34 I [-*ja* omitted]; 35 L maṇī; 36 CL daśana; 37 C saraśādhara; 38 BE palava [E emended to *pallava, sec.m.*]; 39 M [-*ta*- omitted]; 40 A sabanī; G śamanī; 41 A maddhi; 42 I [omitted, added *sec.m.* but with -*ja* removed by folio trimming]; 43 CI saṣi [C emended to *saṣi, sec.m.*]; 44 AB sāvala; C śā̃vala; DEF syāmala; 45 M biṃda°; 46 L [-*ma* omitted, added *sec.m.*]; 47 CDGHIL prāṇa; 48 [A *kucuki*, B *kucakī*, for *kuca kā̆cukī*]; 49 AB [see prec.]; DE kā̆cuki; J kāvukī; 50 CI kaśi; 51 B tatanī; 52 A mrināla; HL mṛṇāla; 53 I bali; 54 BDF harita; G sarata; I harati; 55 A balai-; B balava-; 56 H yuta; 57 CGHL śyāma; 58 H śīśa; I śīsa; 59 GKM tara; I [precedes next: *manõ taru*]; 60 AL manu; BI manau; CK mānaũ; G mānõ; 61 A ṣalana; 62 ABJ kau; CFIM kõ; G ko; 63 A hridanī; D

hṛdinī; G hradanī; 64 A krisi; CEFGHL kṛśa; J kṛśi; 65 C kaṭī; F kaṭa; 66 A prithu; CDEGM prathu; 67 C kiṃkiṇī; D kikiṃṇī; GHL kiṃkiṇi; M kiṃkani; 68 A brita; CEGJL brata; 69 CDGILM kadalī; 70 H °yuta; 71 CGHL bhūṣaṇa; 72 B bhāī; CEFL bhāva; H bhāya; 73 ACEFGHM bilobhi; L bilobhe [emended to *bilobhi*]; 74 I ivabha [-*va*- crossed out]; M ībha [emended to *ibhi*]; 75 I biharati; 76 H karinī; 77 all MSS jai śrī hita; 78 ABEM haribaṃsa; 79 CHL prasaṃśita; GI praśaṃsita; 80 E [omitted, added *sec.m.*]; GHL śyāmā; 81 F kīrata; 82 BCFGHJKL biśada; 83 GH śravaṇani; I śrāvanana [emended to *śravanana*]; 84 A bisu; F bisva; 85 CEFGL durita; HI durati; M duritu; 86 J [*da*- omitted, added *sec.m.*].

Metre: 16+10 *mātrās*.

CP 30.

१ देषत[1] नव निकुंज[2] सुनि[3] सजनी लागत[4] है[5] अति चारु[6] ।
२ माधविका[7] केतुकी[8] लता लै रच्यौ[9] मदन आगारु[10] ॥
३ सरद[11] मास राका[12] निसि[13] सीतल[14] मंद सुगंध समीर ।
४ परिमल[15] लुब्ध मधुब्रत[16] बिथकित नदित[17] कोकिला[18] कीर ॥
५ बहुबिधि[19] रंग[20] मृदुल[21] किशलय[22] दल[23] निर्मित प्रिय[24] सषि[25] सेज ।
६ भाजन कनक बिबिधि[26] मधु[27] पूरित[28] धरे धरनि[29] पर हेज ॥
७ तापर कुशल[30] किशोर[31] किशोरी[32] करत हास परिहास ।
८ प्रीतम पानि[33] उरज बर[34] परसत[35] प्रिया दुरावत[36] बास ॥
९ कामिनि[37] कुटिल[38] भृकुटि[39] अवलोकत[40] दिन प्रतिपद प्रतिकूल[41] ।
१० आतुर अति अनुराग बिबस[42] हरि धाइ[43] धरत[44] भुजमूल ॥
११ नागर नीबी बंधन मोचत ऐंचत[45] नील निचोल[46] ।
१२ बधू कपट हठि[47] कोप कहत[48] कल[49] नेति[50] नेति[51] मधु बोल ॥
१३ परिरंभन[52] बिपरित[53] रति[54] बितरत[55] सरस सुरत[56] निजु[57] केलि[58] ।
१४ इंद्रनील[59]-मणिमय[60] तरु मानौं[61] लसत[62] कनक की बेलि ॥
१५ रतिरन[63] मिथुन ललाट पटल पर श्रमजल[64] सीकर[65] संग ।
१६ ललितादिक अंचल झकझोलत[66] मन अनुराग अभंग ॥
१७ हित[67] हरिबंश[68] जथामत[69] बरनत[70] कृष्ण[71] रसामृत[72] सार ।
१८ श्रवन[73] सुनत[74] प्रापक[75] रति[76] राधा पद अंबुज सुकुवार[77] ॥

1 I deṣati; 2 M nakuṃja; 3 K [omitted, added *sec.m.*]; M suna; 4 AE lāgatu; DI lāgati; 5 A he; 6 A cāra; 7 E mādhavakā; F mādhivakā; M madhavikā [emended to *mādhavikā*]; 8 HKM ketakī; 9 DI racyo; 10 AEGM āgāra; 11 CGHM śarada; 12 E [*ra*- omitted, added *sec.m.*]; K [-*kā* omitted]; 13 CGH niśi; FM nisa; 14 CGHL śītala; 15 A paramala; C parīmala; [emended to *parimala*, *sec.m.*]; I paramali; 16 A °bata; BDIJL °bṛta; C madhū°; K °bṛtta; 17 A nachita; GM nadata;

HI naḍati; 18 A kokila; 19 B bahū°; 20 K [one *akṣara* erased between *raṃ-* and *-ga*]; 21 A mridula; 22 A kiśalai; BH kisalaya; 23 B lada; 24 A prīya; H piya; 25 F saṣī; 26 FHK bibidha; 27 K [omitted, added *sec.m.*]; 28 I [preceded by *pīvata*, crossed out]; 29 CG dharaṇi; M dharana; 30 B kusala; 31 B kisora; 32 A kisorī; 33 BJ pāna [J emended to *pāni, sec.m.*]; C pānī [emended to *pāna, sec.m.*]; FGHL pāṇi; DM prāna [D emended to *pāna*]; 34 B bara ba; 35 D [*-sa-* omitted, added *sec.m.*]; 36 A darāvati; BDEJL durāvati; I [*-ra-* omitted, added *sec.m.*]; 37 C kāminī; FM kāmina; 38 H kuṭina; 39 A bhrakuṭī; B bhrakaṭi; CG bhrakuṭi; EF bhṛkuṭī; 40 AFIL avalokita; [I emended to *avalokati*]; BDE avalokati; M avilokita; 41 A priti°; B prita°; 42 C bibaśa; H bibisa; 43 HM dhāya; 44 I dharati; 45 CI ẽcata; 46 C nīcola; 47 EIKM haṭha; 48 ADEJL kahati; I [*kahata* emended to *kahati*]; 49 B kalu; 50 F neta; 51 F neta; L nete [emended to *neti*]; 52 AB para°; E [*-na* omitted]; 53 A biparati; F [preceded by *cuṃb*[*-ana*], crossed out]; 54 I rata; 55 AJ bitarati; FIL bitarita; 56 IM surati; 57 H nija; 58 B ṣeli; M kela; 59 D [*iṃda*° emended to °*iṃdu*]; 60 A manimiva; BEJ manimaya; 61 ACGIJM māno; 62 ABDEJL lasati; 63 CGHI °raṇa; 64 I [*-jala* omitted]; 65 A śīkara; 66 ABD jhakajholati; CGHM jhakajhorata; IL jhakajhorati; 67 all MSS jai śrī hita; 68 ABEM haribaṃsa; 69 CH yathāmati; FGM jathāmati; 70 A barnata; E [*-ta* omitted, added *sec.m.*]; G baraṇata; I baranati; 71 AB kṛsna; 72 A rasāmrita; 73 CGHI śravaṇa; LM sravana; E śrīvana [emended to *śravana*]; 74 M [*-ta* omitted, added *sec.m.*]; 75 A prāpaya; 76 A karata; FK rata; 77 AHL sukumāra; CG sukũvāra; M sukũvāri.

Metre: 16+11 *mātrās*.

CP 31.

१ आजु[1] अति राजत[2] दंपति भोर[3] ।
२ सुरत रंग के[4] रस मैं[5] भीने[6] नागरि[7] नवल किशोर[8] ।।
३ अंसनि[9] पर[10] भुज दिये[11] बिलोकत[12] इंदु[13] बदन बिवि[14] ओर[15] ।
४ करत पान रसमत्त[16] परस्पर लोचन[17] त्रिषित[18] चकोर ।।
५ छूटी[19] लटनि[20] लाल मन[21] करष्यौ[22] ये[23] याके चित चोर[24] ।
६ परिरंभन[25] चुंबन[26] मिलि[27] गावत सुर[28] मंदर[29] कल घोर ।।
७ पग डगमगत[30] चलत बन[31] बिहरत[32] रुचिर[33] कुंज[34] घन षोर[35] ।
८ हित[36] हरिबंश[37] लाल ललना[38] मिलि[39] हियौ[40] सिरावत मोर ।।

1 H āja; 2 I rājati; 3 B bhore; 4 B [*kara* for *ke rasa*]; 5 A mau; CFGHJKM mẽ; 6 BDL bhīnai; 7 C nāgarī; FILM nāgara; 8 B kisora; 9 HIM aṃsana; L aṃśani; 10 IM pari; 11 AEFJ dīye; BDHL diyai; G diẽ; 12 IJ bilokati; KL bilokita; 13 E chaṃdu; M iṃda; 14 EFM biva; 15 BM aura; 16 J °mata [emended to *matta, sec.m.*]; 17 E tyocana;

18 GILM tṛṣita; F triṣata; 19 AE chuṭī; 20 B laṭāni; I laṭana; M [-*ṭa-* omitted, added *sec.m.*]; 21 A manu; 22 CEL karṣyau; DIJ karaṣyo; 23 AC e; 24 E corī; 25 L pariraṃbhaṇa; 26 A cūṃbana; 27 B mila; C milī; K [one *akṣara* erased between *mi-* and *-li*]; 28 H svara; 29 ABDEHIJL maṃdira; [J emended to *maṃdara*]; 30 M magaḍagata; 31 B mani; 32 E bihārata; 33 B racira; 34 B kūṃja; 35 ABI ghora; 36 all MSS jai śrī hita; 37 ABEM haribaṃsa; 38 B lālanā; M lalinā; 39 C milī [emended to *mili, sec.m.*]; F mila; 40 AIM hiyo.

Metre: 16+11 *mātrās*.

CP 32.

१ आजु[1] बन क्रीडत[2] स्यामा[3] स्याम[4] ।
२ सुभग बनी निसि[5] सरद[6] चाँदिनी[7] रुचिर कुंज अभिराम[8] ॥
३ षंडन अधर करत परिरंभन[9] ऐंचत[10] जघन[11] दुकूल[12] ।
४ उर नष पात[13] तिरीछी[14] चितवनि[15] दंपति रस समतूल[16] ॥
५ वे[17] भुज पीन[18] पयोधर[19] परसत[20] बामदृशा[21] पिय[22] हार ।
६ बसननि[23] पीक अलक आकरषत[24] समर[25] श्रमित[26] सत[27] मार[28] ॥
७ पलु[29] पलु[30] प्रबल चौंप[31] रस लंपट अति सुंदर सुकुवार[32] ।
८ हित[33] हरिबंश[34] आजु[35] त्रन[36] टूटत[37] हौं[38] बलि बिसद[39] बिहार[40] ॥

1 DEHM āja; 2 IM krīḍati; 3 GHL śyāmā; 4 GHL śyāma; 5 EGH niśi; FM nisa; 6 A [*sarada* emended to *saradi, sec.m.*]; GHM śarada; 7 ABIM cā̃danī; D [-*nī* omitted, added *sec.m.*]; 8 B abharāma; 9 L pariraṃbhaṇa; 10 ACJ ẽcata; E ãcata [emended to *aĩcata, sec.m.*]; 11 M [-*gha-* omitted, added *sec.m.*]; 12 B dūkūla; I [omitted, added *sec.m.*]; 13 BIL pāti; K pā̃ti; 14 A tīrīchī; BI tīrachī; L tirichī; 15 M citavana; 16 E samatula; 17 C vai; 18 D [-*na* omitted, added *sec.m.*]; 19 B pavodhara; 20 I parsata; 21 A °disā; BF °dasā; CEM °daśā; GHIJL °dṛśā; 22 F pīya; 23 FIM basanana; 24 BHL ākarṣata; I [followed by *śra*[-*mita*], crossed out]; 25 A surata; 26 A śrīmata [emended to *śramita, sec.m.*]; E śrimata [emended to *śramita, sec.m.*]; 27 GM śata; 28 G bhāra; 29 ADFHM pala; [folio missing in D: text absent from second *palu* to 34.6 *āśakta*]; 30 AFHM pala; 31 ACGK cōpa; 32 AH sukumāra; GLM sukũvāra; 33 all MSS jai śrī hita; 34 AEM haribaṃsa; 35 M āja; 36 A tinu; CGHM tṛṇa; F tṛna; I trina; L traṇa; 37 A ṭūṭatu; E ṭuṭata; I ṭūṭati; K ṭaṭata; 38 ACEFGIM hõ; 39 ABFGHL biśada; 40 E bihara [emended to *bihāra, sec.m.*].

Metre: 16+11 *mātrās*.

CP 33.

१ आजु[1] बन राजत जुगल[2] किशोर[3] ।
२ नँदनंदन[4] बृषभाननंदिनी[5] उठे उनीदे भोर ॥
३ डगमगात पग परत[6] सिथल[7] गति परसत नष ससि[8] छोर ।
४ दसन[9] बसन षंडित मषि[10] मंडित गंड[11] तिलक कछु[12] थोर ॥
५ दुरत न[13] कच करजन[14] के रोके[15] अरुन[16] नैन[17] अलि[18] चोर ।
६ हित[19] हरिबंश[20] सँभार[21] न तन[22] मन सुरत[23] समुद्र[24] झकोर ॥

[Folio missing in MS D.]

1 C aju; HM āja; 2 H yugala; 3 AB kisora; 4 B naṃdanadana; [see note]; 5 BE braṣabhānanaṃdinī; H bṛṣabhānunaṃdinī; IM bṛṣabhānanaṃdanī; 6 F dharata; I uṭhati; 7 AG sithila; H śithila; 8 A siṣa; CG śaśi; M saśi; 9 IL daśana; 10 AM maṣa; 11 E gaṃḍi; CF kachū; 13 A [omitted; *na-* added *sec.m.*]; 14 CEGHL karajani; I karijana; 15 EI rokai [*-k-* is unclear in E: apparently replaces original]; F rauke; 16 B [*-na* omitted]; GIL aruṇa; [*aruna*/*aruṇa* follows next in AFGIM]; 17 ACEFI nena; 18 B ala; 19 all MSS jai śrī hita; 20 AE haribaṃsa; 21 ACF sabhāra; BI sabhāri; JK sābhāri; 22 B tata; 23 K [omitted, added *sec.m.*]; 24 B sumudra.

Metre: 16+11 *mātrās*.

CP 34.

१ बन की कुंज निकुंजनि[1] डोलनि[2] ।
२ निकसत निपट साँकरी बीथिनि[3] परसत नाहिं[4] निचोलनि[5] ॥
३ प्रातकाल रजनी[6] सब जागे सूचत[7] सुष दृग[8] लोलनि[9] ।
४ आलसवंत[10] अरुन[11] अति ब्याकुल[12] कछु[13] उपजत[14] गति गोलनि[15] ॥
५ निर्त्तनि[16] भृकुटि[17] बदन अंबुज मृदु[18] सरस हास[19] मधु बोलनि[20] ।
६ अति आसक्त[21] लाल अलि[22] लंपट बस[23] कीने[24] बिनु[25] मोलनि[26] ॥
७ बिलुलित[27] सिथल[28] स्याम[29] छूटी[30] लट राजत[31] रुचिर कपोलनि ।
८ रति बिपरित[32] चुंबन[33] परिरंभन[34] चिबुक चारु टकटोलनि[35] ॥
९ कबहु[36] श्रमित किशलय[37] सज्जा[38] पर मुष अंचल[39] झकझोलनि ।
१० दिन[40] हरिबंश[41] दासि[42] हिय सींचत[43] बारिधि[44] केलि[45] कलोलनि ॥

[Folio missing in D: text resumes in line 6, *āśakta*.]

1 H nakuṃjana [see note]; 2 M ḍolana; 3 A bithini; CIK bīthani; FM bīthina; 4 C nāhī [emended to *nāhi, sec.m.*]; EFGHJL nāhī; 5 B [*-la-* omitted]; M nacolana; 6 E rajinī; 7 B sūcata sūcata; E sucata; I sūcati; L sūcita; 8 ABM draga; E druga; 9 E locani; 10 L (*-sa-* omitted); 11

GHIL aruṇa; 12 I [*-ku-* omitted]; 13 A kuchu [emended to *kachu, sec.m.*]; 14 A upajati; 15 F [*-la-* omitted]; M golana; 16 CE nṛttani; DGI nirttana; FHJ nirtani; M nṛttana; 17 BFG bhṛkuṭī; M bhrakuṭī; 18 A mridu; B mṛda; 19 B [*-sa* omitted]; 20 M bolana; 21 A āsakti; DFJL āśakta [D: text resumes here after missing folio]; 22 IL rasa; 23 B saba; C baśa; M basi; 24 C kine; BDL kīnai; 25 GHIKM bina; 26 M molana; 27 B bilalita; M bilulata; 28 AG sithila; H śithila; 29 GH śyāma; 30 AE chuṭī; 31 AIJ rājati; 32 A biparati; CEIM biparīta; 33 B caṃbana; 34 D [*-na* omitted, added *sec.m.*]; I pariraṃbhani; 35 JM ṭakaṭolana; 36 CE kabahuka; GIJKLM kabahũ; 37 BH kisalaya; 38 AFH sijyā; BDIJM sejyā; C sajyā; 39 I aṃcali; 40 B dita; C jai śrī hita [emended to *dina, sec.m.*]; I hita; 41 ABEM haribaṃsa; 42 EFIKL dāsa [K emended to *dāsi*]; 43 ABCK sīcata; D sīcati; J sĩcati; 44 FGIKM bāridha; 45 FM kela.

Metre: 16+12 *mātrās.*

CP 35.

झूलत[1] दोऊ[2] नवल किशोर[3] ।
रजनी जनित[4] रंग सुष सूचत[5] अंग अंग उठि[6] भोर ॥
अति अनुराग भरे मिलि[7] गावत[8] सुर[9] मंदर[10] कल घोर ।
बीच[11] बीच[12] प्रीतम चित[13] चोरत[14] प्रिया[15] नैन[16] की कोर ॥
अबला अति सुकुवार[17] डरति[18] मन बर हिंडोर[19] झकोर[20] ।
पुलकि[21] पुलकि[22] प्रीतम उर[23] लागति[24] दै[25] नव उरज अकोर[26] ॥
अरझी[27] बिमल माल कंकन[28] सौं[29] कुंडल सौं[30] कच डोर ।
बेपथजुत[31] क्यौं[32] बनै[33] बिबेचित[34] आनँद[35] बढ्यौ[36] न थोर ॥
निरषि निरषि फूलत[37] ललितादिक[38] बिबि[39] मुष[40] चंद[41] चकोर ।
दै[42] असीस[43] हरिबंश[44] प्रसंसित[45] करि[46] अंचल की[47] छोर ॥

1 E jhulata; I ye doū jhūlata [for *jhūlata doū*]; L jholata; 2 AE dou; 3 AB kisora; 4 BM janata; 5 E sucata; I sūcati; L sūcita; 6 C uṭhe [emended to *uṭhi, sec.m.*]; 7 BF mila; C milī [emended to *mili, sec.m.*]; 8 I gāvati; 9 H svara; K [one *akṣara* erased between *su-* and *-ra*]; 10 ABDEHIJL maṃdira [J emended to *maṃdara, sec.m.*]; 11 M bīci; 12 M bīci; 13 CE citu; 14 EI corati; 15 AC prīyā; L prayā [emended to *priyā*]; 16 AEFIK nena; H nayana; 17 AHJ sukumāri; BG sukũvāri; F sukuvara [emended to *sukuvāra, sec.m.*]; KM sukũvāra; L sukumāra [emended to *sukumāri*]; 18 FGHKLM ḍarata [L emended to *ḍarati*]; 19 BG hiḍora; 20 B ukora; 21 M pulika; 22 M pulika; 23 B pura; 24 CFHKLM lāgata; 25 C de; 26 H ākora; 27 BDEIJ arujhī; HM urajhī; 28 HL kaṃkaṇa; I [*kaṃcana* emended to *kaṃkana,* foll. by *kau* emended to *kī*]; 29 ACFGM sõ; B sau; 30 ACFGIM sõ; 31 CHL °yuta; 32 AH kyõ; B kyau; 33 ACFK banẽ; D banaī; E bani; GILM

bane; I bane hai [*hai* crossed out]; 34 B bibecata; J [-*ta* omitted, added *sec.m.*]; 35 A anaṃda; 36 I baḍhyo; 37 ADHIJL phūlati; E phūlate; 38 K [-*ka* omitted, added *sec.m.*]; 39 JM biba [J emended to *bibi, sec.m.*]; F biṃba; 40 A maṣa; 41 H caṃdra; 42 C de; 43 E [-*sa* omitted, added *sec.m.*]; H aśīsa; 44 B śrī haribaṃsa; EM haribaṃsa; HI śrī haribaṃśa; 45 AGH praśaṃsita; B [-*ta* omitted]; CL prasaṃśita; 46 BDHIJM kara [J emended to *kari*, *sec.m.*]; 47 CEGM ke [E emended to *kī*].

Metre: 16+11 *mātrās*.

CP 36.

१ आजु[1] बन नीकौ[2] रास[3] बनायौ[4] ।
२ पुलिन पबित्र[5] सुभग[6] जमुना[7] तट मोहन[8] बेनु[9] बजायौ[10] ॥
३ कल कंकन[11] किंकिनि[12] नूपुर[13] धुनि[14] सुनि[15] षग मृग[16] सचु पायौ[17] ।
४ जुवतिनि[18] मंडल मध्य स्यामघन[19] सारँग राग[20] जमायौ[21] ॥
५ ताल मृदंग[22] उपंग मुरज[23] डफ मिलि रस सिंधु[24] बढायौ[25] ।
६ बिबिधि[26] बिसद[27] बृषभाननंदिनी[28] अंग सुधंग[29] दिषायौ[30] ॥
७ अभिनय[31] निपुन[32] लटकि[33] लट लोचन[34] भृकुटि[35] अनंग नचायौ[36] ।
८ ताताथेई-ताथेई[37] धरति[38] नौतन[39] गति[40] पति ब्रजराज[41] रिझायौ[42] ॥
९ सकल उदार[43] नृपति[44] चूडामनि[45] सुष बारिद[46] बरषायौ[47] ।
१० परिरंभन[48] चुंबन आलिंगन उचित[49] जुवति[50] जन पायौ[51] ॥
११ बरषत कुसुम[52] मुदित नभ नाइक[53] इंद्र[54] निसान बजायौ[55] ।
१२ हित[56] हरिबंश[57] रसिक राधापति[58] जस[59] बितान जग[60] छायौ[61] ॥

1 E aju; HM āja; 2 ACIGM nīko; 3 ACE rāsu; 4 AM banāyo; L racāyo; 5 M [-*bi*- omitted, added *sec.m.*]; 6 M śubhaga; 7 CH yamunā [C emended to *jamunā, sec.m.*]; 8 I mauhana rāsa racāyau [*rāsa racāyau* crossed out]; 9 B bainu; DK baina; GH beṇu; JM bena [J emended to *benu, sec.m.*]; 10 AM bajāyo; 11 GHL kaṃkaṇa; 12 C kiṃkiṇī; FJ kiṃkina; GHL kiṃkiṇi; M kiṃkanī; 13 M nūpara; 14 B dhuna; C dhunī; H dhvani; 15 FM suna; 16 A mriga; K [omitted, added *sec.m.*]; 17 IM pāyo; 18 BJ juvatinu; C yuvatini; FIM juvatina; H yuvatina; 19 CHJ śyāmaghana; G śyāmaghara; 20 AC rāgu; 21 AIM janāyo; 22 A mridaṃga; 23 E [-*ja* omitted]; 24 M siṃdha; 25 AIM baḍhāyo; 26 GI bibidha; 27 BCGHJL biśada; 28 ABEF braṣabhānanaṃdinī; HK bṛṣabhānunaṃdinī; IM bṛṣabhānanaṃdanī; 29 E sugaṃdha; 30 AIM diśāyo; 31 A abhinai; 32 A nipuni; B napuni; G nipuṇa; 33 F laṭaka; M laṭika; 34 A locani; 35 AG bhrakuṭī; BCFIM bhṛkuṭī; E bhrakuṭi; 36 AIM nacāyo; 37 A tatatheī-tatheī; E tātāthei-tāthei; 38 DFJK dharata; 39 A nūtana; M notana; 40 C gātī [emended to *gati, sec.m.*]; 41 A bṛija° [sic]; DIM bṛja°; 42 AIM rijhāyo; 43 C ūdāra;

44 A nripati; 45 GHIKM °maṇi; 46 CDEH bāridhi; IJ bāridha; 47 AIM baraṣāyo; E bāriṣāyau; F bariṣāyau; I barasāyo; 48 B pararaṃbhana; L pariraṃbhaṇa; 49 I ucati; 50 A jūvati; CH yuvati; 51 GIM pāyo; 52 BIFM kusama; 53 A nāīka; BDHIJ nāyaka; 54 D [emended to *iṃdu*]; M īṃdra; 55 AM bajāyo; 56 all MSS jai śrī hita; 57 EM haribaṃsa; 58 C °patī [emended to °*pati, sec.m.*]; 59 ACEL jasu; H yasa; 60 A jagu; 61 AIM chāyo.

Metre: 16+12 *mātrās*.

CP 37.

१ चलहि[1] किन[2] मानिनि[3] कुंज कुटीर ।
२ तो बिनु[4] कुँवरि[5] कोटि बनिता[6]-जुत[7] मथत मदन की पीर ॥
३ गदगद[8] सुर[9] बिरहाकुल[10] पुलकित स्रवत[11] बिलोचन[12] नीर ।
४ क्वासि[13] क्वासि[14] बृषभाननंदिनी[15] बिलपत[16] बिपिन[17] अधीर ॥
५ बंशी[18] बिसिष[19] ब्याल मालावलि[20] पंचानन पिक[21] कीर ।
६ मलयज[22] गरल हुतासन[23] मारुत[24] साषामृग[25] रिपु चीर ॥
७ हित[26] हरिबंश[27] परम कोमल[28] चित चपल चली पिय तीर ।
८ सुनि भयभीत[29] बज्र[30] कौ[31] पंजर[32] सुरत सूर[33] रनबीर[34] ॥

1 C calahī; 2 ABDJ kini; 3 A manini; C māninī [emended to *mānini sec.m.*]; BDEJM mānani; FI mānina; 4 EFGHIKM bina; 5 A kuvara; BDEIJ kuvari; C kuvarī; L kūvara; 6 C binitā; 7 H yuta; 8 L gadgada; 9 GH svara; 10 ABDHIJ [follows next; DJ emended to *bi° pu°, sec.m.*]; E [emended to follow next]; 11 ABCFGHIJKLM śravata; D śravana; E sravana; 12 B bilocata; FLM balocana; 13 B krāsi; FI kvāsa; 14 B krāsi; E kvasa; FI kvāsa; 15 A briṣabhāna°; B bṛṣaṣabhāna°; E braṣabhāna°; HK bṛṣabhānu°; IM °naṃdanī; 16 CEIKLM bilapati; 17 A bipini; FIM bipana; 18 BCEM baṃsī; 19 ACE biśaṣa; L biśiṣa; M bisaṣa; 20 C mālāvalī [emended to *mālāvali, sec.m.*]; 21 D pīka; 22 E [*-ya-* omitted]; 23 C hutāśana; 24 K mārata [emended to *māruta, sec.m.*]; 25 A °mriga; E °mṛta; L śākhā°; 26 all MSS jai śrī hita; 27 AEM haribaṃsa; 28 M komila; 29 K °bhīti; 30 A bajjara; E babhra; 31 A kō; GIKM ko; 32 BDFIL piṃjara; CJ [emended to *piṃjara*]; 33 E sura; 34 BGHK raṇa°; C [emended to °*dhīra, sec.m.*].

Metre: 16+11 *mātrās*.

CP 38.

१ बेगि[1] चलहि[2] उठि गहर[3] करत[4] कत[5] निकुँज बुलावत[6] लाल ।
२ हा राधा[7] राधिका[8] पुकारत[9] निरषि[10] मदन गज ढाल ॥
३ करत[11] सहाय[12] सरद[13] ससि[14] मारुत फूटि मिली उर माल ।

४ दुर्गम[15] तकत[16] समर अति कातर करहि[17] न पिय[18] प्रतिपाल ॥
५ हित[19] हरिबंश[20] चली अति आतुर[21] श्रवन[22] सुनत[23] तिहि[24] काल ।
६ लै राषे[25] गिरि[26] कुच बिच सुंदर[27] सुरत सूर ब्रजबाल[28] ॥

1 FGM bega; 2 C calahī; I calihi; 3 ABD gaharu; 4 ABCDEF karati [follows next in A]; I [followed by *haṭha,* crossed out]; 5 CK kita; 6 D bulāvati; 7 M radhā; 8 B [*rā-* omitted]; 9 ABIJ pukārati; 10 FH niraṣa; 11 D karati; 12 A sahāī; BCEGLM sahāi; 13 GHM śarada; 14 C śasi; GHLM śaśi; I saśi; 15 A duragama; B dugama; I durggama; 16 M tikata; 17 C karahī; 18 A prīya; 19 all MSS jai śrī hita; 20 AEM haribaṃsa; B harabaṃsa; 21 C ātūra; 22 HIL śravaṇa; 23 B [*-na-* omitted]; 24 C tihī; M tihã; 25 ADFK rāṣai; C rāṣẽ; 26 IM gira; 27 A suṃdari; CE suṃdarī [*-da-* omitted in C, added *sec.m.*]; 28 ALM bṛja°; B bṛjaija°; C [folio damage obscures text: appears to read *sūra°* for *braja°, sec.m.*]; GH brija°.

Metre: 16+11 *mātrās.*

CP 39.

१ षेल्यौ[1] लाल चाहत रवन ।
२ रचि[2] रचि[3] अपने[4] हाथ सँवार्‌यौ[5] निकुंज[6] भवन[7] ॥
३ रजनी सरद[8] मंद सौरभ[9] सौं[10] सीतल[11] पवन ।
४ सो बिनु[12] कुँवरि[13] काम[14] की[15] बेदन[16] मेटे[17] ब कवन ॥
५ चलहि[18] न चपल बालमृग[19]-नैनी[20] तजि[21] ब[22] मवन[23] ।
६ हित[24] हरिबंश[25] मिलि[26] ब प्यारे की आरति[27] दवन[28] ॥

1 ADI ṣelyo; G ṣelau; M ṣelo; 2 I raca; 3 I raca; 4 BDL apanai; 5 AI savāryo; CEFG savāryau [followed by *ki* in E]; H sãmāryau; M sudhāryo; 6 A nikuṃjani; 7 A bana; 8 C [the following are written *sec.m.* over folio repair: *sarada, maṃda, sītala, pavana*]; GH śarada; 9 A sorabha; B sauraba; 10 ACFG sõ; BE sau; 11 HL śītala; 12 BEFGHIM bina; 13 AEI kuvari; BDFJ kuvara [F emended to *kuvari, sec.m.*]; C kũvarī; 14 E kīma; G [omitted]; 15 G [omitted]; 16 AEL bedani; 17 A maiṭẽ; BDKL meṭai; FHJ meṭa; 18 C calahī; 19 A °mriga-; 20 AEFJK nenī [J emended to *nainī, sec.m.*]; 21 I taja; 22 I na; 23 A madana; G bhavana; M mana [emended to *mayana, sec.m.*]; 24 all MSS jai śrī hita; 25 BEM haribaṃsa; 26 A [remainder of line reads *mile rasa lampaṭa rādhikā ravana,* which is from 40.6]; C milī; FGHILM mila; 27 B āīta; 28 EJ vadana [J emended to *davana, sec.m.*].

Metre: 16+7 *mātrās.*

CP 40.

१ बैठे[1] लाल निकुंज[2] भवन[3] ।
२ रजनी[4] रुचिर मल्लिका[5] मुकलित त्रिबिधि[6] पवन ॥
३ तू सषि[7] काम केलि[8] मनमोहन मदन दवन ।
४ बृथा[9] गहर[10] कत[11] करत[12] कृशोदर[13] कारन[14] कवन ॥
५ चपल चली तन की सुधि[15] बिसरी सुनत[16] श्रवन[17] ।
६ हित[18] हरिबंश[19] मिले रस लंपट राधा[20] रवन ॥

1 A bani baiṭhe; 2 M nakuṃja; 3 D [-*na* omitted, added *sec.m.*]; 4 E rajinī; 5 C mallīkā [emended to *mallikā, sec.m.*]; E malikā; 6 F trabidha; 7 AFM saṣī; 8 M kela; 9 A brithā; EG brathā; 10 ABDHJ gaharu; G gahana; 11 E [omitted, added *sec.m.*]; 12 ABDFH karati; L [emended to *karati*]; 13 AL kriśodari; BM kraśodara; C kṛśodarī; GH kṛśodari; J [emended to *kṛśodari, sec.m.*]; 14 G kāraṇa; 15 B sudhe; F sudha; 16 E [-*na*- omitted, added *sec.m.*]; 17 GL śravaṇa; 18 all MSS jai śrī hita; 19 EM haribaṃsa; 20 ACDEFGHIJKLM rādhikā; B rākā [emended to *rādhikā, sec.m.*].

Metre: 16+6/7 *mātrās.*

CP 41.

१ प्रीति[1] की रीति[2] रँगीलौई[3] जानै[4] ।
२ जद्यपि[5] सकल लोक चूडामणि[6] दीन अपनपौ[7] मानै[8] ॥
३ जमुना[9] पुलिन[10] निकुंज भवन मैं[11] मान[12] मानिनी[13] ठानै[14] ।
४ निकट[15] नवीन कोटि कामिनि[16] कुल धीरज मनहि[17] न[18] आनै[19] ॥
५ नस्वर[20] नेह[21] चपल मधुकर ज्यौं[22] आन आन सौं[23] बानै[24] ।
६ हित[25] हरिबंश[26] चतुर सोइ[27] लालहि[28] छाडि मेड[29] पहिचानै[30] ॥

1 BCFIM prīta [C emended to *prīti, sec.m.*]; E prītī; 2 BFI rīta; 3 BK rãgīlau; E rãgīloi na; FGIM rãgīloī; 4 ACFJK jānẽ; DL jānaī; E jāni [emended to *jānẽ*]; G jāne; 5 BE jadapi; CH yadyapi [C emended to *jadyapi, sec.m.*]; DJ jaddapi; FIM jaddipa; K jadipa; L jadyapa; 6 ABEFI cūḍāmani; C cūḍāmanī; M cūḍāmana; 7 AB apunapau; IM apanapo; 8 ACE mānẽ; DJL mānai; G māne; 9 H yamunā; 10 A [-*na* omitted]; G kuṃja; 11 AFGHJKM mẽ; BE mai; 12 A mānu; 13 E māninī; FIM mānanī; 14 AEF ṭhānẽ; B ṭhānau; CGJK ṭhāne [J emended to *ṭhānaī, sec.m.*]; DL ṭhānaī; 15 I nipaṭa [emended to *nikaṭa, sec.m.*]; M nikaṭi; 16 C kāminī [emended to *kāmini, sec.m.*]; FIM *kāmina*; 17 A manahū; C manahī; 18 E [followed by *diya,* crossed out: cf. 42.4 *mana diye*]; 19 ACEFJ ānẽ [J emended to *ānaī*]; DL ānaī; G āne; 20 CFGM naśvara; 21 A nehu; 22 A jyõ; BCK jyau; I jyo; 23 A

so; BEJK sau; GM sõ; 24 ACEGJ bāne; [J emended to *bānaĩ sec.m.*]; DFL bāne; 25 all MSS jai śrī hita; 26 ABEM haribaṃsa; I [*-baṃśa* omitted; *-baṃsa* added *sec.m.*]; 27 ABCDFGHIJKLM soī; 28 B [*-hi* omitted]; E lālahe [emended to *lālahi, sec.m.*]; 29 B maiḍa; K meḍi; DHJL maiḍa; 30 ACFJ pahicānẽ; DIKL pahicānaī; E pahicānõ; G pahicāne; M pahacānai.

Metre: 16+12 *mātrās*.

CP 42.

१ प्रीति[1] न काहू[2] की कानि[3] बिचारैं[4] ।
२ मारग अपमारग बिथकित मन को[5] अनुसरत[6] निवारैं[7] ॥
३ ज्यौं[8] सलिता[9] सावन[10] जल उमगत[11] सनमुष[12] सिंधु[13] सिधारैं[14] ।
४ ज्यौं[15] नादहि[16] मन दियैं[17] कुरंगनि[18] प्रगट पारधी मारैं[19] ॥
५ हित[20] हरिबंश[21] हिलग[22] सारँग ज्यौं[23] सलभ[24] सरीरहि[25] जारैं[26] ।
६ नाइक[27] निपुन[28] नवल मोहन बिनु[29] कौन[30] अपनपौ[31] हारैं[32] ॥

1 F prīta; 2 BDEK kāhu; 3 EFJ kāna [J emended to *kāni*]; 4 AGM bicāre; 5 DK kau; 6 A anasarata; I anusarati; L anusarita; 7 AG nivāre; M nivārẽ; 8 AI jyõ; BDK jyau; 9 CFGHL saritā; M saratā; 10 G sāgara; H śrāvaṇa; 11 BCDGJ umagati; EFL umagita; 12 IKL sanmuṣa; 13 AM siṃdha; 14 AG sidhāre; B sīdhārai; I sudhārai; M sidhārẽ; 15 AI jyõ; BK jyau; 16 C nādahī [emended to *nādahi, sec.m.*]; 17 A dīye; B diai; CEF diyẽ; DHIL diyaī; G die; K dīyaī; M diye; 18 F kuraṃgana; L kuraṃgini; 19 A māre; E marai; M mārẽ; 20 all MSS jai śrī hita; 21 AEM haribaṃsa; 22 A hilagi; 23 A kī; BCEK jyau; H jyõ; 24 F śala [*-bha* omitted]; G śalabha; 25 C śarīrahī; GHL śarīrahi; J sarīraha; 26 G jāre; M jārẽ; 27 BDHIJ nāyaka; 28 BM nipuni; 29 A jyo; 30 EFGM bina; 30 ACFI kona; 31 ABFJ apunapau; I apunipau; M apanapo; 32 G hāre; M hārẽ.

Metre: 16+12 *mātrās*.

CP 43.

१ अति[1] नागरि[2] बृषभान[3]-किशोरी[4] ।
२ सुनि[5] दूतिका[6] चपल मृगनैंनी[7]
आकरषत[8] चितवनि[9] चित[10] गोरी ॥
३ श्रीफल[11] उरज कँचन सी देही
कटि केहरि[12] गुन[13] सिंधु[14] झकोरी ।
४ बेनी[15] भुजँग[16] चंद[17] सत[18] बदनी
कदलि[19] जंघ जलचर गति चोरी ॥

५ सुनि[20] हरिबंश[21] आजु[22] रजनीमुष[23]
बन मिलाइ[24] मेरी निजु[25] जोरी ।
६ जद्यपि[26] मान समेत[27] भामिनी[28]
सुनि कत[29] रहत[30] भली जिय भोरी ॥

1 F [emended to *ati hī, sec.m.*]; 2 BI nāgara; 3 BEFG braṣabhāna-; H bṛṣabhānu-; 4 E kisorī; 5 J suna; 6 DE dutikā; 7 A mraganenī; EFIJ °nenī; 8 ACEI ākaraṣati [E emended to *ākaraṣata, sec.m.*]; FHKLM ākarṣata; G ākarṣati; 9 GHM citavata; DIJ citavana [J emended to *citavata, sec.m.*]; 10 C citta; 11 B śrīkala; 12 M kehara; 13 GHJM guṇa; L rasa; 14 A siṃdha; 15 ABDFL bainī; GHM beṇī; 16 A bhuvāga; 17 DHJ caṃdra; 18 CGM śata; 19 CFGHIM kadalī [I followed by *ṣaṃbha,* crossed out: cf. 29.14 *kadali ṣaṃbha*]; 20 M suna; 21 ABEM haribaṃsa; 22 BHIJLM āja; 23 B [*-ja-* omitted]; 24 A milāī; HI milāya 25 DEGHM nija; 26 A jaddipi; BDJ jaddapi; H yadyapi; F jadipa; IKM jaddipa; L jadyapa; 27 A samaiti; 28 D [*bhāminī* emended to *bhāmini, sec.m.*]; M bhāmanī; 29 E kāta [emended to *kata*]; I kati; 30 ADIL rahati; B rahasi; E rahita.

Metre: 16+16 *mātrās*.

CP 44.

१ चलि[1] सुंदरि[2] बोली[3] बृन्दाबन[4] ।
२ कामिनि[5] कंठ[6] लागि[7] किनि[8] राजहि[9]
तू[10] दामिनि[11] मोहन[12] नौतन[13] घन ॥
३ कँचुकी[14] सुरँग बिबिधि[15] रँग सारी
नष जुग[16] ऊन[17] बने[18] तेरे तन ।
४ ये[19] सब उचित नवल मोहन कौं[20]
श्रीफल[21] कुच जोवन[22] आगम धन ॥
५ अतिसै[23] प्रीति[24] हुती अंतरगति[25]
हित[26] हरिबंश[27] चली मुकलित[28] मन
६ निबड[29] निकुंज[30] मिले[31] रससागर
जीते सत[32] रतिराज सुरत रन[33] ॥

1 LM cala [L emended to *cali*]; 2 BFIJM suṃdara [J emended to *suṃdari, sec.m.*]; C suṃdarī; 3 E ṣoli; 4 E braṃdābana; 5 C kāminī; IM kāmina; 6 B kaṃṭhi; 7 B laggi; K lāgī; 8 EFGILM kina; C kīna [emended to *kīni, sec.m.*]; 9 C rājahī; FGM rājai; 10 A ta; 11 C dāminī; FLM dāmina; 12 I mauhana; 13 A nūtana; I nautama; 14 A kācuki; D kucakī; 15 B [*bi-* omitted]; GH bibidha; 16 H yuga; 17 E una; 18 ACE banẽ; B banai; D banaī; J bana; 19 AC e; 20 ACFKM kō; BJ kau; G ko; 21 B śrīkala; I [followed by *juga,* crossed out]; 22 A [follows

next]; H yobana; 23 FLM atisaya; GH atiśaya; 24 FM prīta; 25 F aṃtaragata; 26 all MSS jai śrī hita; 27 ABEM haribaṃsa; 28 K mukalīta; 29 BFGHJLM nibiḍa; 30 M nakuṃja [emended to *nikuṃja, sec.m.*]; 31 E milẽ; 32 GHM śata; 33 G raṇa.

Metre: 16+16 *mātrās*.

CP 45.

१ आवति[1] श्री बृषभान[2]- दुलारी[3] ।
२ रूप रासि[4] अति चतुर सिरोमनि[5] अंग अंग सुकुवारी[6] ॥
३ प्रथम उबटि[7] मज्जन[8] करि[9] सज्जित[10] नील बरन[11] तन सारी ।
४ गूंथित[12] अलक तिलक कृत[13] सुंदर[14] सेंदुर[15] माँग[16] सँवारी[17] ॥
५ मृगज[18] समान[19] नैन[20] अंजनजुत[21] रुचिर रेष अनुसारी ।
६ जटित[22] लवंग ललित नासा[23] पर[24] दसनावलि[25] कृत[26] कारी[27] ॥
७ श्रीफल उरज[28] कसुँभि[29] कँचुकी[30] कसि उपर[31] हार छबि न्यारी ।
८ कृश[32] कटि[33] उदर गँभीर नाभिपुट[34] जघन[35] नितंबिनि[36] भारी ॥
९ मनौं[37] मृनाल[38] भूषन[39] भूषित[40] भुज[41] स्याम[42] अंस[43] पर डारी ।
१० हित[44] हरिबंश[45] जुगल[46] करनी[47] गज बिहरत बन[48] पिय[49] प्यारी ॥

1 BFGIKM āvata; E avati [emended to *āvati, sec.m.*]; 2 E braṣabhāna-; H bṛṣabhānu-; 3 C dūlārī; 4 B rāsa; G rāśi; 5 BF siromana; EL śiromani; GH śiromaṇi; M siromaṇi; 6 AHL sukumārī; B sukārā; D [-*rī* omitted]; JKM sukũvārī; 7 B upaṭi; I ju ubaṭi; 8 A maṃjjana; BDIJM maṃjana; 9 B kara; 10 E sajjata [emended to *sajjita, sec.m.*]; F sajita; 11 G baraṇa; 12 AD gũthita; FHM guṃthita; 13 AB krata; D kṛtata [-*ta* at beginning of new folio]; K kṛti; 14 CE suṃdari; 15 BDKL saĩdura; C sīdura [emended to *sẽdura, sec.m.*]; 16 AI māga; 17 ADEFI savārī; B sajavārī; C [*sã-* omitted, added *sec.m.*]; 18 A mrigaja; 19 D sāmāna [emended to *samāna*]; 20 AEIJ nena; C nayana; 21 H °yuta; 22 C jaṭīta; 23 HL nāśā; 24 M pari; 25 H daśanāvali; L [-*sa-* omitted]; M darasanāvali; 26 AB krata; 27 I bhārī [emended to *kārī*]; 28 B [-*ja* omitted]; 29 B kasakāsubhī; CDEFIJKLM kasũbhī; G kāsubhī; H kasũbhī; 30 AJKL kācuki; BM kũcakī; 31 A [-*pa-* omitted]; BDGIJKL ūpara [I followed by 5 *akṣaras,* heavily crossed out]; HM ūpari; 32 A kasi; B krasa; FILM kṛsa; 33 C kaṭī; 34 M nābha°; 35 D jaghani; 36 ABCDFGHKL nitaṃbani; E nitaṃbhani; IJM nitaṃbana; 37 A māne; BJ manau [J emended to *mānau, sec.m.*]; CE manõ; D mānau; G māno; IM mano; 38 A mrināla; GHL mṛṇāla; 39 E bhuṣana; GH bhūṣaṇa; 40 A [follows next]; 41 I [followed by *chabi,* crossed out]; 42 GHILM śyāma; 43 L aṃśa; 44 all MSS jai śrī hita; 45 EM haribaṃsa; 46 H yugala; 47 A karani; B karinī; GH karaṇī; I [followed by *basa,* crossed out]; 48 M [omitted, added *sec.m.*]; 49 F pīya.

Metre: 16+12 *mātrās*.

CP 46.

१ बिपिन[1] घन कुंज रतिकेलि[2] भुज मेलि रुचि
स्याम[3] स्यामा[4] मिले सरद[5] की जामिनी[6] ।
२ हृदै[7] अति फूल[8] समतूल पिय नागरी[9]
करनि[10] कर[11] मत्त मनौ[12] बिबिधि[13] गुन[14] रामिनी[15] ॥
३ सरस गति हास परिहास[16] आवेस[17] बस[18]
दलित[19] दल[20] मदन बल कोक रस[21] कामिनी[22] ।
४ हित[23] हरिबंश[24] सुनि[25] लाल लावनि[26] भिदे[27]
प्रीय[28] अति सूर[29] सुष सुरत[30] संग्रामिनी[31] ॥

1 AE bipini; BFM bipana; 2 M °kela; 3 CGH śyāma; 4 GHL śyāmā; 5 GHM śarada; 6 H yāminī; M jāmanī; 7 A hridai; HKL hṛdaya; 8 E phula; 9 A nāgari; 10 A karini; G karaṇī; J [emended to *karini, sec.m.*]; M karanī; 11 AGIM kari; 12 A mana; B manai; CFJ manõ; DHL manaũ; EGIM mano; 13 G bibidha; 14 GH guṇa; 15 G rāgiṇī; I rāsinī [emended to *rāminī, sec.m.*]; M rāmanī; 16 FM parahāsa; 17 A āvaisa; CGHLM āveśa; 18 B [*-sa* omitted]; C baśa; 19 GM dalata; 20 D [*-la* replaces original reading, *sec.m.*]; 21 A basa; E rasi; 22 E kāmili [emended to *kāmilī, sec.m.*]; LM kāmanī [L emended to *kāminī*]; 23 ABCDEFHIJKLM jai śrī hita; G [omitted; *jai śrī* prefixed to *haribaṃśa*]; 24 AEM haribaṃa; 25 A prabhu; M suna; 26 B vanya [*la-* omitted]; CH lāvaṇya; DIJK lāvanya; M lāvana; 27 F bidhe; GM bhidhe; 28 BCDEFGHIJKLM priyā; 29 H śūra; 30 E [*-ta* omitted, added *sec.m.*]; I surati; 31 FM saṃgrāmanī.

Metre 4x / ⏔ ⏑ ⏔, ⏔ ⏑ ⏔ /.

CP 47.

१ बन की लीला लालहि[1] भावै ।
२ पत्र प्रसून[2] बीच[3] प्रतिबिंबहि[4] नष[5] सिष[6] प्रिया[7] जनावै ॥
३ सकुचि[8] न[9] सकत प्रगट परिरंभन[10] अलि लंपट दुरि[11] धावै ।
४ संभ्रम[12] देत कुलकि[13] कल[14] कामिनि[15] रति रन[16] कलह मचावै ॥
५ उलटी[17] सबै[18] समझि[19] नैननि[20] मैं[21] अंजन रेष बनावै[22] ।
६ हित[23] हरिबंश[24] प्रीति[25] रीति[26] बस[27] सजनी[28] स्याम[29] कहावै ॥

1 C lālahī; K sālahi; 2 E prasuna; 3 M bīci; 4 C pratibiṃbahī; 5 K [*-ṣa* omitted, added *sec.m.*]; 6 H śiṣa; K siṣi; 7 I priyahi; 8 B sukuci; C sakūci; FHJ sakuca; 9 I [omitted, added *sec.m.*]; 10 A pariraṃbhita; L pariraṃbhaṇa; 11 B dura; 12 B saṃbhṛma; D [*-ma* omitted, added *sec.m.*]; J saṃbhrata; 13 B phulaka; DIJ kulaka; M kulika; 14 FI kali; 15 C kāminī; M kāmina; 16 BGHJLM raṇa; 17 C ulaṭi; 18 M [follows

next; order emended to *sabai samajhi, sec.m.*]; 19 CD samujhi; FI samujha; J samajha [emended to *samujha, sec.m.*]; 20 AGI nenani; E nena [*-ni* omitted]; 21 ADFGHKM mẽ; BEJ mai; 22 E banīvai [emended to *banāvai, sec.m.*]; 23 all MSS jai śrī hita; 24 AEM hari-baṃsa; 25 A [follows next]; 26 F rīta; 27 C baśa; M basi; 28 E sajana [emended to *sajanī, sec.m.*]; 29 GH śyāma.

Metre: 16+12 *mātrās*.

CP 48.

१ बनी बृषभान[1]– नंदिनी[2] आजु[3] ।
२ भूषन[4] बसन बिबिधि[5] पहिरे[6] तन पिय मोहन हित साजु[7] ॥
३ हाव भाव लावन्य[8] भृकुटि[9] लट हरत[10] जुवति[11] जन पाजु[12] ।
४ ताल भेद अवघर[13] सुर[14] सूचत[15] नूपुर[16] किंकिनि[17] बाजु[18] ॥
५ नव निकुंज अभिराम स्याम[19] सँग[20] नीकौ[21] बन्यौ[22] समाजु[23] ।
६ हित[24] हरिबंश[25] बिलास रास[26] जुत[27] जोरी अबिचल[28] राजु[29] ॥

1 B braṣabhāna-; E braṣabhānu-; H bṛṣabhānu-; I śrī bṛṣabhāna-; 2 IM naṃdanī; 3 H āja; 4 EGH bhūṣaṇa; 5 GT bibidha; 6 ACEFGIJ pahirẽ; BK pahirai; DHL pahiraī; M parẽ [*-ha-* added *sec.m.*]; 7 AHKM sāja [M emended to *sāju, sec.m.*]; 8 CEGH lāvaṇya; 9 AEM bhrakuṭi; CFI bhṛkuṭī; G bhrukuṭi; 10 ACED harati; B harita; J hariti [emended to *harati*]; 11 CH yuvati; 12 AHKM pāja [M emended to *pāju, sec.m.*]; 13 ABDJ aughara [D emended to *avaghara, sec.m.*]; I oghara; 14 GH svara; M [omitted, added *sec.m.*]; 15 C sūcati; E sucata; IL sūcita; 16 M nūpara; 17 BEI kiṃkinī; CGHL kiṃkini; FM kiṃkanī; 18 AHKM bāja [M emended to *bāju, sec.m.*]; 19 GH śyāma; 20 A saga; G sãgi; 21 DGIM nīko; 22 A banyõ; CGM banyo; I banyo hai; FL banyaũ; 23 AHILM samāja [M emended to *samāju, sec.m.*]; 24 all MSS jai śrī hita; 25 AEM haribaṃsa; 26 DL rāsa rasa [D emended to *rāsa* by crossing out of *-sa ra-*]; 27 E rata [*ju-* added *sec.m.*, but *ra-* not cancelled]; 28 M abacala; 29 AHM rāja [M emended to *rāju, sec.m.*].

Metre: 16+11 *mātrās*.

CP 49.

१ देषि[1] सषी[2] राधा पिय[3] केलि[4] ।
२ ये[5] दोउ[6] षोरि[7] षरिक[8] गिरि[9] गहबर[10]
बिहरत कुँवर[11] कंठ[12] भुज मेलि ॥
३ ये[13] दोउ[14] नवल[15] किशोर[16] रूप निधि
बिटप[17] तमाल[18] कनक मनों[19] बेलि ।

४ अधर अदन चुंबन परिरंभन[20]
तन पुलकित आनँद[21] रस झेलि ॥
५ पट बंधन कँचुकी[22] कुच परसत[23]
कोप[24] कपट निरषत[25] कर[26] पेलि[27] ।
६ हित[28] हरिबंश[29] लाल रस लंपट
धाइ[30] धरत उर बीच[31] सकेलि ॥

1 C deṣa; 2 A sī; 3 F pīya; 4 M kela; 5 A e; 6 CDFGHIJKLM doū; 7 GM ṣora; 8 B [*ṣari-* omitted]; C ṣirika; FGM ṣaraka; H ṣiraka; 9 IM gira; 10 L gahbara; 11 ADIJ kuvara; C kũvari; H kumari; 12 E [followed by *ja*]; 13 A e; 14 CDFGHIJKLM doū; 15 F [*-va-* omitted, added *sec.m.*]; 16 A kisora; 17 L biṭapi; 18 D timāla; 19 A mānau; BGM māno; CEI mano; D mānaũ; HJ manaũ; L manu; 20 GL pariraṃbhaṇa; 21 A ānaṃda; B anaṃda; 22 AD kaṃcuki; E kuṃcuki; 23 I parasati; 24 C koka; 25 AI niraṣati; 26 I paga; 27 M pela; 28 all MSS jai śrī hita; 29 ABE haribaṃsa; 30 A dhāī; HM dhāya; 31 M bīci.

Metre: 16+15 *mātrās*.

CP 50.

१ नवल[1] नागरि[2] नवल नागर[3] किशोर[4] मिलि[5]
कुंज कोमल[6] कमल दलनि[7] सज्जा[8] रची ।
२ गौर स्यामल[9] अंग रुचिर तापर[10] मिले
सरस[11] मनि[12] नील मनो[13] मृदुल[14] कंचन[15] षची ॥
३ सुरत[16] नीबी निबँध हेत पिय[17] मानिनी[18]
प्रिया[19] की भुजनि[20] मैं[21] कलह मोहन[22] मची[23] ।
४ सुभग[24] श्रीफल उरज पानि[25] परसत रोष
हुंकार[26]गर्व दृग[27] भंग भामिनी[28] लची[29] ॥
५ कोक कोटिक रभस[30] रहसि हरिबंश[31] हित[32]
बिबिधि[33] कल माधुरी किमपि नाहिन[34] बची[35] ।
६ प्रणय[36]-मय[37] रसिक ललितादि[38] लोचन चषक
पिवत[39] मकरंद[40] सुष रासि[41] अंतर सची[42] ॥

1 K [preceded by *navala nāgarī*, incompletely erased]; 2 BCEIK nāgarī; 3 A nāgari [emended to *nāgara*]; G nagara; 4 AB kisora; 5 BE mila; C milī; 6 M komila; 7 G [*-la-* omitted]; IM dalana; 8 AF sijyā; BIJM sejyā; H śayyā; DL sajyā; 9 BI sā̃vala; CGHJ śyāmala; 10 M tāpari; 11 G sarala; 12 ACGHLM maṇi; J [*ma*[?]*au,* with second consonant unclear, emended to *maṇi, sec.m.*]; 13 A mānõ; B manau; CFH manõ; JKL manaũ; M māno; 14 A mridula; 15 E [preceded by *kaṃ* (at end of folio)]; 16 AM surati; 17 AFM priya; BDGI priyā; 18 FIM mānanī;

19 A prīyā; BJ piyā [J emended to *priyā, sec.m.*]; F pīyā; 20 B bhujana; E bhujanani; M bhugana [emended to *bhujani, sec.m.*]; 12 ACFGHJKM mẽ; BD mai; 22 I mauhana; K [one *akṣara* erased between *mo-* and *-hana*]; 23 K [omitted, added *sec.m.*]; 24 M śubhaga; 25 BDIJM pāna; [J emended to *pāni, sec.m.*]; H pāṇi; 26 CI hūṃkāra; 27 A driga; B daga; EKM draga; 28 FG bhāminī; M bhāmina; 29 BI calī; 30 AH rabhasi; 31 AEM haribaṃsa; H śrī haribaṃśa; 32 B hati; 33 G bibidha; 34 C nāhīna; 35 K bīcī [emended to *bacī*]; 36 A pranai-; 37 A mai; C mẽ; 38 I [*-ta-* omitted, added *sec.m.*]; M lalitādika [*-ka* incompletely erased]; 39 EFGIKLM pīvata; 40 B [*-ṃda*, and *su-* from next, omitted]; 41 BF rāsa; M rāśi; 42 L śacī.

Metre: 4x / ⏕ ⏑ ⏕, ⏕ ⏑ ⏕ /

CP 51.

१ दान[1] दै[2] री नवल किषोरी[3] ।
२ मागत[4] लाल[5] लाडिलौ[6] नागर[7]
प्रकट[8] भई बिन दिन[9] की चोरी ॥
३ नव नारंग[10] कनक हीरावलि
बिद्रुम[11] सरस जलज[12] मनि[13] गोरी ।
४ पूरित[14] रस पीयूष[15] जुगल[16] घट
कमल कदलि[17] षंजन[18] की जोरी ॥
५ तो[19] पै[20] सकल[21] सौंज[22] दामन[23] की
कत सतरात[24] कुटिल दृग[25] भोरी ।
६ नूपुर[26] रव[27] किंकिनी[28] पिसुन[29] घर[30]
हित[31] हरिबंश[32] कहत[33] नहि[34] थोरी ॥

1 BCDJ dānu; 2 C daī; 3 A kīśorī; B kisorī; 4 BDFHLM mãgata; 5 B lāli; E lālu; 6 CDI lāḍilo; M lāḍalo; 7 A nāgari; 8 M praghaṭa; 9 E bina; 10 AG nāriga; B nāragi; CDEIJM nāriṃga; 11 B biṃduma; C bĩdrūma [emended to *bĩdrūma, sec.m.*]; 12 I sajala; 13 C manī; GHLM maṇi; I mati; 14 E purita; M pūrata; 15 AI piyūṣa; EF pīyuṣa; M payūṣa [emended to *piyūṣa, sec.m.*]; 16 H yugala; 17 CM kadalī; 18 M [*ṣaṃ-* replaces original]; 19 CM tau; 20 AE pẽ; CG paī; 21 C [follows next]; 22 AEM sõja; 23 ABCDEGHI dāmini; FL dāmani; J [emended to *dāmani*]; K dāminī; M dāmina; 24 ADHIJL satarāti; 25 A driga; BF daga; DEKM draga; 26 M nūpara; 27 B [omitted]; 28 A kiṃkini; C kiṃkiṇi; GHL kiṃkiṇī; M kiṃkanī; 29 C piśuna; I pisūna; 30 B [*-ra* omitted]; 31 ABCDEFHIJKLM jai śrī hita; G jai hita; 32 EM haribaṃsa; 33 ADI kahati; 34 DEF nahī; HLM nahī.

Metre: 16+16 *mātrās*.

CP 52.

देषौ[1] माई[2] सुन्दरता की सीवाँ[3] ।
ब्रज[4] नवतरुनि[5] कदंब नागरी निरषि करत[6] अध[7]- ग्रीवाँ[8] ॥
जो[9] कोउ[10] कोटि कलप[11] लगि जीवै[12] रसना[13] कोटिक[14] पावै[15] ।
तऊ[16] रुचिर बदनारबिंद[17] की सोभा[18] कहत[19] न आवै[20] ॥
देवलोक भूलोक[21] रसातल[22] सुनि[23] कवि कुल मति डरियै[24] ।
सहज माधुरी अंग अंग की कहि कासों[25] पटतरियै[26] ॥
हित[27] हरिबंश[28] प्रताप रूप गुन[29] बय[30] बल स्याम[31] उजागर[32] ।
जाकी भ्रू[33] बिलास बस पशुरिव[34] दिन[35] बिथकित[36] रस[37]- सागर ॥

1 BCIM deṣo; 2 B [*mā-* omitted, added *sec.m.*]; E māi; 3 BEFK sīvā; CI sīvā; LM sīva; 4 ADM bṛja; 5 B taruna; CG taruṇi; 6 BDJL karati; 7 B ati-; DJKL adhi-; 8 B grāvā; CJK grīvā; FI grīvā; L grīvā̃; 9 ADL jau; 10 A koī; BCDFGHIJKL koū; 11 A kalapi; H kalpa; 12 C jīvaī; G jīve; 13 L rasmā; 14 F koṭaka; 15 G pāve; 16 AE taü; DJ toū [J emended to *taū, sec.m.*]; K taba; 17 M badanārubṛṃda; 18 H śobhā; 19 DIJL kahati [J emended to *kahata, sec.m.*]; 20 G āve; 21 AEIK bhuva°; [*-valoka* and foll. *ras* are written *sec.m.* over folio repair in E]; C bhūva°; 22 L raśātala; 23 M śuni; 24 C ḍariyaī; HJM ḍariye; 25 BE °sau; CDHIJL °saũ; 26 B [*-ta-* omitted, added *sec.m.*]; JM paṭatariye; L [followed by repeat of whole line, crossed out]; 27 all MSS jai śrī hita; 28 AEM haribaṃsa; 29 EGHJ guṇa; 30 A be; E bai; 31 GHK śyāma; 32 B ūjāgara; 33 B bhū; E bhu; M bhru; 34 D pasuri [*-va* added *sec.m.*]; EFL pasuriva; 35 E dena [emended to *dina, sec.m.*]; 36 A biśrakita; D bithakithata [second *-tha-* crossed out]; 37 A suṣa-.

Metre: 16+12 *mātrās*.

CP 53.

देषौ[1] माई[2] अबला कै[3] बल[4] रासि[5] ।
अति गजमत्त[6] निरंकुस[7] मोहन निरषि[8] बँधे[9] लट पासि[10] ॥
अब ही[11] पंगु[12] भई[13] मन की गति बिनु[14] उद्यम[15] अनयास[16] ।
तब की कहा[17] कहौं[18] जब पिय[19] प्रति[20] चाहत[21] भृकुटि[22] बिलास[23] ॥
कच संजमन[24] ब्याज भुज[25] दरसत[26] मुसकनि[27] बदन बिकास[28] ।
हा हरिबंश[29] अनीति[30] रीति[31] हित[32] कत[33] डारत[34] तन[35] त्रास[36] ॥

1 CGHIM deṣo; 2 E māi; 3 BCEFGHI ke; 4 BIM bali; 5 BFH rāsa; GM rāśi; 6 E °mata; 7 A niruṃkusa; CGHM niraṃkuśa; L naraṃkuśa [emended to *niraṃkuśa*]; 8 B niraṣa; 9 AI badhe; B badha; E bāvi [emended to *bādha, sec.m.*]; 10 FH pāsa; G pāśa; 11 FGHLM hī̃; 12 BDFI paṃga; 13 E bhaï; 14 BEFGIM bina; 15 AE udima; BG

uddhima; CDFIJ uddima; 16 AC anayāsi; FGHK aniyāsa; L aniyāse [emended to *aniyāsi*]; 17 L kaha [emended to *kahā* by scribe]; 18 ABEIK kahau; CFGM kahō; 19 AGI priya; 20 G pati; L pata [emended to *prati*]; 21 ABDJ cāhati; 22 A bhrikuṭi; BCEFIK bhṛkuṭī; L bhrakuṭī; M bhrakuṭi; 23 AC bilāsi; L [emended to *bilāsi*]; 24 BCDEJ saṃjamani; H saṃyamana; 25 B bhaja; E bhaji [emended to *bhuji, sec.m.*]; 26 C darasita; E tarasita [emended to *darasita, sec.m.*]; 27 DL musikani; IM musakana; K musikana; 28 A bikasi [emended to *bikāsi, sec.m.*]; CL bikāsi; E bikāśa; 29 ABEM haribaṃsa; 30 BCFHIJKM anīta; 31 ACFHKL rīta; 32 A hiti; 33 M [*-ta* omitted, added *sec.m.*]; 34 ADIJL ḍārati; B ḍarata; C ḍarati [emended to *ḍārati, sec.m.*]; G ḍarāta; 35 A tanu; 36 ACL trāsi.

Metre: 16+11 *mātrās.*

CP 54.

१ नयौ[1] नेह्[2] नव रंग[3] नयौ[4] रस[5]
नवल स्याम[6] बृषभान[7] किशोरी[8] ।
२ नव पीताँबर[9] नवल[10] चूनरी[11] ॥
नइ[12] नइ[13] बू ँदन[14] भीजत[15] गोरी ॥
३ नव[16] बृंदाबन[17] हरित मनोहर
नव चातिक[18] बोलत मोर मोरी ।
४ नव मुरली[19] जु मलार[20] नई[21] गति
श्रवन[22] सुनत[23] आये[24] घन घोरी ॥
५ नव भूषन[25] नव[26] मुकट[27] बिराजत[28]
नई[29] उरप[30] लेत थोरी थोरी ।
६ हित[31] हरिबंश[32] असीस[33] देत मुष[34]
चिर[35] जीवौ[36] भूतल[37] यह[38] जोरी ॥

1 A nao; CDFGIM nayo; 2 A [*-ha* omitted, added *sec.m.*]; 3 A raṃgu; 4 A nao; CFGHIM nayo; 5 A rasu; 6 GH śyāma; 7 BE braṣabhāna; GH bṛṣabhānu; 8 ABE kisorī; 9 AI pītaṃbara; B pītā̃mara; 10 A navalū; 11 E cunarī; 12 all MSS naī; 13 all MSS naī; 14 AD būdani; BC būdana; E bū̃mdanani; GL bū̃dani; 15 ADGHJL bhījati; F [*bhīj-* replaces original reading, *sec.m.*]; 16 E mava [emended to *nava, sec.m.*]; 17 E braṃdābana; 18 B catika; G cātaki; H cātaka; L cātrika; 19 M muralā; 20 A marāla; B mālāra; C mallāra; 21 E maī [emended to *naī, sec.m.*]; 22 GIL śravaṇa; 23 C śunata; 24 AJ āe; 25 GHL bhūṣaṇa; 26 E [*-va* omitted, added *sec.m.*]; 27 E mukuṭa; 28 F [*birājata* replaces original (beginning *ca-*), *sec.m.*]; 29 A [omitted]; 30 B urpa; 31 all MSS jai śrī hita; 32 AEM haribaṃsa; 33 G usīsa; H aśīṣa; 34 D [*-ṣa* omitted, added by scribe]; 35 B ciru; C ciraṃ; 36 A jīyō; BDFGL jīyau; CI

jīvo; 37 A [follows next]; B [-*la* omitted]; E bhutala; M avatala [emended to *bhūtala, sec.m.*]; 38 A ihu.

Metre: 16+16 *mātrās*.

CP 55.

१ आजु[1] दोउ[2] दामिनि[3] मिलि[4] बिहसी[5] ।
२ बिच[6] लै[7] स्याम[8] घटा अति नौतन[9] ताके[10] रंग रसी[11] ॥
३ एक चमकि[12] चहु[13] ओर[14] सषी री अपने[15] सुभाइ[16] लसी ।
४ आई एक[17] सरस गहनी मैं[18] दुहुँ[19] भुज बीच[20] बसी ॥
५ अंबुज नील उभै[21] बिधु[22] राजत[23] तिन[24] की चलन[25] षसी[26] ।
६ हित[27] हरिबंश[28] लोभ भेटन[29] मन पूरन[30] सरद[31] ससी[32] ॥

1 HM āja; 2 BDEFGHIJKLM doū; 3 C dāminī; BFM dāmina; 4 FL mila [L emended to *mili*]; 5 AG bahasī̃; CEFJKM bahasī; H bihãsī; 6 C bīca; 7 A laya; C laye; 8 GHL śyāma; 9 AC nūtana; [C: folio bearing text from *-tana* to 57.14 (*kā-*)*minī* is a replacement, *sec.m.*, of lost folio]; B nautane; E nutana; F naütana; 10 D °kaī; 11 B [*ra-* omitted]; I [omitted, added *sec.m.*]; 12 ABCEFGM camaka; 13 A [with foll.] cahuvora; BHJL cahũ; CFG cahū; D cauhu; 14 M aura; 15 DL apanai; 16 A subhāī; BDHIM subhāva; FJ subhāya; 17 B aika; 18 ACFGHJKM mẽ; BE mai; 19 BIF duhu; E [*du-* omitted; *do* added *sec.m.*]; GM dou; K doū; L duhũ; 20 M bīci; 21 B umai; H ubhaya; 22 B bibidhū; CM bidhi; J bidha; 23 A rājati; 24 C tila; G tini; 25 ABJL calani; 26 C basī; E ṣusī; 27 all MSS jai śrī hita; 28 AEM haribaṃsa; 29 A bhaiṭana; B bhaṭena; JK bhẽṭana; L bheṭani; 30 DGH pūraṇa; E purana; 31 B [*-ra-* omitted]; GH śarada; M sadara [emended to *sarada, sec.m.*]; 32 D [*-sī* omitted, added *sec.m.*]; G śaśi; HM śaśī; I śasī.

Metre: 16+10 *mātrās*.

CP 56.

१ हौं[1] बलि जाऊँ[2] नागरी स्याम[3] ।
२ ऐसै[4] ही[5] रँग करौ[6] निसि[7] बासर
बृंदाबिपिन[8] कुटी अभिराम[9] ॥
३ हास बिलास सुरत[10] रस सींचन[11]
पशुपति[12] दग्ध जिवावत काम ।
४ हित[13] हरिबंश[14] लोल[15] लोचन[16] अलि
करहु[17] न सफल[18] सकल सुष धाम ॥

[Text in C is on replacement folio, *sec.m.*]

1 ACEFGIM hõ; BDK hau; 2 ACEFIJ jāu; HK jāũ; 3 A [followed by approx. 9 *akṣaras,* cancelled by application of paste]; GH śyāma; 4 AI ese; FGJ aise; 5 CFHM hĩ; 6 C karaũ; IM karo; 7 BFM nisa; H niśi; 8 A bṛṃdābipini; E braṃdābipini; FIM bṛṃdābipana; 9 K [*-rāma* omitted, added *sec.m.*]; 10 IM surati; 11 BDFJM sīcana; CEK sīcani; L [emended to *sīcani*]; 12 ABCFJL pasu°; 13 all MSS jai śrī hita; 14 AEM haribaṃsa; B harabaṃsa; 15 A lobha; 16 D [followed by *ma,* incompletely erased]; 17 B karaha; K karahũ; 18 K suphala.

Metre: 16+15 *mātrās.*

CP 57.

१ प्रथम जथामति[1] प्रनऊँ[2] बृंदाबन[3] अति रम्य ।
२ श्री राधिका[4] कृपा[5] बिनु[6] सब के[7] मननि[8] अगम्य ॥
३ बर[9] जमुना[10] जल सींचन[11] दिनही[12] सरद[13] बसंत ।
४ बिबिधि[14] भाँति[15] सुमनस[16] के सौरभ अलि कुल मंत ॥
५ अरुन[17] नूत[18] पल्लव[19] पर कूजत[20] कोकिल[21] कीर ।
६ निर्त्तनि[22] करत सिषी[23] कुल अति आनंद[24] अधीर[25] ॥
७ बहत[26] पवन रुचिदाइक[27] सीतल[28] मंद सुगंध ।
८ अरुन[29] नील सित[30] मुकलित जहँ[31] तहँ[32] पूषन[33]– बंध[34] ॥
९ अति कमनीय[35] बिराजत[36] मंदिर[37] नवल निकुंज ।
१० सेवत सगन[38] प्रीतिजुत[39] दिन मीनध्वज[40] पुंज ॥
११ रसिक[41] रास जहँ[42] षेलत स्यामा[43] स्याम[44] किशोर[45] ।
१२ उभै[46] बाहु परिरंजित[47] उठे उनीदे[48] भोर ॥
१३ कनक[49] कपिस पट[50] सोभित[51] सुभग साँवरे[52] अंग ।
१४ नील बसन कामिनि[53] उर कँचुकि[54] कसूँभी[55] सुरंग ॥
१५ ताल रबाब मुरज डफ बाजत मधुर मृदंग[56] ।
१६ सरस उकति[57] गति[58] सूचत[59] बर[60] बँसुरी[61] मुषचंग[62] ॥
१७ दोउ[63] मिलि[64] चाचरि[65] गावत[66] गौरी[67] राग[68] अलाप[69] ।
१८ मानस[70] मृग[71] बल बेधत[72] भृकुटि[73] धनुष[74] दृग[75] चाप[76] ॥
१९ दोउ[77] करतारिनु[78] पटकत लटकत[79] इत[80] उत जात ।
२० हो हो होरी बोलत[81] अति आनँद कुलकात[82] ॥
२१ रसिक लाल पर[83] मेलत[84] कामिनि[85] बंदन धूरि[86] ।
२२ पिय पिचकारिनु[87] छिरकत[88] तकि तकि[89] कुमकुम[90] पूरि[91] ॥
२३ कबहुँ[92] कबहुँ[93] चंदन तरु निर्मित[94] तरल हिँडोल[95] ।
२४ चढि[96] दोऊ[97] जन[98] झूलत[99] फूलत[100] करत कलोल ॥
२५ बर हिंडोर[101] झकोरनि[102] कामिनि[103] अधिक डराति[104] ।
२६ पुलकि[105] पुलकि बेपथ अँग प्रीतम उर लपटाति[106] ॥
२७ हितचित[107] निजु[108] चेरिनु[109] उर आनँद न[110] समात[111] ।
२८ निरषि[112] निपट नैननि[113] सुष व्रन[114] तोरत[115] बलि जात[116] ॥

२९ अति उदार[117] बिबि[118] सुन्दर सुरत सूर[119] सुकुवार[120] ।
३० हित[121] हरिबंश[122] करौ[123] दिन दोऊ[124] अचल बिहार ॥

[Each couplet is numbered in B. Replacement folio in C ends in line (14).]

1 A brathāmati; F jathāmata; H yathāmati; 2 BDHJ praṇaũ; CFI pranaū; E pranaü; G praṇāũ; M praṇaũ; 3 AE śrī braṃdābana; BCDFGHIJKLM śrī bṛṃdābana; 4 A rādhike; 5 AB krapā; 6 ACFGM bina; 7 E kī; 8 ILM manana; 9 I baru; 10 H yamunā; 11 ABC sīcana; D sīcata; F sī̃cata; K sīcani; L sī̃cani; 12 A hīnahī̃; CDEFLM dinahī̃; 13 GHM śarada; 14 G bibidha; 15 AD bhāti; F bhā̃ta; 16 BDHIJ sumanasi [-*sa*- replaces original in D]; 17 AGHIL aruṇa; 18 E nuta; 19 E palava; 20 B kũjata; CFL kūjita; DH kũjata; E kujita; I [followed by *ali kula kaṃta*, crossed out]; 21 D kokilā; 22 A nirtana; BI nirttana; C narttana; E nirtata; F nṛtani; G nṛtyani; HJ nirtani; K nṛttani; M nṛtyana; 23 C saṣī; HL śiṣī; 24 C anaṃda; 25 C adhāra; 26 A bahatu; B babahata; DG bahati; 27 DFHILM °dāyaka; 28 GHL śitala; K sitala; 29 GHIL aruṇa; 30 LM śita; 31 ABCDEFGHIJKM jahā̃ [followed by one erased *akṣara* in K]; 32 all MSS tahā̃; 33 E puṣana; GH pūṣaṇa; 34 GI baṃdhu; 35 A kavanīya; 36 D [-*ta* omitted]; E birājita; I birājati; 37 M maṃdara; 38 A saghana; GHK sagaṇa; 39 FJM prītajuta; H prītiyuta; 40 AEF mīnadhuja; B mīnadhyaṃja; C minadhuja; 41 C rāsika; 42 ADEGJKL rāsi; C rāja; 43 ABDEFHIKL jahā̃; GM tahā̃; J [(?)*hā̃*: emendment makes first *akṣara* illegible]; 44 GHJL śyāmā; 45 GHJL śyāma; 46 A kisora; E kiśorī; 47 CHM ubhaya; 48 BCK pararaṃjita; M pariraṃbhana [emended to *pariraṃjita, sec.m.*]; 49 E unīdi; 50 C kanika; 51 L paṭu; 52 CGH śobhita; I sobhiyata; 53 A sā̃varai; BIJ sāvare; C sā̃vara; G sā̃vare; 54 C kāminī; FM kāmina; G CE kamini; 55 AE kācuki; 56 AF kasubhi; BE kasubhī; CDEGHIJK kasūbhī; L kasū̃bhī; M kusūbhī; 57 A mridaṃga; 58 E [-*kati* omitted]; K ukata; 59 J [omitted, added *sec.m.*]; 60 AL sūcita; I sūcati; 61 M baru; 62 ABDEFIJK basurī; C bā̃surī; 63 C °cṃada; 64 BCDEFHIJKLM dŏū; 65 F mila; 66 BFM cā̃cara; CGI cācara; J cā̃cari; 67 AI gāvati; 68 gorī; 69 A rāgu; 70 AEIJL alāpi [J emended to *alāpa, sec.m.*]; CD ālāpi; 71 BIJ mānasi; 72 A mriga; 73 I bedhati; 74 A bhrakuṭi; CEFGIK bhṛkuṭī; M bhrakuṭī; 75 A dhanaṣu; M dhanaṣa; 76 A driga; BDM draga; E daga; 77 BCEJL cāpi [J emended to *cāpa, sec.m.*]; F cā̃pa; I cā̃pi; 78 DFGHJKL dŏū; 79 A karatāranī; B karitārinu; CG karatārini; EM karatārani; I karatārina; 80 B laṭakatu; K [omitted, added *sec.m.*]; 18 AM īta; 81 B bolati; 82 B kalakāta; 83 J pari [emended to *para, sec.m.*]; 84 ADJK melati; 85 C kāminī; FM kāmina; 86 E dhuri; G dhūra; 87 A picakāīni; C picakārīni; EGK picakārini; M picakārina; 88 C chīrakata; I chirakati; 89 B takita; K [omitted, added *sec.m.*]; 90 ACEL kuṃkuma; 91 E puri; F pūra; 92 ACDEIJ kabahu; M kabahũ; 93 B kacahu; EIJ kabahu; FM kabahũ; 94 A [-*r*- omitted]; M

niramata; 95 ABDI hiḍola; G hinḍola [sic]; 96 C caḍhī; E caḍi; 97 ABE dou; 98 A mili; 99 E jhulata; J [-*ta* omitted, added *sec.m.*]; 100 BH phulata; 101 ABC hiḍora; FM hiṃḍola; G hiḍola; 102 FM jhakorana [emended to *jhakorani* in M, *sec.m.*]; 103 C kāminī; IM kāmina; 104 FGIKM ḍarāta; 105 L pulaka [emended to *pulaki*]; M pulika; 106 FGHIKM lapaṭāta; 107 L °ciṃtika; 108 A niniju [*ni-* at end of folio]; DGHILM nija; F neju; 109 EK cerini; F ceranu; G corani; I cerunu [emended to *cerinu, sec.m.*]; M cerana; 110 K [omitted, added *sec.m.*]; 111 L samāti; 112 IM niraṣa; 113 ACDEFJ nenani; I nenana; 114 DIJ tṛna; CGHM tṛṇa; 115 HIJL torati; 116 L jāti; 117 C uddāra; 118 IM biba; 119 BE sura; H śūra; 120 BCEFIJ sukumāra; G sukāvāra; KM sukūvāra; 121 ABCDFGHIJKLM jai śrī hita; E śrī hita; 122 AE haribaṃsa; 123 AGM karo; C karaū; IL karahu; 124 AEI dou.

Metre: 12+11 *mātrās*.

CP 58.

१ तेरे[1] हित लेन[2] आई[3] बन तें[4] स्याम[5] पठाई[6]
हरत[7] कामिनि[8] घन[9] कदन काम कौ[10] ।
२ काहे कौं[11] करत[12] बाधा सुनि[13] री चतुर[14] राधा
भेटिकै[15] मेटि[16] री[17] माई प्रगट जगत[18] भौ ॥
३ देषि री रजनी नीकी रचना रुचिर[19] पी[20] की
पुलिन नलिन[21] नभ उदित रोहिनी[22] धौ[23] ।
४ तू[24] तौ[25] ब[26] सषी सयानी[27] तैं[28] मेरी एकौ[29] न मानी
हौं[30] तोसौं[31] कहत[32] हारी जुवति[33] जुगति[34] सौं[35] ॥
५ मोहनलाल[36] छबीली[37] अपने[38] रंग रँगीलौ[39]
मोहत[40] बिहंग[41] पशु[42] मधुर[43] मुरली रौ ।
६ वे[44] तौ[45] ब[46] गनत तन[47] जीवन[48] जोवन[49] तव[50]
हित[51] हरिबंश[52] हरि[53] भजहि[54] भामिनि[55] जौ[56] ॥

1 A [preceded by *māī hau*]; C [preceded by *māī hʊ*]; 2 BDHKL laina; 3 G āi; 4 B tai; DH taī; IL te; 5 GHLM śyāma; 6 E patāī; G pāṭhāī; 7 ABCDEGHILM harati; F harita; J [emended to *harati, sec.m.*]; 8 D kāminī; M kāmina; 9 B dhana; 10 GM ko; 11 FI kō; GM ko; 12 ABCDJ karati; 13 BIM suna; 14 E caturi; 15 A bhaiṭikai; E bheṭekai; GHI bheṭike; 16 A maiṭi; E meṭe; IM meṭa; 17 A rā [emended to *rī, sec.m.*]; 18 G jāgata; L [-*ga-* omitted, added *sec.m.*]; 19 L rucara [emended to *rucira, sec.m.*]; 20 BCDGIJKLM piya; 21 G [omitted]; 22 FIM rohanī; GHL rohiṇī; 23 DHIM dhaū; 24 BE tu; 25 I to; 26 B [omitted]; H 'ba; 27 A syānī; 28 ACDFGIJ tẽ; BE tai; 29 I eko; M yeko; 30 ABDE hau; CFGI hõ; 31 AB tosau; FGIJM tosõ; K tausaū; 32 ACDEJ kahati; 33 AFGI juvatī; E javati; H yuvati; 34 C jugatī;

EF jugata; 35 **ABEHIL** sau; FM sõ; 36 **I** mauhana°; 37 **CDIM** chabīlo; 38 L apanai; 39 A ragīlau; **CDEIM** rāgīlo; 40 E mohita; 41 C bihaga; 42 **ABEFL** pasu; 43 I [omitted]; 44 C vai; 45 DIM to; E gau [emended to *tau, sec.m.*]; 46 H 'ba; 47 E [*ta-* omitted]; FGM [omitted; added *sec.m.* in F]; 48 JL jīvani [J emended to *jīvana, sec.m.*]; 49 H yovana; 50 C dhana; GM tana; 51 all MSS jai śrī hita; 52 AEM haribaṃsa; F [omitted]; 53 A [omitted]; K hiri [emended to *hari*]; 54 F bhajajahi; J bhajaha [emended to *bhajahi, sec.m.*]; G bhaje; M bhajaī; 55 **CGM** bhāminī; FI bhāmina; 56 **I** jyõ.

Metre: 8+8+8+7 *varṇas.*

CP 59.

१ यह जु एक मन बहुत[1] ठौर[2] करि[3] कहि[4] कौने[5] सचु पायौ[6] ।
२ जहँ[7] तहँ[8] बिपति[9] जार जुवती[10] ज्यौं[11] प्रगट[12] पिंगला गायौ[13] ॥
३ द्वै[14] तुरंग पर[15] जोर[16] चढत[17] हठि[18] परत[19] कौन[20] पै[21] धायौ[22] ।
४ कहि[23] धौं[24] कौन[25] अंक पर[26] राषै[27] जो[28] गनिका[29] सुत[30] जायौ[31] ॥
५ हित[32] हरिबंश[33] प्रपंच बंच[34] सब[35] काल[36] ब्याल कौ[37] षायौ[38] ।
६ यह[39] जिय[40] जानि[41] स्याम[42] स्यामा[43] पद कमल सँगी[44] सिर[45] नायौ[46] ॥

1 I bahota; 2 B ṭhauri; EI ṭhora; 3 F kara; 4 **I** kaho; K kahu; 5 BDKLM kaunai; **CGI** kone; E kona; 6 **IM** pāyo; 7 all MSS jahā̃; 8 A tahā; BCDEFGHIJKLM tahā̃; 9 FJK bipata [K emended to *bipati*]; 10 H yuvatī; 11 **AC** jyõ; BEK jyau; D jyo; FIM lõ; GHL laū; 12 BG pragaṭi; 13 **IM** gāyo; 14 B duya; I dve; 15 I pari; K pai; 16 **AC** jabaru; E jaura; F jyaūra; I jori; L joru; 17 **AFL** caḍhatu; 18 **HIM** haṭha; 19 L paratu; 20 **A** kavana; **CF** kona; 21 **ACFGILM** para; 22 **IM** dhāyo; 23 B [lines (4) and (5) are omitted, and added at the foot of the folio apparently in the scribe's own hand but in a different pen]; C kahī; 24 **ABEK** dhau; CFI dhõ; 25 A kaunu; **CFI** kona; 26 E [*-ra* omitted]; I pari; 27 **CM** rāṣe; 28 **AFG** jau; **BCJK** jyau [J unclear; emended to *jo, sec.m.*]; I jyõ; 29 GH gaṇikā; J ginikā [unclear; emended to *ganikā, sec.m.*]; 30 B sutā; 31 **DIM** jāyo; 32 all MSS jai śrī hita; 33 **ABEM** haribaṃsa; 34 B basa; D baca; J baṃci; 35 B [omitted]; 36 B [*-la* omitted]; 37 **CGIM** ko; 38 B dhāyau; **IM** ṣāyo; 39 A yahu; 40 C jīya; 41 C jānī; FH jāna; 42 GHL śyāma; 43 D syāma; GHL śyāmā; 44 B sagī; 45 C siru; H śira; 46 **AI** nāyo.

Metre: 16+12 *mātrās.*

CP 60.

१ कहा कहौं[1] इन[2] नैननि[3] की[4] बात ।
२ ये[5] अलि प्रिया[6] बदन[7] अंबुज रस[8] अटके अनत[9] न जात ॥

३ जब जब रुकत पलक संपुट लट[10] अति आतुर अकुलात ।
४ लंपट लव निमेष[11] अंतर तें[12] अलप कलप सत[13] सात[14] ॥
५ श्रुति[15] पर कंज दृगंजन[16] कुच बिच[17] मृगमद[18] ह्वै न समात ।
६ हित[19] हरिबंश[20] नाभि[21] सर जलचर जाचत[22] साँवल[23] गात ॥

1 ABK kahau; CFGIM kahõ; 2 A īni; G ini; M īna; 3 ACEFK nenani; I nenana; 4 B [omitted]; 5 A e; 6 A priye; 7 B [-*da*- omitted, added *sec.m.*]; 8 B [foll. by *ke*]; 9 L aṃta; 10 E laṭī; G [omitted]; 11 M nameṣa; 12 B tai; DHL taĩ; G te; 13 GLM śata; 14 L śāta; 15 KM śruta; 16 B hagaṃjana; DKLM dragaṃjana; E dṛgeṃjana; 17 G [omitted]; M bīci; 18 A mrigamada; M [-*da* omitted, added *sec.m.*]; 19 all MSS jai śrī hita; 20 BEM haribaṃsa; 21 B naṇi; 22 BF [-*ca*- omitted]; E jocata; H yā̃cata; JK jā̃cata; 23 ABD sāvala; F syā̃mala.

Metre: 16+11 *mātrās*.

CP 61.

१ आजु सषी मन मैं[1] जु बने[2] प्रभु नाचत हैं[3] ब्रज[4]- मंडन[5] ।
२ बैस[6] किशोर[7] जुवति[8] अंसनि[9] पर दिये[10] बिमल भुजदंडन ॥
३ कोमल [11] कुटिल अलक सुठि[12] सोभित[13] अवलंबित जुग[14] गंडन ।
४ मानहु[15] मधुप[16] थकित[17] रस लंपट[18] नील कमल के षंडन ॥
५ हास[19] बिलास हरत सब कौ[20] मन काम समूह बिहंडन ।
६ हित[21] हरिबंश[22] करत अपनौ[23] जस[24] प्रगट अषिल ब्रह्मंडन[25] ॥

1 AB mai; CFGHIJM mẽ; 2 AFG banẽ; BE banai; D banaĩ; 3 AD hẽ; G hai; 4 IM bṛja-; 5 E maṃḍala; 6 CKL baiśa; H bayasa; M baisi; 7 A kisora; 8 A juvatī; H yuvati; 9 DIJM aṃsana; HL aṃśani; 10 ACEIJM diyẽ; BD diyai; G diẽ; HL diyaī; 11 M komila; 12 D suni; 13 C śobhita; 14 EHK yuga; 15 A mānõ; B mānau; D manaũ; HJL mānahũ; I māno; 16 I [omitted]; 17 G [-*ta* omitted]; I bithakita; 18 B [-*ṃpa*- omitted]; 19 E [whole line omitted, added *sec.m.*]; F hāsi; 20 ACFGIM ko; 21 all MSS jai śrī hita; 22 A haribaṃsa; 23 ACFGHIJM apano; 24 AC jasu; H yasa; 25 B bramā̃ũna; FK brahamaṃḍana.

Metre: 16+12 *mātrās*.

CP 62.

१ षेलत रास[1] दुलहिनी[2] दूलहु[3] ।
२ सुनहु[4] न[5] सषी सहित ललितादिक
निरषि निरषि[6] नैननि[7] किन[8] फूलहु[9] ॥
३ अति कल मधुर महा मोहन धुनि[10]
उपजत[11] हंससुता[12] के[13] कूलहु[14] ।

४ थेई थेई[15] बचन मिथुन मुष[16] निसरत[17]
सुनि सुनि देह दसा[18] किन[19] भूलहु[20] ॥
५ मृदु[21] पदन्यास उठत[22] कुमकुम[23] रज
अद्‌भुत[24] बहत[25] समीर दुकूलहु[26] ।
६ कबहुँ[27] स्याम[28] स्यामा[29] दसनाँचल[30]
कच[31] कुच हार छुवत भुजमूलहु[32] ॥
७ अति लावन्य[33] रूप अभिनय[34] गुन[35]
नाहिन कोटि[36] काम समतूलहु[37] ।
८ भृकुटि[38] बिलास हास[39] रस बरषत
हित[40] हरिबंश[41] प्रेम[42] रस[43] झूलहु[44] ॥

1 A rāsu; 2 D [emended to *dulahina*]; FI dulahanī; 3 B dūlahū; EK dulahu; G dūlaha; 4 B sunahū; 5 E [omitted]; 6 B niraṣa; K [omitted, added *sec.m.*]; 7 AEJ nenani; I nenana; 8 BDEF kini; GM kyaũ na; IJ kyõ na [J emended to *kyaũ na, sec.m.*]; 9 B phūlahū; 10 H dhvani; 11 AD upajati; 12 HL haṃśa°; 13 BD kai; 14 B phūlahū; I kūlahū; 15 B [graph similar to Arabic numeral '8' between *the-* and *-ī*; for *avagraha* ?]; 16 B suṣa; 17 E nisurata; L [followed by repeat of *muṣa nisarata*, crossed out]; 18 A disā; CHIL daśā; 19 BDFJK kini; I kyõ na; 20 A bhulavahu [emended to *bhūlahu, sec.m.*]; B bhūlahū; E bhulahu; 21 A mridu; J ṃrda; 22 DJ uṭhati; E uṭati; 23 I kuśamakuma [emended to *kumakuma*]; L kuṃkuma; 24 B adabhuta; 25 B [omitted, added in scribe's own hand]; DIJ bahati; 26 B dukūlahū; C dakūlahu; E dukulahu; 27 A kabaha; B kabahũka; CDEFI kabahu; GM kabahũ; 28 CGH śyāma; 29 CGHL śyāmā; 30 ABDEFJL dasanaṃcala; C daśanaṃcala [remainder of folio in C is a replacement, *sec.m.*; original hand resumes at 63.4]; 31 A kaka; E [omitted, added *sec.m.*]; 32 B °mūlahū; E °mulahu; 33 EGH lāvaṇya; 34 A abhimai; 35 GH guṇa; 36 AE [follows next]; 37 B samatūlahū; E samatulahu; M [*-ma-* omitted, added *sec.m.*]; 38 A bhrikuṭi; CEFGIL bhṛkuṭī; 39 E hāsi; 40 all MSS jai śrī hita; 41 ABEM haribaṃsa; 42 A praima; 43 B [*ra-* omitted, added in scribe's own hand]; 44 B jhūlahū; C jhūmahu; E jhulahu.

Metre: 16+16 *mātrās*.

CP 63[i].

[Text of CP 63 is headed *chaṃda cāri* in BEFGIJKLM, *chaṃda cyāri* in D, *tribhaṃgī chaṃda cāra* in H. The four component stanzas are numbered *1—4* in all MSS except A, in which each is followed immediately by its *ṭīkā*.]

१ मोहन मदन त्रिभंगी[1] ।
२ मोहन मुनि[2] मन[3] रंगी[4] ॥

मोहन[5] सघन[6] प्रगट परमानँद[7] गुन[8] गंभीर[9] गुपाला[10] ।
सीस[11] किरीट[12] श्रवन[13] मनि[14] कुंडल[15] उर मंडित[16] बनमाला[17] ॥
पीताँबर[18] तन[19] धातु[20] बिचिव्रित[21] कल[22] किंकिनि[23] कटि[24] चंगी ।
नष[25] मनि[26] तरनि[27] चरन[28] सरसीरुह[29] मोहन[30] मदन व्रिभंगी[31] ॥

[Text in C is on a replacement – folio, *sec.m.*, up to line (4).]

1 ACEF trabhaṃgī; M [foll. by *lāla*]; 2 A [lacks *daṇḍa* of *i-kāra*]; M muna; 3 M [*mana, sec.m.*, replaces original reading]; 4 E raṃga; 5 ABCDEFGHIJKL [foll. by *muni*]; M [foll. by *muna*]; 6 A *-na* omitted, added *sec.m.*]; 7 E pramānāda; 8 GHM guṇa; 9 A bhaṃgīra; 10 AE gupāla; 11 H śīśa; K sisa; 12 C kirīṭa; M kariṭa; 13 śravani; C [original hand resumes with *-vana* after replacement ½ folio]; GHIL śravaṇa; 14 A mana; FGHL maṇi; M maṇa; 16 M [first two *akṣaras* crossed out, leaving *-ta*; *maṃḍi-* added *sec.m.*]; 17 A °māla; 18 BD pītābara; E pītaṃbara; 19 L taru; 20 AFGIM dhāta; K dhāti; [emended to *dhāta*]; 21 C bicītrita; D bicitrīta; FM bicitrata; 22 I kali; 23 kaṃkana; CHL kiṃkiṇi; G kikiṇi; M kiṃkaṇa; 24 FGI kaṭa; 25 D [foll. by one *akṣara*, crossed out]; 26 CFGHILM maṇi; 27 ACGHM taraṇi; E taraṇa; 28 GILM caraṇa; 29 F sarasīrahu; 30 I mauhana; 31 AEF trabhaṃgī; C tṛbhaṃgī.

Metre: lines (1)–(2), 12 *mātrās*; (3)–(6), 16+11 *mātrās*.

CP. 63[ii].

मोहन बेनु[1] बजावै ।
इहि[2] रव नारि[3] बुलावै ॥
आई[4] ब्रज[5] नारि[6] सुनत बंशी[7] रव[8] ग्रहपति[9] बंधु[10] बिसारे[11] ।
दरसन मदन[12] गुपाल[13] मनोहर मनसिज ताप[14] निवारे ॥
हरषित[15] बदन बंक अवलोकनि[16] सरस मधुर धुनि[17] गावै[18] ।
मधुमय[19] साम[20] समान अधर धरे[21] मोहन बेनु[22] बजावै[23] ॥

1 A bainu; DF baina; E bena; GHIL beṇu; M beṇa [emended to *baina, sec.m.*]; 2 A ihi; DHL ihī; I iha; 3 M nāra; 4 GHJL āī; 5 F [followed by repeat of *braja*]; HI bṛja; 6 M nāra; 7 ABCDEM baṃsī; 8 A ruha; 9 A grihapati; DEGH gṛhapati; M grahapata; 10 D baṃdha; M [second *akṣara* crossed out; *-dhu* added, sec.m.]; 11 C bīsāre; 12 C [text from *-dana* to 63[iii].5 *manohara* is on replacement ½ folio, *sec.m.*]; EM *-na* omitted, added *sec.m.*]; 13 EFM gopāla; 14 C tapata; 15 A haratapra; F harṣita; I haraṣata [emended to *haraṣita*]; M haraṣati; 16 CF avalokana; M avilokani; 17 H dhvani; M sura; 18 C gāve; 19 A °mai; 20 AKM syāma; GH śyāma; 21 ACEL dhari; DHIK dharaī; FGJM

dharẽ; 22 ABDK bainu; E bena; F baina; GHIM beṇu; 23 HJ bajāvaī; I bajauvai [emended to *bajāvai, sec.m.*].

Metre: lines (1)–(2), 12 *mātrās*; (3)–(6), 16+11 *mātrās*.

CP 63[iii].

रास[1] रच्यौ[2] बन माही[3] ।
बिमल[4] कलपतरु[5] छाही[6] ॥
बिमल कलपतरु[7] तीर सुपेसल[8] सरद[9] रैन[10] बर चंदा ।
सीतल[11] मंद सुगंध पवन बहै[12] तहँ[13] षेलत[14] नँदनंदा[15] ॥
अद्भुत[16] ताल मृदंग[17] मनोहर किंकिनि[18] शब्द[19] कराही[20] ।
जमुना[21] पुलिन[22] रसिक रस सागर रास[23] रच्यौ[24] बन माही[25] ॥

[Text in C is on a replacement ½ folio, *sec.m.*, up to line (5).]

1 A rāsu; 2 A racyõ; DI racyo; B racyaū; 3 FGH māhī̃; CLM mā̃hī̃; K mā̃hī; 4 A [line (2) omitted; very rough margin addition, *sec.m.*, reads perhaps *yāmāle kālāpe tā*[?]*o chāhī*]; 5 H kalpataru; 6 CFH chāhī̃; JK chā̃hī; GLM chā̃hī̃; 7 H kalpataru; 8 BGHL supeśala; D [*-sa-* omitted, added *sec.m.*]; 9 GHL śarada; 10 AL raini; BCJ rena [J emended to *raini, sec.m.*]; E reni; 11 GHL śītala; 12 C baha; 13 ABCEFGHJKLM tahā̃; D tahā; I jahā̃; 14 AC ṣele; E ṣalai; 15 AC nadanaṃdā; 16 B adabhuta; 17 AK mridaṃga; 18 B kikini; CGHL kiṃkiṇi [C: original hand resumes with *kiṃkiṇi* after replacement ½ folio]; F kiṃkina; I kiṃkinī; M kiṃkana; 19 A svāda; DM sabda; 20 CFHI karāhī̃; D karāihī [emended to *karāhī*]; K karā̃hī; GLM karā̃hī̃; 21 CH yamunā; 22 M pulana; 23 A rāsu; 24 AB racyaū; CDI racyo; M racau; 25 B mahī; CFH māhī̃; G mā̃hī; LM mā̃hī̃.

Metre: lines (1)–(2), 12 *mātrās*; (3)–(6), 16+11 *mātrās*.

CP 63[*iv*].

देषत मधुकर[1] केली[2] ।
मोहे[3] षग मृग[4] बेली ॥
मोहे मृग[5] धेनु[6] सहित[7] सुरसुंदरि[8] प्रेम[9] मगन[10] पट छूटे[11] ।
उडगन[12] चकित थकित ससि[13] मंडल कोटि[14] मदन मन[15] लूटे ॥
अधर पान[16] परिरंभन[17] अतिरस आनँद[18] मगन[19] सहेली ।
हित[20] हरिबंश[21] रसिक[22] सचु[23] पावत देषत मधुकर[24] केली ॥

1 A madhukura; 2 A keli [emended to *kelī* in scribe's own hand]; 3 E mohi; 4 A mriga; 5 A mriga; 6 ACM dhena; F dhainu; 7 C sahita; M sahata; 8 BDFGIJKM surasuṃdara [JK emended to *surasuṃdari,* sec.

m.]; C surasuṃdarī H svarasuṃdara; 9 A praima; 10 B [*ma-* omitted]; 11 BE chuṭe; 12 GL uḍagaṇa; 13 CEGH śaśi; I śasi; 14 FM koṭa; 15 B [omitted, added in scribe's own hand]; 16 AI pāni; L pāṇi; 17 L parirambhaṇa; M pararaṃbhana; 18 A ānada; D anaṃda; 19 B [followed by one line from *ṭīkā* of 63[i].1, lightly erased]; E rasagana; 20 ABCDEFGHIJKL jai śrī hita; M jai śrī hiti; 21 AE haribaṃsa; M harabaṃsa; 22 B rasaka; 23 B [*sa-* omitted]; 24 A madhukura.

Metre: lines (1)–(2), 12 *mātrās*; (3)–(6), 16+11 *mātrās*.

CP 64.

१ बेनु[1] माई[2] बाजै[3] बंशीबट[4] ।
२ सदा बसंत रहत बृन्दाबन[5]
पुलिन[6] पबित्र सुभग जमुना[7] तट ॥
३ जटित[8] क्रीट[9] मकराकृत[10] कुंडल
मुषारबिंद[11] भवर[12] मानौ[13] लट ।
४ दसननि[14] कुंद कली[15] छबि[16] लज्जित[17]
सज्जित[18] कनक समान पीत पट ॥
५ मुनि[19] मन ध्यान धरत[20] नहि[21] पावत
करत[22] बिनोद संग बालक भट[23] ।
६ दास[24] अनन्य[25] भजन रस कारन[26]
हित[27] हरिबंश[28] प्रगट लीला नट ॥

1 ABF bainu; D baina; GHM beṇu; 2 E māi; 3 C bājẽ; GI bāje; 4 CEFM baṃsī°; 5 IK śrī bṛṃdābana; 6 E pulani; J pulana [emended to *pulina, sec.m.*]; 7 CDH yamunā; 8 C jaṭīta; 9 H kirīṭa; 10 A °ākrita; B °ākrata; L °ākṛti; 11 A muṣārbiṃda; G muṣa arabiṃda; M muṣā arabiṃda [emended to *muṣa arabiṃda, sec.m.*]; 12 GHM bhramara; J [omitted; *bhā̃vara* added *sec.m.*]; KL bhā̃vara; 13 CFGH mānõ; DL mānaū; EIM māno; 14 CHL daśanani; 15 J kali [emended to *kalī, sec.m.*]; 16 A chābi [*chā-* at end of line; *daṇḍa* intended for foll. *i-kāra*]; 17 BF lajita; E [followed by *kai*]; GM lājata; 18 EKM sajjata; F sajita; 19 C munī; M muna; 20 M karata [emended to *dharata, sec.m.*]; 21 A nahi; FHL nahī; 22 M [1st *akṣara* replaces original, perhaps *dha-* for prec. *dharata*]; 23 A raṭa; 24 H dāsi; 25 A [2nd *akṣara* indistinct; perhaps *-nyi-* emended to *-nā-* ?]; 26 GH kāraṇa; 27 all MSS jai śrī hita; 28 BEM haribaṃsa.

Metre: 16+16 *mātrās*.

CP 65.

१ मदन मथन घन निकुंज षेलत हरि[1]
राका[2] रुचिर सरद[3] रजनी ।
२ जमुना[4] पुलिन[5] तट सुर के[6] तरु[7] निकट[8]
रचित रास[9] चलि मिलि[10] सजनी ।।
३ बाजत[11] मृदु[12] मृदंग[13] नाचत सबै सुधंग[14]
तै[15] न श्रवन[16] सुन्यौ[17] बेनु[18] बजनी ।
४ हित[19] हरिबंश[20] प्रभु[21] राधिका रवन[22] मोकौ[23]
भावै[24] माई[25] जगत भगत[26] भजनी ।।

[Stanza omitted in I.]

1 A [omitted]; 2 E rakā [emended to *rākā* in scribe's own hand]; 3 GH śarada; 4 CH yamunā; 5 A [followed by *puli,* lightly crossed through]; 6 BJ kai [follows next]; FHK [follows next]; 7 F [partial emendment of *ta-* to *ke, sec.m.*]; 8 C nīkaṭa; 9 E rāsi; 10 C mīla; F mila; G bhali; 11 DJ bājati; 12 A maghu [for *madhu*?]; E [omitted, *madhu* added *sec.m.*]; M mṛda [emended to *mṛdu*]; 13 A mridaṃga; 14 E sugaṃdha; 15 AK tai; BE te; CGJM tẽ; 16 GHM śravaṇa; 17 A sunyõ; B sunasau; DL sunyaũ; 18 A bena; BD bainu; FK baina; GHM beṇu; 19 all MSS jai śrī hita; 20 AEM haribaṃsa; 21 A prabho; 22 G ravaṇa; HM ramaṇa; 23 CDGHKL mokaũ; EFM mokõ; J [followed by *tau, sec.m.*]; 24 C bhavai; G bhāvaī; M bhāve; 25 C māi [emended to *māī, sec.m.*]; 26 E jagata.

Metre: 8+8+11/12/13 *varṇas.*

CP 66.

१ बिहरत[1] दोऊ[2] प्रीतम कुंज[3] ।
२ अनुपम[4] गौर स्याम[5] तन सोभा[6] बन बरषत[7] सुष पुंज ।।
३ अद्भुत षेत महा[8] मनमथ[9] कौ[10] दुंदुभि[11] भूषन[12] राव ।
४ जूझत[13] सुभट परस्पर[14] अँग अँग उपजत[15] कोटिक[16] भाव ।।
५ भर[17] संग्राम[18] श्रमित अति अबला निद्रायत[19] कल[20] नैन[21] ।
६ पिय[22] के[23] अंक निसंक तंक तन आलसजुत[24] कृत[25] सैन[26] ।।
७ लालन[27] मिस आतुर[28] पिय परसत[29] उरू[30] नाभि[31] उरजात ।
८ अद्भुत[32] छटा बिलोकि[33] अवनि पर बिथकित[34] बेपथ गात ।।
९ नागरि[35] निरषि[36] मदन बिष ब्यापत[37] दियौ[38] सुधाधर[39] धीर ।
१० सत्वर[40] उठे[41] महा मधु[42] पीवन[43] मिलत[14] मीनमिव[45] नीर[46] ।।
११ अबही[47] मैं[48] मुष मध्य[49] बिलोके बिंबाधर सुरसाल[50] ।

१२ जाग्रत[51] ज्यौं[52] भ्रम भयौ[53] पर्‌यौ[54] मन[55] सत[56] मनसिज[57] कुल जाल[58] ॥
१३ सकृदपि[59] मयि[60] अधरामृतम्[61] उपनय[62] सुंदरि[63] सहज सनेह[64] ।
१४ तव[65] पद पंकज कौ[66] निज[67] मंदिर[68] पालय सषि[69] मम देह ॥
१५ प्रिया[70] कहति[71] कहु[72] कहाँ हुते[73] पिय[74] नव[75] निकुंज[76] बर राज ।
१६ सुंदर बचन रचन[77] कत बितरत[78] रति[79] लंपट बिनु[80] काज ॥
१७ इतनौ[81] श्रवन[82] सुनत[83] मानिनि[84] मुष अंतर रह्यौ[85] न धीर ।
१८ मति[86] कातर बिरहज दुष ब्यापत[87] बहुतर[88] स्वास[89] समीर[90] ॥
१९ हित[91] हरिबंश[92] भुजनि[93] आकरषे[94] लै राषे उर माँझ[95] ।
२० मिथुन[96] मिलत जु कछुक[97] सुष[98] उपज्यौ[99] त्रुटि[100] लवमिव भइ[101] साँझ[102] ॥

1 D bihare [-*ta* added *sec.m.*]; K [-*ta* omitted, added *sec.m.*]; M beharata; 2 AE dou; 3 B [followed by *ke madhya* (from *ṭīkā*)]; 4 B anuyama; 5 CGH śyāma; 6 GH śobhā; 7 B [*ba*- omitted]; 8 C maha [emended to *mahā, sec.m.*]; 9 GIKL manmatha; 10 GI ko; M koko [1st *ko* lightly erased]; 11 FGKM dūdubhī; I dūdabhī; 12 E bhuṣana; GHLM bhūṣaṇa; 13 E bujhata [emended to *jujhata, sec.m.*]; 14 AM parasapara; 15 B upajati; 16 EF koṭaka; 17 BDHIJ bhari [J emended to *bhara, sec.m.*]; 18 I sṛṃgāra; 19 A nidrāīta; CEF nidrāita; L nadrāyata [emended to *nidrāyata*]; 20 I kali; 21 B nanai [emended to *nainai* in scribe's own hand]; EI nena; 22 F pīya; 23 E ni [*ke* added *sec.m.*, but *ni* not cancelled]; 24 CH °yuta; 25 AB krata; 26 AEFI sena; B sainai; H śaina; 27 BKM lālani [K emended to *lālana*]; 28 C atura [emended to *ātura, sec.m.*]; 29 I parasati; 30 BCD uru; 31 D nābhī; 32 E [omitted, added *sec.m.*]; 33 M biloka; 34 D bithakīta; G bithakiya; 35 I nāgarī; LM nāgara; 36 B niraṣa; M niriṣi; 37 ACEGLM byāpita; BI byāpyo; DJ byāpyau [J emended to *byāpata, sec.m.*]; 38 A dayau; IM diyo; 39 CFKL sudhādhari; 40 B śatvara; 41 A [foll. by *ju*]; E uṭhi; 42 B madhū; I mi [-*dhu pīvata* omitted, added *sec.m.*]; 43 B pivata; I [see prec.]; 44 B [-*ta* omitted]; 45 A mīnamīva; 46 B nāri; 47 CGLM abahĩ; 48 AB me; CGJ mẽ [J emended to *maĩ, sec.m.*]; 49 F maddha; 50 K surasālā; L suraśāla; 51 A jāgata; D [-*ta* omitted]; 52 ABCG jyau; GI jyõ; 53 IM bhayo; 54 I paryo; 55 A manu; 56 B [-*ta* omitted]; GH śata; 57 A manasila; 58 M [-*la* replaces original reading]; 59 A sakradaṣi; F śakṛdapi; GK sukṛdapi; 60 A mai; BCDIJL maya; F mẽ; 61 A adharāmritam; B adharāmratam; 62 A uṣanaya; 63 ADEFGIK suṃdara; 64 B sneha; 65 M tuva; 66 E kaū; FGM ko; I kõ; 67 ABCEK niju; 68 J maṃdina; M maṃdara; 69 AFGM saṣi; 70 G piyā; 71 E kahatī; FHLM kahata; G kahatu; 72 A kahi; CEJKL kahau; I kaho; M kahū; 73 I [foll. by *mahā,* crossed out]; 74 A pīya; H priya; 75 A navala [cf. foll.]; 76 A kuṃja; 77 B [omitted]; 78 A citarita; EJK bitarati [J emended to *bitarata, sec.m.*]; FIL bitarita [I emended to *bitarati, sec.m.*]; 79 J [omitted, added *sec.m.*]; 80 FGHM bina; 81 A ītanau; CGIM itano; 82 G śravaṇu; HILM śrāvaṇa; 83 I sunati; 84 C

māninī; EF mānani; J [emended to *mānani; sec.m.*]; 85 I rahyo; 86 I mata; 87 ACEGLM byāpita; BK byāpyau; H byāpau; I byāpyo; 88 B bahusara; L bahataru; 89 GM śvāsa; 90 A samāra; I [*sa-* omitted, added *sec.m.*]; 91 all MSS jai śrī hita; 92 AEM haribaṃsa; 93 AFHI bhujana; 94 B ākaraṣai; G ākarṣẽ; HKM ākarṣe; I ākaraṣaī; 95 ABEJ mājha; 96 M mithana; 97 C kachūka; 98 A suṣu; 99 A upajyõ; DI upajyo; 100 ABDFIJ truṭa [J emended to *truṭi, sec.m.*]; E [foll. by one erased *akṣara*]; 101 BCDEFGHIJKLM bhaī; 102 J sājha.

Metre: 16+11 *mātrās*.

CP 67.

१ रुचिर राजत[1] बधू[2] कानन[3] किशोरी[4] ।
२ सरस षोडस[5] किये[6] तिलक मृगमद[7] दिये[8]
मृगज[9] लोचन उबटि[10] अंग सिर[11] षोरी ॥
३ गंड पंडीर[12] मंडित चिकुर चंद्रिका[13]
मेदिनी[14] कवरि[15] गूंथित[16] सुरँग डोरी ।
४ श्रवन[17] ताटंक कै[18] चिबुक पर[19] बिंदु दै
कसुंभि[20] कँचुकी[21] दुरै[22] उरज फल[23] कोरी ॥
५ बलय[24] कंकन[25] दोति[26] नषनि[27] जावक जोति[28]
उदर[29] गुन[30] रेष पट[31] नील कटि थोरी ।
६ सुभग[32] जघनस्थली कुनित[33] किंकिनी[34] भली
कोक संगीत रस सिंधु[35] झकझोरी[36] ॥
७ बिबिधि लीला[37] रचित रहसि[38] हरिबंश[39] हित
रसिक सिरमौर[40] राधारवन[41] जोरी ।
८ भृकुटि[42] निर्जित[43] मदन मंद सस्मित[44] बदन
किये[45] रस[46] बिबस[47] घनस्याम[48] पिय[49] गोरी ॥

1 ACL rājati; D rāja [*-ti* added *sec.m.*]; 2 E badhu; 3 M kānani; 4 BM kisorī; 5 CEHKL ṣoḍaśa; M ṣoḍasi; 6 AB kiyai; DHIL kiyaī; EFGJKM kiyẽ; 7 A mriga°; 8 A dīyẽ; B diyai; EFGKM diyẽ; DHIJL diyaī; 9 A mrigaja; JM [*-ja* omitted, added *sec.m.*]; 10 C ubaṭī; E ubaṭa; 11 HJ śira; 12 CE piṃḍīra; 13 M caṃdrakā; 14 AF modinī; IM medanī; 15 C kavarī; M kūvara [emended to *kavari*]; 16 A guthita; C graṃthita; FM guṃthita; G gaṃthita; 17 CGHL śravaṇa; 18 DHIJ ke; 19 I pari; 20 AE kasubhi; B kusubhī; CDGKM kasũbhī; H kasũbhī; I kasubhī; 21 AJ kā̃cuki; M kācī; 22 CF durẽ; D dūraī; E duri; J duraī; GIM dure; 23 M [*-la* omitted, added *sec.m.*]; 24 A bale; B [*-ya* omitted]; G balai; 25 GHL kaṃkaṇa; 26 A [followed by *deti*]; EG deta [E emended to *dota, sec.m.*]; FIM dota; H dyoti; 27 FI naṣana [I emended to *naṣani, sec.m.*]; 28 F jota; H jyoti; 29 G udāra; 30 B ṇa; GHILM guṇa; 31 GM paṭu; 32 F śubhaga; 33 GHM kvaṇita; 34 A kīkinī; B

kiṃkina; CGHL kiṃkiṇi; M kaṃkiṇi [emended to *kiṃkiṇi, sec.m.*]; 35 A siṃdha; 36 I [-*jhorī* replaces original reading]; 37 G lālā; 38 G rasahi; 39 AEM haribaṃsa; H śrī haribaṃśa; 40 AE siramora; H śiramaura; L saramaura [emended to *sira*°, *sec.m.*]; 41 G °ravaṇa; H °ramaṇa; M °ramana; 42 A bhrikuṭi, CEF bhṛkuṭī; M bhrakuṭi; 43 K nirjjita; M nirajita; 44 C śasmita; 45 A kīyẽ; M kiyẽ; 46 B rāsi; 47 B bibaśa; 48 GHL °śyāma; 49 F pīya.

Metre: (3x/ ⏓ ⏑ ⏓, ⏓ ⏑ ⏓ /) + / ⏓ ⏑ ⏓ / + 4m.

CP 68.

१ रास मैं[1] रसिक[2] मोहन[3] बने[4] भामिनी[5] ।
२ सुभग पावन पुलिन सरस सौरभ नलिन
मत्त मधुकर निकर सरद[6] की[7] जामिनी[8] ॥
३ त्रिबिधि रोचक[9] पवन ताप दिनमनि[10] दवन
तहाँ[11] ठाडे[12] रवन[13] संग सत[14] कामिनी[15] ।
४ ताल[16] बीना[17] मृदँग[18] सरस नाचत सुघँग[19]
एक[20] तैं[21] एक संगीत की स्वामिनी[22] ॥
५ राग[23] रागिनि[24] जमी बिपिन[25] बरषत[26] अमी
अधर बिंबनि[27] रमी मुरलि[28] अभिरामिनी[29] ।
६ लाग[30] कट्टर[31] उरप सप्त[32] सुर[33] सौं[34] सुलप
लेत[35] सुंदर[36] सुघर[37] राधिका नामिनी ॥
७ तत्त[38] थेइ[39] थेइ[40] करत[41] गति ब नौतन[42] धरत[43]
पलटि[44] डगमग[45] ढरत[46] मत्त[47] गजगामिनी[48] ।
८ धाइ[49] नवरँग धरी उरसि[50] राजत[51] षरी
उभै[52] कलहंस[53] हरिबंश[54] घन[55] दामिनी ॥

1 ACFGHJM mẽ; BE mai; 2 A [followed by one *akṣara,* covered with paste]; 3 A mauhana; 4 ACEFJKM banẽ; B banai; D banaī; 5 M bhāmanī; 6 GH śarada; 7 A [omitted, added *sec.m.*]; 8 H yāminī; M jāmanī; 9 K rocika; 10 GHL °maṇi; IM °mana; 11 D tahā; 12 G ṭhoṭhe; 13 G ravaṇa; H ramaṇa; M ramaṇi; 14 CGH śata; 15 M kāmanī; 16 D tāvala [-*va*- lightly erased]; 17 B pīna; CGH bīṇā; 18 A mṛdãga; 19 E sugãdha; 20 I eke [emended to *eka*]; 21 B tai; L te; 22 M svāmanī; 23 B [omitted]; 24 AG rāginī; B rāgani; C rāgīni; FI rāgiṇa; M ragina; 25 AE bipini; F bipana; 26 I barṣata; 27 B bibana; E bibini; G bibani; I biṃbana; 28 CEFGLM muralī; 29 IM abhirāmanī; 30 BDIJ lāgi [J emended to *lāga, sec.m.*]; 31 AC kaṭṭari; B kaṭra; E kadari; F kaṭara; I kaddara; 32 C śapta; 33 H svara; 34 AFGIKM sõ; B sau; 35 AJ leti; 36 ADJ suṃdari; 37 E susughara; J [emended to *sughari, sec.m.*]; 38 A [prec. by *tā*- added *sec.m.*]; 39 ADEGHIKM theī; 40 AEGHIKM

theī; 41 ABDEJ karati; 42 A nūtana; 43 ABDIJ dharati; 44 F palaṭa; G palaṭhi; 45 F ḍagamaḍa; 46 ABEIJ ḍharati [I has illegible *akṣara* added *sec.m.* to follow *ḍha-*]; 47 E mata; 48 M °gāmanī; 49 H dhāya; 50 M ūrasi; 51 ABDEJ rājati; 52 BDFIJ jai śrī ubhai; H jaya śrī ubhaya; 53 L kalahaṃśa; M kalihaṃsa; 54 AEIM haribaṃsa [I emended to *haribaṃśa, sec.m.*]; B harabaṃsa; 55 B dhana; E saghana.

Metre: 4x/ ⏕ ⏑ ⏕ , ⏕ ⏑ ⏕ /

CP 69.

१ मोहनी[1] मोहन[2] रँगे[3] प्रेम सुरंगे[4]
मत्त[5] मुदित कल नाचत सुधंगे ॥
२ सकल कला प्रबीन[6] कल्यान[7] रागिनी[8] लीन[9]
कहत[10] न बनै[11] ये[12] माधुरी अँग अंगे ॥
३ तरनि[13] तनया[14] तीर त्रिबिधि[15] सषी समीर[16]
मनों[17] मुनिब्रत[18] धर्यौ[19] कपोत[20] कोकिल[21] कीर[22] ॥
४ नागरि[23] नव[24] किशोर[25] मिथुन मानस[26] चोर[27]
सरस गावत[28] दोउ[29] मंजुल मंदर[30] घोर ॥
५ कंकन[31] किंकिनि[32] धुनि[33] मुषर[34] नूपुर[35] सुनि[36]
हित[37] हरिबंश[38] रस[39] बरषै[40] नव तरुनि[41] ॥

1 A [half-line reads: *syāmā mohana rāge rāge rasa prema suraṃge//*]; 2 I mauhana; 3 HIJ [followed by double *daṇḍa* as for line end]; 4 ACL [followed by double *daṇḍa* as for line end]; 5 E mata; 6 GH prabīṇa; 7 GH kalyāṇa; 8 F rāginī; H rāgaṇī; I rāgini; 9 E līne [foll. by one crossed-out *akṣara*]; 10 DJ kahati [J emended to *kahata, sec.m*]; 11 ACDFK banẽ; E [*-nai* omitted]; GIM bane; L banaĩ; 12 ACF e; E yai H [omitted]; 13 EFJ tarana [J emended to *tarani*]; GM taraṇi; 14 K tanaiyā; 15 G tribidha; 16 I samīre; 17 ABJK mānau; C mānõ; D manaũ; EGM māno; FHL mānaũ; I [omitted]; 18 A manidatu; CE munibratu; DIK munibṛta; 19 AI dharyo; 20 BCDEFGHIJKLM kapotī; 21 all MSS kokilā; 22 E kora; 23 ACFH nāgarī; IM nāgara; 24 E navala; 25 M kisora; 26 ABCDEGHIJLM manasi; 27 A [foll. by double *daṇḍa* as for line end]; 28 A gāvati; 29B CDFGHIJKLM doū; 30 ABCDEFHIJL maṃdira [J emended to *maṃdara, sec.m.*]; 31 CGHL kaṃkaṇa; 32 BM kīkinī; CHL kiṃkiṇi; G kikiṇi; I kiṃkani [emended to *kiṃkini*]; 33 B dhūni; H dhvani; J dhuna [emended to *dhuni, sec.m.*]; 34 A muṣura; J [*-ra* omitted, added *sec.m.*]; 35 HL nūpurani; J [emended to *nūpurani, sec.m.*]; B nupura; E napura; 36 A [foll. by double *daṇḍa* as for line end]; M suna; 37 ABCDEFHIJKLM jai śrī hita; G jai hita; 38 AEM haribaṃsa; 39 E rasu; 40 CGHM baraṣe; K baraṣi; 41 GM taruṇi.

Metre: 10+10+20 *mātrās*.

CP 70.

१ आजु[1] सँभारत[2] नाहिन गोरी ।
२ फूली[3] फिरत[4] मत्त[5] करनी[6] ज्यौं[7] सुरत समुद्र झकोरी ॥
३ आलस बलित[8] अरुन[9] धूसर[10] मषि[11] प्रगट करत[12] दृग[13] चोरी ।
४ पिय[14] पर करुन[15] अमी रस बरषत अधर अरुनता[16] थोरी ॥
५ बाँधत[17] भृंग[18] उरज अंबुज पर[19] अलक[20] निबंध[21] किशोरी[22] ।
६ संगम किरच[23] किरच[24] कँचुकी[25] बँध[26] सिथल[27] भई[28] कटि[29] डोरी[30] ॥
७ देत[31] असीस[32] निरषि[33] जुवती[34] जन जिनकै[35] प्रीति[36] न[37] थोरी ।
८ हित[38] हरिबंश[39] बिपिन[40] भूतल[41] पर संतत अविचल[42] जोरी ॥

1 DH āja; 2 AI samhārati; BD sabhārati; CFG sabhārata; J sābhārati; 3 E phulī; 4 AB phirati; I phirai; JK [emended to *phirati, sec.m.*]; 5 E mata; 6 G kariṇī; HM karaṇī; 7 AI jyõ; BC jyau; 8 J abalita; 9 GHLM aruṇa; 10 E dhusara; H dhūṣara; 11 A maṣa; M muṣi; 12 BM karati; 13 A driga; B daga; DHK draga; 14 B piyā; 15 CGHM karuṇa; E karuni; L karuṇi; 16 CGHILM aruṇatā [M foll. by *thorī bā̃dhata bhraṃga ura-*, of which *thorī* lightly erased]; 17 D bādhata; 18 A bhriṃga; BK bhṛga; CEGM bhraṃga; 19 E pari [emended to *para, sec.m.*]; 20 E akala; M [-*ka* omitted, added *sec.m.*]; 21 I nabaṃdha; 22 BM kisorī; 23 BDHIJL kiraci; M karica [prec. by one cancelled *akṣara*, and emended to *kiraci sec.m.*]; 24 BDHIJL kiraci; K [emended to *kiraci, sec.m.*]; 25 AGKM kãcuki; L kãcuka; 26 BEFK bāda; 27 A sithila; H śithila; I śithala; 28 D bhaï; 29 I kaca [emended to *kaṭi, sec.m.*]; 30 E jorī [*j*- crossed out]; 31 ABIJ deti; 32 H aśīṣa; 33 M niraṣa; 34 H yuvatī; 35 B jinakau; CF jinake; E jivake; GM tinike; K tinakai; 36 FM prīta; 37 M [omitted, added *sec.m.*]; 38 all MSS jai śrī hita; 39 AEM haribaṃsa; 40 A bipini; FILM bipana; 41 E bhutala; 42 D [foll. by *ca*, lightly erased]; GM avacala.

Metre: 16+12 *mātrās*.

CP 71.

१ स्याम[1] सँग राधिका[2] रास[3] मंडल बनी ।
२ बीच नँदलाल[4] ब्रजबाल[5] चंपक[6] बरन[7]
ज्यौं[8] ब[9] घन तडित बिच कनक मर्कत[10] मनी[11] ॥
३ लेत[12] गति मान[13] तत्त[14] थेई[15] हस्तक भेद
स रि[16] ग म[17] प ध नी[18] ये[19] सप्त[20] सुर[21] नंदिनी[22] ।
४ नृत्य[23] रस पहिर[24] पट नील प्रकटित[25] छबी[26]
बदन जनु[27] जलद[28] मैं[29] मकर की चंदिनी[30] ॥

५ राग रागिनि[31] तान मान संगीत मत
थकित राकेस[32] नभ सरद[33] की जामिनी[34] ।
६ हित[35] हरिबंश[36] प्रभु हंस[37] कटि[38] केहरी[39]
दूरि[40] कृत[41] मदन मद मत्त गजगामिनी ॥

1 DFGHL śyāma; 2 A rādhike; 3 B [*-sa* omitted, added *sec.m.*]; 4 AE nada°; 5 A bṛja°; 6 E [text from *campaka* to *ka*[*-naka*] omitted, added *sec.m.*]; 7 GHI baraṇa; M barṇa [emended to *baraṇa*, *sec.m.*]; 8 ADEI jyõ; BC jyau 9 E; aba; H 'ba; 10 A markati; BI marakata; E rmta [sic, *repha* written above *m*; *-ta* emended to *ka*, and *-ta* added *sec.m.*]; 11 C minī; E sanī; LM maṇī; 12 ACDEJ leti; 13 E mana [emended to *māna*, *sec.m.*]; 14 L tata; 15 CE thei; 16 BGIJM ra [J emended to *ri*, *sec.m.*]; E rī; 17 F m [forming conjunct with next]; 18 ACDEGHIM ni; B nya [understood as forming *dhanya* with prec.?]; F na; 19 A e; M yeha [*-ha* lightly erased].20 A spata; 21 H svara; 22 FIKLM naṃdanī [K emended to *naṃdinī*]; 23 A nirta; DGHK nirtta; I nirtya; 24 C pahirī; GILM pahara; 25 A pragaṭati; BDEFL pragaṭata; CGHM pragaṭita; K prakaṭa; 26 BCJ chabi; 27 EGM jano; F janau; HL janaū; 28 D [*-da* omitted, added *sec.m.*]; M ja [?; 2nd *akṣara* emended to *-da*, *-la-* added *sec.m.*]; 29 ABE mai; CGHJKM mē; 30 AIM cādanī; BDEFGJK cādinī; C cādinī; 31 ABC rāginī; FI rāgina; GHM rāgiṇi: K rāgani [emended to *rāgini*]; 32 CGHJL rākeśa; D [*-sa* omitted, added *sec.m.*]; 33 GH śarada; K [*-da* omitted, added *sec.m.*]; 34 H yāminī; 35 all MSS jai śrī hita; 36 ABEM haribaṃsa; 37 L haṃśa; 38 F kaṭa; M [*-ṭi* is emendment of original reading]; 39 C kehari; 40 AE duri; BFI dūra; M [dū- is emendment of original reading]; 41 AB krata; K [emended to *kṛti*].

Metre: 4x/ ⏓⏓ ⏑ ⏓⏓, ⏓⏓ ⏑ ⏓⏓ /

CP 72.

१ सुंदर पुलिन सुभग सुषदाइक[1] ।
२ नव नव घन अनुराग परस्पर[2]
षेलत कुँवर[3] नागरी नाइक[4] ॥
३ सीतल[5] हंससुता[6] रस[7] बीचिनि[8]
परसि[9] पवन सीकर[10] मृदु बरषत ।
४ बर मंदार कमल[11] चंपक कुल
सौरभ सरस मिथुन[12] मन हरषत ॥
५ सकल सुधंग[13] बिलास परावधि
नाचत नवल मिले सुर[14] गावत ।
६ मृगज[15] मयूर[16] मराल भवर[17] पिक
अद्‌भुत[18] कोटि मदन सिर[19] नावत[20] ॥

७ निर्मित कुसुम[21] सैन[22] मधु पूरित[23]
भाजन कनक निकुंज बिराजत ।
८ रजनीमुष सुष रासि[24] परस्पर[25]
सुरत[26] समर दोऊ[27] दल साजत ॥
९ बिट कुल नृपति[28] किशोरी[29] कर[30] धृत
बुधि[31] बल[32] नीबी बंधन मोचत ।
१० नेति[33] नेति[34] बचनामृत बोलत
प्रणय[35] कोप प्रीतम[36] नहि[37] सोचत[38] ॥
११ हित[39] हरिबंश[40] रसिक ललितादिक
लता भवन रंध्रनि[41] अवलोकत[42] ।
१२ अनुपम[13] सुष भर[44] भरत[45] बिबस[46] असु[47]
आनँद बारि[48] कंठ दृग[49] रोकत[50] ॥

1 A °dāika; BDHIJL °dāyaka; 2 M parasapara; 3 ABDJLM kuvara; H kũvari; I kuvari [followed by 3 *akṣaras,* crossed out]; 4 A nāika; DHIJ nāyaka; 5 BGHJL śītala; 6 L haṃśa; 7 D [*-sa* omitted, added *sec.m.*]; 8 AF bīcana; BD bīcinu; C bīcanī; EGKLM bīcani; I bīcina; 9 DIJM parasa; 10 H śikara; 11 DFI kavala; 12 A mithunu; 13 E sugeṃdha; M sugaṃdhaga [first *-ga-* partially erased]; 14 H svara; I [followed by *va,* lacking top line]; 15 M [*-ga-* replaces original *akṣara, sec.m.*]; 16 A maṣayūra [emended to *mayūra*]; E mayura; 17 KL bhãvara; H bhrãmara; 18 B adabhuta; 19 C siru; H śira; 20 D [*-vata* omitted, added *sec.m.*]; 21 ABFM kusama; 22 CDEI sena; H śayana; 23 B puta [*-ri* omitted]; E purita; M pūrata; 24 FM rāsa; GH rāśi; 25 M parasapara; 26 E [*-ra-* omitted, added *sec.m.*]; 27 AE dou; 28 AM nṛpata; 29 M kisorī; 30 A kala; J kari [emended to *kara*]; 31 IL budha; K buddhi; 32 D balaya; I [followed by *jorī,* crossed out]; 33 D neti neti; FM neta; 34 FM neta; 35 EF pranaya; 36 C pritama; 37 A nahī; 38 C śocata; 39 all MSS jai śrī hita; 40 AEM haribaṃsa; 41 DIFM raṃdhrana [I emended to *raṃdhrani, sec.m.*]; E raṃdhṛni; 42 BDG avalokati; 43 A anūpama; 44 E bhari; 45 ACHJ bharita; E bhariba [emended to *bharita, sec.m.*]; L bharati; 46 CG bibaśa; E batibasa; F bibisa; 47 C aśu; E aṃsu; 48 C bārī; 49 A driga; B daga; DEK draga; 50 BDJ rokati.

Metre: 16+16 *mātrās.*

CP 73.

१ षंजन मीन मृगज[1] मद मेटत[2]
कहा कहौं[3] नैननि[4] की बातें[5] ।
२ सुनि सुंदरी[6] कहाँ[7] लौं[8] सिषाई[9]
मोहन[10] बसीकरन[11] की घातें[12] ॥

३ बंक[13] निसंक[14] चपल[15] अनियारे[16]
अरुन[17] स्याम[18] सित[19] रचे[20] कहाँ[21] तें[22] ।
४ डरत[23] न[24] हरत परायौ[25] सर्बसु[26]
मृदु[27] मधुमिव[28] मादिक दृग[29] पातें[30] ॥
५ नैंकु[31] प्रसन्न[32] दृष्टि[33] पूरन[34] करि
नहिं[35] मोतन[36] चितयौ[37] प्रमदा[38] तैं[39] ।
६ हित[40] हरिबंश[41] हंसकल[42] गामिनि[43]
भावै[44] सु[45] करहु[46] प्रेम[47] के नातें[48] ॥

1 A mrigaja; 2 A maiṭata; D [-*ta* omitted, added *sec.m.*]; 3 ABD kahau; CGM kahõ; 4 AE nenani; I nena; 5 BE bātai; DIKLM bātaĩ; 6 E suṃdara; H suṃdirī; K suṃdari; 7 AJ kahā; E kahaū; 8 AB lau; CGM lõ; DE lo; 9 B siṣāĩ; L saṣaĩ [emended to *siṣaĩ*]; 10 I mauhana; 11 GH baśīkaraṇa; LM baśīkarana; 12 BDE ghātai; HLM ghātaĩ; 13 B baṃkā; E baṃsa [emended to *baṃka*, *sec.m.*]; 14 H niśaṃka; 15 E cupala; 16 C aniāre; 17 CGHILM aruṇa; 18 GHM śyāma [M emended to *syāma*, *sec. m.*]; 19 L śita; 20 GM race haĩ; 21 BCD kahā; 22 BE tai; DHLM taĩ; I te; 23 A urata; 24 M [additional *na hara-*, and (*sarba-*) *su mṛ* (*-du*) written outside indented *mūla* margin: later cancelled]; 25 A parāvo; I parāyo; 26 AF sarabasu; D rabasu [*sa-* added in scribe's own hand]; GHM sarbasa; 27 A mridu; 28 M madhu iva; 29 A driga; BDK draga; 30 DIKL pātaĩ; E pāte; 31 AEFI neku; GHLM naika; 32 AEF prasaṃna; 33 A drisṭi; B daṣṭi; F dṛṣṭa; 34 E purana; GHM pūraṇa; 35 F nahī̃; HJ nahī; L nahā̃ [emended to *nahī̃*, *sec. m.*]; 36 A [follows next]; 37 C cittayau; GIJM citayo; 38 BCDFGHJKLM pramudā; 39 ACEGJM té; 40 all MSS jai śrī hita; 41 AE haribaṃsa; 42 L haṃśa°; 43 CE gāminī; F gāmina; 44 GM bhāvaĩ; I bhāve; 45 EFHLM so; G [*so* is in parenthesis]; 46 F karau; I karo; 47 A praima; 48 DHJKLM nātaĩ; B bātai; EI nāte.

Metre : 16+16 *mātrās.*

CP 74.

१ काहे कौं[1] मान[2] बढावत[3] है[4] बालक मृग[5] लोचनि[6] ।
२ हौं[7] ब[8] डरनि[9] कछु[10] कहि न[11] सकति[12] इक[13] बात सकोचनि[14] ॥
३ मत्त मुरलि[15] अंतर तव गावत
जाग्रत[16] सैन[17] तवाकृति[18] सोचनि[19] ।
४ हित[20] हरिबंश[21] महा मोहन[22] पिय[23]
आतुर[24] बिट बिरहज दुष[25] मोचनि[26] ॥

1 ABE kau; CFGIM kõ; 2 A mānu; 3 ABCDIJ baḍhāvati; M bādhāvata; 4 AFJ hau (J emended to *hai*, *sec. m.*]; BD he; I ho; 5 A mriga;

6 E locanī [emended to *locani*, *sec. m.*]; FM locana; 7 ACGM hõ; BDK hau; 8 H 'ba; 9 FH ḍarana; G urani; 10 CFJ kachū; 11 M ni; 12 CFHKM sakata; I sakita; 13 A īka; 14 B sakaucani; FM sakocana; 15 ABEFGM muralī; 16 A jāgata; E jāgṛta; K tāgrata; 17 CDEFJ sena [J emended to *saina*, *sec. m.*]; H śayana; 18 A tavākrati; B tavākrata; CDEFHJK tavākṛta; 19 F socana; 20 all MSS jai śrī hita; 21 AEM haribaṃsa; 22 I mauhana; 23 B piyā; F pīya; 24 D atura; 25 A duṣu; 26 ADFI mocana.

Metre : (1) 16+10, (2) 14+10, remainder 16+16 *mātrās*.

CP 75.

१ हौं[1] जु[2] कहति[3] इक[4] बात सषी सुनि[5] काहे[6] कौं[7] डारति[8] ।
२ प्रान[9] रवन[10] सौं[11] क्यौं[12] ब[13] करत[14] आगस[15] बिनु[16] आरति[17] ॥
३ पिय चितवत[18] तव चंद[19] बदन[20] तन[21]
तू[22] अधमुष[23] निजु[24] चरन[25] निहारति[26] ।
४ वे[27] मृदु[28] चिबुक[29] प्रलोइ[30] प्रबोधत[31]
तू[32] भामिनि[33] कर[34] सौं[35] कर[36] टारति[37] ॥
५ बिबस[38] अधीर बिरह अति[39] कातर[40]
सर[41] औसर[42] कछुवै[43] न बिचारति[44] ।
६ हित[45] हरिबंश[46] रहसि[47] प्रीतम मिलि[48]
त्रिषित[49] नैन[50] काहे न प्रतिपारति[51] ॥

1 ACEGIM hõ; B hau; 2 B nū; 3 BFKM kahata; 4 GLM eka; 5 H suna; 6 B kahe; E kāhi; M kahě [emended to *kāhe*, *sec. m.*]; 7 A kõ ba; BK kau; CGHM kõ; 8 ABIJKL ḍarāti; FGHM ḍārata; 9 E [conjoined to next as *prānravana*, but with *ra* also added *sec. m.*]; GHIM prāṇa; 10 A ramana; GM ravaṇa; H ramaṇa; L [omitted]; 11 ACFGM sõ; BEK sau; 12 ACI kyo; B kyau; D kyõ; 13 H 'ba; 14 ACDEL karati; 15 E āgama; 16 FGM bina; 17 A ārāti; FGHM ārata; I [*parādha*, crossed out, between *ā-* and *-rati*]; 18 A citavati; 19 K caṃdra; 20 B [*-da-* omitted]; 21 C [omitted]; 22 A tǖ; C tu; E tū; 23 BDIJ adhi°; 24 GHM nija; 25 D [*-na* omitted]; GHM caraṇa; 26 FGHKM nihārata; 27 C vai; 28 A mridu; 29 I [*ka*, lacking top line, between *ci-* and *-buka*]; 30 HI praloya; 31 ACEFGJLM prabodhita; I bodhita; 32 CE tǖ; 33 C bhāminī; F bhāmina; 34 B [*-ra* omitted]; 35 ABEK sau; CFGJM sõ; 36 J kari [emended to *kara*, *sec. m.*]; 37 FGHM ṭārata; 38 G bibaśa; 39 I [replaces original reading]; 40 B kārata [foll. by double *daṇḍa* as for line end]; 41 E (*-ra* omitted, added *sec. m.*]; M rasa; 42 AEFHKL avasara; B osara; 43 BCJL kachūvai; 44 FGHLM bicārata [L emended to *bicārati*, sec. m.]; J bicārita; 45 all MSS jai śrī hita; 46 AEM haribaṃsa; 47 M rahisa; 48 C milī; FM mila; 49 B tripita; GIKM tṛṣita;

L traṣita; 50 EJ nena [J emended to *naina*, *sec. m.*]; H nayana; I maina; 51 FGH pratipārata; M pritipārata.

Metre: (1) 16+10, (2) 14+10, remainder 16+16 *mātrās*.

CP 76.

१ नागरी[1] निकुंज ऐन[2] किशलय[3] दल रचित सैन[4]
कोक[5] कला कुशल[6] कुवरि[7] अति उदार[8] री।
२ सुरत रंग अंग अंग हाव भाव भृकुटि[9] भंग
माधुरी[10] तरंग मथत कोटि[11] मार री[12] ॥
३ मुषर[13] नूपुरनि[14] सुभाव[15] किंकिनी[16] बिचित्र राव
बिरमि[17] बिरमि[18] नाथ बदत[19] बर बिहार री।
४ लाडिली[20] किशोर[21] राजहंस[22] हंसिनी[23] समाज
सींचत[24] हरिबंश[25] नैन[26] सुरस सार री ॥

1 A syāmā nāgarī jū [*jū* crossed out in scribe's red ink]; 2 ACEIJ ena [J emended to *aina*, *sec. m.*]; 3 A kiśalai; EM kisalaya; 4 ACEFJ sena [J emended to *saina*, *sec. m.*]; 5 B kauka; 6 ABJM kusala; 7 C kuvarī; FI kuvara; GL kūvari; H kūmari; M kūvara [emended to *kūvari*, *sec. m.*]; 8 C uddāra; 9 A bhrikuṭi; CEFIM bhṛkuṭī; 10 A madhurī; 11 K koṭe [emended to *koṭi*, *sec. m.*]; M koṭa; 12 C [omitted]; 13 A muṣuru; 14 A nūpuraruna; B nūpūrani; C nūpurani; DF nūpurana; 15 H svabhāva; 16 C kiṃkini; GH kiṃkiṇī; LM kiṃkaṇī [L emended to *kiṃkiṇī*, *sec. m.*]; 17 AEFGM birama; 18 AEFGM birama [A followed by *tha*, crossed out]; 19 ADIJ badati; M badita; 20 FM lāḍalī; I [preceded by *rā*, crossed out]; 21 BM kisora; 22 L °haṃśa; 23 B haṃsanā [emended to *haṃsinī*, *sec. m.*]; L haṃśinī; 24 ABDKL sĩcata; J sĩcati; 25 AEM haribaṃsa; 26 AEIJK nena; C nayana.

Metre: (7 x / ⏓ ⏑ ⏓ ⏑ /) + /—/

CP 77.

१ लटकति[1] फिरति[2] जुवति[3] रस[4] फूली।
२ लता भवन[5] मैं[6] सरस[7] सकल निसि[8]
पिय[9] सँग सुरत हिंडोरे[10] झूली[11] ॥
३ जद्यपि[12] अति अनुराग[13] रसासव
पान[14] बिबस[15] नाहिन गति भूली[16] ।
४ आलस[17] बलित नैन[18] बिगलित लट
उर पर कछुक[19] कंचुकी षूली[20] ॥

५ मरगजी माल[21] सिथल[22] कटि[23] बँधन[24]
चित्रित कज्जल पीक दुकूली[25] ।
६ हित[26] हरिबंश[27] मदन सर[28] जर्जर[29]
बिथकित स्याम[30] सजीवनि[31] मूली ॥

1 BFGHILM laṭakata; K [emended to *laṭakata, sec. m.*]; 2 BCFGKLM phirata; 3 H yuvati; 4 A ati; 5 C bhuvana; 6 ABE mai; FGHJM mẽ; 7 I sakarasa [-*ka*-crossed out]; 8 C nisī; FM nisa; HGM niśi; 9 F pīya; 10 AI hiḍore; B hiḍorai; CFM hīḍorẽ; DKL hīdoraī; G hiḍorẽ [collocation with prec. is *suratahi ḍorẽ*]; 11 E jholī; 12 ABE jadapi; CH yadyapi; DIJK jaddapi; FGM jaddipa; L jadyapi; 13 G anurāsa; 14 IK pāni; 15 C bibaśa; 16 B mūlī; 17 D āsala; 18 ACIJ nena; B [-*na* omitted, added in scribe's own hand]; 19 BC kachūka; D kachu; 20 D [-*lī* omitted, added in scribe's own hand]; I ṣulī,; 21 A mala [emended to *māla, sec. m.*]; 22 A sithila; H śithila; 23 C kaṭī; F kaṭa; 24 M bãdhani; 25 C dūkūlī; 26 A śrī hita; BCDEFGHIJKLM jai śrī hita; 27 AEM haribaṃsa; 28 B rasa; GHL śara; 29 B jajãra; DHK jarajara; 30 GHIL śyāma; 31 BFGHIM sajīvana.

Metre: 16+16 *mātrās*.

CP 78.

१ सुधंग[1] नाचत[2] नवल किशोरी[3] ।
२ थेई[4] थेई[5] कहति[6] चहति[7] प्रीतम दिसि[8]
बदन चंद[9] मनो[10] तृषित[11] चकोरी ॥
३ तान बँधान[12] मान मैं[13] नागरि[14]
देषत स्याम[15] कहत[16] हो हो री ।
४ हित[17] हरिबंश[18] माधुरी अँग अँग
बरबस[19] लियौ[20] मोहन[21] चित[22] चोरी[23] ॥

1 E sugaṃdha; 2 ADIJ nācati; 3 BM kisorī; 4 C thei; 5 C thei; 6 CGHM kahata; F [with next] bacana kahata [-*ca*- and *ka*- lightly erased, *ca*- added *sec. m.*, yielding *bana cahata*]; 7 BFGHKM cahata; J [followed by erased word]; 8 AGH diśi; BDFIM disa; CL diśa; 9 GH caṃdra; 10 A mānai; CJ manõ; D mānaũ; FK mānau; GM mānõ; H manaũ; I māno; L manu; 11 ABCEHM triṣita; 12 AE badhāna; 13 AFGHJKM mẽ; BE mai; 14 B [followed by *visarga* sign (to mark caesura??)]; C nāgarī; FM nāgara; 15 GHL śyāma; 16 L kahati; 17 all MSS jai śrī hita; 18 EM haribaṃsa; J haribaṃdha; 19 B [*bara*-omitted]; 20 A kiyo; EI liyo; M liyau hai [*hai* lightly erased]; 21 A [omitted]; 22 A citai; 23 A muṣa morī.

Metre : 16+16 *mātrās*.

CP 79.

१ रहसि[1] रहसि मोहन[2] पिय[3] के सँग[4]
लडैंती अति रस[5] लटकति[6] ।

२ सरस सुधंग[7] अंग मैं[8] नागरि[9]
थेई[10] थेई[11] कहति[12] अवनि पद[13] पटकति[14] ॥

३ कोक कला[15] कुल[16] जानि[17] सिरोमनि[18]
अभिनय कुटिल भृकुटियनि[19] मटकति[20] ।

४ बिबस[21] भये[22] प्रीतम[23] अलि[24] लंपट[25]
निरषि करज नासापुट[26] चटकति[27] ॥

५ गुन[28] गन[29] रसिकराइ[30] चूडामनि[31]
रिझवत[32] पदिक[33] हार[34] पट[35] झटकति[36] ।

६ हित[37] हरिबंश[38] निकट[39] दासी[40] जन
लोचन चषक रसासव[41] गटकति[42] ॥

1 C [line inverted : *rī . . laṭakati* foll. by double *daṃḍa* and then *rahasi . . sãga*]; 2 I mauhana; 3 A pīya; 4 all MSS sãga rī [foll. in A by double *daṃḍa* as for line end]; 5 A saṃsa [*-sa* replaces original]; 6 FK laṭakata; 7 E sugaṃdha; 8 ABE mai; CGHIJKM mẽ; 9 C nāgarī; 10 C thei; 11 CD thei; 12 FGIJKM kahani; 13 CF paga; I pada pada; 14 FJKM paṭakata [J emended to *paṭakati, sec. m.*]; 15 A [foll. by *guna* (crossed out)]; 16 C kuśala; K [one *akṣara* erased between *ku-* and *-la*]; 17 A jani; 18 C siromanī; GHL śiromaṇi; M siromaṇi; 19 AC bhrakuṭiyani; E bhṛkuṭīyani; F bhṛkuṭiyana; 20 FK maṭakata; 21 CGH bibaśa; 22 AIJ bhae; B bhaai; C bhayẽ; 23 D pītama; 24 C alī; 25 K laṃpaṭi; 26 CHL nāśā°; 27 A laṭakati [emended to *caṭakati, sec. m.*]; FK caṭakata; 28 GHILM guṇa; 29 GHIM gaṇa; 30 ACE rasikarāī; BHJ rasikarāya; M rasakarāi; 31 BE cuḍāmani; C cūḍāmanī; GHLM cūḍāmaṇi; 32 ACL rijhavati; M rijhivata; 33 A padīka; E padeka; H pādaka; 34 A hāru; 35 I pada; 36 DFKM jhaṭakata; 37 ABCDEFGHIJKL jai śrī hita; M jai śrī hiti; 38 AEM haribaṃsa; 39 A niraṣi; 40 I dāśī; 41 K ramāsava; 42 DFK gaṭakata.

Metre : 16+16 *mātrās*.

CP 80.

१ बल्लबी[1] सुकनक बल्लरी[2] तमाल स्याम[3] संग
लागि[4] रही अंग अंग मनोभिरामिनी[5] ।

२ बदन जोति[6] मनो[7] मयंक अलक तिलक छबि[8] कलंक
छपति[9] स्याम[10] अंक मानौं[11] जलद[12] दामिनी ॥

३ बिगत[13] बास हेम षंभ[14] मनो[15] भुवंग[16] बेनि[17] दंड
पिय[18] के कंठ प्रेम[19] पुंज कुंज कामिनी ।
४ सोभित[20] हरिबंश[21] नाथ साथ सुरत अलसवंत[22]
उरज कनक कलस[23] राधिका[24] सुनामिनी[25] ॥

1 E balabī; 2 EF balarī; 3 HL śyāma; 4 G [*lāgi rahī* omitted, though space provided in printed page layout]; 5 A mānõ abhirāminī [*a*- lightly erased]; B manobhirāmīnī; F manõ abhirāminī; JKL manaubhirāminī; M manobhirāmanī; 6 CH jyoti; F jota; 7 A janu; BEHJ manau; CI manõ; DF manaũ; GKM māno; L mānaũ; 8 M chaba; 9 BDIJ chapita; F chapata; L chipati; 10 BGHL śyāma; 11 ACM mānõ; BEFH manau; DIJ manaũ; G māno; K manõ; 12 B jaladi; 13 BDJ bigati; 14 B ṣaṃbhi; 15 AC mānõ; BHJK manau; C manõ; DFL manũ; GM māno; 16 B bhavaga; DGJLM bhavaṃga [J emended to *bhuvaṃga*, *sec. m.*]; 17 ABDFK bainī; CIJ benī; E bīne; GHLM beṇī; 18 A pīya; 19 A praima; 20 ABDEFIJKLM jai śrī sobhita; CGH jai śrī śobhita; 21 AEM haribaṃsa; K [*-baṃ-* omitted, added *sec. m.*]; 22 ABCDFGHIJKLM ālasavāta: 23 BCGHL kalaśa; 24 A rādhike; 25 B susunāminī.

Metre : (7x/ ⏓⏓ ⏑ ⏓⏓ ⏑ /)$^{+}$/—/

CP 81.

१ बृषभाननंदिनी[1] मधुर कल[2] गावै[3] ।
२ बिकट औघर[4] तान चर्चरी[5] ताल सौं[6]
नंदनंदन मनसि[7] मोद उपजावै[8] ॥
३ प्रथम मज्जन[9] चारु चीर[10] कज्जल तिलक
श्रवन[11] कुंडल बदन चंदनि[12] लजावै[13] ।
४ सुभग नक बेसरी[14] रतन[15] हाटक जरी
अधर बँधूक[16] दसन[17] कुंद[18] चमकावै[19] ॥
५ बलय कंकन[20] चारु उरसि[21] राजत[22] हार[23]
कटि ब किंकिनि[24] चरन[25] नूपुर[26] बजावै ।
६ हंसकल[27] गामिनी मथत[28] मद कामिनी[29]
नषनि[30] मदयंतिका[31] रंग[32] रुचि द्यावै[33] ॥
७ नृत्य[34] सागर रभस[35] रहसि[36] नागरि[37] नवल
चंदचाली[38] बिबिधि[39] भेदनि[40] जनावै[41] ।
८ कोक बिद्या[42] बिदित[43] भाइ[44] अभिनय[45] निपुन[46]
भ्रू[47] बिलासनि[48] मकरकेतनि[49] नचावै[50] ॥
९ निबिड[51] कानन भवन बाहु रंजित[52] रवन[53]
सरस आलाप[54] सुष पुंज बरषावै ।
१० उभै[55] संगम सिंधु[56] सुरत पूषन-[57] बंधु[58]
द्रवत मकरंद हरिबंश[59] अलि पावै[60] ॥

1 E braṣabhāna°; H bṛṣabhānu°; IM °naṃdanī; 2 B kalā; I kali; 3 B gavai; CJ gāvaĩ; G lagāvai; 4 A aughaṭa [emended to *aughara*, *sec. m.*]; CEFH avaghara; 5 A cacarī; B caracarī; E carcarā; 6 ACFGM sõ; B sau; 7 A masina; F manasa; M manisa; 8 CJ upajāvaĩ; 9 BEIK maṃjana; F maṃjjana; J majana [emended to *majjana*, *sec. m.*]; 10 I rucira; 11 GHILM śravaṇa; 12 J caṃdana; 13 C lajāvaĩ; 14 A besari; L beśarī; 15 CL ratna; 16 AEI baṃdhuka; B badhūka; 17 CHL daśana; 18 M [*-da* replaces original crossed-out reading]; 19 C camakāvaĩ; 20 GHLM kaṃkaṇa; 21 M [followed by *padakana*, covered with yellow paste]; 22 A rājatu; 23 ACH hāru; B hāṭa; 24 B kikini; CHLM kiṃkiṇi; F kiṃkani; G kiṃkiṇī; 25 GHILM caraṇa; 26 E nupura; 27 L haṃśa°; 28 A mathati; G mathita; M [*mathata mada kāminī* omitted, *maṃthita mada kāminī* added *sec. m.*]; 29 A kāminī; D [*kā-* replaces original reading]; 30 F naṣana; 31 ACKL madaaṃtikā; B madayatikā; E madaatikā; 32 M [*-ga* replaces original reading]; 33 B dhāvai; G dyāve; 34 ABDI nirtta; C nirttya; EHJ nirta; 35 AH rabhasi; F rabhisa; 36 E rahasī; K [emended to *rahasa*]; 37 FGI nāgara; 38 A ciṃdacāli; B caṃdracālī; G cidacālī; J caṃducālī [emended to *ciṃducālī*, *sec. m.*]; M ciṃdacālī; 39 M bibadha [emended to *bibadhi*, *sec. m.*]; 40 F bhedana; 41 B tanāvai; 42 B bidhā; 43 E bidata; 44 AE bhāī; F bhāya; H bhāva; 45 M abhanaya [two *akṣaras* crossed out between *abha-* and *-naya*]; 46 H nipuṇa; M napuni; 47 B bhu; E bhu; 48 FM bilāsana; 49 I mikara°; 50 C nacāvaĩ; 51 CE nibaḍa; 52 E rājita; 53 GM ravaṇa; H ramaṇa; 54 BD ālāpi; F ālapa; H alāpa; 55 AHJL ubhaya; B ūbhai; I ubhe; 56 A siṃdha; B sidha; C siṃdhū; 57 E puṣana; GHLM pūṣaṇa; 58 BC baṃdhū; E baṃdha; 59 AEM haribaṃsa; 60 C pāvaĩ.

Metre: (7x/⏓⏓ ⏑ ⏓⏓/)$^{+}$/4m/.

CP 82.

१ नागरता[1] की रासि[2] किशोरी[3] ।
२ नव नागर कुल मौलि[4] साँवरौ[5]
बरबस[6] कियौ[7] चितै[8] मुष मोरी ॥
३ रूप रुचिर अँग अंग माधुरी
बिनु[9] भूषन[10] भूषित[11] ब्रज[12] गोरी ।
४ छिन[13] छिन[14] कुशल[15] सुधंग[16] अंग[17] मैं[18]
कोक रभस[19] रस सिंधु[20] झकोरी[21] ॥
५ चंचल रसिक मधुप मोहन[22] मन
राषे[23] कनक कमल कुच कोरी ।
६ प्रीतम[24] नैन[25] जुगल[26] षंजन[27] षग
बाँधे[28] बिबिधि[29] निबंधन[30] डोरी ॥

७ अवनी उदर नाभि सरसी मैं[31]
मनहु[32] कछुक[33] मादिक[34] मधु घोरी ।
८ हित[35] हरिबंश[36] पिवत[37] सुन्दर बर
सौंव[38] सुदृढ[39] निगमनि[40] की तोरी ॥

1 BDIJ nāgaritā [J emended to *nāgaratā, sec. m.*]; 2 F rāsa; GH rāśi; 3 M kisorī; 4 EF maula; 5 A syavaro; BD sāvarau; CI sā̃varo; 6 E [*-ba-* omitted]; 7 A liyau; E kiyai; IM kiyo; 8 CI cite; 9 B [followed by double *daṇḍa* as for line end]; EFGIKM bina; 10 A bhūṣina [emended to *bhūṣana*]; E bhuṣana; GHM bhūṣaṇa; 11 A bhūṣata [emended to *bhūṣita*]; E bhṛṣita; I [emended to bhūṣana]; 12 A bṛja; 13 AE chinu; H kṣana; 14 AE chinu; H kṣana; 15 AFM kusala; 16 EM sugaṃdha [M emended to *sudhaṃga, sec. m.*]; 17 B āṃga; 18 ABDJ mai; CGHKM mẽ; 19 H rabhasi; 20 M siṃdha; 21 K jhakajhorī; 22 A mohāna; G [follows next]; 23 AL rāṣyau; 24 B pītama; 25 AEFIJK nena [J emended to *naina, sec. m.*]; 26 H yugala; 27 D [one *akṣara* crossed out between *ṣaṃ-* and *-jana*]; G ṣaṃḍana; 28 ABDI bādhe; 29 M bibidha; 30 E nibaṃdhani; I nabaṃdhana; 31 ABE mai; CGHJKM mẽ; 32 CHL manahū̃; F manaū̃; G mānõ; M māno; 33 C kachūka; 34 CE mādaka; 35 all MSS jai śrī hita; 36 BEM haribaṃsa; 37 FGIM pīvata; 38 ABDK sīva; C sī̃vā; 39 A sudṛḍha; B sudaḍha; F sudiḍha; M sudṛḍhi; 40 I nigamana.

Metre : 16+16 *mātrās*.

CP 83.

१ छाडि[1] दै[2] मानिनी[3] मान मन धरिबौ[4] ।
२ प्रणत[5] सुंदर सुघर प्राणबल्लभ[6] नवल[7]
बचन[8] आधीन[9] सौं[10] इतौ[11] कत[12] करिबौ ॥
३ जपत[13] हरि बिबस[14] तव[15] नाम प्रतिपद[16] बिमल
मनसि[17] तव[18] ध्यान तें[19] निमिष[20] नहि[21] टरिबौ ।
४ घटत[22] पलु[23] पलु[24] सुभग सरद[25] की जामिनी[26]
भामिनी सरस अनुराग दिस[27] ढरिबौ[28] ॥
५ हौं[29] जु कछु[30] कहति[31] निजु[32] बात सुनि मानि[33] सषि[34]
सुमुषि[35] बिन[36] काज घन[37] बिरह दुष[38] भरिबौ ।
६ मिलत हरिबंश[39] हित कुंज किशलय[40] सैन[41]
करत[42] कल[43] केलि[44] सुष सिंधु[45] मैं[46] तरिबौ ॥

1 AHK chā̃ḍi; M chāḍa; 2 CJ daĩ; 3 FIM mānanī; H maninī; J [emended to *mānanī*]; 4 E dharibai; M dharabau; 5 AE pranata; 6 AEF prāna°; 7 E valana [emended to *navala, sec. m.*]; 8 B [followed. by *prayā jī so bacana* (from Lok.'s *ābhāsa* to CP 84)]; 9 B adhīna; 10 ACFG sõ; BK sau; D [omitted]; 11 CI ito; E ītau; 12 A karata; F kita; I kati; 13 K

japati; 14 CGH bibaśa; 15 LM tuva; 16 A priti°; M prata°; 17 M [-*na*- omitted, added *sec. m.*]; 18 L tuva: 19 BE te; HK taĩ; 20 ABCDEFJM nimaṣa; H nimiṣi; I nimaṣi; 21 DHJL nahī̃; G nāhi; 22 ABDEJL ghaṭati; 23 FHKM pala; 24 FHKM pala; 25 GH śarada; 26 H yāminī; M jāmanī; 27 CL diśa; D [-*sa* omitted, added *sec. m.*]; GH diśi; JK disi; 28 ACE ḍaribau; K ḍharibo; 29 ABEK hau; CGIM hõ; 30 A kachū; 31 FHKM kahata; J [emended to *kahata*]; 32 FGLM ika; J [emended to *ika, sec. m.*]; K [2 *akṣaras* erased between *ni*- and -*ju*]; 33 FGHKM māna; 34 AFM saṣī; 35 ABDFIJKLM sumuṣa; C sumuṣi; 36 ABCEJL binu; 37 E dha; J [omitted, added *sec. m.*]; 38 A duṣu; M duṣi; 39 EM haribaṃsa; 40 AEJKM kisalaya; 41 CF sayana; EGIJK sena [J emended to *saina, sec. m.*]; 42 J karati; [emended to *karata, sec. m.*]; 43 AI kali [A emended to *kala*]; 44 AC kelī; M kela: 45 F siṃdha; 46 ABE mai; CFGHJKM mẽ.

Metre : (3x/5+5/) + /5/ + / ⏑⏑⏑⏑ /

CP 84.

१ आजु[1] देषियत[2] है[3] प्यारी[4] रंग[5] भरी ।

२ मोपैं[6] न दुरत[7] चोरी[8] बृषभान[9] किशोरी[10]

सिथल[11] कटि[12] की डोरी नंद के लाल[13] सौं[14] सुरत लरी ॥

३ मोतिन[15] लर[16] टूटी चिकुर चंद्रिका[17] छूटी[18]

रहसि रसिक लूटी[19] गंडनि[20] पीक परी ।

४ नैननि[21] आलस बस अधर बिंब निरस[22]

पुलकि[23] प्रेम[24] परस[25] हित[26] हरिबंश[27] राजत[28] षरी ॥

[Vulgate text is given on next page]

1 all MSS [followed. by *ba*; '*ba* in H]; 2 ABCJL deṣiyati; 3 A hau; F haĩ; I he; 4 all MSS ho pyārī; 5 F [*raṃga bharī* omitted]; 6 CE °pẽ; GM° paī; 7 ACDL durati; E durita; 8 L caurī [emended to *corī*]; 9 E braṣabhāna; GHM bṛṣabhānu; 10 M kisorī; 11 A sithila; H śithila; L [*sithala kaṭi kī ḍorī* omitted]; 12 M takaṭa; 13 ACDEFHKL lālana; JM [emended to *lālana, sec. m.*]; 14 ACFGHIM sõ; BK sau; 15 AL motini; C motīyani; D mutiyanu; E mītiyana; FHM motiyana; G mutiyana; IJ motinu [J emended to *motiyanu, sec. m.*]; K motiyani; 16 M lari; 17 M caṃdrakā; 18 EM chuṭī; 19 B luṭī; 20 FIJK gaṃḍana [K emended to *gaṃḍani*]; 21 A nainā; C nayana; I nenana; J nenani; 22 BGHM narasa [GH printed *na rasa*]; I narasi; 23 BFGHJM pulaka; L [*pulaki prema parasa* omitted]; 24 A praima; 25 A parasi; 26 ABCDEFGHIJK jai śrī hita; M jai śrī hiti; 27 AE haribaṃsa rī; B haribaṃśa i [*i* emended to *rī, sec. m.*]; CDFGHIJKL haribaṃśa rī; M harabaṃsa rī; 28 ABDEJ rājati.

Metre : [10+10+X *mātrās*]

Vulgate text (with orthography standardized)

१ आजु ब देषियत है हो प्यारी रंग भरी ।
२ मोपै न दुरत चोरी बृषभान की किशोरी
सिथल कटि की डोरी नंद के लाल(न) सौं सुरत लरी ॥
३ मोतिन/मोतियनि लर टूटी चिकुर चंद्रिका छूटी
रहसि रसिक लूटी गंडनि पीक परी ।
४ नैननि आलस बस अधर बिंब निरस
पुलकि प्रेम परस हित हरिबंश री राजत षरी ॥

CHAPTER V

THE CAURĀSĪ PADA: ANNOTATED TRANSLATION

The translations offered here attempt the usual compromise between a readable English style and faithfulness to the original, any freedom of rendering usually being acknowledged and explained in a note; no justification has been given, however, for the free rendering of compounds, since literal translation of compounded forms would inevitably lead to an obscure or elliptical sentence in the English. The couplet-based construction of the text, shown in the previous chapter by the use of the traditional single and double *daṇḍas* for alternate lines of the *mūla,* is generally shown by the use of semi-colons and full stops for odd and even lines respectively.

The descriptive and eulogistic themes of the CP do not, for the most part, call for any special contextualization (*pace* the commentators, for whom contextualization is an important device in the imposition of desired interpretations), and introductory comments have therefore been given only when it is necessary to resolve ambiguities or obscurities.

Since the object of the study is to analyse the CP as it stands, rather than from the point of view of developed sectarian *siddhānta,* the translations are intended to be theologically 'neutral'. Sectarian constructions of the *mūla* are discussed in the annotations, where the *ṭīkās* of Dhar., Rasik., Prem., Lok. and LCG are analysed. (These commentaries have been introduced in section II.4.) Clearly it has been neither possible nor desirable to discuss each and every point of interpretation from the lengthy *ṭīkās,* but the annotations aim to show a representative sample, forming the basis for a discussion (in section VII.4) of the sectarian reading of the text. The *ṭīkās* are often referred to in discussions of cruxes such as variant manuscript readings and obscurities of syntax. Translations of quoted extracts from the *ṭīkās* are usually appended only where an annotation seeks to propose a particular reading of the gloss. Annotations are headed by line-number, so that they may be approached either directly from the *mūla* or via the translation. References to dictionary entries are to the word in question *sub voce,* unless specified otherwise.

CP 1.

1 Whatever my beloved does, pleases me
and whatever pleases me, that my beloved does;

2 the place that I cherish is in the eyes of my beloved,
and my beloved seeks to become the apple of my eyes.

3 My beloved is yet dearer to me than body, mind, and life-breath,
and my beloved has given himself up to me ten million times over;

4 Hita Harivaṃśa, as swan and pen are the dark one and the fair—
tell me, who could separate the water from the waves?

Context: Rādhā speaks in the first three lines.

(1)-(4) This first stanza is metrically irregular: the *ṣaṭpadī* formulation found in other stanzas of similar line-length is not apparent here; nor is there any trace of *varṇavṛtta* rhythm, the sequence of *gurus* in the first line being particularly anomalous. The two component couplets of the stanza each have a rough overall coherence in moric length, (1) consisting of 26+26 *mātrās* and (2) of 26+25 while (3) and (4) are of 21+23 and 22+20 *mātrās* respectively. The syntax of line (1) suggests a *pāda* construction of 15+11+11+15 *mātrās*, and an initial *pāda* of 15 *mātrās* may also be discerned in lines (3) and (4); an 11-*mātrā pāda* recurs in the second half-line of (2) and (3), while in (4) the 9-*mātrā* phrase *kahau kauna karai*, with its semantic and alliterative cohesion, may be understood as a catalectic variation on this.

Omission of *ke* from the first half-line of (2) in L may indicate an attempt to achieve a syllabic scansion, yielding a line construction of 14+14 syllables in (1) and (2): but a crude syllabic construction is not preferable to a moric one. (Excision of *tau* would in any case be a preferable emendation if such were sought, since analytical *pyāre ke nainani* is clearly preferable to **pyāre nainani*; and cf. accretion of *tau* in some manuscripts in line (3).

Inclusion in (3) of *to*/*tau* after *mere* in B(E)FGIJM is apparently an attempt to approximate the line length of (3) to the preceding lines, or to achieve two half-lines of equal length within (3), and follows *mokau tau* in the previous line. The superfluous reduplication of *prāna* in the same line in BDIJ (and expansed to *prāne te prāna* in F) may have a similar intention.

The first line, with its repeated relative-correlative construction, bears a close resemblance to the *padas* of Svāmī Haridāsa, in which such constructions are strikingly common. The first line of *Siddhānta ke pada*, for example, reads as follows (Prabhudayāl Mītal 1961:57):

jyõhī jyõhī tuma rākhata hau,
tyõhī rahiyata haũ ho hari.

(With a single exception (*Kelimāla* 33, *op.cit.*, p. 77), all the *padas* attributed to Haridāsa resemble CP 1 in having a construction of four lines; and most have limited metrical coherence.)

(4) *haṃsa haṃsinī*: 'swan and pen', though not a literal translation, preserves in English idiom the intended idea of inseparability.

(4) *taraṃgani*: the BCEF form *taraṃginī* 'river' is an inappropriate Sanskritization, the true reading being an obl. pl. -*ani* form.

CP 2.

1 Now the night is beautiful
with a meeting of lightning and fresh cloud;

2 Mohana is a king amongst lovers: what kind of woman is she
who would show capricious anger towards him?

3 Hearing this, Hita Harivaṃśa, she of elephant gait
joined Rādhāramaṇa.

(1) In all manuscripts the line begins with the phrase *pyāre bolī bhāminī/-anī*, which together with following *āju nīkī jāminī* yields an unprecedented long sequence of *guru* syllables. Given the frequency with which *āju* occurs in line-initial position at the beginning of the stanza (cf. 4.1, 5.1, 7.1, 10.1 etc.), it seems almost certain that *pyāre bolī bhāminī* must be a commentatorial accretion, later confused in the extant commentaries and prefixed to the *ṭeka* on the basis of its *-inī* rhyme. A semantic argument supports the hypothesis that *pyāre bolī bhāminī* is an accretion. Grammatically, *pyāre* can only be vocative here, with *bhāminī* as subject of *bolī*: yet the addressing of such a statement by Rādhā to Kṛṣṇa ('Dear one', said the lady, 'today...') is unattested in the text and cannot be considered likely. Prem. Dhar. and LCG interpret *pyāre bolī* as agentive, with the verb allegedly showing concord with *bhāminī*; such a transitive agentive usage is attested in the phrase *benu dhuni nādalāla bolī* (28.3), but a reference to a specific (human) object as here would normally require transitive *bulā-* (cf. 38.1, 63[ii].2) rather than *bol-*. Lok. and Rasik. attempt to accommodate *bolī* by interpreting this *pāda* as being addressed to Kṛṣṇa by a *sakhī*; but this vocative use of *pyāre* by a *sakhī* is also unattested, and furthermore requires an awkward change of subject later in the stanza.

The whole of the first line is metrically dissimilar to the following lines, the received text of which is readily edited to a consistent 10+10+12 *mātrā ṣaṭpadī* construction as described in the following notes. With its anomalous scansion and anomalous (A)AA rhyme, line (1) is perhaps appended as a heading to the coherent couplet of (2)-(3); such a hypothesis would explain another anomaly, viz. the odd number of lines in the stanza (a feature found in only one other example, CP 69).

(1) *navīna*: excision of this word would reduce the final *pāda* to the 12-*mātrā* form found in subsequent lines (reading *saudāminī*); yet *navīna* is semantically apposite, and general uncertainty about the relation of (1) to the remaining lines prohibits excision on purely metrical grounds.

(1) *saudāminī*: all the commentators read *sau* (in its various spellings) as a post-position, yielding analytical *megha sau dāminī*; yet such a collocation can hardly compete with that involving the semi-*tatsama saudāminī*. (*HŚS* cites Saudāmanī as a *rāginī*, consort (*sahacarī*) to the *rāga* Megha: this is confirmation that the *megha-saudāminī* collocation is an established one.) In view of probable scribal understanding of *sau* as a post-position, nasalization in the MSS is here shown in the apparatus.

(2) All the manuscripts have the semantically redundant *rī māī/-i* after *rasika*. This appears to be an attempt to achieve a *pāda* length roughly coherent with the *pādas* of (1); cf. the accretion of *māī* to the performed version of CP 12, discussed in chapter VI. Excision of *rī māī* reinstates a (weak) *pāda* rhyme, *-ka rāi/karai*.

(3) The *pyārī* which follows *sunata* in all the manuscripts is presumed to be intrusive, since it has no clear place in the syntax of the line, but duplicates the subject function of *gajagāminī*; cf. intrusive *pyāre* (etc.) in (1) above. With *pyārī* excised, the *pāda sunata rādhāravana* has the 10-*mātrā* value of preceding *hita haribaṃśa śravana*.

(3) *rādhāravana*: the manuscripts all read *rādhikā°*. Following a first *pāda* of 10 *mātrās*, and with strong *pāda* rhyme in *-avana*, however, *rādhā°* must surely be intended as the correct metrical form. Elsewhere in the text, *rādhā°* is attested twice (16.5, 19.14), whereas *rādhikā°* occurs only in metrically corrupt passages (40.6, 65.4). In the present line, imposition of *rādhikā* may show an attempt to match the prevailing 12-*mātrā* construction of the *pāda* (first two lines); a sectarian attempt to dissimilate the epithet from *rādhāramaṇa* (as particularly associated with the rival Gauḍīya *sampradāya*) may also be involved.

CP 3.

1 At dawn the two are [still] greedy for love,
rejoicing greatly in their victory in the battle of passion;
2 heavy drops of perspiration are on their faces,
and the adornments on their various limbs are in disarray.
3 Of their *tilakas* but little remains,
curly locks like wayward bees are loose on lotus-faces;
4 Hita Harivaṃśa, their eyes and words are steeped in the colour of love,
and their clothes lie loose at their waists!

(2) *śrama bārija*: all the commentaries take this phrase, with its pleonastically suffixed *-ja*, as qualifying *ghana biṃdu*; thus Prem. *śrama bāri nāma prasveda ko hai. tāsõ ju upajī ghanī bū̃de so muṣa para birāje haĩ.* Prolixity in the *ṭīkā* here reflects pleonasm in the *mūla*. (The collocation *bāri jaghana* in printed text G reappears in the *ṭīkā* in G but appears to be a printer's error.)
(3) *sithala*: since there is an excess of one *mātrā* in the line, M's reading *sthila* may be an ingenuous attempt to correct metre and thereby to allow *rahyau* its full metrical weight of three *mātrās*.
(4) *madana*: this and its derivative *maina*, along with synonyms such as *kāma*, may of course be interpreted as personifications of 'passion' rather than as abstract. Commentators interpret the two senses variously in different locations, but the overall sense is barely affected.
(4) *rãga rãgi*: repetition of *rãg-* may intend a *śleṣa* here, with *rãga* to be taken in its dramatic sense; thus, 'enjoying the theatre of love'. No commentator, however, proposes this.
(4) *dukūla*: a fine cloth made either of cotton or of the bark of the *dukūla* tree (Motīcandra p. 54).

CP 4.

1 Today, young girl, your joyful face
imparts your heart's ease at union with the lover;
2 wrapped in lethargy are your words, tinted in a pretty hue your cheeks,
weary and red your sleepless eyes.
3 Your lovely *tilaka* is but a trace, the blossoms in your hair are scattered,
and your hair-parting is as though you had not adorned it at all;
4 bountiful mine of compassion, when you proffer your lips
you withhold none of their essence!
5 Why do you conceal yourself timidly? You have exchanged garments with your lover,
and subjugated Śyāma, instructing a hundred Kāmadevas;
6 the garland on your chest is wilted and your circlet of bells loose,
Hita Harivaṃśa, in the bed in the house of creepers!

(1)–(6) Readings of *tau/to* are found in all the manuscripts following *āju* in (1); later in the line, the phrase *piya saṃgama sūcata* appears in the manuscripts with analytical *ke* after both nouns, *piya ke saṃgama ke sūcata*. With these accretions excised, a *ṣaṭpadī* construction of 10+10+15 *mātrās* is attained (with the usual licences), the only inconsistencies being (catalectic?) 9-*mātrā* first *pādas* in (3) and (6), matched by a 9-*mātrā* second *pāda* in (3). Accretion of *tau* may reflect an erroneous interpretation of the stanza's construction as *varṇika*, since with *tau* retained in (1), the first two *pādas* of every line each constitute 8 *varṇas*; the fact that no consistent *varṇika* construction persists in the third *pāda* shows, however, that this syllabic scansion is at most a superficial tendency. Accretion of the genitive case-markers in (1) cannot be explained on metrical grounds; rather this expansion of the line must be commentatorial. The redundance of both case-markers is demonstrated in Dhar.'s gloss *piya saṃgama suṣa sūcatai sobhita tana hita sāja*, where they are conspicuously absent: this may even reflect a lost authentic reading.

In all lines except the first, both 10-*mātrā* *pādas* consist of 5 *mātras* + ⏑⏑—⏑ (while the 9-*mātrā* *pādas* in (3) and (6) consist of 4 *mātrās* + ⏑⏑—⏑). The same pattern can only be achieved in (1) by reinstating *tau* and adopting the following hypothetical scansion:

—⏑ ⏑ ⏑⏑ —⏑//⏑⏑⏑—⏑⏑ — ⏑
**iau tau juvati terau badana ānãda bharyau.*

Since standard practice is opposed to the scansion **bhāryau* (scansion: — ⏑), this scansion must ultimately be disallowed, and line (1) regarded as anomalous in respect of its internal rhyme.

No fixed sequence of long and short syllables persists throughout the *pāda*- initial *gaṇas*, though the first *pāda* has occurrences of —⏑⏑⏑ *gaṇas* in (1), (2), (5).

The moric construction of the final *pāda* in this stanza is 5+5+ ⏑⏑—⏑, with the exception that the division between the first two *gaṇas* is transgressed in (6) by -*baṃ*- (and in (5) by *syā*-, if reading *basa kiyẽ syāma siṣai* by analogy with (6)).

(2) Pleonastic *dŏu* is metrically superfluous and may be an accretion.

(4) *karunākara*: while the commentators all construe this as a phrase involving absolutive or postpositional *kara/kari* in composition with *karunā*, the general prevalence of the compound form *karuṇākara* must render such an interpretation unlikely.

(4) *rāṣata kachu na sāra*: the idea is of the lips being drained of colour—cf. 15.4 etc.

(5) *palaṭe prītama cira*: Lok. extends the reference of this phrase, and interprets the whole stanza as being addressed to Kṛṣṇa in Rādhā's guise.

(6) *kīkini*: a reading of the first syllable as short yields the metrical pattern of 9+9+15 *mātrās* found in (3). Cf. notes on 36.3 and 67.6.

CP 5.

1 Today at dawn in the creeper-palace
   joy rains down, and the fine couple is rapturous;
2 the fair and the dark, delightful, brimful with love,
   set their feet upon the ground so unsteadily.
3 Tinged with the saffron of her breasts is the many-stranded garland
   of glorious Śrī Śyāma, lord of amorous pleasure;
4 and the beloved is decorated with the marks of love,
   traced by the very hand of the foremost of the adroit!

5 Greatly delighted by their affection,
the two sing softly and steal each other's heart away;

6 Hita Harivaṃśa, the *ali,* intent on their praise,
imparts a sweeter tone to their singing.

(3) *dhāmadhara*: cf. *dhāma-* forms cited by *MW*, *dhāmabhāj/-adhipa/-vat*. Thus Lok. glosses *prakāsa ke dharanahāre* 'possessed of brilliance' (though Lok. applies this to the *mālāvali*, whereas position indicates that it qualifies *syāma*). (Prem. interprets *dhāma* as 'body', with *-dhara* as absolutive; thus *apane dhāma para dhāre haĩ.*)
(6) *parāyana*: Dhar.'s reading *parāī na* is reflected in his gloss, *gāna parāī na dampati bhāvata*, 'no other singing appeals to the couple'.
(6) *ali* intends the usual pun of *sakhī*/bee.
(6) Rasik. appears to interpret *tara* as *tāla* (cf. *HŚS*, where *tala* is defined as 'slap'): *madhura madhura dai tāla.*

CP 6.

1 Who is the deft young beloved whom you meet, Lāla,
like a thief in the night?

2 —listen dear one, no matter how you try you cannot conceal
your contented eyes, maddened with love.

3 On your chest are moon-shaped nailmarks, your clothes are another's
and your speech is incoherent;

4 Hita Harivaṃśa, Rādhā's lord the lover is devastated by passion!

(1)-(4) A wide variation in the length of second *pādas* suggests that this is a composite stanza formed from diverse sources; no two lines have a common metrical structure, although a first *pāda* of 16 *mātrās* is common to all lines except (3), which has 14 *mātrās*. It is noteworthy that the *pāda, hita haribaṃśa rasika rādhāpati* occurs a further *two* times in the text —in 9.6 and 36.12.

A line construction of 16+14 *mātrās* as found in (1) is not attested elsewhere in the text. Hypothetical excision of the vocative *lāla* would establish a standard 16+11 *mātrā* line, which could be matched in (2) by a similar hypothetical excision of *caina maĩ* (the double locative *raṃga maĩ, caina maĩ*, both analytical, being unusual and inelegant):

(1) **milata cora hvai raina;*
(2) **rãga maĩ gahile naina.*

The hypothetical adjustments are speculative, however, and cannot form the basis for a reconstruction of the text; nor is the incompatibility of the remaining lines, which are both internally coherent, explainable from the manuscript evidence. (G's reading *maĩ na* for *mẽ naina* in (2) is not helpful, since neither as printed nor as **maina* does this collocation cohere semantically.)

In addition to a relatively literal interpretation of the stanza, Lok. gives a second *artha* based on the concept of *antaraṅga vihāra.*
(1) *jāhi*: *-hi* is not regular in composition with *mil-*, which usually takes the postposition *saũ.*
(2) *ba*: though sometimes possibly representing (its etymon?) Sk. *evam, ba* usually appears to be equatable with *aba* 'now'. Of the 16 occurrences in the text (ignoring one excised occurrence in the vulgate of 84.1), six follow *-aũ* in a monosyllable, as

here, while the remainder follow words of two short syllables such as *kasi* (14.3), *suni* (28.3), *kata* (28.4). This pattern suggests that the usage is largely formulaic, perhaps incorporated as a metrical 'filler'.

CP 7.

1 Today in the pleasant bower, sport young boy and youthful
damsel;

2 quite matchless is their mutual attachment—
hear me, the couple [plays] on an incorporeal earth.

3 Fresh camphor and pollen abound
on the ground of divers corals and crystals made;

4 on a beautiful couch of tender shoots
the fair one has been seated by the dark.

5 They are wholly intent on the mirth and merriment of their union
and betel juice gilds their lily-cheeks;

6 an enchanting quarrel of hands fair and dark
loosens the cord of her waistband knot.

7 The artless girl becomes agitated, mistakenly filled with pique
on seeing herself in the mirror on Hari's chest;

8 alluring her [by touching] her comely chin, the lover enlightens her,
coaxing her and showing it is only a reflection.

9 Hearing the ambrosial words 'No! No!',
Lalitā and the others watch furtively;

10 Hita Harivaṃśa, shaking her hands in love's feigned anger
she has broken her garlands!

(1) For a discussion of the *nikuñja* setting see R. Snell 1985.
(1) *maṃju*: A reads *muṃja* in both *mūla* and commentary; and cf. A's *muja* for *maṃju* in 17.3. H. *mũja* < Sk. *muñja* 'a kind of grass' (*CDIAL* 10184) may be intended, but no other textual context associating this with *nikuñja* surroundings has been observed.
(5) *mithuna*: all the commentators gloss as 'pair' (*doū* or *jugala*); yet the whole foot may be read as a determinative compound.
(6) *nībī baṃdhana*: although a usual term for the *nīvi*-knot is *nīvibandha* (G.S. Ghurye, p. 163), it is unlikely that the present form represents *baṃdha* with oblique pl. termination *-na* since direct case is more apposite in this accusative context; *tatsama bandhana* is therefore intended. Support for this view is found in nominative *kaṭi bā̃dhana* (77.5) and in the lack of oblique pl. *-ni* spellings in the manuscripts, while support for the opposite argument must be conceded in the single occurrence of (nominative) *kā̃cukī bā̃dha* (70.6). The crux recurs in a further three instances, all involving accusative case:

nāgara nībī baṃdhana mocata (30.11)
paṭa baṃdhana kā̃cukī kuca parasata (49.5)
budhi bala nībī baṃdhana mocata (72.9)

Cf. also occurrences of *nibaṃdh-/nibā̃dh-*: 50.3, 70.5, 82.6.

(8) *praloi*: < *pralobha*?? No other occurrence of this form has been observed except that in 75.4 referred to in the following note. Touching a person's chin is a gesture of entreaty, which is presumed to be the intention here. In his *ābhāsa* to CP 41, Prem. has the sentence *kabahũ cibuka pralocata haĩ*; but a derivation from *locayati* hardly seems apposite here, and the *-ca-* may be a misreading.
(8) *prabodhata*: this correct (finite) form is found in BDH only. In a similar context at 75.4 (*ve mṛdu cibuka praloi prabodhata*), where the finite sense is not obscured by enjambement as it is in the present line, the °*ata* form is found in K as well as in BDH.

CP 8.

1 Your lotus eyes are very red, my friend!
2 Languid, proud, passion-rapt,
after the night-wake they are no longer collyrium-blacked,
my friend.
3 The flight of the pupil springs from under drooping brow—
Mohana the hart is pierced, and cannot move, my friend!
4 Hita Harivaṃśa: you with the gait of a *kalahaṃsa*
throw [both] bees and *sakhīs* into confusion, my friend!

(2) *maṣi na malina*, 'no longer collyrium-blacked'; this interpretation is necessary in order to accommodate the form *maṣi na* since *maṣina* appears meaningless. The latter form has, however, been taken by the commentators: Rasik., Lok. *kajjala malina*, Prem. *kājara karikẽ malina*, 'smeared with kohl'. LCG's gloss reads *inakā kājala phīkā paḍa gayā hai* 'their kohl has become faded', but bases this on the reading *makhina*.
(3) *golaka*: Lit. '(eye-)ball', but also 'pupil', a sense given in *HŚS*.
(3) The second half-line has an excess of two *mātrās* unless the long syllables in *bidhayau* and *mohana* are scanned as short. Two-*mātrā mṛga* is conspicuously absent from Dhar.'s paraphrase, but no MS reading suggests that this word might be an accretion to the *mūla*.
(4) *hita haribaṃśa haṃsakala gāmini*: the same *pāda* appears again in the same metre at 73.6, and *haṃsakala gāminī* occurs at 81.6. *haṃsakala* is taken as a synonymous inversion of the more usual *kalahaṃsa*: cf. *haṃsarāja/rājahaṃsa*, *MW*. In the present line *haṃsakala*, but not *kalahaṃsa*, accords with 6+4+4+2 *mātrā* metrical construction; similarly at 81.6 *haṃsakala* is the only metrically appropriate form. The inversion here also exploits the alliterative sequence *-baṃśa haṃsa* (which is also found at 1.4 and 27.17).

CP 9.

1 The pair, Rādhā and Mohana, is adorned;
2 Śyāma Manohara is a sapphire gem,
the Fair One has a body of gold.
3 On Hari's broad forehead is a *tilaka,*
the lady has *rorī* amidst her shining hair;
4 the Lord's walk is that of a king elephant,
Vṛṣabhānu's daughter has the gait of an elephant queen.

5 The young girl has a blue mantle, Mohana a yellow garment,
  and a red mark on his head;
6 Hita Harivaṃśa, Rādhā's lord the lover
  is steeped in the dye of sensual love.

(1) The characteristic (x) +12 *mātrā* construction of the *ṭeka* in *Sāra* metre (see section VI.6.(iii)) cannot be attained on the basis of the manuscript readings. If the superfluous case-marker *kī* is excised, then a 12-*mātrā* second *pāda* is achieved with the same cadence [⌣ ⌣ — —] that is found in all successive lines.

— — — ⌣ ⌣ — —
banī // *rādhā mohana jorī*;

— ⌣ — ⌣ ⌣ ⌣ — —
[...] // *sātakuṃbha tana gorī* [etc.]

The shortness of the remaining first *pāda, banī*, may have encouraged the accretion of honorific *śrī* in AHI.

It should also be noted, however, that 15+13 *mātrā* lines are attested in Apabhraṃśa metres of 16+12 *mātrās* (*BhK* p. 49).

(2) *iṃdranīlamani...sātakuṃbha*: only Prem. makes explicit the intended image, which is of the *setting* of the sapphire in the gold.

(3) *rorī*: a turmeric-based powder used for *tilakas* (*HŚS*).

(3)–(5) Unusually for the CP, in three consecutive lines the *Sāra* caesura (after the 16th *mātrā*) is not reinforced by syntax:

bhāla bisāla tilaka hari, kāmini// *cikura caṃdra bica rorī*;
gaja nāyaka prabhu cāla, gayaṃdani// *gati bṛṣabhānakiśorī*.
nīla nicola juvati, mohana paṭa// *pīta aruna sira ṣorī*;

Though unusual in the CP, such enjambement is well attested in Apabhraṃśa (as for example in *BhK* 207.7 and 207.14).

(5) *ṣorī*: the meaning appears to be '*tilaka*' (H. *khaura, khaurī*, '*tilaka* of horizontal shape', *HŚS*); Prem. contrasts *ṣorī* with *tilaka* as regards composition: *māthe para aruna khauri hai. pahile tilaka kahi āye haĩ. so caṃdana ko jāniyai aura tarala jāniyai*'. 'On the forehead is a red *khauri*: previously was said '*tilaka*'—that is of sandal and also of jewel-form.' Lok. glosses *ṣorī* as 'turban' (*pāga*), a sense which is more apposite with *sira*, and in avoiding a repetition of the content of (3), but which is of unknown derivation and is perhaps based on a guess from *paṭa*.

CP 10.

1 Today, the wondrous pair of adroit lady and youth is most pleasing;
  what can I say of their crowning loveliness in every limb?
2 they revel in an embrace as the circle of the round-dance is joined,
  with the sweet touch of slender arms and of cheek against cheek.
3 The sport of Śyāma and the beautiful lady is loud with flute and drum
  and with a sweet tumult of anklets and other ornaments,
  waist-bells and bangles;
4 Harivaṃśa, the hidden *sakhī* sees the step of the *sudhaṅga* dancer,
  and dedicates herself, offering body and soul.

(1) *jora* retains the fem. gender (apparent in the concord of *bhāvatī*) of *jorī*, from which it derives.

(1) *kahā kahaũ*: this is the only irregular *gaṇa* in the stanza, failing to show the regular / ⏖ ⏑ ⏖ ⏑ / construction.

(2) *lāsa*: it is unclear whether or not this term signifies a particular style. In his commentary on CP 65, Rasik. shows *lāsa* as distinct from *rāsa*, and following it:

> *kāliṃdī taṭa pulina yaha suratarū nikaṭa bilāsa;*
> *tahā̃ cali sajanī milana ruci racita rāsa puni lāsa.*

Cf. Rasik.'s gloss to CP 61, where the *nṛtya* precedes the *rāsa*:

> *prathama nṛtya karike bahuri karata rāsa kī keli.*

This sequence of two distinct events brings to mind the contemporary performance of *rāsalīlā*, in which the *rāsa* dance proper is followed by one of a variety of dance-dramas depicting specific incidents in the Kṛṣṇa legend (N. Hein p. 143).

(3) *mṛdaṃga*: the North Indian barrel-drum.

(3) *tāra*: Rasik. and Prem. interpret as *(kara-)tāla* 'cymbal' (cf. the collocation *tāla mṛdaṃga* at 63.13), while Dhar. and Lok. retain the ambiguity of the *mūla*.

(4) *nirttanī*: presumably for Sk. *nartana*. *nṛ-* forms, appearing here in ADELM, are always favoured by M and appear also in CFGK (cf. 12.2 *nirttata*, 34.5 and 57.6 *nirttani*), but can only represent attempted Sanskritization.

(4) *sudhaṃga*: a dance form associated with the *rāsa* but of uncertain description. *Sudhaṃga* appears frequently in the poetry of Harivaṃśa and his contemporaries, often in alliterative contexts (with *mṛdaṃga*, *aṃga* etc.), and often associated with dance-step mnemonics (such as *tatta theī theī*, CP 68) which recreate the strong rhythms of dance styles such as *kathak*. A couplet in a *pada* of Harirāma Vyāsa (Vāsudeva Gosvāmī p. 279) suggests a relevance of eye-movements:

> *naṭavā naina sudhaṃga dikhāvata;*
> *caṃcala palaka saboda ughaṭata haĩ graṃ graṃ tat theī theī kala gāvata.*

Cf. note on the phrase *aṃga sudhaṃga diṣāvata nārī* (19.10).

CP 11.

1 In the autumn night the grove is pleasing and beautiful,
Rādhā and Hari are in radiant attire, and the moon in the night sky is full;

2 he of dark splendour and she of golden body revel together in union,
like lightning flashing amongst sapphire-blue clouds.

3 Red and yellow their fresh fine garments, a matchless source of love
the cool and fragrance-laden breeze, softly blowing;

4 on a bed made from tender shoots, the Lover speaks flattering words
but the lady in capricious pride opposes him constantly.

5 Desire churns Mohana's mind as he touches her breasts, waistband and necklace
and the fervent lady says with trembling voice, 'No! No!';

6 engross yourself to the full in the manifold sports of Naravāhana's Lord,
a river of the essence of amorous joy to purify the world.

(1) *rādhā, rākā*: the predominant /⏗⏑⏗⏑/ *gaṇa* composition is disrupted by these two words and by *narabāhana, nadī* in line (6). Lines (2)–(5) are regular throughout.
(2) *mili eka saṃga*: this tautology is maintained in the translation.
(2) *mani nīla*: manuscript evidence for *mano/-au* is weak and sporadic, though the emendment in MS A suggests some irregularity in the transmission there also. The *mano/-au* reading (to be scanned as two *laghus*) suggests that these scribes regarded the compounded image of *nīrada* and *mani nīla* to be tautological.
(6) The use of the *chāpa 'narabāhana'* has been discussed in VII 2. (i). In his gloss on this occurrence, Rasik. explains away the *chāpa* with an acronym:

> *narabāhana ihi nāma ko artha suṣada ika māni;*
> *a[c]chara prati gunasīla yuta ālī gana madhi jāni.* 18.
> ***na**vala keli **ra**sa darasa hita **bā̃**ḍhata **ha**rṣa sucitta;*
> ***na**mra sadā ati dīna hvai hita pada sevata nitta.* 19.

CP 12.

1 Come, wise Rādhikā! For your sake Śyāma has arranged a round-dance,
a store of joy, on the bank of the Yamunā;
2 groups of young girls dance in great eagerness at the music and merriment
as the joyful flute, source of delight, is playing.
3 In that most pleasing place near the *vaṃśīvaṭa*
a soft breeze blows from the [sandal-clad] Malaya mountain, yielding all joys.
4 the forest is strongly fragrant with half-blown jasmine,
and there is bright moonlight in the full-moon autumn night.
5 Cowherd girl, feast your eyes on Naravāhana's Lord,
whose head-to-toe beauty removes the agony of desire;
6 lady! Experience this ocean of delight, rejoice with your arms joined around his neck,
for Śyāma's sport in the fresh bower is worthy of the world's praise!

(1) *tere hita*: this *gaṇa* is the first of many where the /⏗⏑⏗⏑/ arrangement, more or less regular throughout CP 10 and CP 11, is not sustained; the *gaṇa* of the present stanza is best described as consisting simply of 6 *mātrās*.
(2) *rāga raṃga*: the sense 'arena of love' may alternatively be intended.
(3) *vaṃśīvaṭa*: the 'flute-banyan', the tree under which Kṛṣṇa played his flute.
(3) *jahā̃, tahā̃,* this is the only instance in this metrical type (for which see section VI.2) in which the trochaic value of the last two syllables of the first two *pādas* is dropped in favour of a rising rhythm.
(4) *bikāsa/subāsa/māsa*: this internal rhyme establishes a line construction of 12+12+12+8 *mātrās* as a variation on the predominant 12+12+9+11 construction. The same occurs with the internal rhyme *meli/jheli/keli* in line (6).
(5) *narabāhana*: for a discussion on the use of this *chāpa* see p. 462 and cf. its occurrence in 11.6.
(6) *baṃdinī*: for Sk. *vandanīya*.

CP 13.

1 Nanda's darling son has stolen my heart away!

2 I was threading my pearls on a string,
when he threw pebbles amongst them and left, my friend,
at daybreak.

3 Sidelong his glance and sprightly his step,
this crown-jewel among lovers, Nanda's boy;

4 tell me, how can the heart be withheld, when one hears
the resonance of his sweet and melodious flute?

5 For the sake of the moon of Govinda's face,
my eyes have become a *cakora* longing for a glimpse!

6 Hita Harivaṃśa: Young girl, take the lover's delight,
unite with him, friend, with your life as an offering.

(2) *kā̃kara ḍāri*: the conceit is understood as an amorous teasing, designed to draw attention, by all the commentators. (But Dhar.'s *ṭika* on this stanza is largely illegible, being written in the margins of the folio.)
(2) *ḍāri gayau*: this construction is seen by the commentators as stem *ḍāri* in composition with intensive *gayau*; thus Lok. glosses with *ḍāra dīnau*, Rasik. *ḍāri daye*. Prem. retains the *mūla*'s *ḍāri gayau*. An intensive use of *jā-* is not, however, attested elsewhere in the text, and the construction is better understood as absolutive *ḍāri* with finite *gayau*. The conceit of amorous teasing is strengthened if this sense of 'he threw pebbles, and was off' is allowed; cf. the *Sūrasāgara* version of this stanza (Appendix II), which has the explicit *ḍāri cale* in which no intensive sense is possible.
(4) *kaise*: for A's reading *kāko* cf. the reading *kākau* in the *Sūrasāgara* version of this stanza (Appendix II).

CP 14.

1 How could I hide your red lips?

2 Taking them to be sun and moon, you have subjugated them with
adoration—
could I make them a bloom of wondrous hues?

3 Binding your *kaustubha* gem in auspicious silken cloth
could I smear your limbs with lotus pollen?

4 As the delighted moon leaves the cloud [so your joy will be apparent]—
where could I seek out a delusion [to conceal it]?

5 If [even] the moon burns, then how could I conceal it,
[since even] the ocean of [my] deception has no effect?

6 And Hita Harivaṃśa—O *rasika*, dandy lover,
I would play your eyebrows against the wagtail!

Context: the stanza constitutes a *sakhī*'s words to Kṛṣṇa, who seeks entry to Rādhā's presence; the *sakhī* will only allow Kṛṣṇa to go to Rādhā if he dons the garb of a *sakhī*, and here points out the difficulties of achieving such a disguise.

The commentators are in agreement on the general context of the stanza, but none is able to provide convincing glosses on the various cryptic allusions of lines (2)–(6). All the commentators except Lok. envisage a context in which Kṛṣṇa seeks admission to the privacy of Rādhā's bathing place; Lok. prefers a more usual CP context, in which Kṛṣṇa is suffering from *viraha* and enlists the *sakhī*'s aid in overcoming Rādhā's *māna*. Rasik. gives an extended commentary of 93 *dohās*, referring to the stanza as 'occult' (*sugūḍha*); LCG admits that he cannot deduce a coherent meaning, and simply refers the reader to the *ṭīkā* of Prem. without attempting a gloss himself. It does, indeed, appear that this is a so-called *kūṭa* stanza of the type found in texts attributed to Sūradāsa and discussed by Miltner (1962) and Bhāṭī (1970): cf. also an example in the *Rāsa māna ke pada* of Kevalarāma (Entwistle p. 234), also coincidentally numbered 14. The intended sense of such stanzas lies concealed under a mesh of homonyms which often relate to the already labyrinthine contexts of Hindu cosmology and mythology. Wherever possible, epithets or the names of items are expressed periphrastically, typically by 'patronymics' of the type *paṃkajasuta* exemplified here in the third line; lexical items often stand as symbolic numbers, a device which may be involved here in such words as *rabi* and *sasi* in line (2), *aṃga* in line (3), *iṃdu* in (4) and *aṃbu* in (5) (though the sense of any such interpretation is not apparent in this context). The individual homonyms chosen for a *kūṭa* verse tend to be those with a high number of possible meanings (cf. particularly Sūradāsa's repeated use of *sāraṃga* in its various senses), such that the possible number of *overall* interpretations increases by geometrical progression; there appears to be no single stock of interpretations for individual items, and in the absence of an authentic 'key' such stanzas may be so recondite as to be virtually unintelligible. This appears to be the case in lines (2) to (5) of the present stanza, and the translation given above cannot claim to be definitive. The notes below discuss the principal interpretations offered by the commentators.

(1) *kai*: absolutive from *kar-*, used pleonastically in composition with *kaise* (cf. H. *kyõkar* etc.). Cf. also a second occurrence in line (5), and discussion in note on 67.4.

(2) *rabi sasi saṃka bhajana kiyau apabasa*: this is the most problematic passage of the stanza, and no commentator offers a convincing gloss. Lok. takes 'sun' and 'moon' as representing two categories of love, 'hot' and 'cold':

> *prema kī jāta uśna aru sītala hai. tātai rabi sasi tulya jo prema tākī saṃkā hai. jaba saṣī beṣa tumhāre prema udai hoi āvai taba kahā kījai. taba lāla jī bole prema ne tau apanai basa hoibe kau bhajana kiyau hai. kahā ki vaha tau basa āpa hī hai.*

'The categories of love are 'hot' and 'cold'; thus there is apprehension of that love which resembles the sun and the moon: what is to be done when, with you in *sakhī's* garb, your love dawns? Then Kṛṣṇa said, "Love has performed devotional practice in order to be under its own control"; that is, it is itself in control [?].'

Prem. takes 'sun' and 'moon' as *upamānas* for separation and union respectively:

> *rabi śaśi kī śaṃkā hai. jaba unikõ bhajana karikẽ apane basa karõ taba adbhuta raṃgani ke kusumani sõ ina adharani ko raṃga phiri banāū̃... saṃjoga biyoga rūpī caṃdramā sūrja tumhāre adharani mẽ base haĩ. aba biyoga sūrja kī tapatī sõ adhara sūki rahe haĩ. tini para pāparī bā̃dhi rahī hai. tāte raṃga na caḍhe. aura kyaū̃ hū̃ karike raṃga banāū̃. tau jaba priyā jū sõ saṃjoga hoigo, taba jaise caṃdramā amṛta śrave hai, taise saṃjoga rūpa caṃdramā sõ drava calẽge. heta kahā. ki pānī chuṭana lagego. tāte caṃdramā sūrya kõ basa karõ taba adharani ko raṃga phirike banāū̃.*

'There is apprehension as to sun and moon; having subjugated them with adoration then I shall again colour these lips with blooms of wondrous colours... The moon and sun of union and separation [respectively] reside in your lips. Now the lips are parched from the burning of the sun of separation, and are encrusted and hence devoid of colour; and how indeed could I colour them? Just as nectar flows from the moon, so will fluid ooze from the moon in the form of union when you are united with the beloved. What is the import of this? That perspiration will begin to flow. Therefore I shall subjugate the moon and sun and then re-colour your lips.'

Rasik. takes 'sun' and 'moon' as metaphors for the redness of the lips themselves:

sūraja nita hī hota aruna raṃga jā china udaya;
sasi pūraṇa udyota pūranamā ke dina aruna. 29.

tātẽ duhu ke eka sī rahata arunatā saṃga;
so saba jīti laī aho tuva adharani ke raṃga. 30.

yaha mana me bhaya jānikai ravi sasi doū mitta;
karata bhajanu tuva adhara kau ārādhanu kare nitta. 33.

tātẽ rabi sasi kiye basa tuma hī sahaja subhāi;
tāhī tẽ tuva adhara hī baḍhī arunatā āi. 35.

'(29) The sun is always red at the time of its rising;
and the fully luminous moon is red on the day of its fullness.
(30) Thus a similar redness endures in both of them alike;
[but] the redness of your lips has defeated all of that.
(33) Knowing this fear in their minds, the two friends sun and moon
worship your lips and ever pay homage.
(35) Thus spontaneously you have subjugated sun and moon
and so your lips have increased in redness.'

Dhar. makes 'sun' stand for 'eyes' and 'moon' for 'heart', but offers no gloss on the remainder of the half-line:

locana sūra manõ mana iṃda tihāre hẽ ātura kyõ ju chipāū̃

'Your sun-like eyes and your moon-like mind are distressed—how could I hide them?'

All the commentators' renderings are contrived to a greater or lesser extent. The syntax of the half-line is obscure in the absence of case-markers; but it is likely that *saṃka,* accommodated with difficulty (or not at all) in the glosses quoted above, is used in the sense attributed by *MW* to Sk. *śaṅkā, in fine compositi* as 'belief', supposition, presumption (of or that any person or thing is—)'. Such an interpretation here would yield a sense 'in the belief that [the lips?] are sun and moon...'. It is consequently an attractive hypothesis to take *rabi sasi* as the object of the action of 'subjugation' (*kiyau apabasa*): cf. J's emendment of singular *kiyau* to plural *kiye*, presumably in accordance with this resolution of the syntax as involving an agentive construction (though *rabi sasi* might equally well be regarded as compounded into a singular form and thus requiring singular *kiyau*).

(2) *adbhuta raṃgani kusuma banāū̃*: the sense is still presumably concerned with the disguise of the lips. Prem. adds no further gloss to that quoted above. Lok. and Dhar. introduce a new item, elliptical 'blossom-braided hair'; thus Lok.:

adabhuta raṃga ke kusumani sau ābharana banāi kabarī gū̃thaugī

'Making ornaments with flowers of wondrous colours I shall plait your hair-braids'.

Rasik., more reasonably, retains the *adhara* context:

kusama kahai te puhapa kī lai paṣurī bahu raṃga;
anupama adharani kau ahau ḍhāpo tina ke saṃga. 38.

'(38) Taking many-coloured petals of a *kusuma*—that is, a flower—
I shall cover your matchless lips with them.'

(3) This line presents no great problems of interpretation: the *kaustubha* gem and Kṛṣṇa's complexion both require disguise in the terms of the stanza's conceit.

(3) *sutani*: if the sense 'lotus pollen' is indeed intended, the oblique plural-*ani* ending is unexplained. Given the excess of (two) *mātrās* in the half-line, singular *suta* may

have been the authentic reading; but when the whole context is so uncertain such a hypothetical emendment cannot be incorporated.
(3) *lipāũ*: the AC reading *lipā-*, an attested causative from *lip-* (itself formed from *līp-* < *lipyate*) applies here. No attestation is found (in derivatives of *lupyate*) for a trans. verb **lupā-* to support the DEFGHIJKLM reading. See *CDIAL* 11061, 11083.
(4) *haraṣita iṃdu tajata jaisai jaladhara*: a plausible interpretation is given by Lok. and Prem., who understand the image of the moon peeping out from the clouds as referring to Kṛṣṇa (-candra)'s true identity showing itself through the *sakhī* disguise.
(5) *himakara* is taken by Prem. and Rasik. as referring to Rādhā's *māna*, by Lok. as referring to Rādhā's *svabhāva*; but a more coherent sense is achieved by regarding the expression as gnomic: to disguise Kṛṣṇa is as difficult a task as to extinguish a burning moon.
(6) *bhṛkuṭi bhaũha*: *bhaũha*, which does not appear elsewhere in the text, may be a commentatorial accretion, since (a) it is tautological after *bhṛkuṭi*, and (b) there is an excess of three *mātrās* in this half-line.

This final conceit is intended as the *sakhi's* crowning argument: even if all other parts of the disguise could be achieved, Kṛṣṇa's dancing eyebrows are sure to give him away. The commentators, however, perhaps beguiled by the tautology referred to above, would have the half-line refer to a meeting of Kṛṣṇa's eyes with Rādhā's.

CP 15.

1 Oh tell me your secret, lovely lady—
you stay silent, drunk with pride;

2 I am weary of saying to you, "Listen, dear Rādhikā,
why do you coyly say nothing of the pleasures of the night?"

3 Oh hear me, you with eyes like a doe's! The flowers are fallen from your braided hair,
ringlets fall freely on the border of your shawl, and you speak drowsily;

4 your lips are colourless, your cheeks dyed red,
and you walk, young girl, with an unsteady rolling gait.

5 The handsome one has enjoyed you secretly, your girdle and clothes are loose,
and the red bodice on your breast has a slack fastening!

6 with her heart delighted with these words heard from her friend,
Harivaṃśa, she went into the arbour smiling.

(4) *adhara niraṃga*: the MSS evidently agree on this reading, since the alternative collocation *adharani raṃga* proposed by printed text G would almost certainly lead to readings of the oblique plural *adharana*. The phrase recurs at 21.5 and 23.3, with a single reading of °*na* in M in the latter occurrence. The conceit 'lips drained of colour' occurs several times in the text.
(4) Agreement of *racyau* with singular *raṃga* may imply an assumption of derivation or *rac-* from **racyate*, and not *rajyate*, in this usage, the syntax of the phrase *raṃga racyau...kapolani* being 'colour is disposed on the cheeks'; *rac-* < *rajyate* would require dir. plural *kapola*, with verbal agreement.
(4) *raṃga/kapolani*: absence of internal (*pāda-*) rhyme in *ṣaṭpadīs*, in an alliterative

context such as *niraṃga raṃga*, occurs elsewhere in the text also, and is discussed in VII 2. (i). (Line (1) also has no rhyme between its first two *pādas*, but is in any case metrically irregular.)

CP 16.

1 Come today at my bidding, deer-eyed lady;
2 he sings sweetly amidst the circle of damsels—
   it is good that you join your lover, cuckoo-voiced one.
3 So well versed in the amatory arts,
   skilful of gesture, one who dances the *lāga* step—
4 young girl, amassment of beautiful form, heed my words:
   the moonlit night passes by with every moment.
5 Hita Harivaṃśa, she went to him eagerly,
   this giver of sensual joy to Rādhāramaṇa;
6 and countless dynasties of love-gods became ill-at-ease
   with the ardour of their clandestine embracing and kissing.

(3) *koka*: *HŚS* and *BBhSK* give 'a type of *saṃgīta*' as a secondary definition. *koka* appears in dance contexts in four occurrences in the CP (16.3, 79.3, 81.8, 82.4); yet there is no reason why the primary meaning should not apply here. The '*saṃgīta*' sense is not attested, and may be based (wrongly) on just such a context as the present one.

(3) *lāga*: *lāganṛtya* is described in the *Saṅgītadarpaṇa* as a category of *deśī* dance movements comprising nine different forms (Mandakranta Bose, p. 150). A source closer in time to the CP is the *Nirtta bilāsa līlā* of Dhruvadāsa (Lalitā Caraṇ Gosvāṃ (ed.) 1971: 262), where *lāga* appears in juxtaposition to *alaga* and *hurumaī*, noted by Bose (*ibid*., p. 156) as stepping or jumping movements:

alaga lāga hurumaī ju līnī; pragaṭa kalā nija guna kī kīnī.

'In the *alaga*, *lāga* and *hurumaī* [steps] that she took, she demonstrated her skilful art.'

CP 17.

1 See the forest-sport of the Beauty-of-Vraja and Mohana!
2 Each with an arm on the other's shoulder, the youthful pair is a congest of form,
   as though a lovely golden creeper were entwining a *tamāla* tree.
3 With a sweet tumult of the humming of bees in the fresh bower,
   this amassment of love sings, blending the voices of peacocks and parrots with its own;
4 they are impassioned in every limb in the recurring joy of love-making,
   as at every moment Harivaṃśa drinks it in through the chalices of his eyes.

(1) The scansion of the *ṭeka* does not accord with that of the remaining lines. A line of 12+9 *mātrās* can be attained by reducing feminine *suṃdarī* to masculine *suṃdara*, and by emending diminutive *banī* (for which see following note) to *bana: *āju deṣi braja suṃdara mohana bana keli*; there is, however, no manuscript support for such a hypothesis, which in any case fails to achieve the *varṇika* arrangement of lines (2) to (4).

(1) *banī keli*: an alternative interpretation, taken by Prem., reads *banī* as perfective participle of *ban-*, in concord with feminine *keli*. Lok. and Rasik., however, maintain the compound *banī keli* in their glosses. *banī* is attested by Platts as a diminutive of *bana*; and cf. another occurrence at 32.2, where the existence of *banī* as a substantive is confirmed by Rasik.'s gloss *banī maḍhya*.

(2) *ki-śora:* the caesura between the first and second *pādas*, reinforced by internal rhyme in subsequent lines, is enjambed here where alliteration (*aṃsa aṃsa, kiśora jora, rūpa rāsi*) replaces *pāda* rhyme.

(2) *rahi*: this word provides the only disruption to the stanza's trochaic/tribrachic *gaṇa* composition.

(3) LCG proposes the fanciful notion that the collocation of *bhavara, mora*, and *pika*, as symbolizing the tonic, seventh and fifth (respectively) of the musical scale, shows a connexion with the *rāga* Ṭoḍī which is traditionally allocated to this stanza. It is not apparent how these notes could be said to represent any particular *rāga* (unless they constituted the tonic, dominant and sub-dominant, which is *not* the case here).

(4) The compound *surata raṃga* echoes (but does not actually intend) the parallel form *sura-taraṃg-* (*MW* s.v. *sura*): a juxtapositioning of the two forms appears in consecutive *ślokas* in the *Rādhāsudhānidhi* (Bābā Hit Dās, p. 13):

śloka 19: *śrī rādhike* **suratarangi ni***tamba bhāge*
śloka 20: *śrī rādhike* **surataraṅgiṇi** *divyakeli*

The collocation *surata raṃga* appears again at 31.2 and 76.2.

CP 18.

1 Hear what I say, graceful Rādhā—
  2 you have found a fathomless ocean of joy!

3 You, daughter of the cowherd Vṛṣabhānu,
  4 have joined your lover Mohanalāla in merriment.

5 Before whom Brahmā and Śiva bow
  6 *him* you have made braid woodland flowers.

7 That essence of which holy writ [can only] say, "It is not"
  8 you have tasted as the ambrosial nectar of his lips.

9 Your beauty cannot be told in words—
  10 Hita Harivaṃśa sings a little of your fame.

(1)–(10) Whereas in the majority of stanzas the individual line, enclosed by end-rhyme, is a syntactic whole, in CP 18 and 19 it is the couplet which constitutes the syntactic unit. This is particularly evident in lines 5-6 and 7-8 of the present stanza: each of these two pairs of lines is linked by a relative-correlative construction. To demonstrate this couplet-based construction, the second line of each couplet has been indented in the edited text and the translation.

CP 18 and 19, which together comprise the Āsāvarī *rāga* group, are the only examples in the CP of this *caupāī* verse type. Another couplet-based stanza construction is found in CP 27.

(1) *rādhā*: vocative *rādhe* appears only at 28.1; further occurrences of *rādhā* in vocative contexts follow in 23.1, 38.2, and 58.2.
(2) *agādhā*: arbitrary lengthening of the final syllable in this word anticipates the same feature in six lines of CP 19; cf. note to 19.1 *bhujadaṃḍana*.
(6) °*pai*: the GIM reading °*para* may reflect a preference for a graphically bisyllabic orthography, in deference to the dactylic rhythm which predominates in the stanza (and in this couplet particularly):

— ⌣ ⌣ — ⌣ ⌣ — ⌣ ⌣ — -
tāpara taĩ banaphūla bināye.

(8) The accretion of *taĩ*, found in all MSS except A, is perhaps from a commentatorial paraphrase and/or is subsequent upon the collocation *tāpai taĩ* in 18.6. A's reading *tini terau*, while semantically plausible ('he tasted the ambrosial nectar of your lips'), is metrically no more correct than the majority reading. It is unlikely that the short 16-*mātrā* line could sustain metrical irregularity to the extent of an additional two *mātrās*.

CP 19.

1 The *rasika,* the Ornament of Vraja, sports in the round-dance,
2 placing his staff-like arms on the young girls' shoulders.
3 The moon is resplendent in the clear autumn-night sky
4 and the so-sweet flute plays in mellow tone.
5 Ghanaśyāma is resplendent as a *tamāla* tree,
6 the Vraja damsel adorned as a golden creeper.
7 Cymbal, drum and *upaṅga* resound,
8 and the singing disturbs the minds of myriads of love-gods.
9 Wearing many ornaments and saris of various hues
10 the women demonstrate the *sudhaṅga* dance.
11 Blossoms are scattered by the delighted consorts of the gods,
12 and the low sound of the celestial kettledrum is heard.
13 Hita Harivaṃśa, Śyāmā's heart is enraptured,
14 for Rādhāramaṇa is the dwelling-place of all joys.

(1) *bhujadaṃḍana*: oblique plural termination is for rhyme, since grammar requires direct case (unless a forced sense, 'shoulders are applied to his arms', is to be understood). Further arbitrarily lengthened final forms occur in lines (5), (7), (8), (12) and (14), reflecting a process used also in Ap. metrics (see p. 427). *syāmā* in line (13) is ambiguous: it may be intended either as a genuine feminine form (since Śyāmā/Rādhā has an established role in the context of the stanza), or as an ingenuously extended masculine form. Cf. a repeat of the half-line in 24.6, where the ambiguity of gender recurs also.
(7) *upaṃga*: the name is given to a variety of musical instruments. One has the hourglass shape of the *ḍamarū* drum, and a string attached to one of its two drumheads is plucked at different tensions to produce notes of varying pitch as with the Bengali *ānanda laharī* (Cunnīlāl Śeṣa p. 44). Another type is defined by the *HŚS* as the *nasataraṃga*, and is so described by T.N. Mukharji (p. 95): 'Nyasataranga...a trumpet-shaped instrument, has to be placed upon the vocal chords, sounds from

which produce by vibration a clear reedy note upon the instrument... It is known in Sanskrit as the *Upāṅga*, and is extensively used by Hindus in the North-Western Provinces, and particularly at Muttra and Brindāban.' In the Āīn-i Akbarī, the *upaṃga* is described as a kind of shawm: 'The *upang* is a hollow reed a yard long, the upper part of which has a hole in the centre in which a reed is inserted' (H.S. Jarrett II, p. 256). Finally, H.A. Popley (p. 121) refers to a further application of the word: 'The *nosbug*, or *śruti upāṅga*, or *bhajana śruti* is...used almost exclusively for the drone. This is the Indian bagpipe.'

Although it is not clear which instrument is intended in the CP, a reference from a similar *rāsa* context in the *Sūrasāgara* (Nandadulāre Vājpeyī (ed.), Vol. I, p. 625, *pada* 1677) clearly suggests a wind instrument, perhaps of the shawm type:

> *ughaṭata syāma nṛtyati nārī;*
> *dhare adhara upaṃga upajaī leta haĩ giridhārī.*
>
> 'Śyāma marks the rhythm, the lady dances;
> holding the *upaṃga* to his lip, Giridhārī plays variations.'

(10) *aṃga sudhaṃga diṣāvata nārī*: the collocation *aṃga sudhaṃga* occurs a further three times, at 36.6, 79.2 and 82.4. The latter two contexts, *sarasa sudhaṃga aṃga mẽ nāgari* and *china china kuśala sudhaṃga aṃga mẽ*, show that the sense of *aṃga* here is 'section of *saṅgīta*', or 'type of dance'. In the present context and in its close parallel in 36.6 (*bṛṣabhānanaṃdinī aṃga sudhaṃga diṣāyau*), however, *aṃga* may mean 'limb, body' in an instrumental case; this interpretation has some support in later texts such as the *vāṇī* of Harirāma Vyāsa, but there the collocation of *aṃga* with *sudhaṃga* is usually in a highly alliterative, and hence perhaps formulaic, context: *aṃga aṃga prati sudhaṃga raṃga gati taraṃga saṃga rati anaṃga māna bhaṃga mani mṛdaṃga bājai* (Vāsudev Gosvāmī p. 313).

(12) *duṃdubhi*: D's reading with long final *-ī* reflects familiarity with a late usage, in which the word *duṃdubhī* refers to a pair of one large and one small kettledrum, more commonly known as *nagāṛā* (< Pers. *naqqāra*) (Lālmaṇi Miśra pp. 76-78). The *duṃdubhi*, on the other hand, is described in the *Saṅgītaratnākara*, *ślokas* 1145-47, as being similar to but distinct from the kettledrum *niśāna* (*loc. cit.*). Both *duṃdubhi* and *niśāna* appear in the CP with the intended image of thunder resounding in the heavens (with Indra as percussionist).

CP 20.

1 You are drunk with the essence of Mohanalāla!—

2 Young bride, why do you bashfully conceal from me your secret first love?

3 See, you have covered yourself with a yellow garment—
where is your red dappled mantle?

4 Your broken string of pearls dangles down,
your bosom is marked with the crescent-moon of fingernails.

5 Your bimba-fruit lips are split, your cheeks
decorated with collyrium, and you walk unsteadily;

6 your reddish eyes wander languidly,
the blossoms are fallen from your rows of curls.

7 Today in seclusion Mohana has plundered
the various things he held in trust!

8 Hita Harivaṃśa, hearing these words the lady
went into the arbour smiling.

(1) The masc. concord of the genitive case-marker *ke* precludes the reading of *rasa māti* as an adjectival compound in the received text. The syntax is therefore [*tū*] *mohanalāla ke rasa* [*saũ/maĩ*] *mātī* [*hai*]. A postposition, *saũ* or *maĩ*, does indeed follow *rasa* in all the commentaries except Dhar. Since the *ṭeka* is elliptical without this postposition, and since *rasa mātī* would normally be construed as a compound (cf. 31.4 *rasa matta*), a hypothetical reconstruction may be proposed:

**mohanalāla keli rasa mātī.*

The addition of the syllable *-li* would yield the typical metrical construction of the *ṭeka* in *Sāra* metre, viz. (X)+12 *mātrās*.
(2) *gupata*: readings of *gupati* appear to understand a finite usage (**gup-*), which is not attested elsewhere. Most of the commentators supply a substantive in their glosses (*bāta* or *keli*), with which *gupata* is made to agree; this construction renders the syntax of the line unnecessarily complicated, and *gupata* (for Sk. gupta) is better understood as qualifying *neha*.
(3) *pīta paṭa*: Kṛṣṇa's yellow dhoti or *pītāmbara*.

CP 21.

1 Your two eyes are telling tales!—
2 they are very restless, and will not be contained anywhere—
they have met Kuñjavihārī.
3 Your parting is disordered, its blossoms fall all about,
and a stray curl is hanging down;
4 fingernail scratches are seen plainly on your bosom—
how could you hide them, my dear one?
5 Betel juice has fallen on your blessed cheeks,
and your lips have lost their colour, tender lady;
6 Hita Harivaṃśa, a burdensome languor afflicts every limb
of the lady who savours the essense of love.

(1) *karata dou cārī*: in this context, where Rādhā's attempts to conceal the evidence of her love-making are unsuccessful (as in CP 15 and 20.2 etc.), the primary meaning must derive from the sense of *cārī* as 'tale-telling' (H. *caḍī* ⟨ *cāṭū-*). Hence Lok. and Prem. gloss *cārī* with *cugalī* (for Persian *cuglī*). The dislocation of *dou* from *naina*, however, suggests a deliberate collocation with *cārī* which inevitably invokes the numerical sense *cāra* (with *-ī* for rhyme); (*āṃkhẽ*) *do cāra honā* is an idiom with the sense 'an exchange of glances to take place', and hence 'to meet' (*HŚS* s.v. *do*; cf. also *cāra āṃkhẽ honā/karnā*, *ibid.*, s.v. *cāra*). The expression may therefore be read as anticipating the more explicit *mile haĩ* in the following line; a true *śleṣa*, however, is not involved since the two meanings are in competition rather than complementary. The hypothetical sense deriving from *cārī* as 'four' is nowhere suggested in the commentaries: Lok. and Prem. restrict themselves to the *cugalī* interpretation already mentioned, while Dhar. and Rasik. merely paraphrase the *mūla*, retaining *cārī* but omitting a gloss on *dou* (regarded by them as pleonastic?).
A possible third interpretation of *cārī* as meaning the dancing term (for which cf.

note on *caṃdacālī*, 81.7) and yielding a conceit of 'dancing eyes' is consistent with the content of the second line of the couplet, but must be regarded as too specifically technical a sense to be involved here.
(3) *bithurī*: fem. concord shows agreement with *mãga*, whereas semantically an agreement with *kusuma* would seem more apposite. Such an interpretation would be possible with an absolutive form **bithuri* (which would also repair the overall moric length of the line, allowing *paraī* its full metrical weight), but no such reading is found in the manuscripts, and the received reading is consistent with a caesura after the seventh *mātrā*, strongly favoured statistically in *Sāra* and *Sarasī* metres.

CP 22.

1 I would give up myriads of wagtails for those eyes!—
2 tremulous and nimble, reddish and sharp-pointed,
their foremost part decorated with collyrium.
3 Their bright and captivating sidelong glance
is disdainful of the love-battle's hosts;
4 Hita Harivaṃśa, their splendour cannot be described—
it is an ocean of joy, delightful to the mind.

(1) The eyes are Rādhā's, as in adjacent stanzas.
(1) *vār-*: the sense here is more general than in the expression *vāri pheri* (10.4), and has the sense 'relinquish, cast away'.
(4) *suṣa samudra* may be taken as an epithet of Kṛṣṇa ('delightful to the mind of Kṛṣṇa'), a sense proposed by Prem.

CP 23.

1 Beloved Rādhā, your eyes are playful!—
2 with your adoration and your golden youthfulness of body
you have bought Manohara.
3 Your lips are colourless, your curls and ringlets loose,
stained with betel-juice your cheeks;
4 you have become immersed in joy, and do not realise
that you have on [Kṛṣṇa's] yellow mantle.
5 His nail-scratches are clearly visible on your breasts,
like a group of the moons on Śaṅkara's head;
6 Hita Harivaṃśa: you speak a little, lady,
in such a languorous voice!

(2) *kanaka tana jobana*: in collocation with *mola le-*, a monetary sense may be attributed to *kanaka*—'bought with the gold of your youthfulness of body'; elsewhere in the text, however, (11.2 and *passim*), *kanaka* describes the fair brilliance of Rādhā's body, and may therefore be best understood as qualifying the compound *tana jovana* in the present context. A regular caesura after the seventh *mātrā* of the line suggests that *bhajana* is to be regarded as a separate item, and not compounded with what follows.

(3) *alaka*: the reading *alika* found in M, and probably intended by G's *ālaka*, is understood by Prem. as the *tatsama* word meaning 'forehead', and is consequently glossed with *māthā*. Similarly, Lok.'s and Rasik.'s paraphrases read *muṣa* and *lalāṭa* respectively. These interpretations are presumably intended to avoid the tautology *alaka laṭa*. (The word *alika* itself appears to be some sort of ghost word, perhaps wrongly inferred from a misconstruction of the compound *alikalekha*; *MW* cites an occurrence in the *Bālarāmāyaṇa* only.)

CP 24.

1 Today Gopāla plays in the delight of the round-dance,
on the sandy riverbank near the tree of plenty, oh my companion;
2 the moon of the clear autumn sky is resplendent
and pleasant is the breeze of threefold nature, oh my companion.
3 *Campaka, Bakula* and jasmine are in bud
and cuckoo and parrot are impassioned and enthralled, oh my companion;
4 excellent is the music and merriment of the *deśī sudhaṅga* dance,
in that throng of Vraja damsels, oh my companion.
5 Indra has sounded his kettledrum in delight
and the resolute sage has abandoned his vow, oh my companion;
6 Hita Harivaṃśa, Śyāmā with enraptured heart
removes the deep pain of passion, oh my companion.

(1) *tīra*: there is no reason why the straightforward nominal sense should not apply here, as in the compound *tanayā tīra* (69.3). A postpositional sense, 'near', is, however, taken by Prem. (*ke nikaṭa*) and is also implied by Lok.'s *tarai* 'beneath'. The collocation *kalapataru tīra* recurs at 26.4 and 63[iii].3; for a postpositional usage of *tīra*, see *piya tīra* at 37.7.
(2) *tribidhi*: this formula refers to the conventional description of the breeze given more fully at 57.7: *sītala maṃda sugaṃdha*, 'cool, gentle and fragrant'. Final *-i* presumably indicates a confusion of *-°vidha* with *vidhi*; cf. *bahubidhi* (11.6 and 30.5, with no *-a* readings), for *°bidha*. Manuscript agreement and attestation in *BBhSK* suggests that *-i* forms are established for BrBh; *bahubidhi*, but not *tribidhi*, is attested in Platts also.
(6) *syāmā*: up to this point the stanza has centred on the actions of Gopāla, Rādhā not being mentioned. If the *pāda*, *hita haribaṃśa magana mana syāmā* has been borrowed wholesale from 19.13, where *syāmā* may be an arbitrary extension *metri causa* of the masc. form *syāma*, then the masc. sense may be apposite here also. In this case the context of the stanza would remain restricted to Kṛṣṇa's *rāsa* dance with the *gopīs*, without specific involvement of Rādhā.

CP 25.

1 Today Rādhikā the accomplished is handsomely adorned!—
2 amongst the company of Vraja damsels she is foremost
in beauty and skilfulness, and in qualities of disposition and dress.

3 A lotus in her right hand, her left hand on a *sakhī*'s shoulder,
in unison she sweetly sings a *rāga* of dulcet tones;
4 Hita Harivaṃśa, she who is learned in all knowledge
secretly meets great-fortuned Śyāma in the fine new arbour.

(3) *dakṣina*: a four-*mātrā* form is required for metre, the ten-*mātrā* feet being perfectly maintained throughout the stanza. The *tadbhava* form *dachina*, preferable in terms of manuscript support, has therefore to be rejected. (The forms *dakkhina, dacchina* are not represented in the MSS.)

CP 26.

1 The flute of Madanagopāla is an enchantress!—
2 hear me, O Rādhikā; as one hears her sweetness
she destroys the anguish of Kāma.
3 A full-moon autumn night in the *vṛndā* forest, my friend,
and a very cool and gentle breeze, laden with fragrance;
4 on the most pure sandy riverbank with lotuses attended by bees
is a round-dance performed by Balavīra under the tree of plenty.
5 Best of the whole dance-circle, you have joined Hari—
with what could I compare this bride and groom adorned?
6 you the golden-bodied one and Lāla the emerald
are a pair of *kalahaṃsas,* and Harivaṃśa their votive slave.

(1) *mohana...bā̃surī*: the *ṭeka* establishes a regular *varṇavṛtta* pattern which is maintained throughout the stanza (with a single irregularity in line (5), noted below). A weak caesura may be said to exist after the first syllable to *go-pāla*.
(3) *rajani/sajani*: this lines introduces internal rhyme marking off 10-*mātrā pādas* and establishing a *ṣaṭpadī* pattern. This rhyme is maintained throughout lines (3) to (6), but with varying strength.
(4) *sevita*: finite °*ata* found universally among the manuscripts cannot be intended in this line, where *parama pāvana pulina* and *bhṛṃga sevita nalina* must surely both qualify *kalapataru tīra*. A confusion of participial adjectives with finite participles is commonplace in the manuscripts, but has not elsewhere led to a complete loss of the correct form.
(4) *tīra/balabīra*: cf. the rhyme *kalahaṃsa/haribaṃśa* at the same point in line (6). Both lines show *pāda* rhyme in the first half-line also, and are therefore effectively *pañcapadīs* of 10+10+8+5+7 *mātrās.*
(5) *banī* is the only metrical irregularity in the stanza. Semantically it is satisfactory as meaning 'bride', and no metrically correct alternative suggests itself.
(5) *bara*: Prem. glosses with *śreṣṭha*, understanding *bara* as adjectival. Yet in collocation with *banī* 'bride', the adjectival sense can hardly compete with the nominal sense 'groom' which is surely intended; context supports this reading, with an act of union (*milī*) described immediately beforehand, and a *state* of union alluded to in the following line.
(5) *kāsu*: *su* (for *sũ*) is a variant of *saũ* (*LIO* 3.177), appearing in the CP in this rhyme context only.
(6) *ubhai*: a trisyllabic scansion is required for metre.

tion of lines or couplets from various sources, or deriving from various metrical models; such a hypothesis is supported by the appearance of the standardized 8+6 syllable construction late in the stanza.

(1) *na thora*: A's reading *ghora* is simply a miscopying of *thora*, as shown by another example of the same error in the nonsensical *ānaṃda baḍhyau na ghora* (Dhar.'s introductory *dohā* to CP 19). In the present line, A's omission of the negative particle *na* is presumably to compensate in sense for the reading *ghora*.

(3) Many of the couplets in this stanza are without a finite verb, since they are intended as epithets governing *bṛṃdābana*.

(3) As in certain subsequent lines (see for example note to line (12) below), the commentators tend to regard a caesura after the 8th *varṇa* as intransgressible; here, consequently, they do not permit the compound *rūpa-mañjarī*, preferring instead to read *jugala rūpa* as a compound (qualifying *jūthikā*); thus Prem.:

> *jūthikā nāma cābelī kau hai; so jugala rūpa hai, sveta aura pīta.*

'*Jūthikā* is the name for jasmine, which has two forms—white and yellow.' *jugala*, however, normally comprises the *second* member of compounds (cf. *pīyūṣa jugala* 51.4, *naina jugala* 82.6); the interpretation *jūthikā-jugala, rūpa-mañjarī* is therefore more plausible here.

(3) *rasāla* may alternatively be regarded as an adjective ('succulent'), qualifying *rūpamañjarī*.

(4) *gulāla*: the usual Hindi sense, appropriate here for its seasonal associations, is 'red colour thrown during Holī festivities'. An alternative possibility, closer to its derivation from Pers. *gul-lāla* (*GNG* p. 102), is the sense 'red flower, poppy' which may be intended by Dhar.'s gloss *gulāla dala*, 'leaves of *gulāla*'.

(8) *nūta* is glossed as 'mango' by Prem. and the modern commentators, but has no attested derivation other than < *nūtana*. Similarity to Sk. *cūta* suggests that *nūta* may be a misreading, though it is also possible that conjectural *cūta* may have been deliberately excised from the text at an early stage in its transmission, since its primary sense in Hindi is 'vulva' and its usage is restricted to vulgar or abusive contexts. (In terms of syllabic construction the line is deficient by one syllable, though E's *nutana* and L's *nūtani* (for **cūtani*?) do afford the requisite 14 syllables; in terms of moric construction, on the other hand, the line as it stands is matched precisely by 27.10.) The plausibility of an original reading of (or based on) *cūta* is strengthened by the usage of this word in similar contexts in the *GG*, including one instance showing, as in the present line, collocation with *mukulita*:

> *sphuradatimuktalatāparirambhaṇamukulitapulakitacūte;*
> *vṛndāvanavipine parisaraparigatayamunājalapūte.*
>
> (*GG* 3.7; Stella Sandahl-Forgue p. 165.)

(10) *saina*: a trisyllabic scansion is required in order to attain 8+6 syllable construction; hence the *graphically* trisyllabic forms (*sayana, śayana*) introduced by CFL and H respectively.

(11) *muraja*: a drum, likened to the *mṛdaṅga* by the *HŚS*, but whose precise form is uncertain.

(12) *bara*: although agreements with both following *and* preceding subjects are attested in the CP (exemplified by *uraja bara* (30.8) and *bara bihāra* (76.3) respectively), it is likely that *bara* qualifies *bīnā* here, in accordance with more usual Sk. usage. In deference to the alleged caesura, Rasik. and Lok. interpret *bara muṣacaṃga* as a compound.

(12) *muṣacaṃga*: (*mukha*+Pers. *cang* 'Jew's harp'; Platts cites the forms *moracaṃga, muracaṃga, mucaṃga* and *mūhacaṃga*); the prefixed *mukha-* distinguishes this instrument, the Jew's harp, from various other Indian instruments called *caṃga*, such

(6) *haribaṃśa*: this is the first case in the text where *haribaṃśa* is clearly intended as a third party; it is noteworthy that the context in which this occurs has *vaṃśī* as topic. With reference back to the *ṭeka*, the meaning of the final phrase may therefore be 'Hari's flute is *balidāsa* of the pair of *kalahaṃsas*'.

CP 27.

1 Joy is abundant in springtime Vṛndāvana,
2 resplendent with young skilful lady and adroit youth.

3 [It is rich in] the two jasmines, in *rūpamañjarī* and mango trees,
4 and in bees worn out by *gulāla* and *madhumādhavī*.

5-6 The god of love is delighted by groups of *campaka* and *bakula* flowers,
the various lotuses, and the rapture of *ketakī* and *medinī*.

7 A pleasant and agreeable wind of threefold nature blows,
8 half-opened fresh [blooms] are resonant with cuckoo and parrot.

9-10 A bed of tender leaves is created as a mass of delights
in the dense and lovely bower by the pure riverbank.

11 Anklets, tambourine, frame-drum, flute, barrel-drum,
12 *upaṅga*, noble *vīṇā* and mouth-harp resound.

13-14 Garments are coloured by musk, sandal, saffron,
abīra, *bandana* and sap of aloes.

15 The beautiful one and Hari sing a sweet springtime song;
16 birds and beasts are thrilled, and the river checks its flow.

17 Hita Harivaṃśa, may the assembly of swan and pen
18 rule together thus from age to age!

(1)-(18) In this stanza, all lines except (8) can be scanned as consisting of 14 syllables. It is likely that this 14-syllable form is associated with the springtime song-type *dhamāra* (cf. a direct reference to this form in line (15), and also the seasonal *rāga* heading Vasanta under which the stanza falls), since this is invariably sung in 14-beat *Dhamāra tāla*.

The metre of CP 27 is identified by Rāmcaraṇlāl Śarmā (p. 364) as being *Mukunda*, of 8+6 syllables; but despite the fact that the 14-syllable line does indeed appear to be construed in accordance with this scheme both by the commentators (see notes to lines (3) and (10) below) and by the *samāja* singers (see section VI.5.iii), 8+6 construction only becomes a regular feature in lines (13)ff. (The *chāpa* line, (17), is not fully consistent with this pattern: but since the phrase *haṃsa haṃsinī samāja* occurs also in 76.4 (*rājahaṃsa*~), it may have been included here simply as a convenient formula.)

Lines (3) and (6), both incidentally having a caesura after the 6th, and not the 8th, syllable, share a strong *varṇavṛtta* rhythm: — ⏑ — / ⏖ ⏑ — ⏑ ⏖ ⏑ / ⏖ ⏑ — ⏑. *Varṇavṛtta* rhythm appears again in the trochaic *chāpa* line (17). Other lines have no such consistent rhythm, but rather show a variety of moric patterns ending always with the 6-*mātrā* cadential *gaṇa* ⏖ ⏑ — ⏑ which endures throughout. The variety of metrical formulations in the remainder of the line suggest that the stanza is a compila-

as 'a small timbrel' (L.G. Tewari, p. 260) and a stringed instrument (Abdul Halim Sharar, p. 267 n. 419).
(13) *abīra*: a red powder thrown during Holī festivities (syn. *gulāla* in this sense).
(14) *baṃdana* (= Sk. *vandanī*): a yellow pigment used in the making of *tilakas*.
(14) *cīra*: the sense 'bark', attested by Platts, may equally well apply in this line, though 'garment' is more apposite in all other CP contexts.
(15) *suṃdari*: readings of *suṃdara* (BFGIKM) restrict the reference to *hari*; yet in the light of the context set in line (2), the commentators seem to be right in construing *suṃdari*, thereby making the *dhamāra* a duet.

CP 28.

1 Oh Rādhā, see what goes on in the forest:
2 an eternal spring, with leaves and fruits
  [and yet] blossoms still in the bud.
3 Nandalāla has sounded the call of his flute—
  why do you tarry when you have heard it?
4 Why do you still delay, lovely lady,
  while the chance passes by uselessly?
5 With Lāla the handsome emerald,
  and you who are golden-bodied,
6 Hita Harivaṃśa's pair is well met,
  both being transported by their host of virtues.

(1)-(6) This second stanza to which the *rāga* Vasanta is allocated shows a precise compatibility with the 14-*mātrā Dhamāra tāla* typically used for such springtime songs; it is also compatible with the 7-*mātrā tāla Rūpaka* used in the performance of CP 28 described in section VI.5.iii. The first *pāda* of lines 2-6 is of 14 *mātrās*; analysis of the performance shows how the vocative *rādhe* from line 1 is used throughout as a metrical makeweight to extend the second, ten-*mātrā pāda* to a similar 14-*mātrā* unit. Following this arrangement, the whole stanza fits precisely into the *vibhāgas* of *Rūpaka* and *Dhamāra* (with the *ṭeka* requiring inversion to *deṣi bana kī bāta, rādhe*).

Rūpaka	1	2	3	/4	5	/6	7/	/1	2	3	/4	5	/6	7
Dhamāra	1	2	3	4	5	/6	7/	8	9	10	/11	12	13	14
28.1	*de*	—	*ṣi*	*ba*	*na*	*kī*	—	*bā*	—	*ta*	*rā*	—	*dhe*	—
28.2	*ri*	*tu*	*ba*	*saṃ*	—	*ta*	*a*	*naṃ*	—	*ta*	*mu*	*ka*	*li*	*ta*
	ku	*su*	*ma*	*a*	*ru*	*pha*	*la*	*pā*	—	*ta*	*rā*	—	*dhe*	—

[etc.]

(6) *māta*: LCG glosses '*parājita*', thereby deriving *māta* from Pers. *māt* and not from Sk. *matta* 'intoxicated, delighted'. In the intended image, however, the setting of the emerald in gold produces an effect greater than that of the sum of the two individual components (cf. the modern Hindi idiom with this sense, *maṇi kā̃cana yoga*); an implication of competition is therefore inapposite in this context. Cf. *mātī* < *matta*, 15.1.

CP 29.

1 Crown-jewel of all young Vraja damsels, Śyāmā is adorned today;

2 her sweetness in every limb from head to foot
has enchanted her fortunate Śyāma.

3 The plaited-braid hair of she with a golden lotus-face glistens

4 as though the half-moon between her hair-ornaments
were swallowed by Rāhu.

5 On her head the essence of blessed fortune flows in a channel
established by her lover as her parting;

6 her eyebrows are the bow of passion, her eyes arrows,
collyrium-blacked lines their arrow-points.

7 Her jewel *tilaka,* the ear-ornament on her cheek,
the pearl at her nose,

8 her jasmine[-bud] teeth and sweet blossom lips
are comforters to her lover's heart.

9 Oh *sakhī*, amid her chin is a lovely and natural beauty-spot;

10 and her bosom, a casket for the jewel of her lover's life-breath,
is bound and drawn tight by her bodice.

11 Her lotus-stem arms which rob his strength are bangle-clad,
their sweet touch pleasant to hear;

12 they are, as it were, a lovely and comely watering-pool
made around the tree of Śyāma's head.

13 Her deep navel is a pool for the sporting
of the fish of Mohana's mind;

14 slender her waist, broad her bell-encircled hips,
and her thighs are like plantain trunks.

15 Her lotus feet, decorated with lac and ornaments,
rest on the earth of her lover's chest

16 as with many a new expression and allurement
the elephant sports in passion with his excellent mate.

17 Śyāmā's radiant and mighty fame is praised by Hita Harivaṃśa;

18 the singing or hearing of it is a mine of joy
which appeases the evil of the world.

(2) *naṣa siṣa*: this introduces the conventional *nakhaśikha* description given in lines (3)-(15).

(4) *cikura caṃdrikani bīca aradha bidhu*: the image is not fully clear, but since the syntax must yield the sense 'the half-moon amidst her hair-ornaments', *aradha bidhu* may also refer to an ornament. Prem., Lok. and LCG hold that the *aradha bidhu* is the forehead, as exemplified by Prem.'s gloss *cikurani kī caṃdrikā haĩ. tini maĩ muṣa esẽ rājata hai māno ādho caṃdramā rāh[ū] ne grasyo hai.* But such an interpretation does not cohere: firstly, the previous line has established 'gold' and 'lotus', and not 'moon', as metaphors for the face, secondly, the forehead cannot be envisaged as 'between' the hair-ornaments; thirdly, if Rāhu (the braided plaits) has eclipsed the moon of the face then its golden radiance should have been extinguished! Rasik.'s

gloss is too close a paraphrase to offer any helpful interpretation, while Dhar.'s, conversely, is too loose a rendering.

(5) The allusion is to the act of decorating a woman's hair-parting by her husband. None of the commentaries, however, comments on the implied auspicious state of wedlock, significant to the sectarian view of Rādhā as *svakīyā*.

(10) *tanī*: the verbal sense (H. *tan-* < *tanoti*), is taken by the commentators; nominal *tanī* (<*tanikā*), 'fastening-string of garment', may alternatively apply.

(11) *śravanī*: the sense from *śravanīya* given by Prem. in the second of his two *arthas* is appropriate, following *balayajuta*, as referring to the jingling of bangles. Rasik. and Dhar., and Prem.'s first *artha*, gloss with *śravata* 'giving a flow (of *rasa*)': cf. a confusion of *srav-* with *śrav-* in readings for *sravata* at 29.5 and 37.3. Lok.'s gloss *śroṇī* has no sound basis. A derivation from *śramaṇa-*, by analogy with the rhyme-word *ravanī* < *ramaṇīya-*, is not applicable.

(12) *miḍabārī*: possibly from H. *meḍa* (for which cf. 41.6) < *mariyādā*, +*bārī* < *vāri-*, giving the sense 'dike-water'? Prem. and Lok. gloss *thā̃varau* (H. *thā̃valā*, 'trench dug for water round the root of a tree', Platts); Dhar. glosses *mẽḍa* 'dike, bank'.

CP 30.

1 Listen my companion! As one looks at the new bower
 it appears most lovely;
2 with creepers of *Mādhavikā* and *Ketukī*
 this abode of love is fashioned.
3 On this full-moon night in the autumn month
 there is a cool, gentle and scented breeze;
4 the fragrance-hungry honeybee is satiated,
 parrot and cuckoo are in song.
5 Friend, with tender many-hued leaves of young shoots
 a bed is prepared by the lover;
6 and vessels of gold filled with various sweet intoxicants
 are placed affectionately on the ground.
7 Thereon the adroit youth and damsel sport and make merry;
8 the lover's hand touches her fine breasts,
 the beloved covers them with her clothes.
9 The loving lady peeps from under her crooked brow,
 ever opposed to his every word;
10 restless and quite in the grip of passion
 Hari hurriedly clasps her shoulders.
11 He, the clever one, frees the ties of her waistband
 and draws back her blue mantle;
12 but the bride in feigned obstinate anger tenderly cries
 "No! No!" in a sweet voice.
13 [Then] with embracing in inverted lovemaking
 she bestows her joyful loveplay;
14 it is as though a golden creeper shone on a tree of sapphires.

15 On the brows of the pair engaged in the battle of love
cling droplets of perspiration;

16 and with unceasing love in their hearts, Lalitā and the other *sakhīs*
fan them with the borders of their garments.

17 Hita Harivaṃśa describes as best he can
the quintessence of the nectar of Kṛṣṇa's savour;

18 hearing of it cultivates love for the tender lotus feet of Rādhā.

(5) *saṣi/-ī* appears as a vocative at or near the end of the line or phrase in a number of instances (13.2, 13.6, 29.9, 66.14, 69.3, 83.5), often interrupting the syntax (as *tribidhi saṣī samīra,* 69.3). Such a reading is therefore appropriate here also, although compounded *priya saṣi* is also possible.

(6) *heja*: perhaps < *hṛdya-*, as attested in *CDIAL* for Old Gujarati *heja* with the sense 'affection'. Here glossed *heta sõ* by Prem., *pyāra sõ* by Lok., *heja* does not appear to be attested elsewhere in Hindi but does occur once in Dhar.'s gloss to CP 27.10 (again in rhyme with *seja*): *suvana dalani racī seja bāḍhyo ati heja.*

(10) *dharata bhujamūla*: the image seems unclear, and *-mūla* is perhaps more for rhyme than for sense. Prem., perhaps ignorant of Sk. *bhujamūla* 'shoulder', glosses with *kuca* 'breasts'.

(13) *biparita*: the (metrically correct) shortening of *-īta* to *-ita* is not attested elsewhere, and is perhaps intended to contribute to the alliterative effect of the whole phrase *biparita rati bitarata.*

(13) *rati*: the form *rata* attested in compound with *viparīta* in *MW* is found only in MS I, and is therefore unlikely to represent an authentic reading.

(15) *lalāṭa paṭala*: *l*° *paṭṭa* (*-ka*) is the form attested in *MW*; the present form may reflect familiarity with the sense of *paṭala* as '*tilaka*' (*ibid.*), though it is unlikely that such a specialized sense would be intended here.

(17) The compound *kṛṣṇa rasāmṛta sāra* yields the only occurrence in the entire text of the epithet *kṛṣṇa.*

CP 31.

1 Today the couple is most resplendent, at dawn:

2 steeped in the essence of passion's joy
are the cultivated lady and the youth.

3 With arms round each other's shoulders
each looks at the other's moonlike face;

4 drunk with each other's essence
they imbibe with the eyes of thirsty *cakoras.*

5 Her loosened locks have drawn Lāla's spirit
and he is the thief of her mind;

6 with embraces and kisses they sing together
in voices of low, soft tones;

7 Walking with wavering steps they roam the wood,
through deep dell and lovely grove;

8 Hita Harivaṃśa, Lāla and his lady together
ease my heart!

(5) *ye yāke cita cora*: the general context of the stanza, which describes the *mutual* attraction of the *daṃpati*, suggests that *ye* refers to Kṛṣṇa in reciprocity to the first half of the line where Rādhā is subject; the unusually full pronominal construction would have little purpose if a change of subject were not indicated. All the commentators except Lok., however, retain Rādhā as subject. There is no commentatorial support for a third possibility, where *ye* would refer to *laṭani*, advancing the image established by *karaṣyau*.
(6) *sura maṃdara* (=Sk. *mandrasvara*): uncertainty as to the meaning of this phrase is reflected by the high number of *maṃdira* readings. Lok. reads *mṛdaṃgana kī suṃdara ghora hai*, 'there is a lovely sound of *mṛdaṅgas*'. Prem. maintains, without any attested basis, that *maṃdara*, *kala* and *ghora* are the names of the three musical *grāmas*.

CP 32.

1 Today Śyāma and Śyāmā sport in the forest;
2 the night is made beautiful by the autumn moonlight
    and the grove is bright and lovely.
3 With the splitting of lips and embracing,
    and the drawing back of garments from their thighs,
4 and in the nail-scratches on their chests, and in their slanting glances
    the couple shares an equal joy.
5 He touches her arms and her swelling breasts,
    she of lovely eyes [touches] her lover's garland;
6 betel juice is on their clothes, their locks of hair are drawing [each other],
    making a hundred love-gods battle-weary.
7 The craving of these voluptuaries, so beautiful and tender,
    is stronger with every moment;
8 with a charm to preserve them now, Hita Harivaṃśa,
    I am an offering to their pure revelry.

(2) *banī*: the verbal sense from *ban-* is taken by Prem. and Lok., while Rasik. has the phrase *banī madhya* 'in the wood'; Dhar. has no direct gloss. Cf. 17.1 where *banī* does have a nominal sense.
(5) *bāmadṛsā*: since **vāmadṛśā* is unattested, the present form must be a Hindi form based on Sk. *vāmadṛś* (*MW*) (for **vāmadṛśi*?). Readings of *-da°* (BCEFM) may represent a construing of a *tatsama*, *daśā* 'edge of garment'; but word order makes a sense 'the lady [touches] her lover's hem and garland' unlikely.
(8) *trana ṭūṭ-*: the 'breaking of a straw' is a symbolic act of ritual protection from the effects of the evil eye (*HŚS* s.v. *tṛṇa*, where the citation given is from Svāmī Haridāsa); cf. *vāri pher-* (10.4) with similar sense.

CP 33.

1 Today the youthful pair is resplendent in the forest:

2 Nanda's son and Vṛṣabhānu's daughter
are arisen sleepless at dawn.

3 Their feet fall faltering with languid gait,
the tips of their moon-shaped nails brushing the ground;

4 their lips are torn, their cheeks ornamented with collyrium,
and just a little of their *tilakas* remains.

5 Her locks will not be restrained though her fingers try to hold them,
they are thieving bees for her red [lotus-] eyes;

6 Hita Harivaṃśa, neither body nor mind can be held in check
in the squalls of the ocean of passion.

(2) *nādanaṃdana*; although this form, with regular weakening in the first syllable, is expected, KLM show *candrabindu* in *-nādana* (and cf. B's reading *-nadana*). Elsewhere in the text, the readings *nādanaṃdā* (with final *-ā* for rhyme, (63[iii].4) and etymological *naṃdanaṃdana* (81.2) both appear as metrically apposite forms.
(3) *parasata naṣa sasi chora:* the intended image is of a very languorous gait. Lok.'s gloss, *parasata hai naṣa caṃdrakani kau basana kau chora*, 'the edges of their garments touch their moon-shaped nails', demands that *chora* can of itself have the sense *aṃcala* etc., which is unlikely.

CP 34.

1 In their roamings in the forest's thicket-bowers,

2 they pass through very narrow lanes,
but do not touch them with their garments.

3 At dawn the rolling of their eyes betrays the joy
of their night-long wakefulness—

4 some little movement stirs in their orbs,
languid, reddish and distracted.

5 With her dancing eyebrows, soft lotus face,
joyful laugh and sweet speech

6 she has bought control over Lāla without cost—
the wanton bee who is utterly enamoured of her!

7 Loose and disarranged, dark straggling locks of hair
shine on her lovely cheeks,

8 with a comely stroking of chins in the kissing and embracing
of this inverted lovemaking.

9 Sometimes when she lies wearied on a couch of shoots,
her face is fanned with the hem of his garment;

10 Harivaṃśa ever sprinkles the heart of the slave
with waves from this ocean of revelry!

(1) *kuṃja nikuṃjani*: the collocation of the text in H is *kuṃjana kuṃjana*, in G *kuṃjani kuṃjani*. Prem., however, glosses *nikuṃja tě kuṃja...aura kuṃja tě nikuṃja*. The collocation of the *mūla* suggests that a semantic distinction does exist between

kuṃja and *nikuṃja* (as indeed suggested by Prem.'s gloss), and the most satisfactory sense is attained by reading *kuṃja nikuṃja* as a single unit on the model of *kuṃja kuṭīra* (37.1) etc.

(2) *parasata nāhi nicolani*: the conceit lends emphasis to the supernatural surroundings of the grove, which is the point of the couplet. The commentators, however, make the *couple* the subject of the conceit: Prem. glosses *latā jo haĩ saṣirūpa haĩ, āpa saraka jāi haĩ*, 'the creepers have the form of *sakhīs* and slip back of their own accord'; Lok. glosses *yāmai priyā prītama kā lāghavatā kahī* 'in this the dexterity of lover and beloved is expressed', but concedes *athavā bracha cetana hai. āpatai daunau kau bibasa jāni māraga deta hai* 'or the trees are sentient, and themselves knowing the couple to be helpless, make way for them'.

(3) *sūcata suṣa dṛga lolani*: lit., 'they betray their joy with the rolling of their eyes'.

(6) *kīne*: the context of 'purchase' occurring in the following expression *binu molani* confirms that *kīne* is likely to be from the verb *kīn-* ⟨ *krīṇāti*, rather than from *kī-*; the only perfective forms from *kar-* attested in the CP are *kiyau, kiye*. The expression *basa kar-* is, however, attested in the text (4.5 etc.), which suggests that a *śleṣa* is intended here.

(7) *rājata*: it is possible that a non-finite participle **rājita*, not now attested in the manuscripts, may have been intended; this would allow the whole of line (7), and the next line (similarly without a finite verb), to be read as instrumental in composition with *basa kīne* in the previous line— 'with cheeks adorned...' etc.

(9) *sajjā* derives from *śayyā-* independently of its synonym *seja*⟨ **śeyyā-*. The reading *sejyā* in BDIJM, and perhaps the AFH reading *sijyā*, probably shows a confusion of the two Hindi forms.

(10) *haribaṃśa dāsi hiya sīcata*: interpretation of this phrase depends upon the place accorded to *haribaṃśa* in the syntax of the line (see p. 112 for a discussion of this problem in a wider context). If Harivaṃśa is taken to be Kṛṣṇa, then Harivaṃśa's *dāsī* will clearly be Rādhā; and such a sense will yield the attractive paradox of the *dāsī* Rādhā (line (10)) subjugating her master (line (6)). Furthermore, 'sprinkling the heart' is a logical sequel to 'fanning the face' in the first half of the couplet, and elsewhere in the text it is usually Rādhā, and not Kṛṣṇa, who requires such resuscitation (66.5 *śramita ati abalā*, etc.). An alternative interpretation, favoured generally by the commentators, takes *haribaṃśa dāsi* as 'Harivaṃśa the slave' (with the usual conceit of devotee as female); this is consistent with the construction of other stanzas, where the final line or couplet withdraws from the action and makes a statement about the relationship between the devotee and the divine couple.

CP 35.

1 The two young ones are swinging to and fro;
2 having arisen at dawn, their every limb betrays
the night's merriment and joy.
3 Quite filled with love they sing together
in low tones and musical voice.
4 from time to time the beloved captivates her lover's heart
[with a glance] from the corner of her eye.
5 So delicate, the lady is frightened in her heart
by the rush of the excellent swing;
6 in a thrill of emotion she clings to her lover's chest,
tendering her young breasts in offering.

7 His bright garland is entangled with her bracelets,
and with his earrings her strands of hair;
8 how can they be separated when trembling so?
Their joy has grown in no small measure.
9 Looking on constantly, Lalitā and the other *sakhīs* are overjoyed—
cakoras to the moons of those two faces;
10 taking the hems of their garments, they bless the ones
praised by Harivaṃśa.

(1) *jhūlata*: the rhyme of this participle with others in line (2), (3), (4) and (6) strengthens the caesura before the second half-line in both full line and *ṭeka* alike. Cf. also the weak rhyme with *bibecita* (8) and *prasaṃsita* (10) in respect of the manuscripts' confusion between *-ata* and *-ita* participles elsewhere in the text, and the commentators' confusion over *prasaṃsita* noted below.
(10) *prasaṃsita*: despite a complete lack of **prasaṃsata* forms, Prem. and Lok. both gloss with finite participles (*praśaṃsā kare haĩ* and *baḍāī karata haĩ* respectively).
(10) *kari aṃcala kī chora*: the sense is probably that of the modern Hindi idiom *aṃcala pasāranā* 'to show humility while supplicating (a deity)' (Bholānāth Tivārī p. 3); for such a sense cf. the expression *aṃcala jore* in composition with *bīnatī kar-* in the *Sūrasāgara* (Hardev Bāhrī p. 3, but reference not traceable in the *SS* itself). Such an interpretation sits well in the context of the line. Alternatively, the reference may be to the service of fanning offered by the *sakhīs*, for which cf. 34.9. The commentators all give literal paraphrases which leave the crux unresolved.

CP 36.

1 Today in the forest a fine round-dance is created;
2 on the pure sandbank by the blessed Yamuna's shore,
Mohana has sounded his flute.
3 Hearing the sound of sweet bracelets, waist-bells and anklets
birds and beasts have become joyful;
4 as amidst the circle of damsels
Ghanaśyāma has introduced the Sāraṅga *rāga*.
5 Cymbal, barrel-drum, *upaṅga*, *muraja* and frame-drum
have together swelled the ocean of *rasa*,
6 and with her various radiant limbs
Vṛṣabhānu's daughter has demonstrated the *sudhaṅga* dance.
7 Skilful of gesture, and with eyes overhung by curls,
her eyebrows have set Kāma a-dancing:
8 seizing a new rhythm with a "tātātheī! tātheī!"
she has delighted her husband, lord of Vraja.
9 Best of all illustrious sovereigns,
he has made clouds of joy rain down,

10 and the damsel-folk won delightful embraces,
with clasping and kissing.

11 Rejoicing in the showering of blossoms,
Indra sounded the kettledrum;

12 Hita Harivaṃśa, the canopy of fame of Rādhā's lord the lover
has overspread the world.

(3) *kiṃkini*: although the first four-*mātrā gaṇa* in a line of this type is rarely a dactyl, a manuscript support for *kīkinī* is weak here; alliteration with prec. *kaṃkana* supports the given reading. Cf. notes to 4.6 and 67.6.
(4) *syāmaghana*: the literal sense 'dark cloud' is also suggested by the context, and a reading as 'he has amassed dark cloud' is possible. This exploits the sense of *maṃḍala* as 'sphere (of the skies)', and echoes the lexical sense of *sāraṅga* as 'cloud' (*MW*) which may lend the *rāga* a seasonal connotation; it also accommodates *jamā-* rather more comfortably by giving it a concrete object. The singular *-āyau* of the verb, however, entails singular number for 'cloud', such that a truly satisfactory *śleṣa* is not achieved.
(4) *sārāga rāga*: the present stanza is the first in the sequence CP 36-51 to which Sāraṃga is apportioned in the manuscripts. Lok.'s gloss supplies the two alternatives Bīravai and Dīpaka (*athavā bīravai rāga gāyau. athavā dīpaka rāga gāyau*), perhaps after actual performance usage which is frequently at odds with the *rāga* allocations prescribed in the manuscripts.
(6) *aṃga sudhaṃga diṣāyau*: the phrase is repeated verbatim by all the commentators except Prem., who glosses *bahuta bhātini sõ bṛṣabhānanaṃdinī jū sudhaṃga nṛtya ko aṃga diṣāvata bhaī*, 'Vṛṣabhānunandinī demonstrated the *sudhaṅga* dance section in many ways'. See note to 19.10 for a discussion of the collocation *aṃga sudhaṃga*.
(8) *tātāthei tāthei*: these are mnemonics used to mark time and to stress rhythmic patterns in dancing and drumming: cf. similar occurrences in 62.4, 68.7, 71.3. The metrically long vowels in mnemonic sequences of this kind are usually pronounced short, and must be so scanned here. Cf. the following portion of a *Kṛṣṇa stuti*, annotated in a manual for dance performance, in which long vowels *pronounced* as long by the dancer are followed by a dash (representing *avagraha* in the Nāgarī); the construction is in 12-*mātrā pādas*, and the phrase *tātheithei* constitutes only 6 *mātrās*:

mo-ra mukuṭa sira so-he-; pī-tā̃ bara mana mo-he-.
pā̃-va pai-janī- suhā-ta; rū-pa madana ko- lajā-ta.
tā-theī theī calata cā-la; upajata nava chaṃ-da tā-la.
(*Saṅgīta*, 1970:200)

As in the other CP occurrences, the alliteration of the repeated dental *t* is taken up in the remainder of the line in 36.8. (For *theī theī*, cf. Skt. *thai thai* 'imitative sound of a musical instrument' (*MW*).)
(10) *ucita*: taken by Prem. as 'worthy': *jo juvatī jana ucita hī̃ tini pāyau*, 'those damsels received, who were worthy'. Lok. takes the same sense, but restricts the reference to Rādhā (despite the pluralizing suffix *jana*).
(12) In collocation to the 'Indra' reference, the image of a 'canopy' (*bitāna*) suggests an allusion to the Govardhanadharaṇa myth.

CP 37.

1 Why do you not go to the hut in the grove, proud lady?

2 accompanied by thousands of women, without you, young girl,
the agony of love assails him.

3 His voice is choked, his body trembles in the distress of separation,
and his eyes run with tears;

4 "Where art thou? Where art thou, daughter of Vṛṣabhānu?"
laments the distracted one in the forest.

5 His flute is an arrow, like serpents his many-stranded garland,
and cuckoo and parrot are as lions;

6 sandalwood is venom to him, the wind like fire,
and his clothes are like a prickly plant.

7 Hita Harivaṃśa, the most tender-hearted one
went hastily to her lover;

8 hearing this, he of thunderbolt-body, valiant hero of passion,
became afraid.

(2) *kũvari*: the *-a* reading in A and L must represent loss of *-i*, since a masc. form cannot comfortably be accommodated here. Rasik.'s paraphrase, however, reads *tuma bina hari*, and Lok. glosses his *mūla*'s reading *kuvari* with *prītama*. Dhar.'s paraphrase neither includes nor glosses the A reading *kuvara*; Prem.'s gloss with a vocative (as in the translation) is consistent with the reading *kũvari* found in the Prem. manuscripts GKM. The crux recurs in 39.4 with a repeat of the phrase *to binu kũvari*.

(6) *sāṣāmṛga ripu*: this is glossed by Prem. as *kvaica kī phali* and by Lok. as *kauca kī phalī*, both presumably referring to the pod with stinging hairs of the plant *kaũca*, *kavãca* (> Eng. 'cowage' etc.—*Mucuna prurita*, Platts); in its derivation from *kapi-kacchū* (*ibid.*), this is a synonym for the *śākhāmṛgaripu* conceit (for which cf. the English name 'monkey puzzle' for the Chilean pine). LCG also glosses *kõca*, but equates it with *apāmārga* (*Achyranthes aspera*, *MW*). Dhar. merely reiterates the *mūla*; Rasik. paraphrases with the synonym *bānararipu*. Hardev Bahrī (p. 574) defines *śākhāmṛgaṛpu* (sic) as *kilanī* ('tick, dog-louse', Platts) in his gloss on the *Sūrasāgara* recension of this stanza (see Appendix II). Deśrājsiṃh Bhāṭī (p. 58) defines *śākhā-mṛgaripu* as the prickly shrub *ciraciṭā* in his gloss on an occurrence of the word in *Sūrasāgara* 270 (referred to by Bhāṭī as 2705).

(8) *ranabīra*: the reading °*dhīra* imposed in E as a late emendation appears also in the *Sūrasāgara* recension of this stanza.

CP 38.

1 Arise and come quickly—why do you delay?—
Lāla calls you to the bower;

2 "Ah Rādhā! Rādhikā?" he calls
as he sees the cast of the elephant of passion.

3 The autumn moon and the breeze lend it their support,
and the garland on his chest has defected and joined them;

4 he seeks a place of refuge, most fearful of the conflict—
won't you come to your lover's defence?

5 Hita Harivaṃśa, when she heard this she was much affected,
and went to him that very moment;

6 the Vraja damsel took the passion-hero
and protected him between the beautiful peaks of her breasts.

(2) *ḍhāla*: Prem. glosses with 'banner' (*dhujā*), a sense attested by Platts and *HŚS* and clearly a possibility in this military context. Rasik.'s and Dhar.'s retention of the *mūla* verbatim, and Lok's confused gloss *niraṣi madana gaja kī* [*sic*] *āvana kau*, suggest that the word may have been unfamiliar to these commentators.

(6) *surata sūra*: Prem., Lok. and Dhar. all understand this as referring to Rādhā, as exemplified by Prem.'s gloss: *brajabāla jo śrī priyā jū so surata ke raṇa mẽ sūra haĩ.* Such an interpretation, which seeks to raise Rādhā's status, sacrifices the intended paradox of all-powerful Kṛṣṇa's helplessness. Lok. maintains the ambiguity of the *mūla* by glossing *sūra hai brajabāla*; yet *brajabāla* is intended to have fem. reference, as at 71.2.

CP 39.

1 Lāla desires to play in amorous dalliance;

2 he has decked out the bower-house,
preparing it lovingly with his own hands.

3 It is a night of autumn, and the cool wind
is gentle and fragrant;

4 who but you, young girl,
could now extinguish the agony of his desire?

5 Won't you come swiftly, doe-eyed one,
abandoning now your silence—

6 subduer of your lover's anguish,
unite with him, [begs] Hita Harivaṃśa!

(4) *to binu kũvari:* in this repeat of a phrase already met in 37.2, there are no glosses suggesting masc. gender for *kũvar-*. Prem. and Lok. paraphrase with *kũvari* as a vocative addressed to Rādhā; Rasik. and Dhar. have no direct gloss.

(4) *meṭẽ*: readings of *meṭa* (FHJ) are presumably attempts at metrical 'correction'.

(5) *capala* occurs adjectivally in collocation with *naina* at 22.2, 43.2 and 73.3; but in the present context *nain-* is within the compound *bālamṛganainī*, and *capala* is therefore to be understood in composition with *cal-*, with adverbial force, as at 37.7 and 40.5. Prem. correctly glosses *he bāla mṛga nainī śīghra kyaũ na calau;* Lok. and Rasik., however, take the other sense in their respective glosses *cali nija kuṃja kau, he capala bāla mṛga nainī* and *mṛga sisu caṃcala sama su dṛga calo tajo kina mona*. Dhar. has no gloss on this half-line.

(5) The second *pāda* is short by one *mātrā*; there are no attestations of a Hindi stem **tajj-* or **tāj-* to suggest that *taji* may be a corrupt reading.

(5) *mavana* is formed for rhyme from H. *mauna*, on the model of the (legitimate) spellings *kauna*/*kavana*.

CP 40.

1 Lāla tarries in the bower-house;
2 the night is pleasant, with budded jasmine
  and breeze of threefold nature.
3 Through your love-play, friend,
  you are the subduer of Manamohana's passion;
4 why do you delay uselessly, slender-waisted one?
  What is the reason?
5 Hearing this, she set off swiftly,
  careless of the fate of her body;
6 and, Hita Harivaṃśa, she met
  the love-greedy lover of Rādhā!

(1) *bhavana* etc.: all the rhyme-words in this stanza, except *śravana*, have already appeared in the rhyme-scheme of CP 39.
(6) *rādhāravana*: although the second half-line in this stanza is not of consistent length, the edited reading has a metrical weight consistent with (1) and (4). A possible reason why the form *rādhikāravana* may have been imposed is discussed in the context of a similar crux at 2.3.

CP 41.

1 Only the voluptuary may know the course of love;
2 though he is the crowning glory of the whole world,
  he deems himself wretched.
3 In the bower-house on Yamuna's bank
  the haughty one is intent on jealous indignation;
4 the myriads of groups of young loving ladies near at hand
  can bring no composure to his heart.
5 Transitory is a love which, like the fickle bee's
  arises with a host of others;
6 Hita Harivaṃśa, that person alone is wise
  who abandons all bounds and discerns Lāla.

(2) *jadyapi:* it is unclear how *-dd-* spellings (which are attested in *HŚS*) can have derived from Sk. *yadyapi*, unless simply by miscopying of the *dy* conjunct. A metrical readjustment of H. *jadapi* (which may itself show contamination by *tadapi*) could be a possible explanation in individual occurrences, but can hardly underlie more widespread usage. *-ipa* spellings occurring in the manuscripts here (and cf. further occurrences of the word at 43.6 and 77.2) are presumably metathetical.
(5)–(6) This final couplet, and in particular the final line, appears somewhat out of context: there is a change of subject from a straightforward description of Kṛṣṇa's *viraha* in (1)–(4) to a didactic expression of the desirability of single-mindedness in devotion to 'Lāla' in (5)–(6). The commentators contextualize the stanza as being addressed to Rādhā, thereby allowing the didactic couplet to be interpreted as a recommendation that she abandon her *māna* and join her lover: but Rādhā is referred

to in the *third* person in line (3), and furthermore it is rather unusual for an accusation of promiscuity, such as appears in line (5), to be levelled at a *māninī*.
(5) *nasvara neha capala madhukara jyaũ*: the injunction to respond to Kṛṣṇa's monogamy contained in this couplet is rather at odds with the conceit of Kṛṣṇa himself as a fickle 'bee' elsewhere in the text (e.g. 63 [iv].1 *deṣata madhukara keli*).

CP 42.

1 Love observes nobody's proprieties;
2 who could prevent a love-sick mind
from following its path, good or bad?
3 As when a stream, swelling with monsoon waters,
makes headlong for the sea;
4 or when in the open a huntsman slays a doe
which is intent on his song;
5 And, Hita Harivaṃśa, as when a bird becomes enmeshed
or a moth burns up its body—
6 [yet] who but the clever lord, young Mohana,
would give up his very self?

(4) *nādahi mana diye*: the fascination of the deer for the huntsman's song is a stock image in Hindi verse; cf. *SS* 3906, a *pada* similarly describing the effects of *prīti*, in which the fourth line reads *sārãga prīti karī ju nāda saũ sanmukha bāna sahyau*.
(4) *kuraṃgani*: Prem., Lok. and Rasik. ignore the *-ani* ending and gloss as masc. singular 'deer'; Dhar. glosses *kuraṃganu*. Given the loss of *-i-* in MSS's *nitaṃbani* for *nitaṃbini* at 45.8, it is also possible that L's fem. *kuraṃgini* is an authentic reading (a gnomic singular being attractive here).
(4) *pāradhī*: *HŚS* defines as 'a huntsman who operates from a hide'. The point of the conceit, therefore, is that the doe is engrossed to the extent that the huntsman can leave his hide and kill his prey 'in the open' (*pragaṭa*). This technical sense of *pāradhī* is apparently not familiar to the commentators, who do not so explain the conceit; Lok. even substitutes *badhika* for *pāradhī* in his gloss. (Dhar. has no gloss on the second half of (4) or on the first half of (5)).
(5) *hilaga sārãga*: Lok. and Rasik. take *hilaga* as a (fem.) noun, presumably understanding the sense 'love, attachment' as given by Prem.'s gloss *sārãga sõ āsakta hoike*. This interpretation is based on Prem. and Lok.'s definition of *sārãga* as 'lamp' (*dīpaka*) which is not, however, attested in *MW* even in the long list of meanings from the lexicographers, and is 27th (and still uncited) in the *HŚS* list. Given the *recherché* nature of this alleged definition, therefore, it seems more probable that *sārãga* has the established sense 'bird', and that *hilaga* is the absolutive from *hilag-*, 'become entangled': this sense is attested in Platts, s.v. *hilagnā*. *hilaga sārãga* is therefore separate from, and complementary to, the following image *salabha sarīrahi jārai*.
(6) All the commentators emphasize a contrast between the sacrifice of *apanapau*, achieved only by Kṛṣṇa, and of mere life, achieved more easily; the sense requires the addition of 'yet' in the translation.

CP 43.

1 Vṛṣabhānu's daughter is highly accomplished:
2 listen, messenger-girl: the fair one, nimble and deer-eyed,
attracts the mind with a glance.
3 Her wood-apple breasts, her golden body and her lion's waist
are[but] ripples on the ocean of her qualities;
4 her braided hair is a snake, her face a hundred moons,
her thighs are plantain [stalks], and she has stolen the swan's gait.
5 Hear me, Harivaṃśa: today at nightfall
bring my constant partner to me in the forest;
6 though the lovely lady is beset by jealous pride,
how could she, the virtuous one of guileless heart, linger when she hears [the call]?

(2) *suni dūtikā*: the context of the stanza, agreed by all the commentators, is one in which Kṛṣṇa addresses Harivaṃśa as *sakhī*.

(4) *jalacara*: Rasik. glosses as 'fish' (*mīna*); Prem., too, offers this as an alternative to *haṃsa* and as yielding an image of 'oblique gait' applied to the eyes: *mīna ne ini nainani kī tirachī gati curāi laī hai*. Lok. also glosses with *mīna*, but also contrives an imposition of the sense *gajagati*: *bana nāma jala kau. bana mai hāthī rahe, tākī gati corata hai.*

CP 44.

1 Come beautiful one, he has called you to Vṛndāvana;
2 loving lady, why do you not cling to him and shine—
you the lightning, Mohana the fresh cloud?
3 Your bodice is red, your sari multi-coloured,
your body is decorated with the sixteen [adornments];
4 these are all young Mohana's due,
and the youthfulness of your wood-apple breasts is his legitimate inheritance!
5 Great love was within her, Hita Harivaṃśa,
as she went to him with blossoming heart;
6 the ocean of *rasa* united with her in the dense bower
defeating a hundred love-gods in the battle of passion.

(3) *naṣa juga ūna*: Prem. lists the 16 *śṛṅgāra* in a ten-line *pada* bearing his own *chāpa*. Further references to the conceit appear in CP 45, 67, 81, and a full discussion is given in an extended note to 45.3.

(4) *āgama dhana*: the compound is not retained, nor its technical sense (*āgama*: 'descent of property'—H.H. Wilson 1855: 9) glossed, by any of the commentators. Instead, all read *āgama* in compound with prec. *jovana*, as expressed most simply by

Lok.: *kuca navīna jovana so dhana*. Dhar. adds a conceit of his own, with the dawning of youth's rays behind the mountain of the beloved's breasts: *udai bhayau dinakara nava jovana suṃdara uraja salila tai...* LCG records a practice in which an esteemed person makes a gift of *śrīphala* fruits together with money; he accordingly glosses *āgama dhana* as 'money to be presented'. The technical sense of the compound, however, does not permit these free-ranging interpretations.
(5) *aṃtaragati*: being found only in F, the etymologically correct °*ta* ending does not appear to be authentic. Cf. the CP spelling *bibidhi*, for which readings in °*dha* are similarly doubtful.

CP 45.

1 Śrī Vṛṣabhānu's darling daughter comes;
2 an amassment of beautiful form, crest-jewel of the greatly skilled,
delicate in every limb.
3 Being firstly anointed and bathed,
her indigo-pigmented body is dressed in a sari;
4 her locks are braided, a pretty *tilaka* drawn,
her parting decorated with vermilion.
5 Her fawn-like eyes are marked with collyrium,
following a lovely line;
6 a jewelled nose-pin is on her charming nostril,
her teeth are edged with black.
7 A necklace of rare splendour lies on
her wood-apple breasts bound in a saffron bodice;
8 her waist is slender, deep the navel in her belly,
and the thighs of the full-hipped one are well rounded.
9 As lotus-stems are her ornamented arms,
thrown around Śyāma's shoulders;
10 Hita Harivaṃśa, like the pair of elephant and mate
the lover and beloved besport themselves in the forest.

(3) *prathama*: for adverbial usage cf. 57.1 *prathama jathāmati pranaũ*. In the present stanza, the word introduces a sequence of items which may be construed as the 16 *śṛṅgāras* alluded to in 44.3; *prathama* has this function again in 81.3, and the conceit also occurs in CP 67. In all three stanzas the 16 items follow a general *nakhaśikha* sequence; but the three lists differ broadly, as can be seen from the following tabulation (in which each item is followed by the number of the line in which it occurs):

	CP 45	CP 67	CP 81
1	*ubaṭana* (3)	*tilaka* (2)	*majjana* (3)
2	*majjana* (3)	*ubaṭana* (2)	*cīra* (3)
3	*nīla barana* (3)	*ṣorī* (2)	*kajjala* (3)
4	*sārī* (3)	*gaṃḍa maṃḍita* (3)	*tilaka* (3)
5	*gũthita alaka* (4)	*caṃdrikā* (3)	*kuṃḍala* (3)
6	*tilaka* (4)	*medinī kavari* (3)	*badana* (3)
7	*sẽdura* (4)	*ḍorī* (3)	*besarī* (4)
8	*aṃjana* (5)	*tāṭaṃka* (4)	*adhara* (4)

9	*lavaṃga* (6)	*biṃdu* (4)	*dasana* (4)
10	*dasanāvali kārī* (6)	*kā̃cukī* (4)	*balaya* (5)
11	*kā̃cukī* (7)	*balaya* (5)	*kaṃkana* (5)
12	*hāra* (7)	*kaṃkana* (5)	*hāra* (5)
13	*kaṭi* (8)	*jāvaka* (5)	*kiṃkini* (5)
14	*nābhi* (8)	*udara reṣa* (5)	*nūpura* (5)
15	*jaghana* (8)	*paṭa* (5)	*haṃsakala* [*-gati*] (6)
16	*bhuja* (9)	*kĩkinī* (6)	*madayaṃtikā* (6)

Although the *nakhaśikha* sequence is generally shared by all three lists, the only specific lexical item common to all three is *tilaka*. In the present stanza, none of the commentators allege a 16-*śṛṅgāra* conceit; Prem. and Rasik. both recognise it in CP 67, where both give inventories of the items, while in CP 81 the conceit is recognised by Dhar., who merely mentions the term *navasata siṃgāra*, and by Rasik., who again offers a full inventory. For the purpose of comparison with the *mūla*, these various glosses will be considered here.

At CP 67 Prem. gives a computation of 16 items differing from that given above. He regards certain items as elliptical and inherently implied (*ānuṣaṃgika*) by other items (as for example *aṃjana*, allegedly implied by *mṛgaja locana*, and *snāna*, allegedly implied by *ubaṭana*); other items, included in our list, are regarded by him as inadmissible: e.g. *gaṃḍa maṃḍita*, regarded as general description (*yaha sĩgāra mẽ nāhī, muṣa kī sobhā ko barnana hai*), and *balaya*, *kaṃkana* and *kiṃkini*, classified separately as belonging to the complementary category of *dvādaśa ābharaṇa*. Prem.'s computation of the items in CP 67 is as follows:

1	*tilaka*	9	*ḍorī*
2	*aṃjana* (elliptical)	10	*tāṭaṃka*
3	*ubaṭana*	11	*biṃdu*
4	*snāna* (elliptical)	12	*besarī* (elliptical)
5	*aṃga rāga* (elliptical)	13	*kaṃcukī*
6	*ṣorī*	14	*mālā* (elliptical)
7	*caṃdrikā*	15	*reṣa*
8	*madinī kavari*	16	*nīlāṃbara*

This list may be compared with the sequence of items given by Prem. in a *pada* of his own composition included in his gloss (quoted below from the text in M) on the phrase *naṣa juga ūna* (44.3). Items are given in **bold type**:

rājata śrī bṛṣabhāna dulārī;
jhamaki rahe navaśata aṃgana mẽ trabhuvana kī chabi vārī.
kiyẽ prathama ***maṃjana*** *manaraṃjana diyẽ* ***jalaja*** *nāsā rī;*
nīlāṃbara ***sā̃rī*** *ati rājata* ***nīvī̃*** *sarasa sãvārī.*
benī gūhī bibidhi ***phūlani*** *sõ dipati* ***taraunā̃*** *bhārī;*
amgā̃-rā̃ga *tana cikura* ***caṃdrakā̃*** *guhī lasata sobhā rī.*
ura ***mā̃lā̃*** *kara* ***kamala pā̃na*** *muṣa cibuka syāma* ***bĩdu*** *nyārī;*
draga ***aṃjana*** *muṣa m[u]ṣara* ***patrikā̃ jā̃vaka*** *pagana sudhārī.*
kasatūrī ko ***tilaka*** *bhāla laṣi mohe naṃda lalā rī;*
premadāsa hita yaha suṣa nirașata āṣiyā ṭarata na ṭārī.

Quite apart from discrepancies between individual items in *ṭīkā* and *mūla*, this sequence differs from the CP sequences in having no trace of *nakhaśikha* order.

Rasik. gives two alternative inventories in his gloss on CP 67. Neither is apparently intended as a direct gloss on the items given in the *mūla*; rather, Rasik. broadens the discussion by citing *conventional* listings—as is shown by his phrase *dūsare graṃthāṃtara mata* in introducing the second series. These lists differ from the *mūla's* and that given by Prem. in admitting abstract qualities such as *cāturī* to the conceit. Rasik.'s inventories are as follows:

pahile **maṃjana** *eka jo dūjau suṃdara* **cīra**;
tilaka *tīsarau jāni daga-* **aṃjana** *caturtha dhīra.*
kuṃḍala *paṃcama leṣiye nāsā* **muktā** *saṣṭa;*
hāra *sāta yõ bhāni aru syāma* **ḍora** *soi aṣṭa.*
kāvarī *nava ura āniye daśa* **nūpura** *jhanakāra;*
aṃga lepa **caṃdana** *vahai ekādasa suṣa sāra.*
chudrāvali *dvādasa tathā terahe puni* **tā̃būla**;
kara **kiṃkani** *hī caturdaśa paṃdraha* **caturī** *mūla.*
ṣoḍasa **sugati** *ju jānikai ye soraha byāṣyāna;*
te rādhā tana lase nita dhyābo rasika sujāna.

dūsare graṃthāṃtara mata ṣoḍasa siṃgāra nāma.

ubaṭana maj[j]ana puhapa *puni lepa su* **caṃdana** *aṃga;*
alakāvali masi biṃdukana *ura* **kaṃcukī** *suraṃga.*
caṣa **kājjala** *duti sahi subha ujjala* **cīra** *sarīra;*
sara **ṣorī tābola** *muṣa* **jāvaka** *raṃga gābhīra.*
lāja ju yukta mṛdu **hāsa** *aru* **rasanā** *surāgita cāru;*
sobhita saba bidhi **cāturī** *ye ṣoḍasa si[ṃ]gāra.*

In his gloss on CP 81, Rasik. gives yet another list, this time remaining closer to the *mūla*:

tana ṣoḍasa siṃgāra je bāne priyā ke cāru;
tina kõ barani sunāvaī nāma pragaṭa bistāra.
ādi **sumajjana** *jāniyẽ dvitiya* **cārutā** *māni;*
tritīya su suṃdara **cīra** *mṛdu ati sūchama tana bāni.*
aru **tilaka** *kuṃkuma racita lasata caturtha lalāṭa*
netrāṃjana *paṃcama asita* **kuṃḍala** *ṣaṣṭa sughāṭa.*
nāsā **muktā** *saptayau* **hāra** *aṣṭa hiya dhīra;*
ḍora *su nava* **kabarī** *dasama ekādasa* **maṃjīra**.
tana **caṃdana** *dvādasa laṣahu mili ujjala ghanasāra;*
chudraghaṃṭikā *trayodasa manimaya sabda sudhāra.*
tā̃būla *caturdasa pācadasa kara* **kaṃkana** *jhanakāra;*
atihi **caturatā** *mili sakala ye ṣoḍasa siṃgāra.*

The 16-*śṛṅgāra* convention is widely attested throughout Hindi literature. It is not, however, a feature of Sanskrit poetics, and is also notably absent from the early 14th century Maithilī text *Varṇa ratnākara*, a 'repository of literary similes and conventions' (S.K. Chatterji, ed., 1940: xxi) which contains a large number of other such categories and conceits. The CP's examples do not show a conceit exemplified in the *Padmāvata* (40.4-5; V.S. Agravāl, ed., pp. 588-9), wherein the 16 are divided into four groups of four natural attributes, being variously long (hair, etc.), short (teeth, etc.), slender (nose, etc.) and broad (cheeks, etc.); nor are the present examples restricted to the category 'appliances for decoration' listed by Platts s.v. *siṃgār.* Unlike these other occurrences (and cf. further examples in *HŚS* s.v. *śṛṅgāra*, and Entwistle 1983:422), the CP's sequences are structured only in terms of *nakhaśikha* sequence. It is possible, therefore, that the CP tradition represents an early stage in the development of the Hindi 16-*śṛṅgāra* convention out of the Sk. *nakhaśikha varṇana* (perhaps conflated by the *ṣoḍaśa kalā* conceit as exmplified in the *Varṇa ratnākara*, *loc. cit.*, p. 18).

(3) *nīla barana tana sārī*: the word order suggests that, unless *tana* is simply a pleonasm with *sārī* (as e.g. *tana-cīra*, *BBhSK*), the compound *nīla barana tana* refers to the indigo tattooing listed in Platts (s.v. *siṃgār*) as one of the 16-*śṛṅgāras*. All the commentators, however, take *nīla barana* as qualifying *sārī* (in spite of the description of the *sārī* as 'multicoloured' in 44.3), with *tana* as locative.

A sense of Sk. *tanu* as 'fine in texture' is attested in the *Ṛtusaṃhāra* (*MW*), but a lack of more general attestion makes it unlikely that this sense is intended here.

(7) *upara:* the metrically correct short *u-* is found in ACEF. ACE, however, read *upara* for *correct ūpara* at 20.3, and A does so again at 23.4; the *u-* readings in the present line may, therefore, be only accidentally correct and not represent a genuine preservation of the archetype. A's *ura* probably indicates a simple omission of *-pa-*, perhaps founded on a scribe's misreading of the text as (metrically deficient) **ura hāra*, 'chest garland'.
(8) *nitaṃbani*: an oblique plural cannot be intended here, though Prem.'s ingenuous gloss *jaghana nitaṃbani sahita bhārī hai* attempts to accommodate one by introducing a postposition. As in the case of *kuraṃgani* (42.4), the *-ani* ending must be for fem. singular *-ini*. The fact that the total number of *śṛṅgāras* becomes an excessive 17 if *jaghana* and *nitaṃba* are taken as separate items supports the hypothesis. A reading as *nitaṃba na bhārī* is not plausible.
(9) *ḍārī*: fem. ending shows agreement with *bṛṣabhānadulārī* as stanza subject, *ḍārī* being a non-finite participle. Prem.'s gloss *māno kamala kī mṛṇāla sī bhuj(h)ā bhūṣaṇa sahita śyāma ke aṃsa para ḍārī hai* attempts to explain the fem. agreement by substituting the *mūla*'s masc. *bhuja* with fem. *bhujā*; but this latter form is barely attested.

CP 46.

1 Taking pleasure in their love-play with arms joined in the forest's dense arbour,
Śyāma and Śyāmā are united on an autumn night;
2 lover and accomplished lady rejoice equally in their hearts,
like impassioned elephant and mate delightful in diverse qualities.
3 Being absorbed by the laughter and merriment of their amorous behaviour,
Madana's force is decimated by the lady addicted to dalliance;
4 listen, Hita Harivaṃśa! Lāla is overcome by her loveliness—
the lover is most valiant in gaiety, she a champion in love-making!

(2) *rāminī*: since it is semantically implausible that this should qualify only fem. *karani*, fem. *-inī* is presumably an accommodation for rhyme.
(3) *dalita dala madana bala*: the construction put on this phrase in the translation is consistent with the *gaṇa* construction of the line, and accommodates the relationship of *dala* 'division of an army' with *bala* 'army', but is not represented in the commentaries; in their characteristic unwillingness to recognise determinative compounds, they all take *bala* as an instrumental governed by *kāminī*.
(4) *hita hari-*: this catalectic four-*mātrā gaṇa* is the only instance in this stanza of a deviation from the standard five-*mātrā* (⏓⏑⏓) *gaṇa*. G's omission of *hita*, and A's reading of *prabhu* for *suni*, both suggest some irregularity in the transmission of the *chāpa*, though A's reading may be an assimilation to *hita haribaṃśa prabhu* in 71.6 (again with catalexis in the first *gaṇa*).
(4) *lāvani*: the alternative form *lāvanya*, which has somewhat better manuscript support, is unmetrical as it disallows the established five-*mātrā gaṇa* arrangement given by *lāla lāvani bhide* (—⏑—/⏑⏑⏑—); although the additional *mātrā* provided by *lāvanya* yields the expected 20-*mātrā* value in the half-line, this computation is achieved only on the basis of the received *chāpa*, which the preceding note has shown

to be doubtful. The popularity of the *lāvanya*/*-ṇya* spellings here may show assimilation to the other occurrences at 48.3 and 62.7, where no readings of *lāvani* are found in the MSS.

(4) *prīya*: this metrically correct form, a commonplace spelling for masc. *priya*, is found only in A. The imposition of (fem.) *priyā* found in all other MSS is apparently an attempt to elevate Rādhā's status, in accordance with sectarian theology; but the sense of the stanza as a whole, which seeks to emphasise the mutuality of the relationship between lover and beloved, is damaged by such an interpretation. Readings of catalectic *priya* are not found in the manuscripts.

CP 47.

1 The forest game appeals to Lāla;
2 with a reflection in leaves and flowers
[the forest] simulates the beloved from head to toe.
3 Unable to desist, [Lāla] the greedy bee hastens stealthily for an
open embrace;
4 the loving lady throws him into confusion by calling out in joy,
and excites a commotion in the battle of love.
5 Realising that everything is turned contrarywise,
he draws in [his own] eyes a line of collyrium;
6 Hita Harivaṃśa, in subjection to the usages of love,
he is called 'Śyāma the *sajanī*'!

(1) *bana kī līlā*: the game is a kind of hide-and-seek. In (2) the shiny surfaces of leaves in the forest (which is here praised for *its* special qualities, as in 34.2 etc.) reflect multiple images of Rādhā; Kṛṣṇa (3) hastens to embrace these forms, but is disconcerted to find them counterfeit; Rādhā (4) calls out joyfully from her hiding place and further confuses Kṛṣṇa; Kṛṣṇa (5), (6), finally realises that everything is inverted and adopts a female form, implying that since his own attempts to attain Rādhā are vain, he must assume a *sakhī*'s role. It is rather surprising that the commentaries make little of the theological potential of the conceit, wherein the role of *sakhī* is elevated to the high status constantly alleged by the sectarian view.

(2) *pratibiṃbahi*: the oblique inflexion *-ahi* notwithstanding, Prem., followed by LCG, takes *pratibiṃbahi* as subject. The interpretation given in the translation, in which *bana* from line (1) is the subject of *janāvai* in line (2), is specified by none of the commentators; this is consequent upon their general tendency to gloss individual lines as syntactically and semantically independent units. *bana* is preferable to abstract *līlā* as subject, and analytical *bana kī līlā* allows such an interpretation.

(2) *janāvai*: *janā-* is the causative form of both *jan-* (⟨ *janayati*) and *jān-* (⟨ *jānati*), and it is unclear which is meant here. The former, however, is mostly restricted to the technical sense 'give birth to' (hence *janāī* f. 'midwife', Platts p. 390), which suggests that the derivation from *jān-* is more likely. All the commentators except Rasik., who retains *janā-*, gloss with *diṣā-*; this supports the hypothesis.

(3) *sakuci na sakata pragaṭa pariraṃbhana*: auxiliary *sak-* occurs only in composition with a finite verb, and must therefore relate to *sakuci* (as verbal stem). This sense isgiven by Dhar.'s *chā̃ḍi sakocu* and by Rasik.'s *sakuca sakata nahi neka hū pragaṭa karata pariraṃbha*. Prem. and Lok., however, understand the *mūla* as elliptical and supply *kar-*, reading *sakuci* as absolutive; thus Prem.: *sakucike pragaṭa pariraṃbhana nāhī̃ kari sakata hai.*

(4) *kulaki*: Rasik.'s gloss, *kabahuka saṃbhrama daita tahā̃ pulakita pyārī aṃga* suggests that *pulaki* may have been a variant for *kulaki*. B's *phulaki* appears to be a simple misreading: cf. B's *ph* for *k* in *dukūla* (11.3) and *k* for *ph* in *śrīphala* (43.3, 44.4).
(5) *ulaṭī*: fem. concord is for elliptical *bāta* (Prem.) or *kriyā* (Lok.).
(5) *aṃjana reṣa banāvai*: the conceit, made somewhat clearer by *sajanī syāma kahāvai* in the final line, is of Kṛṣṇa assuming the guise of a *sakhī* in order to be close to Rādhā. Both Dhar. and Prem. confuse the image by alleging a sense in which *Rādhā's* application of collyrium to her *right* eye (the 'male' side) is perceived by Kṛṣṇa in mirror-image as being in the *left* eye (the 'female' side); why this should allow Kṛṣṇa to see through Rādhā's playful disguise, as the commentators intend, is not clear.
(6) The first *pāda* of this *chāpa* line is deficient by one *mātrā*. G notes a variant *biparīta* for *prīti*: though this is semantically appropriate, the collocation of *prīti* with *rīti* is well established (cf. *BBhSK* s.v. *prītirīti*, and CP 41.1), whereas *biparīta*/°*ita* occurs only in composition with *rati* in the CP (30.13 and 34.8: cf. *GG* 11.5 *rati viparīte*). G's variant seems therefore to be merely an attempted correction of metre.

CP 48.

1 Vṛṣabhānu's daughter is adorned today;
2 the divers ornaments and clothes worn on her body
are decorations well suited to infatuate her lover.
3 The loveliness of her gestures and blandishments, and her eyebrows and curls
demolish the empty show of the young womenfolk;
4 the music of anklets and girdle-bells
produces notes in the complex variations of *tālas*.
5 Pleasant is the meeting with Śyāma,
lovely in the fresh grove;
6 Hita Harivaṃśa, the couple holds unbroken sway
in the round-dance of wanton merriment!

(4) *avaghara*: meanings deriving from *CDIAL* 750 **avaghara*- 'flowing down' cannot apply here, unless the form *ogha* attested by *MW* from the lexicographers, and having the sense '(flood, stream), quick time in music' is related. An etymology ⟨ *ava*+*ghaṭa*, proposed by *HŚS*, is a possibility as a parallel development to *sughara* ⟨ *sughaṭa* (as in 68.6, 83.2). *HŚS* cites musical contexts for *aughara* (the spelling found in MSS ABDJ in the present context) from Sūradāsa, where *aughara* is in collocation with *tāna*, and from Haridāsa, in collocation with *tāla*. The commentators' sense 'complex, attained with difficulty' (and hence indicating virtuoso performance) is consistent with such usages.

Since the etymology and sense of this word are so uncertain, the existence of a form *avaghaṭarikā* 'name of a musical instrument' (*MW*) may also be noted.

CP 49.

1 See, my companion, the play of Rādhā and her lover;

2 In dell-pastures and hillside thickets
these two young ones roam with arms around each other's neck.

3 These two fresh youths, a treasure of beauty,
are as it were a golden creeper around a branching *tamāla* tree;

4 there is enjoyment of the savour of bliss, with bodies thrilled
by the tasting of lips, kissing, and embracing,

5 He touches the ties of her garments, and her bodice and breasts,
while she looks at him with feigned anger and pushes his hand away;

6 Hita Harivaṃśa, Lāla is greedy for love and hastens to hold her,
gathering her to his breast.

(2) *ṣori ṣarika giri gahabara*: alliteration of *ṣ*/*ṣ* and of *g*/*g* suggests a pairing into the compounds *ṣori-ṣarika, giri-gahabara*.
(2)–(3) Unusually, adjacent lines from two successive couplets here combine to provide a single conceit, the statement *kaṃṭha bhuja meli* in (2) being illustrated by the simile *biṭapa...beli* in (3). The repeat of demonstrative *ye dou* is also a peculiarity. It is possible that (3) may be an interpolation, meant as an expansion of (1)–(2); and the *kopa* of (5) is a rather incongruous development after the union expressed in (4).
(3) *biṭapa*: L's reading *biṭapi* may represent Sk. *viṭapi*, which occurs *metricausa* for *viṭapin* (*MW*). The word order of *biṭapa tamāla* is consistent with such a derivation.

CP 50.

1 The young accomplished lady and the young adroit youth
have together made a couch of soft lotus leaves in the grove;

2 limbs fair and dark are joined thereon
as it were a lovely sapphire set in tender gold.

3 A charming quarrel between lover and proud lady has broken out in the beloved's arms
over the drawstring for amorous occasions;

4 he touches her blessed wood-apple breasts with his hand—
an angry moan, a haughty oblique glance, and the loving lady yields.

5 Harivaṃśa Hita, thousands of modes of love are vigorously [enjoyed] in seclusion
as in that manifold pleasant sweetness nothing at all is eschewed;

6 The loving voluptuaries Lalitā and the others drink that nectar through the vessels of their eyes,
storing up a hoard of delight in their hearts.

(2) The predominant 5-*mātrā gaṇa* (⏕⏑⏕) is upset by *aṃga* in this line, by *priyā* in line (3), and by the phrase *roṣa huṃkāra* in line (4). In all cases the overall moric count remains correct, and there is no suggestion of irregularity in the transmission of these readings (save in the case of *priyā*, discussed below).
(3) The collocation of *nībī* with *nibaṃdha,* rather than with the usual *baṃdha-* as at 7.6, 30.11 and 72.9, suggests that the technical legal sense of these two terms may be implied. *Nīvī* has the sense of 'capital, stock' (H.H. Wilson 1855:380), and *nibandha* that of 'a *corrody*, or fixed allowance granted by the Rāja or person in authority, to be received from the proceeds of a manufactory, mine, or estate' (*ibid.* p. 375). Such an interpretation would accommodate *surata* rather more happily than is possible otherwise: 'A charming dispute has broken out in the beloved's arms between lover and proud lady, over [the dispensation of] an allowance from the trust of amorous dalliance'. Since the trust called *nīvī* often related to the property of a *deva* managed by shebaits (J.D.M. Derrett II, p. 61), it is quite possible that it would have been a commonplace concept in sectarian circles. (This interpretation is not, however, proposed by any of the commentators. Prem. glosses *nibādha* with *nirbaṃdhana karai*; cf. Dhar.'s gloss *mocata nībī.* But *nibaṃdh-* < *nirbandh-* is not attested in *BBhSK* or *HŚS*.)
(3) *priyā* is unmetrical: a restoration of hypothetical **prīya* as at 46.4 is plausible, but would duplicate *piya* earlier in the same line.
(4) *lacī* is not glossed by Dhar., and is retained verbatim in Lok.'s paraphrase. Rasik. glosses *lajāi*, surely without justification; Prem. proposes that the 'bending' is caused by the oppressive burden (*bojha*) of maintaining the symptoms of anger. The intended sense, however, is that Rādhā gives way under the pressure of Kṛṣṇa's advances.
(6) *sac-*: this unnasalized derivative of **sancayayati* (*CDIAL* 12867) is attested in *BBhSK*, but the only citation is again from a rhyme context. Unnasalized *sac-* is, however, attested in Jāyasī (*HŚS* s.v. *sacanā*). Derivates with *c* from *CDIAL* 13085 (4) *sajyate* are well attested (though not in Hindi), and may have contaminated Hindi *saṃc-* to yield the *sac-* form.

CP 51.

1 O young damsel, make your offering;
2 Lāla the skilful darling demands it,
    for your constant concealment has come to light!
3 Your fresh oranges, gold, string of diamonds,
    lovely corals, and your pearls, fair one—
4 your twin pitchers filled with ambrosial nectar,
    your lotuses, plaintains, and wagtail pair—
5 All the possessions you have are in the form of gifts:
    why speak angrily, artless lady with angled glance?
6 your waist-bells and the ringing of your anklets are inside-informers,
    Hita Harivaṃśa, and say not a little!

(1) *dāna dai rī*: the conceit on which the stanza rests is that of *dāna līlā*, in which Kṛṣṇa extracts a toll from Rādhā and the other milkmaids.
(2) *dina dina kī corī*: the 'concealment' or 'evasion' intended is perhaps that carried out by the *navayauvanāmugdhā nāyikā*, reluctant to admit to her budding maturity.
(3)–(4) The *upamāna* listed in this couplet are mostly traditional ones, and the com-

mentators are in agreement on most of the attributable *upameya* (which generally form a *nakhaśikha* sequence):

nāraṃga = 'cheeks', rather than Dhar.'s suggestion 'breasts' which duplicates *ghaṭa* below. The spellings in °*i*° found in ACDEGIJM derive from the Hindi form *nāriṃgī*.

kanaka = 'body'—i.e. for *nakhaśikha* order, general complexion. Not glossed by Dhar.

hīrāvali = 'teeth'.

bidruma = 'lips'.

ghaṭa = 'breasts'.

kamala: probably 'hands' (for *nakhaśikha* order), rather than 'feet' (Rasik.) or 'face' (remainder).

kadali = 'thighs'; not glossed by Rasik. or Dhar.

ṣaṃjana kī jorī: all the commentators allege the usual *upameya*, 'eyes', (as applicable elsewhere in the text); yet this is quite out of sequence for *nakhaśikha*, and it is possible that some euphemism may be intended. Cf. a sense 'the secret pleasures of the Yatis, cohabitation of the saints' attested by *MW*, from the lexicons, for *khañjanarata*.

jalaja mani is not included in the list since no metaphorical sense is intended. Prem.'s alleged *upameya* of abstract 'smile' (*hasani*) is rather too recherché; Dhar.'s 'bodily splendour' (*tana kā̃ti*) duplicates *kanaka* and is in any case unlikely, since any metaphorical sense of 'pearls' must relate to their plurality—e.g. for 'teeth'. *gorī* is not an item in the list; yet Rasik. reads, in a *soraṭhā*, *gore cibuka rasa kūpa piya cita tahā̃ buḍi buḍi uṭhai*: this use of *gore* is unclear.

(5) *dāmana kī*: for this usage of the oblique plural *-ana* cf. the KhB. expression *in dāmõ* 'at this price'. The *dāmin-* spellings predominant among the manuscripts may show confusion with *dāminī* (< *saudāminī*); and this sense may be intended in Lok.'s obscure gloss *yā bhā̃ti sakala saũja dāmini priyā jī sahita tuma pāsa hai*(?).

(6) *thorī*: fem. concord is for elliptical *bāta*.

CP 52.

1 See, my companion, the utmost bounds of beauty!—

2 the band of young Vraja damsels bow their heads
when they behold the skilful lady.

3 If someone should live for ten million ages
and find ten million tongues,

4 even then the radiance of that bright lotus face
could not be put into words.

5 Hearing of it, poet lineages of all the three worlds
are afeared in their minds;

6 for say, with what could the innate sweetness of those various
limbs be compared?

7 Hita Harivaṃśa, for splendour, qualities of form,
for youthful vigour and strength, Śyāma is celebrated;

8 [Yet even] that ocean of *rasa* is ever stilled by the one
whose eyebrow-play has subjugated him like a sacrificial
animal!

(1)-(6) See section VI.6 for a transcription of this stanza sung in a *samāja* performance.
(1)-(2) A *pada* with a similar first couplet appears in the *Śrī Brajanidhi muktāvalī*, a collection attributed to the 18th century poet Brajanidhi:

> *rādhe suṃdaratā kī sīvā̃;*
> *manamohana kau hū mana mohyo nirakhi karata adha grīvā̃.*
> *citavani calani hasani pyārī kī dekhe bina kyõ jīvā̃;*
> *brajanidhi kī abhilāṣa niraṃtara rūpa sudhā rasa pīvā̃.*

(Purohita Harinārāyaṇ Śarmmā, p. 164.)
(5) *ḍariyai*: with its rhyme-word *paṭatariyai* in the following line, this is the only example in the CP of the BrBh. synthetic passive (for which see *LIO* 3.144-46).
(6) *paṭatariyai*: the verb *paṭatar-* is listed in *BBhSK*, but no attestation is given; none of the commentators retain the verbal form in their paraphrases, preferring *paṭatara de-* (Lok. and Dhar.), *sama kar-* (Rasik.), *barābara kar-* (Prem.). *paṭatar-* is, however, cited in *Rāmacaritamānasa* 3.247 (*HŚS*).
(8) *jākī*: fem. concord is with *bhrū*, showing the latter not to be compounded with foll. *bilāsa*.

CP 53.

1 See, my companion, the mass of strength of this frail maiden–
2 Mohana, an unrestrained elephant quite wild with desire,
is ensnared by the noose of her curls when he beholds her!
3 Already the movement of his mind is lamed,
without endeavour and voluntarily;
4 what [then] can I say of the time when she looks toward her lover
with playfulness in her eyebrow?
5 On the pretext of tying up her hair, she shows off her arms
with a smile on her radiant countenance;
6 alas, Harivaṃśa! Why does she cast his body into such dread
in the iniquitous way of love?

(1) *kai*: derivation is from *kīdṛk*, with the sense 'or'. Interpretation as oblique gender case-marker is precluded by the fem. gender of *rāsī*; interpretation as the interrogative adj. 〈 *kati* cited in *LIO* 3.43 is syntactically unsatisfactory here since *abalā* would presumably require a genitive case-marker for such a construction.
(2) *pāsi*: final *-i* is explained by the Hindi form *pāsī*, specialised from *pāśa* with the sense 'hobble for an animal'. Although **pāsa* (as in FH, with G *pāśa*) would be sufficient to give the sense required, the specialised meaning of *pāsī* is apposite and attractive for the image.

CP 54.

1 New is the love, novel the merriment and new the delight
of young Śyāma and Vṛṣabhānu's daughter;
2 new is his yellow garment and new her many-coloured sari,
and with ever new raindrops is the fair one drenched.

3 Fresh is Vṛndāvana, verdant and captivating,
where the young cuckoo calls with peacock and peahen;

4 new is the flute which [plays] the Malāra rāga with a novel lilt,
and hearing it massy clouds have gathered.

5 Resplendent with new ornaments and new diadems
they take ever new and dainty *urapa* steps;

6 Hita Harivaṃśa utters this benediction:
may this pair live long on the earth!

(2) *naī naī*: this is a necessary metrical emendation of the MSS' *nai nai*.

(3) *mora morī* is not glossed by Dhar., who substitutes *marāla*.

(4) *ghorī* represents *ghora* emended for rhyme.

(5) *urapa*: M. Bose (pp. 149, 150, 152, 161) cites the usage of a term *urūpa*, designating a class of dancing exercise in the *deśī* tradition, in the *Nartananirṇaya* (an unpublished text attributed to Puṇḍarīka Viṭṭhala and allegedly written for Akbar) and the *Saṅgītadarpaṇa* of Dāmodara (V.S. 1704). Present-day *kathak* dance knows *urapa* as the term for a sprightly vertical jump, with knees drawn up and feet held together; such a definition is not inconsistent with that given by Lakṣmīnārāyan Garg (p. 58), again in the *kathak* context, who describes *urapa* as an *aṅga* in which the dancer jumps spryly in a display of impetuous sentiments. In some BrBh. texts such as the *Rāsa-pañcādhyāyī* of Nandadāsa, (cited in *HŚS* s.v. *urapatarapa*), *urapa* commonly occurs in collocation with *tirapa* (or *tarapa*), another term cited by Bose (p. 149) from the *Nartananirṇaya*; Bose cites no particular correspondence between these terms, from which it may be inferred that the collocation is founded on alliteration (in the BrBh. spelling), and not on technical application. Indeed, if Hindi *urapa* does represent Sk. *urūpa*, the *-a-* spelling may be explained by assimilation to the form *tirapa*. In his gloss on the present line, Dhar. introduces *tirapa* alongside *urapa*: *naī naī urapa tirapa naī naī gati leti priyā nava lāla bihārī*; neither he nor any other commentator offers a definition of the term(s).

CP 55.

1 Today two lightnings have shone together;

2 taking between them the so-fresh dark cloud,
they are imbued with its delight.

3 One, O my friend, flashing all around
shone according to its own nature;

4 and one came into a sweet embrace,
settled in the two arms [of the 'dark cloud'].

5 On the blue lotus [of Kṛṣṇa's face] two moons are resplendent,
their roaming stilled;

6 Hita Harivaṃśa, with the eager desire of union in their hearts
are these two full moons of autumn.

(1) *dou*: with short *-u* (as AC only), the *ṭeka* accords with the 6+10 *mātrā* structure regular for this form.

(1) *dou dāmini*: the 'two lightnings' are the natural lightning and, metaphorically,

fair Rādhā; a parallel image is introduced with *ubhai bidhu* in line (5) below. Cf. the note to lines (3)-(4), where the conceit is developed. (Rasik. is much confused by the conceit, and proposes three alternative meanings for the 'two lightnings': (i) Rādhā's arms; (ii) Rādhā, and Kṛṣṇa's yellow mantle; Rādhā and her reflection on Kṛṣṇa's breast.)

(1) *bihasī*: derivation is from *vihasati*. Readings with *ba-* erroneously assume a derivation from Arabic *baḥs* (Hindi *bahasanā, bahasa karanā*, 'to dispute'); this sense, alleging rivalry between the 'two lightnings', is also proposed by Prem. (*bāda karẽ haĩ*) and by Lok. (*bihasi* [sic] *kīnī ki deṣau adhika pyārī kauna hai*). The argument against the acceptance of this derivation is threefold; firstly, the link of lightning with root *has-* is an established one (*MW*); secondly, no sense of rivalry or dispute is evident in subsequent lines—(3) and (4) expand the image of (1) and (2) with a description of the parallel and complementary attributes of two species of the same genus, without any sense of contest; thirdly, Perso-Arabic vocabulary hardly occurs in the text elsewhere (save in the case of certain artefacts).

(3)-(4) This couplet expands the reference *bica lai* of (2); the metaphorical allusion to Rādhā is here combined with a conceit envisaging two kinds of lightning, sheet and forked (respectively spontaneous and cloud-borne), as appearing behind and amidst the 'dark cloud'. Since the couplet in its commentatorial expansion undoes, to some extent, the metaphorical allusion to Rādhā, and since its presence disturbs the balance of the first and last couplets (each of which introduces an image complementary to the other), it may perhaps be an interpolation.

(5) *aṃbuja nīla ubhai bidhu rājata*: *ubhai* qualifies *bidhu*, referring to the natural moon and that of Rādhā's face; the image is therefore parallel to the 'lightning' image above. This parallelism is broken by Dhar. and Lok., who read *ubhai* as qualifying *aṃbuja* and allege the sense 'the two blue lotuses of Kṛṣṇa's hands', understanding *bidhu* as a metaphor for Rādhā's face.

CP 56.

1 I dedicate myself to Śyāma and the accomplished lady;
2 may they revel thus night and day
  in the lovely hut in the Vṛndā forest.
3 With a dousing in the essence of amorous enjoyment
  their mirth and merriment resurrects Kāma, who was burned by Paśupati;
4 Hita Harivaṃśa, will you not consumate the greedy bees of your eyes
  [by feasting them on] this abode of all joys?

CP 57.

1 Firstly I make obeisance as best I can
  to Vṛndāvana the most pleasurable,
2 inaccessible to the minds of all
  but for Śrī Rādhika's favour.
3 With the irrigation of Yamuna's excellent water
  autumn and spring endure there constantly,

4 and swarms of bees are drunk
with the fragrance of many kinds of flowers.

5 On ruddy young shoots cuckoo and parrot warble,

6 while troops of peacocks dance, frenzied with delight.

7 There flows a gentle breeze, cool, gentle and fragrant;

8 reddish, blue and white lotuses are blooming in every place.

9 A most attractive dwelling adorns the fresh bower,

10 and multitudes of love gods
ever serve joyfully with their attendants.

11 Where the youthful Śyāmā and Śyāma play in the lovers' round-dance,

12 the two delighted in each other's arms
arise sleepily at dawn.

13 [His] blessed dark limbs are decorated
in gold and tawny cloth;

14 the blue-clad loving lady has on her breast
a bodice of fine saffron hue.

15 Cymbals, *rabāb, muraja* and frame-drum
resound with the sweet barrel-drum

16 as in sweet proclamations excellent flute and mouth-harp
indicate the rhythm.

17 The two sing a springtime song together,
tuning their voices to the Gaurī *rāga*;

18 The bow of the brow and the arc of the eye
forcibly pierce the deer of the mind [with the arrow of a glance]!

19 Clashing hand-cymbals together,
the two go swaying this way and that;

20 "*Hohohorī*" they cry,
calling out in their great delight.

21 The loving lady smears Lāla the voluptuary
with [yellow] *vandana* powder;

22 taking aim again and again,
the lover sprinkles her with syringes filled with saffron.

23 Sometimes a lively swing is set up
in a sandal tree;

24 the two of them mount it and swing to and fro,
frolicking and blossoming with joy.

25 The loving lady is greatly alarmed
by the lunges of that excellent swing,

26 and with a thrill of delight she wraps her quaking limbs
around the beloved's chest.

27 Their well-wishing constant attendants
feel an overflowing joy;

28 seeing how great is the pleasure of their eyes
they make a charm of protection and dedicate themselves
[to the pair].

29 Most illustrious are these two beautiful ones,
tender heroes of amorous dalliance;

30 Hita Harivaṃśa, may the pair ever perform
their unremitting sport!

(2) *manani*: ILM *manana* may intend the abstract sense 'understanding'; but concrete *mana* with oblique plural *-ni/-na* is semantically preferable, and has the better manuscript support.

(4) *maṃta*: apparently *mā̃ta* (< *matta*) emended for rhyme; this is the sense taken by all the commentators.

(5) *nūta*: cf. the discussion of this word under 27.8.

(8) *jahā̃ tahā̃*: an imposition of unmetrical *ā̃* forms is found in all MSS except L, which reads *jahā̃ tahā̃*; cf. another occurrence of *jahā̃* in line (11).

(10) *mīna°*: final *-a* must be read as a *guru* (before *dhv-* of compounded *-dhvaja*), for metre.

(11) *rasika rāsa*: *-rāsi* readings (ADEGJKL) do not yield a satisfactory sense if derived from Sk. *rāśi*; attempts to explain *rāsi* < *rāśi* by Prem. (*rasika rāja...athavā rasa ke samūha*) and LCG (*rasikatā kī rāsi*) are unconvincing.

(12) *pariraṃjita*: apparently formed by analogy with *pariraṃbhana* etc.; an alternative reading *para raṃjita* is implausible because *bāhu para* is an unlikely rendering for a sense *bāhu mẽ* (though Prem. is happy to gloss *dou hātha para hātha dhare raṃjita*).

(15) *rabāba*: despite an attempt by Ahobala to link *rabāba* with Sk. *rava* (*Saṅgīta-pārijāta* II, 125-28 in an unconfirmed quotation by Cunnīlāla Seṣa p. 17), the word and the instrument—a lute, sometimes bowed—are of Arabic origin.

(16) *ukati*: Dhar.'s gloss with *ughaṭi* 'marking the accents of the *tāla*' does not reflect the *mūla* in A.

(17) *gaurī*: Lok. and Prem. see an inconsistency here, both insisting that Gaurī is an evening *rāga* and therefore inappropriate to the time of day established in line (12): thus Lok. glosses *dhoṣau sā̃ja hī kau mana mai hai*; and Prem. *jahā̃ prema hai tahā̃ marjāda nahī̃ tātẽ...ye samaya ke ādhīna nā̃hī*.

(18) *cāpa* duplicates the sense of *dhanuṣa*; the conceit is perhaps rhyme-*gratia*. Rasik. reiterates the *mūla*; Prem. paraphrases it and adds *kaṭākṣa jo haī so bāṇa haī* in order to complete an elliptical image; Lok. similarly supplies *katācha sara bhai*, but glosses *cāpa* with *cillī* 'bowstring'; Dhar. equally brazenly reads *bhrakuṭī dhanuṣa, draga sara*. LCG reads *cā̃pa* as abs. from *cā̃p-* (<**camp-*) 'press', reading *bhṛkuṭi rūpī dhanuṣa para dṛga rūpī bāṇõ ko cā̃pakara* (*dabākara*), hardly a tenable interpretation but one which may account for the nasalization of the long vowel in FI and the *-i* ending in BCEIJL.

(21) *baṃdana*, (22) *kumakuma*: the exchange of colours complements the sartorial image of lines (13) and (14): fair Rādhā, wearing a red bodice, is coloured with red *kuṃkuma*; dark Kṛṣṇa, wearing a golden garment, is smeared with yellow *vandana*.

(25) *ḍarāti*: an intransitive extended-stem form is attested in *BBhSK* (usually but not always in a rhyme context, as here). The *ḍarā-* form is retained by all the commentators except Dhar., who reads abs. *ḍari*.

(28) *nainani* is not meant pleonastically (with *nirași*), but rather anticipates the idiom *trana torata* (for which cf. *trana ṭūṭata*, 32.8) which expresses the need for protection from the evil effect of admiring eyes.

(30) *acala*: the sense is 'constant' (syn. *abicala* 48.6), though somewhat tautological after *dina*; an interpretation as 'earth' (syn. *bhūtala* in the parallel context *cira jīvau bhūtala yaha jorī*, 54.1) is also feasible.

CP 58.

1 For your sake I am come to take you, sent by Śyāma from the forest—
   loving lady, he removes the grievous pain of desire;

2 Why do you make obstacles? Listen, O wise Rādhā—
   unite with him, my friend, and remove your undisguised fear of the world.

3 O see on this beautiful night the lovely creation of the beloved,
   the moon risen in the sky above lotuses on the sandbank;

4 my friend, you are very artful and have not heeded a single thing I have said—
   I have worn myself out speaking to you, young girl, with all my wit.

5 Handsome Mohanalāla, addicted to his own pleasures,
   entrances bird and beast with the sweet sound of his flute;

6 Hita Harivaṃśa: he deems your youthfulness his very life
   when you worship Hari, O loving lady.

(1)-(6) In its received form the stanza has a regular metrical line of 8+8+8+7 syllables. This syllabic construction may, however, overlie an original moric metre of 12+12+9+8 *mātrās*. This hypothetical moric scansion can be achieved in the first couplet, with a deficiency of one *mātrā* in the second *pāda* of (2), by reading (1) *těre*, *tĩ̆*, (2) *kāhě kaũ̆*, *bheṭikaĩ̆*, and by excising from (2) the superfluous vocative *māī* (in regard to which cf. the accretion of *māī* to line (1) in AC, and to the sung version of CP 12 (section VI.6.ii). An approximation to this scansion can be achieved, with similar licence, in lines (3)-(5), though line (4) requires the excision of the superfluous *ba* (= *aba*) and voc. *juvati*; in line (3), the final caesura would fall after the first syllable of *udita*. Only in the *chāpa* line does the hypothetical moric scansion break down severely in the first two *pādas*, here of ten *mātrās* each (but not showing the regular construction of the ten-*mātrā pādas* in CP 25 etc.). The absence of a 12+12+9+8 model in the CP, and the imperfect scansion of this hypothetical moric construction in comparison with the precise syllabic scansion, argue against the editing of the stanza to the moric form.

(1) *harata*: *-ti* readings interpret Rādhā as subject; but *tere hita* in the first line, and *apane raṃga rãgilau* in line (5) show Kṛṣṇa to be in the ascendant here, with Rādhā the beneficiary of his *līlā*. The high number of *-ti* readings is not typical of fem. contexts, but rather is itself indicative of an attempt at sectarian adjustment of the sense: the process can be seen under way in J, with original *harata* changed to *harati*.

(3) *pulina nalina nabha udita rohinī dhau*: only Lok. comments on this untimely nocturnal blossoming: *eka adabhuta bāta bhaī hai...rāta mai kamala kaba phūlata hai*? This conceit may be intended by the *mūla's racanā rucira pī kī*; cf. also the *dūtikā's* confession, in the following line, of contrivance in her exhortation to Rādhā. The other commentators imply by their silence that the description is simply rhetorical, and understand *racanā* to apply to the usual 'bed of leaves'.

(5) *apane raṃga rãgīlau*: in an attempt to explain this rather puzzling phrase, Lok. discards the reflexive reference of *apane* in his gloss, and substitutes *tere* (*tere raṃga mai rãgi rahyau haĩ*).
(6) *tava*: Lok.'s gloss *jovana kī saphalatā* appears to be based on the reading *dhana*, found only in C. The GM reading *tana* (with *tana* omitted from the first *pāda*) is reflected by Prem.'s gloss *prītama to aba jīvana aura jovana aura tana tumahī kõ ganata haĩ*.
(6) *jau*: Lok. probably understands *jau* as =*jyau* (and reads *bhajahi* as imperative) in his gloss *bhajahi pāsa mai bhāmini jau* 'adore him intimately in the manner of a woman'; similarly Prem., *jaise tuma ko hari bhaje haĩ taiseĩ hari ko tuma bhajau*. A derivation of *jau* from *jaba*, on the model of the rhymes *-au* < *-ava* in lines (2), (3) and (5), is more attractive for sense, and is specified by Dhar.'s *jau lau* 'as long as'. (A correlation of *jau* in the sense 'when' with *tava* (read as *taba*) is not involved, since the pronominal sense of *tava* is semantically necessary.)

CP 59.

1 Tell me, who [ever] found happiness
by applying this his single mind to sundry things?
2 adversity attends a paramour's girl in every place,
as Piṅgalā has plainly declaimed.
3 Who could ride on two horses,
yoking them together and stubbornly mounting them?
4 Tell me then, who would take on his lap
a son to whom a harlot gave birth?
5 Hita Harivaṃśa, all the phenomenal world is deception,
fodder for the predatory beast of Death;
6 knowing this, bow your head to those who are devoted
to the lotus feet of Śyāma and Śyāmā.

(1)-(6) Rasik. gives an extended gloss of 58 *dohās* to this stanza. Most of his interpretations are based on fanciful etymologies, such as his derivation of (2) *bipati jāra* from *vi* 'bird' +*pati*, and *jāla* 'snare'. Prem. gives two glosses, the first (more or less) literal, the second extending the *artha* to extol the virtues of the *svādhīnabharttṛkā nāyikā* over the *kalahāntaritā nāyikā*.
(1) *yaha ju*: Lok. ignores the admonitory purpose of the stanza and restricts the reference of *ju* to *Kṛṣṇa—yaha ju lāla tākau eka mana hai*; the other commentators correctly relate *ju* to *mana*. *yaha ju* may alternatively be understood as relating in a general demonstrative way to the whole phrase *eka mana bahuta ṭhaura*, giving the sense, '(Who found happiness) through this [practice] of applying his single mind to many things?'.
(1) *kaune*: see a discussion of this form in section III.3.(v).
(2) *piṃgalā*: the reference is to an episode in the *Bhāgavata purāṇa* (XI 8.22-44) in which Piṅgalā, a courtesan of Vidiśā city, renounces her promiscuous ways and becomes a single-minded devotee; it is this idea of promiscuity which provides the link with the opening line.
(3) *jora*: the only commentator to offer a gloss is LCG, who reads as Persian *zor* and glosses *jabaradastī*. Reading *jora* as absolutive from *jor-*, the sense 'yoking, harnessing' complements the image and is surely intended; this technical sense is attested in Platts (s.v. *joṛanā*).

(3) *parata*: the syntax is based on *dhāyau par-*, 'a running to occur'.
(3) *pai*: readings of *para* (ACFGILM) show a confusion between the intended sociative ppn. *pai* (< *pārśve*) and loc. *pai/para* (< **uppari*); *pai* with loc. force is not encountered in the CP, a single occurrence in the MSS being found in K, for *para*, earlier in line (3). The ACFGILM readings notwithstanding, none of the commentators propose a locative sense for *kauna pai* ('on which horse...?').
(4) *jo*: *jyo/au* forms are incorrect for sense: *jo suta* is meant.
(4) *jo ganikā suta*: interpretations given by Rasik. are based on a fanciful reading as *jogani kā suta*, 'a son of yogis'. (Genitive *kā* does not occur in the CP.) This interpretation does at least confirm the reading *jo* as existing in Rasik.'s exemplar (see previous note).
(5) *baṃca*: presumably for **vañca*, analogically inferred *metri gratia* for Sk. *vañcana*?
(6) *syāma syāmā...nāyau*: Lok. reads *syāma nai syāmā pada kamala sau lagāikai sira nāyau*, against the didactic intention of the stanza. An interpretation predicating *sãgī* on *syāma* ('bow your head to Śyāma, who is devoted to the lotus feet of Śyāmā') is possible, but unlikely since *syāma syāmā* is usually compounded.

CP 60.

1 What can I say of these eyes?
2 they are like bees engrossed in the nectar of the beloved's
lotus face,
and do not stray elsewhere!
3 Whenever obstructed by an eyelid or a covering curl,
they are quite restless and confounded;
4 seven hundred aeons seem less long to these greedy ones
than the duration of that momentary blinking.
5 They cannot be accommodated as the lotus at her ear,
her collyrium, or the musk between her breasts;
6 Hita Harivaṃśa, they beg to be a dark-bodied fish
in the pool of her navel!

(1) The eyes are Kṛṣṇa's.
(2) *anata na jāta*: the idea of single-mindedness recommended in the previous stanza is perhaps taken up again here.
(5) *hvai na samāta*: a dual image, understood only by Prem., is contained in the final line. Firstly, the eyes *pass over* Rādhā's lotus ear-decoration, her collyrium and the spot of musk between her breasts, and settle only for the navel as their resting-place: in this conceit *hvai* has the sense of KhB. *hokar* as '(passing) through, (going) via'. Secondly, the conventional *upamāna* are one by one denounced as insufficient to their task, until finally the 'fish' metaphor is acknowledged in the final line: here *hvai* has the more literal sense of 'being, becoming'. Cf. 73.1 for another occurrence of this latter conceit, this time in respect of Rādhā's eyes.

CP 61.

1 Today, my friend, the ornament of Vraja—
the lord who is adorned in the forest—is dancing;

2 the youth in his prime has his immaculate staff-like arms
around the young girl's shoulders.

3 His soft and curly ringlets, exceedingly beautiful,
are hanging over his two cheeks

4 like honey-bees stilled in their greed for nectar
on the segments of a blue lotus.

5 His mirth and merriment captivates the minds of all
and is destruction to hosts of Kāmas;

6 Hita Harivaṃśa, he reveals his own glory
throughout the whole universe!

(2) *juvati aṃsani*: the commentators do not read this as a compound, but seek to understand *juvati* as being numerically singular and thereby interpret its meaning as 'Rādhā'. Plurality is, however, explicit in the almost identical phrase of 19.1 (*juvatini aṃsa diye bhujadaṃḍana*) and is quite appropriate here, where no further mention is made of Rādhā.
(4) *ṣaṃḍana*: context requires the sense 'segment, portion' yielded by reading this as oblique plural of *khaṇḍa*, though a technical sense 'segment of a bloom, petal' is unattested. Direct singular *khaṇḍana* is inapposite.
(6) *brahmaṃḍana*: the FK spelling *braha-* may be intended as a (hyper-) correct metrical form, the moric cadence /⏑, 3/2/ being usual in this metre and found in all other lines of this stanza save (4).

CP 62.

1 Bride and groom play in the round-dance;

2 won't you hear me, friend? Why not look on constantly
with Lalitā and the other companions, and rejoice with
your eyes?

3 Most soft and mellifluous, a greatly entrancing sound
arises on the Yamuna shore;

4 hearing again and again the cry "*theī! theī!*" issuing from the
lips of the pair,
why do you not forget your mortal state?

5 Saffron pollen rises up with the delicate alighting of their feet
and a wondrous breeze flows from silken clothing,

6 sometimes Śyāma touches Śyāmā's lips,
hair, breasts, garland and shoulder.

7 Ten million Kāmas have no equivalence
to this most lovely beauty and skill of gesture;

8 the mirth of their eyebrow-play showers down delight—
Hita Harivaṃśa, dally in this sentiment of love!

(1)-(8) *-ahu* rhymes have various derivations, as follows:
(1) *dukūlahu* is a regular nominative form;

(2) *phūlahu*, (4) *bhūlahu* and (8) *jhūlahu* are regular plural imperatives;
(3) *kūlahu* clearly has locative sense, but can represent only Ap. gen./abl. (Jacobi 1918:33);
(5) *dukūlahu* is a regular Ap. abl.;
(6) *bhujamūlahu* and (7) *samatūlahu* are problematic—perhaps for Ap. acc. *-au* (Jacobi *loc.cit.*) with intrusive -h-?

Since these are rhyme forms it is not clear to what extent they represent genuine features of the morphology, except in the imperative forms (which are attested more widely in the CP).

(2) *niraṣi niraṣi nainani kina phūlahu*: Rasik.'s gloss *phūlahu kini diṣi nena* implies wrongly that *nainani* is used pleonastically in composition with *niraṣi*; Prem. and Lok.'s correct interpretation reads *nainani* as instrumental (glossed *nainani saũ*) in composition with *phūlahu*. Dhar.'s non-committal *biloki drigina phūlaha* retains the *mūla's* word order.

(4) *theī theī*: cf. note to 36.8 *tātātheī tātheī* for this dance mnemonic.

(5) *raja:* Platts cites as masc. in Hindi, fem. in Urdu; yet verbal agreement in *-i* in DEJ indicates an understanding of fem. gender; this is supported by Lok. and Prem.'s *kumakuma kī raja*, and by modern H. usage as reflected by *HŚS*.

(5) *bahata samīra dukūlahu*: the conceit of the fanning effect of flying garments in the vigorous dance is reproduced by Lok. and Prem. but misconstrued by Dhar. who reads: *tribidha samīra cira ita uta bhae* 'clothes flew all about in the breeze of threefold nature'. Such an interpretation belies the ablative *-ahu* termination. Rasik. omits any gloss on *dukūlahu* and reads simply *bahata pavana abhirāma*.

CP 63[i].

1 Madanamohana of thrice-bent stance!

2 —Mohana who impassions the hearts of sages!

3 Mohana is the highest bliss, manifest in concrete form,
Gopāla profound in qualities;

4 on his head a diadem, on his ear a jewelled ring,
and his chest is adorned with a garland of wild flowers.

5 His yellow-clad body is coloured with mineral pigments,
sweet bells are at his handsome waist;

6 the gems of his toenails are suns to the lotuses of his feet:
Madanamohana of thrice-bent stance!

(1) Commentatorial treatment of this stanza is discussed in R. Snell 1990.

(1) *tribhaṃgī*: the heading given by H to this composite stanza is *tribhaṃgī chanda cāra*. Although *tribhaṃgī* is indeed the name of a metre, it is according to Kellogg (p. 580) and *MW* a syllabic metre of 32 syllables to the line; there can therefore be no connexion with the present verse type called *chanda*, discussed in section VI.3(i).

(2) *muni*: Lok. declares, unaccountably, *muni priyā jī ke urojani kī upamā hai*. This gloss is representative of the general tenor of the commentaries in their attempt to play down Kṛṣṇa's ascendancy in this *rāsapañcādhyāyī* context.

(3) The first *pāda* of this line has an excess of two *mātrās* in the received text. Although similar 18-*mātrā pādas* occur also in the received text of corresponding lines of 63[ii] and 63[iv], q.q.v., these are not seen as metrically correct forms but rather as irregularities partly consequent upon a confusion over the varying amount of second line material repeated in the third line of this stanza type (see p. 421). In the present line,

muni/-a is semantically superfluous and has been excised on the above hypothesis, viz. that it represents an unwarranted repeat of the phrase *mohana muni* from line (2); the restored text yields, incidentally, the alliterative collocation *mohana saghana*. Note an attempt in E partially to correct the metre by reading *pramānāda* for *paramānāda*; and cf. the version of the text which appears in the *Brajanidhi granthāvalī* (Purohit Harinārāyaṇ Śarmmā (ed.) p. 245) with the following metrically regular wording:

mohana madana tribhaṃgī;
mohe mana munaraṃgī.
mŏhĕ mana suguna pragaṭa paramānāda guna gaṃbhīra gopālā;

(3) *gupālā*: by reading *gupāla* and (4) *banamāla*, A incorrectly converts this couplet to the 16+11 *mātrā* metre Sarasī.

(5) *dhātu*: no attestation of the specific proposed sense has been found. Prem. and Lok. gloss as 'gold', but the former feels the need for an alternative explanation also: *jaise caṃdani karike tana...bicitrita kariyata hai, taise caṃdana ke tulya je suṃdara komala raṃga raṃga kī dhātī haĩ tini karike tana bicitrita hai.*

CP 63[ii].

1 Mohana plays the flute,
2 and with this sound he calls the women.
3 On hearing the sound of his reed-pipe the women of Vraja are come,
dismissing all thought of husbands and kinsmen;
4 a vision of the captivating Madanagopāla
checks the anguish of desire.
5 With gladdened face and oblique glance
he intones a joyous and delightful sound;
6 holding it to his lips, [with music] like honeyed words of persuasion
Mohana plays the flute.

(2), (3) *nāri*: plural number is implied by the *rāsapañcādhyāyī* context, and is understood by all the commentators; only Lok. attempts to restrict the reference to Rādhā, explaining that the (implied!) plural is honorific: *bahuvacana gauravatā mai hai.*

(3) As in the equivalent *pādas* of 63[i] and 63[iv], the first *pāda* of this line has an excess of two *mātrās* in the received text. Pleonastic *rava* in all manuscripts except A may be a 'correction' of A's *ruha*, itself probably mistakenly copied after (*baṃ-*)*sī* from (*sara-*)*sīruha* in 63[i].6, by assimilation to an occurrence of *rava* in (2) above. Since it is uncommon for an authentic reading to be preserved in A alone, the hypothesis must however be regarded as too conjectural to allow the excision of *rava* from the edited text.

(3) *grahapati*: may intend 'patriarch, head of family', as specified by Prem. (*je graha mẽ muṣya haĩ*). Lok. fancifully understands *graha-* in its *tatsama* sense, yielding *grahapati* as 'sun', *baṃdhu* as 'lotus': 'dismissing all thought of (the splendour of) the lotus'!

(3) *bisāre*, (4) *nivāre*: there are no *-ai* readings for these forms; the first is a nonfinite participle, in which *-e* would be expected, but the second is a finite use of the participle for present tense, in which *-ai* is simplified to *-e* for rhyme. It is unlikely that an *-ai/-ai* rhyme is intended, since this would imply finite force for *bisārai* inconsistent with the subsidiary nature of the clause in which it occurs. Such a recons-

truction would, furthermore, yield an AAAAAA rhyme scheme, unattested in the other component stanzas of CP 63.
(4) *madana*: omission of *-na* in EM is a metrical compensation for the (incorrect) reading *gopāla* for *gupāla*.
(6) *sāma*: Sk. *sāman*, one of the four *upāyas* in the art of winning over an adversary, yields the Hindi sense 'sweet (persuasive) talk' (*HŚS* s.v. *sāma*); hence its use in this description of a summons or invitation to the dance. Readings of *syāma/śyāma* are semantically unattractive before *samāna*, LCG's interpretation 'sweet as Śyāma' (describing the flute) being rather contrived. In an unusual acknowledgement of the existence of conflicting readings, Prem. records the preferred *pāṭha: dūsaro pāṭha śyāma kī jāgaha sāma hai;* but Prem., with Lok., interprets *sāma* as the Veda, hardly apposite here.

CP 63[iii].

1 He has contrived a round-dance in the forest,
2 in the shade of the pure tree of plenty.
3 On the fair riverbank with its pure tree of plenty,
an autumn night and a splendid moon,
4 a cool, gentle and fragrant wind blows,
and there plays Nandanandā.
5 Wondrous cymbals, the enchanting drum
and girdle-bells resound;
6 on the Yamuna's sandy bank the lover, the ocean of *rasa*
has contrived a round-dance in the forest!

(1) *rāsa racyau*: 'he' is provided as subject because the stanza is understood as a thematic continuation of 63[ii]; and also in anticipation of the repeat of *rāsa racyau* in line (6), where *rasa sāgara* is subject.
(3) *tīra*: the syntax of Lok.'s gloss *ujjala kalapa kamala bṛcha ke tīra* indicates an interpretation of *tīra* as postposition; see a note to 24.1 for an explanation why an interpretation of *tīra* as substantive is preferred.

CP 63[iv].

1 Watching the honeybee's sport,
2 birds, beasts and creepers are enchanted.
3 With the beasts and cattle, beautiful deities [too] are enchanted,
immersed in love with dress disordered;
4 the constellations are bewildered, the moon's orb stilled,
and the hearts of myriads of love-gods stolen.
5 With that most relishable kissing and embracing
the companion-girls are engrossed in bliss;
6 Hita Harivaṃśa the voluptuary finds joy
watching the honeybee's sport.

(3) As in 63[i].3 and 63[ii].3, an excess of two *mātrās* is found in this third line also. Reading *mõhã* restores the metre: alternatively *mṛga* may be understood as an accre-

tion from line (2) as was *muni* in 63[i].3 (but there with semantic support for the hypothesis).
(3) *mṛga dhenu*: wrongly interpreted as a *tatpuruṣa* in Lok.'s gloss *mṛga kī dhenu mṛgī*.
(3) *surasuṃdari*: following *dhenu* the intended sense must allude to the *gopīs* (figuratively *apsarases*); a fem. ending is therefore required. Lok. and Prem. understand *sura* as 'musical tone': cf. H's reading *svara*.
(3) *paṭa chūṭe*: the image seems a little extreme. The sense 'disordered clothes' is proposed by all the commentators except two: Rasik. retains the *mūla*'s wording, *paṭa chūṭe*; Lok. gives the farfetched interpretation 'opened wide the eyelid' in his gloss *netra ke puṭa ju palaka so pisāra dīnau*. A sense based on *paṭa* as 'throne'—'enchanted deities left their thrones'—is conceivable (and would confirm the masc. ending of *surasuṃdara* found in BDFGIJKM); but elsewhere in the CP *chūṭ-* always has the sense of 'dishevelled'.

CP 64.

1 O friend, the flute resounds under the *vaṃśīvaṭa*;
2 springtime endures forever in Vṛndāvana,
on the pure sandbanks of the blessed Yamuna shore.
3 A studded diadem, and earrings in crocodile's shape,
and curls I deem as bees on the lotus of his face;
4 the splendour of jasmine buds is put to shame by the teeth
[of him] adorned in yellow garments like gold.
5 Sages who meditate inwardly cannot attain him
—he frolics in the company of gallant boys;
6 a source of the sentiment of devotion for his devoted servants,
Hita Harivaṃśa, he is manifest as the *līlā* dancer!

(6) *ananya*: understood by Prem. and Lok. as qualifying *dāsa* (as Prem. *je dāsa ananya haĩ tinike*...); Dhar. and Rasik. maintain the *mūla*'s word order in which qualification of *bhajana* is also possible. The former interpretation is supported by a common Hindi usage as exemplified in *Sevakavāṇī* 12.1.1: *rasika ananyani mukhya guru jana bhaya khaṃḍanā* (Lalitā Caraṇ Gosvāmī ed., 1975:117).
(6) *bhajana rasa kārana*: Lok. and Prem. understand *kārana* as a postposition, glossing *bhajana rasa ke heta*; similarly Rasik., *bhajana hita*. The intended sense of this interpretation is 'in order to enjoy the savour of devotion'; but the *mūla*, lacking any expression of 'enjoyment', lends itself more readily to the interpretation given above.

CP 65.

1 Hari plays in the dense bower which destroys desire,
on the lovely full-moon night of autumn;
2 come, my friend, and join the round-dance
contrived near the *kalpa* tree on the Yamuna's sandy shore.
3 All dance a *sudhaṅga* as the sweet drum resounds,
and [only] you have not heard the flute-playing;

4 Hita Harivaṃśa's lord, Rādhikā's lover, is dear to me
as worthy of worship with the world's adoration, oh my companion.

(1)–(4) In terms of a simple computation of syllables, the first two *pādas* are regular in all four lines. The central lines (2) and (3) show internal rhyme and have a third *pāda* of 12 syllables. Excision of *māī* from line (4), not justified by the MSS but with a possible precedent in 58.2, would yield a final *pāda* in this line of 11 syllables, parallel to that of line (1) with which the lack of full internal rhyme is shared; this hypothetical excision would also restore to the final *pāda* a caesura after the fifth syllable, as found in the other lines. The evidence therefore suggests a linking of (1) with (4) and of (2) with (3).
(2) *sura ke taru*: BFHJK read *surataru ke/kai*. The evidence for the choice of reading is conflicting; *surataru ke* retains the Sk. compound, while *sura ke taru* yields a repeat of the metrical configuration of the first *pāda* of (2), a feature found also in the following line if *sabai* is read as ⏑⏑. Hypercorrection of analytical *sura ke taru* to the compound form seems more likely as a scribal emendation than a metrical re-ordering, and the analytical form has the marginally stronger manuscript support.
(4) *prabhu*: A's reading *prabho* may repeat an attempt to reinforce internal rhyme with *mokau*, on the model of lines (2) and (3); but a partial rhyme already exists between *mokau* and *prabhu*.
(4) *rādhikā ravana*: Lok. dismantles this commonplace compound in his gloss *rādhikā aru unake ravana*; cf. Dhar.'s simple gloss *dou* 'the pair'.

CP 66.

1 The two lovers sport in the grove;

2 fair and dark, their bodily splendour is beyond compare
and rains down a mass of joy in the forest.

3 In the wondrous [battle-] field of mighty Kāma
with the tumult of ornaments for kettledrums,

4 the champions grapple together limb to limb,
and a million passions are aroused.

5 The frail lady is much fatigued by excessive battle,
and her lovely eyes are drowsy;

6 a sleeping place is made for her anguished and wearied body
in her lover's fearless embrace.

7 Longing to caress her, the lover touches
her broad navel and her breasts;

8 beholding such wondrous brilliance on the earth
his body is wearied and trembling.

9 Seeing him suffused with Madana's poison,
the adroit lady has fortified him with her ambrosial lips;

10 straightway he is recovered on drinking this strong draught,
like a fish returned to water.

11 "Just now I beheld in your face
luscious lips like *bimba* fruits" [said he];

12 "[while yet] awake, it was as though delusion overcame my mind,
which fell into a snare set by hundreds of dynasties of
love-gods!

13 Bring near just once the nectar of your lips
with your natural love, beautiful one,

14 and protect my body, oh my mistress,
in the eternal abode of your lotus feet!"

15 Speaks the beloved, "Tell me, my lover, where were you,
king of the fine new bower?

16 why do you offer these pretty fabrications of words,
lascivious and vain?"

17 Hearing this much from the proud lady's lips,
no fortitude remained in his heart;

18 his timid mind was suffused with the pain of separation,
and mighty was the wind of his sighs.

19 Hita Harivaṃśa, she drew him in her arms
and taking him, kept him in her bosom;

20 and in that special pleasure born of the couple's uniting,
evening came in an instant, as though in the twinkling of an eye.

(1)–(20): Rasik. interprets this stanza an enshrining the nine *rasas*, in the following sequence: lines (1)–(2) *śṛṅgāra*; (3)–(6) *vīra*; (7)–(10) *karuṇa*; (11)–(12) *adbhuta*; (13)–(14) *hāsya*; (15)–(16) *raudra*; (17) *vībhatsa*; (18) *bhayānaka*; (19)–(20) *śānta*. This fanciful scheme is preceded by an exegesis explaining how all *rasas* derive from, and are secondary to, *śṛṅgāra*.
(6) *saina*: the B reading *sainai* is consequent upon the scribe's partial correction of *nanai* to *nainai* (for *naina*) in the previous line.
(7) *lālana misa ātura*: *misa* appears not to have its usual sense of 'pretence, pretext' here, since the 'caressing' (*lālana*) is both desired and *openly* carried out. Lok.'s gloss *ṣela ke misa ātura* suggests postpositional usage with the sense 'as to' ('desirous as to a caressing'); cf. the definition given by Platts, 'in the form or character of'. Dhar. has no gloss for *misa*; Prem. and Rasik. follow the *mūla*, with *laḍāibe ke misa* and *lālana misa so* respectively.
(7) *urū*: derivation from Sk. *urū-* 'broad' is more plausible than that from Sk. *ūru-* 'thigh' understood by Prem. (*urūni ko aura nābhi ko*...); the other commentators retain the *mūla*'s word order. D's reading *uru nābhī* is a hypercorrection for metre, this collocation alone providing the usual moric construction:

/ ⌣⌣ ⌣⌣ / —— / ⌣,⌣—/⌣
-sata uru nābhī urajāta

(9) *byāpata*, for Sk. *vyāpta*, is the preferred reading since Sk. *vyāpita* is rarely attested (*MW*); *-ata* provides caesura rhyme with *pīvata* in the following line. The BrBh. participle *byāpyau/yo* in the BDIJ group may derive from an occurrence of this form in Lok.'s paraphrase, or may show confusion with Sk. *vyāpya*. Cf. a repeat of the same usage in line (18).
(10) *uṭhe*: E reads *uṭhi*; the accretion of *ju* in A (*uṭhe ju*) suggests that A's archetype may also have read *uṭhi*, subsequently emended but with the compensating metrical filler *ju* retained.

(13) *sakṛdapi*: *sakṛt* is understood by Prem. and Rasik. as 'a little', by Lok. as 'once'; Dhar. has no gloss on this couplet.
(13) *suṃdari*: the Sanskritic context of this line is a strong case for the acceptance of the *-i* ending, as a Sk. vocative; *-a* readings (ADEFGIK) represent loss of *-i* through weakening of the final vowel, and/or scribal ignorance of the Sk. vocative form.
(20) *kachuka*: the force must be particularizing rather than partitive or generalizing in this hyperbolic context, since any curtailment of *suṣa* would be anti-climactic in this final line; cf. Prem.'s gloss *jo koi eka anirvacanīya suṣa*, 'a certain ineffable joy'.
(20) *truṭi lava:* lit. 'fraction of a second'.

CP 67.

1 Shines the radiant bride, the woodland damsel;

2 she has the lovely sixteen [adornments], with a *tilaka* of musk,—
the doe-eyed one has anointed her body and wears a sandalwood mark on her head.

3 Her pomegranate cheeks are adorned, a moon-ornament is in her hair,
medinī flowers are plaited into her braid with red cord;

4 she has ornaments at her ears and a beauty-spot on her chin,
and her saffron bodice conceals her fruit-like breasts in its border.

5 With the flashing of her bracelets and bangles, the lustre of the lac on her nails,
the three creases on her belly, her blue garment and tiny waist,

6 and with wonderful bells a-jingle on the blessed eminence of her hips,
there is a turbulence on the ocean of the essence of music and lovemaking.

7 Manifold sports are contrived clandestinely, Harivaṃśa Hita,
by the best of lovers Rādhāramaṇa and his spouse;

8 Madana is defeated by her eyebrows, and with a gently smiling face the
fair one has made her lover Ghanaśyāma helpless in passion.

(2) *ṣoḍasa*: see note to 45.3 for a computation of the 16 *śṛṅgāras* given in lines (2) to (6), and for a discussion of the commentators' interpretations.
(3) Here the *pāda*-rhyme which is regular in the first halves of all other lines has given way to *gaṇa*-based alliteration; see a discussion in VI 2, and cf. 26.2 for another example of the absence of *pāda*-rhyme in this metre.
(3) *paṃḍīra*: the intended sense 'pomegranate' (Sk. *piṇḍīra*) is given by none of the commentators; Rasik. and Dhar. give *caṃdana*, Prem. *pā̃dura barana*, Lok. *kesara kau maravaṭa* ('a facial application of saffron given to a bride', Platts), LCG *mahuā ke puṣpa* (*Bassia latifolia*).
(4) *kai*: this is a form of absolutive *kari* for rhyme with regular *dai* on the model of (participial) *kiye/diye* of line (2); usage of *kai* as a verbal absolutive is normally restricted to conjunctive forms of the type exemplified by *bheṭikai* (58.2) (but cf. also the pleonastic use of *kai* suffixed to *kaise* in 14.1, 14.5).

(4) *korī*: apparently *kora/kori* adapted for rhyme. In normal Hindi usage *korī* has acquired the specialised sense 'division, branch, class' (Platts), but the sense 'border, hem' is attested for *kora* (*ibid.*), and is intended here. Strangely, Rasik., Dhar. and Prem. all omit a gloss on this word; Lok. compounds *korī* with prec. *uraja phala*, glossing *uraja phala ke agra*, ('nipple'?), and LCG follows this sense.
(5) *doti, joti*: the metrical formation ⏓ ⏑ ⏓ which prevails throughout the stanza is disrupted by these words, though the five-*mātrā gaṇa* is maintained:

⏑⏑⏑ — / ⏑⏑ —⏑ // ⏑⏑⏑ —/⏑⏑ —⏑
balaya kaṃkana doti naṣani jāvaka joti

(For a further metrical irregularity, see (8) *kiye*.)
(6) *kīkinī*: the *varṇa vṛtta* context clearly requires this spelling, despite weak manuscript support.
(7) *haribaṃśa hita*: unusually, Prem. gives the *chāpa* the lexical meaning of its components, reading *śrī priyā jū bibidha bhā̃ti kī līlā race haĩ ekā̃ta me baṃśī sahita jo hari tinike heta.*
(8) The majority reading *kiye* is metrically irregular, ⏓ ⏑ being otherwise regular. MS A's *kīye* should not be taken as a metrical correction (reading *kīyĕ*), since incorrect *kī-* for *ki-* is a common feature of this manuscript.

CP 68.

1 The lover and the lady are charmingly adorned in the round-dance;
2 in the autumn night, swarms of bees are intoxicated
with the sweetly fragrant lotuses on the blessed and pure sandbank.
3 With a refreshing wind of threefold nature quenching the heat of the day-star,
there stands the lover in the company of a hundred loving ladies;
4 to cymbal, *vīṇā* and drum they dance a pleasant *sudhaṅga*,
each more expert than the last in the musical arts.
5 *Rāga* and *rāginī* are established with the raining of nectar in the wood
as the delightful flute is enjoyed by [Kṛṣṇa's] *bimba*-like lips;
6 graceful and proficient, the one named Rādhikā
takes *lāga, kaṭṭara* and *urapa* steps, and *sulapa* with the seven notes.
7 '*Tatta thei! thei!*' she goes, and seizes a new rhythm—
she turns and rolls with wanton motion in a drunken elephant's gait;
8 the young handsome one has run and seized her, and the pure one adorns his breast—
Hita Harivaṃśa, the two *kalahaṃsas* are as lightning and raincloud!

(1) *bane*: Prem. alleges a second meaning, 'the lover becomes the lady'; such a conceit is not developed in the ensuing lines.

(2) *nikara*: as in line (6), the third *pāda* has no rhyme with the first two *pādas*. Internal rhyme is complete in all three *pādas* in lines (3), (5) and (7) only; in (4) and (8) the third *pāda* alliterates with, but is not metrically equivalent to, the previous two: *mṛdāga/sudhāga/saṃg*[-*īta*]; *dharī/ṣarī/hari*[-*baṃśa*].

(3) *tahā̃ ṭhāḍe ravana*: the first 5-*mātrā gaṇa*, *tahā ṭhā-*, is the only instance of a disruption of the stanza's ⏔⏔ ⏑ ⏔⏔ pattern; being thus isolated, the metrical configuration lends emphasis to the statement 'there stands', and thereby underlines the status of Kṛṣṇa as hero of the poem.

(6) *lāga*: the *Nartananirṇaya* describes a class of *deśī* dance exercises or steps called *lāga* (M. Bose pp. 155-6). While differing in execution, these are apparently characterized by vigorous movement and jumping steps; and the *Saṅgītadarpaṇa* confirms that '*lāga* is jumping in the Karnāṭa style' (*loc. cit.*). In the *kathak* context, Lakṣminārāyaṇ Garg (p. 58) defines *lāga* somewhat obscurely as an *aṅga* of the dance in which '*do aṅg āpas mẽ sundartā ke sāth milte hõ*' (?).

(6) *kaṭṭara*: Bose (p. 160) cites another *deśī* dance movement called *kaṭṭari* as described in both the *Nartananirṇaya* and the *Saṅgītadarpaṇa*; in the former it is also called *kaṭṭaḍidharu* (or *dharukaṭṭaḍi*), and is alleged to derive from Telanga, suggesting a Dravidian source for the CP term. Other senses of H. *kaṭṭara*, listed in *HŚS* s.v. and deriving from H. *kāṭ*- are not involved here.

(6) *sulapa*: another of the *deśī* dance movements described by Bose (*loc. cit.*) from the *Nartananirṇaya* is *sūlupa*, a 'harmonious combination of stringed instruments and drums like *mṛdaṅgas*. This accompanies gay dances.' In his prefatory remarks to the gloss on 62.5 (a description of the dust flying up from the dancers' feet), Prem. offers the comment *aba sulapa ko barnana karata haĩ*. Whether or not this remark tallies with the technical sense given by the *Nartananirṇaya*, its unsolicited use by Prem. does at least suggest that the term had some currency in the language of this commentator. In contrast to the 62.5 context, Garg (*loc. cit.*) defines *sualpa* as an *aṅga* showing great delicacy of expression, performed 'with great elegance' (*viśeṣ nazākat se*).

CP 69.

1 The enchantress and Mohana are joyful and flushed with love—
intoxicated and delighted, they dance sweetly in the *sudhaṅga* step.

2 Skilled in all the arts and engrossed in the Kalyāṇa *rāgiṇī*,
their sweetness in every limb cannot be put into words.

3 On the bank of the Yamuna with a breeze of threefold nature, *sakhī*,
it is as though pigeon, cuckoo and parrot have taken a sage's vow of silence.

4 Skilful lady and fresh youth, a pair to steal the mind,
sing sweetly in a lovely low tone.

5 Hita Harivaṃśa, hearing the sound of bracelets and bells and tinkling anklets,
joy showers down on the young maiden.

(1)–(5) An attempt has been made in six MSS to impose a six-line form on this irregular 5-line stanza: ACL show line-end *daṇḍas* after *suraṃge*, HIJ after *raṃge*. Neither contrivance succeeds in converting the first line into a recognisable couplet form. Variants discussed in the notes below suggest that the stanza has been understood and transmitted in a *varṇika* guise, with a construction of approximately 8+8+8+8 syllables; the underlying *mātrika* construction of lines (2) to (5) can, however, be restored (with the usual licences) in every *pāda* except (2) *kalyāna rāginī līna* and (5) *baraṣai nava taruni*. Line (1) remains an anomaly; the additional material found in A's version of the line appears to be unhelpful commentatorial accretion (though it does not reappear in the Dhar. *ṭīkā*).

Division of the five lines into couplets is problematic, since each line is semantically independent. AA line-end rhyme between (1) and (2) yields a *ṣaṭpadī* AAA̧ BBA rhyme scheme not found elsewhere in the text: the *sudhaṃge/aṃge* rhyme suggests, therefore, a late attempt at forging a link between original and new material, rather than an original genetic connection between the two lines. The self-contained CCC rhyme-scheme of the remaining lines is not attested elsewhere in the CP. A possible thematic link between (3) and (4) has some support from *-u* rhyme in the 3rd *pāda*.

(2) *kalyāna rāginī*: since the *pāda* has an excess of 3 *mātrās*, the fem. *-inī* ending may be an accretion to fit a *varṇika* scansion (Kalyāṇa being a *rāga*, not a *rāginī*, in the earlier literature: (*Saṅgītadarpaṇa* II.82). The only common 2-*mātrā rāga* names, Śrī and Naṭa, are also classified as masc.; a change from a form such as **śrī rāginī* to *kalyāna rāginī* in order to tally with the Kalyāṇa prescription of the sequence CP 66-71 is not, therefore, an attractive hypothesis.

(3) *kapota kokila kīra*: masc. *-a* forms are required for metre. The accretion of fem. *-ā* may show confusion with *kokilā kīra* in 30.4.

(4) *mānasa*: the metrically requisite long vowel has been lost in the MSS. The form *manasi* popular in the manuscripts shows assimilation to such contexts as 81.2, 83.3 where this locative may be genuinely maintained.

CP 70.

1 Today the fair one does not hold herself in check;
2 she wanders joyfully like an impassioned elephant,
plunging in the ocean of amorous pleasure.
3 Wrapped in lethargy, reddened and with their collyrium like dust,
her eyes display her theft [of Kṛṣṇa's love];
4 through showering on her lover the nectarous essence of compassion
the redness of her lips is all but gone.
5 With the tying of her ringlets, the maiden [seems to] bind up
bees on the lotuses of her breasts;
6 in union, the fastening of her bodice has come apart,
and her waistband has become loose.
7 The young womenfolk, who feel no small joy,
invoke a blessing as they look on:
8 "Hita Harivaṃśa, may the eternal pair [remain] constantly
on this world in the forest!"

(1) *sābhārata*: Lok. supplies *apanai tana kau* as object; Rasik., Dhar. and Prem. retain the ellipsis of the *mūla*. LCG imposes an intransitive sense, *besābhāra bana rahī hai*.

(4), (7) *thorī*: a repeat of the same rhyme-word within a single rhyme-scheme is found only twice in the CP; the other example is 36.2/11 *bajāyau*, where the two occurrences are separated by a clear eight lines.

(5) *alaka nibaṃdha*: this collocation, as a determinative compound, is preferred to the alternative *alakani baṃdha* with *-ni* as oblique plural termination; cf. *nībī nibãdha* (50.3) where this collocation is essential to the *śleṣa* involving technical senses of Sk. *nīvi* and *nibandha*. In the present couplet, a differentiation appears to be intended between *nibaṃdha* in (5), as having an abstract sense, and *baṃdha* in (6), as having a concrete sense; a concrete sense is, however, applicable to *nibaṃdha* in 50.3 and 82.6.

CP 71.

1 Rādhikā is decked out with Śyāma in the *rāsa* circle;
2 in the middle are Nandalāla and the Vraja damsel of *campaka* hue,
like gold and emerald amidst cloud and lightning.
3 She adopts dance-steps, [calling] the measure '*tatta theī*'
[making] various hand movements and delighting in the seven notes
of the gamut;
4 In the joy of the dancing, her face with its splendour seen against
the blue dress she wears
is like Capricorn moonlight against a cloud.
5 The moon in the sky of that autumn night is worn out
by the musical precepts of *rāga* and *rāginī*, note sequences
and rhythmic variations;
6 Hita Harivaṃśa's lord is a *haṃsa*, while she has a lion's waist;
he has destroyed Madana's pride and she has the gait of an
enraptured elephant.

(1) Since the second line is primarily a description of the *maṃḍala* and not of Śyāma and Rādhikā, an interpretation of *maṃḍala* as subject of the whole couplet, with *banī* then seen as a noun ('forest': cf. 17.1) in the locative case, is also a possibility. The syntax would then be, 'With Śyāma in the company of Rādhikā, a *rāsa* circle exists in the forest'; for a similar use of *saṃga*, cf. the phrases *saṃga bālaka bhaṭa* (64.5) and *saṃga sata kāminī* (68.3).

(2) *ghana taḍita bica kanaka markata manī*: the most satisfactory interpretation of this double metaphor is the one given by Prem., in which Kṛṣṇa and Rādhā (as gem set in gold) are envisaged as surrounded by the traditional *rāsa* circle composed of alternate Kṛṣṇas and *gopīs* (cloud and flashes of lightning). Rasik. and Dhar., attempting to limit the reference to Rādhā and Kṛṣṇa alone, read both the metaphors as pertaining to these two, ignoring the construction in which *bica* relates to the compound *ghana taḍita*. Lok. also restricts the reference, but bases it on an alleged conceit in which Rādhā sees herself reflected in Kṛṣṇa's bosom (*taḍita* amidst *ghana*) and vice versa (*markata manī* amidst *kanaka*).

(3) *gati*: Bose (pp. 105-6) lists 15 dance movements called *gati*, the list being compiled from the *Nartananirṇaya*, the *Abhinayadarpaṇa* and the *Saṅgītadarpaṇa*. Most are imitative of animal or bird gaits or movements; the list includes *gajalīlā* or *gajagāminī*, and *haṃsī*, for which cf. the zoological references of line (6).

(3) *māna*: the general sense 'measurement' is applicable, though a sense given in the *HŚS* is of a pause (*virāma*) in the *tāla*, having the four varieties *sama*, *viṣama*, *atīta* and *anāgata* (relating respectively to the first beat of the *tāla*, the half-way beat,

and to beats following and anticipating the *sama*). This sense does not appear to have widespread acceptance in musicological texts (though a reference in the *mārga-tāla* section of the *Saṅgītaratnākara* (v. 43) may be relevant).
(3) The predominant ⏕⏑⏕ *gaṇa* arrangement of the stanza is disrupted by the sequences

/⏑⏑ —⏑/   / ⏑ — —/
[*ha-*]*staka bheda*   and   *dha nī ye*

in the present line; further disruption occurs in line (5):

/⏑⏑ — —⏑/
[rā-]gini tāna,

and in the first *gaṇa* of the *chāpa* line (for which see note below).
(3) *naṃdinī*: only Prem. understands a reference to Rādhā here. Rasik. and Lok. read *naṃdinī* as adjectival, qualifying *sura*; this interpretation imposes masc. gender onto the fem. *-inī* ending. The collocation *sura naṃdinī* may reflect familiarity, from another context, with the compound *suranaṃdinī* in the sense of *sura* as 'god'. The crux is further complicated by a citation in *MW* of the sense 'a particular musical composition' for *nandinī*; but no reference to such a term has been traced in *saṅgīta* texts, suggesting that the currency of this meaning must be limited. There is no manuscript reading **nādinī* as a rhyme for *cā̃dinī* in the following line.
(4) *prakaṭita*: syntax requires a reading of *prakaṭita chabī badana* across the caesura; BDEFL apparently view the caesura as a syntactic barrier, and accordingly impose the finite participle *pragaṭata* (with appropriate *tadbhava* $k > g$ change).
(6) The commentators equate *kaṭi keharī* with *prabhu haṃsa* in an attempt to marshall all reference to Kṛṣṇa into the first half-line, thereby again maintaining the caesura as a syntactic barrier. The description 'lion-waisted' however, like its English equivalent 'wasp-waisted', must surely refer to the *female* physique (as at 43.3).
(6) *hita haribaṃśa*: the *chāpa* is unmetrical in lacking one *mātrā* in the first *gaṇa*; cf. a similar occurrence in 46.4. In the present line there is no further evidence of irregularity to suggest a corruption in the transmission of the *chāpa*; the four-*mātrā gaṇa* is therefore understood to be catalectic.

CP 72.

1 On the beautiful sandbank, blessed and joy-giving,
2 with deep and ever-new love for each other,
  the young skilful lady and hero play.
3 After touching the ripples of cool Yamuna water,
  the breeze rains down gentle droplets;
4 the minds of the couple are delighted by the luscious fragrance
  of stands of fine coral trees and lotuses and *campakas*.
5 Acme of all delight in the *sudhaṅga* style,
  the young ones dance and sing with voices joined;
6 fawns, peacocks, geese, bees, cuckoos
  and wondrous myriads of love-gods make obeisance to them.
7 A bed made of blossoms, and golden vessels filled with intoxicants
  adorn the bower;
8 in a mutual abundance of joy at nightfall
  the two parties accoutre themselves for a battle of love.

9 The king of all pleasure-seekers, restrained by the damsel's hand,
frees the ties of her waistband by mental address;
10 "No, no!" she cries in an ambrosial voice—
but the lover heeds not her coquettish anger.
11 Hita Harivaṃśa, the loving voluptuaries Lalitā and the others
look on through chinks in the creeper house;
12 filling brimful with that unparalleled pleasure, they can barely breathe
as tears of joy stop their throats and eyes!

(2) *kũvara*: Prem.'s gloss *kũvari nāgarī jū* presupposes a fem. spelling not found in the Prem. MSS (GKM).
(4) *haraṣata*: understood as transitive by Lok., who glosses *saurabha sarasa mithuna ke mana kau haraṣata hai.*
(6) Prem. explains this line in terms of the intended figure, a *vyatireka*, in which the *upamānas* listed acknowledge the superiority of, respectively, the eyes, dancing skill, gait, humming tone, voice, and sweetness of beauty of the pair.
(9) *kiśorī kara dhṛta*: the sense 'restrained by the damsel's hand' is more literal than the commentators' interpretation represented by Lok.'s *kiśorī kau kara pakarikai*, which detracts from the intended sense of *budhi bala.*

CP 73.

1 They despoil the wagtail, fish and fawn of their pride—
what then can I say of these eyes?
2 Tell me pretty one, how much have you taught them
of the ploys of enchantment and bewitchment?
3 Devious and bold, nimble and sharp-pointed,
red, black and white—how have you made them so?
4 Their tender glances, intoxicating like wine,
fearlessly rob another of all he has.
5 Young woman, you have not looked at me
with even a single benign glance;
6 [Says] Hita Harivaṃśa, you with the gait of a *kalahaṃṣa*
follow your inclination in matters of love!

(1)–(6) *-ātẽ/-ātaĩ* rhymes: etymological *-ẽ* and *-aĩ* endings are represented inconsistently in the manuscripts. The intended rhyme scheme is based on a close phonetic approximation of the two vowels.
(2) *mohana* may be read as the name of Kṛṣṇa, as object of *basīkarana.*
(3) *race* relates to *all* the qualities listed in the line, and not merely the colours of the latter half-line; it is therefore understood as deriving from **racyate* rather than *rajyate.*
(3) *kahā̃ tẽ*: the sense is that of the equivalent KhB. expression *kahā̃ se*, 'how, by what means?'.
(4) *mṛdu* must be understood as qualifying *dṛga pātẽ*, since *mṛdu madhu* would be an unexpected collocation (except for assonance). Prem. apparently reads *mṛdu*

madhu (as does Lok.), and contrives an interpretation of *mṛdu* as 'butter' and *madhu* as 'honey', a mixing of which yields a fatal poison: *heta kahā ki mṛdu kahibe mē̃ māṣana aura madhu kahibe mē̃ sahata. ye doū milē̃ tau biṣa hoi.* Rasik.'s *ṭīkā* (the MS has no *mūla*) reads *mṛgamada* in this context: *mṛgamada sī mādika mahā nena katākṣi calāhi.*

(4) *pātē̃*: *-ē̃* is contrived for rhyme only, *pāta* being masc. A reading **dṛga pātai* as intending Sk. instrumental *dṛkapātaiḥ* has no precedent in the CP and does not seem likely in the general style of the language of the text (even in a context which produces such a form as *madhumiva*).

(5) *naiku...citayau*: lit. 'you have not looked at me having composed [even] a single benign glance'. The line has only 15 *mātrās*.

(5) *pramadā*: though the *-u-* spelling popular in the manuscripts is attested in the *Sūrasāgara* (*BBhSK*) and even in the *Pṛthvīrājarāso* (*HŚS*), it is clearly for *pramadā*, conflated with *pramudita* etc.

(6) *nātē̃*: nasalization is added superfluously, for rhyme.

CP 74.

1 Why do you augment your haughty pride, lady with the eyes of a fawn?

2 —I am now quite afeared and shrink from saying anything at all!

3 With frenzied flute he sings of your heart,
and awake on his bed he is thinking of your form;

4 [begs] Hita Harivaṃśa: free from the pain of separation
the distressed voluptuary, your most beguiling lover!

(1)–(4) The peculiar metrical arrangement of this stanza, in which a couplet of 26, 24 *mātrās* is followed by regular lines of 32 (16+16) *mātrās*, is repeated in CP 75; cf. also the similarity between 74.2 *haũ...kahi na sakati ika bāta* and 75.1 *haũ ju kahati ika bāta*. In both stanzas, (1) is apparently a 16+10 *mātrā* construction, while (2) may be construed either as a 14+10 *mātrā* construction (i.e. of the *Rūpamālā* type exemplified in CP 28) or as an 8+16 construction forming a transition between (1) and the remaining lines.

(2) *kachu* must relate to *ḍarani*, and is not the object of *kahi na sakati* (which governs *ika bāta*).

(3) *tava* is genitive, and must therefore relate to *aṃtara* 'heart' in contiguity with *tavākṛta* in the second half-line. *aṃtara* is omitted in Dhar.'s gloss; Lok.'s reading *muralī ke aṃtara mai* is unconvincing, and Prem.'s *niraṃtara* ingenuous; the intention of Rasik.'s paraphrase, *gāvata muralī matta piya aṃtara tuma hī citta*, is not clear.

(3) *saina*: all the commentators give the sense 'sleep', as the antithesis of *jāgrata*. Such an abstract sense would normally be expressed by a pairing of similar participial forms such as the *jāgrata/sovata* which appear in the glosses of Prem., Rasik. and Dhar.; elsewhere in the text *saina* always has a concrete sense. The *intended* antithesis is between the distinct conceits of the two *pādas* of the line. A precedent for the *saina...socani* idea is found in *Gītagovinda* V.5, showing loc. *-śayane*:

> *vasati vipinavitāne tyajati lalitadhāma;*
> *luṭhati dharaṇiśayane bahu vilapati tava nāma.*

(3) *tavākṛti*: since *ākṛta* is not widely attested, and the negative sense of *akṛta* is inapposite, the phrase must be *tava+ākṛti*.

CP 75.

1 Listen *sakhī*, why do you dismiss what I say?
2 Why do you cause suffering to the darling of your life, for no offence?
3 The lover looks at the moon of your face,
and you gaze at your feet with head bowed;
4 he propitiates you by stroking your soft chin,
and you, lady, put aside his hand with your own.
5 Helpless, unsteady and much distressed by separation,
he does not consider at all the favourableness of the moment;
6 Hita Harivaṃśa, why do you not meet your lover in secret,
and foster his thirsting eyes?

(1)–(2) The metrical arrangement of this first couplet, 16+10 and 14+10 *mātrās*, reproduces that of the first couplet in the previous stanza, and is again followed by lines of 16+16 *mātrās*; see note to 74.(1)–(4).
(1) *ḍarati*: readings of unmetrical *ḍarāti* (ABIJKL) are unexplained, unless there is some confusion with the use of *ḍar-* in a similar context in 74.2.
(2) *ārati*: in composition with *kar-* is attested in Sūradāsa (*HŚS*). Prem., however, reads *ārati* as adjectival and unconnected with *karata*: *kyaũ aba itano karata hau. ve tau aparādha binā haĩ aura āratavaṃta haĩ.*
(3) *tana*: the intended postpositional force ('towards') is understood by all the commentators except Prem., who alleges a nominal sense as *aṃga*: *ye citavata muṣa caṃda tuva aru nava aṃgani kṣā[ṃ]ti.*
(4) *prabodhata*: for a discussion of this reading see note to the phrase *cibuka sucāru praloi prabodhata*, 7.8.
(5) *sara*: a back-formation from *avasara*. Citations in *BBhSK* all involve the collocation *sara avasara*, here yielding the sense *samaya kusamaya* as glossed by Prem.
(6) *triṣita naina*: in the present context (especially following (3)), an interpretation of the 'eyes' as Kṛṣṇa's, and not Rādhā's, seems appropriate; the opposite view is also possible, however, and would echo the sentiment of *Gītagovinda* IX.6:

sajalanalinīdalaśītalaśayane;
harim avalokaya saphalaya nayane.

CP 76.

1 A bed of the leaves of young shoots is made by the skilful lady in the bower,
and most generous is this damsel, skilled in the amorous arts;
2 with the delight of amorous dalliance in every limb,
with passions and alluring gestures and bending of the eyebrows,
the waves of her loveliness assail a million love-gods.
3 Amidst pleasantly tinkling anklets and the wondrous sound of bracelets
she cries "Stop! Stop, my lord!" in the excellent sport;

4 The darling girl and the youth, a union of *rājahaṃsa* and *haṃsinī*,
dampen the eyes, Hita Harivaṃśa, with the quintessence of
their joy.

(1) *nāgarī*: for a further example of the accretion of commentatorial material similar to A's *syāmā nāgarī jū* here, cf. A's version of 69.1.
(1) *aina*: the sense 'place, abode' is established in Hindi, with examples in Sūradāsa, Kevalarāma etc.: cf. attestation of the sense 'place of refuge' in Manu for Sk. *ayana-* (*MW*). A pleonastic usage with the locative sense of *desa* in the compound *kuṃja desa* (11.1) is understood by all the commentators in the present context.
(1) *kalā* disturbs the predominant cretic rhythm.
(2) *taraṃga*: internal rhyme with *aṃga/bhaṃga* confirms the existence of a caesura after the ninth *mātrā* of this half-line; cf. similar confirmation in 80.2, but compare also 12.4 and 12.6 where internal rhyme points to a *pāda* construction of 12+12+12+8 *mātrās*.
(3) *nūpurani*: Rasik.'s paraphrase gives the word *maṃjīra*, unsupported by any *mūla* MS, in this context; *maṃjīra* is not, however, a synonym for *nūpura*, and is unmetrical.
(3) *nātha badata*: Lok. understands as 'the Lord cries'.
(4) *rājahaṃsa*: none of the commentators recognize the possibility of such an enjambement of the caesura (though only Prem. gives a specific gloss, *doū rājā haĩ*).

CP 77.

1 Swaying and turning, the damsel is blooming with joy;
2 she has swung with her lover in the swing of amorous dalliance,
all the sweet night long in the house of creepers.
3 Though helpless through imbibing the spirituous essence of great affection,
she has not strayed from her course;
4 her eyes are wrapped in lethargy, her locks dishevelled,
and the bodice on her bosom lies slightly open.
5 Her garland is crumpled, her waistband loose,
her silken garment decorated with collyrium and betel-juice;
6 Hita Harivaṃśa, she is a restorative herb to wearied Śyāma,
rent by the arrows of the god of love.

(1) *rasa*: A's reading *ati* (perhaps engendered by the alliteration of the preceding three words) reappears in Dhar.'s gloss on the line, where the *mūla* is repeated verbatim.
(3) *nāhina gati bhūlī*: i.e. she has not abandoned the role alluded to in the final line. Prem. glosses *mana kī gati*, Lok. *cāha kī gati*, Rasik. *rati suṣa sugati bidhāna*.
(5) *dukūlī*: this is the masc. *-a* form amended for rhyme.
(5) *bā̃dhana*: a reading of the first syllable as short is necessary to achieve a 16-*mātrā* half-line, but such licence is not attested in other occurrences of *baṃdhana*. Cf. A's ingenuous contraction of *māla* to *mala* in the same half-line.
(6) *mūlī*: *HŚS* attests a sense *jaṛī būṭī* 'medicinal herb' for this extended *-i* form.

CP 78.

1 The young maiden dances a *sudhaṅga;*
2 "*theī*! *theī*!" she calls, looking towards her lover,
like a *cakorī* thirsting for the moon of his face.
3 Seeing the one skilled in well-timed melodic passages
and in rhythmic measurement, Śyāma cries "*Ho ho rī*!";
4 Hita Harivaṃśa, the sweetness of her various limbs
has forcibly stolen Mohana's mind!

(3) *bādhāna*: *HŚS* alleges a technical sense as 'the first beat (*sama*) of the *tāla*'. As in the present line, however, the *HŚS* attestation (from Tulasīdāsa, s.v. *baṃdhāna*) shows the word as following *tāna*; the technical sense is therefore actually yielded only by the compound *tāna-baṃdhāna* as meaning 'the closing of a melodic run [on the first beat of the rhythmic cycle]', and is not inherent in *baṃdhāna* per se. Cf. further occurrence of *tāna bādhāna* in Sūradāsa (*BBhSK* s.v. *bādhāna*) and Kevalarāma (Entwistle p. 244).

(4) The final half-line in A, *barabasa kiyo citai muṣa morī*, is, but for *kiyo*, found again in 82.2. (The gloss in Dhar. is, however, based on the standard text.) Rasik.'s gloss is evidently a conflation of the standard text and A's variant:

aṃga aṃga ati mādhurī hasati mṛdula muṣa mori;
barabasa hī mohana citahi leti hai pyārī cori.

CP 79.

1 In secret solitude with her beguiling lover
the darling sways in an excess of joy;
2 in the sweet *sudhaṅga* dance, the skilful lady
cries "*theī theī*!" as her feet beat upon the ground.
3 Crown-jewel of those skilled in the arts of love,
she makes enticing movements with her eyebrows in dramatic display;
4 seeing her lover rendered helpless like a greedy bee,
she snaps her fingers in front of his nose.
5 He, the crest-jewel of kings among lovers, a very assembly of qualities,
tugs in delight at her clothes and her garland with its pendant charm;
6 Hita Harivaṃśa, the nearby slavegirls
quaff this spirituous essence through the vessels of their eyes.

(1) The second *pāda* of this first line must be corrupt, a 16+13 *mātrā* line being most unlikely: hence the confusion in MS C which inverts the two *pādas*. The particle *rī*, found in all the manuscripts, cannot belong to the first *pāda* (**sāga rī*), which is regular in 16 *mātrās* without it; nor can it belong to the second *pāda* (**rī laḍaitī*), since *rī* is not conceivable in *pāda*-initial position. It must therefore be an accretion incorporated to fill out the defective *pāda*. A metrically satisfactory text cannot be

restored on the basis of the existing readings. (A hypothetical construction involving an enjambed caesura, **piya ke saṃ/-ga rī laḍaitī*, would yield a scansion of 16+16 *mātrās*, but only with a *pāda*-ending in two *gurus*, anomalous in this stanza where all other first *pādas* end — ⏑ ⏑.)
(2) *kahati*: manuscript support for the variant *kahani*, semantically plausible as a verbal noun, exists in two branches of the stemma (FG, IJK); but the collocation of participles with dance *bolas* is regular elsewhere, as for example in 78.2 *theī theī kahati*.
(4) *nāsāpuṭa*: *-puṭa*, giving the sense 'wing of the nose, nostril' (*MW*) is semantically redundant and is perhaps incorporated for alliteration with foll. *caṭa-*. Dhar.'s gloss *gahi nāsā kara caṭakati hai* is obscure, since 'grasping' has no apparent application here. In the intended conceit, Rādhā, with an audacious gesture which mocks Kṛṣṇa's status as *rasikarāi cūḍāmani*, arouses Kṛṣṇa from his swoonlike state of helplessness (cf. 66.12); perhaps disturbed by the impudence implied by this literal sense, LCG alleges a sense in which *karaja nāsāpuṭa* alludes to a 'nostril-like' shape made by the fingers when producing a snapping sound.
(5) *padika hāra*: best read as a determinative compound. *HŚS* notes that a *padika/padaka* is an ornament bearing the mark of a god's footprint, often used as a talisman to protect children.
(6) *nikaṭa*: A's reading *niraṣi* shows assimilation to similar contexts such as 70.7 *niraṣi juvatī jana*.

CP 80

1 Enchanting in every limb, the cowherdess is a creeper of fine gold
clinging to the *tamāla* tree of Śyāma;

2 the brightness of her face is like the moon, her locks and *tilaka* the blemishes on its brightness,
as she lurks in Śyāma's embrace like lightning in cloud.

3 Unclad are the golden pillars [of her thighs], as a serpent her staff-like braid—
the lady of the grove is a mass of love in the lover's embrace;

4 ornamented with her lord, Harivaṃśa, and wearied by amorous dalliance
is she with breasts like golden pitchers, the prettily-named Rādhikā.

(1)-(4) The *gaṇa* pattern / ⏓⏓ ⏑ ⏓⏓ ⏑ / persists throughout, with the exception of *lāgi rahī* in the first line. Internal rhyme in (2) reinforces this line's caesurae, which yield a construction of 12+12+9+11 *mātrās*; but the lack of such a construction in the other lines shows this to be a secondary refinement. (3) shares with (2) the 12+12 *mātrā* half-line; but (1) clearly does not, and syntax suggests that the caesura in (4) falls after *sātha* rather than before it (where it would yield a 12-*mātrā pāda*, but would disrupt the *nātha sātha* composition): (4) appears, therefore, to approximate to the construction of (1), in which the caesura follows *ballarī*, rather than to the central lines. The stanza is characterized by a high degree of alliteration, which may be a factor in the irregular positioning of the caesurae.
(2) *manō̃*: A's synonymous variant *janu* is not attested elsewhere in the text, and is perhaps incorporated in order to avoid repetition of *mānaũ/manō̃* which occurs later in the line and again in (3); alliteration with prec. *joti* may also be sought.

(2) *mānaũ*: only ACGLM have the requisite long initial syllable. Other manuscripts, reading *manau* etc., supply the correct total of *mātrās* but with irregular scansion.
(3) *beni*: the metrically requisite short *-i* is not found in the manuscripts.
(4) *alasavaṃta*: only E preserves (or fortuitously provides) this metrically correct reading.

CP 81

1 Vṛṣabhānu's daughter sings in soft and mellow tone;

2 with exacting and wondrous melodic passages in the *tāla* of Carcarī,
she creates delight in the mind of Nandanandana.

3 Firstly bathing, and charming with veil, collyrium and *tilaka*
and with rings on her ears, her face puts the moonlight to shame;

4 she has a blessed nose-ring of jewel-studded gold,
and her lips like *bandhūka* flowers make her jasmine teeth gleam.

5 Pretty bracelets and bangles, the necklace adorning her heart,
the bells at her waist and the anklets at her feet she makes resound;

6 the lady with the gait of a *kalahaṃsa* stirs desire
as the *madayaṃtikā* of her nails gives a colourful lustre.

7 Impetuous in this ocean of dance, in solitude the young accomplished lady
demonstrates the various movements of *candracālī*;

8 knowledgeable in the amatory arts, skilled in gesticulation and dramatic gesture,
with the sporting of her eyebrow she sets the god of love adancing.

9 In the house in the impenetrable forest, her lover delighted in her arms,
she makes fall a shower of joy with a sweet prelude;

10 Harivaṃśa the *ali* enjoys the nectar oozing
from the lotus of amorous enjoyment on the two confluent oceans!

(1) *bṛṣabhāna*: in the present stanza this metrical formulation (⏑⏑—⏑) occurs seven times alongside the predominant ⏓⏑⏓ *gaṇa*. The other instances are: (2) [*au-*]*ghara tāna*; (3) [*ma-*]*jjana cāru*; (5) [*kaṃ-*]*kana cāru*, [*rā-*]*jata hāra*; (10) [*saṃ-*]-*gama siṃdhu*, [*pū-*]*ṣana baṃdhu*. Four of the seven instances constitute the second *gaṇa* of a line. No other metrical formulations are encountered, and a five-*mātrā* *gaṇa* is maintained throughout.
(2) *bikaṭa*: the general sense 'formidable, difficult' (Sk. *vikaṭa*) may apply, although the same derivation may give a more technical sense intending a note sequence which involves convoluted passages (and not simply a straightforward progression through the *āroha* and *avaroha* of the scale). Prem. glosses *bikaṭa* and *aughara* as *tāla ke bheda*. Cf. also a sense of *vikaṭatva*, cited in the *Sāhityadarpaṇa*, as '(in rhetoric) a sound of words reminding of a dance' (*MW*).

(2) *manasi*: this spelling may reflect familiarity with compound forms (*manasija* etc.) rather than an authentic locative; but there is little evidence to support emendment to *manasa*. Metathesis in A and M shows that *manasi* existed as a reading in the archetypes of these manuscripts at least.
(3) *prathama*: as at 45.3, this word heralds a 16-*śṛṅgāra* list; here it begins with *majjana* in the present line and ends with *madayaṃtikā* in (6). See the extended note to 45.3 for a full list of items, and discussion.
(6) *haṃsakala*: cf. a discussion on this form in the note on 8.4. In the present line, *haṃsakala* (and not the more usual *kalahaṃsa*) accords with the ⏖⏑⏖ *gaṇa* construction.
(6) *madayaṃtikā*: *MW* translates as 'Arabian jasmine' (citing the *Yogayātrā* of Varāhamihira). All the commentators, however, assimilate to more familiar kinds of nail-decoration: henna (*mẽhadī* in various spellings, Prem., Dhar., Rasik.) or lac (*mahāvara*, Lok.).
(7) *caṃdacālī*: presumably for **candracārī*; *HŚS* cites a number of categories of *cārī* in the sense 'an *aṅga* of the dance', but *candra*° is not included in the list (or attested elsewhere). The *ci-* spelling occurring in some of the manuscripts is unexplained.
(9) *ālāpa*: the musical context demands an interpretation as the musical term, rather than as 'conversation'.
(10) *ubhai* may qualify *saṃgama*, with the sense 'two sorts of union' (following *koka bidyā bidita* in (8) above).

CP 82

1 The damsel is a mass of sophistication;
2 with a glance and a turn of the head she has overwhelmed
  the dark one, best of all adroit youths.
3 Radiant with beauty and having sweetness in every limb,
  without adornment is the fair lady of Vraja adorned;
4 at every moment [more] skilful in the *suḍhaṅga* dance,
  she plunges in love's stormy ocean of joy.
5 She holds the mind of that capricious lover, the bee Mohana,
  on the cusps of her golden lotus breasts,
6 and the two wagtail eyes of her dear one
  she binds with the various strings of her fastenings.
7 It is as though a certain intoxicating liquor were mixed
  in the pool of her navel in the ground of her belly;
8 and the most beautiful, Hita Harivaṃśa, drinks it
  and has broken the strict rule of sacred scriptures!

(2) *citai*: regular absolutive (=*cita*) from *cita-*.
(2) *morī*: the absolutive, with *-i* lengthened for rhyme.
(2) *barabasa*: use of this form (< *bala*+*vaśa*?) in composition with *kar-* is unattested elsewhere and is in some doubt. Usual occurrences of *barabasa* are adverbial, having the sense 'forcibly', as in 78.4 *barabasa liyau mohana cita corī* to which A's reading of *liyau* in the present line is perhaps an assimilation. The *Sūrasāgara* version of this stanza (Appendix II) reads *kiyau*. Of the CP commentators, only Rasik. retains the *barabasa kar-* composition, and there too in a virtual paraphrase: *barabasa kiye*

muṣa morī. Prem. and Lok. dismantle *bara-basa* and gloss respectively *balatkāra sõ basa kiyau hai* and *śreṣṭha kari basa karyau hai* (the latter gloss, with *śreṣṭha kari*, evidently understands *bara* as Sk. *vara*, hardly a likely derivation here even if seen as enjambed in a construction **kula maula sāvarau bara/basa kiyau*); LCG glosses *vivaśa banā diyā hai*, while Dhar. has no direct gloss. Given the lack of attestation of *barabasa kar-*, then, there is a possibility that A's *liyau* is the authentic reading.
(3) *bina bhūṣana bhūṣita*: Prem. perceives a reference to the natural 'adornments' described in 16-*śṛṅgāra* lists, and quotes three lines attributed to Dāmodara Hita based on this conceit: see note to 45.3 for a discussion.
(4) *china:* for *-i-* cf. Oriya *ei-khini* (*CDIAL* 3642 *kṣaṇa-*), Panjabi *khinu* (*GNG*).
(5) *korī*: presumably derives from *koṭi-* and intends 'nipple': this specific sense is given only by Lok.'s *kuca agra.*

CP 83

1 Cease this holding of proud anger in your mind, haughty lady;
2 why act thus towards your young dear-as-life,
  who is humble, handsome, adroit, and dependent on your word?
3 Helplessly Hari constantly recites your perfect name,
  his mind straying from contemplation of you not for a second;
4 the blessed autumn night slips by with every moment,—
  lovely lady, set yourself towards joyous love!
5 Listen to what I say, heed your *sakhī*:
  fair-faced one, vain is your suffering in the deep pain of separation.
6 Hita Harivaṃśa, they meet on a bed of leaves in the grove,
  and make sweet sport, swimming in an ocean of pleasure.

(1)–(6) *-ibau* rhyme: forms in (1), (2) and (5) are clearly verbal nouns, and *taribau* in (6) may also be so construed. (3) and (4) diverge from this homogeneous usage in the outer couplets: *ḍharibau* in (4) has a clear gerundive sense, while *ṭaribau* is best understood as a gerund.
(2) *itau kata*: this *gaṇa* alone disrupts the /⏕ ⏑ ⏕/ pattern which subsists in this stanza. The five-*mātrā* value of the *gaṇa* is maintained.
(3) *bimala*: Rasik. reads *bimala manasi* as an enjambment, and glosses *bimala sucitta.* Dhar. has no gloss on *bimala.*
(4) *ḍharibau*: the root *ḍar-* can hardly apply here, and its occurrence in ACE is a clear case of shared error in this group. Dhar. contrives a gloss on the *ḍar-* reading all the same: *mai ju ḍarati mana piya anurāga tai būḍai nahī cita bhrama nidhi māt.*
(5) *niju*: readings of *ika* (FGLM and latterly J, and appearing also in the glosses of Prem. and Lok.) show assimilation to the phrase *haũ ju kahati ika bāta* at 75.1; in the present context *ika* is inapposite, since its particularising sense is at odds with the generalizing sense of *kachu.*
(5) *sumuṣi*: *-i* (for adjectival *-ī*) is preferred to nominal *-a*, since context requires a vocative.
(6) *saina*: metre requires a bisyllabic value for *sai-*, since the ⏕ ⏑ ⏕ *gaṇa* is regular throughout the stanza. (It here yields [*kiśa-*] *laya saina.*)
(6) *haribaṃśa hita*: this form of the *chāpa*, inverted for metre, allows Prem. to take the sense 'for the sake of Harivaṃśa' (*haribaṃśa rūpī saṣī ke heta*). Lok. misunder-

stands Prem.'s reading of *hita* as postpositional, and glosses *hita saṣī ke heta*, retaining *hita* as a proper noun.

(6) *taribau*: the 'redemptive' sense of *tar-* is not involved here; cf. a distinction in *CDIAL* between H. *tar-* (as here) 'surmount, float on, swim' < 5702 *tarati*, and H. *tar-* 'to be saved' formed from trans. *tār-* < 5796 *tārayati*.

CP 84

1 Today, beloved, you appear full of love;
2 daughter of Vṛṣabhānu, your spoliation is not hidden from me—
you have struggled in passion with Nanda's darling boy!
3 Your string of pearls is broken and your moon-ornament slipped
from your hair—
in secret the lover has plundered you—
the betel-juice [of his kiss] lies on your cheeks;
4 your eyes are overcome with languor, your *bimba*-lips sapless—
[declares] Hita Harivaṃśa, you shine in brilliance!

(1)–(4) The vulgate text does not cohere metrically, but appears to assume an arbitrary syllable-count (8+8+8+X) the attaining of which requires the incorporation of superfluous material often detrimental to sense and/or grammar (see following notes). The evidence of L, though of little value elsewhere, cannot be passed over here: L omits from lines (2) and (4) respectively the two *pādas*, *sithala kaṭi kī ḍorī* and *pulaki prema parasa*, whose inclusion in the vulgate text distorts the usual *ṣaṭpadī* line construction. It seems unlikely that L should deliberately or accidentally have excised two out of three additional rhyming *pādas* (*rahasi rasika lūṭī* in (3) being retained in L); and so accretion in the other manuscripts on the basis of incidental caesura rhyme in the single instance of line (3) must be a more logical hypothesis. L's version of the second half-line in (2), (4) brings these closer in metrical weight to the second half-line of (3) than does the vulgate version, though a full equivalence is not achieved; L's version of (4) also locates the *chāpa*, *hita haribaṃśa*, in initial position in the second half-line, which alone is attested in CP *ṣaṭpadī* construction. Scansion of both the edited text and the vulgate shows correspondences between (1) and (3) and between (2) and (4).

(1) *āju* is followed by *ba* in all manuscripts. *ba* is often semantically lightweight, but here is wholly tautological after *āju*, and must have been incorporated into the line in conformity with the erroneous imposition of 8-syllable *pādas*.

(1) *ho* (MSS): inelegant after *hai*, and contributing towards an unusually long sequence of *gurus*, this vocative particle is unattested elsewhere in the text except in the formula *hohorī* (57.20). With *ho* excised, a coherent 10+10 *mātrā* line is achieved.

(2) The first half-line of the vulgate text has a construction of 12+12 *mātrās*. Analytical *bṛṣabhāna kī kiśorī* is unattested elsewhere in the text, whereas *bṛṣabhāna-kiśorī* occurs at 9.4, 43.1, 54.1 (and cf. the similar compound epithets *bṛ° naṃdinī*, *bṛ° dulārī*, again without analytical parallels). The second *pāda* is, therefore, readily reducible to the prevalent 10-*mātrā* length, and may be matched in the first *pāda* by reading *mopai* as two *laghus*.

(2) *naṃda ke lāla*: readings of ~ *lālana* are perhaps intended to achieve a 12-syllable *pāda* as equivalent to the third *pāda* of (4). *lālana* may be accommodated metrically into the correct 16-*mātrā pāda* by reading *ke* as short: but the fact that *lālana* does not appear elsewhere in the text (except as a verbal noun, 66.7) suggests that fully regular *lāla*, attested in BGIJM, is authentic here.

(3) *motina*: an 11-*mātrā pāda* as yielded by readings of *motiyan*° (from the extended H. form *motiyā*) is not attested as first *pāda* of a line; given the prevalence of 10-*mātrā pādas* in this stanza, the choice here appears to be between the 4-*mātrā* readings *motin*° (ABIJL) and *motiyan*° (CEFHKM)/*mutiyan*° (DG). (Variations on *motiyan*° in C and E are taken to be scribal error.) *motina* is preferable as being fully regular metrically, and as having the support of attestation in the similar context of 20.4.
(3) *caṃdra*: both this form and the manuscripts' *caṃdrikā* are attested in collocation with *cikura* (9.3 and 67.3 respectively); *caṃdra* yields a 10-*mātrā pāda* consistent with prec. *motina lara ṭūṭī*. Total lack of manuscript support is a further example of the imposition of the supposed 8-syllable *pāda* onto this stanza.
(4) *naina*: the syntactically unattractive oblique pl. forms found in all manuscripts except A and C again assume an 8-syllable *pāda* construction. Accretion of *-na*/*-ni* is encouraged by a misconstruction, explicit in GH and implied by loss of *ni-*(*rasa*) in BIM, of *biṃba nirasa* as *biṃbana*/*-ni rasa*.
(4) *rī*: inclusion of this expendable vocative particle reflects analytical *naṃda ke lāla* in (2), since with *ke* and *rī* excised a third *pāda* of 14-*mātrās* is obtained in both lines.

CHAPTER VI

METRE IN THE CAURĀSĪ PADA

1. Introduction

The first part of this chapter attempts a metrical analysis of all the prosodic types represented in the CP, and seeks to locate antecedents for these in Apabhraṃśa prosody; *varṇa vṛtta* is discussed first, followed by the *mātrika* metres. The main metrical features of the 84 stanzas are then tabulated, and the disposition of metres discussed. The final section of the chapter examines the way in which CP *pādas* are set to *tālas* when sung in the temple *samāja* tradition; rhythmic analysis of tape recordings of ten stanzas, representative of the main prosodic types, aims to identify the common ground between textual metre and musical *tāla*. Particular attention is paid to the influence that the performance tradition may have had on the composition and transmission of the stanzas analysed. This section includes a complete transcription, in a *tāla* framework, of a performance of CP 52.

The traditional metre names found in taxonomic Hindi *chandaḥ-śāstra* are not, for the most part, of very great value in either the historical or the empirical approach to the subject of prosody; for this reason, they have not generally been followed here. The tabulated summary of CP metres does, however, include the traditional metre names where appropriate: these are taken from the *Chandaḥprabhākara* of Jagannāth Prasād 'Bhānu Kavi'.

2. Varṇa vṛtta

Two basic types occur in the CP: (i) those formed on the 6-*mātrā gaṇa* /⏔⏑⏔⏑/ (CP 10, 11, 12, 17, 76, 80); (ii) those formed on the 5-*mātrā gaṇa* /⏔⏑⏔/ (CP 25, 26, 46, 50, 67, 68, 71, 81, 83). In most cases, the *gaṇa* construction is maintained more or less consistently throughout the stanza, exceptions being mostly limited to the internal arrangement of syllables within the *gaṇa* and not involving transgression of *gaṇa* boundaries. Most metres of this type comprise couplets of lines having seven repeats of the *gaṇa* followed by a final *gaṇa* which is either a *guru*, or a spondee, trochee, or iambus. The only variation on this arrangement is that in which the final *gaṇa* has the same value as those preceding it, that is to say a type comprising eight repeats of the *gaṇa*.

Individual metres within types (i) and (ii) are defined according to their *pāda* construction; *pāda* boundaries do not necessarily coincide with *gaṇa* boundaries, and so in the examples which follow, caesurae are shown by spacing of the text rather than by double obliques //. *Pāda* construction is frequently reinforced by caesura rhyme, although irregularity in this feature shows it to be a secondary development. End-rhyme is found in the last three syllables or, slightly less frequently, in the last two syllables.

Type (i): metres based on the 6-*mātrā gaṇa*

Five stanzas, CP 10, 11, 12, 76 and 80 have the line construction (7× /⏓⏑⏓/) + /–/. The first two lines of CP 10 serve to demonstrate the 12.12.20 *mātrā* construction of the line:

–⏑ – ⏑/–⏑–⏑/ –⏑– ⏑/–⏑ –⏑
10.1 *āju nāgarī kiśora bhāvatī bicitra jora*
⏑– ⏑⏑⏑/– ⏑– ⏑/⏑⏑⏑ – ⏑/–
kahā kahaũ aṃga aṃga parama mādhurī;
⏑⏑⏑ –⏑/ – ⏑ ––⏑/ –⏑–⏑/– ⏑ – ⏑
10.2 *karata keli kaṃṭha meli bāhudaṃḍa gaṃḍa gaṃḍa*
⏑ ⏑⏑⏑⏑⏑/–⏑ ––/ –⏑– ⏑/–
parasa sarasa rāsa lāsa maṃḍalī jurī.

The high degree of alliteration in these two lines is typical of this metrical type in the CP. *Pāda* rhyme (*kiśora/jora*) in the first line is not found in the second line, but reappears in the remaining two lines. *kahā kahaũ* in line (1) provides an example of rising rhythm, in which the predominant trochaic stress pattern of the *gaṇa* is reversed: cf. (*lāgi*) *rahī* in the same line position in 80.1, again in collocation with *aṃga aṃga*:

–⏑ ⏑–/– ⏑ – ⏑/ ⏑⏑ ⏑–⏑/–
80.1b *lāgi rahī aṃga aṃga manobhirāminī*

While the second half-line often appears to have a caesura after the twelfth *mātrā*, yielding a line construction 12.12.12, 8, this is not fixed; internal rhyme elsewhere in this type suggests rather a second half-line of 9, 11 *mātrās* (and cf. a similar tendency towards the 9, 11 configuration in type (ii) below):

⏑⏑⏑ – ⏑/– ⏑– ⏑/ –⏑ ––/ ⏑⏑⏑ – ⏑/
76.2 *surata raṃga aṃga aṃga hāva bhāva bhṛkuṭi bhaṃga*

1. A résumé of the Greek metrical terms may be useful:

amphibrach	⏑–⏑	periambus	⏑⏑
anapaest	⏑⏑–	proceleusmatic	⏑⏑⏑⏑
cretic	–⏑–	spondee	––
dactyl	–⏑⏑	trochee	–⏑
iambus	⏑–		

– ⏑⏑– ⏑/– ⏑ ⏑ ⏑⏑/– ⏑ – – ⏑/–
mādhurī taraṃga mathata koṭi māra rī

⏑⏑⏑–⏑/ ⏑⏑ ⏑– ⏑/ ⏑⏑⏑ ⏑⏑⏑/ ⏑⏑ ⏑– ⏑/
80.2 *badana joti mano mayaṃka alaka tilaka chabi kalaṃka*

⏑ ⏑⏑ –⏑/– ⏑ –⏑/⏑⏑⏑ –⏑/–
chapati syāma aṃka mānaū̃ jalada dāminī

The first couplet of CP 12 again points to a second half-line of 9, 11 *mātrās,* since a caesura after the twelfth *mātrā* would bisect the words *ka-liṃda* and *murali-kā* respectively (because of the high number of *gaṇas* failing to show the /⏓⏑⏓⏑/ arrangement, CP 12 must be regarded as a debased example of the true *varṇavṛtta* type):[1]

⏑⏑⏑ –⏑/– ⏑–⏑/ –– ⏑⏑/⏑⏑ ⏑ – ⏑/
12.1 *calahi rādhike sujāna tere hita suṣa nidhāna*

–⏑ ⏑ ⏑⏑/ – ⏑ ⏑⏑ ⏑/– ⏑ – ⏑/–
rāsa racyau syāma taṭa kaliṃda naṃdinī

–⏑⏑ ⏑ ⏑/– ⏑ –⏑/ –⏑ – ⏑/⏑⏑ ⏑–⏑/
12.2 *nirttata juvatī samūha rāga raṃga ati kutūha*

–⏑⏑ ⏑⏑/–⏑ ⏑⏑⏑/– ⏑–⏑/–
bājata rasamūla muralikā anaṃdinī

In such cases, therefore, the line may arbitrarily assume the construction 12.12.9, 11; but in the absence of any *fixed* caesura in the second half-line, the couplet is to be seen as comprising a *ṣaṭpadī* of 2 × 12.12.20 *mātrās.*

CP 80 shares with CP 10, 11, 12 and 76 the *varṇika* arrangement (7 × /⏓⏑⏓⏑/) + /—/; but with the exception of line (2) quoted above, there is no fixed caesura in either half of the line. A caesura after the twelfth *mātrā* in 80.1a would bisect the word *balla-rī:*

–⏑–⏑/⏑⏑⏑ –⏑/– ⏑–⏑/ –⏑ – ⏑/
80.1a *ballabī sukanaka ballarī tamāla syāma saṃga*

Throughout the stanza, however, hypothetical *pādas* of 12.12 *mātrās* end in the trochaic rhythm which subsists throughout caesura rhyme in this metrical type (with the exception of an instance of rising rhythm, *jahā̃/tahā̃*, in 12.3): 80.1a *balla-/saṃga*; 80.2a *-aṃka/-aṃka*; 80.3a *ṣaṃbha/daṃḍa*; 80.4a *nātha/-vaṃta.* In terms of metrical weight, therefore, if not in terms of rhyme or word division, the coherence of the 12.12 construction is maintained even here.

The absence of true caesurae in this stanza may be explained by one of two hypotheses: either the stanza is a debased example of the type

1. The alternative hypothesis, viz. that since *varṇavṛtta* is a refinement on *akṣara* and *mātrā* prosodies, CP 12 should be regarded as an early prototype representing a stage *before* the inception of 'standard' *varṇavṛtta*, would be difficult to substantiate: in context and content the stanza is of a piece with the remainder of the CP, and it is hard to envisage that its source could be substantially earlier than that of the other stanzas.

and simply fails to show the usual features of *ṣaṭpadī* rhyme, or the *ṣaṭpadī* configuration is itself a secondary development, introduced as a refinement of the alliterative trochaic construction of the individual line. Irregularity in *ṣaṭpadī* rhyme in other stanzas suggests that the latter is more likely to be correct.

CP 17 has the same *gaṇa* construction as CP 10, 11, 12, 76 and 80 but has a final trochee in place of the final *guru* of these stanzas. *Gaṇa*-based alliteration in the first half-lines of (2)—(4) supports the hypothesis that the 12.12 division is more a function of the trochaic rhythm than a fundamental feature of line construction; and, as in 80.1a above, a caesura after the 12th *mātrā* bisects a word (*ki-śora*):

— ⏑ — ⏑/ — ⏑ — ⏑/— ⏑ — ⏑/— ⏑ — ⏑

17.2a *aṃsa aṃsa bāhu dai kiśora jora rūpa rāsi*

⏑⏑ ⏑— ⏑/ ⏑ ⏑⏑ — ⏑/ — ⏑ ——/ — ⏑ — ⏑/

17.3a *nava nikuṃja bhavara guṃja maṃju ghoṣa prema puṃja*

⏑ ⏑⏑ ⏑⏑⏑/— ⏑ — ⏑ — ⏑ — ⏑/⏑⏑⏑ ⏑ ⏑/

17.4a *madana mudita aṃga aṃga bīca bīca surata raṃga*

Type (ii): metres based on the 5-*mātrā gaṇa*

The 5-*mātrā gaṇa* /⏓⏑⏓/ forms the basis of CP 25, 26, 46, 50, 67, 68, 71, 81, 83. This is the Lacchīhara metre of Apabhraṃśa, which appears in the *BhK* as 2 × —⏑——⏑——⏑——⏑— (Jacobi 1918:46). In the CP it is demonstrated mostly clearly in the *ṭeka* of CP 25, where the cretic rhythm is rigorously maintained:

—⏑ —/— ⏑—/— ⏑—/— ⏑ —

25.1 *āju nīkī banī rādhikā nāgarī*

Again in CP 26 it is the *ṭeka* which has the clearest *varṇavṛtta* formation:

— ⏑—/ ⏑⏑⏑ —/—⏑ —/—⏑—

26.1 *mohanī madana gopāla kī bā̃surī*

The / ⏓⏑⏓ / *gaṇa* is maintained without exception throughout CP 25, but in all other stanzas of this class there is at least one *gaṇa* in which the cretic rhythm is disrupted. The *gaṇa* / ⏑⏑⏑— / is prominent in line-initial position. In CP 46 and CP 71 /*hita hari*–/ forms a catalectic 4-*mātrā gaṇa* in the final line, though in CP 46 at least there is some doubt as to the authenticity of this reading (see discussion under 46.4). CP 4 also belongs to this type, but shows a freer arrangement in the construction of its *gaṇas*.

The construction of the line in this type tends to follow the *ṣaṭpadī* couplet pattern, but is not standard throughout: as in type (i) above, *ṣaṭpadī* construction with caesura rhyme is often secondary to strong and frequent alliteration based on the *gaṇa*. The greatest variation is found in CP 26: lines (3) to (6) have internal (*ṣaṭpadī*) rhyme between the first two *pādas,* and line (2) has a similar construction but without the reinforcement of rhyme. Further internal rhyme in the second half of lines (4) (*tīra*/*-bīra*) and (6) (*-haṃsa*/*-baṃśa*) suggest that these two lines are of the *pañcapadī* type (i.e. with an apparent construction of 10.10.8.5.7 *mātrās*). While this additional rhyme is not found in other lines, the alliterative sequences *karata ratirāja* in (2) and *banī bara banita* in (5) suggest that the same third *pāda* of 8 *mātrās* may be developing here also. Here then we should notice the extraordinary diversity of metrical types represented within a single stanza—(1) *varṇavṛtta;* (2) *catuṣpadī*; (3) and (5) *ṣaṭpadī*; (4) and (6) *pañcapadī*:

– ⏑–/ ⏑ ⏑⏑ –/– ⏑ –/ – ⏑ –

(1) *mohanī madana gopāla kī bā̃surī;*

– ⏑– / ⏑ ⏑ ⏑ ⏑⏑/ ⏑ ⏑⏑ ⏑⏑/ – ⏑ –/

(2) *mādhurī śravana puṭa sunata suni rādhike*

⏑ ⏑⏑ ⏑⏑/–⏑ –/ – ⏑ ⏑⏑/ – ⏑ –

karata ratirāja ke tāpa kau nāsu rī.

⏑⏑⏑ –/– ⏑⏑⏑/ ⏑ ⏑⏑ –/ – ⏑⏑⏑/

(3) *sarada rākā rajani bipina bṛṃdā sajani*

⏑ ⏑⏑ ⏑⏑/ – ⏑ –/⏑⏑ ⏑ ⏑⏑/–⏑ –

anila ati maṃda sītala sahita bāsu rī;

⏑⏑⏑ –/ ⏑ ⏑ ⏑⏑⏑/ – ⏑ –/⏑⏑ ⏑⏑⏑/

(4) *parama pāvana pulina bhṛṃga sevita nalina*

⏑⏑ ⏑⏑⏑/–⏑ ⏑⏑/–⏑ ⏑⏑/–⏑–

kalapataru tīra balabīra kṛta rāsu rī.

⏑⏑⏑ –/ ⏑⏑ ⏑–/ ⏑ ⏑ ⏑ ⏑⏑/⏑⏑⏑–/

(5) *sakala maṃḍala bhalī tuma ju hari saũ milī*

⏑– ⏑⏑/⏑ ⏑⏑ ⏑ ⏑/– ⏑ ⏑⏑/–⏑ –

banī bara banita upamā kahau kāsu rī;

⏑ ⏑ ⏑ – /⏑⏑ ⏑–/ –⏑ –/ ⏑⏑ ⏑–/

(6) *tuma ju kaṃcanatanī lāla markata manī*

⏑ ⏑⏑ ⏑ ⏑/– ⏑ ⏑⏑/– ⏑ ⏑⏑/–⏑ –

ubhai kalahaṃsa haribaṃśa bali dāsu rī.

The same formation of 8.5.7 (and 8.5.6) occurs in the following half-lines:

⏑ ⏑⏑ ⏑⏑/ –⏑ ⏑ ⏑/–⏑ ⏑⏑/ – ⏑–/

46.2a *hṛdai ati phūla samatūla piya nāgarī*

⏑ ⏑ ⏑ ⏑⏑/–⏑ ⏑⏑/–⏑ –/–⏑ ⏑⏑/

46.3a *sarasa gati hāsa parihāsa āvesa basa*

⏑ ⏑⏑ ⏑ ⏑/– ⏑ ⏑⏑/– ⏑ ⏑ ⏑/ – ⏑–

68.8b *ubhai kalahaṃsa haribaṃśa ghana dāminī* (cf. 26.6 above)

– ⏑ ⏑ ⏑/– ⏑ ⏑ ⏑/– ⏑ – / ⏑ ⏑ ⏑ ⏑ ⏑/

71.2a *bīca na̐dalāla brajabāla campaka barana*

83.6b (in this example the *pādas* cohere through consonance rather than through caesura rhyme:)

⏑ ⏑ ⏑ ⏑ ⏑ / – ⏑ ⏑ ⏑/ – ⏑ ⏑⏑/ ⏑ ⏑ ⏑⏑

karata kala keli suṣa siṃdhu maĩ taribau

The formation also appears in terms of syntax, without alliterative support; as in 46.2-3 above, the feature often appears in *both* lines of a couplet:

⏑⏑⏑ ⏑ ⏑/ – ⏑ ⏑ ⏑/ – ⏑ ⏑⏑/ – –

67.5b *udara guna reṣa paṭa nīla kaṭi thorī*

– ⏑ –/– ⏑ ⏑ ⏑/– ⏑ ⏑ ⏑/– –

67.6b *koka saṃgīta rasa siṃdhu jhakajhorī*

⏑ ⏑ ⏑ –/– ⏑ ⏑ ⏑/ – ⏑ ⏑ ⏑/– ⏑⏑

81.9b *sarasa ālāpa suṣa puṃja baraṣāvai*

⏑ ⏑ ⏑ ⏑ ⏑/– ⏑ ⏑ ⏑/– ⏑ ⏑ ⏑/ – ⏑⏑

81.10b *dravata makaraṃda haribaṃśa ali pāvai*

Although this configuration appears quite commonly, it is far from being established as a standard *pāda* construction. More commonly, alliteration tends to reinforce the coherence of the individual 5-*mātrā gaṇa*, and consequently 5.5 patterns appear frequently in the second as well as the first half of the line:

– ⏑ – / – ⏑ ⏑ ⏑/⏑ ⏑ ⏑ –/ – ⏑ –

25.2b *sīla siṃgāra guna sabani tẽ āgarī*

– ⏑ – / – ⏑ –/⏑ ⏑ ⏑ –/ – ⏑ –

46.1b *syāma syāmā mile sarada kī jāminī*

⏑ ⏑ ⏑ ⏑ ⏑/ – ⏑ ⏑ ⏑/⏑ ⏑ ⏑ ⏑ ⏑/ – ⏑ –

46.2b *karani kara matta manau bibidhi guna rāminī*

⏑ ⏑ ⏑ ⏑ ⏑/⏑ ⏑ ⏑ ⏑ ⏑/ – ⏑ ⏑ ⏑/ – ⏑⏑

46.3b *dalita dala madana bala koka rasa kāminī*

– ⏑ ⏑⏑/ – ⏑ ⏑ ⏑/⏑ ⏑ ⏑ – / – ⏑ –

46.4b *prīya ati sūra suṣa surata saṃgrāminī*

– ⏑ ⏑ ⏑/⏑ ⏑ ⏑ ⏑ ⏑/⏑ ⏑ ⏑ –/ – ⏑ –

68.2b *matta madhukara nikara sarada kī jāminī*

3. Mātrā Chanda

(i) 16+11/12 *Mātrās*

The most common type of *mātrā chanda* in the CP is that having a line of 16+11 or 16+12 *mātrās*. The two varieties differ in the length of the final syllable,[1] but are in all other respects identical and so may be discussed together; *italicizing* in the following list denotes stanzas of the 16+11 variety, while an asterisk shows that the stanza's first line is short (a *ṭeka*): CP 9*, 20*, 21*, 22*, *23**, *30*, *31**, *32**, *33**, 34*, *35**, 36*, *37**, *38*, 41*, 42*, 45*, 47*, *48**, 52*, *53**, 59, *60**, 61, 63[2], *66**, 70*. Observations made here on the metrical construction of these stanzas do not necessarily hold true for the *ṭeka,* which is dealt with separately.

The connexion with the Apabhraṃśa 28-*mātrā* line is very close. The 6+4+4+4+4+4+2 *mātrā* construction specified by Hemacandra for the *dvipadī* Upabhramarapada (Jacobi 1918:49) is almost always apparent in the CP examples (though Hemacandra does not specify a caesura after the 16th *mātrā*, a marked feature of the CP line).[3] Furthermore, the great majority of lines show the specific construction noted by Jacobi, *loc.cit.*, for this metre (Dovai) in the *BhK* where a caesura after the 16th *mātrā is* a regular feature:

⏓⏓⏓/⏑⏓⏑/⏓–/⏑⏑, ⏓/⏓⏓/⏑.⏓⏑/–
(– ⏑⏑) (–)

Exceptions to the basic 6+(5×4)+2 arrangement total only 19 in the whole group listed above; six of the 19 are from the second line (i.e. part of the first couplet) of a stanza; occurrences are mostly limited to specific collocations, as shown:

(a) collocations involving *kahā* or *kahā̃:*

⏑ ⏑́ – ⏑/– –/–
20.3b *kahā̃ cūnarī rātī*

⏑ ⏑́ ⏑ –/⏑⏑ –/–
21.4b *kahā durāvata pyārī*

⏑ ⏑ – ⏑ ⏑́ ⏑⏑⏑/⏑⏑⏑⏑/⏑⏑
53.4a *taba kī kahā kahau jaba piya prati*

⏑ – ⏑⏑⏑/ ⏑ ⏑ ⏑ ⏑́ ⏑ –/⏑ ⏑
66.15a *priyā kahati kahu kahā̃ hute piya*

(b) collocations involving *priyā:*

⏑ ⏑́ ⏑ –/⏑⏑ – ⏑/
30.8b *priyā durāvata bāsa*

⏑ ⏑́ ⏑⏑⏑/ – –/⏑
35.4b *priyā naina kī kora*

1. The 16+12 type characteristically has a long final syllable, but this may occasionally be represented by two shorts.

2. CP 63 is a composite stanza of the type called *chanda* (discussed below); it predominantly comprises lines of the 16+12 *mātrā* form under discussion here.

3. Bryant (p. 132, footnote) records a construction of '(2)(4)(4)(4)(2)/(2)(4)(4)(2)' *mātrās* as being usual for this metre in the *Sūrasāgara*.

⏑⏑/⏑⏑ ⏑ –́ ⏑ –/⏑⏑
47.2b *naṣa siṣa priyā janāvai*
– ⏑⏑ ⏑ –́ ⏑⏑⏑/– ⏑⏑/⏑⏑
60.2a *ye ali priyā badana aṃbuja rasa*

(c) other:

– ⏑⏑–/ –⏑–́ ⏑–/⏑⏑
30.2a *mādhavikā ketukī latā lai*
– – –/ – ⏑–́ ⏑–/⏑⏑
38.2a *hā rādhā rādhikā pukārata*
⏑–́ – ⏑/⏑⏑–/⏑
66.7b *urū nābhi urajāta*
– ⏑⏑ ⏑–́ ⏑–/⏑⏑⏑⏑/⏑⏑
66.8a *adbhuta chaṭā biloki avani para*

The most frequent transgression of the Dovai construction specified by Jacobi for the *BhK* is in the first and fifth four-*mātrā gaṇas,* which are often anapaests in the CP: Jacobi records no variations on the usual amphibrach/proceleusmatic (⏑–⏑) save a single occurrence of a dactyl. In the fifth four-*mātrā gaṇa* of the CP line the anapaest is a function of end-rhyme cadence, which is always –⏑⏑ (16+12) or –⏑ (16+11) such that the amphibrach is an impossibility in this position; anapaests are notably less common in the first four-*mātrā gaṇa*. Significantly, the first syllable in each of these two *gaṇas* is rarely long in the CP: to this extent at least the CP retains the Apabhraṃśa scansion. As the following examples demonstrate, there is a tendency for a caesura to follow the first *mātrā* of the first four-*mātrā gaṇa*—i.e. the seventh *mātrā* of the line—and, rather less frequently, the first *mātrā* of the fifth four-*mātrā gaṇa* also; frequent occurrence of the *chāpa* '*hita haribaṃśa*' in line-initial position guarantees such a construction:

⏑⏑ ⏑⏑–/⏑, ⏑⏑⏑/⏑⏑ –/ ⏑⏑, ⏑⏑/⏑ ⏑ –/ ⏑⏑–/–
20.8 *hita haribaṃśa bacana suni bhāmini bhavana calī musakātī*
– ⏑⏑⏑ ⏑/⏑,⏑⏑ ⏑/⏑⏑–/–,⏑ ⏑/ – ⏑ ⏑/ ⏑⏑– / ⏑⏑
22.2 *caṃcala capala aruna aniyāre agrabhāga banyau aṃjana*
⏑ ⏑⏑ ⏑–/⏑,⏑⏑⏑/⏑⏑ –/–, –/⏑⏑ –/⏑, ⏑–/⏑
23.3 *adhara niraṃga alaka laṭa chūṭī raṃjita pīka kapola*
– ⏑⏑ ⏑ ⏑/⏑, ⏑–/⏑⏑–/⏑⏑, –/⏑ –/⏑,⏑–/⏑
23.4 *tū rasa magana bhaī nahi jānata ūpara pīta nicola*
– ⏑⏑⏑⏑/⏑,⏑⏑⏑/⏑⏑ – / ⏑⏑, –/⏑⏑ –/⏑, ⏑–/–
45.4 *gū̃thita alaka tilaka kṛta suṃdara sẽdura mā̃ga sā̃vārī*
⏑⏑–⏑⏑/⏑, ⏑ ⏑ ⏑/ ⏑⏑⏑⏑ /⏑⏑, – / ⏑ ⏑ –/⏑, ⏑ –/⏑⏑
47.5 *ulaṭī sabai samajhi nainani maĩ aṃjana reṣa banāvai*
⏑⏑⏑ – ⏑/⏑, –⏑ / ⏑⏑ ⏑⏑/⏑⏑, ⏑ ⏑/⏑⏑
53.5 *kaca saṃjamana byāja bhuja darasata musakani*
⏑ ⏑/⏑, ⏑ – ⏑
badana bikāsa

– ⏑⏑ –/⏑, ⏑⏑⏑/⏑⏑ ⏑⏑/⏑⏑, –/ ⏑ ⏑ –/⏑, ⏑ –/⏑⏑
61.5 *hāsa bilāsa harata saba kau mana kāma samūha bihaṃḍana*

Three other *gaṇa* constructions are frequently at variance with Jacobi's model:

(a) /⏑⏑⏑ ⏑ – ⏑/ (and much less commonly /⏑ – ⏑ ⏑⏑⏑/) in the first *gaṇa:*

– ⏑ – ⏑/⏑⏑ –/ ⏑ ⏑ –/⏑⏑
9.2a *iṃdranīlamani syāma manohara*

⏑ ⏑ ⏑ ⏑⏑/⏑⏑ –/⏑ ⏑ ⏑ ⏑/⏑⏑
30.12a *badhū kapaṭa haṭhi kopa kahata kala*

–⏑ – ⏑/ ⏑⏑–/⏑ ⏑ –/–
34.3a *prātakāla rajanī saba jāge*

⏑⏑ ⏑ – ⏑/⏑ ⏑–/⏑ – ⏑/⏑⏑
48.5a *nava nikuṃja abhirāma syāma sãga*

(b) a frequent occurrence of an amphibrach in the fifth *gaṇa:*

⏑⏑ ⏑ ⏑ – /⏑ ⏑⏑⏑/⏑ ⏑ ⏑⏑/ ⏑⏑ ⏑⏑/⏑ – ⏑/
22.4 *hita haribaṃśa kahata na banai chabi suṣa samudra*

⏑ ⏑ –/ ⏑⏑
manaraṃjana

⏑⏑⏑⏑⏑⏑/– ⏑⏑/⏑⏑–/ ⏑⏑ ⏑ ⏑/⏑ – ⏑/ ⏑–/⏑⏑
34.8 *rati biparita cuṃbana pariraṃbhana cibuka cāru ṭakaṭolani*

⏑ ⏑– ⏑⏑/⏑⏑ – / ⏑ ⏑ ⏑ ⏑/⏑⏑ –/⏑ – ⏑/– –/⏑⏑
41.3 *jamunā pulina nikuṃja bhavana maĩ māna māninī ṭhānai*

⏑⏑ ⏑⏑⏑ ⏑/⏑– ⏑/⏑⏑–/⏑⏑ ⏑ ⏑/⏑ – ⏑/– –/⏑⏑
59.2 *jahã tahã bipati jāra juvatī jyaũ pragaṭa piṃgalā gāyau*

(c) an amphibrach in the third *gaṇa:*

⏑⏑⏑⏑ – / ⏑⏑ – /⏑ – ⏑/⏑ ⏑
36.4a *juvatini maṃḍala madhya syāmaghana*

–⏑ – ⏑/⏑ ⏑ –/⏑ – ⏑/–
37.4a *kvāsi kvāsi bṛṣabhānanaṃdinī*

⏑⏑ ⏑ ⏑– /⏑ ⏑ –/⏑ – ⏑/⏑ ⏑
48.6a *hita haribaṃśa bilāsa rāsa juta*

⏑⏑ ⏑⏑⏑ ⏑/⏑ ⏑ – / ⏑ – ⏑/–
52.2a *braja nava taruni kadaṃba nāgarī*

The *ṭekas* in the stanzas of this group are of between 15 and 20 *mātrās:* nine, or rather less than half the total, have 16 *mātrās.* All but one (20.1 *mohanalāla ke rasa mātī*) consist of the 11/12-*mātrā* second *pada* of a full line, preceded by a short first *pāda* of between 3 and 8 *mātrās.* In most cases, including all the 16-*mātrā ṭekas* save 70.1, the caesura is syntactically as strong as that found in the full line:

⏑⏑⏑⏑/⏑ ⏑ –/⏑⏑–/⏑⏑ –/ ⏑ ⏑
22.1 *nainani para vārau̐ koṭika ṣaṃjana*
–/⏑⏑ –/⏑⏑ –/⏑ ⏑–/–
45.1 *āvati śrī bṛṣabhānadulārī*
–/⏑⏑–/– –/ ⏑ ⏑– /– –/–
52.1 *deṣau māī suṃdaratā kī sīvā̐*
⏑ – ⏑/⏑⏑ ⏑⏑/⏑⏑⏑⏑/– –/⏑
60.1 *kahā kahau̐ ina nainani kī bāta*

Even in the seven *ṭekas* where a verbal caesura is not in evidence, the line can still be scanned as (X)+11/12 *mātrās* except in 20.1 (quoted above):

⏑ –/– –/ – ⏑ ⏑/– –/–
9.1 *banī rādhā mohana kī jorī*
– – –/– –/– ⏑⏑/⏑ ⏑ –/⏑
23.1 *rādhā pyārī tere naina salola*
–/⏑ ⏑ –/⏑⏑ –/⏑⏑ –/–
70.1 *āju sa̐bhārata nāhina gorī*

As may be seen in many of the above examples, the *ṭeka* tends to be marked by a strong anapaestic rhythm; this is not usually maintained so strongly in the subsequent lines of a stanza, although it does appear frequently throughout the text.

CP 63, of which a 16+12 *mātrā* line is the principal component, is a composite stanza of the type known in Hindi prosody as *chanda*. Each of its four sections has six lines, rhyming AABBAA; the first couplet of each section is of 2 × 12 *mātrās,* and remaining lines are all of the 16+12 construction discussed above. Line (3) of each section repeats some material from line (2), and the second *pāda* of the final line is a repeat of the first line.[1] The supposition that the four sections are to be seen as constituting a single unit is confirmed by the fact that the *chāpa* occurs only in the last of the total 24 lines.

(ii) 16+10 *Mātrās*

This metre appears in only two stanzas, CP 29 and CP 55. It is a truncated variant of the 16+11/type, behaving exactly as the examples of that type discussed above, but ending in a four-*mātrā gaṇa* which, as a function of end-rhyme cadence, is always an anapaest:

⏑⏑ ⏑⏑ ⏑⏑/⏑ ⏑ – /⏑ ⏑⏑⏑/⏑ ⏑ –/– –/⏑ ⏑ –
29.1 *braja nava taruni kadaṃba mukaṭa mani syāmā āju banī*

1. A similar arrangement is found in the *chanda* stanzas of the *Rāsa māna ke pada* of Kevalarāma (Entwistle 1983:208-22; 278-80; 316-18); and cf. the *chant* form in the *Ādigranth* (e.g. *Āsā mahalā* 1, *chant* 5, pp. 438-9).

⏑ ⏑ ⏑⏑ –/⏑ ⏑–/⏑⏑ ⏑⏑/⏑⏑ –/– – /⏑ ⏑ –

55.2 *bica lai syāma ghaṭā ati nautana tāke raṃga rasī*

There is only a single exception to the rule of the Apabhraṃśa model for the 28-*mātrā* line, wherein the fifth *gaṇa* is always /≃≃/:

⏑⏑ –⏑⏑/⏑⏑–/– ⏑⏑/⏑ ⏑ ⏑ ⏑/⏑ – ⏑/⏑ ⏑ –

29.3 *yaũ rājata kavarī gũthita kaca kanaka kaṃja badanī*

29.12 is the only line to disrupt the 6+(5×4) *mātrā* construction, the second *pāda* here beginning *racī*: (there are no MS readings for **rucira racī*):

– ⏑ – ⏑/⏑⏑ ⏑ ⏑/⏑⏑ –/– ⏑ ⏑́ ⏑⏑⏑/⏑⏑–

29.12 *syāma sīsa taru mano miḍabārī racī rucira ravanī*

The 16-*mātrā* *ṭeka* of CP 55 follows the pattern described for *ṭekas* above, viz. a full second *pāda* preceded by 6 *mātrās:*

– ⏑⏑ –/⏑⏑ ⏑⏑/⏑⏑–

55.1 *āju dou dāmini mili bihasī*

(iii) 16+6/7 *Mātrās*

The two stanzas in this metre, CP 39 and CP 40, have a similar format of *ṭeka*+5 full lines, and share similar rhymes. Both are irregular in the second *pāda*, variously of 6 or 7 *mātrās*. In the first *pāda*, however, both stanzas follow the pattern established in the types described above; indeed, 39.3-5 and 40.2-3 follow precisely the Apabhraṃśa model, with caesura after the seventh *mātrā* and the second *gaṇa* being an amphibrach:

⏑⏑– ⏑⏑/⏑, – ⏑/⏑⏑⏑ ⏑/⏑⏑

39.3a *rajanī sarada maṃda saurabha saũ*

⏑⏑– ⏑⏑/⏑, – ⏑/– ⏑ ⏑/⏑⏑

40.2a *rajanī rucira mallikā mukalita*

Again, the *ṭekas* consist of a full second *pāda* preceded by a first *pāda* of varying length; the *ṭeka* of CP 40 particularly demonstrates this construction since its second *pāda* also appears as the second *pāda* of 39:2:

⏑⏑– –⏑ ⏑ –⏑ ⏑⏑⏑

40.1 *baiṭhe lāla nikuṃja bhavana*

⏑⏑ ⏑⏑⏑ ⏑/– – /⏑ ⏑ –/⏑⏑ ⏑ – ⏑ ⏑⏑⏑

39.2 *raci raci apane hātha sãvāryau nikuṃja bhavana*

(iv) 16 *Mātrās*

CP 18 and CP 19 have the 4×4 *mātrā* line of the Apabhraṃśa Aḍilā as discussed by Jacobi (1918:47). The following features of the Apabhraṃśa construction are regular in the CP stanzas also: (i) the last *gaṇa* is a dactyl or a spondee; (ii) there is no amphibrach, or proceleusmatic with a caesura after the first *mātrā*; (iii) rhyme is AABB etc.; (iv) 2nd and 3rd *gaṇas* may combine. Jacobi notes frequent combinations of 1st and 2nd *gaṇas* as well as 2nd and 3rd, but here only the latter combination is found (two examples):

– ⏑⏑/ – ⏑ –́ ⏑ –/– –
18.3 *tū bṛṣabhāna gopa kī beṭī*
– ⏑ ⏑/–⏑–́ ⏑ ⏑ ⏑/ –⏑⏑
18.7 *jo rasa neti neti śruti bhāṣyau*

Amphibrachs being absent, every line may alternatively be scanned according to Hemacandra's scheme for the Aḍilā, 6+4+4+2 *mātrās* (Jacobi, *loc.cit.*), or by Jacobi's own proposed alternative of 6+6+4 *mātrās*; both schemes accommodate the two quoted exceptions to 4×4 construction.

(v) 16+16 *Mātrās*

This is the most common metre in the text, accounting for the following 19 stanzas (an asterisk identifies a stanza in which the first line is a short *ṭeka*): CP 5, 7, 8*, 14*, 16*, 43*, 44*, 51*, 54, 62*, 64*, 72*, 73, 74, 75, 77*, 78*, 79, 82*. Nearly all the 16-*mātrā* half-lines follow the 6+4+4+2 Aḍilā construction discussed above under type (iv): the metre is, therefore, a simple doubling of the Aḍilā form, rhyme and syntax showing the single line-length to be of two 16-*mātrā pādas*. More *pādas* fail to yield a scansion of 4×4 *mātrās* than fail to yield a scansion of 6+4+4+2 *mātrās*; in CP 62, for example, a single *pāda* is necessarily 4×4 (with an amphibrach as second *gaṇa*—disallowed in the Aḍilā, but admitted in the Paddhaḍikā (Jacobi, *loc.cit.*)), whereas five *pādas* are necessarily 6+4+4+2 (or 6+6+4):

⏑ ⏑ ⏑ ⏑/ ⏑ – ⏑/⏑ ⏑ ⏑⏑/–⏑⏑/
(4×4): 62.2a *sunahu na saṣī sahita lalitādika*
⏑ ⏑ ⏑ – ⏑/ – –/⏑ ⏑–/⏑ ⏑/
(6+4+4+2): 62.6a *kabahũ syāma syāmā dasanā̃cala*
⏑⏑ – –/⏑ – ⏑/⏑ ⏑ ⏑⏑/ ⏑ ⏑/
62.7a *ati lāvanya rūpa abhinaya guna*
– ⏑ ⏑ –/⏑ – ⏑/⏑ ⏑ –/⏑ ⏑/
62.7b *nāhina koṭi kāma samatūlahu*
⏑ ⏑⏑ ⏑–/⏑ – ⏑/ ⏑ ⏑ ⏑ ⏑/⏑⏑/
62.8a *bhṛkuṭi bilāsa hāsa rasa barasata*
⏑⏑ ⏑⏑– /⏑ – ⏑/⏑ ⏑ –/⏑ ⏑/
62.8b *hita haribaṃśa prema rasa jhūlahu*

Amphibrachic second *gaṇas*, exemplified in the latter four *pādas*, occur 24 times in this type; they tend to occur in pairs—either in successive *pādas*, as above (four such pairings), or in successive lines (three such pairings):

– ⏑ ⏑ –/⏑ – ⏑/ ⏑⏑ –/⏑⏑/
78.3a *tāna bā̐dhāna māna maĩ nāgari*
⏑⏑ ⏑⏑–/⏑ – ⏑/–⏑⏑/⏑⏑
78.4a *hita haribaṃśa mādhurī ā̐ga ā̐ga*

Much less common is the appearance of an amphibrach in the third *gaṇa*; this occurs only six times, three of the examples being from successive lines in CP 82:

⏑⏑ – ⏑⏑/⏑ ⏑ ⏑⏑/⏑ – ⏑/⏑⏑/
82.2a *nava nāgara kula mauli sā̐varau*
– ⏑ ⏑ ⏑ ⏑/⏑ ⏑ – / ⏑ – ⏑/–/
82.3a *rūpa rucira ā̐ga aṃga mādhurī*
⏑⏑ ⏑ ⏑ ⏑ ⏑/⏑ ⏑ –/ ⏑ – ⏑/ ⏑⏑
82.4a *china china kuśala sudhaṃga aṃga maī̐*

In the *BhK*, the final *gaṇa* (in the 4 × 4 *mātrā* arrangement) is a dactyl; this may be represented by a spondee, or occasionally by a proceleusmatic, while an anapaest is exceptional (Jacobi, *loc.cit.*). The same holds true here, but with spondees predominant; the final four *mātrās* of the CP *pāda* are represented as follows:

Spondee: CP 7, 14, 43, 51, 54, 73, 77, 78, 82 (*-orī* rhyme in all except 14, 73, 77);
Dactyl: CP 62, 74, 75;
Proceleusmatic: CP 79;
Dactyl/Proceleusmatic: CP 5, 44, 64, 72;
Anapaest: CP 8, 16.

With the exception of CP 72, which has couplet rhyme of the Apabhraṃśa type, all stanzas have the same end-rhyme throughout; end-rhyme varies in strength from the disyllabic (as 5.1-2 *bara/para*, etc.) to the quadrisyllabic (as CP 7.1-2 *nalina rī/malina rī*, etc.).

All but three *ṭekas* in this group are of 16 *mātrās* and follow the usual *pāda* construction. Of the three exceptions, 51.1 is of 16 *mātrās* and may be understood as the usual *pāda* but with catalectic first *gaṇa*:

– ⏑ ⏑⏑/– ⏑ ⏑/⏑ ⏑–/–
51.1 *dāna dai rī navala kiśorī*

8.1 and 14.1 are both of 19 *mātrās*; both include the collocation *aruna tere*.

In CP 74 and 75 the first couplet comprises lines of 16+10 and 14+10 *mātrās*; this anomaly is discussed in the notes to these stanzas.

(vi) 16+15 *Mātrās*

There are four stanzas in this metre: CP 3, 13, 49, 56. The metre is the same as type (v), viz. 2×(6+4+4+2), but with a single *laghu* in the final *gaṇa* of the second *pāda*: the 15-*mātrā* form is, therefore, that which underlies the 16-*mātrā* line of CP 19, in which a final *laghu* is typically arbitrarily lengthened to give spondee rhyme. In the present type end-rhyme is trochaic, always preceded by a *laghu* except in the following two cases:

⏑ ⏑⏑ ⏑ ⏑⏑/ ⏑⏑– /– –/⏑
13.4b *sarasa madhura muralī kī ghora*
⏑⏑ ⏑⏑ –/⏑ – ⏑/– – / ⏑
56.1 *haũ bali jāũ nāgarī syāma*

The latter example also shows one of the four instances in this group where an amphibrach appears in the second *gaṇa* of a *pāda*; similarities between two of the remaining instances demonstrate a tendency for this feature to become stereotyped:

⏑⏑ ⏑⏑–/⏑ ––⏑/⏑⏑ – / ⏑⏑
49.6a *hita haribaṃśa lāla rasa laṃpaṭa*
⏑ ⏑ ⏑⏑–/⏑ – ⏑/– ⏑ ⏑/⏑⏑
56.4a *hita haribaṃśa lola locana ali*

There is only a single instance of an amphibrach occurring in a third *gaṇa*:

– ⏑⏑ ⏑ ⏑/⏑ ⏑–/⏑ – ⏑/ ⏑ ⏑
49.3a *ye dou navala kiśora rūpa nidhi*

This *pāda* also illustrates the continuing tendency for a caesura to fall after the seventh *mātrā* (cf. CP 56, where this occurs in every *pāda* without exception): here the caesura is strengthened by rhyme (*-la*/*-li*) with the second *pāda* of the line:

⏑⏑⏑ ⏑ –/⏑ ⏑ ⏑ ⏑/ ⏑ ⏑ –/⏑
49.3b *biṭapa tamāla kanaka manŏ beli*

CP 3 has no *ṭeka*; the *ṭekas* of CP 13 and 49, as that of CP 56 quoted above, constitute regular 15-*mātrā pādas*.

(vii) 16+17 *Mātrās*

This arrangement occurs in CP 24 only. Each line ends with the vocative expression *rī sajanī*, preceded by *-īra* rhyme (24.1-2 *tīra/samīra*, etc.); the metre may, therefore, be seen as a form of the 16+11 *mātrā* type, with which it tallies in every other respect, with a refrain appended to every line. In lines (1), (3)-(6) of this six-line stanza a caesura falls after the seventh *mātrā* in the first *pāda*, but not of the second; in line (2) the converse is the case.

(viii) 14+11 *Mātrās*

The single stanza in this metre, CP 28, has six lines including a 14-*mātrā ṭeka*. A consistent scansion of 6+4+4, 6+4 *mātrās* is attainable in all the full-length lines; this form occurs in the Apabhraṃśa *Paümacariu* with the name Ahiṇavavasanatasiri (Abhinavavasantaśrī), but there the first *pāda* invariably ends ⏑⏑⏑ (Bhayani, p. 87). (This Apabhraṃśa type is technically a 13+10 *mātrā* metre, but is readily extended to 14+10 by the lengthening of the final syllable: cf. the same process in 15/16 *mātrā* types discussed above.) 6+4+4 and 6+4 *mātrā pādas* occur also in the *BhK* (Jacobi 1918: 49) but in the inverted order 10+14, and with a rhyme-scheme AB,CD. End-rhyme in CP 28 is trochaic *-āta* within a final amphibrach (in all lines except the *ṭeka*); this scheme tallies with the amphibrachic *gaṇa* at the end of the first *pāda* in the *BhK* metre (which Hemacandra calls Kalahaṃsa). In the *Paümacariu*, however, the line always ends /–⏖/. Neither Apabhraṃśa form, therefore, provides a direct model for the CP form.

Spondaic third *gaṇas* in lines (3) and (6) prohibit the 6+5+4 *mātrā* scansion given in the *Svayambhūcchandas* for a 14-*mātrā pāda* (Bhayani, *loc.cit.*); an amphibrachic second foot is found in lines (2), (3), (4) and (6), and is attested once in the *Paümacariu*.

The CP metre is exemplified by the final couplet:

      – ⏑ – ⏑/⏑ ⏑ ⏑ ⏑/–⏑⏑/ ⏑ ⏑ ⏑ – ⏑/⏑ –⏑
28.5 *lāla markatamani chabīlau tuma ju kaṃcana gāta*
      ⏑– ⏑⏑ ⏑/⏑ – ⏑/––/ ⏑ ⏑⏑ ⏑ ⏑⏑/⏑ –⏑
28.6 *banī hita haribaṃśa jorī ubhai guna gana māta*

The construction of the *ṭeka* is anomalous: although a caesura after *rādhe* yields the expected structure of 4+10 *mātrās*, long *kī* disrupts an otherwise stable line cadence and precludes the 6+4 *pāda* scansion of the other lines:

      – –/ –⏑ ⏑⏑ – – ⏑
28.1 *rādhe deṣī bana kī bāta*

(ix) 12+11 *Mātrās*

CP 57, of 30 lines in rhyming couplets, is the single example of this metre; the line construction is 6+4+2, 6+4+1. Line (2) alone fails to admit a first *gaṇa* of 6 *mātrās:*

— — ⏑ ⏑́ ⏑ — / ⏑ ⏑ ⏑ / ⏑ ⏑ — ⏑ ⏑ / ⏑ ⏑ — / ⏑

57.2 *śrī rādhikā kṛpā binu saba ke manani agamya.*

The second *gaṇa* is an anapaest in 15 lines, a proceleusmatic in eight, a dactyl in four, an amphibrach in one, a spondee in one. The third *gaṇa* is a periambus in all lines except (1) and (4).[1] The fifth *gaṇa* is an anapaest in all lines except (12) and (13), which have a spondee: with the final laghu, therefore, regular rhyme cadence is trochaic. Thus the second *pāda* is identical to that of the the *dohā*, as are 11-*mātrā pādas* in Apabhraṃśa 11+12 and 11+14 *mātrā* metres (type(7) and (8) in the metrical analysis of the *Paümacariu,* Bhavani pp. 86-7).

The 12+11 line may, therefore, be defined thus: 6+4+(⏑⏑ / —), 6+ ⏑⏑ — + ⏑

(x) *Irregular Mātrika Ṣaṭpadīs*

CP 1, 15, 58, 65 and 84 all have an irregular scansion; they have mostly been transmitted in a *varṇika* form, but appear to belong originally to the *mātrika ṣaṭpadī* class. Some general observations common to all five may be made here, but irregularities and suspected corruptions and accretions are discussed in the annotations to the individual stanzas.

Varṇavṛtta rhythm is usually entirely lacking in these stanzas, but *pāda* rhyme usually yields the aab, ccb *ṣaṭpadī* pattern found in the *varṇavṛtta* metres discussed above. Several lines have been subject to an unusual amount of accretion (mostly of vocatives or vocative particles), apparently with the intention of achieving a syllabic scansion in the line: many lines comprise *pādas* which, in their vulgate versions at least, can be scanned as 8 syllables.[2] This kind of syllable-count scansion, in which the length and order of syllables is more or less random, is accepted in Hindi prosody as a discrete metrical species with the label *varṇika muktaka:* Gaurīśaṅkar Miśra cites examples from Sūradāsa and Tulasīdāsa (1975:233 ff; 278ff). Yet such a species of metre lacks any precedent in the earlier literature, and the evidence of the CP suggests that the syllabic coherence of ostensible syllabic lines is secondary to an underlying moric construction. Occasional (random?) syllabic coherence in lines not showing any true *varṇika* pattern does occur, however, and it may be that such couplets as 15.5-6, having a syllabic count of

1. The caesura which follows is strengthened by rhyme in *-ta* in lines (8)-(13), (16)-(22), (24), while of the intervening lines both (15) and (23) have forms in —⏑ *-ta* immediately *following* the caesura.

2. *ai* and *au* vowels usually have to be counted as monosyllabic for such scansion.

$2\times(8+8+13)$ and no consistent moric scansion, represent a transition in Hindi metrics from true *varṇavṛtta* to a degenerate computation of syllables:[1]

15.5 *rahasi ramī chabīle rasana basana ḍhīle*
sithala kasani kaṃcukī ura rātī;
15.6 *saṣī saũ suni śravana bacana mudita mana*
calī haribaṃśa bhavana musakātī.

The irregularity of line length in this minority of CP *pādas* is a feature which appears very commonly in stanzas attributed to Hita Harivaṃśa's contemporary, Svāmī Haridāsa. Gopāl Datta (p. 258) maintains that the only criterion for line length in the *pādas* of Haridāsa is that each line should be containable by a number of complete *tāla āvartas*, the textual caesuras coinciding with the musical *sam* (the first beat of the *āvarta*).[2] Irregularity of this kind is commonplace in *dhrupada* songs, for which the only formal requirement is that the text should comprise the four lines needed to correspond to the four *dhrupada* sections of *sthāyī, antarā, sañcārī* and *ābhoga*.[3] In the CP, most stanzas do maintain at least an approximate regularity in terms of line length, even when the internal arrangement of individual lines fails to show any true metrical coherence: but even if the wilder metrical extravagancies of *dhrupada* texts are not apparent here, it is important to note the existence of such a tendency within the *pada* genre, since it is within this same context that the CP has been transmitted through the sung tradition.

4. Note on the Derivation and Transmission of Metrical Types in the CP

A conclusion which may be drawn from the metrical analysis in the above pages is that Hindi *pada* metres of the CP type have closer correspondences to Middle Indo-Aryan metrics than is generally acknowledged. While the Jain Apabhraṃśa texts cited here can hardly have constituted a model for verse forms of the CP type, it would appear that both genres share elements inherited from a common source. It is

1. Syllabic *pādas* are also attested in Bengali verse (*akṣaravṛtta*), as for example a so-called *dīrgha tripadī* of 8 + 8 + 10 *akṣaras* cited by Tārāpada Bhaṭṭācārya (p. 73); but here too the underlying form is moric (with long open vowels read as short, as an extension of Apabhraṃśa prosodic licence: Nilratan Sen, p. 11).

2. Datta's example of a *dhamāra tāla* setting shows the correlation between syllable length and musical beat to be very loose; it would appear that a line of almost any length or composition could be structured according to the 14 *mātrā dhamāra* format according to this system.

3. For an extreme example of such metrical irregularity, cf. *Brajanidhi pada saṃgraha* no. 140 (Purohit Nārāyaṇ Śarmmā, pp. 224-5).

also clear that scribes tend to overlook Middle Indo-Aryan metrical features, and increasingly to present the text in the guise of a simplified prosody preoccupied with *pāda* length (moric or syllabic) at the expense of *gaṇa* construction. This same tendency is promoted further by the commentators who, as is shown in annotations to the text, attribute disproportionate importance to the *pāda* as a semantic and syntactic unit.

5. The Disposition of Metres in the CP

The table below shows the main metrical features of the 84 stanzas. An asterisk against a *pada* number in the first column indicates that a musical performance of that *pada* is discussed in section 6 of this chapter. The *rāga* names given in the second column are those given in the majority of manuscripts; some variations are given in brackets, but for a full comparative tabulation of the *rāga* allocations in each manuscript the table on pp. 314-6 should be consulted. In the fourth column, the construction of the *ṭeka* (if any) is given: where a *mātrika* stanza shows a clear caesura in the *ṭeka*, then this is indicated (e.g. CP 36, '5+12 *m*[*ātrās*]'); if no caesura is apparent, then the overall moric value of the *ṭeka* is given (e.g. CP 20, '15 *m*[*ātrās*]').

Table 3: The metres of the CP

Pada	*Rāga*	*Lines*	*Construction*	*Ṭeka*	*Rhyme*	*Metre name*
1	Lalita/ Vibhāsa	4	Irregular *mātrika*	—	*-āre*	
2	[Lalita]	3	[10+10+12m]	—	*-āminī*	
3		4	16+15	—	*-ūla*	Bīra
4		6	10+10+15m	—	*-aina*	
5		6	16+16m	—	*-ara*	Savaiyā
6		4	16+(X)m	—	*-aina*	
7	Vilāvala	10	16+16m	—	*-orī*	Savaiyā
8		4	16+16m	19m	*-alina rī*	"
9		6	16+12	3+12m	*-orī*	Sāra
10		4	(7x/⏖⏑⏖⏑/)+/—/	—	*-urī*	Vinaya
11		6	"	—	*-āminī*	"
12*		6	(7x/6m/)+/—/	—	*-aṃdinī*	"
13		6	16+15	15m	*-ora*	Bīra
14	Toḍi	6	16+16m	3+16m	*-ā̃ū̃*	Savaiyā
15		6	8+8+13v	—	*-ātī*	
16		6	16+16m	3+16m	*-ainī*	Savaiyā
17*		4	(7x/⏖⏑⏖⏑/)+/—⏑/	—	*-eli*	Naṭa-nāgara
18	Āsāvarī	10	16m	—	AABBCC etc.	Pādā-kulaka
19		14	"	—	AABBCC etc.	"

Pada	*Rāga*	*Lines*	*Construction*	*Ṭeka*	*Rhyme*	*Metre name*
20	Dhanāśrī	8	16 + 12m	15m	*-ātī*	Sāra
21		6	”	4 + 12m	*-ārī*	”
22		4	”	6 + 12	*-aṃjana*	”
23*		6	16 + 11m	8 + 11m	*-ola*	Sarasī
24		6	16 + 17	—	*-īra rī sajanī*	Sarasī + refrain
25		4	4x/——⏑——,	2x/——⏑——	*-āgarī*	Vijayā
26*		6	——⏑——/	—— ——	/*-āsurī*	”
27*	Vasanta	18	14v	—	AABBCC etc.	
28*		6	14×10m	4 + 10m	*-āta*	Rūpamālā
29	Deva-gandhāra/ Gujarī	18	16 + 10	—	*-anī*	Viṣṇupada
30		18	16 + 11m	—	AABBCC etc.	Sarasī
31		8	”	5 + 11m	*-ora*	”
32		8	”	”	AABBCC etc.	”
33		6	”	16m	*-ora*	”
34		10	16 + 12	4 + 12m	*-olana*	Sāra
35		10	16 + 11	4 + 11m	*-ora*	Sarasī
36	Sāraṃga	12	16 + 12m	5 + 12m	*-āyau*	Sāra
37		8	16 + 11m	5 + 11m	*-īra*	Sarasī
38		6	”	—	*-āla*	”
39		6	16 + 7m	7 + 7m?	*-avana*	Niścala?
40		6	16 + 7–7m	14m	*-avana*	”
41		6	16 + 12m	19m	*-ānai*	Sāra
42		6	”	18m	*-ārai*	”
43		6	16 + 16m	16m	*-orī*	Savaiyā
44		6	”	16m	*-ana*	”
45		10	16 + 12m	4 + 12m	*-ārī*	Sāra
46		4	4x/——⏑——, ——⏑——/	—	*-āminī*	Vijayā
47		6	16 + 12m	4 + 12m	*-āvai*	Sāra
48		6	16 + 11	16m	*-āju*	Sarasī
49		6	16 + 15m	15m	*-eli*	Bīra
50		6	4x/——⏑——, ——⏑——/	—	*-acī*	Vijayā
51		6	16 + 16m	15m	*-orī*	Savaiyā
52*	Malāra	8	16 + 12m	8 + 12m	AABBCC etc.	Sāra
53		6	16 + 11m	8 + 11m	*-āsa*	Sarasī
54*		6	16 + 16m	—	*-orī*	Savaiyā
55		6	16 + 10m	6 + 10m	*-asī*	Viṣṇupada
56*	Gauḍa-malāra/Gaurī	4	16 + 15m	15m	*-āma*	Bīra
57		30	12 + 11m	—	AABBCC etc.	Raudrārka group
58		6	[8 + 8 + 8 + 7v]	—	*-au*	
59	[Gaurī]	6	16 + 12m	—	*-āyau*	Sāra
60		6	16 + 11m	6 + 11m	*-āta*	Sarasī

Pada	*Rāga*	*Lines*	*Construction*	*Ṭeka*	*Rhyme*	*Metre name*
61		6	16 + 12m	—	*-aṃḍana*	Sāra
62		8	16 + 16m	16m	*-ūlahu*	Savaiyā
63	[Gaurī]	6 + 6 + 6 + 6	Each stanza (1)-(2) 12m, (3)-(6) 16 + 11m	—	AABBAA	(Chanda)
64		6	16 + 16m	16m	*-aṭa*	Savaiyā
65		4	8 + 8 + (x)v	—	*-ajanī*	
66	Kalyāṇa	20	16 + 11m	4 + 11m	*-uṃja*	Sarasī
67		8	(3x/⏔⏔◡⏔⏔, ⏔⏔◡⏔⏔/) + /⏔⏔◡⏔⏔/ + 4m)	(3x/⏔⏔◡⏔⏔ + 4m	*-orī*	
68		8	4x(⏔⏔◡⏔⏔, ⏔⏔◡⏔⏔)/	2x(⏔⏔◡⏔⏔, ⏔⏔◡⏔⏔/)	*-āminī*	Vijayā
69		5	10 + 10 + 20m	—	AABCD	,,
70		8	16 + 12m	16m	*-orī*	Sāra
71		6	4x(⏔⏔◡⏔⏔, ⏔⏔◡⏔⏔/)	2x/(⏔⏔◡⏔⏔, ⏔⏔◡⏔⏔/)	*-anī*	Vijayā
72*	Kānharau	12	16 + 16m	16m	AABBCC etc.	Savaiyā
73		6	,,	—	*-ataī/ -ātī*	,,
74		4 }	(1) 16 + 10m	—	*-ocana*	
75		6 }	(2) 14 + 10m remainder 16 + 16m	—	*-ārata*	
76		4	(7x/⏔⏔◡⏔⏔◡/) + /—/	 —	*-ārarī*	Vinaya?
77		6	16 + 16m	16m	*-ūlī*	Savaiyā
78		4	,,	16m	*-orī*	,,
79		6	,,	—	*-aṭakata*	,,
80		4	(7x/⏔⏔◡⏔⏔◡/) + /—/	 —	*-āminī*	
81	Kedārau	10	(7x/⏔⏔◡⏔⏔/) + /4m/	10 + 9m	*-āvai*	
82		8	16 + 16m	16m	*-orī*	Savaiyā
83		6	(3x/5 + 5/) + /5/ + /◡◡◡◡/	—	*-aribau*	
84		4	[10 + 10 + X]m	10 + 10m	*-arī*	

Although the order of stanzas within the text is not governed exclusively by metrical types, certain patterns and sequences of metres do emerge from the above table. These may be summarised as follows:

(i) It is common to find sequences of stanzas in a single metre, e.g.:

Vinaya	CP 10-12;
Sāra	CP 20-22;
Vijayā	CP 25-26;
Sarasī	CP 30-33;
Savaiyā	CP 77-79.

(ii) Longer, mixed sequences of two similar metres are also found, e.g. Sarasī and Sāra CP 30-38.

(iii) Couplet rhyme schemes (AABBCC etc.) are found only in the longer stanzas, and rarely in stanzas having a short first line (*ṭeka*):

CP			
CP	18	10 lines	
	19	14 ,,	
	27	18 ,,	
	30	18 ,,	
	32	8 ,,	(including *ṭeka*)
	57	30 ,,	
	63	24 ,,	
	72	12 ,,	(including *ṭeka*)

(iv) The central portion of the text generally comprises stanzas with moric metres of 16+(X) *mātrās*, usually having a short first line (*ṭeka*). A sequence of such stanzas from CP 29 to CP 62 is interrupted only three times by other types. Greater variation in metrical types is found at the beginning and the end of the text, where *ṣaṭpadīs* and *savaiyās* predominate. Four of the first six stanzas are metrically problematic, with considerable variations in line length in the vulgate version.

(v) The first stanza of a *rāga* sequence usually has a longer than average number of lines:

CP	7	Vilāvala	10 lines
	18	Āsāvarī	10 ,,
	27	Vasanta	18 ,,
	29	Gujarī/Devagandhāra	18 ,,
	36	Sāraṅga	12 ,,
	57	Gaurī	30 ,,
	66	Kalyāṇa	20 ,,
	72	Kānharo	12 ,,
	81	Kedāro	10 ,,

(The exceptions are: CP 1, Vibhāsa—4 lines; CP 14, Toḍī—6 lines; CP 20, Dhanāśrī—8 lines.)

(vi) A new *rāga* sequence always coincides with a change of metre.

(vii) Sequences of stanzas with the same number of lines are found: CP 11-16 are all of six lines, though they represent four different metrical types.

(viii) Conversely, sequences of stanzas with alternate line lengths are found: CP 73-80 have alternately six and four lines each.

Two conclusions may be drawn from these observations. Firstly, the fact that the order of stanzas is not entirely random suggests that either certain groups of stanzas share a common origin and have maintained a structural cohesion after being incorporated into the text, or that in his selection and ordering of material (perhaps from diverse sources), the original compiler of the text has been motivated to some extent by considerations of metrical structure. Secondly, a connexion between *rāga* allocations and distribution of metres is clearly established. The implications of these factors will be discussed in chapter VII.

6. The Metres of the CP in Musical Performance[1]

(i) *The Samāja Tradition*

The general features of the metres used in the CP have been outlined above, and parallels have been drawn with the metres of Apabhraṃśa literature. A second approach to the structure of the CP *pada* is possible through an analysis of its application in musical performance, since the sectarian institution of *samāja*, the singing of devotional literature in a semi-liturgical context, is still alive today in the temples of Vrindaban. Because of its attribution to Hita Harivaṃśa, the CP is regarded as the most authoritative and prestigious text of the great body of Rādhāvallabhī literature sung in *samāja*, and it is largely through this tradition that the CP is so well-known in the Rādhāvallabhī community. As will be seen below, aspects of musical performance may reflect certain structural features of the CP *pada*, and may also be responsible for some of the corruptions found in the vulgate text. Although the *pada* is universally acknowledged as being a sung form, little attention has been paid to the connexion between literary metre and musical *tāla*; analysis of recordings of ten CP stanzas[2] show this to be a profitable approach to the subject, since a correlation between the number of *mātrās* (or *varṇas*) in the textual line and the number of *tāla mātrās* in the rhythmic cycle (*āvarta*) is clearly maintained in performance.

Rādhāvallabhi *samāja* is held twice daily in Vrindaban. The main location is the principal temple of Rādhāvallabha jī, but another *samāja* tradition is maintained in the temple of Choṭī Sarkār, where the recordings on which the present analysis is based were made in 1977. The morning performance of the Choṭī Sarkār *samājīs* is held in a sectarian *āśrama* known as Śyāmākuñja. Participation in *samāja*, which is usually held in front of the shrine and lends a congregational aspect to temple *sevā*, is open to all comers. Women and children traditionally sit separately from the men, but this is not a formal requirement; the whole procedure is characterised by a spontaneity and informality which, to the outside observer, is in marked contrast to the intense and often fervent devotion which the singing generates in the devotee. In addition to the daily sittings of *samāja*, special sessions are organized on sectarian feast days, for which traditional sequences of *padas* are specified in the published hymnal *Śṛṅgāra rasa sāgara*,[3] a modern compilation based on the *varṣotsava* format found in some manuscript anthologies.

1. Much of the material contained in this section is included in R. Snell 1983. (I am grateful to Dr. Richard Widdess for his comments on the musical examples quoted here, and to Mr. Devdan Sen for his comments on the *tālas* used in the performances.)
2. The stanzas recorded are CP 12, 17, 23, 26, 27, 28, 52, 56, 72, 73.
3. Bābā Tulsīdās V.S. 2013.

Samāja singing is led by the *mukhiyā*, who sings the text from memory or with reference to a published or manuscript copy. The 'performance' or liturgy begins with the recitation of one or more Sanskrit *ślokas*, usually drawn from the *Rādhāsudhānidhi* attributed to Harivaṃśa or from such texts as the *Karṇānanda* attributed to his son Kṛṣṇadāsa; this is sung by the *mukhiyā* alone, who accompanies himself on the ubiquitous harmonium.[1] This is followed by the singing of a number of *padas*, each section of text being first sung by the *mukhiyā* alone, and then repeated by the assembled chorus. The chorus usually constitutes a central core of regular votaries (this group being called the *jhelā*[2]) together with a number of more casual participants. Each versicle comprises, in a typical *pada*, a *pāda* or a half-line sung to a single *āvarta* of the appropriate *tāla*; when each such section has been sung by the *mukhiyā* and repeated by the chorus, the full line is then sung and repeated. If the *pada* has a *ṭeka*, this will be sung several times at the beginning and the end of the performed *pada*, and may also appear during the course of the *pada*, sung as a refrain between lines or couplets. Rhythmic accompaniment is provided by the *Pakhāvaj*, or in the case of the Choṭī Sarkār performances by the less traditional *tablā*; one or more members of the *jhelā* point up the rhythm of the *tāla* with small cymbals (*jhā̃jha*). While additional melody instruments may be added to this ensemble—as is the *esrāj*, for example, in the *samāja* of Rādhāvallabha temple—this is not the case in the recordings discussed here. Devotees visiting the temple for *darśana* of the deity may make a small cash offering to the *samājīs* while the singing is in progress. When the last *pada* has been sung, the session is brought to a close by a traditional round of *jayakāras*, led by the *mukhiyā*, which celebrate sectarian figures both historical and contemporary; the assembled company then receives *prasāda* from the shrine before taking its leave.

(ii) *The Performance of Varṇavṛtta Stanzas*

The first metrical type discussed above, the *varṇavṛtta ṣaṭpadī*, is represented in the recorded performances by CP 12, of which the first couplet reads as follows:

12.1 *calahi rādhike sujāna tere hita suṣa nidhāna*
rāsa racyau śyāma taṭa kaliṃda naṃdinī;
12.2 *nirttata juvatī samūha rāga raṃga ati kutūha*
bājata rasa mūla muralikā anaṃdinī.

1. The more traditional accompanying instrument is the *sāraṅgī*, but this is being replaced more and more by the hand-pumped harmonium.

2. *jhelā*: generally understood as deriving from H. *jhel-*, the implication being that the chorus 'catches' the sung phrase from the *mukhiyā*. In the Nimbārka tradition, the word *jhelā(-jī)* refers to a specific member of the chorus, viz. he who plays the *jhā̃jha* cymbals (I owe this piece of information to Mr. David Crawford); this suggests a connexion with Bhojpurī *jhāla*, H. *jhallī*, and other words for 'drum' and 'cymbal' derived from Skt. *jhallī-* (*CDIAL* 5358). (Cf. also a word *jhīla* (Platts s.v.), 'The bass (in music or singing); — the treble'?)

This stanza, having a line construction of 12+12+20 *mātrās*, is set in the recorded performance to the 12-beat *tāla Cautala*. Each of the 12-*mātrā pādas* occupies one *āvarta* of *Cautāla*, and the first 12 *mātrās* of the 20-*mātrā pāda* (i.e. up to *murali-*) occupy a third *āvarta*. Thus only eight *mātrās* remain for the fourth *āvarta*, which is then filled by the protraction of the final (long) syllable over one extra beat, and by the addition of a non-textual vocative, *māi*, over a further three beats.[1]

In the transcription which follows, the numbers 1-12 in the top line designate the *mātrās* of the *tāla* cycle; strong and weak beats are shown in the second line in the traditional manner:

x	the primary stressed beat, *sam*;
2,3,4	the secondary stressed beats, *tālī*;
0	the weak (literally 'empty') beat, *khālī*.

The third line shows the strokes of the *jhā̃jha*. (Transcriptions given in this section are of the performed version and show some divergencies from the edited text.)

Cautāla:	1	2	3	4	5	6	7	8	9	10	11	12
	x		o		2		o		3		4	
Jhā̃jha	♩				♩				♩		♩	
12.1	*ca*	*la*	*hi*	*rā*	—	*dhi*	*ke*	—	*su*	*jā*	—	*na*
	te	—	*re*	—	*hi*	*ta*	*su*	*ṣa*	*ni*	*dhā*	—	*na*
	rā	—	*sa*	*ra*	—	*cyau*	*syā*	—	*ma*	*ta*	*ṭa*	*ka*
	li	—	*ṃda*	*naṃ*	—	*di*	*nī*	—	—	*mā*	—	*i*
12.2	*ni*	*ra*	*ta*	*ta*	*ju*	*va*	*tī*	—	*sa*	*mū*	—	*ha*
	rā	—	*ga*	*raṃ*	—	*ga*	*a*	*ti*	*ku*	*tū*	—	*ha*
	bā	—	*ja*	*ṭa*	*ra*	*sa*	*mū*	—	*la*	*mu*	*ra*	*li*
	kā	—	*a*	*naṃ*	—	*di*	*nī*	—	—	*mā*	—	*i*

This is the only instance among the recorded stanzas of extraneous non-textual material being introduced to extend a metrical foot. The section of the musical form *dhrupada* known as *mukhaṛā* not infrequently includes a vocative of this kind; a parallel is evident between the *māi*

1. The need to prolong a textual line in order to fill a musical measure has been noted in older forms of Indian verse also, as for example in the Prakrit and Sanskrit *ākṣiptikās* preserved in the 13th century *Saṅgītaratnākara* of Śārṅgadeva (D.R. Widdess 1980:132). According to Velankar, the same feature is found in Apabhraṃśa metre where feet of two, three or five beats at the end of a line of four-beat feet require a similar extension (discussed by Widdess, *loc. cit.*). Another example of the phenomenon is described by Nilratan Sen (p. 16) in his analysis of the Bengali *Caryāpada*. Similarly in the *jhūlanā* metre of the Gujarātī *prabhātī* form, comprising five-*mātrā* feet divided 3 + 2, the last feet of the second and fourth (final) line 'consist of only one syllable which during the recitation is lengthened to 5 *mātrās*' (F. Mallison, p. 97 footnote 40). The use of meaningless non-textual syllables to fill out metrical patterns is also attested in North Indian folk-song (E. Henry, p. 103).

of CP 12 and the *mukhaṛā* '*māi rī*' in a *dhrupada* text (also set to *Cautāla*) analysed by Richard Widdess. Widdess describes the *mukhaṛā* as comprising 'the first sam or emphasised beat of the sthāyī [first musical and textual line], preceded by an anacrusis of several beats'.[1] In the present example, therefore, the *mukhaṛā* consists of the three beats occupied by the vocative *māi*, together with the following *sam* on which may be sung either the first syllable of the subsequent line or, in the case of a repeat, the first syllable of the line just completed.

The disposition of the final textual syllable *-nī* over three beats, followed by that of non-textual *māi* (in which a euphonic glide between the word's two syllables suppresses its trochaic stress) over another three beats provides a cadence in this last *pāda* which lends a sense of closure to the line: only here is a syllable sustained over three beats of *tāla*.

The trochaic rhythm which predominates in this stanza is found in all the six CP stanzas based on a 12-*mātrā pāda*. It is emphasized by the internal trochee rhyme between many first and second *pādas*: 12.1 *-jāna/-dhāna*. The prevalence of thus rhythm in CP 12 induces the *mukhiyā* to sing the participle *racyau* in line (1) as a trochee; the tendency is, therefore, to impose the prevalent rhythm even when it is not apparent in the text, and thereby to emphasize the *varṇavṛtta* rhythm of the stanza.

The arrangement of each *pāda* in 6-*mātrā gaṇas* is contrary to the theoretical division of *Cautāla* into six *vibhāgas* of two beats each; metre and *tāla*, therefore, correspond only in total moric quantity and not in internal construction. Most lines of the melody to which the *pada* is sung, however, suggest a basic 6+6 construction; in the 1st and 2nd melodic lines each 6-*mātrā* section starts on a high note and progresses down the scale; in the third line the second 6-*mātrā* section is introduced by a jump to the upper tonic (*sā*), which is held like a reciting-note until the end of the line; in the fifth melodic line the sustaining of the second (*re*) of the upper register over two beats reflects a similar sustaining of the fourth (*mā*) of the upper register at the beginning of the line. The melodic construction *is*, therefore, based on a notion of two six-*mātrā* groups, which is not an established feature of *Cautāla*.

Despite the predominance of trochaic rhythm in this stanza, the theoretical divisions of *Cautāla* are of course maintained throughout the performance by the *ṭhekā* (drumming pattern) played by the *tablā* and emphasized by the *jhā̃jha* which, except in fast repeats, are sounded only on the strong *tālī* beats of the cycle—i.e. beats 1 (*sam*), 5, 9 and 11: the *ṭheka* of the *tablā* is particularly apparent in this performance where it is frequently played in its basic undecorated form, or in simple double time.

1. D.R. Widdess 1981:160.

(It may be noticed that the theoretically 'empty' (*khālī*) beat, 7, carries a long syllable in performance; this apparently contradictory feature occurs again in CP 26, and is explained below in the discussion of that stanza.)

The sequence in which the *pādas* of CP 12 are sung and repeated appears to be influenced by purely musical considerations. Two melodic compositions, A and B, are used; A is sung for lines (1), (3) and (5) of the stanza, and B for lines (2), (4) and (6). Each composition consists of four melodic sections, each occupying one *āvarta* of the *tāla*; B is a re-ordering of three of the sections already used in A, with the introduction of one new section.[1] The melodic construction of each couplet is, therefore, as follows:

1st line (composition A): sections I, II, III, IV;
2nd line (composition B): sections III, IV, V, I.

In the recorded text, only sections I and II of 'A' lines are sung and repeated separately as single *āvartas*: all other sections are sung and repeated in pairs—A III with IV, B III with IV, and V with I. In other words, *viṣama* lines are sung as three units (I and II separately, III and IV together), while *sama* lines are sung as two units (III and IV together, V and I together). This may be explained by the melodic construction of I and II, both of which begin and end on the tonic *sā* (albeit an octave apart in I), and are therefore more self-contained than the remaining sections. This sense of *pāda* closure is emphasized by the internal rhyme at the end of sections I and II in A.

The singing of the first two sections separately and the second two together, as in A, bears a resemblance to a similar practice in the performance of *dhrupada* song (also commonly sung in *Cautāla*), where the first two sections *sthāyī* and *antarā* are sung separately, and the second two *sañcārī* and *ābhoga* as one unit.[2] Although each of these sections in *dhrupada* constitutes a whole line of text rather than a single *pāda*, some similarity of melodic composition can be found between the *dhrupada*

1. The five lines of melody to which CP 12 is sung are as follows:

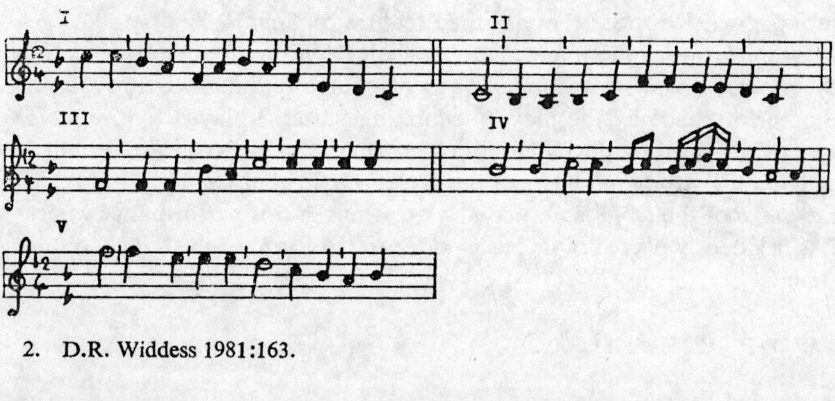

2. D.R. Widdess 1981:163.

and the CP forms: in 'A', the rising phrase of section III to a sustained upper tonic (*sā*) resembles a similar feature in the *antarā* section of the *dhrupada* (and the *khyāl*) style;[1] and a further resemblance is found in composition B, where the new melodic section, V, begins with a sustained upper fourth (*mā*), which is a higher note than has been achieved previously in the composition. This feature in both 'A' and 'B' suggests that the first two *pādas* of each line constitute a kind of *sthāyī*, with the second half-line resembling an *antarā*. As in *dhrupada*, a return to the first *pāda* of the first line (sung in section I) brings a sense of closure to the performance: the performance ends with the syllable *ca-*, sung to the tonic (*sā*) and on the first *tāla* beat (*sam*), from which point the stanza began.

Similar in construction to CP 12 is CP 17, which differs only in having a final trochee in place of CP 12's final *guru*. This *pada* in the version recorded is performed in 6-*mātrā Dādrā tāla*, and is sung in quite a fast tempo with a minimum of repeats. As in CP 12, each sung textual line is divided into four parts, of which the first three are of 12 *mātras* (i.e. *pādas* a and b, and the first 12 *mātrās* of *pāda* c), the last part here being of 9 *mātrās*. In the last, 9-*mātrā* section the long penultimate syllable is extended over 5 beats in order to fill the *tāla āvarta*; there is, therefore, no inclusion of any non-textual 'makeweight' in this instance. With the exception of this accommodation for *tāla*, there is an almost exact correlation between syllable length and musical beat in this performance.

The predominant trochaic rhythm of this stanza, already emphasized by alliteration or internal rhyme, is further strengthened by the 3+3 *mātrā* construction of *Dādrā tāla*, either (a) within individual *gaṇas*, or (b) between two *gaṇas* falling at the same point in successive *āvartas:*

Dādrā	1	2	3	4	5	6	1	2	3	4	5	6
	x			0			x			0		
	|—		⌣	—		⌣|						
(a) 17.2	*-śo*	—	*ra*	*jo*	—	*ra*						
	⌣	⌣	⌣	—		⌣|	⌣	⌣	⌣	—		⌣|
(b) 17.3	*na*	*va*	*ni*	*kuṃ*	—	*ja*	*bhra*	*ma*	*ra*	*guṃ*	—	*ja*

The pattern played by the *jhãjha*, however, detracts from the trochaic stress:

Dādrā	1	2	3	4	5	6
Jhãjha	♩	♫	♩	♫	♩	♫

A recurring feature of the setting of the CP *pada* to *tāla* is that the long third syllable of the name *harivaṃśa* is frequently emphasized by

1. D.R. Widdess 1981: p. 162.

being sung of a strong *tāla* beat, usually the *sam*. In this instance the emphasis is strengthened by a succession of short syllables in the previous *gaṇa*:

⌣ ⌣ ⌣⌣ ⌣⌣/— ⌣ ⌣⌣⌣/

17.4b *palu palu harivaṃśa pivata*

In the performance of this *pada* the honorific *śrī* is prefixed to the *chāpa*, the two syllables *hari-* being compressed into a single beat: the resultant syncopation adds further emphasis to the long syllable *-vaṃśa* which follows:

Dādrā	1	2	3	4	5	6	1	2	3	4	5	6
	⌣	⌣	⌣	⌣	(—)	⌣⌣/	—		⌣	⌣	⌣	⌣/
17.4b	*pa*	*lu*	*pa*	*lu*	*śrī*	*hari*	*vaṃ*	—	*śa*	*pi*	*va*	*ta*

The recorded stanza which illustrates the second *varṇavṛtta* type (that based on the five-*mātrā gaṇa* / ⏕ ⌣ ⏕ /) is CP 26. This stanza, consisting of a 20 *mātrā ṭeka* followed by 5 full lines of 10+10+20 *mātrās*, is set to the 10-beat cycle *Jhapatāla*. The first couplet of CP 26 reads as follows:

26.1 *mohanī madana gopāla kī bā̃surī;*
26.2 *mādhurī śravana puṭa sunata suni rādhike*
karata ratirāja ke tāpa kau nāsu rī.

In performance the line is divided into 10-*mātrā* sections:

Jhapatāla	1	2	3	4	5	6	7	8	9	10
	X		2			0		3		
Jhā̃jha	♩	♫	♩	♫	♫	♩	♫	♩	♫	♫
26.1	*mo*	—	*ha*	*nī*	—	*ma*	*da*	*na*	*go*	—
	pā	—	*la*	*kī*	—	*bā̃*	—	*su*	*rī*	—
26.2	*mā*	—	*dhu*	*rī*	—	*śra*	*va*	*na*	*pu*	*ṭa*
	su	*na*	*ta*	*su*	*ni*	*rā*	—	*dhi*	*ke*	—
	ka	*ra*	*ta*	*ra*	*ti*	*rā*	—	*ja*	*ke*	—
	tā	—	*pa*	*kau*	—	*nā*	—	*su*	*rī*	—

As is shown above, the theoretical *vibhāga* construction of *Jhapatāla* is 2+3+2+3 *mātrās*; in practice, however, an ictus occurs on the sixth beat, *khālī*, as well as on the *sam*, such that the *āvarta* is effectively divided into the same 5+5 *mātrā* construction as the textual line.[1] 5+5

1. The sixth beat of *Jhapatāla* is theoretically weak or 'empty' (*khālī*); yet in the performance of this stanza it is marked by considerable emphasis. This may be explained by the fact that the function of the *khālī* beat is not so much to provide a 'weak' beat or to mark the beginning of a 'weak' *vibhāga* as to provide an asymmetrical arrangement of emphasis over the whole *tāla* cycle: the *khālī* contrasts the beginning of the second half-cycle of five beats with the *sam* at the beginning of the

construction is reinforced by the *jhãjha*, which play a pattern of *two* cycles per *āvarta*. This stress serves to underline the *gaṇa* rhyme and alliteration found in this stanza, as for example in the last line where the long syllable of *haṃsa*, though falling on the *khālī*, alliterates strongly with *vaṃśa* on the following *sam*; (here again the *chāpa* receives syncopated emphasis in performance by the insertion of honorific *śrī* in time borrowed from *hari*-:)

Jhapatāla	1	2	3	4	5	6	7	8	9	10
26.6b	*u*	*bhai*	—	*ka*	*la*	*haṃ*	—	*sa*	*śrī*	*hari*
	vaṃ	—	*sa*	*ba*	*li*	*dā*	—	*su*	*rī*	—

(iii) *The performance of mātrika stanzas*

In the *mātrika* metres of the CP, the predominant *pāda* is of 16 *mātrās*; correspondingly, the most frequently used *tāla* in the *samāja* recordings (as, indeed, in Hindustani music generally) is the 16-*mātrā* *Tīnatāla*. There is a straightforward correspondence between the *āvarta* or *Tīnatāla* and the 16-*mātrā pāda* of such metres; in performance, however, this correspondence is more likely to be disrupted by syncopation than is the case with the *varṇavṛtta* metres with their stricter rhythms. This tendency is illustrated in the following extract from CP 72, which has a line construction of 16+16 *mātrās*, and a 16-*mātrā ṭeka*:

72.1 *suṃdara pulina subhaga suṣadāika*;
72.2 *nava nava ghana anurāga paraspara*
ṣelata kũvara nāgarī nāika.

Tīnatāla

	1	2	3	4	5	6	7	8	9	10	11	12	13	14	15	16
	x				2				0				3			
Jhãjha	♩	♩	♩		♩	♩	♩		♩	♩	♩		♩	♩	♩	
									suṃ	—	—	*dara*	*pu*	*li*	*na*	*-su*
	bha	*ga*	—	*sukha*	*dā*	—	—	*yaka*	—	*nava*	*na*	*va*	*gha*	*na*	*a*	*-nu*
	rā	—	—	*ga*	*-pa*	*ra*	—	*spa*	*ra*	*khe*	*la*	*ta*	*-ku*	*va*	—	*ra*
	nā	*-ga*	*rī*	—	*nā*	—	—	*yaka*	—							

The beats of the *jhãjha* illustrate a practice also found in recordings of other stanzas, wherein each stage in the repetition of a *pāda* or line leads further towards a rhythmic climax. On the first vocalization and repeat of each separate *pāda* the *jhãjha* sounds the simple pattern transcribed above, showing the division of the *āvarta* into four equal

---

whole cycle. Thus the *khālī* is weak only in comparison with the strong *sam*, and may well be the second strongest beat in the whole cycle. Without this distinction between *sam* and *khālī*, 10-mātrā *Jhapatāla* would consist of two identical 5-*mātrā* sections. In *tālas* of this type the wave of the hand which traditionally marks the *khālī* beat in the counting of *tāla*, therefore, merely advises that "this is not the *sam*".

vibhāgas of four beats each. The same pattern is followed during the subsequent singing and repeating of the whole line. When the *mukhiyā* then sings the whole couplet, the *jhā̃jha* sound a more complex rhythm which stresses the *sam* and the ninth beat of the *āvarta*, thereby presenting *Tīnatāla* as a double cycle of 8+8 *mātrās*. Finally when the whole couplet is repeated by the chorus, the *jhā̃jha* play a fast continuous pattern in semiquavers, the *sam* sometimes being marked by an emphasis in volume. The three successive stages in the *jhā̃jha* rhythm may be shown as follows (each stage continues past the end of the textual line and ends on the *sam*):

This separate repetition of each couplet as a discrete unit is a feature not found in the recording of other stanzas; it may reflect the couplet-based rhyme scheme (AABBCC etc.) of CP 72, (though it is not followed in other examples of a similar rhyme scheme).

An unusual setting of a 32-*mātrā* stanza is found in the performance of CP 54. This is a six-line stanza of 16+16 *mātrās*, beginning as follows:

54.1 *nayau ṇeha nava raṃga nayau rasa*
navala syāma bṛṣabhāna kiśorī;

Despite the 16-*mātrā* base, this stanza is sung to 12-beat *Cautāla*. This performance is exceptional amongst all those recorded in that the sung text is given a rhythmic emphasis which derives neither from the internal construction of the *tāla* nor from the construction of the textual line. Against the *tāla* structure of six *vibhāgas* of two beats each, the text is sung to a predominant three-beat rhythm without regard for syllable length:

Cautāla	1	2	3	4	5	6	7	8	9	10	11	12
	X		0		2		o		3		4	
Jhā̃jha	♩				♩				♩		♩	
	na	—	—	*yau*	—	—	*ne*	--	*ha*	*na*	—	*va*
	raṃ	—	—	*ga*	—	*na*	*yau*	—	—	*ra*	—	*sa*
	na	*va*	—	*la*	—	—	*syā*	—	*ma*	*bṛ*	—	*ṣa*
	bhā	—	—	*na*	—	*ki*	*so*	—	—	*rī*	—	—

It must be considered likely that stanzas of this type would more usually be set to a 16-*mātrā tāla*.

In stanzas having a line construction of 16+15 *mātrās,* the penultimate syllable of the second *pāda* is extended in performance to fill the 16-beat *āvarta*; an example is in 56.2b, *bṛṃdābipina kuṭī abhirāma*:

Tīnatāla

	1	2	3	4	5	6	7	8	9	10	11	12	13	14	15	16
56.2b	*bṛṃ*	—	*dā*	—	*bi*	*pi*	*na*	*ku*	*ṭī*	—	*a*	*bhi*	*rā*	—	—	*ma*

Tīnatāla is also used for the 16+11 and 16+12 *mātrā* types. As in the *varṇavṛtta* metres discussed above, the unequal lengths of the constituent *pādas* of these metres call for the use of a metrical 'makeweight' in order to complete the *tāla avarta.* Here, however, no non-textual material is incorporated, since the *ṭeka* itself is usually of a construction which allows its first *pāda* to perform this function; the method is described below.

In length, the *ṭeka* corresponds approximately, and often exactly, to the first *pāda* of a full line; but in its internal construction it typically comprises a full second *pāda* preceded by a short first *pāda* of approximately 5 to 8 *mātrās.* The way in which the *ṭeka* corresponds in *length* to the first *pāda* and in *construction* to the second may be seen clearly in the example of CP 37 (a stanza of the 16+11 type):

(a) showing correspondence of overall length:

37.1 *calahi kina mānini kuṃja kuṭīra*; (16 *mātrās*)

37.2 *to binu kũvari koṭi banitā juta mathata madana kī pīra.* (16+11 *mātrās*)

(b) showing correspondence of construction:

37.1 *calahi kina mānini kuṃja kuṭīra*; (5+11 *mātras*)

37.2 *to binu kũvari koṭi banitā juta mathata madana kī pīra.* (16+11 *mātrās*)

Thus the full *ṭeka* acts as a first *pāda* (of 16 *mātrās*) in that it fills an *āvarta* of *tāla*; the first *pāda* of the *ṭeka*, when appended to the second *pāda* of a full line, has the 'makeweight' function of the non-textual vocative *māi* in CP 12 discussed above. Each *āvarta* of the *tāla* will, therefore, contain one of the following three section of the *pāda*:

(i) the complete *ṭeka*; or
(ii) a first *pāda* of a full line; or
(iii) a second *pāda* of a full line, +the first *pāda* of the *ṭeka.*

In terms of the CP 37 example, these three possibilities will appear as follows:

(i) *calahi kina mānini kuṃja kuṭīra* (16 *mātrās*);
(ii) *to binu kũvari koṭi banitā juta* (16 *mātrās*);
(iii) *mathata madana kī pīra calahi kina* (11+5=16 *mātrās*)

It is, therefore, the first *pāda* of the *ṭeka* which acts as a true refrain, being repeated continuously throughout the performance of the *pāda*. Hence the first *pāda* is commonly syntactically and semantically independent,[1] commonly comprising a vocative (23.1 *rādhā pyārī*), an imperative and vocative (52.1, 53.1 *deṣau māī*), a rhetorical interrogative (60.1 *kahā kahaũ*), or some other fragment which is introductory to the main substance of the *ṭeka*. The above example *calahi kina*, 'Why don't you go...', is typical of such independent phrases which admit of repetition in any line of the stanza.

Not all stanzas have a *ṭeka* whose length corresponds exactly to that of the full line's first *pāda*; in CP 52 and 53, the first *pāda* of the *ṭeka* comprises the 8-*mātrā* phrase *deṣau māī*, each syllable of which occupies one *tāla mātrā* in the performed version (see transcription, pp. 300-303 below).

The varṇika stanza CP 27

CP is the only stanza to show a consistent construction based on the number of syllables per line (though even here moric elements are present, as discussed in the annotations to the edited text). It is included in this section because of a correspondence with the *mātrika* stanza CP 28, discussed below. The 14-syllable line is divided in the sung version into *pādas* of 8 and 6 syllables, as exemplified here in the first two couplets:

27.1	*madhuritu bṛṃdāvana*	*ānaṃda na thora;*
27.2	*rājata nāgarī nava*	*kuśala kiśora.*
27.3	*jūthikā jugala rūpa-*	*maṃjarī rasāla;*
27.4	*bithakita ali madhu-*	*mādhavī gulāla.*

In the performance of CP 27 there is no precise correlation between syllable length and musical beat, although there is a tendency for long syllables to be sustained over more beats than short ones. Two successive *tālas* are used in the performance, both showing a connection with the 14-syllable arrangement but neither reflecting the 8+6 construction of *pādas* within the line. The first *tāla*, *Dīpacandī* of 14 *mātrās*, is used only for the first couplet, and has a different melodic setting from the remainder of the stanza. One *āvarta* covers one *pāda* of text, with syllables being extended as required to fill the 14-*mātrā* cycle; the disposition of syllables over the 14 beats is determined by the internal construction of the *tāla* in four *vibhāgas* (3+4+3+4 *mātrās*). The textual line begins not on the *sam* but on the eleventh beat, so that the words *madhuritu* act as a *mukhaṛā* leading to the *sam* at the beginning of the stressed thematic label *bṛṃdāvana*. The *jhā̃jha* sound on all beats except the last beat of each *vibhāga*; the *khālī* (beat 8) is, therefore, again stressed, as discussed above.

1. But not necessarily: the use of a non-independent phrase presents no problem to the performer; cf. the often elliptical *mukhaṛās* used in Hindustani music generally.

Dīpacandi	1	2	3	4	5	6	7	8	9	10	11	12	13	14
	×			2				o			3			
Jhā̃jha	♩	♩		♩	♩	♩		♩	♩		♩	♩	♩	
											ma	*dhu*	*ṛ*	*tu*
27.1	*bṛṃ*	—	—	*dā*	—	—	—	*va*	*na*	—	*ā*	—	—	—
	naṃ	*da*	—	*na*	—	*tho*	—	—	—	*ra*				

The second and subsequent lines of CP 27 are sung to a different melody in the seven-*mātrā tāla Rūpaka*, eight *avartas* of which cover each line. The rhythmic tempo is therefore increased, though the tempo of the sung text remains almost unchanged. The use of *Rūpaka* is maintained throughout the stanza from line 3, including the final repeat of line 1.

As in the *Dīpacandī* section, it is the position of the *tālīs* of *Rūpaka* which generally govern the rhythm of the sung syllables here, and again this rhythm is stressed by the *jhā̃jha* which sound on the same principle as in the *Dīpacandī* cycle. The second *pāda* of each line is sung to a different melodic structure from the first, rising to a higher note than is found in the first and therefore having something of the quality of an *antarā*. The short second *pāda* is extended to balance the first by the addition of (usually) five syllables from the first *pāda*: the words *jugala rūpa* constitute this repeat in the transcription of line 2 below. After the singing and repeating of the two *pādas* separately, the whole line is sung as one and the 'makeweight' syllables (*jugala rūpa* etc.) are here re-

Rūpaka	1	2	3	4	5	6	7
	×			2		3	
Jhā̃jha	♩	♩		♩		♩	
27.2				*jū*	—	*thi*	—
	kā	—	—	—	—	—	*ju*
	ga	—	—	*la*	—	—	—
	rū	—	—	—	—	*pa*	—
				maṃ	—	—	*ja*
	rī	—	—	—	—	—	*ra*
	sā	—	—	{ *la*	—	*ju*	—
				{ —	—	—	—
	{ *ga*	*la*	—	*rū*	—	*pa*	—
	{ —	—	—	—	—	—	—
	{ —	—	—		—		
	{ —	*la*	—		—		

placed by a prolongation of the line's penultimate syllable (*-ā-*) as shown on page 295. The coincidence of the long syllable in the *chāpa* '*hari-baṃśa*' with the strong beat *sam*, already familiar from other stanzas, is again found in CP 27.

The use of two *tālas* for the single stanza is evidently not fortuitous, as a second recording of the same stanza made on a separate occasion shows exactly the same change from *Dīpacandī* to *Rūpaka* after the first couplet. The change may be based on thematic considerations: the first couplet is a statement of the *pāda's* subject—the presence of the *nāgarī* (*Rādhā*) and the *kiśora* (Kṛṣṇa) in the vernal environment of Vṛndāvana—while the remainder of the stanza is a description of that environment with no further reference to the two protagonists until nearly the end of the stanza (27.15 *gāvata suṃdari hari*...). The use of several *tālas* during one musical piece is not unknown in the *dhrupada* style.

The recorded performance of CP 27 was followed immediately by a performance of CP 28, also on a springtime theme. Again the *tāla* used was *Rūpaka,* but in this case the 14-beat cycle corresponds to a *mātrika* metre, and not a *varṇika* one: CP 28 is composed in the 14+10 *mātrā* metre Rūpamālā. The first couplet is as follows:

28.1 *rādhe deṣi bana kī bāta;*
28.2 *ritu basaṃta anaṃta mukulita kusuma aru phala pāta.*

The order of the *ṭeka* is inverted in performance:[1]

deṣi bana kī bāta radhe,

1. A similar inversion of the *ṭeka* is found in other traditions also. A *Tīnatāla* setting of a *śabad* of Gurū Arjan from the *Ādi granth* (*Toḍī Mahalā* 5, *Ādi granth* p. 717) shows the relocation of initial *māī* at the end of the textual line. The first two lines of the text and their transcription as *asthāyī* [*sthāyī*] are as follows (Gyān Singh 1971:64):

māī carana gura mīṭhe;
vaḍai bhāgi devai paramesaru koṭi phalā darasana gura ḍīṭhe. (*rahāu*).

asthāyī (*tīnatāla*)

1	2	3	4	5	6	7	8	9	10	11	12	13	14	15	16
x				2				0				3			
			ca	*ra*	*na*	*gu*	*ra*	*mī*	—	*ṭhe*	—	—	—	*mā*	—
ī	—	—	*ca*	*ra*	*na*	*gu*	*ra*	*mī*	—	*ṭhe*	—	—	—	*va*	*ḍe*
—	*bhā*	—	*ga*	*de*	—	*vai*	—	*pa*	*ra*	*me*	—	*sa*	*ra*	*ko*	—
ṭa	*pha*	*lā*	—	*da*	*ra*	*sa*	*na*	*gu*	*ra*	*ḍī*	—	*ṭhe*	—	*mā*	—

The first syllable of *māī* is repeated here at the end of the *sthāyī* (fourth line, beats 15 and 16); it appears again in the same position at the end of the *antarā* which carries the third and subsequent textual lines.

but the use of *rādhe* as a filler for the short second *pāda* on the model of CP 52 is not resorted to. Instead, the second *pāda* of 10 *mātrās* is extended by the same two methods as were used in CP 27, that is (a) by the borrowing of four *mātrās* from the first *pāda* of the line (*mukulita* in the example transcribed below) and (b) by the prolonged vocalization of the long penultimate syllable in the line.

The internal construction of the textual line follows precisely the internal construction of *Rūpaka tāla*. Each first *pāda* of fourteen *mātrās* may be scanned as corresponding to the *vibhāga* division of two cycles of *Rūpaka* (3+2+2, 3+2+2); each second *pada* of ten *mātrās* corresponds similarly to one cycle of *Rūpaka* plus one additional *gaṇa* of three *mātrās* (3+2+2, 3):

⏑⏑ ⏑/–/⏑ ⏑/– ⏑/⏑ ⏑/⏑⏑/ ⏑ ⏑ ⏑/ ⏑⏑/ ⏑⏑/– ⏑
28.2 *ṛtu basaṃta anaṃta mukulita kusuma aru phala pāta*
–⏑/ ⏑⏑/⏑⏑/–⏑ –/–/ ⏑⏑ ⏑/ –/⏑⏑/–⏑
28.3 *benu dhuni nā̆dalāla bolī suni va kyǒ arasāta* etc.

Only in its inverted form does the *ṭeka* conform to this *gaṇa* sequence:

–⏑/ ⏑ ⏑ /–/ –⏑/ –/⏑
28.1 *deṣi bana kī bāta ˊrādhe*

The rhythm of the textual line is therefore transmitted faithfully by the *Rūpaka* structure:

Rūpaka	1	2	3	4	5	6	7
	×			2		3	
Jhā̃jha	♩	♫	♫	♩	♫	♩	♫
28.1	*de*	—	*kha*	*ba*	*na*	*kī*	—
	bā	—	*ta*	*rā*	—	*dhe*	—
28.2	*ṛ*	*tu*	*ba*	*saṃ*	—	*ta*	*a*
	naṃ	—	*ta*	*mu*	*ku*	*li*	*ta*
	ku	*su*	*ma*	*a*	*ru*	*pha*	*la*
	pā	—	{*ta*	(*mu*	*ku*	*li*	*ta*
			{—	—	—	—	*ta*)

The strong *tāla* beat 4 duplicates the stress of the *sam*; the resulting paired emphasis is particularly effective in the alliteration of *basaṃta/anaṃta* in 28.2 above. The pattern played by the *jhā̃jha* is slightly more complex than that used in the *Rūpaka* section of CP 27; two quavers sound to the unstressed beats, while a crotchet sounds to the *sam* and the two *tālīs* (beats 1, 4, 6).

CP 27 and CP 28 are the only two stanzas in the text with a '14'-unit base—14 *varṇas* in CP 27, 14+10 *mātrās* in CP 28. This feature, and the springtime theme of the two stanzas (coupled with their allocation to the *Rāga Vasanta*) identifies them as *dhamāra* texts; but, as noted above, the *Dhamāra tāla* associated with this species of springtime song has not been used in the recorded performance.

Performed versions of the text do not necessarily follow the close correspondence of *tāla mātrā* to textual *mātrā* seen in most of the examples given above. The number of beats taken to pronounce a given syllable may be determined by cadential, melodic or semantic criteria rather than simply by the length of the syllable: a syllable of one textual *mātrā*, for example, may be sustained melismatically over several beats of the *tāla*, or conversely two or more syllables may be vocalized within one beat of *tāla*. Furthermore, as the example of CP 28 shows, *tāla vibhāgas* do not necessarily correspond to textual *gaṇas* even when an overall correspondence of *tāla* and metre is apparent. Yet the basic correlation of text to *tāla* endures,[1] and it is often the case that syncopations or other variations introduced by the *mukhiyā* are not followed by the less adventurous chorus.

In order to demonstrate these points, and to show in detail the use of the *ṭeka* as a metrical 'filler' as discussed above, a full transcription of a performance of CP 52 is given below. The performance lasted about 17½ minutes, and is from an evening *samāja* session lasting about 1½ hours. The orthography of the transcription reflects the pronunciation of the *samājīs* rather than forms given in the edited text; lines in Roman type are sung by the *mukhiyā*, those in italics by the chorus. The transcription is arranged according to *tāla* structure and not as a musical score;[2] it may simply be noted that each melodic line begins, with the textual line, on the 10th *mātrā* of the *āvarta*, and that the last 'bar' of the melodic lines which carry the refrain *dekho māī* is always occupied by the same four-crotchet rising figure. A small numerical before each tenth beat indicates which of five melodic lines (given in the footnote) is sung in the following line; a dash in square brackets represents a rest of one *mātrā*. The *jhā̃jha*, which are struck on the first three beats of each *vibhāga* throughout most of the performance, play a faster and continuous rhythm from the point marked by an asterisk in the margin, from which point the tempo increases by about a third. It may be noticed that both *mukhiyā* and chorus often anticipate their entry on the

1. This does not mean that a given metrical configuration can only be contained by one specific *tāla*, see for example the *tāla aṅka* of *Saṃgīta* (January 1940, pp. 161-77), where transcriptions of a single text attributed to Tānsen are given in seven different *tālas*. Cf. also Peter Manuel's transcription of a ghazal in *Rūpaka*, *Dādarā* and *Kaheravā tālas* (1969:106-7).

2. The basic musical transcription may be given separately. The *pada* is sung to six lines of melody in the *rāga Bilāvala*, the second line (la) being simply a variation on the first.

tenth *mātra* by singing one or more syllables from beats eight or nine; this is usually a meaningless utterance (rendered *a* or *ā̃* in the transcription), but sometimes takes the form of the last word of text of the expiring section. Twice the exclamatory expression *e rī hā̃!* replaces part of the text, for emphasis.[1]

1. An exclamation of this kind is a common feature of various *kīrtana* traditions. In the *Ādi granth*, for example, the formula *hari hā̃* appears (as a textual filler?) in the fourth verse of every *phunhe śaloka*. (Surindar Singh Kohli, p. 79)

Tinatāla	1 x	2	3	4	5 2	6	7	8	9 0	10	11	12	13 3	14	15	16
Jhā̃jha	♩	♩	♩		♩	♩	♩		♩	♩	♩		♩	♩	♩	
										[1]sun	da	ra	tā	—	—	kī
	sī	—	—	mā	[-]de	kho	mā	ī	—	[1]*sun*	*da*	*ra*	*tā*	—	—	*kī*
	sī	—	—	*mā*	*de*	*kho*	*mā*	*ī*	[—]	[2]sun	—	dara	tā	—	—	kī
	sī	—	—	-mā	de	kho	mā	ī	— *ā*	[2]*sun*	*da*	*ra*	*tā*	—	—	*kī*
	sī	—	—	*mā*	*de*	*kho*	*mā*	*ī* [-]mā	— ī	[1a]sun	da	ra	tā	—	—	-kī
	sī	—	—	mā	[-]de	kho	mā	ī	*māī* —	[2]*sun* sun	da	ra	tā	—	—	kī
	sī	—	—	mā	[-]de	kho	mā	ī	*hā̃*	[1]*sun*	—	*dara*	*tā*	—	—	*kī*
	sī	—	—	*mā*	*de*	*kho*	*mā*	*ī*	—	[2]*sun*	—	*dara*	*tā*	—	—	*kī*
	sī	—	—	*mā*	*de*	*kho*	*mā*	*ī*	—	[3]braja	na	va	ta	ru	ni	-ka
	dam	—	—	-ba	nā	ga	rī	—	—	[3]*braja*	*na*	*va*	*ta*	*ru*	*ni*	*ka*[-]
	dam	—	—	*ba*	*nā*	*ga*	*rī*	—	[—]	[3]braja	na	va	[-]ta	ru	ni	-ka
	dam	—	—	ba	nā	ga	rī	—	—	[3]*braja*	*na*	*va*	*ta*	*ru*	*ni*	[-]*ka*
	dam	—	—	*ba*	*nā*	*ga*	*rī*	—	[—]	[1]nira	kha	-ka	ra	ta	—	adhi
	grī	—	—	vā	[-]de	kho	mā	ī	— *ā̃*	[1]*nira*	*khi*	*-ka*	*ra*	*ta*	—	*adha*
	grī	—	—	*vā*	*de*	*kho*	*mā*	*ī*	*a*	[3]braja	na	va	ta	ru	ni	-ka
	dam	—	—	ba	nā	ga	rī	—	—	[3]nira	kha	-ka	ra	ta	—	adha
	grī	—	—	vā	-de	kho	mā	ī	— *ā̃*	[3]*braja*	*na*	*va*	*ta*	*ru*	*ni*	*ka*[-]
	dam	—	—	*ba*	*nā*	*ga*	*rī*	—	[—]	[1]*nira*	*khi*	*ka*	*ra*	*ta*	—	*adha*
	grī	—	—	*vā*	*de*	*kho*	*mā*	*ī*	*ā̃*	[4]jo	—	kou	ko	—	ṭi	—
	kal	pa	—	lagi	jī	—	—	ve	—	[4]*jo*	—	*kou*	*ko*	—	—	*ṭi*
	kal	*pa*	—	*lagi*	*jī*	—	—	*ve*	—	[5]rasa	nā	—	ko	—	—	ṭika
	pā	—	ve	—	-de	kho	mā		*ā̃*	[5]*rasa*	*nā*	—	*ko*	—	—	*ṭika*

1	2	3	4	5	6	7	8	9	10	11	12	13	14	15	16
pā	—	—	*ve*	*de*	*kho*	*mā*	*ī*	— *a*	^{4}jo	—	kou	ko	—	ṭi	—
kal	pa	—	laga	jī	—	—	ve	[—]	^{5}rasa	nā	—	[-]ko	—	—	ṭika
pā	—	ve	—	-de	kho	mā	ī	— ā̃	^{4}*jo*	—	*kou*	*ko*	—		*ṭi*
kal	*pa*	—	*lagi*	*jī*	—	—	*ve*	—	^{5}*rasa*	—	*nā*	*ko*	—	*ṭi*	*ka*
pā	—	—	*ve*	*de*	*kho*	*mā*	*ī*	—	^{3}taū	—	*-ru*	ci	ra	—	bada
-nā	—	—	-ra	vin	da	kī	— ā̃	— ā̃	^{3}*ta*	*ū*	*-ru*	*ci*	*ra*	—	*bada*
nā	—	—	*ra*	*vin*	*da*	*kī*	—	[—]	^{1}*śo*	bhā	—	ka	ha	ta	-na
ā	—	—	ve	—de	kho	mā	ī	—] ā̃	^{1}*śo*	*bhā*	—	*ka*	*ha*	—	*ta na*
ā	—	—	*ve*	*de*	*kho*	*mā*	*ī*	[—]	^{3}taū	—	-ru	ci	ra	—	bada
nā	—	—	-ra	-vin	da	kī	—	—	^{1}śo	bhā	—	ka	ha	ta	-na
ā	—	—	ve	[-]de	kho	mā	ī	— ā̃	^{3}*ta*	*ū*	*-ru*	*ci*	*ra*	—	*bada*
nā	—	—	*ra*	*vin*	*da*	*kī*	—	—	^{1}*śo*	*bhā*	—	*ka*	*ha*	—	*ta na*
ā	—	—	*ve*	*de*	*kho*	*mā*	*ī* [-]mā	— ī	^{4}de	—	valo	—	ka	—	bhū
lo	—	—	ka	—ra	sā	ta	la	—	^{4}*de*	—	*valo*	—	*ka*	—	*bhū*
lo	—	—	*ka ra*	*sā*	—	—	*tala*	—	^{5}suna	—	kavi	ku	la	ma	-ti
ḍa	ri	ye	—	—de	kho	mā	ī	— ā̃	^{5}*suna*	—	*kavi*	*ku*	*la*	—	*mati*
ḍa	*ri*	*ye*	—	*de*	*kho*	*mā*	*ī*	[—]	^{4}de	—	valo	—	ka	—[-]	bhū
lo	—	—	ka ra	sā	—	—	tala	—	^{5}suna	—	kavi	ku	la	—	mati
ḍa	ri	ye	—	[-]de	kho	mā	ī	— ā̃	^{4}*de*	—	*va*	*lo*	*ka*	—	*bhū*
lo	—	—	*ka ra*	*sā*	—	—	*tala*	—	^{5}*suni*	—	*kavi*	*ku*	*la*	*ma*	*ti*
ḍa	*ri*	—	*ye*	*de*	*kho*	*mā*	*ī*	—	^{3}saha	ja	mā	—	dhu	rī	—
aṃ	—	—	ga	aṃ	ga	kī	—	—	^{5}*saha*	*ja*	*mā*	—	*dhu*	*rī*	e

1	2	3	4	5	6	7	8	9	10	11	12	13	14	15	16
rī	hā̃	—	—	—	—	—	o	—	[3]saha	ja	mā	—	dhu	rī	*e rī*
hā̃	—	—	—	—	—	—	o	—	*[3]saha*	*ja*	*mā*	—	*dhu*	—	*-rī*
aṃ	—	—	*ga*	*aṃ*	*ga*	*kī*	—	[—]	[1]kahi	kā	—	sõ	—	—	paṭa
ta	ri	—	ye	-de	kho	mā	ī	— *ā̃*	*[1]kahi*	*kā*	—	*sõ*	—	—	*paṭa*
ta	*ri*	—	*ye*	*de*	*kho*	*mā*	*ī*	— *ā̃*	[3]saha	ja	mā	—	—	dhu	rī
aṃ	—	—	ga	aṃ	ga	kī	—	—	[1]kahi	kā	—	sõ	—	—	paṭa
ta	ri	—	ye	-de	kho	mā	ī	—	*[3]saha*	*ja*	(*mā*)	(—) *mā*	*dhu*	—	*rī*
aṃ	—	—	*ga*	*aṃ*	*ga*	—	*kī*	—	*[1]kahi*	—	*kā*	*sõ*	—	—	*paṭa*
ta	*ri*	—	*ye*	*de*	*kho*	—	*māī* jaiśrī	— —	[4]hita	—	hari	vaṃ	—	—	śa pra
tā	—	—	-pa	—	rūpa	guna	*jaiśrī*	—	*[4]hita*	—	*hari*	*vaṃ*	—	—	*śa pra*
tā	—	—	*pa*	*rū*	*pa*	*gu*	*na*	—	[5]vay	ba	-la	śyā	—	—	m u
jā	—	ga	ra	-de	kho	mā	*ī* *a*	— —	*[5]vay*	*ba*	*la*	*śyā*	—	—	*m u*
jā	—	—	*gara*	*de*	*kho*	*mā*	*i* jaiśrī	—	[4]hita	—	hari	vaṃ	—	—	śa
pratā	—	—	-pa	rū	pa	gu	na	[—]	[5]vay	ba	-la	śyā	—	—	m u
jā	—	—	gara	-de	kho	māī	*jaiśrī*	—	*[4]hita*	—	*hari*	*va*	—	—	*ṃśa pra*
tā	—	—	*pa*	*rū*	*pa*	*gu*	*na*	—	*[5]vay*	*ba*	*la*	*śyā*	—	—	*m u*
jā	—	—	*gara*	*de*	*kho*	*mā*	*ī*	—	[3]jā	kī	—	bhrū	—	-vi	lā
—	-sa	—	basa	pa	śu	ri	va	—	*[3]jā*	—	*kī*	*bhrū*	—	—	*vilā*
—	*sa*	—	*basa*	*pa*	*śu*	—	*riva*	— ehā	[3]jā	kī	—	bhrū	—	-vi	lā
—	sa	—	basa	pa	śu	ri	va	—	*[3]jā*	—	*kī*	*bhrū*	—	*-vi* e rī	—
ha	—	—	—	—	—	—	o	—	[3]jā	ki	—	-bhrū	—	—	*e rī*
hā̃	—	—	—	—	—	—	*o*	—	*[3]jā*	—	*kī*	*bhrū*	—	*-vi*	*lā*

	1	2	3	4	5	6	7	8	9	10	11	12	13	14	15	16
	—	*sa*	—	*basa*	*pa*	*śu*	—	*riva*	—	[1]dina	vi	tha	ki	ta	—	rasa
*	sā	—	—	gara	de	kho	mā	ī	—	[1]*dina*	*vi*	*tha*	*ki*	*ta*	—	*rasa*
	sā	—	*ga*	*ra*	*de*	*kho*	—	*māī*	—	[3]jā	kī	—	bhrū	—	—	-vi
	lā	sa	—	basa	pa	śu	ri	va	—	[1]dina	vi	tha	ki	ta	—	rasa
	sā	—	—	gara	de	kho	mā	ī	—	[3]*jā*	—	*kī*	*bhrū*	—	*vi*	*lā*
	—	*sa*	—	*basa*	*pa*	*śu*	—	*riva*	—[-]	[1]*dina*	*vi*	*-tha*	*ki*	*ta*	—	*rasa*
	sā	—	—	*gara*	*de*	*kho*	*mā*	*ī*	—	[2]sun	—	dara	tā	—	—	kī
	sī	—	mā	—	[-]de	kho	mā	ī	— } ã	[2]*sun*	—	*dara*	*tā*	—	—	*kī*
	sī	—	—	*mā*	*de*	*kho*	*mā*	*ī*	— } māī	[1]sun	da	ra	tā	—	—	kī
	sī	—	mā	—	de	kho	mā	ī	— } *ã*	[1]*sun*	—	*dara*	*tā*	—	—	*-kī*
	sī	—	—	*mā*	*de*	*kho*	*mā*	*ī*	—	[2]*sun*	—	*dara*	*tā*	—	—	*kī*
	sī															

CHAPTER VII

THE COMPOSITION AND CONTENT OF THE CAURĀSĪ PADA

1. The Title of the Text

Modern editions of the CP usually bear the title *Hita caurāsī*, some preferring the Sanskritized form *Hita caturāśī*, and it is under these titles that the text is usually discussed in histories of Hindi literature. The evidence of the manuscripts studied for the present edition, however, is that these titles are relatively modern, and represent a literary formalization of the epithet *Caurāsī pada* which simply describes the text as a collection of 84 stanzas.

It is recognised even within the *sampradāya* that the CP was compiled after the death of Hita Harivaṃśa. Early references to Harivaṃśa's collected *padas* do not mention any specific number of stanzas or any title, but refer to the text in such general terms as *vāṇī*, *girā*, etc. The most striking example of this is the 16th century text *Sevaka vāṇī* of Dāmodaradāsa 'Sevaka': the entire fourth *prakaraṇa* of this text is devoted to a eulogy of Harivaṃśa's *vāṇī*, but nowhere does an actual title appear.[1] Dāmodaradāsa seems, therefore, to have known the *vāṇī* only as a loose collection, since he would surely have referred to any formal title current at the time of his writing.

The oldest manuscript collated for the present edition is MS A, dated v.s. 1749 (A.D. 1693). Dharaṇīdharadāsa, author of the *ṭīkā* which this manuscript contains, makes no allusion to the number of stanzas in the text, referring to it simply as *bāṇī*; and strictly speaking the CP as borne by this manuscript does not originally consist of 84 stanzas, since CP 13 is present only as a margin addition, and the numbering sequence does not, consequently, reach 84. The scribal colophon to the manuscript does, however, introduce the 'title' *śrī caurāsī*, and thereby assumes a total of 84 stanzas; similar forms appear in MSS EIL, with *śrī caturāśī* appearing in two of the Premadāsa *ṭīkā* manuscripts, K and M. The title *caurāsī pada* appears in the colophons of BCDFJ: of these, the earliest dated is MS C, whose colophon bears the date v.s. 1794 (A.D. 1737). Nowhere in the manuscripts collated does the title *Hita caurāsī* appear; among the other manuscripts examined, the title appears once only, and then too in a modern copy (described in section II.2.(iv)).

1. Citations of the CP in the *Sevaka vāṇī* are discussed in section VII.3.(ii) below.

The earliest attestation of the epithet (*Śrī*) *caurāsī* in the available sources is, therefore, in the colophon of MS A (A.D. 1693), while the earliest occurrence of the form *Caurāsī pada* is in MS C (A.D. 1737).

A reference from the hagiographic work *Rasika ananya māla*, quoted on p. 11, provides a slightly earlier attestation of the form *caurāsī*: the hagiography is tentatively dated to the mid-17th century. (Though this reference links the title *Caurāsī* with a *gosvāmī* interpreted as Harivaṃśa's eldest son Vanacandra, there is no reason to believe that Vanacandra himself was specificially acquainted with an integral text composed of, or referred to as, a unified corpus of 84 stanzas.)

Since the CP represents a sectarian compilation of individual stanzas or groups of stanzas, it is not surprising to find the lack of a consistently applied title in the earlier sources. In the absence of truly early manuscripts, the aim of the edition cannot go beyond the establishment of an authentic form of *this* compilation, since by definition there can have been no consolidated 'archetype' contemporaneous with the composition of its component parts. In this context, it is reasonable to adopt the descriptive label *Caurāsī pada* as a relatively early title for the anthology: but only after recognising the place of this form in the gradual development zero > *caurāsī* > *caurāsī pada* > *hita caurāsī*.

Discussion of the modern title *Hita caurāsī* invites some comment on the word *hita* itself. 'Harivaṃśa' is a reasonably common name in Vaiṣṇava circles, and it was perhaps in order to differentiate himself from others of the same name that the Rādhāvallabhī Harivaṃśa incorporated the *upanāma hita* into his *chāpa*: this usage established a style which was followed by later sectarian figures—'Hita' Dhruvadāsa, 'Hita' Rūpalāla etc. The meaning of *hita* in Hindi extends beyond its Sanskrit sense of 'good, welfare' etc., and becomes roughly synonymous with *prema*; Rādhāvallabhī authors adopt the term to refer specifically to their own sectarian conception of divine love which, notwithstanding the eroticism of the Rādhā-Kṛṣṇa paradigm through which it is expressed, is purely transcendental and untained by lust (*kāma*). Despite the attribution of this concept to Hita Harivaṃśa, however, this usage only becomes apparent in the works of later authors and is not explicit in the works of Harivaṃśa himself: the term occurs independently of *chāpa* contexts only four times[1] in the CP, and in none of these occurrences does the sectarian sense apply. (The term does not appear in the Sanskrīt text *Rādhāsudhānidhi*, while in its three occurrences in the *Sphuṭa vāṇī*[2] it does not have the sectarian sense.)

Of the early eulogistic works surveyed above in chapter I, only the *Sevaka vāṇī* attaches the *upanāma hita* to Harivaṃśa's name. The absence of the *upanāma* elsewhere does not necessarily prove ignorance

1. CP 12.1, 48.2, 57.27, 58.1.
2. *Sphuṭa vāṇī* 16.2, 18.6, 24.1 (Lalitā Caraṇ Gosvāmī (ed.) 1972:157, 161, 166).

of it, but rather implies, perhaps, that it was regarded as having purely literary reference and that its use outside the context of the *chāpa* was not appropriate or necessary; alternatively, it may have been used only to distinguish the Rādhāvallabhī poet from others of the same name. In the primary sources analysed, the first attestation of the *upanāma hita* serving as a personal name in its own right is in the phrase *hita jū kī rīti* from Priyādāsa's eighteenth century *Bhaktirasa bodhinī*, quoted on p. 14 above (while Nābhādāsa's *mūla*, which this reference glosses, refers only to *harivaṃśa gusā̃ī*).

2. Authorship of the 84 Stanzas

It is by no means certain that all the 84 stanzas are the product of a single author. Six of the 84 appear, with some differences, in the *Sūrasāgara*; a further two bear the *chāpa* not of Harivaṃśa but of one Naravāhana, and the second of these, CP 12, is also attributed to the Aṣṭachāpa poet Kumbhanadāsa. This last attribution, recorded by Lalitā Caraṇ Gosvāmī (1957:376) cannot be discussed here since no text of the Kumbhanadāsa version has been available;[1] the other two attributions are discussed in the following paragraphs.

(*i*) *The 'Naravāhana' Stanzas*

The consecutive stanzas CP 11 and 12 bear the *chāpa 'narabāhana'*. Rādhāvallabhī hagiographies such as the *Rasika ananya māla* (Lalitāprasād Purohit (ed.) 1960:1–4) identify Naravāhana as a 'robber- baron' figure who held the whole of Braj under his sway, but who latterly became a disciple and follower of Hita Harivaṃśa; the sectarian view of the origin of these stanzas is that they were written by Harivaṃśa but 'dedicated' to Naravāhana as a reward for his devoted allegiance. An early example of this ascription is found in the following couplet from the seventeenth century text *Bhaktanāmāvalī* of the Rādhāvallabhī poet Dhruvadāsa:

> *kahā kahaũ nahī̃ kahi sakata narabāhana ko bhāga;*
> *śrīmukha jākau nāma dharyau nija bānī anurāga.*[2]
>
> 'What can I say? I cannot describe the happy lot of Naravāhana, whose name the sweet-voiced one placed affectionately in his own scripture.'

This description of events is frequently recounted by the hagiographical literature.[3] Such a dedication would represent a reversal of the more

1. The stanza does not occur in the anthology of Kumbhanadāsa's *padas* included in Prabhudayāl Mītal (ed.), 1949:105-16.
2. Lalitā Caraṇ Gosvāmī (ed.) 1971:30.
3. See, for example, the following references, all treating of the life of Naravāhana:

usual practice, in which the devotee or admirer of a poet himself composes a stanza in that poet's style and bearing the latter's name, and adds it as an apocrypha to the existing corpus (examples of such *padas* bearing the *chāpa* of Harivaṃśa are given in Appendix III). If the hagiographers' story lacks a ring of authenticity, however, it remains unchallenged by any conflicting evidence; the historical position remains obscure.

The two stanzas bearing the *chāpa narabāhana*, CP 11 and 12, are linked by a strong stylistic resemblance. Both are six-line stanzas and share, with preceding CP 10, a particular metrical structure; both have *-inī* end-rhyme (CP 11 *-āminī*; CP 12 *-āṃdinī*); both share similar internal rhymes in the final couplet, and furthermore share the same rhyme-word *jheli* in the second *pāda* of line (6). The two stanzas also end with similar compound epithets: 11.6 *jagata pāvanī*, 12.6 *jagata baṃdinī*.

In both stanzas, the *chāpa* '*narabāhana*' is followed by the word *prabhu*, yielding the compound epithet 'Naravāhana's Lord, Kṛṣṇa'.[1] In both instances, MSS DI read *prabhū* (though neither manuscript is prone to the arbitrary lengthening of short vowels, and both consistently read *prabhu* elsewhere in the text); lengthening of the vowel here suggests, therefore, a possible metrical compensation for a five-*mātrā chāpa* (i.e. a form metrically shorter than *narabāhana*). Furthermore, the metrical configuration [⏑⏑—] introduced by *narabā-* at the beginning of the line upsets the predominantly trochaic rhythm which subsists throughout these stanzas: no other line (or half-line) begins with such a configuration. Variation of this kind is not without precedent, however (see for example catalectic *hita haribaṃśa* in 46.4 and 71.6), and is not proof, *per se*, of a corrupt reading.

Although similarities between the two stanzas suggest a shared source, there is no specific evidence to show that they may not share

---

(a) Bhagavata Mudita, *Rasika ananya māla* (Lalitāprasād Purohit (ed.) 1961:4):
guru prasanna hvai dvai pada gāyau; naravāhana ke bhoga lagāyau.

(b) Uttamadāsa, *Harivaṃśa caritra* (N.P.S. Āryabhāṣā Pustakālaya, MS 4822 ff. 9v-10r):
niju vihāra ke dvai pada daye; śrīmuṣa vānī madhya liṣi laye.

(c) Priyādāsa, *Bhaktirasa bodhinī* (S.Ś. Bhagvān Prasād (ed.) p. 663):
daī maṃgavāya vastu rākhi yõ durāya bāta
āya dāsa bhayau kahi rījhi pada diyau hai.

(d) Vṛndāvanadāsa, *Rasika ananya paracāvalī*, *Hita Saurabha* VI, No. 2 (April 1973), p. 53:
śrī guru bhaye kṛpāla dekhi tihi̐ carita navīnai;
caurāsī pada mā̐hi jugala pada tākau̐ dīnai.

1. This collocation disallows the interpretation offered by C.S.J. White (pp. 60-61), in which the *chāpa* is broken down into its lexical components and translated 'The Lord....is a vehicle for man'/'The Lord, the Vehicle of Salvation for men'. G.R. Niemann's interpretation (1977:44-45) of *prabhu* as syntactically distinct from the *chāpa* is similarly untenable.

authorship with the remainder of the text. Pairings of stanzas of like kind occur elsewhere in the text (e.g. CP 39, 40; CP 74, 75); further examples of the metre used here occur in CP 10, 76 and 80; and the phrase *kiśalaya dala racita saina* from 11.4 is also found in 76.1.

(*ii*) *The 'Sūrasāgara' Stanzas*

CP 13, 33, 37, 50, 54 and 82 all appear in editions of the *Sūrasāgara* (*SS*). The fact that none of these six appears in the earlier manuscripts of the *SS*[1] shows them to be late accretions to the expansive Sūra tradition; but, far from proving that the stanzas necessarily have their origin in the CP, this evidence suggests the (unprovable) hypothesis that they may have belonged to some independent body of material—perhaps fostered and transmitted by a sung tradition—from which individual *padas* might easily have been borrowed and developed variously along sectarian lines. The omission of CP 13 from the original draft of MS A, and the different locations in the overall stanza sequence allotted to two more of the disputed stanzas (CP 33 and 50) by MS A *vis-à-vis* the other manuscripts, supports this view.

Nothing in the style or content of the six stanzas can prove beyond doubt an original identity with either the CP or the *SS*. The stylistic and thematic grounds on which Vijayendra Snātak bravely concludes[2] that all six stanzas are attributable to Harivaṃśa are superficial and general; and since an overall consistency of style and theme would naturally be sought by any compiler when assembling disparate material for an anthology, the use of such general criteria to resolve the problem of authorship begs the question fundamentally.

The *SS* texts on which the following discussion of the six stanzas is based are given in Appendix II.

CP 13: *SS* 2489/1871. Though substantial divergences between the two versions occur only in the last couplet, the minor variations in line (4) are significant in terms of the transmission of the text. Here two variant readings in the CP manuscripts follow the *SS* version: A reads *kāko* for *kaise*; C reads *rahe*, E *rahi*, L *rahai*, for *rahata* (*SS rahai*). The subjunctive mood accommodated by the *SS* reading *rahai* could be said to be more appropriate here: cf. subjunctive verbs in the similarly rhetorical contexts of 35.8 and 42.6.[3] Line (6) in the *SS* version is a more logical conclusion to the stanza, since it maintains the theme of a *sakhī* describing the effect on herself of a vision of Kṛṣṇa. Snātaka concludes on lexical grounds that the text is attributable to Harivaṃśa; but the 'teasing' motif with which the stanza opens is more akin to *SS* contexts than to the CP, where it has no precedent. The absence of this stanza from MS A clearly casts some doubt as to its origins.

1. J.S. Hawley 1979:8.
2. Vijayendra Snātak 1968:324-30.
3. 35.8 *kyaũ banai bibecita*; 42.6 *kauna apanapau hārai*.

CP 33: *SS* 1817/1119. The first line is held in common by the two versions; in the *SS* text this forms a couplet with line (4) of the CP text. The first half of the third line is also shared, but for the distinction between the participles *parata* (CP)/*dharata* (*SS*); here, MS F falls in with the *SS* reading (but possibly through assimilation to a context in 5.2, rather than as a result of any genetic connexion with the *SS* tradition). The *SS* text contains the unlikely rhyme *bhora*/*bhora* in the third and fourth lines. In the stanza order unique to MS A, this stanza follows CP 31 with a similar first line:

31.1 *āju ati rājata dampati bhora*
33.1 *āju bana rājata jugala kiśora.*

A further correspondence with the remainder of the CP text occurs in line (6), where the phrase *surata samudra jhakora* echoes 70.2 *surata samudra jhakorī.*

CP 13 and CP 33 together account for two of the three CP stanzas with *-ora* end-rhyme (the third being CP 31 quoted above).

CP 37: *SS* 3070/2452. CP 37 stands at the beginning of a sequence of five stanzas whose main theme is the *viraha* endured by Kṛṣṇa during Rādhā's *māna*. There are a number of differences between the two versions, of which the following demand comment.

In line (3), where the *SS* text reads *saṃbhrama ati ātura*, the CP reading is *birahākula pulakita* in CEFGKLM, *pulakita birahākula* in ABDHIJ (original drafts); the coincidence of this variation among the CP manuscripts with the different *SS* version suggests diverse replacement in the CP of an earlier reading. Both recensions yield metrically and semantically sound versions. The orthographic similarity between the two versions of the seventh line suggest the possibility of deliberate scribal superimposition of one reading onto the other at some time during the transmission:

CP *hita haribaṃśa parama komala cita capala calī piya tīra*
SS *hiya maĩ harași prema ati ātura catura calī piya tīra.*

The CP reading *ranabīra* in the final line has been altered, in MS C, to *ranadhīra*, the *SS* reading. The appearance of the word *sūra* in this line has no doubt facilitated attribution of the stanza to Sūradāsa: but *sūra* also appears, again in collocation with *surata*, in the last line of CP 38, and again at 46.4 and 57.29. A further connexion with the remainder of the CP is found in the phrase *to binu kũvari* (37.2), which occurs again at 39.4.

CP 50: *SS* 1809/1191. Four of the five points of difference between the two versions show the *SS* text to be inferior, and presumably therefore to represent a corrupt recension. The first divergence is in line (2);

here the CP reads *sarasa mani nīla mano mṛdula kaṃcana ṣacī*, for which the *SS* has the equally satisfactory *sarasa mani mṛdula kaṃcana su ābhā khacī*. In the following line, however, the *SS* text fails to yield an effective *śleṣa* dependent upon the CP reading *nibǎdha* (and discussed in the annotation to 50.3), and furthermore fails to show the *varṇika gaṇa* /≍⏑≍, ≍⏑≍/which is regular for this metre:

⏑ ⏑ ⏑ –/– ⏑ ⏑ ⏑/ – ⏑ ⏑ ⏑/ – ⏑ –
CP *surata nībī nibǎdha heta piya māninī*
⏑ ⏑ ⏑ –/– – ⏑/⏑ ⏑ ⏑ ⏑ ⏑/ – ⏑ ⏑ ⏑
SS *sũdara nībī baṃdha rahati piya pāni gahi*

In the fourth line, the inclusion in the *SS* text of superfluous *kari* may be consequent upon an inversion of the two words *roṣa, hũkari* (the latter being a miscopying of correct *huṃkāra*). In the fifth line the *SS* reading must be an ingenuous replacement of the *chāpa* '*haribaṃśa hita*', since the *SS* text is again unmetrical (catalexis not being a regular feature in this position):

– ⏑ –/⏑ ⏑ ⏑ ⏑ ⏑/⏑ ⏑ ⏑ ⏑⏑/– – ⏑ ⏑
CP *koka koṭika rabhasa rahasi haribaṃśa hita*
– ⏑ –/⏑ ⏑ ⏑ ⏑ ⏑/⏑ ⏑ ⏑ ⏑ ⏑/– ⏑⏑
SS *koka koṭika rabhasa rasika hari sūraja*

In the final line, the *SS* reading *prāna mana* for CP *praṇayamaya* is semantically inferior.

CP 54: *SS* 1303/685. The first couplet only of the CP six-line stanza is shared by the *SS* four-line stanza. The *SS* reading *nayau geha* in the first line is metrically inferior to the CP's *nava raṃga*. *SS kũvari* in the same line is semantically inferior to the CP's *syāma*, since restriction of the context to Rādhā in the *SS* text damages the correspondence with the following line, where the reference to *pītǎbara* as well as *cūnarī* (both versions) involves *nāyaka* as well as *nāyikā* in the action of the stanza. (*SS kũvari* may, however, represent masc. *kũvara*, in which case this argument does not stand.)

The final line of the CP text contains the phrase *cira jīvau bhūtala yaha jorī*, which echoes further collocations of *bhūtala* and *jorī* at 7.2 and 70.8.

CP 82: *SS* 1819/1201. The resemblance of the two versions is very close. The *SS* readings *mūla*, *sugaṃdha* and *madhurau rī* (second, fourth, and seventh lines) are errors for *maula*, *sudhaṃga* and *madhu ghorī* respectively. (The reading *sugaṃdha* appears here in MSS EM also (either by metathesis or by thoughtless confusion of the two words); but this error is commonplace in E, and occurs in M also at 24.4 and 72.5.) The six-*mātrā* *chāpa* '*sūradāsa*' which appears for seven-*mātrā* '*hita haribaṃśa*' in the final line requires a lengthning of the following *pivata* (CP) to *pīvata* (*SS*): citations in the *Sūra śabdasāgara* (Hardev Bāharī 1981) show the former to have wider currency in the *SS* generally.

There are several collocations in CP 82 which have parallels elsewhere in the text: for 82.2 *barabasa kiyau citai muṣa morī* cf. 78.4 *barabasa liyaũ mohana cita corī*; for 82.3 *ãga aṃga mādhurī* cf. similar collocations at 10.1, 29.2, 69.2, 78.4; for 82.4 *rasa siṃdhu jhakorī* cf. 43.3 *guna siṃdhu jhakorī*. The dance context of this stanza, with Rādhā predominant, is found in the broken sequence CP 78, 79, 81, 82.

The above comparisons of CP and *SS* versions yield no definitive conclusions. The cited parallels between the stanzas under discussion and the remainder of the CP are often striking, but cannot, for two reasons, be taken as proof of an original identity of source: firstly, a detailed search of the *SS* would no doubt yield similar parallels with *SS* contexts; and secondly, the tendency in BrBh verse to the conscious or unconscious use of literary formulae in the construction of a line is commonplace, and is likely to obscure original diversity of authorship. In the case of the last three stanzas discussed, a more coherent text in the CP versions suggests that these stanzas have been preserved more accurately in the Rādhāvallabhī 'recension', and may therefore be regarded as holding a position closer to the archetype than that held by the relatively corrupt *SS* versions; the alternative explanation, viz. that the coherent CP texts represent (hyper-)corrections of original *SS* stanzas, does not seem tenable. In the case of the first three stanzas, however, an open verdict must be returned, the origin of CP 13 remaining particularly doubtful.

3. The Structure of the Text

A cursory survey of the 84 stanzas shows that the collection is not rigidly ordered under any classification scheme except that of *rāga* headings. *Rāga* allocation is, therefore, the first aspect of the text's structure to be discussed below. Subsequently, the factors of metrical type, word use and theme are analysed in an attempt to perceive any possible diversity of sources amongst the component stanzas of the text; existing classification schemes promoted within the sectarian tradition are also assessed.

(*i*) *Rāga allocations in the CP*

All manuscripts allocate a sequence of *rāgas* to the 84 stanzas of the text; the *rāga* distribution varies, but the table below shows that a large degree of agreement exists. The stanza order of MS A, discussed in section II.1(i), differs from that of all other manuscripts in that a group of nine stanzas (CP 27 to 35 in the majority order) precedes a group of seven stanzas which comes first in all other manuscripts; the fact that these two blocks of text constitute discrete *rāga* sections suggests that the *rāga* allocation does at least antedate the dislocation of the text in MS A *vis-à-vis* the other sources.

In table 4, cross-hatching indicates a lost folio (of which details are given in II.1); manuscript orthographies are preserved in the tabulated *rāga* names.

The *mūla* of the CP is usually followed by a stanza in *kavitta* metre, giving the distribution of the 84 stanzas under 14 *rāga* headings. The date of this *kavitta* is unknown, but its authorship has been attributed by the CP's commentator Premadāsa to one 'Harijī Mallajī'.[1] The name 'Śrī Harijū (Harijīmala)' appears in a list of eighteenth century Rādhāvallabhī authors,[2] but even this vague indication of a *floruit* remains unsubstantiated. Of the sources collated for the present edition of the CP, only MS C (v.s. 1794) is without the so-called *rāga saṃkhyā kavitta*, though in the oldest manuscript collated, MS A (v.s. 1749), the *kavitta* is a later addition which supplements an earlier stanza (reproduced in the description of MS A) listing the *rāga* sequence peculiar to that manuscript.

The fact that the original drafts of two oldest manuscript collated, A and C, are without the *rāga* stanza suggests that the stanza was written after the date of these two manuscripts. If this is the case, then the *kavitta* must have been composed to describe an already existing allocation of *rāgas*, rather than to prescribe such an allocation, since even in A and C the order of *rāgas* is very close to that which becomes more or less standard in later manuscripts. The *kavitta*, quoted in section II.3, yields the following computation of the numbers of stanzas allocated to each *rāga*:

Vibhāsa	6	Sāraṅga	16
Vilāvala	7	Mallāra	4
Toḍī	4	Gauḍa	1
Āsāvarī	2	Gaurī	9
Dhanāśrī	7	Kalyāṇa	6
Vasanta	2	Kānharo	9
Devagandhāra	7	Kedāro	4

Except in printed text H, where each *pada* is individually headed with the *rāga* name, only the first *pada* of a sequence bears the *rāga* name. If a *rāga* name is omitted, therefore, the following stanzas seem to be

1. This attribution is quoted in the description of MS G, section II.1(i).
2. Kiśorīśaraṇ 'Ali' 1950: 42.

Table 4: The Rāgas of the CP

CP	A	B	C	D	E	F	G	H	I	J	K	L	M
1	*Lalita*	*Bibhāsa*	*Bibhāsa Lalita*	*Bibhāsa*	*Bibhāsa*	*Bibhāsa*	*Bibhāsa*	*Bibhāsa*	*Bibhāsa*	*Bibhāsa*		*Bibhāsa*	*Bibhāsa*
2								,,					
3								,,					
4								,,					
5								,,					
6								,,					
7	*Bilāvala*	*Bilāvala*		*Bilāvala*	*Bilāvala*		*Bilāvala*	*Bilāvala*	*Bilāvala*	*Bilāvala*	*Bilāvala*	*Bilāvala*	
8								,,					
9								,,					
10								,,					
11								,,					
12								,,					
13								,,					
14	*Toḍī*	*Toḍī*	*Toḍī*	*Toḍī*	*Toḍī*	*Toḍī*	*Toḍī*	*Toḍī*	*Toḍī*	*Toḍī*	*Toḍī*	*Toḍī*	*Toḍī* [changed to *ṭoḍī, sec.m.*]
15								,,					
16								,,					
17								,,					
18	*Asāvarī*	*Asāvarī*	*Āsāvarī*	*Asāvarī*	*Asāvarī*	*Asāvarī*	*Āsāvarī*	*Āsāvarī*	*Āsāvarī*	*Āsāvarī*	*Asāvarī*	*Āsāvarī*	*Āsāvarī*
19								,,					
20	*Dhanāśrī*	*Dhanāśrī*	*Dhanyāsī*	*Dhanāsirī*	*Dhanāśrī*	*Dhanāśrī*	*Dhanāsirī*	*Dhanāśrī*	*Dhanāśrī*	*Dhanāsirī*	*Dhanāśrī*	*Dhanāśrī*	*Dhanāsarī*
21								,,					
22								,,					
23								,,					
24								,,					

CP	A	B	C	D	E	F	G	H	I	J	K	L	M
25								„					
26								„					
27	*Basaṃta*	*Basaṃta*	*Basaṃta*	*Basaṃta*	*Basaṃta*	*Basaṃta*	*Basaṃta*	*Basaṃta*	*Basaṃta*	*Basaṃta*	*Basaṃta*	*Baśaṃta*	*Basaṃta*
28								„					
29	*Gujarī*	*Deva-gaṃdhāra*	*Gujjarī*	*Deva-gaṃdhāra*	*Deva-gaṃdhāra*	*Deva-gaṃdhāra*		*Deva-gaṃdhāra*	*Deva-gaṃdāra*	*Deva-gaṃdhāra*	*Deva-gaṃdhāra*	*Deva-gaṃdhāra*	
30								„					
31								„					
32								„					
33								„					
34								„					
35								„					
36	*Sāraṃga*	*Sāraṃga*	*Sāraṃga*	*Sāraṃga*	*Sāraṃga*		*Sāraṃga*	*Sāraṃga*	*Sāraṃga*	*Sāraṃga*	*Sāraṃga*	*Sāraṃga*	*Sāraṃga*
37-51	Ditto												
52	*Malāra*	*Malāra*	*Malāra*	*Malāra*	*Malāra*	*Malāra*	*Malāra*	*Malāra*	*Malāra*	*Malāra*	*Malāra*	*Malāra*	*Malāra*
53								„					
54								„					
55								„					
56	*Gorī*			*Gauḍa-malāra*	*Gauḍa-malāra*	*Gauḍa-malāra*	*Gauḍa-malāra*	*Gauḍa-malāra*		*Gauḍa-malāra*	*Gauḍa-malāra*	*Gauḍa-malāra*	*Gauḍa-malāra*
57		*Gaurī*	*Gaurī*	*Gaurī*	*Gaurī*	*Gaurī*	*Gaurī*	*Gaurī*	*Gaurī*	*Gaurī*	*Gaurī*	*Gaurī*	*Gaurī*
58								„					
59			*Gaurī*					„					
60								„					
61								„					
62								„					
63			*Gorī*					„					
64			[*sec.m.*]					„					

CP	A	B	C	D	E	F	G	H	I	J	K	L	M
65								,,	*pada* om.				
66	*Kalyāna*		*Kalyāṇa*	*Kalyāna*	*Kalyāna*	*Kalyāna*	*Kalyāṇa*	*Kalyāṇa*	*Kalyāṇa*	*Kalyāni*	*Kalyāṇa*	*Kalyāna*	*Kalyāna*
67								,,					
68								,,					
69								,,					
70								,,					
71								,,					
72	*Kānarau*	*Kanharau*	*Kānharo*	*Kānharau*	*Kānarau*	*Kānarau*	*Kānaro*	*Kānharau*	*Kānharau*	*Kānharau*	*Kānharau*	*Kānharau*	*Kānarau*
73								,,					
74								,,					
75								,,					
76								,,					
77								,,					
78								,,					
79								,,					
80								,,					
81	*Kedārau*	*Kedārau*	*Kedāro*	*Kedārau*	*Kedārau*	*Kedārau*	*Kedārau*	*Kedārau*	*Kedārau*	*Kedārau*		*Kedārau*	*Kedāro*
82								,,					
83								,,					
84								,,					

automatically subsumed under the previous *rāga* heading. Thus it is impossible to tell (except from the secondary evidence of the *rāga saṃkhyā kavitta*) whether the absence of any individual *rāga* heading represents a scribal omission or a substantive difference in *rāga* allocation.

The distribution of *rāgas* accords with the specifications of the *rāga saṃkhyā kavitta* in only five of the sources collated here; even in these five (DEHJL) there is one minor divergence from the *kavitta*, in that Gauḍa is represented by Gauḍa-malāra. (The same is the case with FGK, which variously differ from the *kavitta's* specifications in other ways also.) Divergences from the specifications of the *kavitta* are as follows:

(a) MS A has Lalita for Vibhāsa (CP 1–6); C has Lalita from CP 2 (—6 or —13?: the folio bearing 6–8 in C is missing; Vilāvala may begin at CP 7, as in ABDEHIJKLM). K lacks a heading for the first six stanzas.

(b) Vilāvala is lacking in FG (folio missing in C).

(c) A and C have Gujarī for Devagandhāra (CP 29–35 in majority order, 19–27 in MS A order); GM have no heading here.

(d) F lacks Sāraṅga.

(e) ABCI lack Gauḍamalāra: of these, BCI include CP 56 in the previous group (Malāra), while A begins the Gaurī section with this stanza.

(f) C repeats the Gaurī heading at CP 59, and again at 63 (though this latter is *sec. m.* over a folio repair).

(g) B lacks Kalyāna.

(h) K lacks Kedārau.

The sample may be broadened by adding data given by Uṣā Gupta[1] in a survey of CP manuscripts. The first manuscript referred to by Gupta is our MS C (despite a discrepancy in library catalogue numbers); her second accords with our MS K; her third and fifth with our DEHJL; her fourth, seventh and eighth accord with our DEHJL but also lack Kedārau; her sixth accords with DEHJL but also lacks Kānharau.

Before considering the implications of the *rāga* sequence, it is relevant to record the existence of a similar sequence in the *vāṇī* of Hita Harivaṃśa's alleged associate, Svāmī Haridāsa. The *padas* there are headed by the following *rāgas*: Vibhāsa, Gaurī, Vibhāsa, Vilāvala, Vasanta, Sāraṅga, Malāra, Gaurī, Naṭa, Gauḍamalāra, Kalyāṇa, Avārau (?), Kānharau, Kedārau (R.D. Haynes p. 266).

The commentator Rasikalāla, when cross-referencing from his gloss on one stanza to a parallel context elsewhere in the *mūla*, refers to the latter context by *rāga* section rather than by *pada* number;[2] thus the

1. U. Gupta pp. 199-203.
2. Rasikalāla's commentary on CP 14 includes the following cross-reference :
tākaũ hõ ju kahaũ maramu tuma kaũ sudhi karavāi;
kedāre mẽ padu ju hai tāko bheda batāi. 79.
The commentator subsequently quotes from CP 82.6, from the Kedārau sequence.

rāga headings are seen as having some substantive structural function (although this has not become as formalized as it is in such texts as the *Ādi grantha*, where a new numbering sequence begins with each *rāga*[1]). The *rāga* groupings in the CP do not show any thematic or contextual coherence, except that the two *padas* under Vasanta, CP 27 and 28,[2] do have a specifically vernal theme, and the name of the rainy-season *rāga* Mal[l]āra is specifically linked to a monsoon context in 54.4. This latter reference is one of three instances in the text in which *rāga* names allocated to a particular section appear in the *mūla* itself:

36.4 *juvatini maṃḍala madhya syāmaghana* ***sāraga rāga*** *jamāyau;*[3]
54.4 *nava nuralī ju* ***malāra*** *naī gati śravana sunata āye ghana ghorī;*
57.17 *dŏu mili cācari gāvata* ***gauri rāga*** *alāpa.*

There are many contexts in which springtime and monsoon contexts and themes occur independently of the seasonal *rāga* classifications: these classifications do not, in other words, encompass all examples of the themes they describe. Nor do the *rāga* sections coincide with any other classifiable aspect of the stanzas' form except that, as has been shown in section VI.5, new *rāga* sequences coincide with a change of metre and tend to start with a stanza of longer than average length. The implication of this is that the *rāga* names were imposed on a pre-existing text, taking *some* note of seasonal themes in the text and possibly preferring longer stanzas to bear the *rāga* titles, but otherwise without regard for textual considerations. The basis for the *rāga* sequence must, therefore, be sought outside the text itself.

The usual context in which *rāgas* might be expected to constitute a coherent sequence is that of the literary *rāgamālā*. The *Pañcamasāra-saṃhitā*, dated A.D. 1440[4] and regarded as one of the earliest texts to give *rāga-rāginī* sequences, lists the following 'families'[5] (*rāgas* corresponding to those of the CP being given here in ***bold type***):

Rāga	*Rāginīs*
Mālava	Dhānuṣī [=***Dhanāśrī?***], Mālasī, Rāmakīrī, Sinduḍā, Aśvavārī [=***Āsāvarī***?],[6] Bhairavī.
Mallāra	Velāvalī [***Vilāvala***], Pūravī, Kānaḍā [=***Kānharo***], Mādhavī, Koḍā, Kedārikā [=***Kedāro***].
Śrī	Gāndhārī [=***Devagāndhāra***], Subhagā, ***Gaurī***, Kaumārikā, Veloyārī, Vairāgī.

1. W.H. McLeod p. 71.
2. 28.2 is one of three contexts where the word *basaṃta* appears (though *not* as a *rāga* name); the other two are 57.3 and 64.2.
3. The possibility that Sāraṅga may have a 'monsoon' connotation is discussed in a note to 36.4 *syāmaghana*.
4. E. te Nijenhuis p. 20.
5. S.C. Banerji p. 92.
6. *Var. lect. āśoārī* (*op.cit.*, p. 100).

Rāga	*Rāginīs*
Vasànta	Tuḍī [=***Toḍī***], Pañcamī, ***Lalitā***, Paṭhamañjarī, Gurjarī [=***Gujjarī***], Vibhāṣā [=***Vibhāsa***].
Hindola	Māyurī, Dīpikā, Deśakārī, Pāhiḍā, Vārāḍī, Mārāṭhī.
Karṇāta	Nāṭikā, Bhūpālī, Rāmakelī, Kāmodī, Kalyāṇī [=***Kalyāna***], Gatā.

Of the CP *rāgas*, only Sāranga and Gauḍa-malāra (for which cf. Mallāra) do not appear here. Comparison of this list with the CP sequence of *rāgas* seems to show that our text does not derive its *rāga* classifications *directly* from the *rāgamālā* tradition: but the CP's juxtapositioning of Vibhāsa with Lalita (and with Toḍī in MSS FG, perhaps also in MSS CD), of Āsāvarī with Dhanāśrī, and of Kānharo with Kedāro may represent a distant echo of *rāgamālā* order.

A more striking connexion is apparent between the CP's *rāga* sequence and the so-called 'time theory' of Indian music, which associates the performance of *rāgas* with particular times of day and night. This theory is the subject of much controversy, and hardly any two authorities or any two regional traditions (*gharānās*) agree on its exact application. The principles of the 'time theory' may here be outlined before its implications for the CP tradition are considered.

The earliest textual authority for the identification or *rāgas* with times of day or seasons of the year appears to be the *Saṅgītamakaranda* of Nārada (14th or 15th century),[1] wherein certain *rāgas* are allocated to broad time categories—morning, noon, afternoon, night; a similar system is found in the *Pañcamasārasaṃhitā*.[2] The allocation of times becomes rather more specific in later texts such as the *Saṅgītadarpaṇa* of Dāmodara (c. 1625)[3] and the *Saṅgītapārijāta* of Ahobala (c. 1665).[4] The most developed form of the theory is that propounded earlier this century by V.N. Bhātkhaṇḍe, who divides the day into two 12-hour periods (midnight to noon, noon to midnight), each of which is further divided into three sections.[5] The parent scale (*ṭhāṭa*) of a *rāga* determines the section to which a *rāga* belongs, while the location of its sonant (*vādī*) in the upper or lower tetrachord determines whether the *rāga* belongs to the first or second 12-hour period respectively. On the basis of this theory Bhātkhaṇḍe describes individual *rāgas* as belonging to a specific 'watch' (*prahara, pahara*). Bhātkhaṇḍe's theory has gained wide (but not universal) acceptance amongst Indian musicologists and musicians.

1. E. te Nijenhuis p. 20. According to Svāmī Prajñānānanda (p. 114, cited by E. te Nijenhuis, *loc.cit.*), the 'Nārada' to whom the *Saṅgītamakaranda* is attributed is not the same as the alleged author of the *Pañcamasārasaṃhitā*.
2. S.C. Banerji p. 84.
3. E. te Nijenhuis p. 27.
4. *Ibid.*, p. 28.
5. N.A. Jairazbhoy p. 62.

The table on pp. 321-322 shows the performance times variously ascribed to those *rāgas* which appear in manuscripts of the CP. It may be noticed that despite several exceptions, broad agreement as to the performance times of these *rāgas* exists between the authorities already mentioned and the findings of Fox-Strangways and Daniélou, representing the Poona and Benares *gharānās* respectively. Numerals in the table refer to the various watches of the day, designated on the following traditional basis:

1:	6 a.m.—	9 a.m.	5:	6 p.m.—	9 p.m.
2:	9 a.m.—	12 noon	6:	9 p.m.—	midnight
3:	12 noon—	3 p.m.	7:	midnight—	3 a.m.
4:	3 p.m.—	6 p.m.	8:	3 a.m.—	6 a.m.

(For the sake of clarity this table does not show variations in orthography. For the equivalent *rāga* names appearing in the *Pañcamasāra-saṃhitā*, see the *rāgamālā* list quoted above.)

Although it is not known when the *rāgas* associated with the CP were first allocated to the text, the fact that they appear in the earliest manuscript collated here shows them to be chronologically more closely related to the Sanskrit treatises referred to above than to modern texts and traditions of musical theory. That the actual scales of many *rāgas* have changed considerably over the last three centuries or so has been shown by N.A. Jairazbhoy on the basis of the (16th or 17th century?) *Rāgataraṅginī* of Locana Kavi.[1] It follows that the traditional performance times may have become associated with the *rāgas*' names *per se*, rather than with actual modal characteristics of the *rāgas* themselves;[2] thus performance time is just one among many such extra-musical associations which form part of the traditional *rāgadhyāna*, and is at some remove from the musical character of the individual *rāga*.[3]

The time-sequence of the CP *rāgas* has been noted by P.D. Mītal[4] and by G.R. Niemann, who remarks that the *rāgas* 'more or less follow Rādhā and Kṛṣṇa through the day and seasons.'[5] The seasonal sequence is hardly borne out, however, since the only *rāgas* to which Niemann is able to attribute seasonal associations are Vibhāsa (autumn), Toḍī (late spring), Vasanta (spring), Malāra (rainy season): this hardly constitutes a sequence. The association with times of the day and night, however,

1. N.A. Jairazbhoy pp. 92 ff.
2. I owe this suggestion to Dr. D.R. Widdess.
3. The *rāga* names do not, for the most part, have any intrinsic sense of 'time of day'. Rather, they appear largely to derive etymologically from the iconographic/romantic personifications of *rāgas* and *rāginīs* in the *rāgadhyānas*; cf., for example, descriptions of Vibhāṣā as *samastabhāṣākuśalā*, and of Gandhārī as *gandhamālyāni*, in the *Pañcamasārasaṃhitā* (S.C. Banerji pp. 96, 94).
4. P.D. Mītal 1975: 482.
5. G.R. Niemann 1977: 30.

Table 5: Performance times of the CP Rāgas

Rāga	*Saṅgīta-makaranda*[1]	*Saṅgīta-darpaṇa*[2]	*Saṅgīta-pārijāta*[3]	*Pañcamasāra-saṃhitā*[4]	Fox-Strangways[5]	Daniélou[6]	Bhātkhaṇḍe[7]	*Rāgakośa*[8]
(Lalita)	Morning	Dawn	Any time	Morning	—	Dawn (before sunrise)	Dawn	Dawn
Vibhāsa	—	—	Dawn	Morning	Dawn	Dawn (at sunrise)	Dawn	Dawn
Vilāvala	Morning	Dawn	2-3	Noon	—	2	Dawn	Dawn
Toḍī	—	2	—	Morning	2	1	2	2
Āsāvarī	3-4	—	—	Noon	3	1	2	2
Dhanāśrī	Morning	Dawn	Dawn	Noon	4	4	3	3
Vasanta	Morning	Dawn	Dawn	Spring	8	Spring	8/Spring	8
(Gujarī)	Morning	Dawn	2-3	Morning	—	1	—	—
Devagandhāra	Morning	[Gāndhārī] 2	3-4	Evening	—	—	Dawn	2
Sāraṅga	—	3-midnight	3-4	—	Noon	Noon	[Śuddha-sāranga] 2	5

1. O.C. Gangoli, vol. I pp. 83-4.
2. K. Vasudeva Sastri (ed.) pp. 28-9.
3. Ahobala Paṇḍita pp. 98-9.
4. S.C. Banerji p. 84.
5. A.H. Fox-Strangways, chart facing p. 151.
6. A. Daniélou: citations of performance times taken from *rāga* descriptions s.v.
7. V.N. Bhātkhaṇḍe: citations of performance times taken from *rāga* descriptions s.v.
8. R. Gupta 'Vasant': citations of performance times taken from *rāga* descriptions s.v.

Rāga	*Saṅgīta-makaranda*	*Saṅgīta-darpaṇa*	*Saṅgīta-pārijāta*	*Pañcamasāra-samhitā*	Fox-Strangways	Daniélou	Bhatkhaṇḍe	*Ragakosa*
Malāra	Morning	[Mallārī] Dawn	Any time	Any time/ rains[9]	[Myāchā-malhāra] 3	Rains	[Megha-mallāra] Rains	6
Gauḍa malāra	Afternoon	—	—	—	—	Rains	Rains	Rains
Gaurī	—	3-midnight	—	Evening	4	—	Evening	Evening
Kalyāṇa	—	—	5-6	—	5	5	5	5
Kānharau	—	—	—	Evening	[Kānaḍā] Midnight	—	[Darbārī-kānaḍa] Midnight	[Darbārī-kānaḍā] Midnight
Kedārau	—	—	—	Evening	[Kedāra-Kalyāna] 6	5	5	5

9. *Var. lect. sarvasu sarvadā/varṣāsu sarvadā* (the latter is preferred). S.C. Banerji p. 85.

is of considerable significance, since it may indicate that the *rāgas* were allocated to the text in order to apportion it for the purposes of *aṣṭayāma sevā*, the worship of the deity through the various watches of the 24-hour period.

The requirements of *aṣṭayāma sevā* are laid down in such sectarian texts as the modern *Śrīhita rādhāvallabha aṣṭayāma* compiled by Yugalavallabh Gosvāmī. This text describes a sequence of seven sacraments in which the deity is worshipped with lights (*āratī*) after the ritual presentation of food (*bhoga*). It is during the *āratī* rite that the temple congregation is able to take *darśana* of the deity, an act which constitutes the principle expression of devotion on the part of the devotee. The correspondence between the number of *rāgas* given in most manuscripts of the CP (14) and the number of ritual services in the *Rādhāvallabhī* pattern of *sevā* (7) suggests an allocation of two *rāgas* to each sacrament: this remains conjectual, however, since there is no apparent connexion between the number of *padas* under each *rāga* group and the activities prescribed for each sacrament. The apparent emergence of a secondary time-sequence from (approximately) *rāga* Vasanta (see table above) may perhaps relate to the *utthāpana* sacrament at which the deity is roused from the siesta which divides his day into two parts. This conjecture, too, must remain unproven, because the CP is no longer used in straight-through sequence as the daily liturgy for sectarian worship; present-day performances by *samāja* singers in the Rādhāvallabha temple and elsewhere mainly follow the four-volume anthology of sectarian verse entitled *Śṛṃgāra rasa sāgara*,[1] which includes stanzas from the CP amongst others by different poets.

The *Śrīhita rādhāvallabha aṣṭayāma* describes in some detail the mental attitudes and ritual procedures to be adopted during *aṣṭayāma sevā*. These attitudes and procedures derive from the imagined 'activities' of the deity through the day—his eating, resting, *nikuñja līlā* and so on. The times prescribed for each part of the ritual refer to the hours appropriate to each stage in the devotee's daily worship, and do not necessarily correspond to the relatively short periods for which the deity is presented for *darśana* in the temple. The seven divisions of daily *sevā* are as follows:[2]

1.	*Maṃgala samaya*	5.00—7.00 a.m.
2.	*Śṛṃgāra samaya*	8.15—10.30 a.m.
3.	*Rājabhoga samaya*	10.30—11.00 a.m.

1. Tulsī Dās, Bābā (ed.) This anthology is ordered according to annual festivals (*utsava*); where *padas* from the CP are included they usually retain the *rāga* headings from the CP *mūla*, regardless of the *rāgas* allocated to their neighbours in the anthology. One short section entitled *Śrī rādhāvallabhajī kau aṣṭayāma sevāgāna* (Vol. I, pp. 412-24) gives collections of *padas* for use at each *āratī*; here, exceptionally, no *rāgas* are allocated to the stanzas. Only 5 stanzas from the CP appear in this section: under *Maṅgalā* are CP 13, 25, and 10; under *Śṛṅgāra* is CP 9; and under *Saīna* (=*Śayana*) is CP 76.
2. Yugalavallabh Gosvāmī pp. 1-5.

4. *Utthāpana*	4.00—6.00 p.m.
5. *Sāyaṃkāla*	Evening
6. *Śayana bhoga*	1½ hours after *sandhyā ārati* (=No. 5)
7. *Śayana samaya*	9.30 p.m.—4.00 a.m.

The term *aṣṭayāma sevā* in Rādhāvallabhī tradition, relating to a sequence of seven (and not eight) sacraments, is presumably to be interpreted as referring to 'round-the-clock' service rather than to a division of the day into eight equal *yāmas.* In the Vallabhī tradition, however, (from which the concept of *aṣṭayāma sevā* was probably borrowed) there are indeed eight rituals in the daily round[1]—though here too there is no direct correspondence between ritual and three-hour portions of the day. The following list of *rāgas* used in Vallabhī *sevā*[2] shows a striking correspondence to those found in the CP: 10 of the CP *rāgas* (here shown in **bold type**) appear in the Vallabhī list, and in much the same order.

	Time	*Rāga*
1. *Maṃgalā*	6.30—7.00 a.m.	**Lalita,** Bhairava, **Vibhāsa**
2. *Śṛṃgāra*	7.30—8.00 a.m.	**Bilāvala,** Rāmakalī Guṇakali
3. *Gvāla*	8.30—9.00 a.m.	**Devagaṃdhāra, Toḍī, Āsāvarī**
4. *Rājabhoga*	10.00—10.30 a.m.	**Āsāvarī, Sāraṃga**
5. *Utthāpana*	3.30—4.00 p.m.	**Dhanāśrī**, Bhīmapalāsī
6. *Saṃdhyā bhoga*	4.30—5.00 p.m.	**Gaurī**, *Pūriyā*, *Pūrvī*
7. *Saṃdhyā āratī*	5.30—6.00 p.m.	Śrī, Jaitasrī
8. *Śayana*	6.30—7.00 p.m.	Yamana, Kāmoda, Vihāga **Kedārā**

This correspondence between the CP *rāga* sequence and contemporary Vallabhī practice supports the hypothesis that the CP *rāga* order reflects an apportionment of the text for the purposes of *aṣṭayāma sevā.* Discussion in the above pages suggests that this apportionment may itself derive ultimately from the *rāgamālā* model.

(*ii*) *The Structure of the Text in the Commentary Tradition*

The most ambitious attempt at imposing a structure on the text is that of the commentator Premadāsa: this envisages a sequence of 23 'series' (*śṛṃkhalā*) running through the 84 stanzas.[3] These series do not,

1. The additional Vallabhī sacrament is *gvāla*, a period during which Kṛṣṇa is imagined to be in the pastures tending the herds of cattle. This concept is not favoured by the Rādhāvallabhī tradition, which generally discounts the *gopāla* aspect of Kṛṣṇa's character.
2. P.D. Mītal 1975: 469.
3. The *śṛṃkhalās* are designated in the headings to individual stanzas; thus the *ābhāsa* to CP 1 is preceded by the words *atha prathama pada. prathama āṭha pada kī śṛṃkhalā hai.*

however, represent discrete categories of theme or of any other classifiable criterion, except in the case of *śṛṃkhalās* 7 and 16 which correspond to the Vasanta and Malāra *rāga* sections respectively. 13 of the 23 *śṛṃkhalās* comprise only two stanzas each, and a full 14 individual stanzas are not accommodated by the arrangement. In an apologia for Premadāsa's system the editors of his text try to show that each *śṛṃkhalā* is a structural unit built up around the core theme of *sajjā* (<*śayyā*, implying a *nikuñja līlā* context);[1] but the variety of thematic combinations is wide, and the looseness of structure found in the various *śṛṃkhalās* shows Premadāsa's system to be a rather artless attempt at imposing order on the amorphous collection.

The commentator Rasikalāla, who lays great emphasis on the temporal context (*samaya*) of the *padas*, attempts to forge a narrative link between successive themes. This is readily achieved between stanzas of like content (which are sometimes glossed together in little sequences sharing a common introduction, as for example CP 20-23, 39-40, 41-42, 52-53) but elsewhere calls for a more blatant imposition of a bridging device. Thus CP 15, which describes the *suratānta* beauty of Rādhā, is linked with the previous stanza (identified by Rasikalāla as a context wherein a disguised Kṛṣṇa seeks entry to Rādhā's bathing place) by a sequence of introductory couplets beginning with the following:

pāchai pada ke samai me   pyārī ke ḍhiga syāma;
lai āī ālī jahā̃   majjana kari uṭhi bhāma. 2.
vaha bāsara bītyau tahā̃   uhi bikāsa ke mā̃jha;
hasata lasata vaha kuṃja mẽ   chinaka mā̃ha bhaī sā̃jha. 3.

This is clearly a rather ingenuous method of providing a narrative continuity, and underlines the lack of any true thematic organisation in the text as a whole. Lokanātha, by contrast, is generally content to identify individual contexts without imposing any structural scheme on the collection: his contextualizations comprise extremely formulaic descriptions of the various *nikuñjas* conceived as the settings for the various stanzas, oddly classified by the number of their entrances (e.g. CP 5 *hīrana kī bhūma mahala pāṃcadvārī* (App. I)). Dharaṇīdharadāsa's *ābhāsas* to each stanza consist of the briefest contextualizations, usually within a single *dohā*. Printed text H also prefaces each stanza with a contextualization, as quoted for CP 1 in section II.1.(i). Finally may be mentioned a classification proposed by the eighteenth century author Rūpalāla Gosvāmī (quoted by Vijayendra Snātak[2] from an unspecified source): this is a mere listing of the 84 stanzas under 11 thematic headings, and implies no structural arrangement or thematic order.

1. Vijaypāl Siṃha and Candrabhān Rāvat (eds.) pp. 49-57.
2. Vijayendra Snātak 1968: 294.

(iii) *Formal and Thematic Elements of Composition*

Although the overall pattern of the text in terms of form and content is one of a more or less random distribution of stanzas, some limited coherence appears in sequences of stanzas sharing similar metrical forms (as discussed in section VI.5) and in sequences of shared theme. Examples of the latter are in CP 3, 4, 5, 6, all based on the dawn *suratānta* conceit (and hence showing a connexion with the 'dawn' *rāgas* Lalita and Vibhāsa allocated to this section?), CP 21, 22, 23, sharing *naina* motifs, and CP 61, 62, 63, 64, sharing a *rāsa*/flute context. It can be argued, of course, that such patterns are likely to be thrown up, under the law of averages, as chance juxtapositions in a random order; and alongside such sequences there are places in the text where themes change with every new stanza. More formal correspondences between stanzas occasionally yield more definite groupings unlikely to be born of chance: examples are CP 27 and 28 with shared vernal theme and *dhamāra*-song connexion (discussed in the first annotation to CP 27), CP 39 and 40 with shared *māna* theme and *-avana* rhyme, CP 74 and 75 with shared *māna* theme and anomalous short first couplet with *kah- ika bāta* rhetoric. Since there is no specific evidence of such correspondences representing, historically, pairings of *mūla* with pastiche or commentatorial expansion, it seems that here at least we have evidence of an identity of origin shared by specific stanzas.

Problems in assessing the significance of repeated literary formulae have already been alluded to in the discussion of the *Sūrasāgara* attribution. Even bearing in mind the danger of regarding the sharing of textual phrases as proving a common source, however, the patterns produced by a tabulation of shared formulae in the CP do point to a possible dichotomy of sources for certain homogenous sections of the text. The following tabulation, which aims to be a fairly complete list (but has *not* been compiled with a computer search) shows that textual phrases from a central portion of the CP comprising stanzas 39 to 49 very rarely show correspondences with the remainder of the text, while CP 1-38 and 50-84 very frequently contain phrases which are repeated either within these individual groups or over the two groups as a whole. Thus four distinct categories of formulaic repetitions can be perceived:

(*a*) correspondences within CP 1-38;
(*b*) correspondences of CP 1-38 with 50-84;
(*c*) correspondences within CP 39-49 (one only);
(*d*) correspondences within CP 50-84.

The only exception to this in the tabulated data is the correspondence 43.3/82.4.

(*a*) 6.4 *hita haribaṁśa rasika rādhāpati*
9.6 " " " "
36.12 " " " "

(*b*)	7.2	*suni abhūta bhūtala para jorī*
	54.6	*cira jīvau bhūtala yaha jorī*
	70.8	*bhūtala para saṃtata avicala jorī*
(*b*)	7.6	*nībī baṃdhana mocata*
	30.11	,, ,, ,,
	72.9	,, ,, ,,
(*b*)	7.8	*cibuka sucāru praloi prabodhata*
	75.4	*ve mṛdu cibuka* ,, ,,
(*b*)	7.9	*neti neti bacanāmṛta*
	72.10	,, ,, ,,
(*b*)	10.1	*aṃga aṃga parama mādhurī*
	29.2	*ãga aṃga mādhurī*
	69.2	*mādhurī ãga aṃge*
	78.4	*mādhurī ãga ãga*
(*b*)	11.4	*kiśalaya dala racita saina*
	76.1	,, ,, ,, ,,
(*b*)	15.2	*haũ tosaũ kahata hārī*
	58.4	,, ,, ,, ,,
(*a*)	15.6	*suni śravana bacana mudita mana calī haribaṃśa bhavana musakātī*
	20.8	*hita haribaṃśa bacana suni bhāmini bhavana calī musakātī*
(*b*)	16.4	*palu palu ghaṭati*
	83.4	*ghaṭata palu palu*
(*a*)	16.5	*hita haribaṃśa calī ati ātura*
	38.5	,, ,, ,, ,,
(*b*)	19.2	*juvatini aṃsa diya bhujadaṃḍana*
	61.2	*juvati aṃsana para diye bimala bhujadaṃḍana*
(*a*)	19.3	*sarada bimala nabha caṃda birājai*
	24.2	,, ,, ,, ,, *birājata*
(*a*)	19.10	*aṃga sudhaṃga diṣāvata*
	36.6	,, ,, *diṣāyau*
(*a*)	19.13	*hita haribaṃśa magana mana syāmā*
	24.6	,, ,, ,, ,, ,,
(*a*)	20.5	*adhara biṃba ṣaṃḍita maṣi maṃḍita gaṃḍa*
	33.4	*dasana basana* ,, ,, ,, ,,
(*b*)	22.4	*kahata na banai*
	69.2	,, ,, ,,
(*b*)	25.4	*rahasi haribaṃśa hita*
	50.5	,, ,, ,,
	67.7	,, ,, ,,
(*b*)	26.6	*ubhai kalahaṃsa haribaṃśa*
	68.8	,, ,, ,,
(*b*)	27.17	*haṃsa haṃsinī samāja*
	76.4	,, ,, ,,

(*b*) 29.1 *braja nava taruni kadaṃba*
52.2 „ „ „ „
(*b*) 30.3 *sītala maṃda sugaṃdha*
57.7 „ „ „
63[iii].4 „ „ „
(*b*) 30.6 *bhājana kanaka bibidhi madhu pūrita*
72.7 *madhu pūrita bhājana kanaka birājata*
(*a*) 30.8 *prītama pāni uraja bara parasata*
32.5 *ve bhuja pīna payodhara parasata*[1]
(*a*) 31.1 *āju ati rājata*
33.1 „ *bana* „
(*a*) 31.6 *mili gāvata sura maṃdara kala ghora*
35.3 „ „ „ „ „ „
(*b*) 33.2 *uṭhe unīde bhora*
57.12 „ „ „
(*b*) 33.6 *surata samudra jhakora*
70.2 „ „ *jhakorī* (cf. 43.3/82.4)
(*b*) 36.2 *pulina pabitra subhaga jamunā taṭa*
64.2 „ „ „ „ „
(*b*) 36.8 *tātāthei-tāthei dharati nautana gati*
68.7 *tatta thei thei karata gati ba nautana dharata*
(*a*) 37.2 *to binu kũvari*
39.4 „ „ „
(*a*) 37.8 *surata sūra ranabīra*
38.6 „ „ *brajabāla*
(*b*) 38.6 *lai rāṣe giri kuca bica suṃdara*
66.19 „ „ *ura mā̃jha*
(*c*) 40.6 *hita haribaṃśa mile rasa laṃpaṭa*
49.6 „ „ *lāla* „ „
43.3 *guna siṃdhu jhakorī*
82.4 *rasa* „ „ (cf. 33.6/70.2)
(*d*) 57.15 *bājata madhura mṛdaṃga*
65.3 „ *mṛdu* „
(*d*) 60.1 *kahā kahaũ ina nainani kī bāta*
73.1 „ „ *nainani kī bātẽ*
(*d*) 68.2 *sarada kī jāminī*
71.5 „ „ „
83.4 „ „ „
(*d*) 70.6 *sithala bhaī kaṭi ḍorī*
77.5 „ *kaṭi bā̃dhana*
84.2 „ „ *kī ḍorī*
(*d*) 73.6 *haṃsakala gāminī*
81.6 „ „ „

1. Similar collocations occur at 11.5, 49.5, 50.4, 62.6, and 66.7, but these lack the specific alliterative correspondences of the passages quoted.

The evidence of this data, although not conclusively revealing distinct strata of accretion, does suggest that the central section of the text has some degree of independence from the remainder. A thematic homogeneity over a similar section must also be considered here: it is in approximately the same sequence that the predominance of Rādhā becomes established for the first time in the text. *Padas* earlier in the CP mostly have themes based either on *dampati* themes (*passim*), or on Kṛṣṇa alone (CP 13, 29): but the protracted thematic sequence CP 37-42 introduces themes in which Kṛṣṇa is dependent on Rādhā and suffering in her absence; and CP 43, 45 and 48 are descriptions of Rādhā alone, while CP 47 returns to the theme of Kṛṣṇa's *viraha*.

If this evidence, admittedly circumstantial, is indeed symptomatic of a diversity of sources, then the implication is that the loosely identifiable central section of the text represents an accretion to a pre-existing collection of *padas*: the inclusion in the early collection of stanzas of imperfect metrical composition (itself allowing further degeneration in the manuscripts) may be evidence of its having derived in part from oral tradition,[1] while the 'accretion' may have been composed on a more formal and standardized literary base as a complement to achieve the desired quota of 84 stanzas.[2] The argument against the reverse hypothesis—that the beginning and end parts are accretions onto a central nucleus—is that it is the central section of the text which establishes the *developed* sectarian priorities in theme and content, as relayed by the commentators.

After the establishment of themes with Rādhā predominant in CP 37-42, a freer mixture of themes subsists throughout the rest of the text. Rādhā continues to feature as protagonist in many stanzas, especially in the 50's (e.g. CP 52, 53, 55), while a temporary return to more 'orthodox' *rāsapañcādhyāyī* themes (with Rādhā absent, or peripheral to the main action) follows in the 60's (e.g. CP 60, 61, 63-65). The final stanzas introduce a new combination of conceits, namely a conflation of *rāsa* and *nikuñja* contexts: earlier in the text, a degree of formal separation of these two contexts has been maintained within the individual stanza (though the two may occur consecutively, as in CP 10-11, respectively showing *rāsa* and *nikuñja* themes).

Extant textual references to certain stanzas in the CP give an earlier attestation of these stanzas than is available through the CP manu-

1. The relatively high number of four-line stanzas in the beginning and end sections may reflect a connexion with the *dhrupada* style of song, for which, as discussed in VI.3. (x), a four-line stanza usually provides the text.

2. The special significance attached to the number '84' in Hindu thought obviously lends a holistic unity to the text; since titles including the word *caurāsī* have been shown to be relatively late, however, Snātak's argument (1975: 32) that the very existence of the title constitutes proof of Harivaṃśa's authorship of the whole work is untenable.

scripts themselves (whose *raison d'être*, after all, is to promote a consolidated corpus). The *Sevaka vāṇi* (*SV*) of Dāmodaradāsa 'Sevaka', and the exegetical prose work *Siddhānta vicāra līlā* (*SVL*) of Dhruvadāsa both refer to the CP, either in literal quotations or in close paraphrases. Citations from the *SV*, the earlier of the two texts according to sectarian dating,[1] do include one reference to the central section of the CP (CP 49), but since this reference is the sole example among 15 cited passages, the evidence of the *SV* is not wholly incompatible with the hypothesis that the central section has a later origin than the rest of the text. The nine citations in *SVL* show a more even distribution over the CP *mūla*. In the following transcriptions from the two texts[2] quotations or paraphrases from the CP are given in bold type.

SV 8.8.2; **CP 7.8**

āpa viloki *hṛdaya kiyau māna* ***cibukka sucāru praloya*** *manāī.*

SV 4.3.2-3 *and* 8.8.1; **CP 31.3-4**

aṃsana para bhuja diye vilokata *tṛpita na suṃdara mukha avalokata;*
indu vadana dīkhata vivi orā *cāru sulocana* ***tṛṣita cakorā.***
bhuja aṃsana dīne viloki *rahe* ***mukha candra*** *ubhai madhupāna karāī.*

SV 16.4.1; **CP 32.4**

śrī harivaṃśa ju krīḍahī ***dampati rasa samatūla.***

SV 4.10.1-2; **CP 34.1-2**

kahī nita keli rasa khela vṛndāvipina ***kum̐ja te kum̐ja ḍolani*** *bakhānī;*
paṭa na parasaṃta nikasaṃta vīthinu *saghana prema vihvala su nahi deha mānī.*

SV 4.11.4; **CP 36.8** and **68.7**

tatta theī theī karata gati va nūtana dharata
rāsa rasa racita harivaṃśa bānī.

SV 4.5.2; **CP 49.2**

pariraṃbhana cumbana rasa kelī ***viharata kūvara kaṃṭha bhuja melī.***

SV 4.3.3; **CP 57.23-24**

kabahūka nirmita tarala hīḍolā jhūlata phūlata karata kalolā.

SV 4.5.3; **CP 63[*iii*].1-2**

sundara ***rāsa racyau vana mām̐hī*** *yamunā pulina* ***kalpataru chām̐hī.***

SV 8.7.3; **CP 66.10**

satvara uṭhe mahāmadhu pīvata *mādhurī vāṇī mere mana bhāī.*

SV 4.4.2; **CP 70.1**

āja sam̐bhārata nāhina gorī *aṅga aṅga chavi kahaū su thorī.*

SV 16.5.1; **CP 75.1**

kāhe kaum̐ ḍārata *bhāminī* ***haum̐ jū kahata ika bāta.***

1. The dates of Dhruvadāsa and Dāmodaradāsa are discussed on pp. 8 and 10 respectively.

2. SV references are from Lalitā Caraṇ Gosvāmī (ed.) 1975; SVL references are from Lalitā Caraṇ Gosvāmī (ed.) 1971.

SV 16.7.2.; **CP 75.2**

prāna ravana so̐kata karata binu āgasa *aparādha.*

SV 16.6.1-2; **CP 75.3-4**

ve citavata tuva vadana tū nija carana nihārata;

ve mṛdu cibuka pralovahĩ tū kara so̐kara ṭarāta.

SV 8.7.2; **CP 76.3**

nātha viramma viramma kahī *taba so rati taisī dhaū kaise bhulāī.*

* * *

SVL p. 46; **CP 1.1**

jo bāta priyā jū kaū bhāvai, soī inakaū bhāvai. tahā̃ śrī jī kī bānī. **joī joī pyārau karai soī mohĩ bhāvai bhāvai mohī joī soī soī karai pyāre.**

SVL p. 48; **CP 8.3**

tana mana kī bṛtti jaba prema rasa mẽ thakai taba āśakta kahiye. tahā̃ śrī jī kī bānī. **bīdhayau mohana mṛga sakata cali na rī.**

SVL pp. 49-50; **CP 31.4**

nitya china china prīti rasa siṃdhu tẽ taraṃga rucike uṭhata rahata haĩ naye naye. tahā̃ śrī svāmī jī ko pada. jaba jaba dekhaū terau mukha taba taba nayau nayau lāgata.[1] *aru śrī jī kī bānī.* **karata pāna rasamatta paraspara locana triṣita cakora.**

SVL p. 50; **CP 31.8**

yā prema kī sūkṣma gati hai. khāi aura tripita hoi aura. tahā̃ śrī jī kī bānī. **jai śrī hita harivaṃśa lāla lalanā mili hiyo sirāvata mora.** *yaha sāra kau sāra.*

SVL p. 46; **CP 41.1**

priyā jū kau aṃga aṃga chā̃ḍi aura thauṛa mana na calai prīti aisī hai. tahā̃ śrī jū kī bānī. **prīti kī rīti raṃgīlauī jānai.**

SVL pp. 52-53; **CP 59.5-6**

yaha siddhāṃta kari rākhyau hai. tahā̃ śrī jū kī bānī. **jai śrī hita haribaṃśa prapaṃca baṃca saba kāla byāla kau khāyo;**
yaha jiya jāni śyāma śyāmā pada kamala saṃgī sira nāyau.

SVL p.47; **CP 60.1-2** and **82.5**

jaba jaba ṭhaūra tẽ caṃcalatā chuṭai taba āsakti ke rasa mẽ aṭakai. tahā̃ śrī jī kī bānī. **kahā kahaū ina nainani kī bāta.**
ye ali priyā bādana ambuja rasa aṭake anata na jāta. *aru.* **caṃcala rasika madhupa mohana mana rākhe kanaka kamala kuca korī.** *ityādi.*

SVL p. 49; **CP 60.5-6**

aru deha hū̃ apanī nyārī nāhĩ sahi sakata yaha bhī biraha mānata haĩ. tahā̃ kī bāta śrī gusā̃ī jū gāī. tahā̃ śrī jī kī bānī. **śruti para kaṃja dṛgaṃjana kuca bica mṛgamada hvai na samāta. jai śrī hita harivaṃśa nābhi sara jalacara jā̃cata sā̃vala gāta.**

1. The reference to *śrī svāmī jī ko pada* is to Svāmī Haridāsa, *Kelimāla* 34.1 (Prabhudayāl Mītal 1961: 78).

SVL p. 46; **CP 76.3**

śrī priyā jū bilāsa karaĩ saba lāla jū ke heta aura lāla jū jāmẽ lāḍilī jū sukha pāvaĩ soī karaĩ apane chāha kachū nāhī. tahā̃ bhara keli mahāmadana ke sukha rasa mẽ lāla jū ke bacana. tahā̃ śrī jī kī bānī. ***virama virama nātha baḍata barā bihāra rī.***

4. Sectarian Interpretation of the Themes of the Text

Previous sections of this chapter have hinted at a possible diversity of sources for the 84 stanzas, and although such diversity cannot be proved, the hypothesis stands that the text as transmitted through extant manuscripts may represent the work of more than one author. The commentators, needless to say, work on the assumption that the CP is an integral text deriving directly from the inspiration of Hita Harivaṃśa, and the reverence with which they regard Harivaṃśa—fountainhead of the Rādhāvallabhī tradition—itself becomes a cohesive force in the transmission of the text. The most urgent motivation behind their interpretations of the stanzas is to mould them in accordance with developed sectarian attitudes, and to play down any references which have lost favour since the time of the *padas'* original composition or compilation. For the most part the commentators do not resort to the wilful invention of false etymologies in order to achieve a forced sense from a straightforward context (though examples do occur—see for example the first note to CP 59), nor do the conventional contexts of the CP give much scope for a dramatic adjustment of themes: but the characteristically ambiguous syntax of BrBh verse often allows the commentators to pursue their own interpretations without resorting to artifice, and by assimilating one context to another they are able to side-step the few unfavoured motifs which present obstacles to a sectarian reading of the text. The rather petulant charge of 'wearisome prolixity', which Growse (1883: 208) levels at the commentaries of Rasik. and Lok., disallows the sectarian prerogative to extract as much *rasa* from each context as it may yield and implies an unreasonable expectation of a literal rendering of the *mūla*; while it would clearly be wrong to look to sectarian *ṭikās* for an objective reading, analysis of the *modus operandi* of the commentators does provide a useful insight into the transmission of the text, complementary to that which is gained from analysis of the language of the text as represented in the manuscripts.

M. Corcoran's analysis (p. 78 ff) of the thematic content of selected BrBh texts draws a distinction between sectarian literature, with its pre-occupation with *nitya vihāra*, and non-sectarian literature, which follows more closely the mythological structure of the *Purāṇas*. The CP falls into the former category, but nevertheless contains a number of features which the sectarian (i.e. Rādhāvallabhī) commentators regard as still too 'mythological' in tone, and commentatorial treatment of such references shows an attempted assimilation to 'approved' Rādhāvallabhī priorities. CP 63, which retails the central elements of the *rāsapañcā-dhyāyī* section of the *Bhāgavata purāṇa*, provides the clearest example of this process. The setting of the stanza, with river, tree, cows, birds, deer and deities (and lack of mention of Rādhā) closely reflects the *Bhāgavata purāṇa* account. Of course, a degree of selectivity has already been involved in the compilation of the CP by admitting the *rāsa* context itself while omitting adjacent motifs, such as the *gopīs' viraha* on Kṛṣṇa's disappearance and the *līlānukaraṇa* which ensues: the poet (or compiler) has had the freedom to pick and choose those parts of the *carita* which best evoke appropriate sentiment, without having to commit himself as to the theological implications of the precise narrative contexts from which his chosen motifs derive. A specific example of an omitted episode is that in which a *gopī* who is unable to join the *rāsa* achieves *mukti* through the great intensity of her *viraha*:[1] despite being popular in vernacular versions such as the *Sūrasāgara*[2], this motif is not harmonious with developed Rādhāvallabhī priorities[3] and does not find a place in the CP versions.

The very appearance of the *rāsa* episode motivates Rasik., often the least catholic of the CP commentators, to assert a distinction between two forms of Kṛṣṇa. In his introductory couplets to CP 63 Rasik. explains that Kṛṣṇa, having first obtained sanction from Rādhā, manifests a *vijaya rūpa*[4] to perform the *rāsa* with the *gopīs* (for their benefit), while his *nija rūpa* remains lying with Rādhā in the *nija mandira*.[5] The birth

1. F. Hardy (p. 502) points out that the *Bhāgavata* discusses the theological implications of this episode (which emphasizes the potency of *viraha*).

2. E.g. *SS* 1625/1007.

3. Later Rādhāvallabhī authors regard the *viraha* born of prolonged absence as a *sthūla* concept when compared to the constant apprehension of absence felt during union. Thus Dhruvadāsa, in the *Sidhānta vicāra līlā*, asserts that depictions of *sthūla viraha* (whose episodic nature is contrary to the sectarian conception of divine *prema* as outside space and time) exist solely to initiate the first stages of an understanding of the more subtle conception of *prema* and *viraha:*

> *yā prema mẽ na sthūla prema kī samāī na sthūla viraha kī samāī na māna kī. ekarasa yaha prema hī viraha rūpa hai...jo koū kahai ki māna viraha mahāpuruṣana gāyau hai so sadācāra ke liye. aurani ke samujhāibe kaũ kahyau hai. pahale sthūla prema samajhai taba āge calai.*
> (Lalitā Caraṇ Gosvāmī (ed.) 1971: 49.)

4. Lexical meanings of *vijaya* listed in *MW* include a number of references to Kṛṣṇa, including the hour and also the lunar day of his birth: these senses may intend a specific reference to Kṛṣṇa as *avatāra* as opposed to *aprakaṭa* divine principle. *MW* also records an attestation of *vijaya* as meaning 'a kind of flute', perhaps relevant in this *rāsa* context.

5. Rasik.: *priyā āgyā pāike bije rūpa pragaṭāya;*
tahā̃ dhāi saba ke manahi āsā pūrī jāi. 18.
nija sarūpa āpuna tahā̃ rahe ju pyārī pāsa;
pauḍhe seja subhāi dou nija maṃdira āvāsa. 19.

in Kṛṣṇa's mind of the notion of a *rāsa* is designated an *apūrava bāta*, which Kṛṣṇa dares not at first mention to Rādhā, and which can be arranged only through the offices of the *nija sakhī* (=Harivaṃśa, as discussed below).[1] Having fulfilled the desire of the *gopīs* (for whom the *rāsa* is the fruit of many lives' devotion[2]) the *vijaya rūpa* is reabsorbed into the *nija rūpa*, as are all *prakaṭa* forms of Kṛṣṇa.[3] Rasik. further explains that *līlās* associated with the various (mythical/geographical) locations of Vraja are the province of the *vijaya rūpa*, and he makes a clear distinction between this and the eternal nature of the *nitya vihāra* aspect of Rādhā and Kṛṣṇa's *keli*.[4] The determination with which this interpretation is pursued by Rasik. shows a fundamental distinction to be perceived between *rāsa* and *nikuñja* contexts; and change in context is reflected in Rasik.'s gloss by a change in form, as the commentary switches from the usual *dohā* to *arilla* metre for the paraphrase of CP 63.

With the exception of Dhar., who mentions the *pañcādhyāyī* and thereby actually acknowledges the *Purāṇa* origins of the *rāsa* episode,[5] the other commentators are equally determined to re-interpret the context of CP 63. (Dhar.'s assertion that meditation on the *rāsa* described by Harivaṃśa has a redemptive power may itself be regarded as marking it off from *nitya vihāra* contexts.) Prem.'s *ābhāsa* insists, in the face of the *mūla*, that Kṛṣṇa's fluting calls Rādhā to the *rāsa*;[6] and Lok., adding that it is to overcome Rādhā's petulance that Kṛṣṇa calls her with flute and not voice, assimilates the whole *rāsa* episode to a *māna* context.[7] Prem. takes the words *braja nāri* (63[ii].3) to mean Rādhā alone, and both he and Lok. impose on the phrase *darasana madana gupāla manohara* the sense 'a vision of *her* is charming to Madana Gopāla'.[8]

1. Rasik.: *tabahi lāla ke hiya me upajī apūrava bāta;*
   pyārī sõ kahi sakata nahi saṃkita manahi ḍarāta. 3.
2. Rasik.: *aneka janma sādhana sukṛta bhakti sahita nisi dinna;*
   tinake phala ko samaya braja gopini ko sohi chinna. 7.
3. Rasik.: *sakala kāmanā pūrikai nija sarūpa mẽ āi;*
   rahata rūpa saba lāla ke hvaikai pragaṭa samāi. 20.
4. Rasik.: *braja mẽ mathurā̃ dvārakā aure sabahī ṭhāu;*
   bijaya rūpa saba ṭhā̃ pragaṭa līlā hita bahu bhāu. 22.
   nija sarūpa nija priyā pīu nija bana maṃdira mā̃jha;
   sadā eka rasa rahata he keli magana dina sā̃jha. 23.
5. Dhar.: *paṃcādhyāī ko samai baranyõ śrī haribaṃsa;*
   avagāhai duṣu nāsaī pāpa hoi bidhvaṃsa.
6. Prem.: *tini ke kara kamalani mẽ suṃdara muralī birājata hai.*
   tāko bajāvata haĩ. ...tāke bajāibe mẽ śrī priyā jū kõ bulāvata haĩ.
7. Lok.: *taba lāla jī ne ḍhiṭhāyau jāna bacanani sau priyā jī kau na bulāyau. tribhaṃga hvai benu nāda kīnau. taba priyā jī nai lāla jī kau manoratha jāni maṃḍala para padhāribe kau mana kīnau.*
8. Prem.: *priyā jī ke muṣa aura vākī citavani ko deṣikẽ śrī lāla jū haraṣata bhaye.*
   (A more literal rendering is also offered.)
   Lok.: *so priyā jī kaisī hai. jina kau darasana madana guāla kau manohara hai.*

Similar contrivances are employed to evade the mythological implications of the *rāsa* context of CP 24. Prem. follows a close paraphrase of the final line with the words *heta kahā ki rāsa ke pāchẽ sajjā ko sukha hota bhayau*, implying that the climax of the episode derives not from the *rāsa* itself but from a subsequent withdrawal into the *nikuñja*: *rāsa* is passed over in favour of *śayyā* as the highest bliss. For Lok., too, the *rāsa* is a mere prelude to a *nikuñja* context; as in CP 63, Lok. introduces an element of *māna* into his interpretation—Rādhā scorns Kṛṣṇa's suggestion that they enter the *nikuñja*, until a clap of thunder startles her and demolishes her contrariness.[1] The image of Indra sounding the kettledrum (*maghavā mudita nisāna bajāyau*, 24.5) is weakened into a simile by Lok.'s gloss *bādara garajana lāgyau. soī mānau iṃdra nai nisāna bajāyau.* Rasik. is more brazen in his dismantling of the Indra reference, and by the association of the parallel epithets 'Maghavā' = 'Indra' = 'Surapati' arrives at a form which can be taken to refer to Kṛṣṇa (in terms of a sectarian ordering of divine hierarchy); thus Rasik. converts the *mūla*'s image of celestial kettledrums/thunder into a more comfortable picture of Kṛṣṇa, 'Lord of the gods', providing drum accompaniment for the dance.[2]

Parallel with this restriction of 'mythological' references is a restriction of geographical references relating to locations outside the *vana/nikuñja*; here the commentators draw the distinction between Vṛndāvana and Braj which Corcoran (p. 94) observes in the poetry of the Rādhāvallabhī Dhruvadāsa. Thus when Rādhā is described in the *mūla* of 29.1 as *braja nava taruni kadaṃba mukaṭa maṇi*, Lok. quickly offers the assurance that Vṛndāvana, and not a wider context, is being alluded to here: *braja hī ke madhya śrī bṛṃdābana hai*; and descriptions of Rādhā and Kṛṣṇa's countryside *vihāra* in 49.2 move Rasik. to assert that the 'dell-pastures and hillside thickets' referred to in the *mūla* are merely features of the grove itself.[3]

For most of the commentators the role of Hita Harivaṃśa as bestower to the devotee of *darśana* of the divine sport is of central importance to their interpretations of the text. Rasik., Prem. and Lok. designate Hita

1. Lok.: *priyā jī mauna gahī rahī māna kīnau tāhī china megha udai hoi āyau bījalī camakī. bādara garajana lāgyau. soī mānau iṃdra nai nisāna bajāyau. taba priyā jī ...prītama ke ura lāgī. taba kuṃja mai padhāre.*
2. Rasik.: *maghavā kahiyata iṃdra sõ surapati hū tihi nāma;*
soi ihā̃ yõhī jāniye saba devani ke prabhu syāma. 18.
tina prabhu hī rasa keli juta mudita hoi mana māhi;
duṃdubhi bajaye āpuhī saṣi mana juta cita cāha. 19.
3. Rasik.: *tina kuṃjani kī uccatā soī giri kai tūla;*
jihi madhi bahu bidhi mṛdula ati phūla rahai nava phūla. 8.
gahabara kahiyai saghanatā tini kuṃjani ke mā̃ha;
ati saṃkiranatā soī (galī) ṣori sā̃karī ṭhā̃ha. 9.
tātẽ hyā e kuṃja hī ucca ju giri kai māna;
yahai artha hyā̃ māniyai bane nahī kou āna. 11.

Harivaṃśa as *sakhī*, and interpret the poet's *chāpa* accordingly as *hita haribaṃśa rūpī saṣī, hita saṣī* or *nija saṣī*. (Dhar. occasionally involves part of the *chāpa* in his paraphrase, as in the *ṭīkā* on CP 5 given in Appendix I, but usually omits any reference to it.) Prem. and Rasik. develop the conceit of Harivaṃśa as *sakhī* by a contextualization, in the *ābhāsas* to individual stanzas, wherein the descriptive or narrative content of the stanza is addressed by the *hita sakhī* to another favoured attendant, the *kṛpāpātra sakhī*. In the terms of this device of which an example can be seen in Appendix I, only the *hita sakhī* has access to the *nikuñja*, such that 'she' has a monopoly of *darśana* of the *nitya vihāra*. The *hita sakhī* also has a role in marshalling the action, and acting as *dūtikā*; numerous contextualizations in Prem., Lok., and especially Rasik. emphasize the *sakhī*'s function as go-between and negotiator[1] (but never participant in the sport). As already noted, some *rāsa* contexts in the *mūla* imply a democratic participation in the action by the *gopīs*; the commentators constantly erode this allegation of direct involvement, insisting that the function of the *sakhīs* is service, and that the enjoyment they derive from the *nitya vihāra* is vicarious. In fact the term *gopī* is almost anathema to the commentators since it implies an equality of status between Rādhā (who is, however, described as *bṛṣabhāna gopa kī beṭī* in 18.3)[2] and 'Lalitā and the others', who constitute the *sakhī* group. Although these roles are already established in the *mūla*, the assiduity with which the commentators insist on the secondary role of the *sakhīs* is a further symptom of their dislike of the 'mythological' implications of the *gopī* image. Furthermore, the conceit of the *hita sakhī* enjoying monopoly of access to the *nikuñja* is a new development, introduced by the commentators to enhance the status of Harivaṃśa (and his text) as the sole channel through which the devotee may receive the *rasa* of the *nitya vihāra*.

Contexts in which the commentators feel constrained radically to modify the intention of the *mūla* occur in only a minority of stanzas; alongside *rāsa* motifs of the *Purāṇa* type, for example, are stanzas such as CP 12 where Rādhā has an established place in the action of the stanza. Throughout the text, however, the general drift of the commentators is towards a sectarian reading—a tendency of which the ingenuous re-casting of CP 63 discussed above is an extreme but not untypical example.

Thus the process of the commentaries can be added to a list of aspects of the text's transmission in which a gradual development of 'modern' forms and meanings takes place: in orthography, with the imposition

1. Rasik.: *nija saṣi sõ śrī lāla jū kahata rahata nija heta;*
soī nija saṣi priye sõ samai pāi kahi deta. 20. [CP 38.]

2. All the commentators except Prem. omit the term *gopa* from their glosses on this phrase.

of Sanskritized forms; in language, through simplification and loss of case terminations (with resultant semantic ambiguity tending to encourage the introduction of analytical constructions); in prosody, with the obscuring and loss of original forms, and their replacement with simplified syllabic metrical arrangements; in composition, with a *rāga* sequence possibly deriving from a literary *rāgamālā* being pressed into service for liturgical hymnody; in ascription of authorship, with early allusive references developing into a full-blown hagiography; in designation, with original epithets referring simply to the number of stanzas in the text becoming formalized as a literary title; and finally in theme, with originally puranic motifs being reinterpreted along sectarian lines. Thus the development and transmission of the CP is a truly 'medieval' process, constituting a gradual metamorphosis of classical and post-classical elements into a modern form.

APPENDIX I

Examples of the commentaries of Premadāsa, Lokanātha, Dharaṇī-dharadāsa and Rasikalāla.

The extracts which follow are transcriptions from texts G, F, A and the Rasikalāla manuscript respectively. The use of dotted characters (य़, व़) in MSS F and A has been retained in the transcriptions. In the transcription from G, all punctuation except *daṇḍas* has been ignored.

CP 5; the commentary of Premadāsa. Vijaypāl Singh and Candrabhān Rāvat, pp. 15-16. (Text G.)

अथ पञ्चम पदस्याभास:

सखी को बचन सखी प्रति

सुंदर माधवी ले फूलनि की लता को मंदिर है जाके रंध्रनि में गुलाब के फूल धरे हैं। ते दोऊ ओर फूल हैं जिनिकी डाँडी दिखाई देत नाँही। नाना प्रकार के मणिनि के लहरिया भूमि में झिलमिलाइ रहे हैं। श्री बिहारी बिहारिनि जू मंद मंद मुसिकात परस्पर ग्रीवानि में भुजा दियें लताभवन में जाइ कें सोभा देखन लगे। तिनि के मुख पर सुंदर सुख श्रमजल कण जगमगाइ रहे हैं। सो मानों कंचन मणि और मर्कतमणि में काम जरिया नें जगमोती जटे हैं। चहूँ ओर सखी झमकि रही हैं सो मानों रूप की कनात ठाढ़ी करि दई है। तहाँ श्री हित सखी जू कृपा पात्र सखी सों जोरी जू के रूप को प्रकट बर्णन करें हैं। श्री। [Followed by *mūla*.]

आजु प्रभात लता मंदिर में सुख बरषत अति हरषि जुगल बर इति। हे सखि आजु प्रभात लता के मंदिर में सुख की बरषा होइ है। जो सज्जा मंदिर में सुरतांत को सुख होत हो सोई लता मंदिर में है। क्यौंकि दोऊ श्रेष्ठ अत्यंत आनंदित हैं इति। गौर श्याम अभिराम रंग भरि लटकि लटकि पग धरत अवनि पर इति। गौर श्याम परम सुंदर हैं और परम सुंदर रंग सों भरे हैं। महा मधुर सुकुंवार हैं। ता रंग को जु भार भयो हैं तातें लटकि लटकि कें अवनी पर पगनि कों धरे हैं इति। कुच कुंकुम रंजित मालावलि सुरत नाथ श्री श्याम धाम धर इति। प्रिया जी के श्री अंग की केसरि सों रँगी गई है मालावलि। ता कों सुरत नाथ जो श्याम सो अपनें धाम पर धारें हैं धाम स्वरूप वक्षस्थल इति ज्ञेयं। अथवा लाल जू नें स्वकर गूथी ही जो माला श्याम फल और पीत फूलनि की सो प्रिया जू कों पहिराई ही। प्रिया जू के कुच कुंकुम सों रंजित ही। लाल जू को मन जानि प्रिया जू नें पहिराई ही रीझि कें ताकों धरे हैं। अपनी माला तौ प्रीतम अंतराइ मानि कें उतारि धरत हैं इति। प्रिया प्रेम के अंक अलंकृत चित्रित चतुर शिरोमणि निज कर इति। प्रिया जू प्रेम के अंकनि सों अलंकृत हैं। सो चतुर शिरोमणि ने अपने करनि सों चित्रित करीं हैं। उर बिषें जो नख लगे हैं सोई प्रेम के अंक हैं। अथवा प्रिया जू हृदय में प्रेम के अंकनि सों अलंकृत हीं। तिनि अंकनि कों

चतुर शिरोमणि नें अपने कर चित्रित कियौ प्रिया जू को बक्षस्थल इति। दंपति अति अनुराग मुदित कल गान करत मन हरत परस्पर इति। दोऊ अति अनुराग सों मुदित हैं। सुंदर गान करे हैं। परस्पर मन कों हरे हैं। जोरी जू के रूप गुण सों मिश्रित गान है। तातें परस्पर को गान सुनि कें परस्पर मोहित भए हैं इति। जै श्री हित हरिवंश प्रशंस परायण गाइन अलि सुर देत मधुर तर इति। प्रशंसा विषें जु परायण भ्रमर हैं सोई गाइन हैं। सो संग मधुर तें मधुर सुर देत हैं। अथवा प्रशंसा पराइण जु गान बिषें सखी सोई संग मधुर तें मधुर सुर देइ हैं। दोऊ परस्पर को गान सुनिकें प्रेम रूप मोह के समुद्र में परे। जैसें कोऊ डूबते कों डोरी देइ है तैसें सखी नें मधुर तें मधुर सुर देइ करि वा गहर में सों काढि लये तब दोऊ महाआनंद कों प्राप्त भये इति।

इति श्री हाससमये पंचमो निकुंजविलास :

CP 5; the commentary of Lokanātha. MS F, ff.21v-24r.

अथ पांचै पद कौ आभास। हीरन की भूम महल पांचद्वारी परदा साएवान जरी के। हौद नहर जलजंत्र जल भरे छूटत हैं। वूटा ता भूम महल मैं हरतमनि के। फुलवार नरगस की सुपेद फूल तामें कटोरी री। ब्रछ लता और लता मंदिर नाना रंग के फूलन सों फूले। पछी मृग मोर भृमर पचरंग तहाँ प्रीया प्रीतम सैंन करी। प्रात उठ कुंज विहार लता मंदर में करन लागे। तहाँ सषी के सषी सों वचन। अथ पद मूल। [Followed by *mūla*.]

अथ अर्थ। आजु प्रभात लता के मंदिर में जुगल वर अति हरषकें सुष कों वरषत हैं। यह अद्भुत रीत है कि मेघ तौ वाहर वरषत है ये लता मंदिर मै वरषत है। ओर मेघ पानी वरषत है। ये सुष वरषत है। और सब ठाँउ एक घन वरषत है। ये घन दामिनी जुगल वरषत हैं। तहाँ सज्या सोई भूम है। अरु मनोरथ की डोरी अनुराग कौ हिडोरा। ता पर वैठ विहार के झोटान सों लटकि लटकिकें पग अवनी पर धरे झूलत हैं। कुच कुमकुम कर सातुक के जल सों भीज रंगी है मालावली सुरत नाथ श्री स्याम की। सो कैसे हैं परकास के धरनहारे है। अरु प्रिया जी प्रेम के नषांक सों अलंकृत हैं। सो चित्रित है लाल जी के निजु कर सों। दंपति अति अनुराग सों गान तुल्य सीताकार प्रिया मुष तें। अरु अनुनै बचन प्रीतम मुष तें कहत है सो परसपर मन कौं हरत हैं। तब हित सषी वा विहार की अस्तुत परायन है। अरु वा गान को तहाँ भवर सुर देत है मधुरतर। ५।

CP 5; the commentary of Dharaṇīdharadāsa. MS A, ff. 4r-4v.

दोहा।
लता भुवन में आजु जुग राधे नवल किसोर।
सुष वरषत हरषत मनहि आनंद निधि उठि भोर॥
जथा सवैया।
भोर ही आजु लता मंदिर सुष वरषत रस आनंद भरि दोऊ।
गौर स्याम अभिराम जुगल वर लटकि लटकि पग धरत है सोऊ॥
उरज वाँम पर मुक्त[1] दाम छवि रंजित कुंकुम मृगमद व⟨ो⟩ऊ।

1. Emended from *mukti* by scribe.

कल कर धर वर सोहत मोहत नाहि निकट सजनी जन कोऊ ॥
अन्यच्च ।
परिरंभन अंक अलंकृत प्रीतम चित्रित अंग महा छवि पावत ।
प्रिया प्रेम वस अंस वाहु कसि परम मुदित दोऊ मिलि गावत ॥
सहचरि मन हित परम प्रसंसित गान पराई न दंपति भावत ।
रीझि रीझि मन हरत परस्पर मधुप संग सर भेद सुनावत ॥
मू । ५ । वो । ५ । स । १० ।

CP 5; the commentary of Rasikalāla. Ff. 11ʳ-12ʳ.

पंचम पद सु विलास कछु आनत चित के माँहि ।
जाकों निरषत ही सषी क्यों हू दृग न अगाँहि ॥ १ ॥
प्रीतम दोऊ मिलि करो ऐसो नित्य बिलास ।
यह आली के बचन सुनि बोलति प्रिया हुलास ॥ २ ॥
तहाँ सषी सों राधिके प्रसन वदन मुसिक्याइ ।
कह्यो चलो आली तहाँ प्रीतम जहाँ लसाहि ॥ ३ ॥
यह कहिके प्रीये चली (उठि) पहिरें मरगजे बास ।
सज्जा मंदिर तें जहाँ प्रगट केलि आवास ॥ ४ ॥
निज मंदिर के द्वारे ही लता भवन सरसात ।
जहा श्री मोहन जू लसत कछुक अंग अलसात ॥ ५ ॥
प्यारी जू कों देषिके उठे स्याम अकुलात ।
दरसन कों समयो भयो तब लों कछुक प्रभात ॥ ६ ॥
मिलि ठाढे दोऊ ललन ललनाँ संग कर जोरि ।
कबहुक दृग सों दृग निरषि हसत मृदुल मुष मोरि ॥ ७ ॥
चलत डगमगे पगनि सों मंद २ अंग घूमि ।
कुंज सदन अंगन जहाँ कोमल कंचन भूमि ॥ ८ ॥
हित सहचरि तहाँ पास है ओर अली कछु दूर ।
निज सषी के मन में दुहुनि सोभा रही जु पूरि ॥ ९ ॥
जे सषी कछुवक दूरि ही तिन में तें अलि एक ।
आई जाके चित रहै पहल दरस की टेक ॥ १० ॥
तिन सब सोभा जुगल की देषी नीकी भाति
तौ लों ओर अली तहाँ आइ गई मुसकाति ॥ ११ ॥
जो पहिलें आई हुती तासों पूछति बात ।
जो पाछे पहुची अली सो चित वहु हुलसात ॥ १२ ॥
तासों सोभा जुगल की कहति जु सषि ह्वै ओट ।
कुंज भवन के निकट ही गढी दोउ इक जोट ॥ १३ ॥
पहिलें आई जो सषी तासों कृपा प्रभाव ।
ताको बचन जु सषी सों यह पद समयो भाव ॥ १४ ॥

सषी को बचन सषी सों। पदु। दोहा।
प्रात हीं आजु अहो सषी कुंज मध्य गहें बाँह।
सुष बरषत ह प्रिया पिय हरषत हें मन माँह ॥ १५ ॥
दोऊ प्रीतम रंग भरे लटकि २ हर<ष>इ।
गौर स्याम अभिराम वर अवनी पर धरि पाइ ॥ १६ ॥
उरज कुंकमा सो रगित मुक्तावलि कछु सेत।
रति पति सम श्री स्याम कें हिय में छबि अति देत ॥ १७ ॥
प्रिया प्रेम के अंक सों भूषित करत सुभाँति।
चतुर सिरोमनि निजु करनि चित्रित है बहु भाँति ॥ १८ ॥
अति अनुराग सों मोद भरि दंपति चित्त हुलास।
गान करत मन कों हरत हसत परस्पर हास ॥ १९ ॥
निकट प्रसंसा करत तहाँ गाइन श्री हित आलि।
बीच २ सुर देत हें मधुर २ दै ताल ॥ [२० ॥]
ऐसो समयो देषिकै हों गढी इहि ठौर।
अति अद्‌भुत यह छन सषी राजत जुगल किशोर ॥ २१ ॥
इति श्री चौरासी रहस्य पद अर्थ। ५।

APPENDIX II

Stanzas in the Sūrasāgara (ed. Nandadulāre Vājpeyī) corresponding to stanzas in the CP.

SS 2489/1871, (Vol. II, pp. 27-28); cf. CP 13.

Rāgas: SS Bilāvala, CP Bilāvala.

नंद के लाल हर्‌यौ मन मोर ।
हौं बैठी मोतिनि लर पोवति   कांकरि डारि चले सखि भोर ॥
बंक बिलोकनि चाल छबीली   रसिक सिरोमनि नवल किसोर ।
कहि काकौ मन रहै स्रवन सुनि   सरस मधुर मुरली की घोर ॥
बदन गुबिंद इंदु कैं कारन   तरसत नैन बिहंग चकोर ।
सूरदास प्रभु के मिलिबे कौं   कुच श्रीफल हौं करति अँकोर ॥

SS 1817/1119 (Vol. I, p. 684); cf. CP 33.

Rāgas: SS Bilāvala, CP Devagandhāra/Gujarī.

आजु बन राजत जुगल किसोर ।
बसन बसन खंडित मुख मंडित   गंड तिलक कछु थोर ॥
डगमगात पग धरत सिथिल गति   उठे काम रस भोर ।
रति पति सारंग अरुन महा छबि   उमँगि पलक लगे भोर ॥
स्रुति अवतंस बिराजत हरि सुत   सिबुध बरस सुत ओर ।
सूरदास प्रभु रस बस कीन्ही   परी महा रन जोर ॥

SS 3070/2452 (Vol. II, p. 140); cf. CP 37.

Rāgas: SS Devagandhāra, CP Sāraṅga.

चलौ किन मानिनि कुंज कुटीर ।
तुव बिनु कुँवर कोटि बनिता तजि   सहत मदन की पीर ॥
गदगद स्वर संभ्रम अति आतुर   स्रवत सुलोचन नीर ।
क्वासि क्वासि बृषभानुनंदिनी   बिलपत बिपिन अधीर ॥
बंसी बिसिष माल व्यालावलि   पंचानन पिक कीर ।
मलयज गरल हुतासन मारुत   साखामृगरिपु चीर ॥
हिय मैं हरषि प्रेम अति आतुर   चतुर चली पिय तीर ।
सुनि भयभीत बज्र के पिंजर   सूर सुरति रन धीर ॥

SS 1809/1191 (Vol. I, p. 681); cf. CP 50.

Rāgas: SS Soraṭha, CP Sāraṅga.

नवल नागरि नवल नागर किसोर मिलि
कुंज कोमल कमल दलनि सज्या रची।
गौर साँवल अंग रुचिर तापर मिले
सरस मनि मृदुल सु आभा खची॥
सुंदर नीबी बंध रहति पिय पानि गहि
पीय के भुजनि मैं कलह मोहन मची।
सुभग श्रीफल उरज पानि परसत हुँकरि
रोषि करि गर्ब दृग भंगि भामिनि लची॥
कोक कोटिक रभस रसिक हरि सूरज
बिबिध कल माधुरी किमपि नाहिंन बची।
प्रान मन रसिक ललितादि लोचक चषक
पिवत मकरंद सुख रासि अंतर सची॥

SS 1303/685 (Vol. I, p. 501); cf. CP 54.

Rāgas: SS Kāmoda, CP Mallāra.

नयौ नेह नयौ गेह नयौ रस
नवल कुँवरि बृषभानु किसोरी।
नयौ पीतांबर नई चूनरी
नई नई बूंदनि भीजति गोरी॥
नये कुंज अति पुंज नये द्रुम
सुभग जमुन जल पवन हिलोरी।
सूरदास प्रभु नव रस बिलसत
नवल राधिका जोबन भोरी॥

SS 1819/1201 (Vol. I, p. 684); cf. CP 82.

Rāgas: SS Kedārau, CP Kedārau.

नागरता की रासि किसोरी।
नव नागर कुल मूल साँवरौ
बरबस कियौ चितै मुख मोरी॥
रूप रुचिर अँग अंग माधुरी
बिनु भूषन भूषित ब्रज गोरी।
छिन छिन कुसल सुगंध अंग मैं
कोक रभस रस सिंधु झकोरी॥
चंचल रसिक मधुप मोहन मन
राखे कनक कमल कुच कोरी।

प्रीतम नैन जुगल खंजन खग
बाँधे बिबिध निबंधनि डोरी ॥
अवनी उदर नाभि सरसी मैं
मनहुँ कछुक मादक मधुरौ री ।
सूरदास पीवन सुंदर बर
सीव सुवृढ़ निगमनि की तोरी ॥

APPENDIX III

Additional stanzas bearing the name of Hita Harivaṃśa

[Add. 1]

गोस्वामी श्रीहित हरिवंश महाप्रभुजी के भेट के पद । राग वसंत ।

प्रथम समाज आज वृंदावन विहरत लाल विहारी ।
पंचमी नवल वसंत बँधावनि उमंगि चली व्रज नारी ।।
कंचन थार लिये जुवती जन मधि वृषभान दुलारी ।
फल दल जब नव नूत मंजरी कनक कलस सुभकारी ।।
गावत गीत बजावत बाजे मैंन सैंन उनहारी ।
दरस परस मन मोद बढावत राजत वर छवि भारी ।।
चोवा चंदन अगर कुमकुमा भरि लीनी पिचकारी ।
छिरकत फिरत छवीली गातनि रंग अनूप अपारी ।।
विपुल विलास हाँस रस वरसत उत प्रीतम इत प्यारी ।
(जै श्री) हित हरिवंश निरखि यह शोभा अँखियाँ टरत न टारी ।।

Śṛṃgāra rasa sāgara (Bābā Tulsīdās (ed.), 1956-62) Vol. I, p. 6.

[Add. 2]

नवल वसंत नवल वृन्दावन नवल लाल खेलै होरी ।
नवसत साज नये रंग पहिरै नौतन केशरि घोरी ।।
नव नव साखि जवावि कुमकुमा अवीर भरें भरि झोरी ।
नई नई सखी नई छवि पावै नवल नवल बनी जोरी ।।
नई सहनाई नई डफ वाजनि नवल मुरली धुनि थोरी ।
नवल सखी मिलि चाचरि गावत नवल राधिका गोरी ।।
कालिंदी तट नौतन सोभा नवल चकोर चकोरी ।
(जै श्री) हित हरिवंश प्रेम रस क्रीडत नवल किशोर किशोरी ।।

Ibid., p. 7.

[Add. 3]

गो. श्री हित हरिवंश चन्द्र महाप्रभु जी कृत (यह पद भेट है) ।
राग मलार ।

प्रीतम दोऊ झूलत हैं संकेत ।
उतहिं कुँवर इत कुँवरि राधिका ललिता झोटा देत ।।
दोऊ मिलि मुदित परस्पर गावत अलापत राग मलार ।
खिसि खिसि परत नील पीतांवर नाहिन अंग सम्हार ।।
वरषत मेह सकल वन रंजित अवलोकत छबि देत ।
(जै श्री) हित हरिवंश परस्पर झूलत सखी वलैया लेत ।।

Ibid., Vol. II, p. 141.

[Add. 4]

मिल जैवत लाडिली लाल दोऊ षट विंजन चारु सवै सरसै ।
मन मै रस की रुचि ज्यौ उपजे सखि माधुरी कुंज सवै वरसै ॥
हसिकै मन मोहन हार रहे निज हाथ जिवावन कौ तरसे ।
कर कंपत वीचहि छूटि परे कवहूक गसा मुख लौ परसे ॥
दृग सौ दृग जोर दोऊ मुसक्याय अरे अनुराग सुधा वरसै ।
मनु हार विहार अहार करे तन में मन प्राण परे कर से ॥
सखि सौंज लिये चहु ओर खरी हरखे निरखे दरसे परसे ।
सुख सिंधु अपार कह्यौ न परे अवशेष सखी (श्री) हरिवंश लसे ॥

Vrindaban Research Institute Hindi MS 7848, f. 219r (See discussion on p. 45)

Discussion

There is no actual attribution of these stanzas[1] to Hita Harivaṃśa, their status as *bhẽṭa pada* being acknowledged even within the Rādhāvallabha *sampradāya*: yet their existence is relevant to the present study, since it is evidence of the process by which diverse material may become associated with Harivaṃśa through the use of his *chāpa*. The inclusion of such stanzas in sectarian anthologies may represent an initial stage in the accretion of new *padas* to an existing corpus.

Although the CP is itself not stylistically uniform, certain features of the present stanzas suggest that they are not wholly successful imitations of the general CP style. References to the *sakhīs* in Add.1.3, Add.3.2 and Add.4.7 attribute to them a servile role which is familiar from the CP *ṭikās* but not prominent in the *mūla*; Add.1.2 refers to the festival of *Vasanta Pañcamī*, whereas the CP makes no reference to any calendrical observance, keeping to supramundane contexts throughout; and a number of lexical items found here are absent from the CP, despite being invited by commonplace contexts.[2] Such stylistic criteria may have prevented these stanzas from being included in the corpus of material attributed to Hita Harivaṃśa.

1. Add. 1 and Add. 2 appear also in a miscellany of Braj bhāṣā verse following Bhūpati's *Bhāgavata daśama skandha*, in a manuscript in the University Library, Cambridge. The manuscript, OR MS 57, is in the Perso-Arabic script. I am grateful to Dr. G.R. Niemann for supplying this reference and a transcription of the *padas*.

2. Examples are *ãkhiyã* (Add. 1.10), *gīta*, *bāje* (Add. 1.5), *javādi* (add. 2.3.), *sahanāī* (Add. 2.5), *meha* (Add. 3.5).

BIBLIOGRAPHY

Primary texts are listed under the name of an editor wherever possible. In cases of ambiguity as to authorship/editorship, an editor is designated '(ed.)'. Multiple works under a single author's name are listed chronologically (by date of publication).

1. *Editions and translations of primary texts*

Agravāl, Vāsudev Śaraṇ (ed.) *Padmāvata* [of Malik Muhammad 'Jāyasī'] Cīrgāv, Sāhitya Sadan, V.S. 2018 (A.D. 1961).

Ahobala Paṇḍita, *Saṃgīta pārijāta.* 3rd edition. Hathras, Saṃgīt Kāryālay, 1971.

Alsdorf, Ludwig (ed.), *Der Kumārapālapratibodha.* Hamburg, Friederichsen De Gruyter & Co., 1928.

Anantadāsa Bābāji (ed.), *Śrīśrīrādhārasasudhānidhi.* Radhakund, Śrīkṛṣṇacaitanya Śāstramandir, Caitanyābda 496 (A.D. 1982).

Banerji, Sures Chandra, *Fundamentals of ancient Indian music and dance.* Ahmedabad, L.D. Institute of Indology, 1976. [Includes Skt. text of *Pañcamasārasaṃhitā* of Nārada.]

Bhagvān Prasād, Sītārām Śaraṇ (ed.), *Śrībhaktamāla* [of Nābhādāsa], Lucknow, Tejkumār Press, 1962.

Bhayani, Harivallabh C., *Paümacariu of Kavirāja Svayambhūdeva.* 3 vols. Bombay, Bhāratīya Vidyā Bhavan, 1953.

Caturvedī, Rāmlāl Śyāmsundar (ed.), *Śrī hita sudhā siṃdhu.* 2nd edition. Vrindaban, The author, V.S. 2022 (A.D. 1965).

Chatterji, Suniti Kumar, & Misra, Babua, *Varṇa-ratnākara of Jyotirīśvara Kaviśekharācārya.* Calcutta, Royal Asiatic Society of Bengal, 1940.

Dās, Vrajaratan *Bhāratendu granthāvalī* Vol. III. Varanasi, Nāgarī Pracāriṇī Sabhā, 1953.

Dāsa, Sundarānanda, 'Vidyāvinoda' *Śrī Devakīnandanadāsa kṛta śrī śrī vaiṣṇava vandanā o śrī śrī vaiṣṇavābhidhānam.* Navadvip, Navīnakṛṣṇadāsa Vidyālaṅkāra, 1961.

Entwistle, A.W. The *rāsa māna ke pada* of Kevalarāma. Groningen, Rijksuniversiteit te Groningen, 1983.

Gauḍ, Kālīcaraṇ Caurāsiyā (ed.), *Bhaktamāla arthāt bhaktakalpadruma* [of Pratāpasiṃha]. Lucknow, Tejkumār Press, 1952.

Gauḍ, Nirañjandev Śarmā (ed.), *Do sau bāvana vaiṣṇavana kī vārtā* [of Gokulanātha]. Mathura, Śrī Govardhan Granthamālā Kāryālay, V.S. 2029 (A.D. 1972).

Gosvāmī, Lalitā Caraṇ (ed.), N.d. : *Śrī hita caurāsī.* Vrindaban, Veṇu Prakāśan, n.d.

1971: *Śrī bayālīsa līlā* [of Dhruvadāsa]. 2nd edition. Vrindaban, Bābā Tulsīdās, v.s. 2028 (A.D. 1971).

1972: *Śrī hita caurāsī evam sphuṭa vāṇī*. Vrindaban, Veṇu Prakāśan, v.s. 2029 (A.D. 1972).

1975: *Śrī sevaka vāṇī* [of Dāmodaradāsa 'Sevaka']. Vrindaban, Veṇu Prakāśan, v.s. 2032 (A.D. 1975).

1978: *Śrī rādhāvallabha jī kā varṣotsava*. 3 vols. Vrindaban, Rādhāvallabh Mandir Vaiṣṇav Committee, 1978.

Gosvāmī, Vāsudev, *Bhakta kavi vyāsa jī*. [*Pada* collection edited by Prabhu Dayāl Mītal.] Mathura, Agravāl Press, v.s. 2009 (A.D. 1952).

Gosvāmī, Yugalvallabh, *Śrī hita aṣṭayāma sevā*. Vrindaban, Vṛndāvipin Prakāśan, v.s. 2032 (A.D. 1975).

Gupta, R.D., *Studies in the Bhaktirasa-Bodhinī of Priyā Dāsa*. Ph.D. thesis, University of London, 1967.

[Harirāya]. *Caurāsī kī vārtā* [Lithographed edition]. Aligarh, n.p., 1968.

Hit Dās, Bābā (ed.), *Śrīrādhāsudhānidhi*. Jabalpur, Sundarlāl Indurakhyā, 1950.

Jacobi, Hermann, 1918: *Bhavisatta kaha von Dhaṇavāla*. München, Verlag der Königlich Bayerischen Akademie der Wissenschaften, 1918.

1921: *Sanatkumāracaritam ein Abschnitt aus Haribhadras Nemināthacaritam*. München, Verlag der Bayerischen Akademie der Wissenschaften, 1921.

Jarrett, H.S. (trans.), *The Ain i Akbari by Abul Fazl Allāmi*. 3 vols. [First vol. trans. H. Blochmann.] Calcutta, Asiatic Society of Bengal, 1873-94.

Jhā, Narendra (ed.), *Bhaktamāla: pāṭhānuśīlana evam vivecana*. [Text of Nābhādāsa.] Patna, Anupam Prakāśan, 1978.

Kielhorn, F., *The Vyākaraṇa mahābhāṣya of Patañjali*. 3 vols. 3rd edition. Poona, Bhandarkar Oriental Research Institute, 1962-72.

McGregor, R.S., *The Language of Indrajit of Orchā*. Cambridge, Cambridge University Press, 1968.

Miller, Barbara Stoler, *Love song of the dark lord: Jayadeva's Gītagovinda*. New York, Columbia University Press, 1977.

Mītal, Prabhu Dayāl 1949: *Aṣṭachāpa paricaya*. 2nd edition. Mathura, Agravāl Press, n.d. [Preface dated v.s. 2006 (A.D. 1949)].

1961: *Svāmī Haridāsa jī: jīvanī aura vāṇī*. Mathura, Sāhitya Saṃsthān, v.s. 2018 (A.D. 1961).

Mukhopādhyāya, Upendranāth, *Śrī śrī bhaktamāla grantha* [of Kṛṣṇadāsa Bābā jī]. 5th edition. Calcutta, Basumati Sāhitya Mandir, Caitanyābda 464 (A.D. 1950).

Nāhaṭā, Agarcand, *Rāghava dāsa kṛta bhaktamāla* (*caturadāsa kṛta ṭīkā sahita*). Jodhpur, Rājasthān Prācyavidyā Pratisṭhān, 1965.

Niemann, Grahame Ralph, *Hita Harivaṃśa: a study of the founder of the Rādhāvallabha sect with a translation of his Hita Caurāsī.* B.A. dissertation, A.N.U. Canberra, 1977.

Parīkh, Dvārkādas (ed.), *Caurāsī vaiṣṇavana kī vārtā* [of Gokulanātha]. Mathura, Śri Govardhan Granthamālā Kāryālay, v.s. 2027 (A.D. 1970).

Pollet, G., *Studies in the Bhakta Māla of Nābhā Dāsa.* Ph.D. thesis, University of London, 1963.

Prabodhānanda Sarasvatī, *Śrī vṛndāvanamahimāmṛtam.* [Editions seen as follows: Vol. I, 3rd, 1978; Vol. II, 2nd, 1967; Vol. III, 2nd, 1975; Vol. IV, 1st, 1964.] Vrindaban, Śrīharinām Saṅkīrtan Maṇḍal, v.s. 2021-32 (A.D. 1964-78).

Purohit, Lalitāprasād 1960: *Rasika ananya māla* (*mahātmā bhagavat mudita kṛta*). Vrindaban, Veṇu Prakāśan, n.d. [Preface dated v.s. 2017 (A.D. 1960)].

1971: *Śrī svāmī caturbhujadāsa praṇīta dvādasa yaśa.* Vrindaban, Rādhāvallabh Granthamālā, v.s. 2028 (A.D. 1971).

Raghurājasiṃha, *Bhaktamālā: rāmarasikāvalī.* Bombay, Gaṅgāviṣṇu Śrīkṛṣṇadās, v.s. 2013 (A.D. 1956).

Sandahl-Forgue, Stella, *Le Gītagovinda: tradition et innovation dans le kāvya.* Stockholm, Almqvist & Wicksell International, 1977.

Śarmmā, Purohit Harinārāyaṇ, *Brajanidhi granthāvalī.* Varanasi, Nāgarī Pracāriṇī Sabhā, v.s. 1990 (A.D. 1933).

Shukla, N.S., *Le Karṇānanda de Kṛṣṇadāsa.* Pondichéry, Institut Français d'Indologie, 1971.

Siṃha, Vijaypāl & Ravat, Candrabhān (eds.), *Hitacaurāsī aura usakī premadāsakṛta brajabhāṣā ṭīkā.* Varanasi, Nāgarī Pracāriṇī Sabhā, v.s. 2028 (A.D. 1971).

Śukla, Priyādās, *Śrī hita rādhāvallabha bhaktamāla arthāt vṛhat ananyarasikāvali.* Mathura, Vrajvallabhdās Mukhiyā, v.s. 1986 (A.D.1929).

Tulsīdās, Bābā (ed.), *Sṛṃgāra rasa sāgara* (*śrī rādhāvallabha jī kau varṣotsava*). 4 vols. Vrindaban, the editor, v.s. 2013-19 (A.D. 1956-62).

Vājpeyī, Nandadulāre (ed.), *Sūrasāgara.* 2 vols. 5th edition. Varanasi, Nāgarī Pracāriṇī Sabhā, v.s. 2033-35 (A.D. 1976-78).

Vasu, Nagendranāth (ed.), *Saṃgīta rāgakalpadruma* [of Kṛṣṇānanda Vyāsadeva 'Rāgasāgara']. 3 vols. Calcutta, Baṅgīya Sāhitya Pariṣad, 1914-16.

Vasudeva Śāstrī, K., *Saṅgīta darpaṇam* of Catura Dāmodara. Tanjore, Saraswathi Mahal, 1952.

Vṛndāvanadāsa 'Cācā Jī' 1962: *Śrī hita harivaṃśa sahasranāma.* Vrindaban, Bābā Rādhikādās, v.s. 2019 (A.D. 1962).

1972: '*Rasika ananya paracāvalī*', in *Hita Saurabha* V.4 (October 1972)—VI.4 (October 1973).

White, Charles S.J., *The Caurāsī pad of Śrī Hit Harivaṃs.* Hawaii, The University Press of Hawaii, 1977.

2. *Secondary Sources*

Agravāl, Śakuntalā, *Prabodhānanda Sarasvatī: eka adhyayana*. Ph.D. thesis, Agra University, 1978.

Bāharī, Hardev, *Sūra śabdasāgara*. Allahabad, Smṛti Prakāśan, 1981.

Barz, R., *The bhakti sect of Vallabhāchārya*. Faridabad, Thompson Press, 1976.

Bhāṭī, Deśrājsiṃh, *Sūra kā kūṭakāvya*, Delhi, Aśok Prakāśan, 1970.

Bhātkhaṇḍe, Viṣṇu Nārāyaṇ, *Hindustānī saṃgīta paddhati kramika pustaka mālikā*. [Translated from the Marathi.] 6 vols. Hathras, Saṃgīt Kāryālay, 1953-58.

Bhaṭṭācārya, Tārāpada, *Chandovijñāna*. Calcutta, B.G. Printers and Publishers, 1948.

Bloch, Jules, *L'Indo-Aryen du veda aux temps modernes*. Paris, Librairie d'Amérique et d'Orient, 1934.

Bose, Mandakranta, *Classical Indian dancing: a glossary*. Calcutta, General Printers and Publishers, 1970.

Bryant, Kenneth E., *Poems to the child-god: structures and strategies in the poetry of Sūrdās*. Berkeley, University of California Press, 1979.

Callewaert, Winand M., 'Manuscripts of some Bhaktamālas, Pañcavāṇīs and Sarvāṅgīs', in *Bulletin of the International Association of the Vrindaban Research Institute*, No. 3 (Dec. 1976) pp. 5-12.

Conybeare, H.C., Fisher, F.H. & Hewett, J.P., *Statistical, descriptive and historical account of the North-Western provinces of India*. Vol. VIII, Part I—Muttra. Allahabad, North-Western Provinces and Oudh Government Press, 1884.

Corcoran, Maura, *Vṛndāvana in Vaiṣṇava Braj literature*. Ph.D. thesis, University of London, 1980.

Cunnīlāl 'Śeṣa', *Aṣṭachāpa ke vādyayaṃtra*. Mathura, Akhil Bhāratīya Braj Sāhitya Maṇḍal, v.s. 2013 (A.D. 1956).

Danielou, Alain, *The rāga-s of Northern Indian music*. London, Barrie and Rockliff, 1968.

Dās, Śyāmsundar, *Hindī śabdasāgara*. 11 vols. Revised edition. Varanasi, Nāgarī Pracāriṇī Sabhā, 1965-75.

Datta (Gopāl), *Svāmī Haridāsa jī kā sampradāya aura usakā vāṇī sāhitya*. New Delhi, National Publishing House, 1976.

De, Sushil Kumar, *Early history of the Vaisnava faith and movement in Bengal, from Sanskrit and Bengali sources*. 2nd edition. Calcutta, Firma K.L. Mukhopadhyay, 1961.

Derrett, J. Duncan M., *Essays in classical and modern Hindu law*. 4 vols. Leiden, E.J. Brill, 1976-78.

Fox Strangways, A.H., *The music of Hindostan*. Oxford, Oxford University Press, 1914. [Reprinted 1970.]

Gangoly, O.C., *Rāgas and rāginīs: a pictorial and iconographic study of*

Indian musical modes based on original sources. 2 vols. Bombay, Nalanda Publications, 1935 [reprinted 1948].

Garg, Lakṣmīnārāyaṇ, *Kathaka nṛtya*. 4th edition. Hathras, Saṃgīt Kāryālay, 1981.

Ghurye, G.S., 'Some notes on Hindu costume', in *Bulletin of the Deccan College Research Institute*, VIII (1946-47), pp. 97-172.

Goetz, Hermann, & Ilse-Munk, Rose, *Gedichte aus der indischen Liebesmystik des Mittelalters* (*Krishna und Rādhā*). Leipzig, Verlag der Asia Major, 1925.

Gosvāmī, Lalitā Caraṇ, *Śrī hita harivaṃśa gosvāmī: sampradāya aura sāhitya*. Vrindaban, Veṇu Prakāśan, v.s. 2014 (A.D. 1957).

Grierson, George Abraham, 1889: *The modern vernacular literature of Hindustan*. Calcutta, The Asiatic Society, 1889.

1909: 'Bhaktimārga', in James Hastings (ed.), *Ѐncyclopaedia of Religion and Ethics*, Vol. II [1909] pp. 539-551.

1916: *Linguistic Survey of India*, vol. IX, Part I (Indo-Aryan Family, Central Group—Western Hindi and Panjabi). Calcutta, Superintendent of Government Printing, 1916.

1918: 'The Rādhāvallabhīs', in James Hastings (ed.), *Encyclopaedia of Religion and Ethics*, Vol. X [1918] pp. 559-60.

Growse, F.S. 1878: 'Mathurā notes', in *Journal of the Asiatic Society of Bengal*, Vol. XLVII (1878), pp. 97-113.

1883: *Mathurá: a district memoir*. 2nd edition. Allahabad, North-Western Provinces and Oudh Government Press, 1883.

Gupta, Govind Rām, 'Vasant', *Rāga koṣa*. 2nd edition. Hathras, Saṃgīt Kāryālay, 1970.

Gupta, Uṣā, *Hindī ke kṛṣṇabhakti kālīna sāhitya mẽ saṃgīta*. Lucknow, Lucknow University, 1959.

Hardy, Friedhelm, *Viraha bhakti: the early history of Kṛṣṇa devotion in South India*. Delhi, Oxford University Press, 1983.

Hastings, James, *Encyclopaedia of Religion and Ethics*. 13 vols. Edinburgh, T. & T. Clark, 1908-26.

Hawley, J.S., 1979: 'The early *Sūr Sāgar* and the growth of the Sūr tradition', in *Journal of the American Oriental Society*, 99.1 (1979), pp. 64-72.

1984: *Sūr Dās: poet, singer, saint*. Seattle, University of Washington, 1984.

Haynes, Richard D., *Svāmī Haridās and the Haridāsī sampradāy*. Ph.D. thesis, University of Pennsylvania, 1974. [Ann Arbor, University Microfilms International, 1983.]

Hein, Norvin, *The miracle plays of Mathurā*. New Haven, Yale University Press, 1972.

Henry, Edward Oscar, *The meanings of music in a North Indian village*. Ph.D. thesis, Michigan State University, 1973. [London, University Microfilms International, 1978.]

Jairazbhoy, N.A., *The rāgs of North Indian music: their structure and evolution.* Middletown, Wesleyan University Press, 1971.

Kellogg, S.H., *A grammar of the Hindī language.* 3rd edition. London, Kegan Paul, Trench, Trubner & Co., 1938.

Kohli, Surinder Singh, *A critical study of the Adi Granth.* New Delhi, The Punjabi Writers' Cooperative Industrial Society, 1961.

Lal, Kishori Saran, *Twilight of the sultanate.* London, Asian Publishing House, 1963.

Majumdar, A.K., *Bhakti renaissance.* Bombay, Bhāratīya Vidyā Bhavan, 1965.

Majumdār, Bimānbihārī, *Śrīcaitanyacaritera upādāna.* Calcutta, Calcutta University, 1939.

Mallison, F., '*Bhakti* in Gujarāt: some problems', in W.M. Callewaert (ed.), *Early Hindī devotional literature in current research.* Leuven, Katholieke Universiteit, 1980. pp. 88-102.

Manuel, Peter L., 'The relationship between prosodic and musical rhythms in Urdu ghazal-singing', in Muhammad Umar Memon (ed.), *Studies in the Urdu ġazal and prose fiction.* Madison, University of Wisconsin, 1969. pp. 101-19.

McLeod, W.H., *The evolution of the Sikh community.* Oxford, Oxford University Press, 1976.

Miltner, Vladimir, 'A note on a peculiarity in some verses of Sūrdās', in *Archiv Orientalni*, 30 (1962), pp. 634-37.

Miśra, Gaṇeśbihārī, Śyāmbihārī & Śukdevbihārī, *Miśrabandhu vinoda.* Allahabad, Hindī Granth Prasārak Maṇḍalī, 1913.

Miśra, Gaurīśaṅkar, *Hindī sāhitya kā chandovivecana.* Patna, Bihār Hindī Granth Akādemī, 1975.

Miśra, Lālmaṇi, *Bhāratīya saṃgīta vādya.* New Delhi, Bhāratīya Jñānpīṭh Prakāśan, 1973.

Mītal, Prabhu Dayāl 1968: *Braja ke dharma sampradāyõ kā itihāsa.* Delhi, National Publishing House, 1968.

1975: *Braja kī kalāõ kā itihāsa.* Mathura, Sāhitya Saṃsthān, 1975.

Monier-Williams, M., *A Sanskṛit-English Dictionary.* Oxford, Oxford University Press, 1899 [reprinted 1974].

Motīcandra, *Prācīna bhāratīya veśa-bhūṣā.* Allahabad, Bhāratī Bhaṇḍār, v.s. 2007 (A.D. 1950).

Mukharji, T.N., *Art manufactures of India.* New Delhi, Navrang, 1974. [Reprint of 1888 Calcutta edition.]

Niemann, G.R., 'Uncatalogued Indian manuscripts of Corpus Christi College, Cambridge: the Honner collection', in *Bulletin of the International Association of the Vrindaban Research Institute*, No. 9 (Dec. 1980) pp. 3-15.

Nijenhuis, Emmie Te, *Musicological literature.* Wiesbaden, Otto Harrassowitz, 1977. [*A history of Indian literature*, Vol. VI Fasc. 1.]

Platts, John T., *A dictionary of Urdū, classical Hindī, and English.* 5th impression. London, Oxford University Press, 1930. [Reprinted 1968.]

Popley, Herbert A., *The music of India*. 3rd edition. New Delhi, Y.M.C.A. Publishing House, 1966.

Prajñānanda, Svāmī, *A history of Indian music*. Vol. I. Calcutta, Ramakrishna Vedanta Math, 1963.

Prasād, Jagannāth, 'Bhānu Kavi', *Chandaḥprabhākara*. 8th edition. Bilaspur, The author, 1935.

Prasad, Rajiva Nain, *Raja Man Singh of Amber*. Calcutta, The World Press, 1966.

Saksena, Baburam, *Evolution of Awadhi*. 2nd edition. Delhi, Motilal Banarsidass, 1971.

Saṃgīta [Periodical], *Tāla aṅka*. Hathras, Saṃgīt Kāryālay, January 1940. (7th edition, 1972.)

Śarmā, Nārāyaṇ Datt, *Nimbārka sampradāya aura usake kṛṣṇabhakta hindī kavi*. Mathura, Aśoka Prakāśan, 1978.

Śarmā, Rāmcaraṇlāl, *Hindī sāhitya mẽ aṣṭachāpī aura rādhāvallabhīya kāvya*. Mathura, Javāhar Pustakālay, 1978.

Śarmmā, Gopālprasād n.d., *Bhramocchedana*. Calcutta, Gosvāmī Brothers, n.d.

1919: *Śrī hita caritra*. Calcutta, Gosvāmī Brothers, V.S. 1976 (A.D. 1919).

Sen, Nilratan, *Early Eastern new Indo-Aryan versification: a prosodical study of Caryāgītikoṣa*. Simla, Indian Institute of Advanced Study, 1973.

Shackle, Christopher, *A Gurū Nānak glossary*. London, School of Oriental and African Studies, 1981.

Sharar, Abdul Halim, *Lucknow: the last phase of an Oriental culture*. (Translated and edited by E.S. Harcourt and Fakhir Hussain.) London, Paul Elek, 1975.

Sherring, M.A., *Hindu tribes and castes as represented in Benares*. Calcutta, Trubner & Co., 1872.

Simon, R.L., *Bhakti ritual music in South India: a study of the bhajana in its cultural matrix*. Ph.D. thesis, University of California, 1975. [Ann Arbor, University Microfilms International, 1978.]

Singh, Gyān, *Gurbānī saṃgīta*. Part 1. Amritsar, Śromaṇī Gurdvārā Parbandhak Committee, 1971.

Smith, Vincent A., *The Oxford history of India*. 3rd edition. Oxford, Oxford University Press, 1970.

Snātak, Vijayendra 1968: *Rādhāvallabha sampradāya: siddhānta aura sāhitya*. 2nd edition. Delhi, National Publishing House, 1968.

(ed.) 1975: *Śrī hita harivaṃśa mahāprabhu paṃcaśatābdi smṛtigrantha evaṃ samāroha smārikā*. Vrindaban, Śrī Hita Harivaṃśa Mahāprabhu Paṃcaśatābdi Samāroh Samiti, 1975.

Snell, Rupert 1980 (a): 'History versus hagiography in early Hindi literature: the biography of Hita Harivaṃśa', in *Purvadesh*, Vol. 1 no. 2 (Winter 1980), pp. 109-35.

1980 (b): '*Śrī hita caurāsī aura usakā ṭīkā sāhitya*' in *Rasa Vṛndāvana* Year 2 No's 2-4 (April-June 1980), pp. 91-8.

1983 'Metrical forms in Braj bhāṣā verse: the *Caurāsī pada* in performance', in Monika Thiel-Horstmann (ed.), *Bhakti in Current Research*, 1979-82. Berlin, Dietrich Reimer Verlag, 1983, pp. 353-83.

1984: *The Caurāsī pada: a Rādhāvallabhī text in medieval Hindi.* Ph.D. thesis, University of London, 1984.

1985: 'The *nikuñja* as sacred space in poetry of the Rādhāvallabhī tradition'. Paper read at the Third Conference on Early Devotional Literature in New Indo-Aryan Languages, Leiden, 1985. [Forthcoming in conference proceedings].

Śukla, Rāmcandra, *Hiṃdī sāhitya kā itihāsa.* Revised edition. Varanasi, Nāgarī Pracāriṇī Sabhā, v.s. 2029 (A.D. 1972).

Tagare, Ganesh Vasudev, *Historical grammar of Apabhraṃśa.* Poona, Deccan College, 1948.

Ṭaṇḍan, Prem Nārāyaṇ, *Braja bhāṣā sūra kośa*, 2 vols. Lucknow, Lucknow University, 1962.

Tewari, Laxmi Ganesh, *Folk music of India: Uttar Pradesh.* Ph.D. thesis, Wesleyan University, 1974. [Ann Arbor. University Microfilms International, 1978.]

Tivārī, Bholānāth, *Hindī muhāvarā kośa.* 3rd edition. Allahabad, Kitāb Mahal, 1977.

Turner, R.L., *A comparative dictionary of the Indo-Aryan languages.* London, Oxford University Press, 1973.

Upādhyāy, Baldev, 1953: *Bhāgavata sampradāya.* Varanasi, Nāgarī Pracāriṇī Sabhā, v.s. 2010 (A.D. 1953).

1978: *Vaiṣṇava sampradāyõ kā sāhitya aura siddhānta.* Varanasi, Chaukhamba Amarabharati Prakashan, 1978.

Verma, Dhirendra, *La langue Braj.* Paris, Librairie d'Amérique et d'Orient, 1935.

Widdess, D.R. 1980: *Early Indian musical forms: a study of examples in notation from sources c.* 600-1250. Ph.D. thesis, Cambridge University, 1980.

1981: 'Aspects of form in North Indian alap and dhrupad', in D.R. Widdess and R.F. Wolpert (eds.), *Music and tradition: essays on Asian and other musics presented to Laurence Picken.* Cambridge, Cambridge University Press, 1981. pp. 143-81.

Wilson, H.H. 1855: *A glossary of judicial and revenue terms.* London, W.H. Allen, 1855.

1862: *Essays and lectures, chiefly on the religion of the Hindus.* 2 vols. London, Trubner & Co., 1862.

3. *Manuscripts*

(This list does not include manuscripts of the CP: these are listed in sections II.1 and II.2.)

Bhagavat Mudita, *Rasika ananya māla.* v.s. 1837 (A.D. 1780). Nāgarī Pracāriṇī Sabhā (Mayāśaṅkar Yājñik collection), MS 332.

Rasika ananya māla. v.s. 1817 (A.D. 1760). Nāgarī Pracāriṇī Sabhā (Mayāśaṅkar Yājñik collection), MS 4822.

Bhagavaṃta Mudita & Uttamacaṃda, *Rasika māla.* v.s. 1835 (A.D. 1778). Vrindaban Research Institute, MS 4398. (Cat. no. 409.)

Hita Harivaṃśa, *Phuṭakara pada.* v.s. 1982 (A.D. 1925). Vrindaban Research Institute, MS 7848 (Cat. no. 826; catalogued in error as *Hita caurāsī*).

Rādhārasasudhānidhi. Undated. Vrindaban Research Institute, MS 344. (Cat. no. 2259).

Rādhārasasudhānidhi. v.s. 1848 (A.D. 1791). Vrindaban Research Institute, MS 2309. (Cat. no. 1338.)

Rādhārasasudhānidhi. v.s. 1956 (A.D. 1899). Vrindaban Research Institute, MS 8836. (Cat. no. 8786.)

Rādhāsudhānidhi. Undated. Vrindaban Research Institute, MS 3263. (Cat. no. 2260.)

Rādhāsudhānidhi. Undated. Vrindaban Research Institute, MS 4358.

Rādhāsudhānidhi. v.s. 1829 (A.D. 1772). Vrindaban Research Institute, MS 4410. (Cat. no. 5472.)

Śrī hita jū ke pada. v.s. 1829 (A.D. 1772). Vrindaban Research Institute, MS 4410.

Yamunāṣṭaka. Undated. Nāgarī Pracāriṇī Sabhā, MS 8983.

Prabodhānanda, *Rādhāsudhānidhi.* Undated. Vrindaban Research Institute, MS 6626. (Cat. no. 5475.)

Vṛndāvanamahimāmṛta [with Braj bhāṣā commentary of Bhagavat Mudita]. v.s. 1773 (A.D. 1716). Vrindaban Research Institute, Hindi MS 61.

Rasika Lāla, *Śrī caurāsī rahasya artha samaya nirūpana.* Incomplete, lacks colophon folio. Collection of Bābā Hit Dās, Vrindaban.

[Uttamadāsa], *Śrī harivaṃśa caritra.* v.s. 1835 (A.D. 1778). Vrindaban Research Institute, Hindi MS 4398. (Cat. no. 409.)

Śrī hita caritra. [Author not named in colophon.] v.s. 1817 (A.D. 1760). Nāgarī Pracāriṇī Sabhā (Mayāśaṅkar Yājñik collection), MS 4822.

Śrī hita caritra. v.s. 1837 (A.D. 1780). Nāgarī Pracāriṇī Sabhā (Mayāśaṅkar Yājñik collection), MS 332.

[attrib. Hita Harivaṃśa/Prabodhānanda], *Rādhāsudhānidhi.* Incomplete, lacks colophon folio. Vrindaban Research Institute, Sanskrit MS 3263. (Cat. no. 2260.)

4. *Catalogues*

Aufrecht, Theodor (ed.), *Catalogus catalogorum: an alphabetical register of Sanskrit works and authors.* Wiesbaden, Franz Steiner Verlag, 1962.

Gupta, R.D., & Gupta, M.L. (eds.), *A catalogue of Sanskrit manuscripts in the Vrindaban Research Institute.* Part I. Vrindaban, V.R.I., 1976.

Gupta, R.D., & Wright, J.C. (eds.), *A catalogue of Sanskrit manuscripts in the Vrindaban Research Institute.* Parts II & III. Vrindaban V.R.I., 1978 [II], 1981 [III].

Gupta, R.D., & Gupta, M.L. (eds.), *A catalogue of Hindi manuscripts in the Vrindaban Research Institute.* Part I. Vrindaban, V.R.I., 1979.

Kiśorīśaraṇ 'Ali' (ed.), *Sāhitya ratnāvalī.* Vrindaban, Premdhām Press, V.S. 2007 (A.D. 1950).

Misra, Shyam Behari (ed.), *The second triennial report on the search for Hindi manuscripts (for the years* 1909, 1910 *and* 1911). Allahabad, Nāgarī Pracāriṇī Sabhā, 1914.

Miśra, Vidyābhūṣaṇ (ed.), *Khoja mẽ upalabdha hastalikhita hiṃdī graṃthõ kā satrahavā̃ traivārṣika vivaraṇa (san 1938-41 ī.).* Varanasi, Nāgarī Pracāriṇī Sabhā, V.S. 2012 (A.D. 1955).

INDEX

This index is largely restricted to pre-modern works, authors and sectarian figures appearing in the discussion of the text and its history. Some other items have been included on a more *ad hoc* basis.